The Degrees of Knowledge

THE COLLECTED WORKS OF JACQUES MARITAIN
Volume 7

Honorary Editor-in-Chief
Theodore M. Hesburgh, C.S.C.

Editors
Ralph McInerny
Frederick Crosson   Bernard Doering

Acknowledgments

A grant from the Homeland Foundation enabled this series to get under way.

The following Notre Dame graduate students worked on some stage of the production of this book: John O'Callaghan, Michael Waddell, Melissa Pirelli, Christopher Kaczor, Michael Letteney, Randall Smith and Brendan Kelly. Mrs. Jean Oesterle served as proofreader of several chapters.

DISTINGUISH TO UNITE

or

The Degrees of Knowledge

JACQUES MARITAIN

Translated from the fourth French edition
under the supervision of
Gerald B. Phelan

Presented by
Ralph McInerny

University of Notre Dame Press
Notre Dame, Indiana
1995

Manufactured in the United States of America

Library of Congress Cataloging-in-Publication Data

Maritain, Jacques, 1882-1973
  [Degrés du savoir. English]
  The degrees of knowledge / Jacques Maritain : presented by Ralph
McInerny : translated from the fourth French edition under the
supervision of Gerald B. Phelan.
      p.   cm. — (The collected works of Jacques Maritain : v. 7)
  Includes bibliographical references and index.
  ISBN 0-268-00876-0 (alk. paper)
  1. Knowledge, Theory of. 2. Philosophy of nature.
3. Metaphysics. 4. God—Knowableness. 5. Mysticism. 6. Wisdom.
I. McInerny, Ralph M. II. Title. III. Series: Maritain, Jacques,
1882-1973. Works. 1995.
BD162.M273 1995
121—dc20   94-45159
                                                            CIP

∞The paper used in this publication meets the minimum requirements of the
American National Standard for Information Sciences—permanence of Paper for
Printed Materials, ANSI Z39.48-1984

TABLE OF CONTENTS

Second Part: *The Degrees of Suprarational Knowledge*

PREFACE TO THE ORIGINAL FRENCH EDITION

THE TITLE OF THIS WORK suffices to declare its plan and purpose.[1] To scatter and to confuse are both equally inimical to the nature of the mind. "No one," says Tauler, "understands true distinction better than they who have entered into unity." So, too, no one truly knows unity who does not also know distinction. Every attempt at metaphysical synthesis, especially when it deals with the complex riches of knowledge and of the mind, must distinguish in order to unite. What is thus incumbent upon a reflexive and critical philosophy is above all to discriminate and discern the degrees of knowing, its organization and its internal differentiations.

Idealism usually chooses a particular order of sciences as the univocal type of the world of knowing and constructs its whole philosophy of knowing with reference to that chosen type. Not only does it thus systematically neglect vast areas of knowledge but it also tends to reduce the diversities of the life of the mind to a noetic monism, more sterile, no doubt, and less excusable than the ontological monism of the first philosophers. (For, after all, the mind knows itself; and what excuse can idealism offer when it deceives itself about the very structures of thought?)

In retaliation, many realists seem disposed to abandon the problems proper to the mind as the price they pay for the possession of things. And we are witnessing today a new "cultural"
" dogmatic identifying the anti-idealism of which it makes profession with dialectical materialism.

We hope to show in this book that Thomistic realism, in preserving, according to a truly critical method, the value of the knowledge of things, opens the way to an exploration of the world of reflection in its very inwardness and to the establishment of its metaphysical topology, so to speak; thus, "philosophy of being" is at once, and *par excellence*, "philosophy of mind."

The mind, even more so than the physical world and bodily organisms, possesses its own dimensions, its structure and internal hierarchy of causalities and values—immaterial though they be. Contemporary idealism, in the last analysis, refuses to recognize that mind has any nature or any structure. It sees it only as a pure movement, a pure freedom. Hence, it never really gets beyond spreading it out, whole and entire, upon a single plane of intellection, like a two-dimensional world, infinitely flat. One is, however, justified in thinking that the four dimensions of which St. Paul speaks *"quae sit latitudo et longitudo et sublimitas et profundum,"* (Eph. 3. 18) belong not only to the sphere (or super-sphere) of the contemplation of the saint, but, generally, to the fundamental organization and structure of the things of the mind, both in the natural and in the supernatural order.

From the noetic point of view which we have adopted, let us say that

---

1   The French title of this book is *Distinguer pour unir, ou Les Degrés du Savoir* (tr.).

"length" symbolizes for us the manner in which the formal light that characterizes a particular type of knowing falls upon things and defines in them a
certain line of intelligibility; to "breadth" corresponds the ever-increasing
number of objects thus known; to "height" corresponds the difference of level
created among different sorts of knowing by the degrees of intelligibility and
immateriality of the object and from which there follows for each difference
of level an original and typical mode of procedure; as to the fourth dimension,
"depth," it represents, in our view, those more hidden diversities which
depend upon the manner in which the mind, in its freedom, still further
diversifies its objects and its ways of conforming to the real, according to its
own proper finalities. The difference between speculative and practical philosophy offers the simplest example of such diversities, but it is not the only
one.

However, it is important to bring to light not only the structure, but also the
movement and *élan* of the mind, as well as that admirable law of unsatisfac-
toriness, even in the security of acquired certitudes, in virtue of which the
mind, starting with sense experience, enlarges, heightens and transforms its
own life step by step by involving itself in diverse worlds of knowledge,
heterogeneous, indeed, yet solidary, and by bearing witness that to tend
towards infinite amplitude is, for an immaterial life, to tend towards an infinite
object, an infinite reality which it must needs, in some way, possess. We have
endeavored to point out in this book the principal reasons and modalities of
this movement and of those phases through which it passes.

It is easy to see why this work must explore the most varied domains. After
a sort of general introduction dealing with the question of the Majesty and
Misery of Metaphysics, the first problems to be treated will be those of the
experimental sciences, and the degree of knowing which they represent.
Before pressing on, it is necessary to turn our attention to knowledge itself and
as such, and to establish (Ch. III) the principles of a philosophy of the intellect;
there we shall cross the threshold of critical metaphysics and thenceforth keep
to that point of view. The two following chapters will deal with the philosophy
of nature considered notably in its relations with the sciences, particularly
physics, and with metaphysical knowledge, especially in its noetic structure
and in its relations to negative theology. When we come to knowledge by faith
and the "superanalogy" proper to it, we shall rise to the super-rational degrees
of knowing, whose highest form is mystical experience. Chapter VI is devoted
to problems concerning mystical experience and Chapters VII and VIII consider two eminent cases involving what we have called above the "depth" of
the things of the mind. Therein we shall inquire first, what is the nature of
Augustinian wisdom? And then, what are the distinctive features and the
proper perspective of the "practico-practical" science of contemplation such
as it is found in a St. John of the Cross? The last chapter forms the conclusion
of the whole work. It deals with the doctrine of the "All and Nothing,"

expounded by the same mystical Doctor, St. John of the Cross, and with the highest degree of knowledge and wisdom accessible to man in this life.

We have purposely run through so vast a range of problems and sketched a synthesis (starting with the experience of the physicist and ending with the experience of the contemplative), the philosophical stability of which is guaranteed by the rational certitudes of metaphysics and critique. Only thus could we show the organic diversity and the essential compatibility of those zones of knowledge through which the mind passes in its great movement in quest of being, to which each one of us can contribute only tiny fragments, and that at the risk of misunderstanding the activity of comrades devoted to other enterprises equally fragmentary, the total unity of which, however, reconciles in the mind of the philosopher, almost in spite of themselves, brothers-in-arms who knew not one another. From this point of view it may also be said that the work which metaphysics is called upon to do today is to put an end to that kind of incompatibility of temper which the humanism of the classical age had created between science and wisdom.

Some there are who will reproach us, no doubt, for not remaining throughout on the plane of pure philosophy and for having taken into account, in the second part of the present book, certitudes that depend upon lights of another order. We shall do nothing to turn aside that sort of reproach since we are convinced, in fact, that when a philosopher adopts as the object of his study, something which impinges upon the existential conditions of man and his activity as a free person—and that is just what happens when he studies those degrees of knowledge which are themselves beyond philosophy and imply, in their very essence, a personal relation of the knowing subject with his final end—he can proceed scientifically only if he respects the integrity of his object and, consequently, the integrity of those realities of the supernatural order which are, as a matter of fact, implied in it. We have explained our views on this point in an essay on the notion of Christian philosophy.[2] No philosophical pretension can do away with the fact that man does not exist in the state of pure nature but in the state of fallen and redeemed nature. The first obligation of the philosopher is to recognize what is. And if, in some cases, he can only do so by adhering by faith to the First Truth—which though it be reasonable to do so, is nevertheless due to a grace which transcends reason—he is still a philosopher (though not purely a philosopher) when he uses this very adherence to discern and examine the essential characteristics and the explicative reasons of what lies before his eyes. Then, although he borrows higher lights which he combines with those of reason, he carries through according to his own proper mode of procedure—not as a theologian but as a philosopher—analyzing his data in order to rise to their ontological principles and integrat-

---

2   *Revue Néo-Scolastique de philosophie*, Louvain, May 1932, pp. 178–180. See our book *On Christian Philosophy* [in Volume IV of the Notre Dame edition]. As I have pointed out in an appendix to this little book, moral philosophy *adequately understood* is necessarily *subordinate* to theology.

ing within his investigation of causes, points of information which he gets from the theologian, just as, on other occasions, he likewise integrates points of information that he gets from the biologist or the physicist.

Whenever an unbeliever who reads these pages finds that he cannot grant the truth of the principles of solution which we have assumed, he can at least understand the methodological reasons which make it necessary to have recourse to those principles, and can judge from the outside, as it were, the logical structure of the whole which is presented to him. Moreover, many parts of this whole—to wit, all that deals with the degrees of rational knowing—rely on reason alone. And the doctrines of science which are here proposed, notably those which concern the physico-mathematical knowledge of nature, the philosophy of nature, the divine names and the rational knowledge of God, although they do not constitute the loftiest parts of that edifice, are yet its central parts, just as the doctrine of critical realism is its foundation.

Let it be added that this work has not been conceived as a didactic treatise but rather as a meditation on certain themes linked together in a continuous movement. That is why certain degrees of knowing of major importance in themselves, such as mathematical knowledge and theological knowledge, have not been made the object of a special chapter, although we have not, therefore, refrained from considering and characterizing them. A special study, alien to the philosophical purpose we aim to pursue in this work, would be required for each of them. As far as the foundations of mathematics in particular are concerned, we are of the opinion that many preliminary studies are needed before Thomistic philosophy is in a position to propose a systematic interpretation in which all the critical problems raised by modern developments of the mathematical sciences may find solution. Nevertheless, we have tried on several occasions (Chs. II, IV, V) to give precision in this connection to a certain number of doctrinal points which appear to us to be of particular importance and which already indicate quite definitely, in what spirit, it seems to us, a philosophy of mathematics should be elaborated.

Those who agree to read these pages attentively will, perhaps, notice that while we rigorously maintain the formal line of Thomistic metaphysics, rejecting any sort of compromise or watering-down designed to render Thomism acceptable to irrational prejudices, we have tried to clear the ground on several points and to push back the frontiers of the Thomistic synthesis. The drawback that haunts works of this sort, in which many indications and allurements clamor to be taken up again and followed through, is that they demand, in order to be fruitful, a spirit of collaboration and a philosophical continuity which it is generally futile to count on. Be that as it may, these works abide within the spiritual tradition of Thomism, which is an essentially progressive and assimilative doctrine. (Does it not offer us singular proof of its irrepressible vitality in having resisted for centuries, and in always resisting, the treatment it gets at the hands of a pedagogy bent upon short-changing it?)

Incomparably coherent, closely knit together in all its parts, Thomism is, nevertheless, not what is called a "system." When it is said that Thomism is distinguished from all other philosophical doctrines by its universalism, that should not be understood as a mere difference of extent but, on the contrary, as a difference of nature. The word "system" evokes the idea of a mechanical linking-up, or, at the very least, of a quasi-spatial assemblage of parts and, consequently, of a personal, if not arbitrary, choice of elements, as is the case in all artistic constructions. A system unfolds or travels along bit by bit, starting with its initial elements. On the contrary, it is essential to Thomism that it require whatever has to do with its construction or its "machinery" to be rigorously subordinated to what belongs to the immanent activity and the vital movement of intellection: it is not a system, an artifact; it is a spiritual organism. Its inner connections are vital ties where each part exists by the existence of the whole. The principal parts are not initial parts but, rather, dominant parts or central parts, each one of which is already, virtually, the whole.[3] Thought makes no personal choice therein among the elements of the real, it is infinitely open to all of them.

In truth, Thomism is a common task. One is not a Thomist because, in the emporium of systems, one chooses it as if one were choosing one system among others just as you try one pair of shoes after another in a shoestore until you find a pattern that fits your foot better. If that were the way it was done, it would be more stimulating to cut a system to one's own measure. One is a Thomist because one has repudiated every attempt to find philosophical truth in any system fabricated by an individual (even though that individual be called *ego*) and because one wants to seek out what is true—for oneself, indeed, and by one's own reason—by allowing oneself to be taught by the whole range of human thought, in order not to neglect anything of that which is. Aristotle

---

3   Such, for example, are the *tria principia* on which the Dominican Reginald in the seventeenth century wrote a remarkable book (left unfinished, however): *ens est transcendens; Deus solus est actus purus; absoluta specificantur a se, relativa ab alio.* These three principles embrace the whole of Thomism; but the whole of Thomism is needed to understand them. So Reginald's work, with its inevitable didactic fragmentation, is, in respect to the doctrine it expounds, nothing more than an anatomical chart in respect to the living organism. It is doubtless the same for every great philosophical doctrine. Not one of them is a system, an artifact; thought tends of its very nature to be organic and living. But in all of them the price they pay for unity and coherence is that the "system" aspect prevails over the "living organism" aspect. And, what appears to us to be most remarkable in Thomism, what, in our opinion, should be regarded as its privilege, is that while it is sovereignly one and linked together in its parts, the character of organism prevails, on the contrary, over its systematic aspect. Thence it results that nowhere else is the difference between the doctrine itself and the didactic exposition of it so deep and so marked.

and St. Thomas occupy a privileged place for us only because, thanks to their supreme docility to the lessons of the real, we find in them the principles and the scale of values through which the total effort of this universal thought can be preserved without running the risk of eclecticism and confusion.

Can those philosophers, for whom the category of the obsolete is a metaphysical criterion and for whom thought is in duty bound to grow old by forgetting, understand that when we consult the ancients, we do so because we want to hark back to a freshness of vision that is lost today? No treasuring up of experience, none of the advantages, none of the graces of thought's advancing age can possibly replace the youth, the virginity of observation, the intuitive upsurge of intellect, as yet unwearied, towards the delicious novelty of the real.

Distinguishing, as they do, between the *per se* and the *per accidens*, Thomists hold that the progress of philosophy goes forward not only in the bosom of the doctrine they regard as well-founded, but also, by accident, through the proliferation of all the ill-founded systems whose less solid underpinning permits them to precipitate themselves more rapidly—but to perish in the effort!—upon the new aspects of truth which the surge of time discloses.

Yet, after all, it is surely necessary that that which so progresses have some sort of nature at least, like becoming, movement, potency; there needs must be a philosophy, virtual and flowing perhaps, and incapable of being grasped in its integrity at any given moment of its progress, since at each moment it overlaps opposed formulations and hostile systems, a philosophy carried along by that measure of truth which they all possess.

Is philosophy no more than that? Does it know nothing but that state of virtuality? If a doctrinal organism, wholly assured on the basis of true principles, should by good luck happen to exist among men, it will sooner or later incorporate into itself, and realize within itself, that virtual philosophy, which will thereby and to that extent become seizable and demonstrable, formed and organically articulated. It is thus, we feel, that Thomism is destined in the course of its progress to actualize the progress of philosophy.

June 11, 1932.

POSTSCRIPT TO THE SECOND EDITION

THE TEXT OF THE SECOND EDITION conforms with that of the first in practically every detail. A few alterations and additions have been made in the notes. These have been put in brackets to set them off, typographically, from the rest.

Certain works published since the first edition have been referred to in footnotes in the appropriate contexts.

In order to forestall a possible misunderstanding with regard to Chapters II and IV, we think that it is, perhaps, useful to underline the fact that in alluding to the new physics, we consistently adopt the point of view of the philosophical and critical problems which constitute the object of this book. Had we adopted the point of view of the history of the sciences, and had we sought to characterize the development of contemporary physical theories from that point of view, we should have had to emphasize the name of Planck and Quantum Physics more strongly than the name of Einstein and Relativity Physics.

There is good reason to think that although Einstein went beyond and renewed the Newtonian classical physics, he nevertheless remained (as did Lorenz and Poincaré, before him) in the same curve,[1] so that the relativistic revolution is, in respect to the development of physics, less radical and essentially less an innovation than Planck's discovery of the irradiation of quanta. It was in leaving the macroscopic point of view to enter into the quantum-world of the atom that the new physics broke away most decidedly from the old physics and mechanics. Whence the exceptional importance of the theories of Louis de Broglie, Schroedinger and Heisenberg.

But our concern has been to consider the new physics only in relation to our critical researches concerning the proper noetic structure of the physico-mathematical knowledge of nature, and the relations and distinctions that need to be pointed out between that knowledge and the philosophy of nature. Moreover, we had to attach particular importance to Relativity Physics because it called into question the validity of certain conceptions which, in a different context, play a fundamental role in the philosophy of nature—for

---

1   "The theory of relativity constitutes, on the whole, the crowning of the old macroscopic physics, while, on the contrary, the Quantum Theory arose out of the study of the corpuscular and atomic world." (Louis de Broglie, "Relativité et Quanta," *Revue de Métaphysique et Morale*, July–September, 1933). In these few very suggestive pages M. Louis de Broglie recalls how the Theory of Relativity and the Quantum Theory had to confront each other as a result of their having grown up almost independently, and he points out some of the difficulties that arise in trying to reconcile them. The philosopher will keep in mind with particular interest his remarks concerning the necessity in which the physicist finds himself of recognizing "the existence of a privileged direction for the variable, time, and the persistence of physical units in time"; whence there follows, even in *non-quantum relativity*, a certain asymmetry between time and space.

instance the notion of space and the notion of time— and because it opened the door to a serious and facile confusion between the two disciplines.

May 1, 1934.

POSTSCRIPT TO THE THIRD EDITION

SINCE THE SECOND EDITION of this book appeared, M. Etienne Gilson has explained and confirmed his positions in a book that is at all points remarkable, *Réalisme thomiste et critique de la connaissance* (Paris, Vrin, 1939), and in which the dangers of Cartesian-Thomism and Kantian-Thomism are laid bare with implacable lucidity and in which the author's own thought is set forth with the most felicitous precision and shading. Between M. Et. Gilson's position and ours there is no substantial difference. Nevertheless, we maintain that the expression "criticial realism" is a well-founded expression; for if "in such a case, the word *'critical'* means nothing more than *'philosophical,'"* it still characterizes in a very exact fashion a special function of first philosophy, to wit, to judge itself and to judge its own proper principles.

Two other books by the same author, *Christianisme et philosophie* (Paris, Vrin)[2] and *The Unity of Philosophical Experience* (New York, Scribners, 1937), provide a precious contribution to the study of some of the problems dealt with in the present work.

On the question of "Christian Philosophy," and particularly practical philosophy in its relations to theology, clarifications and more precise statements as well as answers to some objections are to be found in our *Science et sagesse* (Paris, Labergerie, 1935).[3]

Our *Quatre essais sur l'esprit dans sa condition charnelle* (Paris, Desclée de Brouwer et Cie, 1939) are in certain respects a supplement to *The Degrees of Knowledge*. In particular, the third Essay completes Chapter VI and the fourth completes Chapter IV of the present work.

July 25, 1939.

---

2   [*Christianity and Philosophy*, translated by Ralph MacDonald, New York, Sheed and Ward, 1939 (Tr.)]

3   [*Science and Wisdom*, translated by Bernard Wall, New York, Scribners, 1940. (Tr.)]

FOREWORD

IT IS WITH PARTICULAR PLEASURE that I am writing this Foreword. For a number of years I have been yearning for a new translation of *Les Degrés du Savoir*, and now my dream has been realized. To tell the truth, the former translation was quite unsatisfactory, marred as it was by a great many misinterpretations and oversights. Moreover, all the Appendices (Annexes), which are an integral part of the book, were lacking. Today we have a genuine translation performed with competent scholarship and a constant concern for accuracy—and which includes all the Appendixes.[1] This was a difficult, long and exacting task. Its accomplishment could be the fruit only of deep intellectual understanding and friendship. I should like to express my warmest thanks to the translators, who are all doctors of philosophy from the University of Toronto, and with all of whom I am, moreover, on familiar terms—they were among my best students at the Pontifical Institute of Mediaeval Studies in Toronto: the Reverend Ralph MacDonald, C.S.B., Dr. Lawrence E. Lynch, both professors at St. Michael's College; Mrs. Lawrence E. Lynch and Mrs. Alfred Byrne.

I am happy to extend my very special gratitude to the captain of the team, Dr. Gerald B. Phelan, who directed, supervised and revised the whole work. I deeply appreciate the great testimony he bore to our long and affectionate collaboration in spending thus so much of his time for my book's sake, and allowing this new translation to profit not only by his mastery of the subject matter but also by his mastery of the French and English languages. I avail myself of the present opportunity to pay my tribute of loving gratitude to this incomparable friend. When I first came to this continent, some twenty-five years ago, it was because, in his capacity as President of the Institute of Mediaeval Studies, he had invited me to give a series of lectures. I was immediately captivated by the eminent qualities of his mind and the charity of his heart and by the way in which were united in him love for truth and philosophical wisdom, in all their objectivity, and evangelic love of one's neighbor. This was the beginning of an intellectual fellowship which has been especially dear to me. And from that time on, I cannot count the proofs of steadfast support and generous cooperation I have received from him. The last, and not the least, is the present translation.

About this translation I have a few particulars to point out. It was made from the fourth French edition, 1946, which was subsequently reprinted but not changed. It has been collated with the former translation throughout the whole work (with, of course, the exception of the Appendices, none of which appeared in the former translation) and with the English translation of the chapter on Augustinian wisdom, which appeared, with some changes, in *The Monument to St. Augustine* (London, Sheed and Ward, 1930, pp. 197–223) and

---

1   I availed myself of this new edition to insert in it a completely new redaction of Appendix IV (on the notion of Subsistence).

which was revised where necessary. Quotations in the text as well as in the notes have been made from either the original English works (e.g., Eddington), or from English translations of the French, German or Spanish works quoted in the original, wherever these were available. This applies especially to Allison Peers' translations of St. John of the Cross and St. Teresa. With one exception (in the chapter on Augustinian wisdom), no references have been given to subsequent writings of the author on the subjects dealt with in this work.

I think it is relevant to add a few words about the guiding rules adopted from the very start for the work of translation, and which I note here on the basis of conversations with Dr. Phelan. Careful attention has been paid to English style and diction; but, on principle, elegance has sometimes had to yield to clearness; idiomatic English has been sacrificed wherever vagueness of language would spoil clarity of thought; and preoccupation with the meaning and sense of the text has predominated over considerations of rhetoric. Furthermore (and here I must make amends for my fondness for parenthetical incidental clauses and carefully articulated but interminable sentences), periodic sentences have frequently been broken up into shorter ones for a less complex English form.

A last remark concerns more important points, relating to the content of the book. First, on the matter of quotations, I used, in writing my book, the rather off-hand manner which is customary among French authors, so that no uniform method of citing authors or quoting texts was followed in the original. An improvement in this regard would doubtless be desirable, but would have considerably delayed publication, and was surely not necessary. No uniform method, therefore, has been introduced into this translation. In each case, however, the reference to an author or to a work, or the source from which a quotation is taken, is amply clear.

Secondly, it would perhaps also have been desirable to take into account, or to submit to critical examination, the various studies dealing with the diverse subjects treated in the book which have appeared since its publication, and especially since the fourth French edition. Yet, here again, considerable delays would have been involved. A philosophical work, moreover, must stand the changing scene which develops around it, and does not need to be recast every season. So no attempt has been made to bring references to relevant studies up to date (1957). Literature on the subjects treated, subsequent to 1946, has not been referred to.

I could not finish this foreword without acknowledging my indebtedness to Mr. Scribner, and especially to Mr. William Savage, for their great kindness and courtesy in deciding to undertake the heavy task of having a new translation made of so voluminous a book, and of publishing it with such care. I extend to them my most sincere thanks.

Jacques Maritain.

July, 1958. Princeton, New Jersey.

INTRODUCTION

JACQUES MARITAIN WAS FIFTY YEARS OLD in 1932 when he published *Distinguer pour unir, ou Les degrés du savoir*, the book that in English is known by the subtitle of the original. It is universally recognized as Maritain's *chef d'oeuvre*. When it appeared, it was regarded as the culmination of its author's career. Few would have guessed then that he had more than forty more years to live, during which he would publish thirty-odd more books. Despite the size and extent of his *oeuvre*, the *Degrees* remains both his major achievement and a convenient summary of his thought.

Maritain's first publication, an article, appeared in 1910 and his first book in 1913. On the face of it, there does not appear to be any focus in his early work. He wrote on scientific method, on the philosophy of Henri Bergson which had so influenced him and Raissa, he wrote *Theonas*, *Antimodern*, and, certainly one of his most influential works, *Art and Scholasticism*. It is this last work that makes crystal clear what Maritain was about, what the commanding inspiration of his work was.

A convert to Catholicism who had studied philosophy at the Sorbonne (and followed Bergson's lectures at the College de France), Maritain did not immediately connect his faith and his philosophy, save perhaps negatively. As a Catholic, he knew he could not be an unequivocal cheerleader for the times. But it was only when he began to study St. Thomas Aquinas that he found his proper line.

The Angelic Doctor, published the same year as the *Degrees*, makes clear that Maritain took with utmost personal seriousness the Church's recommendation of Thomas Aquinas as our principal mentor in philosophy and in theology. In 1919, Jacques and Raissa formed the Thomist Circle, a group of fluctuating membership which met in their home, first in Versailles, then in Meudon, and which sponsored retreats as well. In his *Notebook*, Maritain devotes a chapter to the Thomist Study Circle and includes in an appendix its constitution. The little book he co-authored with Raissa, *Prayer and Intelligence* (*La vie d'oraison*), develops the theme of the interdependence of the spiritual and intellectual lives. Philosophy was not a career for Jacques Maritain, it was not a profession, it was a vocation, his way of salvation. The influence that he had on generations of Catholic scholars, artists, writers cannot be understood apart from this fact. Raissa's memoirs, written during their war-time exile in New York, conveyed to American readers what an authentically Catholic intellectual was like.

From Thomas Aquinas, Maritain adopted the classical conception of philosophy, not as a discipline among others, but as a name for all the disciplines acquirable by natural powers in the quest for wisdom. How was it possible, in the twentieth century, to adopt such a view? The whole intellectual *zeitgeist* was in conflict with it.

The realism of Aristotle and Thomas Aquinas had been rejected by the Father of Modern Philosophy, René Descartes, and its definitive alternative set forth by Immanuel Kant.

The idea that the philosophy of nature, a science of the natural world different from experimental science, could be maintained in our day seemed risible.

That the dream of wisdom, a science of being as being, metaphysics, could still be entertained seemed archaic in a Kantian world.

Maritain's belief that philosophy, far from calling into question the intellectual respectability of religious faith, was both compatible with the faith and an important means of defending it seemed a medieval throwback to many of his contemporaries.

That there is a wisdom beyond metaphysics, beyond theology, the gift of the Holy Ghost, was not a common theme even among Thomists.

In *The Degrees of Knowledge*, Jacques Maritain provides a panorama of human intellectual activity, first distinguishing philosophy of nature and experimental science, making clear the distinctiveness of metaphysics, writing with authority of the mystical life as different from all of the above, and, in the very course of making these distinctions, showing how they are hierarchically related and united. It is a magnificent and sapiential achievement. It has rightly been called Maritain's *Summa*.

Leo XIII's *Aeterni Patris*, issued in 1879, was addressed to the intellectual world in which Maritain was to work. The encyclical was not an invitation to retreat from contemporary reality into a medieval nostalgia. The Christian philosophy that had been developed within the ambience of the faith over the centuries was to be regained with an eye to the intellectual confusions of the time. No Christian could accept the view that the truths men can gain about themselves and the world are in conflict with the truths God has revealed. Thomas Aquinas is the paramount example of a Christian thinker who in his own day, in a time of crisis, went about showing the compatibility of faith and reason and the way in which they mutually help one another. Leo wanted Catholic thinkers to replicate in our times the achievement of Thomas Aquinas in the thirteenth century. Jacques Maritain's long life was a response to that challenge. *The Degrees of Knowledge*, better than any other single work of Maritain, displays the comprehensiveness and range of his interests. Its author takes his inspiration from Thomas Aquinas, reargues his basic positions in the light of the problems posed for them in the twentieth century, and ends by writing a profoundly original work.

If the *Degrees* represents twentieth-century Thomism at its best, this is not to say that it did not have its critics. Samuel Johnson said the Irish are an honest race because they never speak well of one another. This is a libelous remark, of course, if taken literally, but as a joke it has its point. One might apply it, *mutatis mutandis*, to followers of St. Thomas. To single out merely one issue:

Maritain's argument for critical realism ran afoul of Etienne Gilson's attack on the Louvain school's defense of critical realism.

Of course, Gilson agreed with Maritain that our mind's ability to know reality is a fundamental assumption of Thomism. But Gilson felt that a defended realism in the manner of "critical" realism suggested that the mind's ability to grasp the real had to be shown. The reader can judge Maritain's response to this concern. Typically, he sees merit in what Gilson says but uses the criticism to make a more forceful statement of his own position. Noel, Gilson's target, reviewing the *Degrees* in the *Bulletin thomiste*, unsurprisingly devotes much attention to this controversy.

Maritain's teaching on the relation between philosophy of nature and experimental science, surely one of the most carefully worked out of the Thomist solutions, was not thought adequate by Charles DeKoninck of Laval or by the River Forest Dominicans. But DeKoninck had begun by maintaining a version of Maritain's view, and all who dealt with this issue owed a lasting debt to Maritain.

It would not be too much to say that twentieth-century Thomists, both European and North American, have measured their grasp of the common master against Maritain's interpretations. Many have found themselves in agreement with him on all or most major points of contention; some have reluctantly parted ways with him. But whether ally or opponent, Jacques Maritain was acknowledged to be one of the two or three foremost leaders of the Thomistic revival. Widely respected prior to its publication, he secured that reputation once and for all with *The Degrees of Knowledge*.

This Notre Dame edition reproduces the translation which was supervised by Gerald B. Phelan and published by Charles Scribner and Son in 1959. A very few changes have been made, and those chiefly of obvious typographical errors. The French edition consulted was that in Jacques et Raissa Maritain, *Oeuvres Complètes*, Vol. IV, Editions Universitaires, Fribourg, Suisse, 1983.

Ralph McInerny, Director
The Jacques Maritain Center
University of Notre Dame

MARITAIN CHRONOLOGY

1882

November 18, Birth in Paris, son of Paul Maritain and Genevieve Favre.

1883

September 12, Birth of Raïssa Oumansov in Rostov-on-the-Don.

1893

The Oumansov family arrives in Paris.

1898–1899

Jacques studies rhetoric at Lycée Henri IV and meets Ernest Psichari.

1900

Jacques meets fellow student Raïssa Oumansov at Sorbonne

1901

Jacques meets Charles Peguy
Peguy, in the winter of 1901–1902, prompts Raïssa and Jacques to take
Henri Bergson's course at the Collège de France

1902

Jacques and Raïssa engage to marry.

1904

November 26, Jacques and Raïssa marry.
They come upon the writings of Leon Bloy.

1905

June 25, first visit to Bloy.
Jacques passes *agrégation* in philosophy.

1906

June 11, Jacques and Raïssa (and Vera Oumansov) baptized in the church
of St. John the Evangelist in Paris.
August 25, Jacques and Raïssa leave for Heidelberg, where they will
spend two years studying biology. Raïssa's sister Vera comes to live with
them and remains for the rest of her life.

1907
September 8, Encyclical *Pascendi* deals with Modernism.

1908
June, returns to France.
September, Peguy regains his faith.
The Maritains acquire P. Clerissac as their spiritual director.
Jacques's employment consists in work on Orthographic Dictionary.

1909
October, Maritains take up residence in Versailles, where they will remain until 1923.

1910
June, "Reason and Modern Science," Jacques' first published article appears in the *Revue de Philosophie*.
September 15, Jacques begins to read the *Summa theologiae* and is enthralled.

1912
Jacques becomes professor of philosophy at the Lycée Stanislas.

1913
February 13, conversion of Ernest Psichari.
October, Jacques's first book *Bergsonian Philosophy* is published.

1914
June, Jacques named adjunct professor of the History of Modern Philosophy at the Institut Catholique.
August 2, outbreak of World War I.
August 22, death of Ernest Psichari.
September 5, death of Charles Peguy.
November 15, death of Pere Clerissac.

1917
Jacques called up, spends brief time at Camp Satory, is not kept.
November 3, death of Leon Bloy.
March 26–April 8, first visit to Rome; audiences with Benedict XV and with Cardinal Billot on the subject of the apparitions at La Salette.

1918
Becomes joint heir, with Charles Maurras, of Pierre Villard. Takes 1918–1919 year off to work on first volumes of a projected Manual of Philosophy.

1919

Associated with new *Revue Universelle*, in charge of philosophy; contributes many articles at first, tapers off and stops in July 1926.
The Thomist Circle meetings begin.

1920

Art and Scholasticism published.

1921

Theonas published.

1922

Jacques and Raïssa privately print *Prayer and Intelligence (La vie d'oraison)*.
July 20, first meeting with Charles Journet in Switzerland.
October 4, Reginald Garrigou-Lagrange preaches the first retreat of the Thomist Circle at Versailles.
Antimodern published.

1923

June 5, Jacques and Raïssa installed at 10 rue de Parc, Meudon, where they will live until the outbreak of World War II.
September 26–30, second retreat of Thomist Circle, at Meudon. These will be held every year except 1936 that the Maritains are in residence in Meudon.
December 14, Jacques tries to persuade André Gide not to publish Gide's homosexual work *Corydon*.

1924

Réflexions sur l'intelligence et sur sa vie propre published.

1926

Published exchange of letters with Jean Cocteau, who had regained his faith at Meudon.
Meets Olivier Lacombe and Julien Green.
December 20, Action Française condemned by Pius XI after several months of discussion with Charles Maurras in which Maritain and Garrigou-Lagrange took part.

1927

Primauté de spirituel published.
Charles de Bos converted. (Eventually would teach for a few years at Notre Dame.)
Jacques Maritain called to Rome by Pius XI.

1927 (cont'd)

Pourquoi Rome a parlé published with essays by Maritain and others on the condemnation of Action Française.

1928

Peter Wust, German Catholic philosopher, visits Meudon.
Emmanuel Mounier becomes regular participant at Meudon.
Jacques's chair changed from History of Modern Philosophy to that of Logic and Cosmology.

1929–1930

Maritain on leave while he writes *Distinguer pour unir, ou Les degrés du savoir.*
The Angelic Doctor and *Religion and Culture* published.

1931

March 21, meeting of the Société française de Philosophie on the topic of Christian Philosophy. Brehier, Gilson,and Maritain among participants.

1932

Le songe de Descartes published.
Distinguer pour unir published.
De la philosophie chrétienne published.

1933

First visit to Toronto and Chicago.
Du régime temporel et de la liberté published.
Sept leçons sur l'être published.

1934

Pour le bien commun manifesto.

1935

Frontières de la poésie published.
Science et Sagesse published.
La philosophie de la nature published.
Maritain writes "Pour la justice et pour la paix," prompted by Mussolini's invasion of Ethiopia.
Lettre sur l'indépendance published.

1936

Humanisme Intégral published.
Jacques and Raïssa visit Argentina (July 26–November 7).

1938

October 1, departs for United States, returns at Christmas.
Questions de conscience published.
Situation de la poésie, written in collaboration with Raïssa, published.

1939

La Crépuscule de la civilisation published.
Quatre essais sur l'esprit dans sa condition charnelle published.
August 5, death of Charles de Bos.
September 3, declaration of war.

1940

With Raïssa and Vera, leaves for America. Spends January and February
in Toronto, in March move to New York. After the fall of France and the
formation of the Vichy government, decides to remain in U.S. In September, Maritains installed at 30 Fifth Avenue.

1941

January 4, death of Bergson.
A travers le désastre published.
Confession de foi published.
La pensée de saint Paul published.
First volume of Raïssa's *Grandes Amitiés* published.

1942

Les Droits de l'Homme et la loi naturelle published.

1943

The Thomist devotes a jumbo issue to Maritain.
Christianisme et Démocratie published.
Education at the Crossroads published.

1944

Principes d'une politique humaniste published.
De Bergson à Thomas d'Aquin published.
June 6, Normandy beachhead established.
September, *A travers la victoire.*
November 10, return to France, appointed French ambassador to the
Vatican.

1945

Second volume of *Grandes Amitiés* published.
April 1, departure for Rome.

1947

Court Traité de l'existence et de l'existant, La personne et le bien commun published.
November 6, Maritain president of French delegation to UNESCO conference in Mexico.
Resigns as ambassador to accept appointment at Princeton.

1948

Raison et raisons published.
June 27, arrives in New York.
August 19, arrives in Princeton.

1949

La signification de l'athéisme contemporain published.
Revue thomiste devotes a number to the work of Maritain.
June 4, death of Maurice Blondel.
Buys 26 Linden Lane, Princeton, where he will live until 1960 and bequeath to the University of Notre Dame.

1951

Man and the State published.
Neuf leçons sur les notions premières de la philosophie morale published.

1952

June, retires from Princeton University.

1953

Creative Intuition in Art and Poetry published.
Approches de Dieu published.

1954

Suffers coronary thrombosis in March. Begins *Carnet de notes*.
February, death of Paul Claudel.

1957

Reflections on America published.
Founding of the Jacques Maritain Center at the University of Notre Dame.

1959

Liturgie et contemplation, written in collaboration with Raïssa, published.
December 31, death of Vera.

1960

Le Philosophe dans la Cité published.

The Maritains return to France, where the ailing Raïssa dies July 7 in Paris. She is buried at Kolbsheim.

La Philosophie morale published.

1961

Visits U.S. in January, in March installs himself at Toulouse near the Little Brothers of Jesus. In autumn, again visits U.S.

1962

October 11, opening of first session of Vatican II.

1963

June, death of Pope John XXIII and election of Paul VI.

1965

February, *Carnet de notes* published.

September, visits Paul VI at Castel Gandolfo.

December 8, close of Vatican II. The Pope presents Maritain with a message addressed to intellectuals.

1966

Autumn, last trip to the U.S.

November 3, *Le Paysan de la Garonne* published.

1967

De la grâce et l'humanité de Jesus published.

1970

De l'Eglise du Christ published.

October 15, Maritain dons the habit of the Little Brothers of Jesus at Toulouse and in 1971 takes his vows.

1973

April 28, death of Jacques Maritain at Toulouse. On May 2, he is buried at Kolbsheim with Raïssa.

CHAPTER I

THE MAJESTY AND POVERTY OF METAPHYSICS

To Charles Du Bos

1. IN PERIODS WHEN SHALLOW speculation is rife, one might think that metaphysics would shine forth, at least, by the brilliance of its modest reserve. But the very age that is unaware of the majesty of metaphysics, likewise overlooks its poverty. Its majesty? It is wisdom. Its poverty? It is human science. It names God, Yes! But not by His Own Name. For it is not possible to paint a picture of God as it is to draw a tree or a conic section. You, True God, the Savior of Israel, are veritably a hidden God! When Jacob asked the angel early in the morning: "Tell me, what is your name?" (Gen. xxxii, 29), He replied: "Why do you ask My Name?" "It is impossible to utter this truly wondrous name, the name that is set above every name that is named either in the present world or in the world to come."[1]

2. A deep vice besets the philosophers of our day, whether they be neo-Kantians, neo-positivists, idealists, Bergsonians, logisticians, pragmatists, neo-Spinozists, or neo-mystics. It is the ancient error of the *nominalists*. In different forms, and with various degrees of awareness, they all blame knowledge-through-concepts for not being a supra-sensible intuition of the existing singular, as is Spinoza's *scientia intuitiva*, Boehme's theosophic vision, or that of Swedenborg, which Kant so regretfully denounced as illusory. They cannot forgive that knowledge for not opening directly upon existence as sensation does, but only onto essences, possibles. They cannot forgive it for its inability to reach actual existence except by turning back upon sense. They have a basic misunderstanding of the value of the abstract, that immateriality which is more enduring than things for all that it is untouchable and unimaginable, that immateriality which mind seeks out in the very heart of things. But why this incurable nominalism? The reason is that while having a taste for the real indeed, they nevertheless have no sense of being. Being as such, loosed from the matter in which it is incorporated, being, with its pure objective necessities and its laws that prove no burden, its restraints which do not bind, its invisible evidence, is for them only a word.

How is it possible to speculate about geometry in space if figures are not

---

1   Denys, *On the Divine Names* I, 6, St. Thomas' lect. 3. Cf. St. Paul, Eph. i, 21.

seen in space? How is it possible to discourse on metaphysics if quiddities are not seen in the intelligible? Difficult acrobatics are undoubtedly required of the poet; so, too, are they demanded of the metaphysician. In both cases, however, no venture is possible without a primary gift. A Jesuit friend of mine claims that since the fall of Adam, man has become so ill suited to understanding that the intellectual perception of being must be looked upon as a mystical gift, a supernatural gift granted only to a few privileged persons. That is obviously a pious exaggeration. Yet, it does remain true that this intuition is, as far as we are concerned, an awakening from our dreams, a step quickly taken out of slumber and its starried streams. For man has many sleeps. Every morning, he wakes from animal slumber. He emerges from his human slumber when intelligence is turned loose (and from a sleepy unconsciousness of God when touched by God). There is a sort of grace in the natural order presiding over the birth of a metaphysician just as there is over the birth of a poet. The latter thrusts his heart into things like a dart or rocket and, by divination, sees, within the very sensible itself and inseparable from it, the flash of a spiritual light in which a glimpse of God is revealed to him. The former turns away from the sensible, and through knowledge sees within the intelligible, detached from perishable things, this very spiritual light itself, captured in some conception. The metaphysician breathes an atmosphere of abstraction which is death for the artist. Imagination, the discontinuous, the unverifiable, in which the metaphysician perishes, is life itself to the artist. While both absorb rays that come down from creative Night, the artist finds nourishment in a bound intelligibility which is as multiform as God's reflections upon earth, the metaphysician finds it in a naked intelligibility that is as determined as the proper being of things. They are playing seesaw, each in turn rising up to the sky. Spectators make fun of their game; they sit upon solid ground.

3. "You are," I was once told, "a sort of dispenser of black magic, one who would bid us to fly with our arms." "No! I am asking you to fly with your wings." "But we have only arms." "Arms? No! They are really atrophied wings. And that is quite another matter. They would spring up again if you had but the courage, if you but understood that the Earth is not our sole support, and the air is not the void."

To raise a simple factual impossibility, a certain historical state of intelligence, as an objection against a philosopher's undertaking, and say to him: "Perhaps what you are offering on our market is the truth, but our mental structure has become such that we can no longer think in terms of that truth of yours because our mind 'has changed as well as our body,'"[2] that, as an argument, is strictly null and void. It is, however, the best objection that can be raised against the present revival of metaphysics. True, timeless metaphys-

---

2   Ramon Fernandez, "L'intelligence et M. Maritain," *Nouv. Revue Française*, June 1, 1925.

ics no longer suits the modern intellect. More exactly, the latter no longer squares with the former. Three centuries of empirio-mathematicism have so warped the intellect that it is no longer interested in anything but the invention of apparatus to capture phenomena—conceptual nets that give the mind a certain practical dominion over nature, coupled with a deceptive understanding of it; deceptive, indeed, because its thought is resolved, not in being, but in the sensible itself. By advancing in this fashion, not by linking new truths to already acquired truths, but by substituting new apparatus for outmoded apparatus; by handling things without understanding them; by gaining ground against the real bit by bit, patiently, through victories that are always piecemeal and provisory—by acquiring a secret taste for the matter with which it conspires—thus has the modern intellect developed within this lower order of scientific demiurgy a kind of manifold and marvelously specialized touch as well as wonderful instincts for the chase. But, at the same time, it has wretchedly weakened and disarmed itself in the face of the proper objects of the intellect, which it has abjectly surrendered. It has become quite incapable of appreciating the world of rational evidence except as a system of well-oiled gears. Henceforth, it has to take its stand either against all metaphysics (old-fashioned positivism) or in favor of a pseudo-metaphysics (new-styled positivism). Indeed, intellect must choose one of those counterfeits for metaphysics in which the experimental process stands revealed in its grossest form, among pragmatists and pluralists, in its subtlest guise, in Bergsonian intuition, in its religious habit, in the integral action of the Blondellians and their attempt to suffer all things in a mystical fashion and thereby invade the realms of pure understanding.

That is all very true. The slope of modern intelligence is slanted against us. Well, slopes are made to be climbed. The intellect has not changed its nature; it has acquired habits. Habits can be corrected. Second nature? But the first nature is always there; and the syllogism will last as long as man does. It is less bothersome for the philosopher to be out of intellectual step with his time than it is for the artist. Besides, things happen quite differently in the one case than in the other. The artist pours out his creative spirit into a work; the philosopher measures his knowing-spirit by the real. It is by leaning for support, at first, on the intellect of his age, by concentrating all its languors and fires in a single focal point, and then driving it to the limit, that the artist has the opportunity to refashion the whole mass. But the concern of the philosopher is, above all, to seize upon the object, to cling to it desperately, with such tenacity that a break-through is finally effected in the mass which confronts him, achieving a regrouping of forces and a new course of action.

4. It is also very true that metaphysics is of no use in furthering output of experimental science. Discoveries and inventions in the land of phenomena? It can boast of none; its heuristic value, as they say, is absolutely nil in that area.

From this point of view, there is nothing to be expected of it. There is no tilling of the soil in heaven.

For several thousand years we have known that herein precisely lies the majesty of metaphysics. Old Aristotle said that metaphysics is useless; it is of no service because it is above and beyond all service; useless because super-useful, good in and for itself. Note, then, that if it were to serve the science of phenomena, to assist in its output, it would be vain by definition since it would aim to go beyond such science and yet would not be better than it. Every metaphysics that is not measured by the mystery of what is, but by the state of positive science at such and such an instant, is false from the beginning, whether it be the metaphysics of Descartes, Spinoza or Kant. True metaphysics can, in its own way and in due proportion, also say: My kingdom is not of this world. As for its axioms, it seizes upon them in spite of this world, which strives to hide them from it. What does the world of phenomena say, that false flux of the raw empirical, if not that what is, is not, and that there is more in the effect than in the cause? As for its conclusions, metaphysics contemplates them by ascending from the visible to the invisible; it hangs them from a stable order of intelligible causation found enmeshed, indeed, in this world but none the less transcending it, an order which in no way runs counter to the system of sensible sequences studied by experimental science, yet which remains strictly alien to it. The movement of my pen on paper, hand, imagination and internal senses, will, intellect, the first Agent, without whose impulse no created thing would act—such a series of causes is in no way opposed to, but is, on the other hand, of no assistance in determining, the vasomotor changes or the associations of images at work while I am writing. Metaphysics demands a certain purification of the intellect; it also takes for granted a certain purification of the will and assumes that one has the courage to cling to things that have no use, to *useless* Truth.

However, nothing is more necessary to man than this uselessness. What we need is not truths that serve us but a truth we may serve. For that truth is the food of the spirit. And, by the better part of ourselves, we are spirit. Useless metaphysics puts order—not any sort of police order, but the order that has sprung from eternity—in the speculative and practical intellect. It gives back to man his balance and his motion, which, as is well known, means to gravitate, head first, to the midst of the stars, while he hangs from the earth by his two legs. Throughout the whole extent of being, metaphysics reveals to him authentic values and their hierarchy. It provides a center for his ethics. It binds together in justice the whole universe of his knowledge by guaranteeing the natural limits, harmony and subordination of the different sciences. And that is more important to the human being than the most luxuriant proliferation of the mathematics of phenomena. Indeed, what does it profit to gain the whole world and lose the integrity of reason? Besides, we are so weak that the limpid peace dispensed by a healthy metaphysics may quite well be less favorable to experimental discovery than the musings or the eagerness of a mind buried deep in the sensible. The sciences of nature may very well enjoy fishing in troubled waters; but perhaps, too, we have a right to deem ourselves amply surfeited by the benefits of that dissipation.

Metaphysics sets us down in the midst of the eternal and the absolute; it causes us to pass from the show of things to the knowledge of reason (in itself stronger and more certain than mathematical certitudes, even though less adapted to our grasp), to the knowledge of the invisible world of divine perfections spelled out from their created reflections.

Metaphysics is not a means; it is an end, a fruit, a good at once self-justifying and delightful, a knowledge for the free man, the finest and naturally most regal knowledge, the door to the leisure of that great speculative activity in which intellect alone can breathe, set, as it is, on the very peak of causes.

5. And yet that is not even the most remote outline of the joys of the fatherland. This wisdom is acquired after the manner of science: and there is in it a great burden of toil and affliction of the spirit. For the old curse, *maledicta terra in opere tuo*, weighs more tragically upon our reason than upon our hands. Yes, apart from a privilege given by that good Fortune upon which the pagans did well to meditate, what the explorations of the highest intelligibles chiefly holds out to us is the useless toil and frightful sadness of messed-up truths.

The gods envy us metaphysical wisdom (the doctrinal inheritance which alone allows us to attain that wisdom without too grievously mingling error with it, is itself constantly misunderstood); man never holds it except on a precarious claim. And how could it be otherwise? What more beautiful paradox than a science of things divine achieved by human means, an enjoyment of liberty, proper to spirits, gained by a nature which is "a slave in so many ways"? Metaphysical wisdom is at the purest degree of abstraction because it is farthest removed from the senses; it opens out onto the immaterial, onto a world of realities which exist or can exist separately from matter. But our means of making the ascent must also mark our limits. By a kind of natural necessity, abstraction, the lot of all human science, brings with it, along with a multiplicity of partial and complementary insights, the rigid law of logical movement, the slow elaboration of concepts, the complexity and vast mechanism, weightier than air, of the winged apparatus of discourse. Metaphysics would like to contemplate in the purest way, to reach beyond reasoning and to enter the realm of pure intellection; it aspires to the unity of simple vision. It comes close to it, as to an asymptote. It does not reach it. What metaphysician, not to mention the old Brahmins, has more keenly felt this burning desire for sublime unity than Plotinus? But Plotinus' ecstasy is not the highest exercise of metaphysics, it is rather its vanishing-point. And metaphysics, left to itself alone, is not able to achieve it. This happy event, which Plotinus knew four times during the six years Porphyry lived with him, seemed like a brief contact with an intellectual light naturally more powerful, the spasm of a human spirit brushed by a pure spirit in its passage. If we believe Porphyry when he tells us that his master was born in the thirteenth year of the reign of Severus, that he listened to Ammonius at Alexandria, that he came to Rome at the age of forty, that he died in the Campagna; if we believe him when he tells us of his rules of health and his way of living, his kindness towards orphans entrusted to his care, his way of teaching, of composing works, of pronouncing Greek, of arranging his spelling, and the rest, why should we not believe him when he tells us that the philosopher was inspired by a higher daemon who dwelt within him and who showed himself upon his death in sensible guise? "At that moment, a serpent glided under the bed upon which he was reclining and slid into a hole in the wall; and Plotinus gave up his soul."[3] Indeed, it would be surprising if the metaphysical *eros*, wherever Christ does not dwell, did not call for some kind of collusion with superhuman intellectual natures, the *rectores hujus mundi*.

But let us take up our task once more. I am saying that metaphysics suffers not only from the common necessity of abstraction and discourse; it also suffers a weakness proper to itself. It is a natural theology; its object is, above all, the Cause of causes. The Principle of all that is—that is what it would know. And since that alone is fully satisfying, how could it help wanting to know it in itself, in its essence, in that which properly constitutes it? If the desire of seeing the first Cause is natural to man (while remaining "conditional" and "ineffectual," precisely because it does not arise from a source within us naturally proportioned to its object), it is natural to the metaphysician for a special reason because he, if he is worthy of his name, cannot fail to feel its spur. Now metaphysics makes God known to us only by analogy, known, I say, not in those things which are His very own, but in the commonness of transcendental perfections which exist at once in Him and in things—though in infinitely different modes. It is true knowledge, certain and absolute, the highest pleasure of reason, and worth being a man for; but it still falls infinitely short of vision and makes mystery all the more crushingly felt. *Per speculum in aenigmate*. We can all too readily understand that the most perfect fruit of the intellectual life still leaves man unsatisfied.

---

3   Porphyry, *Life of Plotinus*, II, 25. A little further along (Chapter 10) Porphyry tells us how an Egyptian priest, who had come to Rome, had suggested to Plotinus that he would let him see the spirit that dwelled within him, and that he had called up this daemon, who turned out to be a god. "It was impossible," he adds, "to question the daemon or keep him present to sight for long because one of his friends, a spectator at the scene, and to whom the birds had been entrusted, and who was holding them in his hand, suffocated them in jealousy or, perhaps, in terror. Plotinus, then, was attended by one of the most divine daemons; he constantly directed his mind's divine eye towards him. It was for this motive that he wrote his treatise *On the Daemon We Have Received as Our Portion*, wherein he was compelled to give reasons for the differences between the beings that attend man."

It is true to say, then, as a general thesis, that intellectual life is not enough for us. It needs a complement. Knowledge draws all forms and all that is good into our soul. But there they are stripped of their proper existence and reduced to the condition of objects of thought. They are there as so many graftings upon us, but in a mode of being that is essentially incomplete. They demand completion. They arouse forces of gravity within us. We desire to rejoin them in their own real and proper existence, to possess them no longer in an idea but in reality. Love thus arising, impels the soul to a union in the real order, a union which intellect, left all to itself, cannot achieve except in the extreme case of the vision of God.[4] It is inevitable then—unless some inhuman deviation intervene—that intellectual life, as it is in us, must finally admit its poverty and, one day, pour itself out in desire. It is the problem of Faust. If human wisdom does not spill upwards into the love of God, it will fall downwards towards Marguerite. Mystical possession in Eternal love of the Most Holy God, or physical possession, in the fleetingness of time, of a poor fleshly creature (for, great wizard as one may be, that is where it all ends up)—there lies the choice that cannot be avoided.

6. That, then, is the poverty of metaphysics (and yet its majesty, too). It awakens a desire for supreme union, for spiritual possession completed in the order of reality itself and not only in the concept. It cannot satisfy that desire.

We preach a different wisdom—scandal for the Jews, madness for the Greeks. This wisdom, far surpassing all human effort, a gift of deifying grace and free endowments of Uncreated Wisdom, has as its beginning the *mad love* that Wisdom Itself has for each and all of us, and as its end, the union of spirit with it. Only Jesus crucified gives access to it—the Mediator raised up between heaven and earth. When al Hallâj, his hands and feet cut off, and crucified on the gibbet like Him, was asked: "What is mysticism?" he replied, "You see here its lowest stage." "And its highest level?" "You cannot gain entrance to it; and yet tomorrow, you will see what it will become. For it is in the Divine mystery, wherein it exists, that I bear witness to it and that it remains hidden to you."[5]

---

4   In that vision the soul becomes God "intentionally" (*secundum esse intelligible*), not substantially. But it is joined to him in a real (*secundum rem*) union, inasmuch as *through the very infinite essence of God*, immediately actuating the intellect in the intelligible order, it grasps Him and sees Him. Once the intellect has been rendered supernatural by the light of glory it is as the hand by which the blessed grasp God.

5   Louis Massignon, *Al Hallâj martyr mystique de l'Islam, exécuté à Bagdad*, le 26 mars 922 (Paris, Geuthner, 1922, t. I, pp. 9, 306). We are quoting al Hallâj at this point because, insofar as a conjecture may be ventured about the secrets of the heart, everything leads us to think that this great Moslem mystic, who was condemned because he taught the union of love with God and who gave testimony to the very end of his desire to follow Jesus, had grace and infused gifts (and belonged to the "soul" of the Church) and could, as a result, have been raised to authentic mystical contemplation. Fr. Maréchal rallies to this conclusion in his review of

Mystical wisdom is not beatitude, the perfect spiritual possession of Divine reality. But it is a beginning of it. It is an entering into incomprehensible life even here below, a taste, a touch, a sweetness of God that will not pass away, for the seven gifts will continue in vision what they here begin in faith.

We cannot pardon either those who deny it or those who corrupt it, led astray as they are by an inexcusable metaphysical presumption, for while recognizing the Divine transcendence, they will not adore it.

Those doctrines that certain Occidentals suggest to us in the name of the wisdom of the Orient (I am not speaking of Oriental thought itself, whose interpretation requires a whole host of distinctions and shades of meaning), arrogant and facile doctrines, are a radical negation of the wisdom of the saints. In claiming to attain supreme contemplation by metaphysics alone, in seeking the soul's perfection outside of charity (the mystery of which remains impenetrable to them), in substituting a so-called secret tradition inherited from unknown masters of Knowledge in the place of supernatural faith and the revelation of God by the Incarnate Word (*unigenitus Filius, qui est in sinu Patris, ipse ennaravit*)—in all this they are lying, for they are telling man that he can add to his own stature and gain entrance into the super-human by himself. Their esoteric hyperintellectualism, apt in its very structure to put true metaphysics on the wrong scent, is but a specious and harmful mirage. It leads reason to absurdity, the soul to a second death.

Vain philosophy can also be an enemy of wisdom in still another way: not, indeed, by suppressing the wisdom of the saints by metaphysics, but by more-or-less mixing the two together and, in the most serious instances, by brashly confusing it with metaphysics—and that is to fundamentally corrupt its nature. It is thus that an attentive and penetrating mind, after fifteen years of zealous research and unstinted efforts devoted to the most careful and intense erudition, has been led to disfigure in a tragic way the mystical hero whose inner drama he had undertaken to retrace. Alas! How could a philosopher with the sole help of a fund of historical information, even supposing it were exhaustive, and aided by the most intuitive Bergsonian sympathy, penetrate the heart of a saint? How could he relive John of the Cross in himself? Every one of philosophy's false keys is shattered for the very good reason that there is no lock; entrance to it is gained only through a wall. Despite my friendship for you, my dear Baruzi, I must confess that in turning a Leibnizian light on John of the Cross, you have erred. In wrenching his contemplation from that which was the life of his life (infused grace and the working of God within him), in making of him some sort of ineffectual giant of the metaphysics to come, still held in "extrinsicist" superstitions, yet aiming above all to reach (through a process of self-spoliation, in which man's mind did the whole job) a less and less crude intellectual comprehension of God, and succeeding so

---

Mr. Louis Massignon's admirable work. (J. Maréchal, *Recherches de Science Religieuse*, May–August 1923). Cf. below, Ch. VI, § 26.

well in that task that he has led us "to some extent beyond Christianity"[6]—in all this you have traced out a picture of the saint which the latter would have held in abomination and one whose glaring falsity, coupled with such great zeal, is a subject of astonishment and sadness[7] for us. Your just man *does not*

6   Jean Baruzi, *Saint Jean de la Croix et le problème de l'expériénce mystique*, 2nd ed., p. 230.

7   Cf. Dom. Phil. Chevallier, *Vie spirituelle*, May 1925, and R. Garrigou-Lagrange, *ibid.*, July–August 1925; and Roland Dalbiez's little work, *Saint Jean de la Croix d'après M. Baruzi* (Editions of *Vie Spirituelle*).

[In the second edition of his book, Jean Baruzi has deserved commendation for suppressing certain shocking passages, and his preface indicates that today he is more appreciative of the difficulty and scope of the problems he had approached. Yet, at its roots, his thought has not evolved one whit. Does he not tell us (p. 674, n. 4) that "when the mystic attains this noetic purity, he cuts himself off from what Léon Brunschvicg, in his profound observations . . . calls "naturalistic psychism" and on the contrary, joins hands with "intellectualistic idealism"? By misunderstanding the very essence of St. John of the Cross' mysticism, it is not surprising that he compares his mysticism (by accidental analogies that are taken to be basic analogies, pp. 676–677) with Plotinus' mysticism (and that is still farther removed from what Mr. Léon Brunschvicg calls "Intellectualistic idealism"), and that he believes that John of the Cross, quite independently of any problem of influence, joins up once more with Neo-Platonism "through his thought's most secret movement." (p. 677).

In the preface to the second edition, he defends himself forever having intended to "transfer the mystical level to a metaphysical level" (p. iii) or to represent "John of the Cross as absorbing himself in a Deity that would be quite opposite to the living God of Christianity" (p. xiii). As far as we are concerned, we have not criticized his intentions: we have criticized his philosophy and the interpretations it inevitably suggests to him.

Whereas he has honestly pointed out that "this divine genesis is accomplished at the very heart of Christianity" (p. 656), his whole book has been conceived on the theme that (as regards John of the Cross' mystical experience itself) it has been so accomplished in a *contingent* manner: that that experience is in fact Christian, but that a combination, a synthesis, between what essentially and necessarily arises from mysticism and what derives from Christianity, has produced it. "The soul is, however, without limits, and God is Himself without bounds. But here the soul stripped bare and the God without mode *combine* with the soul touched by mystical grace and the God in Three Persons of theological Christianity. . . . The *synthesis* is accomplished in him, more lovingly than in any other Catholic mystic, perhaps, because to an intense love of God, who is Father, Son and Holy Ghost, *is joined* a pure adherence to essential Divinity, to the 'Deity,' and, although the term does not occur in his language—to the One." (pp. 674–675. Italics mine.) Cf. below, Ch. IX, § 16.

When a philosopher is retracing and rethinking the history of another mind, it is a dangerous temptation to believe that it is his task to lead that mind up to the full truth of its own nature, a truth to which it is supposed never to have attained by itself. History reminds the philosopher it has no other God besides God and that it is not in our power to re-engender creative ideas. And then, too, in such a game one runs the risk of imposing obedience to one's own gods on the hero

live by faith. This *theopath* does not suffer things Divine, but a disease of the Sorbonne.

The contemplation of the saints is not the line of metaphysics; it is the line of religion. This supreme wisdom does not depend on the intellect's effort in search of the perfection of knowing but on man's gift of his entire self in search of a perfect rectitude in respect to his End. It has nothing to do with the "stultification" which Pascal advised the proud to cultivate (if it is there, it is because pride has already fallen). Rather, it knows so well that it no longer dreams of knowing. This highest kind of knowing supposes that knowing has been forgone.

The saints do not contemplate to know, but to love. They do not love for the sake of loving but for the love of Him whom they love. It is for the love of their first beloved, God, that they aspire to that very union with God that love demands whilst they love themselves only for Him.[8] For them, the end of ends

that is admired. In Baruzi's eyes, John of the Cross' most authentic drive tended towards a pure knowledge, one that infinitely surpassed every mental condition and every perceptible datum in a constant self-destruction of knowing. It would make us transcend our own natures, not indeed in entering a "thickness" of *supernatural realities* that are to be attained mystically according to their own mode, but by merely entering a *mode* (without modes) of knowing (cf. pp. 454, 600–601, 612–613)—a realm of unknowing superior to our own way of experiencing and understanding, wherein we would better understand the same realities that are the object of metaphysics and philosophy: "Being" (p. 448), "things" (p. 584), "the universe" (pp. 584–585), "the Divine One" (p. 675). (Pp. 639 and 645, it is a matter of "cosmic ecstacy" and "cosmic discovery.") Baruzi separates "mystical faith" from dogmatic faith (p. 448, cf. pp. 510–511, 600–601, 659), and that is directly contrary to John of the Cross' thought and experience. And although he does not ignore the role of love in the latter's mysticism, he singularly reduces its role and does not show its content: his explanation gives the invincible impression that in this mysticism, as in Neo-Platonism, love would be a kind of metaphysical *striving* destined to make us "enter a new world" (p. 611) and a mere means of a transcendent "noetic." Thus, he finds himself misunderstanding something that is most personal and central to St. John of the Cross; I mean, of course, the sovereignty and living certainty of love's primacy.

Certain lines written by Jean Baruzi (*Final Note* in the second edition) forced us to make these precisions. And if we have criticized him with some vigor, it is because in our opinion the problems he is attacking—problems that also have a capital importance for him—do not belong to the field of pure erudition. They involve, rather, essential truths. And it is also the high esteem in which we hold Baruzi's great effort—in spite of all the troubles we experience with it—that makes us deplore the fact that such human labor should run the risk of hiding from him the message of the saint he wanted to honor.]

8 But then the love of self *secundum rationem proprii boni* does not vanish, but its act gives place to the act of the love of charity wherein man loves himself *propter Deum et in Deo. (Sum. Theol.*, II–II, 19, 6; 19, 8 and 2; 19, 10), an act which, by perfecting him and raising him up, contains in itself the natural love that every man bears towards his own being and even more than his own being towards God. (I, 60, 5; II–II, 25, 4.)

is not to bring exultation to their intellect and nature and thus stop at themselves. It is to do the will of Another, to contribute to the good of the Good.[9] They do not seek their own soul. They lose it; they no longer possess it. If in entering into the mystery of Divine filiation and becoming something of God, they gain a transcendent personality, an independence and a liberty which nothing in the world approaches, it is by forgetting all else so that they do not live, but the Beloved lives in them.

I would willingly agree that the antinomies the "new mystics"[10] discover in traditional mysticism (because they construct an artificial idea of it, an idea vitiated by solemn modern prejudices about the life of the spirit) actually do characterize many philosophical pseudo-mysticisms. (And the new mysticism itself will have difficulty avoiding them.) But when referred to an authentically mystical life, those antinomies lose all meaning. In genuine mystical life there is neither "creative will" seeking direct exaltation in pure adventure or endless surpassing, nor "magic will" seeking self-exaltation in mastery over the world and in complete possession. Here there is love (our philosophers forget it, yet it is the very thing that does accomplish everything); here there is charity, which uses knowledge—which love itself makes delectable and present through the action of God's spirit—to adhere more fully to the Beloved. Here the soul does not wish to exalt itself and it does not want to be destroyed: it wishes to be joined to Him who first loved it. For here there is a God who is not a name, but a reality; there is a Real, and indeed, a Super Real which first exists, before us and without us—one that is capable of being grasped neither humanly nor angelically, but divinely, and one who makes us divine for that very purpose—a Super spirit the attaining of Whom does not limit us but removes the limits from our finite spirit—You the living God, our Creator! Before discussing mysticism, there is a question, John Brown, that you must first answer: "Has your Mr. Peter Morhange been created?"

The contemplation of the saints does not issue from the spirit of man. It issues from infused grace. (Let us talk theology, since we cannot answer the questions troubling our day except through recourse to notions from sacred science.) I say that contemplation is indeed the perfect fruit of our own acts, but only according as we are born of Water and the Spirit. A supernatural work in its very essence, as indeed it is, it none the less truly emanates from the depths of our substance and from our natural powers of activity only, however, to the extent that our substance and our activity (which are passive before the

---

9   Cf. St. Thomas Aquinas, *Sum. Theol.*, II–II, 26, 3 ad 3: "Hoc quod aliquis velit frui Deo, pertinet ad amorem, quo Deus amatur amore concupiscentiae; magis autem amamus Deum amore amicitiae, quam amore concupiscentiae; quia majus est in se bonum Dei, quam bonum, quod participare possumus fruendo ipso; et ideo simpliciter homo magis diligit Deum ex charitatem quam seipsum." Cf. also Cajetan, in II–II, 17, 5.

10   Cf. Henri Lefebvre, "Positions d'attaque et de défense du nouveau mysticisme," *Philosophies*, March 1925.

omnipotent God) are, through Him and the gifts He engrafts upon them, raised up to face a divine object which in itself is absolutely inaccessible to the energies of nature if left to themselves.[11] It is a supremely personal work, a free and active work, a life which springs up to eternity. Yet it is a life that is more like an inactivity and a death because being supernatural, not only in its object but also in its very way of proceeding, it emanates from our spirit moved by God alone and depends upon *operative grace* in which the whole initiative belongs to God. And because faith is the root and foundation of all supernatural life, such a work is inconceivable without faith, "outside of which, there is no proximate and proportioned means" of contemplation.[12]

Finally, the contemplation of the saints is not only *for* divine love; it is also *through* it. It not only supposes the theological virtue of Faith, but the theological virtue of Charity and the infused gifts of Understanding and Wisdom as well; and these do not exist in the soul without charity. Love as such attains immediately and in Himself the very God attained in faith in an obscure manner and, as it were, at a distance. This is so because as far as understanding is concerned, there is distance when there is not vision, while love unites us in our heart to Him who is hidden in faith. Mystical wisdom, moved and actually regulated by the Holy Ghost, experiences the Divine things thus imbedded in us by charity, God becomes ours by charity. Through and in that Love which, so to speak, gives itself to us within our very selves, and, "in virtue of an incomprehensible union,"[13] it knows that Love affectively. It knows it in a night above all distinct knowledge, above every image and every idea, as though infinitely transcending all that any and every creature could ever think of Him. *Vere tu es Deus absconditus, Deus Israel Salvator.* This secret wisdom which secretly purifies the soul attains God as a hidden God, a saving God, one who is the more a savior the more hidden He is. It remains, however, all the while under the supervision of theology.[14] It constantly depends in respect to its

---

11   Philosophers who speak of the *supernatural being superimposed*, in connection with the doctrine of "obediential power," have never read the Thomist theologians—or, if they have read them, they have not understood them. Cf. John of St. Thomas, *Curs. Theol.*, I P., q. 12, disp. 14, a. 2 (Vivès, t. II).

12   Cf. St. John of the Cross, *Ascent of Carmel*, II. See below, Ch. VIII, § 16.

13   Denys, *On the Divine Names*, VII, 3.

14   At least in the communicable expressions in which human language translates mystical experience—i.e., as regards that which is no longer, properly speaking, mystical experience but, rather, the theology with which it is pregnant (*see below* Ch. VIII, § 13)—it is a fact that mystical wisdom may be under the supervision of theology. Thus, the theologian does not judge the contemplative as contemplative, but only to the extent that the contemplative comes down to the level of conceptual expression and rational communication. An astronomer can, in the same way, judge a philosopher who is talking astronomy.

      But mystical wisdom of itself is superior to theological wisdom, and the spiritual man is the one who judges the speculative theologian, not, to be sure, in the order of doctrine but in the realm of experience and life. *Spiritualis judicat*

earthly human conditions and foundations on many notions and conceptual signs wherein Divine Truth is revealed to our understanding (without, of course, abandoning revealed dogma in the least! Quite the contrary!). It knows better than by concepts that very thing in which the conceptual formulae of dogma communicate to human understanding. How, then, could it help but surpass every distinct notion and expressible sign so as to cling, in the very experience of love, to that reality which is the first object of faith? In this, we are poles apart from Plotinus. Here it is not a question of mounting intellectually beyond the intelligible, of climbing by metaphysics and its cleverly regulated dialectical scale right up to the abolition—still natural—of natural understanding in a superintelligible, or to an angelic ecstasy. Rather, is it a question of rising lovingly beyond the created, of renouncing self and all else so as to be carried off by charity into the transluminous night of faith, transported by a Divine activity, and borne to a sovereign supernatural knowledge of the unlimited supernatural, or of being transformed into God by love. For "in the final analysis we have been created for this love alone."[15]

No, metaphysics is not the doorway to mystical contemplation. That door is Christ's humanity, for by Him we have been given grace and truth. *I am the way,* He has said of Himself, *if anyone enters by Me, he will be saved, and he will pass inside, and he will pass outside and he will find pasture.* Having gained

---

omnia, et a nemine judicatur (I Cor. ii, 15).

As far as really judging the secret and incommunicable substance of mystical experience itself is concerned, and discerning spirits, that is not in itself the speculative theologian's business. It is the concern of spiritual men and of the theologian only insofar as he is himself a spiritual person and possessed of a practical knowledge (cf. Chap. VIII, §§ 7 and 8) of mystical ways: "This is really," wrote John of St. Thomas, "the apostolic rule: *'Believe not every spirit, but try the spirits if they be of God.'* (I John iv, 1). And again: *'Despise not prophecies. But prove all things: hold fast that which is good.'* (I Thess. v, 20–21). . . . This examination should usually be made in common. . . .

"This does not mean that therein the gift of the Holy Ghost is subject to the virtue of prudence or that it is inferior to it or receives its determination from it. For those who judge such revelations or virtues should not do so in accordance with the reasons of human prudence but, rather, according to the rules of faith to which the gifts of the Holy Ghost are subject, or according to the gifts themselves which can be more excellently present in some men than in others. But if human reasons or theological reasons are still used in examining things of this sort, they are taken into secondary consideration only, and then merely by acting as aides assisting in providing a better explanation of that which concerns faith or the instinct of the Holy Ghost.

"That is why, in examining things of the spirit, and matters mystical, recourse must not only be had to the scholastic theologians, but to spiritual men as well, to men who possess mystical prudence, who know spiritual paths and how to discern spirits." (John of St. Thomas, *Gifts of the Holy Ghost*, V, 22. French tr. by R. Maritain, pp. 201–202).

15   St. John of the Cross, *Spiritual Canticle*, 2nd ed. str. 28 (19), ed. by Allison Peers (London, Burns Oates, 1934) Vol. 2, pp. 341 ff.

entrance through Him, the soul climbs and penetrates the dark and bare contemplation of pure Divinity, and it descends once more and goes out to the contemplation of sacred humanity. And in both instances, it finds pasture and is nourished by its God.[16]

7. There are two things to consider in every sign, concept or name: the object it makes known and the way in which it makes it known. In all the signs our intellect uses to know God, the way of signifying is defective and unworthy of God since it is not proportioned to God but to that which is not God, i.e., to the way in which perfections, which in their pure state pre-exist in God, exist in things. In the same imperfect way in which created things represent God from Whom they proceed, our concepts (which primarily and directly attain the created) make God known. The perfection they signify, the perfection which—if it belong to a transcendental order—can exist in an uncreated state as well as in a created state, must be signified essentially as it exists in a created, limited and imperfect condition. So, too, all the names by which we speak of God, while signifying a single self-same reality which is inexpressibly one and simple, are still not synonyms because they signify according to the mode in which those perfections, pre-existing in God in a state of sovereign simplicity, are participated and divided in creatures. God is subsistent Goodness just as He is subsistent Truth and subsistent Being. Yet, if the Idea of Goodness, of Truth and of Being subsisted in a pure state, it would not be God.

Whence it follows that names and concepts which properly belong to God, in being applied to Him, retain their whole intelligible value and all their meaning: the thing signified is entirely in God, and in Him it is present with all that constitutes it for the intellect ("formally" say the philosophers): in saying that God is good, we qualify the Divine Nature intrinsically and we know that everything that goodness necessarily implies is to be found there. But within this perfection as it is in pure act (which is God Himself), there is still infinitely *more* than is signified by its concept and name. It exists in God in a way which infinitely surpasses our way of conceiving ("eminently," say the philosophers). For in knowing that God is good, we still do not know what Divine Goodness is because He is good as nothing else is good, true as nothing else is true; He is as nothing else we know is. "Thus," says St. Thomas, "when the name wise is said of man, it in some way *describes* and envelops the thing signified: but not so when it is said of God; for then, it leaves the thing signified, as it were, uncontained and uncircumscribed, and exceeding the signification of the name."[17]

Thus, all knowledge of God by notions or concepts, whether acquired, as

---

16   Cf. St. Thomas Aquinas, *Quodlib.* VIII a. 20; Joseph of the Holy Ghost, *Cursus theologiae mystico-scholasticae*, Disp. prima prooemialis, q. 2, § 1 (Bruges, Beyaert, 1924 ed., t. I, p. 117).

17   St. Thomas Aquinas, *Sum. Theol.*, I, 13, 5.

in metaphysics and speculative theology, or infused, as in prophecy, in short, all purely intellectual knowledge of God, short of the Beatific Vision, even though it be absolutely true, absolutely certain, and constitute an authentic wisdom, desirable above all things, is still irreparably defective, lacking due proportion to the object known and signified, in its very manner of grasping and signifying.

It is clear, then, that although we can be given a knowledge of God, not *sicuti est*, that is, by His essence and in vision, but at least in accordance with the very transcendence of his Deity, that is, by making use of a mode of knowing appropriate to the object known, such a knowledge cannot possibly be obtained in a purely intellectual way. To transcend every method of conceiving while still remaining in the line of human understanding, and, consequently, of the concept, is a contradiction in terms. We must pass through love. Love alone, and I am speaking of supernatural love, can effect this overreaching. Here below, intellect can enter the realm that lies beyond all method only by a renunciation-of-knowing in which God's Spirit, by making use of the connaturality of charity and the effects produced in affection by Divine Union, grants the soul a loving experience of that very being which no notion approximates or can approximate. "And then, released from the world of sense and intellect, the soul enters into the mysterious darkness of a holy ignorance, and, renouncing every scientific datum, it loses itself in Him who cannot be seen or grasped. It now belongs entirely to this sovereign object without belonging either to itself or to others. It is united to the unknown through its noblest part because it has renounced knowledge. Finally it draws from this absolute ignorance a knowledge that understanding could never win to."[18]

8. It seems that the trend of modern times is set under the sign of a disjunction between flesh and spirit, or a progressive dislocation of the shape of human things. It is only too clear that the march of humanity under the sway of money and mechanics[19] marks a progressive materializing of intellect and of the world. On the other hand, as though in compensation for this phenomenon, the spirit (with which our discursive and social activity has less and less

---

18   Denys, *Mystical Theology*, Ch. 1, 3.
19   Material techniques of themselves should have prepared the way for a life much more completely freed of matter, but in virtue of man's fault they actually tend to oppress spirituality. Does that mean that technique must be forsaken or that we must give ourselves up to vain regrets? That has never been our view. But in this case reason has to impose its human regulation. And if it succeeds in this without having to have recourse to purely despotic and, for quite other reasons, inhuman solutions, the materialization of which we have been speaking would have been overcome—at least for a time, anyway. We are not making any claim here to express the law of a necessary curve in events, we are merely trying to sift out, from the point of time in which we now exist, the significance of a tendency in the form of a curve which these have followed down to the present moment—and a tendency that human liberty *can* rectify.

to do and is thus freed from guaranteeing the organic functions of human life) undergoes a kind of deliverance—at least, a virtual one. "Photography has set the art of painting free." This expression of Jean Cocteau can be applied to every realm. Printing has freed the plastic arts from the pedagogical function that was incumbent upon them in the days of the cathedrals. Sciences of phenomena have freed metaphysics from the trouble of explaining things of sensible nature, and from so many illusions which had followed upon it for Greek optimism. We must congratulate ourselves on this purification of metaphysics. It is less pleasant to state, however, that in the practical order, the government of earthly things, to the extent that it demands a heavier material work of intellect, is more and more separated from the life it leads beyond time. The earth is no longer in need of a moving angel; man pushes it by the strength of his arm. Spirit ascends to heaven.

Yet, man is flesh and spirit, not held together by a thread, but substantially united. The fact that human affairs cease to be cut to the measure of man (since some of those affairs take their rhythm from the energies of matter, while others look for their standards to the exigencies of a disincarnate spirituality) constitutes for man a frightful metaphysical disjunction. It is quite believable that the shape of this world will pass away on the day that this tension becomes so great that our heart will break.

As for the things of the spirit themselves, "to liberate" them is to run the risk of perpetuating an illusion—even worse than slavery. The constraints imposed on spirit in its service of man were good for it; they hampered it but they gave to it its natural weight. But the "angelizing" of art and knowledge? Will all this purity, possible to the spirit, be lost in a brutal frenzy? No! But it will be found and truly exist only in the sheepfold of Spirit. There where the Body is, the eagles will gather. Although the Christendom of days gone by has been undone, yet Christ's Church has continued to rise. It, too, has been set free little by little and delivered from the care for civil communities that reject it, from the temporal providence it once exercised in accordance with its rights to heal our wounds. Despoiled, stripped of everything, when She flees into a solitude She will take with Her all that remains in the world not only of faith and charity and true contemplation, but of philosophy, poetry and virtue. And all these will be more beautiful than ever.

9. The pressing interest of the present crisis arises from the fact that, being more universal than any other, it forces us all to make decisive choices. Here we have come to the parting of the ways. In virtue of the West's failures (for it has abused Divine graces and allowed the gifts it had to render fruitful for God to be lost) it discovers that, being no longer supported by the order of charity, the order of reason is corrupted through and through and is no longer good for anything. The evil wrought by the rationalist has produced a tension between nature and the *form of reason*. Thenceforth, it has become very difficult to cling to what is human. Its stake must either be set above reason and still

on its side, or below reason and against it. Now the theological virtues and the supernatural gifts are the only things that are above reason. On all sides—even in the ranks of the new humanists or the partisans of dialectical materialism (as in days gone by amongst the followers of Barrès)—the cry is heard: spirit, spirituality! But upon what spirit are you calling? If it is not the Holy Spirit, you might just as well call upon the spirit of wood alcohol or the spirit of wine. The whole so-called spiritual, all the self-styled suprarational which does not exist in charity only serves animality in the final reckoning. Hatred for reason will never be anything but a revolt of the genus against its specific difference. Dreaming is quite the contrary to contemplation. If purity consists in a perfect releasing of life in accordance with the trends of its own mechanisms, it exists more truly in the brute than in the saint.

The world—that world for whom Christ did not pray—has made its choice in advance. To be delivered from the *forma rationis*, to flee far from God in an impossible metaphysical suicide, far from the cruel and saving order set down by eternal Law—that is the desire with which the flesh of the old man tingles; it was the desire of the Devil of old when he fell from heaven like thunder. To express it in an absolute fashion and as fully as possible to a being who, most of the time, does not know what he is doing, a kind of heroism is required. (The Devil has his own martyrs.) A testimony without promise, a testimony given to what is worse than death! . . . As for the great mass of men, if we can judge it by the ordinary conditions of human nature, it would be easy to believe that they would follow the same downward course, but without will or courage, hypnotized by the ideal. This course is such an easy one!

It is a mistake, however, to judge according to nature alone. Grace is there and it always holds in reserve its own surprises. For even as this old world continues to slip, the true new world comes forth—the secret, invincible coursing of Divine sap in the Mystical Body which endures and does not grow old, the blessed awakening of souls under the sign of the Virgin and the Spirit. O Wisdom which reaches with strength from one end of the world to the other and makes extremes one! O promise which makes beauty of these times of misery, and renders us joyful! Though baptized nations, unfaithful to their calling, cut themselves off from the Church, blaspheme the name of Christ on all sides by presenting as a Christian civilization what is nothing but its corpse, the Church still loves those nations. She has no need of them. They are the ones that need the Church. It is for their welfare that the Church, by using the only culture in which human reason very nearly succeeded, has tried for so long to impress a Divine form on earthly matter, to raise man's life and reason and so to maintain them in their perfection, under the most gentle sway of grace. If European culture comes to the brink of danger, She will save its essentials and will know how to lift up to Christ everything that can be saved in other cultures. She hears, rumbling at the roots of history, an unforeseen world, a world that will undoubtedly persecute Her as much as the ancient world did.

(Is not Her mission a mission of suffering?) But She will find in it new possibilities of action.

If Hilaire Belloc means that Europe would be nothing without the faith and that its very reason for being has been, and still is, to dispense faith to the world, he is right in saying that Europe is the faith. But absolutely speaking, No! Europe is not the faith and the faith is not Europe; Europe is not the Church, and the Church is not Europe. Rome is not the capital of the Latin world; Rome is the capital of the world. *Urbs caput orbis.* The Church is universal because it is born of God. All nations are at home in it. Their Master's arms on the cross are stretched out over all races and all civilizations. It does not bring *the benefits of civilization* to people, but rather, Christ's Blood and supernatural beatitude. It seems that a kind of wondrous epiphany of its catholicity is being readied in our times, and the steady growth in missionary countries of a native clergy and a native episcopacy can be considered a prophetic sign of it.

For a long time the East has remained asleep on the fringes of history, but now, touched by madness, it is today as sick as the West. But, East or West, wherever the living faith has taken root, we shall see that adherence to what is truly beyond reason, to uncreated Truth, to the wisdom of the saints, will bring in its train a restoration (not, it is true, without some effort) of the very order of reason itself, a restoration implied by supernatural life as a condition of its existence. Thus do the Gospel and philosophy, mysticism and metaphysics, the Divine and the human, go hand in hand. The great plan of Brahmanandav, taken up once more by his disciple, Animananda, is not the plan of a European, but of a Bengali. This plan was to establish in Bengal a contemplative congregation whose members, religious mendicants on the order of the Hindu *sannyasis*, would set, for the whole of India, an Indian example of Catholic holiness, and, without overlooking the Vedanta, would base its intellectual life on the doctrines of Thomas Aquinas.[20] I cherish this tribute to the strength of Thomism. Though a gift made to the whole world by mediaeval Christianity, it neither belongs to one continent nor to one century; it is universal as is the Church and truth.

10. I would never scorn the distress nor the waiting of those who feel that all is lost and await the unexpected. But what is it they really expect? That is the important thing. Is it anti-Christ or the Parousia? We look for the resurrection of the dead and the life of the world to come. We know what we are waiting for and that it surpasses all understanding. There is a difference

---

20   Michel Ledrus, S.J., *L'Apostolat bengali* (Louvain, 1924). A completely Chinese Catholic congregation, the Little Brothers of St. John the Baptist, was founded in China in 1928 by Fr. Lebbe. In a general way, those who know China best think that in our day what is finest in its ancient spiritual tradition has, in Catholicism, its only chance of escaping the basic materialism youth goes on seeking in the West.

between not knowing what one hopes for and knowing that the thing one hopes for cannot be conceived.

"Adrian, while still a pagan, asked the martyrs, 'For what reward do you hope?' They replied, 'Our mouth cannot speak it nor our ear hear it.' 'And so, you have learned nothing of it? Neither by the law nor the prophets? Nor any other writing?' 'The prophets themselves did not know it as it should be known, for they were only men who adored God, and they have told in words the things they received from the Holy Ghost. But concerning that glory, it is written: "Eye has not seen, nor ear heard, nor has it entered into the heart of man what the Lord has prepared for those who love Him." ' . . .

"On hearing that, Adrian immediately jumped down into their midst and said, 'Count me among those who confess the faith with these saints, for behold I, too, am a Christian.' "[21]

---

21   Boninus Mombritius, *Sanctuarium seu vitae sanctorum*, new ed. by the monks of Solesmes (Paris, Fontemoing, 1910): *Passio sancti Adriani M. cum aliis 33 MM.*

FIRST PART

THE DEGREES OF RATIONAL KNOWLEDGE: PHILOSOPHY AND EXPERIMENTAL SCIENCE

CHAPTER II

PHILOSOPHY AND EXPERIMENTAL SCIENCE

I
THE OBJECT OF THIS CHAPTER

1. IN HIS IMPORTANT WORK on *Explanation in the Sciences*, Émile Meyerson says: "True science, the only one that we know, is in no way, and in none of its parts in accordance with the positivist scheme."[1] At this point in our work, we are not undertaking to show that the critical-intellectualist or critical-realist[2] scheme, while maintaining for philosophy and metaphysics their eminent character as science, corresponds more exactly to the vast logical universe of whose modern development the sciences offer us some picture. A whole treatise would be needed for that. We would only like to propose, in summary fashion and from the point of view of the philosopher, a general sketch of this scheme—such at least as it appears to us in the light of the history of the sciences. We are not unaware of the gaps in our outline: it is subject to many retouchings and many additions. Such as it is, however, and in spite of its inadequacies, we hope it will permit the reader, in reference to his own experience, to estimate the worth of a doctrine which the indolence of many of its defenders and the neglect of modern critiques of science have for a long time caused to be misunderstood.

This chapter is devoted to the relations of scientific experience and philosophy. In other words, the experimental level of knowing (wherein knowing is further specified according to the diverse sciences of the phenomena of nature) is here considered, especially in its relation to the higher levels (wherein knowing is universalized and unified). This will be a kind of introduction to the three following chapters, in which an attempt will be made to envisage the conception that critical realism fashions of philosophic knowing in all its generality. And, indeed, this point of view will at one and the same time

---

1   Émile Meyerson, *De l'explication dans les sciences* (Paris, 1921, t. I, p. 31.
2   These seem to us the most appropriate terms to designate a philosophy that no overly simplified label can define for the very reason that its proper objective is so lofty that empiricism and idealism, realism and nominalism are all transcended at one stroke and reconciled within it. Concerning the notion "critical realism," see below, Ch. III.

include a more profound treatment as well as a larger synthesis of the problems herein involved.

While reserving for the next chapter an examination of the foundations of Thomistic noetic, we will at this point take the principles and metaphysical structure of that noetic as granted by hypothesis. It is a noetic that recognizes the existence of things outside the mind and the possibility of the mind's attaining these things and constructing within itself and by its own activity, beginning with the senses, a knowledge which is true or in conformity with what is. Those of our readers who might still be doubtful about these principles may, in any event, provisorily suppose them as postulates. Moreover, they will recall that even for science they are not doubtful. Science is naturally realistic. If experimental science does not in itself constitute an ontology of nature, nevertheless, according to the remark of the very discerning philosopher cited above, a background of ontological values is at least, and in fact, inevitably demanded of it.

Science in General

2. What notion should we have of science in general, understood in the sense of that specific form of knowledge at which the mind aims when it is aware that it is striving towards what men call knowing scientifically?[3] The concept that Aristotle and the ancients had of it is very different from the one that moderns have constructed because, for the latter, it is the eminent dignity of the experimental sciences, the positive sciences, the sciences of nature, the sciences of phenomena as we say, which appropriates the notion of science.

---

3   It is perfectly clear that only by reflective abstraction can such a specific form be disengaged from the various sciences already constituted among men. It is not, however, a mere residual mean (statistical "totality") set forth in *abstractio totalis* or abstraction of a logical generality, but it is, rather, a question of a pure type (ideal "formality") disengaged in *abstractio formalis* or abstraction of a formally constitutive element (see below, Ch. II, § 12). The different existing sciences in which such a pure type has been disengaged still leave much to be desired in offering an adequate presentation of it, as those sciences are at present constituted.

E. Husserl has recourse to a substitute for *abstractio formalis* (all notion of which is lacking in most modern philosophers) when he sets about "living" the scientific task in his meditation (cf. *Méditations cartésiennes*, pp. 7–11), and thereby grasping the "intention" of science. That is really possible only through a reflection (which is at least implicit) upon sciences as really given. On the other hand, the Cartesian method followed by Husserl compels him to brand with temporary invalidity those sciences whence he has drawn the idea of science. If, on the contrary, we maintain the perspective of spontaneous realism actually required by the sciences themselves, it is because we presuppose that critical reflection (which will be treated in the following chapter) can achieve an awareness of knowledge in general and subsequently of the validity of the different sciences, at least their general and undetermined validity.

For the ancients, on the contrary, it was the eminent dignity of metaphysics which oriented this notion. It is necessary, then, to avoid applying haphazardly and without due precaution the Aristotelian-Thomist notion of science to the whole vast noetic material that our contemporaries are accustomed to call by that name. One would only expose oneself to worse mistakes. However, for both the ancients and the moderns—and in this sense they are in agreement— the clearest, the most perfect type of science, the one most perfectly within our grasp[4] is provided by mathematics. It may, then, be considered conditionally— I do not mean that it has to be corrected and adapted, but rather that it must be adequately dwelt upon and refined—that the critical-intellectualist or critical-realist theory of science, whose principles have been set down by the metaphysicians of antiquity and of the middle ages, alone provides us with the means of seeing clearly into epistemological problems that have in our day become a veritable chaos.

How, then, define science in general and in accordance with its ideal type? We would contend that science is a knowledge perfect in its mode, or more precisely a knowledge in which, under the compulsion of evidence, the mind points out in things their reasons for being. For the mind is not satisfied when it merely attains a thing, i.e., any datum whatever, but only when it grasps that upon which that datum is founded in being and intelligibility. *Cognitio certa per causas*, the ancients would say: knowledge by demonstration (in other words mediately evident) and explanatory knowledge. We see at once that it is a knowledge so rooted as to be necessarily true, that it cannot not be true, or is in conformity with what is.[5] For it would not be a knowledge perfect in its mode, an infrangible knowledge, if it could be found false. That holds good for the pure type of science, whatever may be the role of hypothesis in its development and of the vast element of conjecture and probability upon which the most concrete sciences rely for their certitude and which, moreover, they rigorously determine.

---

4   The contention that mathematics constitutes the kind of science that is most perfectly within the grasp of the human intellect (there are infant prodigies in this science) is exactly correct, especially as regards classical mathematics. But it is no longer correct with reference to a mathematics from which axiomatics have almost entirely eliminated intuition. It is true that the axiomatic method, no matter how precise it may be, "can never be self-sufficient" nor "justify its own existence by itself alone. . . . An abstract science cannot be isolated from its intuitive origins—even though it be mathematics—without depriving it of its deepest meaning and its inner life" (F. Gonseth, *Les fondements des mathématiques*, Paris, 1926, pp. 13, 96).

5   Taken in itself and abstracting from its systematic connections, the notion of scientific truth proposed by Husserl and "conceived as an ensemble of well-founded predicative relations or relations founded in an absolute fashion" (*Méditations cartésiennes*, 1931, p. 10) does not seem very far removed from such a conception.

3. If, however, this knowledge is necessarily true, should not the object on which it lays hold be just as necessary? How could a changeable and contingent object give rise to a stable knowledge, one which could not be false? Furthermore, would a thing be explained, would we be giving a reason for it, if, once its reason for being were posited, it could be otherwise? That is the problem which from the very beginning has been thrust upon philosophical reflection; it is the problem which led Plato, when confronted with the fact of certain knowledge, to set up a world of Divine Ideas. Let us not try to escape with any timid reply in which the primary demands of scientific knowledge would be obscured. Let us grant from the beginning—and we will immediately see how this statement must be understood and restricted—that there is knowledge of the necessary only, and that the contingent, as such, is not the object of science. Science bears directly and of itself on a necessary object.

The difficulty is immediately evident. The object of science is necessary. But the real, the concrete, flowing world of things, involves contingency. This table could not—exist there in front of me today, and I who am writing could not—be here at this very hour. Does science, then, not deal with the real? No, it does not bear directly upon the real in all its nakedness, on the real taken in its concrete and singular existence. (In this sense, Mr. Goblot is right in insisting on the difference between *reality* and *truth*.) But, on the other hand, it does not deal with a Platonic world separated from things. It is absolutely necessary to distinguish the *thing* with which science is concerned (this table, for instance) and the perfectly precise *object* ("the formal object") upon which it lays hold and from which it derives its stability (for instance, the geometric properties of this table when considered in its shape or the physico-chemical properties of the wood from which it is made or the laws of its manufacture). The latter (the object) does not exist when separated from the thing (except in our mind) and yet it is not confused with it.[6] Science bears directly and of itself upon the abstract,[7] on ideal constancies and supramomentary determinations—let us

---

6   It is distinguished from it by a distinction of reason.

7   We are well aware that the notions "abstraction" and "abstract natures" are quite repulsive to the nominalism, confessed, or not, admitted by many of our contemporaries. Yet are they unaware of the curious spectacle they themselves present when, while denouncing such notions as vain and old-fashioned, they themselves have on their lips such notions as *science, spirit, method, mathematical reasoning*, and so forth—all of which are objects of thought in which it is difficult not to recognize abstract natures? You might as well pursue a phantom. For the critical intellectualism of an Aristotle or a St. Thomas has never, as they imagine, made scientific abstraction consist in placing an individual in a logical class, or beneath the hypostasized generality of its proper characteristics, but rather in disengaging from it the reality that may be thought by, and consistent with, the mind, that is to say, in disengaging from it the whole complex of intelligibility of which it is the bearer. That is what the Scholastics called *abstractio formalis* (see below, Ch. II, § 12).

Scientific understanding cannot do without this *abstractio formalis* in any way

say, on the intelligible objects that our mind seeks out in the real and sets free from it. They are there, they exist there, but not at all in the condition of abstraction and universality that they have in the mind. On the contrary, they exist in a concrete and singular condition. Human nature exists in each of us. But only in the mind is it a universal nature common to all men. In each of us, it is Paul's or John's nature.

Let us note that scientific law never does any more than express (in a more-or-less direct way, or more-or-less devious way) the property or requirement of a certain ontological indivisible which of itself does not fall under the senses (is not observable) and which for the sciences of nature remains an X (albeit indispensable), and which is nothing other than what the philosophers designate by the name *nature* or *essence*.[8] In virtue of an ontology immanent to our reason (or spontaneous philosophy) we *know in advance* that the network of phenomena or relations selected by us as an object of observation has as its support just such natures or essences, such ontological X's. The experimental sciences do not penetrate these essences in their intelligible structure. And, more often than not, it still remains doubtful whether the more-or-less provisory and unstable categories that those sciences construct, and on which their rational task operates, correspond to those essences. It is, however, exactly within these *ontological non-observables*, which are taken for granted, that there resides the reason for the necessity of those stable relations, which are formulated by science, among the elements the mind selects from phenomena or

---

whatsoever. Whatever may be the way knowing proceeds, even though it proposes only to put phenomena into equations and establish their empiriological connections and so gives up any thought of seeking the essence, abstraction is always at hand. It is abstraction that permits us to establish the rules of measurement and calculation thanks to which phenomena are mathematicized; and it is abstraction that disengages the empirical specificity of phenomena which is a substitute for essence and which presupposes the existence of that essence.

8   Following E. Meyerson, let us quote two significant texts here: "Whatever may be said in modern scientific schools (wherein the great fear, above all other, is to seem to be constructing a metaphysics), moderate atomism, as well as pure atomism, implies the claim that they grasp the essence of things and their inner nature in some way" (Cournot, *Traité de l'enchaînement . . .* Paris, 1861, p. 264). "We are in search of each thing's essence or necessity and these two expressions are equivalent because, when we know the essence, we see that the thing to which it belongs could not . . . be other than it is" (Sophie Germain, "Considérations générales sur l'état des sciences et des lettres aux différentes époques de leur culture," *Oeuvres Philosophiques*, Paris, 1878, p. 158). And in his own turn, Mr. Bertrand Russell writes: "Logic and mathematics force us to admit a kind of realism in the scholastic sense, i.e., to admit that there is a world of universals and truths that do not bear directly on this or that particular existence. This world of universals has to subsist, even though it could never exist in the same sense as that world exists in which particular data exist" ("L'importance de la logistique," *Rev. de Meta. et de Mor.*, xix, May 1911.

which it builds on their foundation. The necessity of laws derives from the fact that they properly and in the final reckoning concern essences or natures, and from the fact that essences or natures are the locale of intelligible necessities. For every nature or essence, as a result of its intrinsic structure, necessarily possesses certain properties (for example, the diagonal of a square is incommensurable with a side) or necessarily tends to produce a determined effect in certain conditions (for example, heat tends to expand solids). What does the law of the expansion of solids by heat mean? Does it mean that a certain concrete event, the expansion of a certain bit of iron placed over a certain flame, is a necessary and inevitable affair? No! This flame might not have been kindled; this bit of iron might not have been placed there; it could have been protected by an insulator, cooled by a stream of water, and so forth. The law means that *solid* (an abstract object which I see in this fragment of iron) has within the secrets of its nature a certain something, I know not what, which (at least, within the conditions of my sphere of observation, which experience will perhaps one day compel me to make more precise)[9] necessarily and unfailingly determines it to expand according to certain specific coefficients under the action of *heat* (an abstract object which I see in this flame and which I can define thanks to a difference in certain calibrated readings). It goes without saying that I may not realize these abstractions as such. Heat may rather appear to me to be the kinetic energy of a multitude of molecules whirling around in disarray; so that, in the corpuscular scale, the law in question becomes a statistical law and only states the stability of a mean result. But if essence or nature with its *determinatio ad unum* thus recedes (and perhaps continually) before the scientist's gaze, it would still not disappear from the field of the real. Absolute chance is a contradictory notion. A crossing of preordained things, which itself is not preordained, supposes the things which are preordained. To know that at a certain age death occurs according to a certain percentage, the actuary depends on statistics alone and on the law of large numbers. But behind this very law and behind the statistics, there is the nature of the human body and the natures of all those physical, moral and social beings in the midst of which this body is placed and whose action it accidentally undergoes. Chance gives rise to fixed numbers only because at the outset there are elements which are not determined by chance, and amongst these chance can be at play. As primary laws or specific determination are, for experimental science, substitutes for natures and essences that are not attained in themselves, so statistical laws are second degree substitutes for them, and like the others, they, too, presuppose that there are natures, the final foundation for the stability of knowing.

9   Such a reservation must necessarily be presupposed in the case of every law established by induction. And the law of the expansion of solids by heat has been established in purely inductive fashion before it was tied in once more with a physical theory of heat.

To the question why does not the necessity of laws—and these are the objects of science—extend to each of the particular events that takes place here below? this answer must be made: the world of actual existence and concrete reality is not the world of pure intelligible necessities. Essences or natures do exist within existing reality; from it they (or their substitutes) are drawn by our mind, but they do not exist there in a pure state. Every existing thing has its own nature or essence. But the existential positing of things is not implied in their nature, and amongst them there are encounters which are themselves not natures, the necessity for which is not prescribed in any nature. Existing reality is therefore composed of *nature* and *adventure*. That is why it has a direction in time and by its duration constitutes an (irreversible) *history*—these two elements are demanded for history, for a world of pure natures would not stir in time; there is no history for Platonic archetypes; nor would a world of pure adventure have any direction; there is no history for a thermodynamic equilibrium.

Necessity and Contingency

4. It is clear, then, that the precise notion of abstraction and the universal will provide the explanation we were seeking. Unless individual thing and universal essence are distinguished, it is impossible to understand how the *event* can be *contingent* while the *law* known by science is *necessary*; how things flow and change while the object of science is of itself immutable and enduring. But so it is precisely because contingency depends on the singular as such (more exactly, in this visible world, on matter, the principle of individuation), whereas of itself science bears not upon the singular as such but on universal natures that are realized in the singular and which the mind draws out of the singular by abstraction.

Science deals with things, but, thanks to abstraction, by "considering apart"—whether it perceives them clearly or lays hold of them in a blind fashion—the universal natures which are realized in things and the necessities proper to these natures. This, then—and not the flux of the singular—constitutes its object. Contingency properly concerns singular events; it is only "according to the intelligible constituents of universal natures" that the necessities known by science apply to singular things.[10] That is why the necessary laws of science do not impose any necessity on each of the singular events in the world of nature. A certain workman has fashioned this stone into a cube; it is necessary that it have the geometric properties of a cube; but it could have had a different shape. This bridge has been constructed in a faulty way because the engineer calculated the stresses inaccurately, or with faulty materials, or because the contractor cheated the government. Inevitably, by reason of the

---

10   "Illa proprie ad singularia pertinent quae contingenter eveniunt; quae autem per se insunt vel repugnant, attribuuntur singularibus secundum universalium rationes" (St. Thomas, *In Perihermeneias*, lib. I, cap. 9, lect. 13, n. 6).

nature of iron or stone, one day this bridge will collapse. But the fact that the engineer calculated inaccurately, or that the contractor lacked integrity, or that a prudent inspector did not give the order to strengthen the work, or that a certain stroller crossed the bridge at the moment of the accident—all that is entirely independent of this natural necessity. It is contingent. These contingencies of the singular escape science. The necessities of the universal are the proper objects of its grasp.[11]

Thus, the *universality* of the object of knowledge is the condition of its *necessity*, the very condition of perfect knowledge or science. By the very fact that there exists scientific knowledge only of the necessary, there is scientific knowledge only of the universal.[12]

5. In this sense Aristotle, following Plato, taught that there is science, absolutely speaking, only of things incorruptible and eternal. However, he corrected Plato by adding that these incorruptible and eternal things (incorruptible and eternal as essences, or negatively) are universal natures which exist outside the mind only in things singular and perishable. Thus, as a result, there can "accidentally" be science of corruptible things, insofar as we apply to the singular the universal truths of science, and to the extent that understanding, "leaving, so to speak, its own sphere, returns, through the ministry

11   It can be predicted with certainty that a certain number of children born today will pass the age of *n* years; but none the less that does not tell what age this particular youngster *X* will attain. The eclipse of 1999 is as certain as an insurance company's schedule of life-expectancy; the leap that an atom will take is as uncertain as my life or yours" (A. S. Eddington, *The Nature of The Physical World*, Cambridge, University Press, 1929, p. 300). It seems that the greater and greater importance assumed by statistical laws in science (and here we are not speaking of "relations of uncertainty" in corpuscular mechanics, for we will have to treat of them later on; we are only speaking of the host of chance shocks on which, in the last analysis, "the leap that an individual atom or individual molecule will take" depends) can be looked upon as an illustration of Aristotelian ideas about the bond between the contingent and the singular. Statistical law seems, then, as we have pointed out above, to be a substitute at second hand for the intelligible necessities inscribed in the universal, which experimental science cannot quite succeed in deciphering.

12   On this point certain rather easy misunderstandings should be avoided. We are stating that there is no science of the individual *as such*. And that does not mean at all that there cannot be an *indirect intellectual knowledge* (by "reflection" upon the senses—or by means of affective connaturality) of the individual as such. From this point of view, we even admit with John of St. Thomas, that there is a proper (indirect) concept of the singular.

Nor does it mean that there could not be a science of the individual—but not as such (i.e., in its singularity, in its very incommunicability). Study of character, graphology, the science of temperaments, etc., are sciences of the individual which, in order to grasp the singular, grasp it under a network of subspecific universal notions and, over and above that, fortify themselves with an art in which experience and the *ratio particularis* play an essential part.

of the senses, to things corruptible in which the universal is found realized."[13] "Although sensible things," says St. Thomas on this score, "are corruptible when taken in their individual existence, they have, however, a certain eternity if they are taken universally."[14] And thus, just as there is no knowledge and demonstration of sensible things except when taken in their universal nature and not in their individuality, it follows that science and demonstration only bear indirectly and "accidentally" on the corruptible; of themselves, they deal with what is "eternal." The immutability and the necessity of the object of knowledge are conditioned by its universality.

This whole doctrine is admirably summarized by St. Thomas in the following text: "The understanding knows the universal and necessary reasons of contingent things. That is why, if the universal reasons of the objects of knowing be considered, all science is of the necessary," although to take things materially, and "to consider the very things about which science is practiced, certain sciences," such as mathematics, for example, "have for their matter necessary things, and others," physics, for example, "have contingent things."[15]

A Digression on "Determinism in Nature"

6. The error of pseudo-scientific mechanism clearly supposes and involves the error of nominalism. If the universal does not directly or indirectly designate an essence or nature but only a collection of individual cases, it is not at all possible to understand how scientific law can be necessary and the succession of singular events contingent. The point that mechanists misunderstand is that law expresses nothing else but the order of a cause, *taken abstractly in its universal nature*, to its effect. And even though the positing of that cause in actual existence is contingent or though, in the flux of particular events, another cause comes along to interfere with the realization of its effect, that order always remains.

If it be supposed that there are no *free* (intelligent) agents in the universe, it is clear that a certain event which has occurred here below (for example, the fact that a certain squirrel is climbing up a certain tree at a certain moment, or that lightning struck a certain mountain at a certain moment) was infallibly predetermined in the configuration of *all* the factors in the universe posited at the beginning. But in that case, there is only a necessity *of fact*, no necessity *of right*. Not only

could this configuration of factors have been otherwise at the beginning, but also none of the numberless meetings between the diverse causal series produced in the course of the world's evolution down to the production of this

---

13   Cajetan, *In Anal. Post.*, lib. I, cap. 8.
14   "Etsi enim ista sensibilia corruptibilia sint in particulari, in universali tamen quamdam sempiternitatem habent" (St. Thomas, *In Anal. Post.*, lib. I, cap. 8, lect. 16).
15   *Sum. Theol.*, I, 86, 3.

event had its sufficient reason in the essential structure of the universe nor in any essence whatsoever. The proximate causes involved in the production of this event *could of themselves* (even though they could not with regard to the whole multitude of situations that in fact preceded and accompanied it, supposing that they themselves were not disturbed) have been prevented from producing it without violating any rational necessity. Of itself, it was a *contingent* event.[16] (And as a result, the supposition that a free agent intervened to modify or prevent it does not imply any impossibility.)

These remarks indicate the sense in which one may speak of the determinism of nature. This expression is quite legitimate if it means that every cause in nature is necessarily determined or ordered by its essence to an effect (which can in fact fail if the cause is not posited or if other causes intervene), and that such necessary determinations are the object of the sciences of nature, or rather their foundation (for the more they free themselves from ontology in their own structure, the more do they escape causality in the philosophical sense of that word).[17] But it is a mistake and a complete blunder to say that science supposes "the universal determinism of nature" if that means that all the events that take place in nature are made necessary and inevitable by right from the very instant that nature itself is posited. Again, it is an error to suppose that such a universal necessity is the object of science which should, from that moment onward, deal with all the individual events occurring in nature, when, on the contrary, if dealt with in this way, they escape it by nature.

7. It is curious to note that Fichte, for example, was led to his "theory of science" and to vast delicate constructions in his metaphysics of liberty, largely by his desire to escape this "universal determinism," a more rigorous criticism of which would have been enough to show him that it is only a murky idea and posits only a pseudo-problem. The same melancholic remarks can be made about Renouvier's philosophy and, more generally, about most of the modern systems that have sprung from Kantianism.

The Aristotelian-Thomist view, on the contrary, by showing how contingency in the course of singular events is reconciled with the necessity of laws known by science, shows how it is possible to insert into nature the liberty proper to spirits which, as such, do not form part of sensible nature and of the corporeal universe but which do, however, act in that universe.

Another Digression. How Do We Attain Essences?

8. Let us close this parenthesis to open a new one. We have just been speaking of natures and essences. Does that mean that, from our point of view, the first intellectual operation, abstraction, immediately yields the *essence of*

---

16 Concerning this question, cf. our *Philosophie bergsonienne*, 2nd ed., pp. lxix–lxx, and 217.

17 See below, Ch. IV, § 10.

things in its intrinsic structure? Is it enough to form the idea of fire, or better still of fieriness, to penetrate the ontological secret of combustion? That would surely be chemistry at a bargain.

Such a reproach forms the basis of criticisms levelled by many contemporary philosophers at what one of the more serious of them calls pre-Cartesian thought. It is rather humiliating to have to reply to it. It may come partly from the misdeeds of decadent scholasticism, partly from a superficial reading of an elementary textbook. Above all, it comes from a profound ignorance of philosophic tradition.[18]

Abstraction (as has been explained very often), from the very fact that it transfers us from the level of sensible and material existence to the level of objects of thought, introduces us into the order of intelligible being, or of *what things are*. But at first it only attains the commonest and poorest aspects of this intelligible being. The idea of fire only represents to us *something, some determined being*, which produces certain sensible effects, for example, burning and glowing. Abstraction reveals certain intelligible aspects which really are in things. But the very essence of things, i.e., the notes that properly constitute their intelligible being and explain their properties, is only attained—when it is attained—at the expense of hard labor. For the discovery of that essence must always be in keeping with the imperfect manner of knowing suited to man, and only in virtue of the properties which reveal it. And I hasten to add that in a whole vast area, that of the inductive sciences, we do not attain it and we have to content ourselves with substitutes, manageable equivalents.[19]

---

18   The philosophers of whom we are thinking, if they undertake to speak of St. Thomas without taking the time to read him (and to read him with scrupulously scientific objectivity and the desire for information they have a right to expect of others and would have even more right to demand of themselves), would only have to cast their lofty glances over some very clearly written pages on this subject—the work of L. Noel (*Notes d'épistémologie thomiste*, p. 142) and J. de Tonquédec (*La critique de la connaissance*, pp. 42, 138; *Immanence*, Appendix I)—and their illusions would be dispelled. Also, see A. Forest, *La structure métaphysique du concret selon saint Thomas d'Aquin*, Ch. III, pp. 72–97; and below, Ch. V, §§ 1–6.

19   On this score let us quote a remarkable page written by Mr. Gaston Rabeau (*Realité et relativité*, Paris, 1927, p. 203) in connection with Mr. Leon Brunschvicg's work on *Expérience humaine et la causalité physique.* "The analysis of causality, facts and the connections between facts, which science seeks, gives us the idea of an interpretation of the real that would not coincide at any point with a more refined Kantianism, a Kantianism without fixed categories and in which functions of judgment are indefinitely flexible. Basically, Mr. Brunschvicg has brought to light the fact that essence (and by that term let us understand laws and theories) is not achieved all at once, that experience suggests truths more than it imposes them, that processes of knowing do not allow themselves to be isolated from the object of knowing, that it is necessary from time to time to turn back by an act of reflection upon the processes that have been used with a view to putting them in a condition to help in more complicated tasks. But all of that is undeniably

We succeed in gaining an intimate knowledge of the real in philosophy, wherein we study things not from the particular point of view of their specific diversity, but from the universal point of view of transcendental being soaked into them. But are we then dealing with a knowledge which is particularized even to the very specific essences themselves? As regards physical realities, we succeed in attaining quidditative definitions only of ourselves and of things belonging to man. And only of these things can we intelligibly attain the nature to a specific degree. For all the rest of the corporeal world, for everything that is below us, since we are unable to attain a perception of their intelligible structures themselves, we are forced to have recourse to a knowledge inductively built on sensible effects alone, one that does not provide us with the essence, but only with simple outward *signs* of it.

It is all too often forgotten that if a metaphysics appears incapable by right (if not in fact) of giving recognition to the process proper to inductive sciences and shows itself imbued with an outrageous ambition and dogmatic intemperance as regards the science of the corporeal universe (to the very point of admitting an exhaustive knowledge of the essence of matter which is thus supposed to lie naked before our mind), then it is the metaphysics of Descartes and Malebranche. This is the very metaphysics from which flows, more-or-less camouflaged by experimentalism, the ever-present mechanist ideal of many contemporary scientists; it is not the critical realism elaborated by the ancients.

That is the end of our second parenthesis. We can now determine more accurately what we had been setting forth above.

Sciences of Explanation (In the Full Sense of the Word) and Sciences of Observation

9. We have said that science as such, and thus every science, by its direct[20]

---

true and we find no difficulty in it, only it is opposed to the phantasmagory of a world of essences made entirely in the mind and to the naiveté of a philosophy that would think it had the divine plan of the world in its head. Besides, in the *Transcendental Analytic*, Mr. Brunschvicg sets forth as a concrete element that stands in the way of a deduction of the categories, irreversible duration which is the matter of real causality: he points out certain invariables that may serve as points of reference in diverse systems; he speaks of something irreducible that is the very basis of experience. In short, he points out the *fact* to us, along with the intelligible nature that constitutes it, and the *spirit*, too, which, in its attempt to compare facts, works at reconstructing the table of essences through separate threads that are only joined together with difficulty. This history of the drama of thought at grips with nature for the purpose of stripping it of its secrets is a powerfully attractive one; and it only seems a bit removed from our own doctrines because these analyses are connected with postulates they (i.e., our doctrines) do not make."

20   In opposition to the movement of *return* whereby it turns back upon the singular.

movement, deals with universal natures or essences; by its very nature it is directed towards these natures. Let us now make the following distinction:

There are sciences which deal with these essences as known; not known in any exhaustive fashion (for indeed we do not know all about anything)[21] but nevertheless known or revealed (by their externals).[22] These are deductive sciences, philosophical or mathematical—deductive, however, for very different reasons. In the latter case, mathematical knowledge, the mind grasps entities it has drawn from sensible data or which it has built on them. It grasps them through their constitutive elements, and constructs or re-constructs them on the same level. These things in the real (when they are *entia realia*) are accidents or properties of bodies, but the mind treats them *as though* they were subsistent beings and *as though* the notion it makes of them were free of any experimental origin. In the former case, on the contrary, in philosophic knowledge, it does not lay hold of substantial essences by themselves but through their proper accidents and it only proceeds deductively by being constantly revitalized by experience (the "analytic-synthetic" method).

These sciences are properly sciences of explanation, διότι ἐστιν, *propter quid est*, in the terminology of the ancients. They reveal to us intelligible necessities immanent in the object; they make known to us effects by principles, or reasons for being, by causes, taking this latter term in the quite general sense that the ancients gave to it. It can happen, it is true, that when confronted by a very exalted reality, one whose essence can be known only by analogy, they must limit themselves (and this is the case of metaphysics when confronted by God) to a knowledge of simple factual (supra-empirical)[23] certi-

---

21 As far as Thomists are concerned, if we knew essences exhaustively (*adequate ut sunt in se*), there would be *as many specifically different sciences* as there are essences so known. Thus, our science, from the mere fact that it embraces a multitude of different natures under one and the same light and on the same level of abstraction, bears witness to the fact that the real remains inexhaustible for it. Cf. John of St. Thomas, *Curs. Phil.*, Log. II P., q. 27, a. 1, ed. by Reiser, t. I, pp. 819 and 824: "Et hoc totum ex eo tandem provenit, quia nostrae scientiae imperfectae sunt et non omnino adaequantur ipsis rebus neque eas adaequate comprehendunt. Nam si quaelibet res perfecte comprehenderetur, quaelibet res fundaret scientiam sibi propriam et specie distinctam ab alia, neque scientia requireret coordinationem specierum, sed quaelibet res per suam speciem adaequatam perfecte repraesentata suas passiones demonstraret."

22 See below, Ch. V, §§ 1 and 2, 4 and 5.

23 *Scire an sit* or *quia est* (knowing in the range of or within the perspective of fact) is not at all limited to knowing of an inductive type, for in a general way (in opposition to *scire quid est* or *propter quid est*, knowing in the range or perspective of a reason for being) this expression designates any knowledge that does not succeed in laying hold of the essence itself in all its intelligible constitution. Thus, for example, in a discipline of the deductive type like metaphysics, *scire quia est* plays a very important role since all the knowledge of God we have here below issues from this sort of knowing.

As for sciences that are termed inductive, they belong to *scire quia est*, to the

tude. But at that very moment they transcend explanation. It remains true, however, that of themselves they still yearn to discover the essence.

And then there are sciences which have to do with essences *as hidden* without ever being able to uncover in themselves the intelligible necessities immanent in their object. These are inductive sciences, sciences which (to the extent, at least, that they remain purely inductive—and that is not the case with physics and the experimental sciences of the moderns: Bacon and Mill are quite wrong on that score) are of themselves only sciences of empirical observation (a particular case of knowledge in the simple line of fact, ὅτι ἐστιν, *quia est*, and which fall short of explanation properly so called. It is by effects that they make causes, or reasons for being, known to us and so these causes or reasons are not made known in themselves but in signs which, for us, are substitutes for them. We know that heat expands metals, that ruminants have cloven hooves. We grasp thereby in a rather blind fashion a necessity whose reason we do not see since a well-established experimental constancy is a sign of necessity, and this latter a sign of some essential connection. Inductively established law is thus much more than a simple general fact; it enfolds an essence but without revealing it; it is the practical equivalent of the essence or cause which in itself remains hidden to us.

The former sciences, sciences of explanation, set before the mind intelligibles freed from the concrete existence that cloaks them here below, essences delivered from existence in time. Even though no triangle existed, it would always be true that the sum of the angles of the Euclidian triangle is equal to two right angles. In that sense, these sciences can be said to give us eternal truths.

The other sciences, sciences of observation, do indeed tend to such truths, but they do not succeed in emerging above existence in time, precisely because they attain intelligible natures only in the signs and substitutes that experience furnishes for them, and therefore in a manner that inevitably depends on existential conditions. Thus, the truths stated by them affirm, indeed, a necessary bond between subject and predicate, but also suppose the very existence of the subject, since the necessity they evince is not seen in itself but remains tangled with existence in time—and to that extent, if I may say so, garbed in contingency.

10. To sum up, we can say that science in general deals with the necessities immanent in natures, in universal essences realized in individuals, in the world of concrete and sensible existence. We have distinguished sciences of explanation or deductive sciences which attain these essences openly (by construction in the case of mathematics, by proceeding from the outside inward in the case of philosophy), and sciences of observation or inductive sciences, which attain these natures only in signs and substitutes, blindly, if

---

very extent that they are inductive, and constitute the supreme type of this kind of knowing in the realm of knowledge of nature.

one may so speak. These latter do indeed have a certain explanatory value, for without that, they would not be sciences. But this consists in noting necessities in things by means of sensible experience, not in assigning their reasons by intelligible means.

The distinction between these two categories of science is absolutely sharp: they are not reducible to each other.

But it is plain that sciences of the second category, sciences of observation, inductive sciences, since they are less perfectly sciences and do not succeed in realizing the perfect type of scientific knowledge, are not sufficient unto themselves. Of their very nature, they tend to sciences of the first category, to sciences of explanation properly so called, deductive sciences. *They are necessarily attracted to them.* In virtue of their very nature as sciences, they invincibly tend to rationalize themselves, to become more perfectly explanatory. In other words, they tend to take on a deductive character, and to that extent they are subject to the regulation of one of the disciplines which are properly deductive, that is to say, either philosophy or mathematics. This point, one should never forget.

11. Let us try now to go even further into the domain of the sciences and discover their essential divisions and hierarchy.

To that end, what we must consider are the diverse degrees of intelligibility in objects of knowledge. If we reflect that what philosophers call matter (Plato's existing non-being) is in the final analysis nothing but the ontological principle of relative unintelligibility (or irrationality to use modern parlance) which affects the very substance of things in nature and signifies, so to speak, the distance separating them from the intelligibility in pure act proper to uncreated Being, then the fundamental thesis that intelligibility goes with immateriality, so forcibly propounded by St. Thomas Aquinas, is immediately understood. The essential divisions of the sciences will therefore have to be established in accordance with the different ways or degrees in which the objects of thought discovered in things by intellectual operation are free of matter. We shall restrict our attention to these essential divisions without pretending to enter in detail into the sub-divisions of the classification of sciences. Moreover, we shall consider only speculative sciences and leave aside the moral sciences which, concerned as they are with the practical order, and proceeding by way of synthesis to the very concrete determinations of action,[24] belong to quite a different chapter of epistemology.

II

THE DEGREES OF ABSTRACTION

12. On this problem we find the guiding thread in the doctrine of the three degrees of abstraction, i.e., the three degrees according to which things present

---

24   See below, Ch. VIII, and Appendix VII.

to the mind the possibility of attaining in them a more-or-less abstract and immaterial object, I mean abstract and immaterial as regards the very intelligibility which flows from premise to conclusion and, in the final analysis, as regards the mode of defining.[25] The mind can consider objects abstracted from, and purified of, matter but only to the extent that matter is the basis of diversity amongst individuals within a species, i.e., insofar as matter is the principle of individuation. In this way, the object remains; and remains to the very extent that it has been presented to the intellect, impregnated with all the notes coming from matter, and abstracts only from the contingent and strictly individual peculiarities, which science overlooks. The mind thus considers bodies in their mobile and sensible reality, bodies garbed in their empirically ascertainable qualities and properties. Such an object can neither *exist* without matter and the qualities bound up with it, nor can it *be conceived* without matter. It is this great realm that the ancients called *Physica*, knowledge of sensible nature, the first degree of abstraction.

Secondly, the mind can consider objects abstracted from, and purified of, matter insofar as matter is the general basis for the active and passive sensible properties of bodies. In this case, it considers nothing more than a certain property which it isolates within bodies—a property that remains when everything sensible is left aside—quantity, number or the extended taken in itself. This is an object of thought which cannot *exist* without sensible matter, but which can be conceived without it. For, nothing sensible or experimental enters into the definition of the ellipse or of square root. This is the great field of *Mathematica*, knowledge of Quantity as such[26] according to the relations of order and measure proper to it—the second degree of abstraction.

---

25   Cf. John of St. Thomas, *Curs. Phil.*, Log. II P, q. 27, a. 1, ed. Reiser, t. I, pp. 822–823.
26   Certain clarifying remarks will be found below on the notion of quantity and the proper object of mathematics (cf. Ch. IV, § 6, and Ch. V, § 2). But let us note at once that, in making quantity as such, or ideal quantity, the object of mathematics in general, we do not have it in mind to exclude every qualitative determination from the mathematical order. Quite the contrary! For whether it be a matter of qualities or formal determinations that are included in the notion of the entities under consideration, or of the "irrational" entities from which they originate (for example, the primary specifications that serve to define the structure of the continuum or which, in the final analysis, rest upon a factual datum—as is the case with the specification "three-dimensional" concerning the space of classical geometry), it is clear that no science of quantity would be possible without qualities. *Analysis situs*, the theory of abstract spaces, the properties of order that are at the basis of topological concepts are excellent witnesses, to the importance of the qualitative element as it essentially affects the domain of mathematics. But then the qualities proper to quantity itself are in question, rather than qualities that refer to the nature of the radical principle of activity in bodies, i.e., qualities that can be reduced to the sensible order (physical qualities).
      On the other hand, it will be noted that, for the scholastics, the science of the continuum and the science of number, while belonging generically to the second degree, or the second order, of abstraction, none the less do present a difference

Finally, the mind can consider objects abstracted from, and purified of, *all* matter. In this case it considers in things only the very being with which they are saturated, being as such and its laws. These are objects of thought which not only can *be conceived* without matter, but which can even *exist* without it, whether they never exist in matter, as in the case of God and pure spirits, or whether they exist in material as well as in immaterial things, for example, substance, quality, act and potency, beauty, goodness, etc. This is the wide domain of *Metaphysica*, knowledge of that which is beyond sensible nature, or of being as being—the third degree of abstraction.

We should note here with Cajetan and John of St. Thomas that these three degrees of abstraction refer to the abstraction called *abstractio formalis*.[27] Actually, there are two kinds of abstraction. First, there is *abstractio totalis*. Let us call it an abstraction, or an extraction, of the universal whole whereby we get

at the very heart of that order—and a specifying difference at that—in the level of immateriality they achieve: the second is higher in abstraction and immateriality than the first (cf. John of St. Thomas, *Curs. Phil.*, Log. II P., q. 27, a. 1. ed. by Reiser, t. I, p. 825; *Phil. Nat.*, I P., q. 1, a. 2, Vives, t. II, p. 16). Modern mathematics, while striving to overcome this difference and amassing in the process the most fruitful discoveries, has only succeeded in the final reckoning in making its significance more marked and precise. For if geometry and arithmetic have become co-extensive, it is still right to think that the numerical continuum presupposes the first and irreducible notion of extension, and that irrational number, in virtue of which "the body of numbers" acquires "the same amplitude or the same continuity as the straight line" (Dedekind), is in reality an arithmetic symbol of a point arbitrarily designated on a straight line, an indivisible common to two segments that are continuous through it [(cf. F. Gonseth, *op. cit.*, p. 40). The vicious circle (that Mr. Weyl denounces) apparently involved in the way the existence of irrational numbers is ordinarily established would only result if an attempt were made to establish that existence in a purely arithmetical way, beginning with rational and whole numbers]. At all events, we are forced to fall back upon the distinction between two "schools" in mathematics, and two only, to wit, "the school of the numerable, Arithmetic, and the school of the continuum, Geometry" (Gonseth, *op. cit.*, p. 72).

Generally speaking, it is important to notice that the three basic degrees of abstraction which are taken *ex parte termini a quo*, according as the mind lets these or those material conditions slip aside, only define the primary, bold determinations of speculative knowledge, and within them discriminations of a specific kind can be found which are taken *ex parte termini ad quem*, according as the mind further sets up the object on a certain fixed level of immateriality (John of St. Thomas, *Log.*, *loc. cit.*). One and the same specific knowledge, for example, the Philosophy of Nature, can consider objects of very different universality (cf. St. Thomas Aquinas, *Comm. in de Sensu et Sensato*, lect. I) which are still on the same level of intelligibility as long as the *modus definiendi* is the same for all of them. But if it is a matter of a different mode of defining, of a different way of establishing scientific notions, then a specifically different type of speculative knowledge is involved.

27   Cajetan, *In de Ente et Essentia*, Prooemium, q. 1; John of St. Thomas, *Curs. Phil.*, Log. II P., q. 27, a. 1, ed. by Reiser, t. 1, pp. 822, 829.

"man" from "Peter" and "Paul," "animal" from "man," etc. In this way we proceed to wider and wider universals. This kind of abstraction, whereby the mind rises above simple animal knowledge of the singular perceived by the sense *hic et nunc*, and which in reality begins with more general and undetermined notions, is at the root of all human knowing. It is common to all the sciences. At this level, every science proceeds towards the greatest possible determination, demanding that its object be compressed, so to speak, into a proper notion, and not enveloped in a more-or-less variable common notion. Second, there is a kind of abstraction, *abstractio formalis*, which we may call an abstraction, or extraction, of the intelligible type whereby, from contingent and material data, we separate what belongs to the formal reason, or essence, of an object of knowing. The speculative sciences differ from one another according to the degrees of this *abstractio formalis*, the objects of the higher science being, as it were, a form or regulating type, with respect to the objects of the lower science. The objects of metaphysics are undoubtedly more universal than those of physics, but it is not on this score, that is, as more common notions on the same level, that the metaphysician considers them, but in virtue of an intelligible form or type on a higher level. The metaphysician considers an object of knowing of a specifically higher nature and intelligibility, and from it he acquires a proper knowledge, a scientific knowledge, by means that absolutely transcend those of the physicist or mathematician.

If a figure of speech be permitted here, let us say that the work of the intellect can be compared to an immaterial magic. From the flux of singular and contingent things, as given to the apprehension of the sense, a first glance of the intellect reveals the world of corporeal substances and their properties. A second glance reveals quite another universe, the ideal world of the extended number. A third glance discloses still another, wholly different, universe, the world of being as being and all the transcendental perfections common to spirits and bodies, wherein we can attain purely spiritual realities, and the very principle of all reality, as in a mirror.

13. Now how are we going to classify the sciences which only a short time ago we called sciences of observation, those, namely, that do not succeed in clearly attaining the natures at which they aim? They are clearly on the lowest level of abstraction. They form a part of *Physica*. From now on, therefore, we can distinguish, within this *Physica*, two classes of science as opposite extremes: sciences of observation (sciences which are above all inductive and which we may call empirical sciences of sensible nature),[28] and a properly explanatory science of corporeal being (the philosophy of sensible nature).

28   They can also be called *physico-physical* sciences, as we call them in our *Réflexions sur l'intelligence*, Ch. VI, or even *empirio-schematic* sciences, as we will call them below (Ch. IV). Generally speaking, that was the science among the ancients which had to do with the details of phenomena (i.e., when they were not absorbed in philosophical pseudo-explanations). And even in our own day they

To be more exact, let us note that all our concepts are resolved in being which is the first object attained (*in confuso*) by intellectual apprehension. The concepts of METAPHYSICS are resolved in being as such, *ens ut sic*; those of MATHEMATICS in that sort of being (isolated within the real) which ideal quantity is; those of PHYSICS in mobile or sensible being, *ens sensibile*. But for the philosophy of nature, the accent must be on *ens* in the expression *ens sensibile*. As a science of explanation, it discovers the nature of its object and the reasons for its being. And, since it is true that the nature of substances below man is not clearly accessible to us in its specific diversity, it must be said that the proper object of the philosophy of nature does not extend to that specific diversity of bodies, nor to the whole multitude of their phenomena, and is constituted only by transcendental being as determined and particularized in the corporeal, mobile and sensible world. We thereby note two things: First, that the philosophy of nature is in a certain continuity with metaphysics, in spite of the essential difference separating them, and that, on this score, it is above mathematics. Second, we note that philosophy does indeed provide a deductive science of corporeal being, but that it is incapable of providing a deductive science of the phenomena of nature.

As regards the empirical science of nature, on the other hand, in speaking of *ens sensibile*, the stress will have to be put on *sensibile*, not on ens. It will tend to resolve all its concepts in the sensible itself, in the visible itself, in observable determinations, at least to the extent that it strives to constitute an autonomous science of *phenomena*. Every definition, for example, the definition of geosynclinal, or of word-blindness, is then taken with reference to sensible observations and indicates something which presents certain well-determined observable properties. Empirical science will, to the same extent, tend to set up a conceptual lexicon entirely independent of the conceptual lexicon of sciences which, like the philosophy of nature and metaphysics, determine their definitions by referring to intelligible being.

Table of the Sciences

14. To sustain our interest in so complex and abstract a matter, we will arrange the notions we have so far derived in a synoptic table.

What do we see in this table?

I. The second degree of abstraction is not only depicted, as it should be, on a level midway between the first and third: it has also been drawn along another vertical line set off to the right of the table.

Why? Because mathematical abstraction is of a type quite apart. Although they differ specifically, *physica* and *metaphysica* have this in common, namely, that they deal only with intelligible objects which *can exist* in things, let us say *real* beings, insofar as the word *real* not only designates actual existence but

---

constitute those vast scientific areas that escape the rule of physico-mathematics and the way in which it rationalizes.

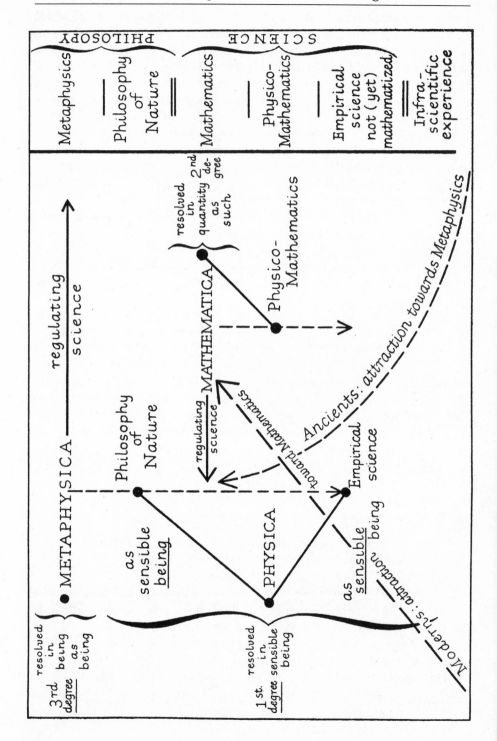

possible existence outside the mind as well. Mathematics, on the contrary, deals with an object which is not necessarily real, but one that may be an imaginary or fictive being (*permissive*, the ancients said),[29] a being of reason as well as a real being. As a result of this main difference, the three degrees of abstraction are not three steps on the same line of ascent, and the first and third, on the one side, the second on the other, require opposite ways of approaching things.

II. On the other hand, empirical science, philosophy of nature and metaphysics are along the same hierarchical line. Although specifically different, the light of the first degree of abstraction is, as it were, a participation in that of the third degree.[30] It is a lower and divided light, but still capable, in the

---

29   Cf. John of St. Thomas, *Curs. Theol.*, I P., q. 6, disp. VI, a. 2, n. 20, *Mathematica an sint bona* (Vivès, t. I, p. 680).

30   In our synoptic sketch we have placed the philosophy of nature at a higher level than mathematics insofar as it shares in the light of the third degree of abstraction. It still remains true, however, that the first degree of abstraction, to which it in itself is reduced, is inferior in immateriality to the second degree, and this point has also been depicted in the table.

On the one hand, these remarks enable us to understand that the sciences of nature presuppose mathematics. "Scientia quae se habet ex additione ad aliam, utitur principiis ejus in demonstrando, sicut geometria utitur principiis arithmeticae; magnitudo enim addit positionem supra numerum, unde punctus dicitur esse unitas posita. Similiter autem corpus naturale addit materiam sensibilem super magnitudinem mathematicam: et ideo non est inconveniens si naturalis in demonstrationibus utatur principiis mathematicis . . ." (St. Thomas Aquinas, in lib. I, *de Caelo et Mundo*, lect. 3). "Quaecumque impossibilia accidunt circa mathematicalia corpora, necesse est quod consequantur ad corpora naturalia; et hoc ideo, quia mathematica dicuntur per abstractionem a naturalibus; naturalis autem se habent per appositionem ad mathematica: superaddunt enim mathematicis naturam sensibilem et motum, a quibus mathematica abstrahunt: et sic patet quod ea quae sunt de ratione mathematicalium, salvantur in naturalibus, et non e converso" (*ibid.*, lib. III, lect. 3). From this point of view, the fact that real space has three dimensions is certified by necessities discovered in the course of construction in mathematical intuition—which is always the privilege of classical geometry. "Naturalis praesupponit a mathematico ea quae circa dimensiones considerat. Et ideo probare demonstrative, esse solum tres dimensiones, pertinet ad mathematicum, sicut Ptolomaeus probat per hoc, quod impossibile est conjungi simul lineas perpendiculares plures quam tres super idem punctum; omnis autem dimensio mensuratur secundum aliquam lineam perpendicularem" (*ibid.*, lib. I, lect. 2). If the notion of displacement is brought in, then we will say: "Let us consider a free solid, fix it at three points, it is immobile, fix it at two only, and each point along the axis of the other two describes a circle; fix it at only one point, and every point at a finite distance from that point can be moved on a sphere" (R. Poirier, *Essai sur quelques caractères des notions d'espace et de temps*, Paris, 1931, p. 105).

On the other hand, we can also understand that the philosophy of the continuum and of numbers returns to the philosophy of nature, to such a point that, according to St. Thomas, the mathematician's "postulates" would have to be

case of the philosophy of nature, of penetrating inside things, but in the case of empirical science, halted on the surface and at signs.

We know that, among the ancients, following the universal law of attraction of the lower by the higher, the empirical sciences of nature have undergone the attraction of the philosophy of nature and metaphysics. And, since only by being informed by a deductive science could they be established as sciences, they have sought this information from notions elaborated by the philosophy of nature and metaphysics.

III. Every higher discipline is regulative with respect to its inferiors. Since metaphysics considers the highest reasons for being, it will, as a result, be the regulating science par excellence, *scientia rectrix*. But mathematics is also a deductive science, a science of the *propter quid*. It will also tend to rule the lower sections of knowing, if not to encroach upon metaphysics itself. We thus understand the struggle for dominion so often engaged in by these two sciences in the course of history.

IV. The great discovery of modern times, foreshadowed by the Parisian doctors of the fourteenth century and by Leonardo da Vinci, and achieved by Descartes and Galileo, is the discovery of the possibility of a universal science of sensible nature informed not by philosophy but by mathematics: *physico-mathematical* science. This tremendous discovery has changed the face of the world (without, apparently, being able to change in any way the essential order of the things of the mind as we have tried to discover it here),and has given rise—as we have tried to show elsewhere[31]—to the terrible misunderstanding

---

proved by the philosophy of nature. "Sunt enim quaedam propositiones, quae non possunt probari nisi per principia alterius scientiae; et ideo oportet quod in illa scientia *supponantur*, licet probentur per principia alterius scientiae. Sicut a puncto ad punctum rectam lineam ducere, supponit geometra et probat naturalis; ostendens quod inter quaelibet duo puncta sit linea media" (St. Thomas Aquinas, *In Anal. Post.*, Lib. I, cap. 2, lect. 5, n. 7). If this way of looking at the matter is correct, then the rational necessities seen by philosophy in the analysis of the continuum as it is set free by abstraction from sensible and mobile reality (in other words, in the axiomatic analysis of the continuum insofar as it can be constructed in imaginative intuition), necessities that would be the basis for the postulates of Euclidian geometry, i.e., that would "discover" the Euclidian axiomatic in the notion of the continuum that can be represented intuitively (as Mr. Hamelin has tried to do from an idealistic point of view in several noteworthy pages of his *Essai*), and that would by the same token justify the non-Euclidian geometries, would give the mind complete security insofar as the compatibility of their axioms is concerned—inasmuch as these geometries, which contain Euclid's geometry and are contained by it, can always be translated into Euclidian language by the addition of extra dimensions; and inasmuch as the compatibility of Euclidian axioms, the absence of any contradiction hidden in their origin, is certified by the fact that the Euclidian continuum can be constructed in intuition: *ab actu ad posse valet consecutio*; for if the Euclidian continuum can be constructed in imaginative intuition and thus given as a fact, it is because there is no hidden incompatibility in its notion.

which, for three centuries, has embroiled modern science and the *philosophia perennis*. It has given rise to great metaphysical errors to the extent that it has been thought to provide a true philosophy of nature. Of itself, it was an admirable discovery from an epistemological point of view, and one to which we can quite easily assign a place in the system of sciences.

It is a *scientia media*, of which geometric optics and astronomy were typical examples among the ancients. It is an intermediary science, straddling mathematics and the empirical sciences of nature, a science for which physical reality provides the matter (through the measurements it permits us to gather from it) but whose formal object and method of conceptualization remain mathematical: a science *materially physical* and *formally mathematical*.[32] In such sciences, the rule of explanation leaves aside physical principles and causes with their proper intelligible value (as Duhem saw very clearly). And yet these sciences remain preponderantly physical, as St. Thomas notes in his commentary on the second book of Aristotle's *Physics*[33] (and as Einstein and Meyerson saw very clearly), because they have their terminus in sensible nature.

---

31 Cf. *Réflexions sur l'intelligence*, Ch. VI.

32 Cf. *Réflexions sur l'intelligence*, Ch. VI, and the texts we have quoted from St. Thomas on page 286, especially In Boet. de Trin., q. 5, a. 3, ad 6: "Quaedam vero sunt mediae, quae principia mathematica ad res naturales applicant, ut musica et astrologia, quae tamen magis sunt affines mathematicis, quia in earum consideratione id quod est physici, est quasi materiale, quod autem mathematici, quasi formale." See also below, Ch. II, § 29.

33 This is the way he has understood the expression : τά φυσικώτερα τῶν μαθμάτων. (*In Phys.* II, 2, 194a, 7), used by Aristotle concerning geometric optics (*perspectiva*), harmony and astronomy. "Hujusmodi autem scientiae, licet sint mediae inter scientiam naturalem et mathematicam, tamen dicuntur hic a Philosopho esse magis naturales quam mathematicae, quia unumquodque denominatur et speciem habet a termino: unde, quia harum scientiarum consideratio terminatur ad materiam naturalem, licet per principia mathematica procedat, magis sunt naturales quam mathematicae" (*In Phys.*, lib. II, lect. 3).

St. Thomas has written elsewhere (*Sum. Theol.*, II–II, 9, 2, ad 3) "Quilibet cognoscitivus habitus formaliter quidem respicit medium per quod aliquid cognoscitur; materialiter autem id, quod per medium cognoscitur; et quia id quod est formale, potius est, ideo illae scientiae quae ex principiis mathematicis concludunt circa materiam naturalem, magis cum mathematicis connumerantur, utpote eis similiores, licet quantum ad materiam magis conveniant cum naturali; et propter hoc dicitur in II Physic. quod sunt magis naturales." In his Commentary, Cajetan has these remarks to make about this text: "Non dicitur quod scientiae mediae sunt magis mathematicae quam naturales: cum falsum sit absolute loquendo; quia simpliciter sunt scientiae naturales, utpote non abstrahentes a materia sensibili. Omnis enim scientia non abstrahens a materia sensibili, est naturalis, ut patet VI Metaph. Sed dicitur quod connumerantur magis cum mathematicis, utpote eis similiores."

Thus, physico-mathematical science is at once *formally mathematical* (through the principles and *means* of demonstration it uses) and more physical than mathematical through the *terminus* or matter in which it verifies its propositions.

These two characteristics are in no way incompatible and are simultaneously affirmed by St. Thomas and Cajetan concerning *scientiae mediae*. Perhaps the more complete explanation of our thought which we are giving in the present work will satisfy Fr. Pierre Hoenen's scruples, for he seems to confuse our position with that of Duhem ("Maritain's Rede te Amsterdam," in *Studien*, May 1927) and he does not see that as far as we are concerned physico-mathematics is, indeed, a science of the *physical real*, but a science that knows that real only by transposing it, and *not as the physical real*. In any event, the distinguished professor will, we hope, find some consolation in making his own the lines with which Cajetan concludes the commentary we have already quoted(in II–II, 9, 1 and 2): "Verum, quia medium utrumque sapit extremum, et scientiae istae ex parte formae ex mathematica veniunt et pendent, ex parte vero materiae physicae sunt, sermones doctorum pie interpretandi sunt, si quando ad alterum extremum nimis declinant."

Moreover, it seems that Fr. Hoenen has read the texts he is criticizing rather rapidly. In our *Réflexions sur l'intelligence* (p. 198), we really have not said that physico-mathematical science is a logical monstrosity; we have said that a *false* notion of this science, one that would confuse it with a philosophy of nature, would make a logical monstrosity of it.

By contending, as he does in his communication to the Thomist Congress in Rome (*De Valore theoriarum physicarum*, Rome, 1925, pp. 61–74, 269–275; cf. also the interesting articles published in the review *Gregorianum*, 1925, pp. 248–265; 1927, pp. 229–242; 1928, pp. 417–460), that physical theories furnish knowledge of physical reality *by analogy*, without stating exactly what kind of analogy he is referring to, Fr. Hoenen seems to take the risk either of giving rise to serious misunderstandings regarding analogy or of giving himself up to a quest for some deceptive sort of concordism. As a matter of fact, what is it that is primarily understood in philosophy by "analogical knowledge"? It is that knowledge by analogy of proper proportionality which metaphysicians employ in order to reach some understanding of spiritual beings. This kind of knowledge teaches or informs us clearly, no doubt, but from a certain stage of conceptualization onward, symbolically, about mathematized physical reality, i.e., physical reality transposed to a level other than its own. The perpetual renewals in science (for instance, at this very moment, the recent ideas on photons and the new mechanics of Louis de Broglie and Heisenberg) show that it is prudent not to ask the philosopher to decide what is true and false in the physical theory of light or in the theory of the atom; all that he needs is to hold as true those experimental facts on which such theories are based and borrow from those very theories a provisional *picture* of things, intended to sustain his thought, rather than to shape it.

One point remains true, and this is what we would have liked to see Fr. Hoenen bring out. It is this: On each side of that knowledge which grasps the object in its essence (and which, later on, we shall call "dianoetic") there is seen to correspond symmetrically (a) the knowledge *by analogy* of proper proportionality (for things above) which metaphysics employs when it rises to the First Cause and (b) the knowledge *by signs* (for things below) which the sciences of phenomena provide us with concerning nature, especially that *symbolic* knowledge with which physico-mathematical theories end up in their loftiest deductive elaboration of the experimentally "given." We realize only too well that this latter kind of knowledge, as the word "symbolic" indicates, belongs to the logic of analogy

[The point that Émile Meyerson has so strongly made against positivism (and also against Duhem), is that a concern for "ontology"—explanation by physical causes—cannot remain foreign to science. But the encounter between the law of causality, which is immanent to our reason, and the mathematical conception of nature, has as its result the construction in theoretical physics of more and more remote and geometrized universes. In these universes, fictive causal entities based on the real (*entia rationis cum fundamento in re*), whose sole function is to serve as a support for mathematical deduction, come to include a very detailed account of empirically determined real cases or conditions. Actually, more often than not, physico-mathematical science will be thus led to revive the old hypotheses of mechanistic metaphysics (while at the same time it radically transforms them, or else, as is evident in our own day, it introduces into them vast areas of displacement and irrationality). This does not happen, however, in virtue of the essential requirements of causal explanation. Émile Meyerson thinks it does because he seems to conceive the rational process only on the Eleatic type; he remains a rationalist in spite of everything. The reason is, rather, that mechanism is the only way of representing causality that can stand up, however precariously, within a general reduction of physics to geometry.

Pierre Duhem, on the other hand, as Amyl Picard recalled in his lecture of December 16 1929 at l'Académie des Sciences,[34] thought that a physical theory is not an explanation; it is a system of mathematical propositions which have, for their purpose, to represent, as completely and simply as possible, a whole complexus of experimental laws."[35] It does, indeed, actually happen that in some of its parts (for example, energetics as Duhem conceived it, or in our own day, wave mechanics according to the interpretation that Heisenberg proposes and to which Louis de Broglie has rallied) physics makes use of pure mathe-

taken in the widest sense of the word: but then, properly speaking, it is a question of a metaphorical analogy the use of which it is the privilege of mathematics to permit for the sake of knowledge of the physically real (cf. below, Ch. IV, §§ 16 and 17). With Fr. Hoenen it can be said: "Secundum maximam Cajetani (*De Nom. Anal.*, cap. 4): *quidquid assimilatur simili ut sic assimilatur etiam illi cui illud tale est simile*, concludendum est: causa quam hypothesis verificata proponit assimilatur causae verae; quod nihil aliud est ac principium analogiae theoriae physicae quod supra delineavimus" (*De valore . . .* , p. 69). But then the *assimilatio* in question is either (a) a univocal substitution insofar as physical theory translates facts and shows us observable and measurable structures and causations (co-determinations) that have the value of *entia realia*, or (b) a symbolic or metaphorical substitution, insofar as physical theory constructs beings of reason on its own, that help it to gather and interpret such data in a deductive explanation. This combination (in many, many varied degrees) of the univocal description of experimental reality and the symbolic interpretation of this same reality appears to us characteristic of physico-mathematical knowledge.

34   *Un coup d'oeil sur l'histoire des sciences et des théories physiques* (Paris, Gauthier-Villars, 1929).

35   See particularly Duhem's book on *La théorie physique*.

matical symbols without therein attempting either *causal explanation* or the constructing of figurative hypotheses through which the mind may in some way take the mechanism of phenomena apart. But to tell the truth, when it does refrain from doing so, it makes a virtue of necessity because it cannot do otherwise. Where Duhem went wrong was in seeking the very model of physical theory in these rather exceptional cases, which he regarded as pure cases. Actually, these cases stand at the very limit of physical theory and in them the mathematical transposition of phenomena is momentarily sustained all alone in the mind without any supporting physical image. So little are they typical of physical theory that the mathematical symbols they use are just awaiting a chance to leave the realm of pure analytical forms and become explanatory entities. (This is what happened in the case of energy. For, "almost all scientists today admit that it is not merely an abstract conception," let us say a pure mathematical symbol. The somewhat crude case of atomic number could also be cited, for it has finally ended up by designating the charge of an atomic nucleus and the number of electrons gravitating about it, when at the outset it was simply a periodic number.) On the other hand, causal entities, and the structural patterns built by the physicists, derive their noematic consistency only from the mathematical symbolism they, so to speak, embody. The interpenetration of mathematics and entitative representations thus seem essential to physico-mathematical knowing. Whence it happens that, in accordance with Amyl Picard's remark, "These academic quarrels seem quite outmoded and the two points of view are curiously mingled in the work of scientists today."[36] Let us say, rather, that they constitute but one point of view. Moreover, Duhem's over-rarefied conception would have destroyed the main incentives arising from the discovery of facts, without which physics would not exist at all.

These explanations were necessary; we hope they will eliminate any misunderstanding concerning the positions herein maintained. Let us now return to our business.]

V. A science of *phenomena* as such became possible with the physico-mathematical *scientia media*, materially physical and formally mathematical. We no longer have to deal with a science of sensible nature which tries to find, as best it can, beneath phenomena, the intelligible connections that philosophy feeds on—philosophy which can explain phenomena only by already transcending them. We now have a science of sensible nature that applies to the details of phenomena themselves, just as they are coordinated in space and time, the formal connections of mathematical relations; and which, thanks to the science of ideal quantity, approximates the deductive character to which it aspires and without which it would not be a perfect science. Thus, to be at once experimental (in its matter) and deductive (in its form, but above all as regards the laws of the variations of the quantities involved), is the proper ideal of modern

36   *Op. cit.*, p. 37. Cf. below, Ch. II.

science. It provides truly scientific knowledge and devises wonderful means of utilizing sensible nature (from the point of view of quantity indeed, but not from the point of view of being). It has given up the direct search for real causes in themselves and aims to translate, first and foremost, its measurements of things into a coherent system of equations. In all these ways physico-mathematical science is evidently bound to end up by inserting itself, like a wedge, between pure empirical science and the philosophy of nature and so to rupture the continuity in which the optimism of the ancients delighted.

For the ancients, it was the philosophy of nature and metaphysics that drained, so to speak, the whole terrain of empirical science and infra-scientific experience and strove to bring it to the level and nature of science. This is the point we depict on the chart by an arrow pointing in the direction of metaphysics.

For the moderns, it is mathematics that performs this function. Thus, an arrow has to be drawn whose direction will be quite the opposite, its trajectory must mark a break, a very clear split, an irremediable fracture, between science and philosophy.

The intersecting of these two arrows symbolizes the epistemological drama of modern times.

As regards the science of the phenomena of nature, the ancients' attempt ended up in a resounding failure, at least, in respect to all that concerns matter and motion. Let us say that it has come a cropper over physics (in the modern sense of the word).

The moderns' effort has been a brilliant success in physics; and in our own day we are witnessing in this realm a crisis of growth which is a prelude to even more brilliant successes. But what will happen—even without quitting the realm of the scientific knowledge of phenomena—in the case of sciences whose objects do not so easily lend themselves to mathematization? They cannot be satisfied with algebraically symbolizing nature; and the real will continue to hold sway over them in the mind, in function of the notion of being. It could well be that the modern conception of science has been brought up short in face of biology and experimental science (to say nothing of the moral sciences which concern philosophy even more closely), just as the ancient view was in face of physics.

VI. We have given a very brief survey of the organic relations obtaining between the principal categories of science. If we now list these categories in a single column, we will see that they rank one above the other in a hierarchical order. Thus we get back to the classical distinction between sciences, in the strict sense of the word, and philosophy.

Science in general includes two great areas. First, there is the realm of wisdom, which knows things through first causes and the highest reasons for being; then there is the domain of science in the narrow sense, which knows things through second causes or proximate principles. Metaphysics is a wisdom. It is *the* wisdom pure and simple of the natural order, that order which is of itself accessible to natural reason. In a certain respect, the philosophy of nature is wisdom, because it deals with the first principles and first causes *in a given order*, to wit, in the order of corporeal nature. (I note, parenthetically, that the study of the basic ontological roots of mathematics, the philosophy of number and the continuum, enters into the sphere of the philosophy of nature, because inasmuch as mathematical abstraction does not of itself deal with real being, it does not include a wisdom in its own proper order.)

We shall, therefore, group these two wisdoms—wisdom pure and simple and wisdom in a certain respect, metaphysics and philosophy of nature—under the name PHILOSOPHY.

As for the other sciences—mathematics, physico-mathematical sciences, experimental sciences or historical sciences (paleontology, linguistics, etc.) which have not (as yet) been, and will likely never be informed, in their essential structure and scope, by mathematics—these we shall group under the name SCIENCE in the narrow sense of the word.

III
SCIENCE AND PHILOSOPHY

15. Although it may happen that the *material object* of philosophy and science are the same—for example, the world of bodies—nevertheless, the *formal object* is essentially different in each case; and it is this that determines the specific nature of intellectual disciplines. In the world of bodies, the scientist will study the laws of phenomena by linking up one observable event with another. If he is trying to discover the structure of matter, he will do this by representing to himself—through molecules, ions, atoms, etc.—how, in accordance with what laws, the ultimate particles (or the mathematically conceived entities that take their place) with which the whole edifice is constructed behave in the framework of space and time. The philosopher will seek to learn *what*, definitively, that matter *is* whose behavior is thus depicted, and what is the nature of corporeal substance as intelligible being. (The fact that, in view of a spatial or spatio-temporal reconstruction, it may be broken down into molecules, ions, atoms, etc., or into protons and electrons whether or not they are linked together in a wave system is irrelevant to the philosopher's problem.)

The scientist proceeds from the visible to the visible, from the observable to the observable (I mean "to what is at least indirectly observable"; I do not mean "to what is always able to be pictured or represented in imagination." For the imagination represents things as they appear to us in our scale of large dimensions, that is, as possible objects of full and continuous observation. But the moment the scientist passes to an order [the atomic order] in which the

very possibility of full and continuous observation of phenomena is eliminated,[37] he passes from a world of objects imaginatively representable to a
world of objects without any imaginable form. Such a world is unimaginable
by default, or "privatively").

The philosopher proceeds from the visible to the invisible, I mean to what
is *of itself* outside the order of sensible observation (for the simple reason that
the principles which he reaches are in themselves pure objects of understanding and not objects of sensible apprehension or imaginative representation. Here is a world unimaginable by nature, or "negatively").

Since they have utterly different formal objects, other principles of explanation, diverse conceptual instruments, and, on the part of the knowing
subject himself, quite distinct intellectual virtues or discriminating lights, the
domain proper to philosophy and the domain proper to the sciences do not
overlap. No explanation in the scientific order will ever be able to displace or
replace an explanation belonging to the philosophical order, and vice versa.
One would have to be very naive to imagine that recognizing, on the one hand,
an immaterial soul in man, and studying, on the other hand, the glycogenic
function of the liver or the relations between idea and image are two explanations that both belong to the same field and run counter to each other.

Truth to tell, scientific explanations do not reveal the very being of things.
Since they explain only proximate causes or even that kind of formal cause
which is the conformity of phenomena to mathematical law (and such more-
or-less arbitrarily constructed entities fashioned as a support for this type of
law), they can never satisfy the mind. For the mind will always, and necessarily, raise questions of a higher order and strive to penetrate into the purely
intelligible.

16. From this point of view, we can say there is a certain dependence of the
sciences on philosophy. Inasmuch as they seek the *raison d'être* and yet reveal
it only imperfectly, the sciences themselves inspire the mind with a desire for
philosophy and look for support to a higher knowledge. It is quite remarkable
how strongly this need has been felt, after the positivistic period of the
nineteenth century, in every domain of science. It is no less remarkable that
the need manifested itself in a most disorderly fashion. For, those who dealt
with philosophy without adequate philosophical equipment inevitably lacked
competence in this field, even when they were scientific geniuses like Henri
Poincaré.

Let it be clearly understood that the sciences do not depend on philosophy
for their intrinsic development. They only depend upon it in principle (not,
indeed, in the sense that they would need philosophy to know their own
principles and use them, but in the sense that it belongs to philosophy to
explain and justify those principles). Perhaps scientists sometimes miscon-

---

37   See below, Ch. IV, §§ 10, 13.

ceive the sort of dependence we are speaking of precisely because they have no need of express recourse to philosophy in order to exercise their properly scientific activity. Yet, if they reflect carefully upon the very activity they exercise (and this is, in truth, to philosophize), they cannot help recognizing that a whole philosophy is involved, so to speak, in practical guise.

The whole use of experimental methods and critique, as for example, the determining of the degree of approximation of acquired results, constitutes an applied or lived logic (*logica utens*). This only becomes pure logic, and the object of a particular science and a speculative art studied for its own sake (*logica docens*) when the logician reflects upon it. But in itself, this is nothing but logic, a properly philosophical discipline, in the state of exercise.

On the other hand, every scientist as a scientist, whatever the conscious or unconscious metaphysical opinions may be which lie at the root of the conception of the world on which he bases his life as a man, in the very exercise of his science, asserts practically (*in actu exercito*) a certain number of eminently metaphysical propositions (M. Meyerson should be thanked for having so forcibly called attention to this point), and he does so with a dogmatism that is all the more intransigent the less it is reflected upon. These propositions may concern the reality of the sensible world, the existence of *things* outside us, stable ontological nuclei, substantial x's, that serve to support phenomena.[38] They may raise the question of the power of our knowing faculties to lay hold of things—with difficulty, no doubt, and in a way that brings with it all sorts of more-or-less obscurely experienced limitations, but that can also enclose incontestable certainties—or, to put it otherwise, they may raise the question of a kind of intelligibility of the world, badly determined, perhaps, and felt to be imperfect, but one which they do not scruple to presuppose. Or again they may raise the question of the value of principles, especially the principle of

---

38   "The habit of calling a spade a spade keeps the scientific fraternity from too much vain quarrelling. It is splendid to agree on words and on the perceptions they designate. This remarkable accord creates among scientists an atmosphere of confidence, a unison from which they derive a certitude that is only a robust belief. There is perhaps not a single chemist who confuses the reality of barium sulfate with the idea he has formed of it. I was once curious enough to put the question to some of them. They all found it rather queer. From the startled looks they gave me I could see they all thought me mad to ask such a question. This, then, is settled: the modern chemist thinks bodies are the absolute substratum of their properties, without bothering his head about the hypothetical character of this conception" (G. Urbain, "Essai de discipline," *La Grande Revue*, March 1920). This remark made by a scientist of unquestioned authority, as M. Meyerson points out (*op. cit.*, II, p. 235), and phrased as it is in language that suggests quite different philosophical opinions, constitutes a testimony that is all the more precious as "this scientist professes, in theory, a quite orthodox positivism and evidently finds the type of thinking he so accurately depicts, utterly blameworthy."

causality,[39] in connection with the world of experience, that is to say, the inadequacy of change to explain itself by itself. . . .

Finally, every scientist has a certain idea of nature proper to his own science. Perhaps it is often explained in a very partial or a most confused way but it is one that is in practice very active and efficacious. It is an idea that undoubtedly plays a major part in the intellectual orientation of the great innovators. From this point of view, what is more remarkable than the aphorisms about the nature of physics that so often came to the lips of Mr. Einstein? Now these considerations about the proper nature of this or that science do not, frankly, appertain to that science itself, but to philosophy; it is a lived *gnosiology*.

In short, there is no science without first principles to which all our reasoning must be reduced, since an infinite regress in this order clearly renders all demonstration impossible. Every scientist, from the very fact that he applies himself to deciding any question, already clings in a very positive, although not conscious way, to an important number of philosophical data. It is evident, then, that it would be well to bring into clear light, to face squarely and see as an object of a perfect mode of knowing, everything that is involved, in a merely implicit fashion, in the mind of the scientist: that is, to philosophize. The objective bonds that link the sciences to philosophy would then be explicitly noted. Their axioms are determinations of the principles of metaphysics; for example, the mathematical axiom: two quantities equal to a third are equal to one another, is a particularizing of the metaphysical axiom: two things identical with a third are identical with one another. Philosophy justifies and defends their principles. It is philosophy that determines the nature of the primary objects the sciences work on and, consequently, their own very nature, value and limits. For example, philosophy, not mathematics, will tell us whether or not irrational numbers and transfinite numbers are real beings or beings of reason; whether non-Euclidian geometries are constructions of reason based on Euclidian geometry and so leave a privileged value to the latter, or whether, on the contrary, they constitute a much vaster whole of which Euclidian geometry is but a species; whether the frontiers between

---

39   We mean that the scientist affirms *in actu exercito*, in the very exercise of his scientific activity, the value of the principle of causality (prior to any philosophical reflection on the meaning, the import of the various modes of verifying that principle, and still less, its critical justifications). For if he were not convinced in practice that everything that happens has a cause, he would never give himself over to his work of research, he would never even begin it. But it so happens that as it makes progress into the meaning of what we call below its empiriological autonomy, science has to re-establish or transpose the concept of cause, and perhaps even admit into the picture of the world it is constructing lacunae that leave many gaps in the field of what is, for it, "causality" (cf. below, Ch. IV, §§ 10 and 33). Thus, between the scientific picture of the world and the energies of the mental work from which it emanates there is a disparity analogous to the one we have explained elsewhere between the scientific universe of the physicist as physicist and the universe familiar to the same physicist as a man.

mathematics and logic are invariable, etc. Finally, philosophy assigns the order reigning among the sciences: *sapientis est ordinare.*

In all of this, philosophy in no way encroaches on the proper scope and method of the respective sciences. For, as we have just seen, it would be absurd to treat a problem belonging to the scientific order by the methods of philosophy, and vice versa. Philosophy acts as a superior science.

17. Since philosophy is superior, and consequently independent—at least, in that which formally constitutes it—it is of itself independent as regards the sciences.

Let it be understood that there is no formal dependence of philosophy on the sciences. Never will a result in the scientific order, never will a scientific theory, never, in short, will science suffice, by its own means, to settle a philosophical question, for such questions depend on principles and on a light which are beyond the scope of science.

There is, to be sure, a great MATERIAL dependence of philosophy on the sciences. In the first place, within the hierarchy of knowledge, philosophy is like a culminating point, one that consequently comes last pedagogically. The philosopher, if he is to judge the value, limits and subordination of the sciences to each other, must obviously know them from that angle and closely follow their development. Moreover, scientific data normally serve the philosopher as illustrations to exemplify his ideas and render them more concrete. Finally, and above all, the progress of science (at least, as regards the established facts, if not the theories) should normally renew and enrich the material it provides for the philosopher's elucidations, especially in all that has to do with the philosophy of nature. Thus, for example, modern discoveries in cell structure, of the ovum in particular and its sexual elements, about artificial parthenogenesis, etc., give new and valuable precisions on the approach to the problem of the education of the vegetative soul. In like fashion, the renewal of geometry since Lobatchevski and Bolyai compels the philosopher to purify many of his notions on quantity. Nevertheless, such a dependence remains material. The changes involved affect, above all, the imaginable representation, so important in respect to terminology and the aura of associations that surrounds didactic terms. To imagine that philosophical doctrines have to be changed with every scientific revolution would be as absurd as to think that the soul is transformed with every change of diet.

Clarifications on the Notion of Fact

18. This is the place to deal briefly with the question of the role of experience and experimental fact in the realm of philosophy.

According to St. Thomas, philosophy rests on facts. It has to accept facts. It begins by humbling itself before the real, first known by the senses, and which we experience by our fleshly contact with the universe. So the philosophy of nature, in contrast with metaphysics, not only takes its origin in sense-experience, but finds there the terminus in which its conclusions must be verified. Yet, it does this in quite another way than the experimental sciences.

What, then, is a fact? It is a well-established existential truth. A certain connection in the objects of our concepts exists in the real. That very fact implies that this existence confronts a mind which can grasp therein those objects. A fact engaging human knowledge is not created by the human mind. A fact is given. But it is given to someone. And if it is given, it is received. A stone is not given to a stone. A fact is given to a mind. That is to say, it is discerned and judged. To conceive it as a pure and simple copy of the external real, devoid of any discrimination, is a deceptive simplification due to the unconscious materialism of the imagination.

Even at the level of the external senses, there is a sense judgment, as St. Thomas says. Sensible perception is itself educed. It is either an instinctive or acquired priming of the internal senses and the *ratio particularis*. Every fact is discriminated. It supposes a judgment either of the sense or of the understanding. Every fact is a witness to the activity of the mind. Idealists are right on that score. They are wrong in thinking that the activity of the mind cannot demand of things or take from them any information expressed by the mind but at the same time *given* by things. Their error is to believe—and this is a gratuitous and, ultimately, an absurd postulate—that every interpretation, or more exactly, every judgment made by our faculties of knowledge, is a deformation or a creation, rather than a more-or-less perfect and profound mode of becoming assimilated to the object and conformed to what is.

19. The error of the idealists is at the same time to challenge the primordial value of sense-intuition. In one way or another, every existential apprehension originates in this intuition, even when the fact in question transcends the whole order of the empirical and the sensible. (The same is true of the experience of our own existence, an experience which, though it is spiritual, not empirical, supposes a reflection on our own acts. This is true, also, of our knowledge of God's existence, which is established from visible things.) In the physical order (knowledge of corporeal nature) facts are given by the sense itself under the discriminating and critical judgment of the intellect. In order to distinguish the register of *fact* from the register of *theory* within this physical order and in the common procedures of the sciences of nature, let it not be said that theory arises from intellect and fact from sense. That would be a very superficial view. Rather, let it be said that, in the register of fact, the intellect intervening with its own natural or artificial resources, even its most scientific stratagems and delicate theoretical constructions, still aims to discern and formulate that which is furnished by sense-intuition.[40] In the register of theory,

---

40   In orders above the physical order, which will come up for consideration later
      on, this work of the intelligence which is characteristic of the "factual register"

on the other hand, working with those same resources, the intellect aims to discover essences or laws and explanatory reasons.

The activity of the mind does not intervene in the complex whole perceived by sense in order to create, but rather to pick out that which is of interest to intellectual knowledge. And because at the very moment a science is born, its characteristic point of view as well as the first facts on which it is based stand revealed; because before any advance is made in a science or any new facts are discovered, the mind must first enter that science and acquire the *habitus* proper to it; because before it approaches any particular scientific realm, the mind has already begun to philosophize, has already explicitly disengaged from the real a notion of being as such and the principles pertaining to it—therefore, the discrimination we have been talking about will already have taken place at a certain level of abstraction, and in the light of certain principles with reference to which the fact has a definite value, I mean a value for knowledge and truth. We may therefore conclude that all facts are not of the same *rank*. They do not constitute an indistinct and disorderly agglomeration gathered together in the market of sensible experience, to which the diverse sciences have to come to look for the commodities they need. Facts themselves belong to various orders or hierarchies of knowledge; there are common-sense facts, scientific facts (facts of interest to the sciences of nature), mathematical facts[41] (facts like the existence—the ideal existence—of underived continuous functions), logical facts, philosophical facts.

20. Speaking materially, it may also be said that philosophy is "experimental" and founded on facts. This is true in the sense that for philosophy experience has not the uniquely pre-scientific and infra-scientific role that it has for mathematics. For mathematical science is established entirely by axiomatic and deductive means, beginning with an imaginative intuition and with notions that abstraction simply forms and reconstructs on the basis of experience. On the contrary, the method of philosophy is an analytico-synthetic one. And because it deals with real being, being that is truly apt to exist outside the mind, experimental observations form an integral part of philosophical knowledge.

For philosophy, however, as opposed to the sciences of nature, all this provides nothing more than a material foundation from which the philosopher may rise through a formal deduction to first intelligible truths, known in themselves, to the consideration of the essences and the necessities they imply. Philosophy turns back to experience only incidentally—in natural philosophy, only to verify, within the sensible, the conclusions deduced, and to seek therein ever new data; in metaphysics, only to garner fresh points of departure and

is ordered to the disclosing of an existential position that we conceive by *analogy* with those furnished by an intuition of the sense.

41   Cf. Pierre Boutroux, *L'idéal scientifique des mathématiciens*, Ch. IV.

materials for analogy, not to verify its conclusions which belong to an entirely immaterial order. For metaphysics, formally speaking, is by no means an experimental science; as knowledge, it is far more purely rational than mathematics.

The Structures and Methods of the Principal Kinds of Knowledge

21. Many important consequences flow from the preceding considerations. At this juncture, we can point out only a few of them rather briefly. We shall especially try to give a glimpse of the sort of instrument of epistemological analysis that St. Thomas' principles can provide and to call attention to one of the characteristic marks of his noetic, to wit, the order and organic differences he establishes among the sciences and the care he takes to recognize and respect the structure and method proper to each.[42] Here St. Thomas' theory of knowledge stands in contrast with many modern systems which rank all sciences on the same level.

It must be kept in mind that every science has to answer two questions: first, the question, AN EST—whether the thing exists; and then the question, QUID EST—what is its nature.

22. Experience plays only a pre-scientific role in mathematics in the sense that one would not have formed the notion, "circle," or "straight line" if one had never seen a ring or a staff. If we had never pointed out with our finger the parts of a concrete collection one after the other, we would never have formed the notion, "number." However, once we get the notions, thanks to the abstractive power of intellect, they present us with objects of thought in themselves quite independent of experience, so independent in fact, that we can generalize them analogically and set them free from the intuitive structure in which they were first revealed. Although mathematical entities can exist only in matter—to the extent that they can exist outside the mind—nevertheless they do not exist in matter as mathematical entities, or in a mathematical

---

42   On this point we draw inspiration from certain ideas developed by St. Thomas Aquinas in his commentary on the *Posterior Analytics* of Aristotle (Bk. II) and in his commentary on the *De Trinitate* of Boethius (q. 5 and q. 6). Let us call to mind here the basic text from the *De Trinitate*, q. 6, a. 2: "In qualibet cognitione duo est considerare, scilicet principium, et finem sive terminum. Principium quidem ad apprehensionem pertinet, terminus autem ad judicium, ibi enim cognitio perficitur. Principium igitur cujuslibet nostrae cognitionis est in sensu. . . . Sed terminus cognitionis non semper est uniformiter: quandoque enim est in sensu, quandoque in imaginatione, quandoque in solo intellectu. . . .

"Deduci autem ad aliquid est ad illud terminari: et ideo in divinis neque ad sensum, neque ad imaginationem debemus deduci; in mathematicis autem ad imaginationem, et non ad sensum; in naturalibus autem etiam ad sensum. Et propter hoc peccant qui uniformiter in tribus his speculativae partibus procedere nituntur."

state. "Straight line," "circle," "whole numbers" are all realized in sensible things, but only by lacking the conditions of ideal purity that the mode of existing mathematically imposes upon them.

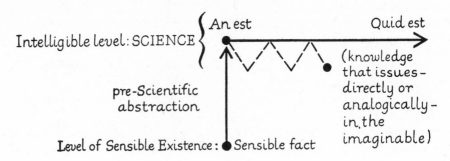

Mathematics

In the mathematical order, the question, AN EST, deals with the ideal existence (*possible existence* or *existence of reason*)[43] of the entity under consideration; and beginning with the notion of this entity, once posited as capable of mathematical existence, the truths concerning it (*quid est*) are deductively established by means of constructive operations which may play a very obvious role but which still remain material. Mathematical deduction formally proceeds in virtue of intelligible connections. These intelligible connections may either guide and determine at each instant the constructive operations, or once and for all establish and justify all the rules for a system of symbols which have simply to be applied by the art so determined. The ancients taught that in mathematics the judgment—whereby knowledge is perfected—does not open upon the sensible, but upon the imaginable. This does not mean that each of the conclusions it establishes must be directly verified in imaginative intuition. They must be verified in it either directly or analogically. That is to say, they either can be constructed in imaginative intuition, or they belong to a system of notions (as, for example, non-Euclidian, non-Archimedian, etc., geometrical entities) stemming from one which may be constructed in intuition (for example, Euclidian entities), and in which they may find an analogical interpretation.[44]

23. In the experimental sciences, experience is essential to the science itself and completely controls it. Here, the question, AN EST bears on facts subject to experimental critique. And the science does not succeed in seeing in itself or

---

43   The meaning of the word "ideal existence" is determined in keeping with the following division: *real being* { *actual* / *possible* / *being of reason* } *ideal being*

44   See below, Ch. IV, § 18.

dianoetically,[45] but only blindly, the essence which is wrapped up in these facts. It does not grasp it in its constitutive notes, but in the vicarious signs with which *perinoetic* [46] understanding is satisfied (especially in the *constancy* of a well-established relation). It grasps the essence in a substitute which is scientific *law*—the judgment wherein knowledge is perfected thus opens upon experience itself, or, to state it otherwise, every newly acquired conclusion must be verified in sensible fact.

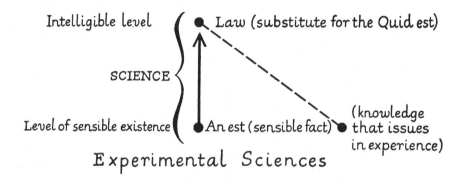

In the physico-mathematical sciences, deductive theory and the system of notions they elaborate hark back to experimental results to verify whether that theory is apt accurately to express those experimental results in an appropriate technical vocabulary. Here the substitute for the ontological *quid est* is not an inductively established law, but a mathematics *quid est*, an algorithm of the physical real.

24. In the philosophy of nature, the sensible fact materially belongs to the science, which still essentially depends upon experience, but it does not formally constitute its medium of demonstration. The question, AN EST, bears on the *real existence* of a nature to which abstraction has been able to rise and to consider in itself—the vegetative soul, for example. Beginning with this nature, once it has been posited, reason establishes its properties by an inductive-deductive coming and going, all the while opening on experience and verifying the conclusions it thus attains in sensible fact.

25. Finally, in metaphysics, sensible fact also belongs materially to the science, because one rises to the invisible only from the visible. But it does not formally constitute its medium of demonstration and *does not verify its conclusions*. The judgment wherein knowledge is perfected opens upon the pure intelligible. For it is not because (as in the case of the philosophy of nature) it

45   See below, Ch. V, § 1.
46   See below, Ch. V, § 3.

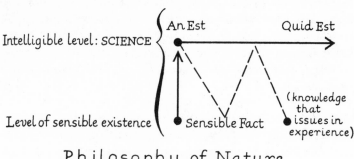

Philosophy of Nature

depends essentially on sensible experience, but rather because of its transcendence, that metaphysics descends (as mathematics does not) to the world of sensible existence. And it also climbs up to the world of supra-sensible existence. Thus, in natural theology, the question, AN EST bears on the *real existence* of an immaterial object to which knowledge by analogy (*ananoetic understanding*)[47] has been able to rise. Beginning with the existence of such an object, once it has been recognized, reason establishes conclusions about the nature (as analogically known) and the perfections of pure Act through the three-fold way of causality, eminence and negation and without any verification either in the sensible or the imaginable, because it deals with the purely immaterial.

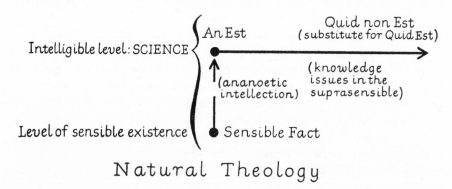

Natural Theology

The Proper Conditions for Philosophy. Its Relation to Facts

26. Philosophy, whether it be the philosophy of nature or metaphysics, emerges from experience and empirical knowledge just as the positive sciences do. But philosophy transcends experience and empirical knowledge in a much purer and more perfect fashion than the positive sciences. First, the proper

---

47   See below, Ch. V, § 13.

experimental material upon which philosophy operates is much simpler, more universal, immediate and incontestable than the experimental material of the sciences. The facts upon which philosophy rests are absolutely general, primordial facts, not such facts as are observable only with more-or-less difficulty—and which, as science progresses, become more and more points at which the real coincides with the (always more and more complex and refined) constructions previously set up by scientific reason—but absolutely general and absolutely first facts.

Secondly, these absolutely general and primordial facts do not arise out of "vulgar experience" (which is, however, in a sense already more certain than scientific experience).[48] Vulgar experience intervenes in philosophy only as a substitute, when no scientific experience is available. Its claim to be admitted is the same as, though secondary to, that of scientific experience. The material proper to philosophy arises from an experience which is already philosophically elucidated and consequently quite superior to vulgar experience. For philosophy judges and criticizes this material *in its own light* in such a way as to establish it with entire certitude inasmuch as, in virtue of being a wisdom, it can defend its own principles. And so it defends and justifies (in an indirect way) the value of sensible perception itself. It is due to this point of view that the fact *that something exists, the fact that a multitude exists, that change and becoming exist, that knowledge and thought exist, that desire exists,* are properly PHILOSOPHICAL FACTS.

27. As for scientific experience, *scientific facts,* it is clear that although they can, as we said a little while ago, provide new materials for philosophy and be taken over by it (for philosophy can batten even on alien matter), of themselves they do not constitute its proper matter. In any case, they should be judged and criticized under the proper light of philosophy, even as its proper matter is, before they can be put to philosophical use.

Of itself, a scientific fact belongs to the realm of the sciences of nature. If it is true, then, that what characterizes these sciences is the fact that their cognitions are resolved into the sensible, then a scientific fact by itself will only be of concern to this type of explanation. So long as it is illumined only by that light which first revealed it within the real and placed it at the disposal of the scientist, it is of interest only to the scientist, and not to the philosopher. It is also an illusion to believe that by appealing to scientific facts without first illuminating them by a higher light, any philosophical debate—the debate

---

48   "The layman believes that the result of a scientific experiment is distinguishable from common observation by a higher degree of certitude; he is mistaken, for an account of an experiment in physics lacks that immediate certitude, comparatively easy to check up on, which characterizes common, non-scientific testimony. Though less certain than the latter, scientific certitude has the advantage over it in the number and exactitude of the details it makes known to us; there lies its true and essential superiority" (Pierre Duhem, *La théorie physique*, p. 265).

about hylomorphism, for instance—may be settled. Of themselves, they have nothing to say on that score. Let them not be tortured in order to wring pseudo-confessions from them! Let them never be cajoled! Yet let them be interrogated, however! But that presupposes that one is already provided with certain relevant points of information. Let them be summoned to appear, and in as great a number as possible. But one must refer to the scientist for assurance regarding all that pertains to their "citizenship," i.e., their experimental meaning and the way in which they are established. They must all be respected, and one must be always on the look out for all the new ones that come to light. However, it is only by relating them to philosophical knowledge already acquired from another source and with philosophical principles, that an intelligible content appropriate to philosophy can be drawn from them. Only then is it possible to discover and judge whatever ontological value they may possess and to use them either to put the conclusions of philosophy in contact with sensible verifications and the latest results of experimental science, or to confirm or establish properly philosophical facts—the starting points of philosophical demonstrations.

A whole nest of critical problems is revealed here, but we will be content to point them out in passing. We pointed out above how to distinguish in a general way, within the domain of the sciences of nature, the category of fact from that of theory. But because in the concrete these two orders constantly overlap (since science, in order to build itself up, is constantly going back and forth from facts to the new theories they serve to construct, and from theory to the new facts it serves to discern) it becomes necessary to set up a hierarchy among scientific facts themselves from the point of view of their factual value and to make a division between those "facts" which truly merit the name and those that in some way usurp it. Facts immediately provided by scientific observation themselves presuppose a certain number of theoretical propositions which have already been admitted (the first of which find their origin in the perception of the senses): these include propositions that have to do with the thing to be measured and the means of measuring it, the apparatus that has to be constructed to achieve this effect. As for other scientific facts which are mediately established, they either result from an encounter between an observed datum and a previously constructed theoretical network, or else they flow from the explanation itself when that explanation is seen to be the only possible one. From that point on, the philosopher has to make many distinctions. So, when modern astronomy established the fact that the earth turns about the sun, or when modern physics establishes the existence of atoms, these "facts," because mediately established, have value as data which is incomparably higher (higher, in fact, in the first case than in the second) than the hypothetical "fact" of the Lorentz-contraction or of the curvature of space postulated by Einstein's synthesis. Where can one look for the principle for such a distinction? Nowhere else than in a critical analysis of the rational processes used in each particular case. The more the mathematical is reduced to the role of enabling one by measurement and calculation to get a surer grasp of the undiluted physical and of those causes and conditions whose character as *entia realia* the philosopher has no reason to question, the more does the result deserve to be considered a fact. But the more the physical is reduced to the role of intervening only as a mere instrument for discriminating between theoretical constructions whose proper value is constituted by their mathematical amplitude and coherence or as simple foundational entities which the philosopher has good reason to regard as beings of reason, the more should the result be transferred to the order, not of fact, but of explanatory image.

28. Given that philosophy is in its own right independent of the sciences, is it not true, nevertheless, that the sciences may indirectly reveal the falsity of this or that philosophical doctrine since a consequence deduced from a principle reveals the falsity of the principle if that consequence is recognized to be false?

That is true if and when a philosophical doctrine happens to encroach upon science itself or to have, as a necessary consequence, a certain scientific conception, or rather a certain general framework imposed on science, whose emptiness is demonstrated.

Despite what certain popularizers may say (and even those thinkers who attribute to the ancients their own carelessness in distinguishing the intelligible from the topographical, and metaphysics from astronomy), these charges do not stand up in the case of the philosophy of Aristotle when carried back to its authentic principles. First, let us consider the human subject. It should be recognized that too great a confidence in the intelligibility of things and in the processes of reason (functioning in an order which is not properly the order of philosophy but the order of experience—an order in which essences are not revealed to us) has played its part (and perhaps an overwhelming part) in the errors of ancient science. On this score, we would quite willingly go very far, for we are convinced that, on the one hand, modern science has rendered philosophy a great service in delivering it from burdens not its own, but which have for a long time oppressed it, namely, the burden of explaining phenomena. And we are convinced, on the other hand, that whereas a loss or weakening of the metaphysical spirit is an incalculable damage for the general order of intelligence and human affairs, it still happens that a predominance of the metaphysical spirit, when it is not accompanied by rigorous critical rectifications, accidentally harms the particular interests of experimental research. And this accident costs us dearly. Experimental research and the smallest step forward in the matter of the tiniest truth of fact is also an affair of the mind. And the mind brooks no interference.

Now let us consider the object. There is no necessary link between the mechanics, the physics and the astronomy of the ancients on the one hand,

and the metaphysics or natural philosophy of the scholastic tradition on the other. The whole structure of the experimental science of the ancients has doubtless crumbled and its collapse may well appear to anxious minds to spell the ruin of everything the ancients had thought. But in reality, their metaphysics and their philosophy of nature, in their essential principles at least (as they can be gathered from the Thomistic synthesis), have no more been affected thereby than the spiritual soul is changed when the body disintegrates.

Now that pure philosophical and metaphysical wisdom has been freed from many foreign elements, it is obviously desirable and necessary that, after this purification, it once more discover its organic relations, broken by three centuries of neglect and misunderstanding, with the total life, the activity, the actuality, of the sciences. For here below, the condition of a soul without a body is a rather uncomfortable one. The prison of the body is good for the soul. (As for the metaphysical systems of modern thinkers, more often than not they have been really nothing but an oppression of metaphysics by the hypostasized ambitions of the science of the sensible world.)

The ideas brought together in the course of this chapter give a glimpse of the conditions under which the work of integration, already begun at several points, can be furthered and brought to a happy conclusion. Whoever seeks to work towards the integrating of philosophy and experimental science must be at once on his guard against both a lazy separatism and a facile concordism and re-establish a vital bond between them without upsetting the distinctions and hierarchies which are essential to the universe of knowing.

To that end, two cases should, it seems, be very clearly distinguished: the case of physico-mathematical science and the sciences of which it is the type on the one hand, and the case of sciences like biology and psychology on the other.

Knowledge of the Physico-Mathematical Type and Philosophy

29. In respect to the explanation of reality, there can be no hope, in our opinion, of ever finding a continuity or dovetailing of the conceptual elaborations of physico-mathematics and the proper texture of philosophical and metaphysical knowledge. That would violate the very nature of things. I am not speaking of a continuity or a dovetailing among facts (to the extent that they can be separated from theories) but among the respective theories themselves. The discontinuity is clear and definite; and it is due to the very essence of these knowledge. Physico-mathematical science is not formally a physical science. Although it is physical as regards the matter in which it verifies its judgments, and although it is oriented towards physical reality and physical causes as the terminus of its investigation, physico-mathematical science does not, however, aim to grasp their inner ontological nature itself. In Chapter IV, we will come back to this observation. It is an observation that has very often

been made by scientists[49] as well as by philosophers, but it may lead to misunderstanding; its epistemological meaning is a delicate matter to determine. But as it stands, it is sufficient for our purpose.

Physics rests upon ontological reality; it is concerned with causes; it is set in motion by a love for the nature of things. But it looks upon this ontological reality, these physical causes, from an exclusively mathematical point of view. It considers them only in respect to certain analytical translations, certain cross-sections effected by mathematics. It retains only the measurable behavior of the real, namely, measurements made by our instruments. (These measurements are, indeed, real and, thanks to them, the entities and symbols of mathematical physics are grounded in reality.) But it is to the measurable that physics reduces all its concepts; for it, only the measurable has meaning.[50] Once in possession of its measures, its essential aim is to weave a network of mathematical relations among them. These relations are deductive in form and constitute the formal object of physics. They undoubtedly need to be completed by a certain hypothetical reconstruction of the physical real, but physics only demands that their final numerical results coincide with the measurements made by our instruments.

There is no pragmatism here. We do not suggest in any sense that in that sort of science useful achievement is substituted for truth. In our estimation, that would be a barbarous notion. As every other science, physics only exists to be true; and the definition of truth—the conformity of our judgments to things—holds good for it just as much as for other sciences. In this case, however, that definition has the following meaning: a physico-mathematical

---

49   "The object of mathematical theories of physical phenomena is not to reveal to us the true nature of things; that would be an unreasonable claim. Their sole aim is to co-ordinate the physical laws that are made known to us by experiment, but which we could not even express without the aid of mathematics. It is of little importance to us whether ether really exists. That is the concern of metaphysicians. As far as we are concerned, the essential point is that everything happens as if it did exist. . . ." (H. Poincaré, *La science de l'hypothèse*, pp. 245–246).

50   "The whole of our physical knowledge is based on measurement. . . . The physical world consists, so to speak, of groups of measures resting on an obscure foundation that is outside the realm of physics. . . . The whole object of the exact sciences consists of pointer-readings and similar indications. We cannot at this point enter into an examination of what can be classified as 'similar indications'; observing the approximate coincidence of a needle with a division on a scale can, in a general way, be extended to include every sort of coincidence or, according to the customary expression used in the language of relativity, an intersection of lines of the universe. This is the essential point: even though we would appear to have very definite conceptions of the objects of the external world, these conceptions form no part of the realm of exact science and are in no way confirmed by it. Before exact science can begin to handle the problem, it must replace them with quantities representing the results of physical measurements" (A. S. Eddington, *The Nature of the Physical World*, Cambridge, University Press, 1929, pp. 252–253).

theory will be called "true" when a coherent and fullest possible system of mathematical symbols and the explanatory entities it organizes coincides, throughout all its numerical conclusions, with measurements we have made upon the real; but it is in no wise necessary that any physical reality, any particular nature, or any ontological law in the world of bodies, correspond determinately to each of the symbols and mathematical entities in question.[51]

51   This is a generalized application of the method which the ancients designated as consisting in "saving sensible appearances," and first made explicit apropos of astronomic theories and, later, of certain parts of physics. As Pierre Duhem has pointed out in a very noteworthy page, the Aristotelian astronomy with its homocentric spheres, even though it was destined very soon to be seen to be irreconcilable with observed facts, was the first application of this method, "the first of the physical theories." For the first time, indeed, in setting up this theory, the geometrician starts with a certain number of simple principles that were given to him from other sources and, following those principles, constructs a hypothetical mathematical system, touches up and complicates that system to the point where it saves the appearances described by observers with sufficient exactness.

"When observation had made us aware of phenomena which the whole system of homocentric spheres was quite incapable of ever saving, then the geometer-astronomers accepted other principles and with the help of these new principles fashioned new hypotheses; but the method they followed in constructing their new astronomic systems was not different from the method they had used in building up the system of homocentric spheres.

"There was no delay in transferring that method of astronomy to the other parts of physics; the author of the *Mechanical Questions*, attributed to Aristotle, tried to apply it to the equilibrium of weighty solids, and Archimedes gave a rational form of rare perfection to this science of the equilibrium of weighty solids; and, following the same method, he extended that admirable form to the equilibrium of liquids and of floating bodies.

"And in turn, Euclid showed how the single hypothesis of the equality between the angle of incidence and the angle of refraction was sufficient to save the phenomena presented by plain, concave and convex mirrors.

"Thus, two centuries before our era, astronomy, the science of equilibrium of weights and a part of optics, had taken the form of precise mathematical theories in their desire to satisfy the demands of experimental control; many parts of physics, in their turn, took on this form only after long centuries of groping about; but to do so they only had to follow the method whereby the first sciences had achieved the status of rational theories.

"Attribution of the title 'creator of the method of the physical sciences' has given rise to many squabbles; some have wished to give it to Galileo, others to Descartes, still others to Francis Bacon, who died without ever having understood anything about this method. Frankly, the method of the physical sciences was defined by Plato and the Pythagoreans of his day with a clarity and precision that have not been surpassed; it was applied for the first time by Eudoxus when he tried to save the apparent movement of the stars by combining the rotation of homocentric spheres" (P. Duhem, *Le système du monde*, t. I, pp. 128–129).

The same discussions, moreover, must have taken place among the Greeks and among the medieval Arabs and Christians concerning the significance of the

The need for causal physical explanation, still immanent to the mind of the physicist finally issues (in the highest of his syntheses) in the construction of a certain, number of beings of reason based on the real and providing an image of the world (or a shadow of an image) apt to support his mathematical deduction. It would betray a quite uncritical optimism, a truly naive optimism, to hope to establish any continuity between the way in which physico-mathematical theories get hold of things and the way philosophical theories do. (For philosophy sets out to grasp ontological principles according to their very reality.) As we have tried to show elsewhere,[52] the conceptions introduced by Einstein must accordingly be admired to the extent that they constitute a

results obtained in this way, as occur in our day concerning "the value of science." St. Thomas has clearly pointed out the bearing of the method in question in the following text: "Ad aliquam rem dupliciter inducitur ratio. Uno modo, ad probandum sufficienter aliquam radicem. . . . Alio modo inducitur ratio non quae sufficienter probet radicem, sed quae radici iam positae ostendat congruere consequentes effectus; sicut in astrologia ponitur ratio excentricorum et epicyclorum, ex hoc quod, hac positione facta, possunt salvari apparentia sensibilia circa motus caelestes; non tamen ratio haec est sufficienter probans, quia etiam, forte, alia positione facta salvari possent" (*Sum. Theol.*, I, 32, 1 ad 2).

To avoid any misunderstandings, let us add that σώζειν τά φαινόμενα does not in any sense imply the rejection of causal research and explanatory hypothesis that Duhem, on his part attributes to physical theory (cf. above, Ch. II, § 4). These are causal explanations themselves and the depictable entities which the physical sciences elaborate, and which are ordered to *the saving of phenomena* and are true (but not in the absolute sense in which a metaphysical doctrine is said to be true) to the extent that they succeed in doing so, without making any claim to penetrate the nature of things by themselves. From that point on it becomes a secondary question to find out whether a scientist attributes to a theory the value of a mere mathematical representation or the value of a causal explanation, or both at once, or whether he moves back and forth from one point of view to the other (as Ptolemy had already done in astronomy; or as, in our own day, in physics "some wonder whether or not the electron does not have a purely analytical existence since it is only a center of vibration in a wave-system to which reality truly belongs. For others only the waves have an analytical existence; a fictitious continuous field has been substituted mathematically for a discontinuous surrounding field" [E. Picard, *op. cit.*, p. 44]); for, this "causal" explanation itself remains within the "empiriological" order and does not have a properly and directly "ontological" significance (cf. Ch. IV, §§ 8 and 9, and Ch. IV, n. 95). As Mr. René Poirier has written, from a viewpoint that is withal very different from our own, "there is no essential difference between the way in which a logical or numerical allegory rationalizes the real, and that in which a structural plan, a figurative hypothesis does so. . . . The most abstract designs of statistical dynamics and general relativity do not issue from a different spirit; they do not correspond to another type of understanding than do mechanical models of the atom or the solar system; the difference between abstract theories and intuitive theories does not belong to an order different from that between painting and sculpture" (*Essai*, pp. 145–379).

52 *Réflexions sur l'intelligence*, Ch. VII.

powerful physico-mathematical synthesis; but they must be rejected if given properly philosophical meaning.

30. Does that mean to say that every organic link between philosophy and mathematical physics is broken? Certainly not! In the very order of the explanation of reality, there exists a continuity between the philosophy of nature and mathematical physics, not indeed in respect to the explanatory theories elaborated by physics, but rather from the fact that, as we have said above, science provides philosophy with a vast supply of facts; and this is an acquired gain which appears to remain permanent through all the changes in theory. Thus, for instance, the existence of atoms (and they no longer have anything in common with those of Democritus) has reached a degree of probability bordering on certitude. I say "The existence of atoms." I do not say "The nature and structure of atoms which science attributes to them." These latter are subject to constant alterations; and scientific symbolism plays a very great role in that. Today, for example, the Rutherford-Bohr atom is vanishing to make room for the Schroedinger atom and (while awaiting other avatars) to become "a wave center having *psi* as its probability." Nevertheless, the existence of those elements called "atoms" which constitute the molecule (and the existence of their own constitutive elements, "protons," "electrons," "neutrons," or whatever other name science may use tomorrow to designate them), although they be thus conceived successively according to different models and although they be thought of only as mathematical symbols, does not seem shaken in the least.

On the other hand, in the epistemological order, the order of the theory of knowledge, the organic link between mathematical physics and metaphysics is exceedingly close. In determining the nature and true value of physico-mathematical science, the place, role and extent of its explanations, not only does metaphysics keep the system of our cognitions in order, but it renders mathematical physics the essential service of protecting it against distortions that would be almost inevitable without it; above all, against the harmful illusion that leads it to regard itself as a philosophy of nature and to believe that things begin to exist only when they are measured by our instruments. Let physico-mathematical explanations use dislocated times and non-Euclidian spaces; they are free, they do well, they must always progress along their own line; the mind settled about their meaning knows its limits.

Perhaps there is something a bit sad about thus observing that the image of the universe, or, more exactly, the images or shadows of images (more-or-less discordant amongst themselves), in which the effort of physical theories to give an explanation, in the final analysis, results, could not be, as was believed for so long, the natural extension of ontological explanations provided by philosophy. Yet for the latter, all this is an excellent purification. It must give up being satisfied with images, whether they be the explanatory but fictional images of science, or the natural but untenable image of common sense (untenable, at least, from the moment it is given an explanatory meaning). In a later chapter,[53] we shall try to show how it is, however, quite proper for philosophy to have recourse to the images of science and to incorporate them into itself, but only in an order quite different from the order of wisdom properly so called.

Knowledge of a Biological and Psychological Kind

31. In the realm of life and of organic wholes, the distinction between the point of view of philosophy and that of the experimental sciences becomes very clear, inasmuch as their respective conceptual vocabulary, their ways of verification and their laws for resolving concepts and organizing knowledge are necessarily heterogeneous. But in such a realm, a certain "continuity" or solidarity between the specifically rational part and the specifically experimental part of knowledge can be established—in spite of an essential epistemological difference—in that which concerns the explanatory theories furnished by the sciences and the ultimate explanation provided by the philosophy of nature. For, while resolving their concepts in sensible and observable being, inasmuch as it is sensible and observable, experimental biology and experimental psychology do not undertake to reconstruct a closed universe of mathematicized phenomena, and it is quite normal that the type of deductive explanation whose attraction they undergo should be of a philosophical type and not of a mathematical type.

It is not that we would want to deny or belittle *a priori* the role of physico-chemical explanations (which are themselves directed towards the ideal of an integral mathematicization of the real) in biology. If it is true that in the living thing physico-chemical forces are the *instruments* of a superior ontological principle, then it is possible to conceive the field of these explanations as stretching out indefinitely, even though they must stop short at certain specific "irrationals" which inevitably arise all by themselves.[54] But it might also be held that, to the extent that the biologist retains a feeling for the reality proper to the living thing, and demands, in the study of the phenomena themselves, a type of explanation which, in the final analysis, does not dissolve that reality into constructed elements (an explanation, in short, that harks back to the very notion of a living being), he would subordinate the physico-chemical explanations thus discovered to a conception "autonomous" to biology. Such an explanation, in which the penetration of the details of phenomena and their grouping under more and more general experimental laws—without thereby claiming to resolve them in the universally explanatory mathematical deduction aimed at by physics (and without at all leaving the level of the observable

53   See below, Ch. IV, § 28.
54   See below, Ch. IV, §§ 34 and 35.

and measurable)—would still be built upon an *understood* ontological structure of concepts supplied by philosophy.

On the other hand, unless the biologist and psychologist put blinkers on their intellect, they will inevitably be led by the very object of their science to ask metaphenomenal questions to which they might try to reply with their own conceptual equipment and their proper methods of analysis; then they will obtain, in the most favorable cases, and by indirect paths and the delimitation of unknowns, solutions that resemble philosophical solutions and are tangential to them. It is thus that in his remarkable works Driesch[55] has realized that embryonic development depends on a nonspatial *factor E*, which maintains the specific type; or, again, that the actions of animals also depend on a non-spatial factor, thanks to which stimulations coming from without are individualized, and that the functioning of the animal-machine is enriched by its exercise—a non-spatial factor that the scientist prudently calls *psychoid*.

But it is only by using the equipment of the philosopher, by becoming philosophers themselves, that they will be able to give a proper and adequate solution to supraexperimental problems that their own experience compels them to envisage; only then will they be able, for example, to learn the true name for the *psychoid* and the *factor E*.

Conclusion

32. One is right in holding that Thomistic philosophy is, more than any other philosophy, in a position to provide the sciences with metaphysical frameworks within which they may deploy their own necessities unhampered and suffer no violence. This is so not only because Thomistic philosophy is essentially realistic and gives a critical justification for the extramental reality of things and the value of our powers of knowing, which every science implicitly takes for granted, but also because it guarantees the autonomy and specific character of each and because its metaphysical explanations of the real have as their necessary consequence no systematic deformation tyrannically imposed on experience.

And here the reproach levelled at Scholasticism by poorly informed minds recoils against modern systems. For it is indeed from these systems that necessarily and *per se* derive such systematic prejudices as mechanism, monism, psycho-physical parallelism, the Cartesian theory of consciousness, universal evolutionism, etc. These systems impose on science the most deplorable metaphysical shackles.

It is not a question of seeking between the sciences and Aristotelian-Thomistic philosophy the concordance of detail that we rejected just a moment ago, but rather of noting a general over-all agreement, a good understanding, a natural friendship, of which the very freedom of science, the ease with which

---

55   Cf. our preface to the French translation of *La philosophie de l'organisme*, by Hans Driesch (Paris, Reviere, 1921).

it develops, is the best indication. This statement is explicitly made by many representatives of the sciences of nature, while elsewhere, a striking renewal of themes proper to the moral philosophy of Thomas Aquinas is evinced in the moral and legal sciences of which we have not spoken in this essay.

If workers are not wanting, if unreasonable prejudices (due above all, it seems, to a morbid fear of ontological research and of all philosophy ordered to a knowledge of things—as though a philosophy of being could not also be a philosophy of mind) do not turn them back from the study of the only philosophy that claims to face the universality of the extramental real without at the same stroke pretending to absorb all knowing into itself, it might well be hoped that we will see a new dawn break upon a new and glorious scientific era—putting an end to misunderstandings engendered in the realm of experimental research by the conflict between Aristotle and Descartes—in which the sciences of phenomena would finally achieve their normal organization, some, physics above all, undergoing the attraction of mathematics and continuing their remarkable progress along this line, others, biology and psychology especially, undergoing the attraction of philosophy and finding in that line the organic order they need and the conditions for a development that is not merely material, but truly worthy of the understanding. Thus there would be a general redistribution springing from the natural growth of the sciences of phenomena, but one that would also suppose—and this point is quite clear—the supreme regulation of metaphysical wisdom.

The divine good of intellectual unity, shattered for three centuries now, would thus be restored to the human soul.

33. Kant denied to metaphysics the character of science because for him experience was the product and the terminus of science, since science built it by applying to sensible data necessities which are pure forms of the mind. But St. Thomas recognized in metaphysics the supreme science of the natural order because for him experience is the starting point of science, which, reading within the sensible "given" the intelligible necessities that surpass it, can transcend it by following those necessities and thereby achieve a supra-experimental knowledge that is absolutely certain.

Being is, indeed, the proper object of the intellect; it is embowelled in all its concepts; and it is to being, wrapped up in the data of the senses, that our understanding is first of all carried.

Should it set this object of its concept free so as to look at it in itself, insofar as it is being, it sees that it is not exhausted by the sensible realities in which the intellect first discovered it; it has a supraexperimental value. So, too, have the principles based on it. In that way, the intellect, if I may say so, "loops the loop," in coming back, to grasp it metaphysically and transcendentally, to that very same being which was first given to it in its first understanding of the sensible.

And so, because it has in its metaphysical concepts, such as being and the transcendentals, an intellectual perception of objects which can be realized otherwise than in the matter in which it perceives them, it will also attain these objects (this time, without directly perceiving them, and, as it were, by the mirror of sensible things) wherever they are realized without matter, as facts established in the world of experience compel us to infer. Thus, the suprasensible cannot be, at least in the natural order, the object of an experimental science. Nevertheless, it is the object of a science properly so called, and indeed, of the science par excellence. For if the universe of being as being, set free by the mind when it delivers its objects from all materiality, does not fall under the senses, intelligible necessities, on the other hand, are discovered there in the most perfect manner. Thus, the knowledge ordered to such a universe of intelligibility is most certain in itself even though we find it difficult to acknowledge it. For we are an ungrateful and mediocre race which only asks to fail in the highest in what it is capable of, and which, of itself, even when higher gifts have strengthened its eyes, will always prefer the dark.

SPECULATIVE PHILOSOPHY

CHAPTER III

CRITICAL REALISM

I
"CRITICAL REALISM"

1. BY THE TERM "CRITICAL REALISM" in the present context we have no intention of designating the ideas of contemporary philosophers who, especially in America and Germany, have chosen that term to characterize their positions.[1] Rather, we use it to designate the Aristotelian-Thomistic conception of knowledge, for it seems to us deserving of the title with much better reason.

Etienne Gilson has raised an interesting and useful controversy on this point by upholding[2] the position that Thomistic realism does, indeed, constitute a "methodical" realism and not a "naive" realism. He says that it could only be made to be a "critical" realism by giving in to the illusions of idealism in the very act of attacking them.

Etienne Gilson's study is recommended because of the many correct and penetrating observations it contains, and it shows in excellent fashion that it would be a vain task to look for the principle of a realistic noetic from the Cartesian *Cogito*, no matter what changes are suggested in it. "Whoever begins as an idealist," he writes, "will necessarily end up an idealist. One does not make a passing acquaintance with idealism. That fact should have been suspected, since history was there to teach it. *Cogito, ergo res sunt*: that is Cartesianism, the very antithesis of what is looked upon as Scholastic realism, and the very cause of its ruination. No one has worked harder than Descartes to build a bridge from thought to thing. He rests his case on the principle of causality; he was the very first one who tried to do it because he was forced to, inasmuch as he placed the starting point of knowledge in the mind's intuition. Thus, it is strictly true to say that every scholastic who considers

---

1   And it is certainly not—definitely not—the theory of the perception of the external world upheld by both Kulpe and many Neo-scholastics as well, a theory quite rightly attacked by J. Gredt (*Unsere Aussenwelt*, 1921, pp. 5 ff., 207 ff., 322 ff.), in which sensation would only attain a subjective term made objective in a secondary manner, thanks to an inference.

2   "Le réalisme méthodique," in *Philosophia Perennis* (Regensburg, Mélanges Geyser, 1930), t. II, pp. 745–755. L. Noel's reply will be found in *Revue Néo-scolastique*, Nov. 1931 ("Le méthode du réalisme"). E. Gilson, "Réalisme et Méthode," *Revue des Sciences Philosophiques et Théologiques*, XXI, 1932, pp. 161–168.

himself a realist because he accepts that way of stating the problem, is in reality a Cartesian. . . . The Cartesian experiment was an admirable metaphysical undertaking and borders on the purest genius. We owe him a great deal, even though his achievement is that he gave brilliant proof of the fact that every experiment of this kind is doomed to defeat in advance. It is, however, the height of naiveté to take up the task once more in the hope of gaining results opposite to those which have always been produced, for it is the very essence of this task to yield just such results. . . . One may start with Descartes but can only end up with Berkeley or Kant. There is an internal necessity about metaphysical essences, and philosophy's progress consists in the very fact of gaining clearer and clearer insight into the content of those essences. . . . Justification for St. Thomas' realism will never be obtained from any *Cogito*."[3] *Aurea dicta!* Let us extend our thanks to a philosopher nourished by the disciplines of history who, in the name of history itself, has given such rigorous testimony to the intelligible necessities that rule the historical growth of thought even amid all the accidents of material causality.

The criticism he offers of idealism[4] from this point of view is most pertinent. History at one stroke bears witness to the essential inability of idealism "to pass from criticism to positive construction" while yet maintaining a proper content for philosophy, distinct from the content of the particular science that is chosen to be the regulative science. It is a witness to the necessity, in which idealism finds itself, of substituting for the real, beings of reason "which are only counterfeit coins" (because it does not want to start from the thing but from thought).[5]

On the other hand, it is perfectly true that neither Aristotle nor St. Thomas, thorough-going and conscious "realists" *in actu exercito* as they were, felt the need of characterizing themselves as "realists," in the sense we give the term today, for the very reason that the error to which realism is opposed had not as yet arisen in the West; I mean it had not achieved the status of a doctrine and a system. But the realism that Thomists profess today merely represents a transition from the implicit to the explicit. In itself such an unfolding represents a real step forward. In this movement, idealism may even be considered to have played a necessary historic role. Because the aptitude of our knowing-faculties to lay hold of the real is an endowment of nature, and because man's mind, in virtue of its native strength, comes to bear on what is real the more spontaneously, the healthier the mind is, so the pathogenic upheaval, so to speak, of the Cartesian *Cogito* was necessary and man's mind needed the aberrant way in which idealism set up the critical problem in order that philosophical intelligence might be compelled to look back upon that problem in calm deliberation, to enter upon a reflexive phase with resolution—

---

3   *Art. cit.*, pp. 747–748, 751.
4   *Ibid.*, pp. 753–754.
5   *Ibid.*, p. 754.

a phase which helped to indicate more clearly the spirituality of reason, whatever the price reason has had to pay for it.

Idealism is indeed a tragic experience for the mind (an experience in which, as in every true tragedy, suicide provides the final dénouement of the drama). But it also offers the mind, in setting up a new problem, fresh possibilities of deepening vision which the mind cannot afford to miss, provided, of course, the mind has completely cleansed itself of that idealism. But from that point on, a two-fold danger must be carefully avoided. First, the danger of accepting, for whatever reason, in even the slightest degree, the idealistic setting of the critical problem. On that score I am in complete agreement with Mr. Gilson. The second danger arises from the rejection of every conceivable possibility of stating the critical problem in any way that would be susceptible of philosophical elucidation. It is on this point that I cannot go along with Mr. Gilson. I believe it is possible—and, indeed, that therein lies the very task of wisdom—to state the problem in a manner quite different from the way idealism states it.

In our opinion, it is not correct to say that realism only exists in virtue of idealism.[6] At that rate, no true thesis would exist except through the error it refutes, no dogmatic definition would exist except through the heresy to which it is opposed; nor is it correct, in my opinion, to say that realism, in order to be critical, would have to "borrow the positing of the problem" from idealism. Moreover, it is not enough merely to note that realism succeeds where idealism fails, or to point out the latter's inability to construct a liveable philosophy.[7] That is unquestionably an indirect sign and its value is far from negligible. But the mind must rather be led consciously to recognize the fact that idealism is an absolute impossibility—impossible *in itself*. On top of that, there is no reason to leave to idealism the exclusive use and possession of the word "critical" with all it signifies. "In the strict sense of the word, to criticize is *to judge*, in conformity with the requirements of the object under examination."[8] How could self-judgment and self-examination be foreign to a philosophy for which spirit is marked by the capacity of completely turning back upon itself? To be candid—as we have noted in a former work[9] and J. de Tonquédec has indicated so strongly[10]—the reproach above all other reproaches to be addressed to the critical realist is that he is not critical enough.

2. The critical problem is not: "How does one pass from *percipi* to *esse*? Since mind is the only object attained in a way that is beyond doubt, can it be

---

6   *Art. cit.*, p. 751.
7   *Ibid.*, p. 753.
8   R. Garrigou-Lagrange, "Le réalisme thomiste et le mystère de la connaissance," *Revue de Philosophie*, Jan.–Feb., March–April 1931, p. 12 of the off-print (an article that is reproduced in the work, *Le réalisme du principe de finalité*, Paris, Desclée de Brouwer et Cie, 1932).
9   Cf. *Réflexions sur l'intelligence*, Chs. 1 and 2.
10   J. de Tonquédec, *La critique de la connaissance*, pp. 21–22.

demonstrated that mind also reaches things, a reality that measures it? No! It is, rather, to be stated in these terms: "On the different levels of elaborating knowledge, what value must be assigned to *percipere* and what to *judicare*? Since the mind, from the very start, reveals itself as warranted in its certitude by things and measured by an *esse* independent of itself, how are we to judge if, how, on what conditions, and to what extent it is so both in principle and in the various moments of human knowledge?" It is absurd to demand that philosophical thought begin, even before it knows anything validly, by proving that it can know (for it could only do so if it did know). It is absurd to suppose at the very start that anything which cannot help but be judged true by the mind can, as a result of some evil genius, not be true, so that then that self-same mind might be asked to show that, as a matter of fact, it is not so. It is absurd to admit that the mind could only attain phenomenal objects and then ask it to prove that such objects are extramental realities.[11] These are some of the *stultae quaestiones* St. Thomas, following in the wake of St. Paul,[12] urges us to avoid.

But once the mind has begun to exert itself (to know and philosophize) in order to gain certainty, by science and wisdom, about things and the soul and their first cause, it must then turn back upon itself and upon what it has acquired, and apply itself to knowing knowledge, to judging it and testing its truth (then to advance once more, and then to turn back again upon itself . . .). Such is the task of metaphysical wisdom[13] which, inasmuch as it stands at the natural peak of spirituality among the sciences, can return to the principles of those sciences and to its own proper principles in order to justify them (if not by direct demonstration—for it is *apaedeusia, idest ineruditio,*[14] to want to demonstrate everything—then at least by a *reductio ad absurdum*) and in this way achieve that perfect reflection upon self which is proper to spirit.

In one sense, as is clear enough, this is a thankless and risky job, as is everything that is of the nature of a census and enumeration, an inventory or reflex evaluation, and which goes against the grain of the direct movement of nature; yet, it is an indispensable job because intelligence, even more so than the hand, should control its tools and that instrument which it itself is. The soberness and humility of true science, however, are particularly favorable to

---

11   Cf. *Réflexions sur l'intelligence*, p. 41.
12   "Stultas quaestiones devita" (Tit. III. 9); "Item quando manifestum proponitur ut dubium, sc. quaecumque debet aliquis per se tenere in scientia." (St. Thomas's *Expositio*, lect. 2).
13   "Considerandum est in scientiis philosophicis, quod inferiores scientiae non probant sua principia, nec contra negantem principia disputant, sed hoc relinquunt superiori scientiae; suprema vero inter eas, scilicet metaphysica, disputat contra negantem sua principia, si adversarius aliquid concedit, si autem nihil concedit, non potest cum eo disputare, potest tamen solvere rationes ipsius" (St. Thomas, *Sum. Theol.*, I, 1, 8). Cf. R. Garrigou-Lagrange, *art. cit.*, p. 101.
14   St. Thomas, *In Metaph.*, lib. IV, lect. 6.

it; so, too, is respect for the object, which in this case is the very mystery of knowledge. Through the performing of this task fundamental truths, especially the general validity of knowledge and first principles, are humbly confirmed—by reason of the impossibility of their contradictories. After that comes the main task. Now the search can advance and refine itself endlessly. This task consists, on the one hand, in analyzing and describing—due regard being had for its integrity—the objective content of knowledge in its various phases[15] and the witness it bears to itself; on the other hand, it consists in metaphysically penetrating its own nature and causes, and making it, properly speaking, know itself. After that one can proceed, in particular instances, to distinguish gnoseological values and to discriminate within the work of knowing, what depends on the real and what on our mind's constructive activity. (Thus, the treatise in the *Summa* concerning the divine names is a critique of theological knowledge; so, too, every search for the true meaning of physical theory is an attempt at a critique of physico-mathematical knowledge.) And, finally, one may embark upon the discovery of the laws of that transcendental "Topica" which crops up again and again throughout the present work.

In all this, the mind gains a true understanding of the object it proposes to deal with, and it judges it in virtue of the intrinsic necessities proper to wisdom. What it thus sets up is a critique of knowledge in the most proper sense. Yet its work will always and essentially be fully conscious of what it really is, a pure reflection upon another activity, to wit, the knowing of things, a purely reflexive enterprise. If this condition is fully understood, the main danger is eliminated: such a critique of knowledge will never be contaminated by idealism. It is, indeed, essential to every idealism to mix a preoccupation for constructiveness with what is an affair of pure reflexivity (even though this preoccupation be not admitted and even be hidden beneath the appearances of methodical rigorousness); a preoccupation, at least, with making the setting up of philosophy depend on that reflexive enterprise as on its preamble, if not with making philosophy itself consist in that very step. As soon as one considers that the task of critique is purely and exclusively reflexive and secondary (not only in the order of time but by its very nature as well) and that, from that moment on, it cannot for one single instant dispense with the knowledge of reality without having recourse to an illusory autophagic process, one is thenceforth immune to the ferment of Cartesianism.

Scio aliquid esse

3. If the foregoing remarks are correct, a Thomistic critique of knowledge must needs be recognized as distinct from every sort of idealistic critique both

---

15   This is what will undoubtedly remain of phenomenological method once it has been sifted by time and reduced to more modest proportions.

by reason of its starting point and by reason of its mode of procedure. Above all, it will be so distinguished by the three following points:

1⁰ The pure *cogito*, closed upon itself, can in no sense provide its starting point. Critique, as a philosophical work, implies the self-consciousness of the mind philosophically turning back upon its previous work of knowing. What must constitute its starting point is not the factually (*de facto*) and chronologically first self-consciousness (which moment of childish experience would we have to go back to?), but that *self-consciousness* which is shown to be by right (*de jure*) and *logically first* by the philosopher who lays bare the simplest roots of knowledge. But how are we to determine it exactly? In our opinion three primordial factors, each of which reciprocally implies the other, are involved in this basic apprehension, and impose themselves on philosophical analysis. First, there is the irrefutable evidence of the principle of identity, a primary fact to which the analysis of already acquired cognition[16] leads, and one in which we find the very first (necessary) living connection between the mind and things. Second, there is the general veracity of our powers of knowing, which is, as it were, the first but still quite undetermined testimony which the intellect renders to itself. Third is the notion of truth, the elucidation of which forms the first problem for critique to solve. Consequently, in attempting to formulate, on reflection, the experience that serves as a starting point for critique, one would have to say: *I am aware of knowing—I am aware of knowing at least one thing, that what is, is; not: I think.*

The *Cogito ergo sum* is ambiguous: it appears to be at once the starting point of philosophy as a whole and also the starting point of critique. An equally

---

16   "Hujusmodi autem principia naturaliter cognoscuntur, et error qui circa hujus-
      modi principia accideret, ex corruptione naturae proveniret. Unde non posset
      homo mutari de vera acceptione principiorum in falsum, vel e converso, nisi per
      mutationem naturae" (St.Thomas, *Cont. Gent.*, IV, 95).
         Cf. R. Garrigou-Lagrange, *art. cit.*, pp. 12–23. "This primordial evidence be-
      longs to the first *intellectual apprehension* of being or the real and to the necessary
      and universal judgements that immediately follow it; these direct acts are
      necessarily prior to reflection made upon them. And then this first, indestructible
      evidence is confirmed by the intellect's reflection upon its own act, on the nature
      of its act and on its own nature, whose *essential finality* it then discovers even as
      it beholds the finality of the eye or ear. By the same token the intellect sees that
      the idea of being imprinted on it and then expressed by it, is also essentially
      relative to *extramental being*, either actual or possible, and quite different from
      being of reason . . ." (*ibid.*, p. 17).
         "It is not true that we are first aware of our certitude as 'permanent subjective'
      states from which we would then conclude (no one has ever been able to explain
      by what right we do so) to a reality distinct from knowledge, to an 'objective
      truth'. No! *Immediate evidence gives us the object*; if it did not give it to us, no amount
      of reflection upon it—that is only too clear—would discover it among its acqui-
      sition." (J. de Tonquédec, *La critique de la connaissance*, p. 444).
         "The real is given at the very outset, in the presence of a knowing activity" (L.
      Noel, *art. cit.*, p. 446).

ambiguous formula, which could stand for these two ends, would be: *"scio aliquid esse (seu esse posse)"*; but we would immediately have to break that statement down into the two meanings it involves. These *must* be distinguished because one of those meanings has to do with direct knowledge and the mind's first movement, while the other concerns reflex knowledge and the mind's second movement. When I say, "I know that something exists (or can exist)," I may intend to state simply that *something exists* (or can exist), *aliquid est.* In this case, my statement has to do with the mind's first movement, and so refers to the *starting point of philosophy as a whole.* The concrete experience it conveys also includes the entire complex of my cognitive activities, since in that experience my intellect seizes intelligible being, which is its direct and proper object. Moreover, because by the very fact that it is possible, that being is seen by the intellect as involving eternal necessities (i.e., rigorous demands that transcend time), it becomes the object of the intellect's very first purely intellectual certitude (the principle of identity). The intellect grasps that being, however, by turning back *in fact* to some singular thing presented by the senses from which the intellect made it spring forth,[17] and also by turning back (even though in a quite implicit fashion, by the mere fact of judgment) to its own act of knowing and its relation to the thing and to the ego that knows and whose actual existence (the most unquestionable of all actual existences, as far as I am concerned) is thus known to me each time I know,[18] though only seminally (*in actu primo*) and not as yet effectively.

If after that I say: "I know something exists (or can exist)" and, being explicitly aware of what was only implicit in my direct knowledge, I now intend to state that *I know* something exists or can exist (*ego cognosco aliquid esse*), then my statement bears upon the mind's second movement and refers to the starting point of *critique.*

The position we are defending should be clear. Inasmuch as the intellect primarily bears neither on itself, nor on the *ego,* but on being, then the very first evidence (I mean first in the order of nature, I am not talking about the chronological order, in which, what is first in itself is often only implicit), the evidence that is *first in itself* for the intellect, is that of the principle of identity "discovered" in the intellectual apprehension of being or the real.

We have said that the reality in question does not necessarily belong to the actual (existential) order, even though the intellect does first grasp the principle of identity as incarnate in some example of sensible existence. Of itself that principle bears upon the whole range of being and especially on the order of essences, or the possible real.[19] At the same time, we have said that in the intelligible order itself a certain actual reality is given to the intellect in this first act of perception and judgment, namely, from the side of the subject: the

---

17 Cf. below, Ch. III, n. 49.
18 Cf. below, Ch. III, n. 45; and § 15, and Appendix V, § 2.
19 See below, Ch. III, §§ 10 and 15.

existence of the thinking subject itself. However, it is given only in an implicit, preconscious way and in first, or initial act,[20] and not yet as the object of explicit knowledge.

Thus, the intellect embraces at one and the same time, and in its own proper sphere, both the possible real (the object "all being . . ." set before the mind and grasped by it and signified in the statement of the principle of identity),[21] and the actual real (the reality of the thinking subject, though as not yet attained in final act [*in actu secundo*]). *Intelligible being* and the self are given to the intellect together and from the very start. But *being* is given in the foreground and up-stage; the self is in the background, behind the scenes, as it were. It is only with the mind's second movement, in the reflex intuition that serves as a starting point for critique, that it moves to the front of the stage.

2^0. An authentic critique of knowledge does not imply a single instant of real or universal doubt.[22] Such an instant of doubt in effect includes *in actu exercito* the negation of something about which we pretend not to know anything as yet (I mean the essential ordination of the intellect to being). And that is a

---

20   On the distinction between initial act (*actus primus*) and final act (*actus secundus seu ultimus*) in the order of knowledge, see below, Ch. III, § 22. When the object of intellection is a thing other than the self, it is known (directly) in initial act from the very fact of the intellect's being actuated by the *species impressa*, and in final act (i.e., as purely and simply known) by the very act of intellection itself and in the *species expressa* or mental word. When the object is the intellect's act, the intellect itself or the existence of the self, it is known (reflexively) in initial act from the very fact that the intellect is in direct act of knowing the thing, and thus it is intelligible in act to itself. It is known in final act (effectively known) by an act of reflex understanding and in a reflex concept. Cf. below, Ch. III, n. 45; *ibid.*, n. 119; and Appendix V, § 2.

21   "Every being is what it is."

22   "Indeed, the evidence grasps us by the throat without leaving us time to defend ourselves; it hits a person right in the eye, not like a blind force, but, rather as an irresistible light. As soon as the mind ventures to reflect, it feels its shock; not a single moment is given to it for deliberation. From the very first step, its reflection falls upon evidence it cannot dispute, that it does not have to 'justify' but only to confirm and mark down. At the beginning of the critique of knowledge there is not, and there cannot be any time to pause. There cannot be a single moment of uncertainty, forbearance, ignorance or real doubt" (J. de Tonquédec, *op. cit.*, p. 444).

"This is a point that Descartes, the founder of modern idealism, did not see when he wrote that God could have made square circles and mountains without valleys if He had wanted to do so. Descartes did not understand that at that point in the philosophical order he was committing a sin against the Holy Ghost or the redeeming light in the spiritual order. From the dawn of our intellectual life we have this absolute certitude: neither God, if He exists and is as powerful as possible, nor an evil genius, no matter how perverse or cunning he is supposed to be, can make a square circle because that is not only *inconceivable* to us; it is *really impossible in itself*" (R. Garrigou-Lagrange, *art. cit.*, p. 14).

vicious circle.[23] As we have pointed out elsewhere,[24] the *universalis dubitatio de veritate* of which St. Thomas, following Aristotle,[25] speaks, this calling into question, this universal *aporia* (the privilege of metaphysics), this *videtur quod non* whereby all scientific research begins and which, in metaphysics, stops at nothing, is in no way a lived or exercised doubt. Nor, indeed, is it the phenomenological epoche.[26] It is an epoche that is not lived but signified as a hypothesis that should be examined. It is a conceived or represented doubt (and, for that reason, much stricter and more sincere than the Cartesian doubt because it does not imply any sham, any arbitrary "forcing" arising from the will, any pseudo-drama). The terminus the mind reaches after following through with such a universal problematizing is, precisely, the clear and reflex awareness of (1) the absolute impossibility of realizing a universal doubt (or a universal "bracketing" of all certitude about the being of things), and (2) the knowledge which the mind already possesses in respect to its essential ordination to lay hold of things. Even though that knowledge lies buried deep in the inner recesses of the exercise of its own basic activity and remains unformulated, it is still present from the very start. For in every judgment the intellect knows itself tacitly and virtually, *in cujus natura est ut rebus conformetur.*[27] Realism is lived by the intellect before being recognized by it.

---

23   And that is not the only one. The value of certitude cannot be cast into doubt in reflection without expressly referring to an absolute and incontestable ideal of certitude, to a notion of certainty that is already acquired and held to be guaranteed, to a strict principle that will command the entire discussion that follows, namely, that valid, scientific certitude—certitude that has objective truth as its correlative—bears certain characteristics, and demands certain conditions. There is at least something for reflection which cannot be at all doubtful! That is a *reflex and, indeed, philosophical certitude*, one that may easily be recognized and that has to be put outside universal doubt. And it implies all the elements of critical philosophy: a notion of truth, reality, objectivity, etc. Critical philosophy has, therefore, begun even before the start assigned it. (Cf. Du Roussaux, "Le Néo-dogmatisme," *Revue Néo-scolastique*, Nov. 1911, pp. 555–556.)

"It is perfectly legitimate to make an inventory and critical revision of the kinds of human knowledge. And that is the very thing we have tried to do in the present work. But there is no room for universal doubt in such an undertaking. 'Despoiling the mind to such a point that it does not even have the barest power of knowing anything about anything is quite impossible even for the split-second of a lightning-flash. . . . Every attempt at universal doubt is a still-born activity, dead in its very seed. In all reality—and even as a possibility—it is simply a non-entity. Such a biased question is an idle question; it is solved in the asking'" (Du Roussaux, *ibid.*, p. 557). (J. de Tonquédec, *op. cit.*, pp. 446–447.)

24   *Réflexions sur l'intelligence*, p. 42.

25   Aristotle, *Metaph.*, B, c. I (St. Thomas, Bk. III, lect. 1). J. de Tonquédec has indicated the true meaning of this expression in the first pages (pp. 436–441) of the conclusion of his book on *La critique de la connaissance*.

26   On this epoche, see below, Ch. III, § 15.

27   St. Thomas, *De Verit.*, I, 9; cf. below, Ch. III, § 9.

3^0. Finally, an authentic critique of knowledge, recognizing as it does that it is foolish to regard the retracing of its own footprints as the first step along its path, does not pretend to be a prerequired condition of philosophy.[28] From this point of view, the conception which Cartesians and Neo-Cartesians form of "philosophical radicalism"[29] appears to be the very epitome of presumption in the matter of human knowing. Critique of knowledge presupposes a long effort of knowing, knowing which is not only spontaneous but scientific, too, and not only scientific (in the modern meaning of the word 'science'), but philosophical, psychological, logical and metaphysical knowledge as well.[30] Critique of knowledge forms part of metaphysical knowledge which is the highest wisdom in the natural order. And if, in the outward and visible order of a written treatise (in which we must act, alas, as though knowledge were possessed and already achieved), it is fitting to place critique at the start of metaphysics as a kind of apologetic introduction (as a matter of fact, critique, ontology and natural theology grow together), it is so because they are even more closely bound together than the moral virtues, inasmuch as they integrate a single specific habit. "The necessary factor is that, instead of being a condition for ontology, epistemology grows in and with it, being at once explanatory and explained, as what supports and what is supported by it, just as the parts of a true philosophy lend mutual support to one another."[31] Critique of knowledge or epistemology does not exist as a discipline distinct from metaphysics. To give it a separate existence is to set a third term between realism and idealism, between yes and no. And that is the whole claim of those moderns with their unthinkable notion of a "pure phenomenon"[32] which empties the very concept of being, the most general of all our concepts, of all being.

---

28   "First one must extricate himself from the obsession that epistemology is the primary condition of philosophy" (E. Gilson, *art. cit.*, p. 754). On that score we are in complete agreement with E. Gilson.

29   Cf. E. Husserl, *Méditations cartésiennes*, First Meditation.

30   "According to the true thought of Aristotle and St. Thomas, critique of knowledge should come at the start of metaphysics (or, if you like, at the end of it by way of reflection) but only after Natural Philosophy and Psychology. For to make a critique of the value of knowledge, it is first necessary to know what it is psychologically. We must first know how to distinguish the intellect's formal object (being and the *raison d'être* of things) from the formal object of the senses (sensible phenomena)" (R. Garrigou-Lagrange, *art. cit.*, p. 11, note); cf. *Revue Thomiste*, Jan. 1924, pp. 18–25, "Dans quel ordre proposer les sciences philosophiques."

     L. Noel (Notes d'épistemologie thomiste, p. 126, note) endorses this thesis noting (and he is very correct in so doing) in turn that critique serves the progress of the philosophical sciences. For in this case as in the case of every organic growth, *causae ad invicem sunt causae.*

31   E. Gilson, *op. cit.*, p. 755.

32   There is a perfectly legitimate notion of phenomenon, but it is one that does not *separate* phenomenon from "the thing in itself." Phenomenon is the sensible appearance of the thing that exists for itself.

Thus, a Thomistic critique of knowledge is distinct from every idealistic[33] pseudo-critique in the very way in which it poses the question and in its first starting point.

4. After these explanations, Mr. Gilson will perhaps agree that his objections against the possibility of a Thomistic critique of knowledge were not unanswerable and that the notion of a critical realism is not a contradictory one, like the notion of a square circle?[34]

At all events, the reasons are now quite clear as to just why we cannot regard Thomistic realism as a naive realism. (At least, this is true if we understand by naiveté the absence of scientific doubt and care for verification; for naiveté can also indicate a certain naturalness of method, a recognition of the primacy of

33   To be able to label itself properly Thomistic, a critique should maintain that the being of sensible things, the proper object of our intellect, is "first known by the human intellect,"and that there is a first intellectual apprehension that may be called a "seeing" (cf. D. Roland-Gosselin, "Peut-on parler d'intuition intellectuelle dans la philosophie thomiste," *Philosophia Perennis*, t. II, p. 730) or a "perceiving" or an "abstractive intuition." (Cf. our *Réflexions sur l'intelligence*, Appendix II, and our *Philosophie bergsonienne*, p. 154, n. 2, and L. Noel, *op. cit.*, pp. 154-155.) The word is of very little importance; the essential thing is to recognize that the object is attained immediately (see below, § 26, and Appendix I, § 4, VIII), and that our intellect does not merely "conceive" being, as some Neo-scholastics (Zamboni, for instance) have claimed, but in conceiving it, the intellect "perceives" it. Such a critique should also maintain that the *species intelligibilis* (*impressa* and *expressa*) is a *quo* and not a *quod* (cf. § 24 and Appendix I), and that the knower becomes the other as other in initial or "first" act (through the *species impressa*) as well as in final or "second" act (by the knowing act itself).If one does not defend all these points, the critique of knowledge then constructed will be one that breaks with the principles of Aristotle and St. Thomas.

34   E. Gilson, *art. cit.*, p. 751. To tell the truth, Etienne Gilson had in mind a certain view of realism that various Neo-scholastics have fashioned. But we think that whereas his objections are well taken against positions like those of Jeannière (whom he does not name), or Picard, or even against the positions of Phenomenologists (cf. especially his remark on pp. 750–751), his disagreement with L. Noel has less to do with the doctrine than with method. And perhaps Mgr. Noel himself would agree that the role he gives the *cogito* in his *Notes d'epistemologie thomiste* (particularly p. 88) is in the final reckoning quite secondary to the essential point in his thought. Mgr. Noel's thought should be sought, rather, in the very resolute criticisms he has directed against Picard (*op. cit.*, pp. 128 ff.) and Zamboni (pp. 133 ff.). On this score, we are pleased to note that on fundamental things, for example on points as important as the *immediacy* of intellectual perception and the points we have singled out above (Ch. III, n. 32), an essential agreement is affirmed between authors like the late Fr. Gény, R. Garrigou-Lagrange, J. de Tonquédec, E. Peillaube, L. Noel, A. Masnovo, M. Cordovani, R. Kremer, E. Gilson. The differences that remain between them are of the sort that is embroidered upon an agreement about basic thoughts; such divergences bear witness to the possibility of a collective work that can help philosophic queries move forward.

nature over reflection.) We think that it is a "conscious, deliberate and voluntary," "methodical" realism, while yet truly and properly a critical realism; indeed, we think it the only gnoseological doctrine fully deserving of that name.

These remarks about the notion of critical realism are only a foreword. Now we have to touch upon some of the central questions of critique itself. To attempt to form an exact idea of speculative philosophy and the two typically different degrees of knowing it contains—philosophy of nature and metaphysics—one must first go through noetic and establish a certain number of positions that have to do with the much more general problem of the relation between thought and the real. Hence, we will start by outlining the solution that, we feel, may well have to be given to this problem according to the principles of Thomas Aquinas' critical realism. Perhaps this explanation will have the good fortune to make it easier to compare Thomistic thought with the various tendencies in England and America that are grouped under the name "Neo-realism." Again, it may be of help in making a comparison with those tendencies to which the name "phenomenological philosophy" is given in Germany. These trends are most interesting to us and we greatly esteem the intellectual stimulation they provide. However, it does seem that they have been somewhat too dominated by the need to react against certain prevailing prejudices. On the one hand, they are too overloaded with *a priori* gratuitousness, and on the other, they are rather too indifferent to metaphysical inquiries. The points we shall have occasion to mention in this regard are but simple indications and mere suggestions spoken in passing. For our purpose is not to embark upon an analysis of these various trends but to deal with the two degrees of knowing, philosophy of nature and metaphysics. As a preamble, we propose to settle in advance the gnoseological positions this plan requires.

II

REALISM AND COMMON SENSE

5. In modern times (suffering as cruelly as they do from the division of the mind against itself), and at a time when common sense has received so many rebukes, a realistic philosophy usually begins with an attempt to give some sort of rehabilitation to common sense and to renew our ties with it. That is a laudable undertaking since it teaches the philosopher a certain humility. It leads him back to the path of nature and tends to re-establish intellectual unity at a most thoroughly and modestly human level—I mean at the very point at which the thought of the man in the street is articulated with the thought of the philosopher. But it is also a risky undertaking since common sense is not something homogeneous, and since a great deal of scientific progress—espe-

cially modern scientific progress—has been made, to tell the truth, in opposition to it.

If one adopts a pure notion of common sense, then it must be said that for Thomists there is complete solidarity between common sense and philosophy; and yet, at the same time, there is a clear distinction between the two. By "a pure notion of common sense," we mean the understanding of truths that are known in themselves, and of the principles of reason (*habitus principiorum*); we mean a metaphysics still unformed, but yet an understanding rich in some of the certitudes absolutely fundamental to human life—certitudes that reason, with the help of experience, draws from these principles of reason. For philosophy is a knowledge in which the basic certainties of common sense are rediscovered but, in this case, fashioned by critical reason and scientifically enunciated. It is a knowledge which extends those convictions of common sense without limit by ever-new discoveries and new demonstrations. It is a knowledge based entirely on the inescapable evidence of the principles which the intellect intuits[35] rather than on the authority of common sense. While St. Thomas' position very forcibly and with great respect maintains the coherence between common sense and philosophy, it is quite different and much more critical than that of Reid.

Let us note parenthetically, naiveté and the superstitious fear of being naive are the two foes of a sound critique. Insofar as philosophy is a wisdom, it has to verify its organs and instruments in proportion to its advances. It should accept nothing from nature or culture without examining and judging it for itself. But to claim "to justify itself from its very roots"[36] and to accept nothing whatever from nature, to make the passage to the world consist in its being verified, these contentions shut philosophy up in a pure artificiality that is much the worst kind of naiveté, for it is the naiveté of the professor. That is

35   Cf. R. Garrigou-Lagrange, *Le sens commun, la philosophie de l'être et les formules dogmatiques* (Paris, Desclée de Brouwer et Cie, 3rd ed.).

36   E. Husserl, *Meditations Cartesiennes*, p. 2. It is a kind of singularly naive credulity about the possibilities of philosophy to think that from the very outset it should be constituted by a "radical" awareness of self (*ibid.*, p. 131), and built up step by step on the "fundamental basis of a full, entire and universal awareness of self" (*ibid.*, p. 134). The human mind will never achieve an awareness of self. For such a self-awareness presupposes a self above all else, and that holds for all degrees of knowing: in the highest level of knowing (metaphysical) as well as at the lower stages (the particular sciences) there is a reversion upon the self, a critique (in the latter case a partial and limited critique, in the former a universal and radical one) that presupposes a direct knowing. If philosophy is to help the human mind gain a more and more profound awareness of self in any very effective way, it is on the condition that philosophy itself is first founded, and then built up step by step. This is similar to a knowledge of being that thus allows the mind to become more aware of itself (through a reflexive process which, in the wake of the idealist's deflection, has actually shown itself, now, for nearly two centuries to be corrosive and destructive of the very knowledge of being upon which it was reflecting).

what those philosophers do who apply themselves in this fashion to the task
of "putting an end to all naiveté" so that one often wonders how they could
have been born. They will find it just as difficult to be born to wisdom (and,
hence, to critique). Let us add that, on the whole, naive naiveté is much better
than anti-naive naiveté; it follows the paths of nature and may be healed. In
the course of the history of thought, it is actually naiveté that has little by little
become more critical through self-reflection. And such a critical progress is
destined to last forever. A Socrates, a Plato, an Aristotle—these men were in
no sense unaware of the critical problem. Book IV (*gamma*) of the *Metaphysics*
is pregnant in spirit with a critique;[37] there is more penetrating critique in
Albert the Great, St. Thomas or Cajetan than in Kant. However, they never
dreamed of setting up the reflexive and critical part of metaphysics as a special
body of doctrine, thereby leaving wide areas of knowing as a kind of waste-
land. Indeed, as we noted above, it should be said that the state of philosophy
in their time involved a much less explicit and less complete isolation of critical
problems and of the technique that goes with them. It remained for Thomists
of the modern era, of the "age of reflection," to bring that technique to a level
more worthy of their master's thought. The microscopic equipment usually
applied to the examination of primary notions and first principles will always
have to be perfected further; so, too, we will never be able to have done with
precritical "naiveté" once and for all. Knowledge comes before reflection just
as nature precedes knowledge. Critical reflection will not cease to increase any
more than the knowledge of nature will.

6. Now, we have said that common sense is not something homogeneous.
Indeed, there exists not only the intellectual content of common sense, of which
we have just been speaking, but there is a complete imagery as well. Thus, for
instance, according to that imagery, the sun turns around the earth, high and
low are absolute determinations of space, our antipodes have their head
downwards, etc. It is absolutely necessary to distinguish the intellectual values
of common sense from its imagery. Philosophy and science can move forward
only on condition that they rid themselves of that imagery.

Finally, according to one of the basic maxims St. Thomas never tires of
repeating, the human intellect is at the lowest level in the scale of spirits. For
that reason, the word "natural" has two quite opposite meanings where man
is concerned. Insofar as common sense is natural, i.e., as it conforms to an
intellect's essential inclinations, it is naturally right, agile and intuitive, it goes
towards being and God with a sort of spiritual phototropism. And in that
sense, philosophy should be its continuation. On the other hand, insofar as the
word "natural" is taken in quite a different second sense and signifies "exposed

---

37   Cf. R. Garrigou-Lagrange, "Le réalisme thomiste et le mystère de la connais-
      sance," *Rev. de Phil.*, Jan.–Feb. and March–April, 1931, p. 10 of the off-print; *Le
      sens commun*, Part I.

to the ordinary perils that menace our intellect," common sense has a kind of natural propensity for stupidity, materialism and a misunderstanding of what is living and spiritual. And in that sense philosophy constantly has to set it right.

Thus it is clear that the history of thought, at least to the extent that it is progressive, is composed of a series of scandals for common sense, each of which is followed by a higher reintegration, conquest and victory for common sense. Each of our steps upon earth is itself an incipient fall followed by a regaining of balance.

Truth

7. One of the very first scandals for common sense in this matter concerns the relation between things and the mind, the very notion of truth. Common sense thinks (and it is not wrong) "what I think is what is." But it immediately materializes that statement; it crushes the life out of it in a facile picture and imagines that thought is a kind of copy or material tracing of the thing, that coincides with it at every point, in such fashion that whatever conditions attach to the one likewise attach to the other.

Reflection soon gives rise to some bitter disillusions. If thought or knowledge were a copy or a tracing of the thing, and if both are identically conditioned, how would error be possible? It would be absurd to conceive of error as the tracing of what does not exist. Moreover, how could we know a thing that was one in itself, for example, what we call "man," by means of a complex thought like the idea "living being" joined to the idea "capable of sensation" and the idea "capable of understanding"? And how could we know by universal ideas a thing that is singular in its proper existence? How, for example, could we know the geometric properties of this table by means of theorems about the rectangle? And how could we look at this weed or apple without ourselves sharing, through our sensation, in their vegetable existence?

In such cases we are compelled to effect a certain disjunction between the thing and thought, to recognize that the conditions that attach to the one do not attach to the other. The way things exist in our thought, so as to be known, is not the same as the way they exist in themselves. (As soon as the mind reflects upon itself it perceives that there is an *inside* to thought, constituting a world apart, even though it is open to things. It is supremely important to be on the watch for any attempt to reduce the things of thought to spatial imagination,[38] but it would be vain to try to get rid of the conditions of human

---

38 On this score, L. Noel quite correctly comments that the idealistic formula "a beyond-thought is unthinkable" arises, to tell the truth, from just such an imagination. Or it merely indicates that thought cannot attain a term without it being, for that very reason, in some way thought about, and that is "a rather useless truism." (*Notes d'épist. thom.*, p. 92; cf. pp. 33–34, 73–76). Also see below, Ch. III, n. 51.

language. The expressions "in the mind," "outside the mind" have no more
spatial significance than the word "spirit," which originally signified breath,
or the word "God," which originally indicated light. Just as when we speak of
creatures existing "outside God," spatiality is purely metaphorical, so, too, in
the present instance. What is meant is that a thing sometimes exists for
itself—either actually or possibly—in the universe we see. In a more general
way it exists in the order of being merely posited or existentially realized, and
at other times it does not exist for itself or in this universe or in space, or in the
order of simple *positio extra nihil*, but rather, under quite different conditions.
It may exist under the conditions of thought, and as either the beginning or
termination of the act of thought. And in that case we say: it exists in thought.[39]
The hackneyed sophism of idealism is to draw its argument from the spatial
and material meaning metaphorically evoked by this "in" and by the "outside"
that corresponds to it. But to refuse to use the expressions "in consciousness"
and "outside consciousness"[40] on the plea that consciousness is neither a circle

---

39   Cf. St. Thomas, *Sum. Theol.*, I, 59, 2; I–II, 86, 1 ad 2; *Cont. Gent.*, IV, 11, n. 3; *In IV
      Sent.*, dist. 49, q. 1, a. 1, sol. 2.
           If, on the other hand, the word *in* is taken, I don't say in a spatial sense, but
      only of an entitative inhering in a subject, then St. Thomas warns us that
      knowledge, taken not as an *accident* of the knower (a condition for the entitative
      order implied by all creative knowledge) but as a *relation* to the thing known and
      in the pure line of knowing, is not in the soul as in a subject in the *entitative* sense
      of the word "in." (This is so because it is outside any and every order of the
      entitative.) "Secundum quod comparatur ad cognoscentem, [notitia] . . . inest
      cognoscenti sicut accidens in subjecto, et sic non excedit subjectum, quia nun-
      quam invenitur inesse alicui nisi menti. . . . Secundum quod comparatur ad
      cognoscibile, . . . sic non habet quod insit, sed quod ad aliud sit. Illud autem quod
      ad aliquid dicitur, non habet rationem accidentis ex hoc quod est ad aliquid, sed
      solum ex hoc quod inest . . . propter hoc notitia secundum considerationem istam
      non est in anima sicut in subjecto; et secundum hanc comparationem excedit
      mentem inquantum alia a mente per notitiam cognoscuntur. . . . Et secundum
      hoc etiam est quaedam aequalitas notitiae ad mentem, inquantum se extendit ad
      omnia ad quae potest se extendere mens" (*Quodlib.*, VII, a. 4). This does not,
      however, prevent things known being in the soul in the intentional meaning
      indicated in the text, and not in any entitative sense.
40   Cf. Georges Gurvitch, *Les tendances actuelles de la philosophie allemande* (Paris, Vrin,
      1930, p. 47) (regarding Edmund Husserl). The point in Husserl's observations
      that is very true is that the object *as such* is neither in the mind nor outside the
      mind. But that is precisely the reason it can exist both in the mind and outside
      the mind. However, Husserl himself cannot express himself without saying
      every minute that the object or *cogitatum* is "immanent to consciousness" (*Médi-
      tations cartésiennes*, Paris, A. Colin, 1931, p. 36), constituted "inside the ego" (p.
      71), that it exists "in us, in me" (p. 73), "in me while the *ego* meditates" (p. 111)
      etc. Moreover, let us observe that if the spatiality metaphorically connoted by all
      the roots of our human words does not constitute a redhibitory fault when we
      say "in the mind," it obviously is not by itself a redhibitory fault when we say
      as a correlative "outside the mind."

nor a casket, would be to deny from the very outset the interiority to self, proper to spirit. It would be to be condemned to describe knowledge by abstracting from spirit; in other words, it would be to forbid every method of penetrating what knowledge is. And now that we have made this observation once and for all, we will pursue our stated purpose without letting ourselves be held up over words and without fearing to use forms of language which connote spatiality only metaphorically, as all metaphysical words do.)

There are two different *esse*'s, two levels of existence, for things: the proper existence they possess in order to maintain themselves outside nothingness, and the existence that supervenes upon them in their apprehension by the soul in order that they may be known. In order that the bindweed and apple may enter the sense of sight, they leave at the door the proper matter in which they subsist; and they lay aside their individuality in order to be able to enter understanding and reasoning. In the inner world of our understanding there is a whole multitude of distinct views or distinct concepts for things that exist undivided in the world of nature, and they lead quite a different life in the latter world than they do in the former. In the world of nature the lion eats the antelope; in the world of understanding the lion receives the predicate carnivorous by means of the copula. And the possibility of error arises simply from the disparity in the way things exist in these two worlds. That indicates that thought is not referred to the thing as a material transfer that coincides with its model: there is a gulf between the conditions or mode of thought and the conditions or mode of the thing.

8. But it also indicates that there is an incomparable unity, a unity deeper than that between a model and a transfer, between the thing and thought, thought in act, I mean. For if things were modified or changed in any way by sensation or intellection (I do not mean in the conditions in which they exist, in their *way of existing*, I mean in regard to those things that properly constitute them, in what they are), then there would no longer be any truth or knowledge. Then the theorist of knowledge could not even express himself by wagging his finger because in such a case there would be left but two equally impossible recourses: either to say that knowledge implies a relation to things but deforms those things, and as a result they are never known; or else to say that knowledge implies no relation to things and that it is an absolute unfolding of thought having only itself as object. This is a position which is quite incompatible with the fact of error and negative ideas. Moreover, it is manifestly *self-refuting* because knowledge itself can only be affirmed to be this or that if it is taken to be something distinct from the act by which it is thought. As has been shown very well in England and America,[41] the principle whereby every relation would have to modify or alter its extreme is a pure postulate of which

---

41   Cf. René Kremer, *Le néo-réalisme américain* (Paris, Alcan, 1920); *La théorie de la connaisance chez les néo-réalistes anglais* (Paris, Vrin, 1928).

proof has never been given and which it is incumbent entirely upon idealism to prove. All efforts to demonstrate that principle are reduced to the statement that a thing cannot be known without being known. And that is what everybody rather suspected.

The relation of knowledge is precisely a relation that does not deform, that neither alters nor modifies its term. The scholastics said that the relation between the soul that knows and the thing known is a real relation (because it puts something new in the soul) but that the relation between the thing known and the soul that knows is a relation of reason, which does not in any way affect or change the thing known. The fact that the mind makes things pass into a state of immateriality and universality, that it divides the various aspects which those things involve, that it handles and manipulates them, separates them, joins them and compares them within itself—this entire task has to do with the conditions of their existence within the mind and the preparations *for* knowing. It does not constitute the *knowing itself* and leaves what the thing is intact. There is a secret, mysterious and holy substance in this great machinery of logic that no treatment can change—the essence or nature, the inmost ontological depth of the things, made present to the mind through the idea.

This distinction between the mode of existing of the thing and the thing itself, or its nature, is of capital importance in the theory of knowledge. And the exigence, immanent in knowledge, to leave the thing, insofar as it is known, intact and unaltered, is so great that it does not even admit that thing and mind are two things in the act of knowing. For then there would be some difference or other between thing and thought; from the very fact the thing is thought about, it would not be purely what it is. In the act of knowing, the thing (in the very measure in which it is known) and mind are not only joined, they are strictly *one*, according to Aristotle's phrase, the intellect in act is the intelligible in act. That is the reason why we said a little while ago that the notion of knowledge as a copy or transfer is utterly inadequate, not only on the side of the disparity between the conditions of the mind and those of the thing, but also on the side of the unity between thing and mind.

9. Thus the sense is clear in which we must understand the definition of truth which St. Thomas has made classic: *adaequatio rei et intellectus*, adequation or conformity between intellect and thing.[42] This adequation or conformity

---

42   Cf. *Réflexions sur l'intelligence*, p. 24; J. de Tonquédec, *La critique de la connaissance*, pp. 225 ff. and 512. According to Fr. Muckle's researches, this famous definition of truth was not in Isaac Israeli, Jewish doctor and philosopher who lived in Egypt between 845 and 940. St. Thomas attributed it to Isaac's *De Definitionibus*. Handed on by some compiler or other, it must go back rather early and the way for it was, at any rate, prepared by Aristotle.

It goes without saying that such an adequation should only be understood as it has to do with what is formally attained of the thing and does not imply at all

has nothing to do with a copy or material transfer. Inasmuch as our knowledge comes originally from the senses, all our words, as we noted a little while ago, are drawn from the order of visible and tangible things: the words "adequation" and "conformity" are no exception. But in this case what they designate should be thought of as completely purified from what is visible and tangible. It is a question of a certain conformity,[43] quite unique in its class, between the way the mind declares itself on the thing and posits it in existence in its own inner act of judgment, and the way the thing exists. It is a correspondence that amounts to an identity, not in relation to the mode of existing in the thing and in the mind, but in reference to the existing of the thing taken in its pure value as intelligible object. This is an existing that is realized (or may be realized) outside the mind, but in the correspondence mentioned, it is lived in the mind by the mind as it is realized (or may be realized) outside the mind. For judgment is like an imitation of the creative act, an imitation that cannot create, and it brings the mind's content into existence outside the mind—not by creation *ad extra*, but by affirmation *ad intra*.[44]

"Truth," says St. Thomas,[45] "is the conformity of the mind with being, according as it says that what is, is, and that what is not, is not." That

that the mind equates itself to everything the thing is. Compared with all the ontological wealth of the least reality, human knowledge must always be said to be unequal to the real (cf. above, Ch. II, n. 21); not only is it not exhaustive, but it achieves the real only through the humblest of means—very often those means are most indirect and precarious—because it is the knowledge of the weakest of spirits.

43 "Secundum proportionalitatem," St. Thomas says (*In IV Sent.*, d. 49, q. 2, a. 1 ad 7).

44 On the nature of judgment see below, § 13.

45 *Cont. Gent.*, I, 59; cf. *In Metaph.*, IV, 1. 8, n. 651; *In Perih.*, I, 1. 3, n. 7; 1. 13, n. 12. It is notable that this notion of truth, which only makes explicit what the mind, from the moment of its first critical reflection and first awareness of itself, intuitively perceives that it is vitally experiencing, in fact, imposes itself even upon those who reject it in theory. Not only does idealism come a cropper over the fact of error, from the very start—for error is a complete scandal and utter impossibility from the very moment that knowing means that the mind grasps itself or posits itself or engenders itself—but also all those who, while claiming to transcend ordinary idealism, continue to reject the "thing" posited outside the mind in its own right, still go on using the idea of truth in fact, but only after reconstituting, as an afterthought and in a quite artificial way, an equivalent for the *adaequatio rei et intellectus*. Such a reconstitution really and necessarily presupposes this primary notion of *adaequatio*. Thus, in E. Husserl's new "transcendental idealism" (and the same holds true for L. Brunschvicg's quite different idealism) the verified takes the place of the true (a thing is true which is presented by a "verifying confirmative synthesis," *op. cit.*, p. 51; cf. pp. 76, 88, 106, 109), as though "to verify" were anything different from "recognizing as true." Thus, to define truth by verification is nonsense. And correlatively Husserl, after the manner of Descartes, takes evidence to be a characteristic of the object of thought (*cogitatum*) taken as separate from the thing, instead of saying that it comes from

conformity is established between the being possessed by the thing and the being affirmed by the mind. When the mind's act (by reason of which things within it are referred to existence in a certain determined way) agrees with the way things behave in existence (actual or possible), and more particularly, when the identification effected by the mind between the two terms of a proposition corresponds to an identity in the thing, then the mind is true.[46]

the thing itself (*ens intelligibile*) according as it is objectified in the mind as the object of judgment.

46   It is a well-known Thomistic thesis that the intellect possesses truth or says what is true or false only in the judgment. (Cf. *Réflexions sur l'intelligence*, pp. 68–69, 74–75.) A commentary on the texts in which St. Thomas treats this question, and especially that classic text from the *De Veritate*, I, 9, may be found in L. Noel's *Notes d'epistemologie thomiste* (Ch. V) and in J. de Tonquedec's *La critique de la connaissance* (Ch. VI). Cf. also D. Roland-Gosselin, "Sur la théorie thomiste de la verité," *Rev. des Sciences Phil. et Théol.*, April 1921, and R. Garrigou-Lagrange, *art. cit.*, p. 16. St. Thomas' text from *De Veritate*, I, 9 is:

Veritas est in intellectu et sensu, licet non eodem modo. In intellectu enim est sicut consequens actum intellectus, et sicut cognita per intellectum; consequitur namque intellectus operationem, secundum quod judicium intellectus est de re secundum quod est; cognoscitur autem ab intellectu secundum quod intellectus reflectitur supra actum suum, non solum secundum quod cognoscit actum suum sed secundum quod cognoscit proportionem ejus ad rem: quod quidem cognosci non potest nisi cognita natura ipsius actus, quae cognosci non potest, nisi cognoscatur natura principii activi, quod est ipse intellectus, in cujus natura est ut rebus conformetur; unde secundum hoc cognoscit veritatem intellectus quod supra seipsum reflectitur.

At this point let us recall, or bring into sharper focus, certain points that seem particularly important to us. To be in conformity with the real ("logically true") is the very "ontological truth" of the senses and intellect in act. All true knowledge is a knowledge that is true. Simple apprehension is only true in this way. But that truth is only possessed as such, when it itself is known, and it is only known through the judgment whereby the mind, in giving its assent to the mental statement it has constructed for this effect, makes its pronouncement about the thing and declares it is so, *ita est*. "Quando judicat rem ita se habere, sicut est forma quam de re apprehendit tunc primo cognoscit et dicit verum. Et hoc facit componendo et dividendo. Nam in omni propositione aliquam formam significatam per praedicatum, vel applicat alicui rei significatae per subjectum, vel removet ab ea" (*Sum. Theol.*, I, 16, 2. Cf. *De Verit.*, I, 3).

From the mere fact that the mind makes its pronouncement about what is, there is a reflection *in actu exercito* of the mind upon itself and upon its own conformity with the thing ("super ipsam similitudinem reflectitur, cognoscendo et dijudicando ipsam," *In Metaph.*, lib. VI, lect. 4. Cf. below, Ch. III, n. 60). But that reflection is still not the logical or critical reflection (cf. Ferrariensis, *in C.G.*, I, 59) in which the mind knows *in actu signato* its own act and concept through a new act and a new concept (reflexive); it is but the mind "taking hold" of itself, and *that is nothing but the very act of judging*. Thus, Cajetan can define judgment as *illa cognitio quae sui ipsius conformitatem cum re cognoscit* (*In*, I, 16, 2).

St. Thomas himself says that very clearly in those precious explanations he has given, *In Perih.*, lib. I, lect. 3, n. 9: "Cognoscere autem praedictam habitudinem [conformitatem suae ad rem] nihil est aliud quam judicare ita esse in re vel non esse; quod est componere et dividere; et ideo intellectus non cognoscit veritatem, nisi componendo vel dividendo per suum judicium."

And in that way there are already known in first act (cf. above, Ch. III, n. 16): the nature (i.e., the finality, which is to conform itself to the being of things) of the act and the nature of the power or faculty from which it emanates (*De Verit.*, I, 9)—this latter will be known in second act by an explicit reflection, as will the nature of the *habitus* (*De Verit.*, X, 9) whence the act proceeds and the very existence of the soul (*De Verit.*, X, 8). See below, Ch. III, n. 63, and Ch. III, n. 111.

Let us also take notice of the following points: [1]. If the nature of the act, habitus and powers is known in this way at the same time as their existence through an explicit reflections and an immediate experience, it is precisely and uniquely to the extent that the act is specified by the object and as the *habitus* (*De Verit.*, X, 9) and power (*ibid.*, I, 9) are more-or-less proximate principles of act and essentially ordered to it (here it is a matter of an experience of my act, *habitus*, intellect, mind in their concrete singularity). "Cujuslibet potentiae animae virtus est determinata ad objectum suum; unde et ejus actio primo et principaliter in objectum tendit. In ea vero quibus in objectum tendit, non potest nisi per quamdam reditionem. . . . Sed ista reditio incomplete quidem est in sensu, complete autem in intellectu, qui reditione completa redit ad cognoscendum essentiam suam. . . . Unde actio intellectus nostri primo tendit in ea quae per phantasmata apprehenduntur, et deinde redit ad actum suum cognoscendum, et ulterius in species et habitus et potentias et essentiam ipsius mentis. Non enim comparantur ad intellectum ut objecta prima, sed ut ea quibus in objectum feratur" (*De Verit.*, X, 9) . [2]. By the same concrete experience and explicit reflection my soul is, on the contrary, only known in its *existence* and not in its nature because it is not a proximate and operative principle but only a radical and substantial principle of its operations; this is true, too, because its essence is not specified by them. "Cujus diversitatis est haec ratio, quia tam habitus quam animam non percipimus in nobis esse, nisi percipiendo actus quorum anima et habitus sunt principia. Habitus autem per essentiam suam est principium talis actus; unde si cognoscitur habitus prout est principium talis actus, cognoscitur de eo quid est; ut si sciam quod castitas est per quam quis cohibet se ab illicitis cogitationibus in venereis existentibus, scio de castitate quid est. Sed anima non est principium actuum per suam essentiam, sed per vires suas; unde perceptis actibus animae, percipitur inesse principium talium actuum, utpote motus et sensus; non tamen ex hoc natura animae scitur" (*ibid.*).

It may even be added that this implicit or lived, but as yet inexplicit, reflection whereby, even before any logical or critical reflection, the mind knows, in its judgment *in actu exercito*, that it is true or in conformity with the real, this reflection, we say, is also the one whereby (even more than by the simple apprehension of the objects of the concept wherein it has already become intelligible in act to itself), even before any introspective reflection, the mind knows the existence of the thinking self in germ or in first act and in a preconscious manner. That existence will only become an object of actual knowledge through an explicit reflection (cf. above, Ch. III, § 3, 1^0.). Thus, in judging things, we have, at one and the same time, an implicit experience of the truth of the mind as well as the germ (still hidden and preconscious) or *intuition* of the experience of ourselves. That is why in reading the text (*De Verit.*, X, 8) wherein St. Thomas explains how each person has an actual knowledge of his soul's existence by reflection (explicit) upon his operations—and especially upon his acts of intel-

And in each individual case we have only one means of knowing whether it is so or not, that is, by resolving our thought into the immediate assertions of sensible experience and the first principles of the understanding in which our knowledge cannot be false because it is intuitively and immediately ruled by that which exists.

For the moment, however, the point we should gather from these researches is that truth is had by referring to the actual or possible existence possessed by the thing: *verum sequitur ESSE rerum.*[47] 1 But then a new problem rears up to confront us.

Thing and Object

10. If the foregoing analysis is correct, the same thing is clearly seen to be at one and the same time in the world of nature, in order to exist, and in the world of soul or mind, when it is known. Thus, we must distinguish between the thing as thing—as existing or able to exist for itself—and the thing as object[48]—

lection—it is important, we believe, to understand by those operations not only simple apprehension but also and above all *judgment*, the act of complete intellection. Let us reread this important text: "Quantum ad actualem cognitionem, qua aliquis considerat se in actu animam habere, sic dico, quod anima cognoscitur per actus suos. In hoc enim aliquis percipit se animam habere, et vivere, et esse, quod percipit se sentire et intelligere, et alia hujusmodi vitae opera exercere; unde dicit Philosophus in *IX Ethic* (cap. 9): *Sentimus autem quoniam sentimus; et intelligimus quoniam intelligimus; et quia hoc sentimus, intelligimus quoniam sumus.* Nullus autem percipit se intelligere nisi ex hoc quod aliquid intelligit: quia prius est intelligere aliquid quam intelligere se intelligere; et ideo pervenit anima ad actualiter percipiendum se esse, per illud quod intelligit, vel sentit."

47 St. Thomas, *De Verit.*, I, 1, 3rd sed contra. Cf. *In I Sent.*, d. 19, q. 5, a. 1: "Cum autem in re sit quidditas ejus et suum esse, veritas fundatur in esse rei magis quam in quidditate, sicut et nomen entis ab esse imponitur; et in ipsa operatione intellectus accipientis esse rei sicut est per quamdam similitudinem ad ipsum, completur relatio adaequationis in qua consistit ratio veritatis"; *ibid.*, ad 7. "Prima operatio respicit quidditatem rei; secunda respicit esse ipsius. Et quia ratio veritatis fundatur in esse, et non in quidditate, ut dictum est, ideo veritas et falsitas proprie invenitur in secunda operatione . . ."; *In Perih.*, lib. I, lect. 5, n. 20; lect. 7, n. 3; lect. 15, n. 4: "Hoc modo se habent orationes enuntiativae ad veritatem sicut et res ad esse vel non esse"; *In Boet. de Trin.*, q. 5, a. 3: "Prima quidem operatio [intellectus] respicit ipsam naturam rei, secunda operatio respicit ipsum esse rei."

48 In this case, the word "object" is taken in the strictest scholastic sense (formal object). It is superfluous to point out that in current modern language it has received a very different meaning inasmuch as the opposition of objective to subjective has finally made the values proper to "thing" or the "real" pass on to the object. In our own day English neo-realist and German phenomenological philosophy tends to restore the authentic meaning to the word "object."

As for the word "thing," it is taken here in as wide a meaning as possible. Whereas it primarily refers to the "sensible and visible thing" in which our

when it is set before the faculty of knowing and made present to it. Our intellect's *objects* as such abstract from actual existence and in themselves involve only a *possible* existence. The objects of our senses as such connote, on the contrary, an existence in act and one that is grasped *ut exercita*, as possessed in the present moment (if it is a matter of the objects of the outer senses), or without temporal[49] determination or in a vague time (if it is a question of objects of imagination), or in the past (if objects of memory are under consideration). The tragedy of modern noetic began when the scholastics of the decadent period—with Descartes in their wake—separated the *object* from the *thing*; from that point on, the *thing* became a problematical "lining" concealed behind the *object*. What are we to think of the value of the notion *thing* we have been using in our analysis up to now? This question is all the more important in view of the fact that, in the face of it, the most remarkable efforts to rise above idealism attempted in our own day in England and Germany have broken down.

In general, moderns take *object* as pure object, cut off in itself from any *thing* in which it has existence, I mean an existence independent of my *cogito*, an existence posited in its own right before my act of thinking and independent of it: existence which is called, in that sense, extramental without the "exteriority" having the slightest spatial meaning; it might as well be termed premental, i.e., preceding the knowledge we have of it, or even metalogical. In using this last designation, I do not mean that in order to know it, logic would have to be forsaken or that a logic different from logic would have to be used. I mean metalogical in the sense that it itself does not belong to the realm of logic or to that which is properly constituted by the life of reason. It does not belong to the order of *the known as known*. It is "beyond" that sphere. It must be added, however, that when we speak of extramental existence we are thinking not only of actual existence but also and primarily of simply possible existence because our intellect, in simple apprehension, abstracts from existence in act and in its judgments it does not only judge of that which exists but also of a thing that can or cannot exist and of the *de jure* necessities contained in those essences. Thus it is primarily with reference to the possible real[50] that the value

intellect naturally finds, as it were, the simplest paradigm of reality (because its concepts come from the senses), it also refers to any reality, whatsoever it may be, whether spiritual or corporeal, to any actual or possible datum that is or can be put into existence independently of our mind.

49 Inasmuch as the existence in act they connote is not determined in time, the objects presented by the imagination are either integrated into the sensation they complete (since they are then but one with the perceived object), or else displaced by sensation and the flux of the present, and cast back into unreality. When such a reduction does not take place, they may themselves be taken for real objects, or at least involved in an illusory interpretation (cf. Pierre Quercy, *Etudes sur l'hallucination*, Paris, Alcan, 1930, t. II, Chs. XV and XVI). And inversely, when the feeling for the present is weakened in consequence of a failure in the synthetic activity of consciousness, sensation takes on a look of unreality!

of intellectual knowledge "is justified" or, better, confirmed or made explicit reflexively, and it is in reference to this that the critique of knowledge should primarily proceed. The noetic of so many modern authors wavers at the very start because they misconceive this basic point in confusing a possible real with a being of reason and in recognizing the actual real as the only real.[51]

Object, then, was taken as a pure object separate from any extramental or metalogical thing. But from that moment, even though the objects of sense and intellect be recognized not as subjective modifications or products of thought (because objects as such have their own irreducible value, constitution and intrinsic stability and resistance), but rather typical structures given to intuition, the question will arise: how to explain the stable connections and regularities these pure objects present among themselves? The idea that objects are distributed in discontinuous groups because they are aspects (it would be better to say "inspects") or elements of knowability in certain ontological nuclei called *things*, the idea that they are capable of extramental existence, the idea that the law of connection between the different shapes our eyes perceive when they look at this table from different points of view is explained by the existence of a thing (precisely this table)—all this will look like a simple explanatory hypothesis among many other equally possible hypotheses. Some men even think, along with Messrs. Russell and Whitehead, that according to

---

50   Cf. R. Garrigou-Lagrange, *art. cit.*, pp. 17–20; *God: His Existence and His Nature* (St. Louis, Herder, 1934), Vol. I, pp. 325–327. "Essentiae rerum antequam existant sunt *entia realia, ut ens reale distinguitur contra fictivum* (being of reason), non tamen ut distinguitur contra non existens in actu, secundum distinctionem Cajetani in I de Ente et Essentia, c. IV, q. 6" (Banez, *In Sum. Theol.*, I, 10, 3).

We have already indicated (Ch. III, § 3, 1^0) that the irrefutable certainty of the principle of identity, the first law of metalogical being before it is the first law of logic, is involved in the intellect's first becoming aware of itself. In fact, the intellect, *in virtue of its own proper activity*, perceives that *necessary* law of all *possible* being in an actual (and contingent) existent grasped by it *through* the sense (cf. Cajetan, *In II Anal.*, II, 13; *Réflexions*, p. 70, n. 3). From this point of view—and provided that a clear distinction is made between the problem of the existence of the external world (which arises out of the critique of sensation) and the problem of simply possible extramental being (which arises from a critique of intellectual knowledge)—it can be said with L. Noel (*Revue Néo-scol.*, Nov. 1931, p. 446) that "the real given is the sensible given," and factually and concretely, it is intelligible at the same time. In the concrete network of our cognitive operations, sense and intellect work together; our *direct knowledge* has its start in a sensible perception that is shot through with an intelligibility that is still not explicitly aware of itself. But for *critical reflection* it is well to give distinct consideration to the primary datum (revealed by psychological and logical analysis) of the intellectual perception *as such*. And that is why we say (cf. above, Ch. III, § 3, 2^0) with R. Garrigou-Lagrange, that awareness of the irrefutable certitude of the principle of identity as the law of all *possible* being is part of the first conscious (philosophical) grasp that constitutes the starting point of critique.

51   Cf. below, Ch. III, § 15.

the principle of economy (Ockham's razor), it is better to do without this hypothesis. To tell the truth, that amounts to a return (in virtue of a kind of Leibnizean view, this time heroically pushed to the absolute) to the view that eliminates natural or subjective causality. It is equivalent to reducing reality to a shower of predicates without any subjects, predicates that fly around in the vast dome of heaven and that have to be tied to one another by purely formal laws. Other men, like E. Husserl, will try to reabsorb the thing and its existentiality into transcendental subjectivity, one function of which will be to constitute the thing inside the self. But that is just another way of suppressing the thing in the authentic meaning of the word, the extramental or metalogical thing.

11. We must say that that is a basic mistake. Philosophical reflection has neither to reconstitute the *thing* starting with the *object* as a necessary hypothesis, nor to suppress the *thing* as a superfluous thesis. Such a thesis is even self-contradictory. Philosophical reflection has to affirm that the thing is given with and by the object, and that it is even absurd to wish to separate them. On this point, a truly critical critique of knowledge, a critique that is fully faithful to the immediate data of reflexive intuition, is in accord with common sense in providing an apology for the *thing*. We would say in Thomistic language that the *thing* is the "material object" of the sense and intellect, whereas what we are calling *object* in this context (i.e., on the one hand, the colored thing, the sounding, cold, warm thing, etc.; on the other, the intelligible *quid*) is their "formal object": material object and formal object are grasped at a single stroke and indivisibly by the very same perceptions.

If, however, the word *thing* seems suspect in this connection, inasmuch as it already belongs to the vulgar tongue, there is nothing to prevent one from adopting a word that is in greater conformity with modern scientific customs (i.e., more artificial and didactic), but a word that evinces a greater care to guard against the non-critical preconceptions of ordinary knowledge. Availing ourselves in our turn of the jargon of pedantry, we will say that just as the object is the correlative of a knowing subject, an ontological "for itself," to which it shows itself and which, by reflecting upon its own acts of thought immediately perceives, not its own essence (as Descartes believed) but the fact of its own existence—we may call this the cisobjective subject—it is also not correlative to, but inseparable (because it is itself) from, an ontological "for itself" which precisely takes the name "object" from the fact that is presented to the mind and this we may call the *objectifiable subject* or *transobjective* subject—not, certainly, because it is hidden behind the object but, on the contrary, because it is itself grasped as object and yet constitutes something irreducible in which the possibility of grasping new objects always remains open (for it can give rise to an endless series of necessary or contingent truths).[52] The transobjective is not a field of shapeless unknowns which shrinks in proportion as new objects are grasped; it is a field of known subjects, and subjects interminably knowable as objects. Whether cisobjective or transobjective, the subject is never grasped as pure subject; it is, rather, precisely what is attained as object.[53] The process of knowledge consists in making it object.

Every act of knowledge tells us this is so, so that if we admit that the mind does truly attain an object that is valid for itself and by which the mind is measured, we should also, and to the same degree, admit that it attains a thing (be it actual or possible), a transobjective subject, which is one with that object (or which is its basis or occasion, if the object is a being of reason). Indeed, being (the being enveloped in sensible things) is the first object attained by our intellect.[54] And what is signified by the name "being," if not *what exists or can exist*; and what is thereby first and immediately presented to the intellect, if not what exists or can exist for itself outside the mind? All anyone has to do is to take counsel with himself and experience within himself the absolute impossibility in which the intellect finds itself: how can it think the principle of identity without positing the extramental being (as at least possible) whose behavior this first-of-all-axioms expresses? A prime object, intelligible extramental being without which nothing is intelligible:[55] that is the irrefutable factual datum that is thrust upon the intellect in the heart of its reflection wherein it becomes aware of its own movement towards its object. That apprehension of being is absolutely first and is implied in all other intellectual apprehensions. From that point on, an object incapable of existing (a being of reason) can, indeed, be conceived, but only on the condition that it is referred

---

52 Let us reproduce at this time J. de Tonquedec's very exact arguments on a most common sophism, of which a typical formula is given in Fonsegrive: "The concept of an object that would at the same time exist in itself and be the object of knowledge is quite dearly contradictory. . . . For, to speak of the object of knowledge is to speak of the thing known. . . . Now, it is only too clear that the known as known does not exist in itself, since it exists as thing known" (*Essais sur la connaissance*, p. 186). J. de Tonquedec correctly replies: "This rather formal argument proves only one thing: the fact of existing in itself is different from the fact of being known. But because the one is not the other, it does not follow that the one excludes the other. The concepts are different but it is not "quite clear" that they cannot be realized together and in the same being. By pitting abstractions one against the other in this way it could just as well be proved that the 'concept' of a moon that was at once round and shining 'is clearly contradictory' because the moon is not round insofar as it is shining" (J. de Tonquedec, *La critique de la connaissance*, p. 32, note). The known as known is the definition of the sphere of logic; the known or, rather, the knowable (*quoad se*) as extramental being defines the sphere of the real.

53 Insofar as it is attained either by reflection upon its own acts, in the case of man, or primarily, and before any other object, as in the case of the angel, the cisobjective subject is also transobjective.

54 Cf. Cajetan, *In de Ente et Essentia*, q. 1.

55 Cf. Garrigou-Lagrange, *art. cit.*, p. 16.

to being or to objects that are capable of existing. That is to say that it must be referred to transobjective subjects (possible subjects) which the mind has made objects and after the manner of which the former object (i.e., one incapable of existing) is conceived and without which it could not have been constructed by the intellect. If the notion "being" can be extended to that which does not exist and which can only exist in the mind, it is only as an afterthought and by a repeat performance, as it were, a second improper use of that first notion, something that makes a thing that does not exist, signify—something conceived on the pattern of being.

12. Push the correct analysis of the immediate content of knowledge even further: it will be ascertained that in the very order of sensitive knowledge itself the content of a sense-perception is not only a certain sensible quality or some stimulation, but also—insofar as we can describe in terms of the intellect something that belongs to a level of non-intellectual knowledge—*some thing* that invades us like an extensive field of a determined, sensory-affective hue and thereby calls forth our motor response. Animal behavior, even at the very lowest levels, can only be explained if the stimulations that are received are not only individualized in the subject in an act of sensation,[56] but even individualized on the side of the object in something sensible and stimulating that the animal perceives. Mounting the zoological scale, this something (delivered by sensation as purely undetermined under the proper sensible) is seen gradually to be determined, solidified and distinguished by the joint effort of all the outer and inner senses, and by the effect either of hereditary instinctive estimates or of individual experience. A dog does not merely know various visual, audible, etc., variables linked together in some way; he knows his master, without the knowledge or power of saying it to himself. On a purely sensitive level, and thanks to numberless comparative associations, he has an analogate of the knowledge we have—of that thing, that transobjective subject we call his master.[57] (In our case, of course, the knowledge is presented to an intellect.) And if the sheep flees from the wolf, it is not, as St. Thomas points out, because the colored object he has seen at that moment has wounded the retina of his eye; it is because the sheep sees in the wolf "his natural enemy."

That presupposes that from the very start the outer senses have presented the animal not only with their "proper sensible" and, simultaneously, with their "common sensibles," such as extension. In addition, albeit in quite an implicit and potential manner (and in a way indiscernible to the sense itself), the outer

---

56   Cf. Hans Driesch, *Die "Seele" als elementarer Naturfactor* (Leipzig, Engelmann, 1903).

57   Concerning animal knowledge and the difference between grasping an object of a concept (that properly belongs to the intellect) and grasping the sensible complexes wherein the object of the concept is realized, see Roland Dalbiez's important remarks in section 4 of the Philosophy of Nature (*Vues sur la psychologie animale*, Paris, Vrin, 1930, pp. 95 ff.).

senses have presented a thing of which the sense's proper object is one aspect. In giving a reason for this fact, the ancients explained that the external sense's act of perceiving opens out upon the thing itself or is terminated in the thing itself, *terminatur ad rem*. They said it does so insofar as the thing exists outside the knower, i.e., insofar as it exercises *hic et nunc* an effective action upon the knower's sense-organs. And they spoke of a *judicium sensus*, with reference to the thing thus grasped, whereby the sense at one and the same time clings to the perceived object as to an existing reality,[58] and is able to deceive us when it is affected in a way different from that in which the thing exists.[59]

Existence is not a sensible object *per se*, but, although the sense is incapable of revealing or "discovering" existence as such, what the intellect discovers (precisely thanks to the perception of the sense) and expresses to itself as existence (not only possible existence but existence in act) is nevertheless actually grasped by it, being buried deep within its object. An analysis of consciousness bears witness to this fact in a way that cannot be denied: consciousness is unavoidably brought to bear on the data of external sense when it seeks the original type to which the notion of actual existence corresponds. It is impossible to find the first origin and the first thing signified by this notion in any other place. The intellect has brought down its first judgments about existence under the constraining evidence of the sense's intuition. As for the animal, even though it does not have this notion, at least the unleashing of its motor power by sensation, the urge of desire or aversion, that makes it seek or flee the sensibly perceived object through space is like a practical equivalent of this notion. This also testifies to the value of existential certitude (not known as such) with which the sense's act is impregnated.

13. If, then, the existence in act of an actually acting thing is implied by sensation, the possible existence, at least, of a possible thing, of a possible transobjective subject, is equally implied by intellectual knowledge. On the one hand, indeed, every predicate not only signifies such or such an intelligible determination, but *that which has* that intelligible determination. Intellectual simple apprehension, in perceiving what I call "triangular" or "conic," "musician" or "philosopher" perceives *something* (possible) which is made its object

---

58   Cf. St. Thomas Aquinas, *In III Sent.*, dist. 23, q. 2, a. 2, sol. 1. "Intellectus noster determinatur ad assentiendum ex praesentia intelligibilis . . . et hoc quidem contingit in his quae statim . . . intelligibilia fiunt, sicut sunt prima principia; et similiter determinatur *judicium sensitivae partis ex hoc quod sensibile subjacit sensibus*." See also the text from the *De Potentia* cited in n. 107.

59   Thus, a feverish person's tongue, covered with a sour coating, perceives sweet beverages to be sour. "Per hoc quod sensus ita nuntiant sicut afficiuntur sequitur quod non decipiamur in judicio quo judicamus nos sentire aliquid. Sed ex eo quod sensus aliter afficitur interdum quam res sit, sequitur quod nuntiat nobis aliquando rem aliter quam sit. Et ex hoc fallimur per sensum circa rem, non circa ipsum sentire" (*Sum. Theol.*, I, 17, 2 ad 1. See J. de Tonquedec's very exact commentary on this text, *op. cit.*, p. 67, n. 2).

under the formal aspect in question. On the other hand, and above all, intellectual knowledge is completed in the judgment. And what is judgment if not an act by which the mind asserts that a predicate and a subject, which differ in notion or in their intramental existence, are identical *in the thing*, or outside the mind? For in every true judgment the two terms that are identified differ in notion, *sunt idem re seu subjecto, diversa ratione.*[60] The notion "whole" is formally quite different from the notion "greater than the part"; the notion "Bernard Shaw" is formally different from the notion "dramatist." And yet when I judge that "Bernard Shaw is a dramatist," or that "the whole is greater than the part," I put in actual existence a thing in which the object of thought "Bernard Shaw" and the object of thought "dramatist" are identified; I place in possible existence a thing in which the object of thought "whole" and the object of thought "greater than the part" are identified. I perform an operation upon my *noemata*, in the very womb of my mind, which has no other meaning than that it refers to the way in which those *noemata* exist (at least possibly) outside the mind. Thus, the proper function of judgment consists in making the mind pass from the level of simple essence or simple object signified to the mind, to the level of thing or subject possessing existence (actually or possibly), a thing of which the object of thought (predicate) and the subject of thought (subject) are intelligible aspects.[61] If it is not admitted that our objects of thought are aspects (or "inspects") of actual or possible things; if it is not admitted that each of them contains, if I may say so, an ontological or

---

60 St. Thomas, *In I Sent.*, dist. 4, q. 2, a. 1; *Sum. Theol.*, I, 13, 12; *Sum. Theol.*, III, 16, 1 and ad l; *Cont. Gent.*, I, 36; John of St. Thomas, *Curs. Phil.*, Log. II P., q. 5, a. 2.

61 In modern times, the notion of judgment has been obscured since Descartes. In brief form, the Cartesian theory amounts to this: judgment consists in an act of the will consenting to the *quod* immediately attained by the mind (to the idea), as to an object conforming with its double (the real *quod*, the ideated). Thus, to see in the judgment (following a trend to which some contemporary scholastics are giving way) a comparison between the mental word and the object thought about, and an affirmation of the mental word's conformity with the object, would be to involve oneself in the Cartesian path of thought in spite of oneself. On the contrary, the thing is declared to be what the *object* (the predicate) attained in the mental word is. The text from the commentary on the *Metaphysics*, which was cited before, Ch. III, n. 45, and which follows: ("Cum intellectus concipit hoc quod est animal rationale mortale, apud se similitudinem hominis habet, sed non propter hoc cognoscit se hanc similitudinem habere, quia non judicat hominem esse animal rationale et mortale; et ideo in hac sola secunda operatione intellectus est veritas et falsitas, secundum quam non solum intellectus habet similitudinem rei intellectae, sed etiam super ipsam similitudinem reflectitur, cognoscendo et dijudicando ipsam" [St. Thomas, *In Metaph.*, lib. VI, lect. 4]), does not mean that in the judgment the mind judges that the concept is conformed to the thing. It means, rather, that the mind in judging knows *in actu exercito* that it itself is true or in conformity with the thing, i.e., that it possesses within itself the likeness of the thing known ("Ex hoc quod cognoscens habet similitudinem rei cognitae, dicitur habere veram cognitionem," *ibid.*).

metalogical charge, then the proper function of judgment becomes unintelligible. Thus, an analysis of intellectual knowledge forces us to consider the same basic testimony in favor of the thing or transobjective subject as did the analysis of sensitive knowledge.

In a sense quite different than that which Locke intends, it might be said with him that every judgment supposes "a perfect harmony" (on the side of the thing) and—effected by the judgment itself—"a reconciliation after a struggle."[62] The "embrace" which precedes "the state of unfettering" which the judgment has as its function "to conquer," is given within the thing; it is given in the transobjective subject.[63] The judgment restores to the transobjective subject the unity that simple apprehension (by laying hold of different objects of thought in it) has shattered. That unity could not hold precedence in the mind since, quite to the contrary, the mind undoes it only to reconstitute it afterwards. It held precedence outside the mind, in existence (actual or possible) which, insofar as it is possessed, is outside the order of mere representation or simple apprehension.[64] And finally, in order that judgment may

---

62   E. Laske, *Die Lehre vom Urtheil* (cited by Gurvitch, *Les tendances actuelles de la philosophie allemande*, p. 173).

63   And it is seen there. The mind really does not bring together, as from the outside, "distant and solitary" (J. de Tonquedec, *op. cit.*, p. 188) concepts which it would then apply to the real. When it directs itself to the thing in an attempt to penetrate it, the mind sees and lays hold in it of a diversity of objects of its concepts into which it divides the thing (that is the preparation for judgment, and rests within the jurisdiction of simple apprehension). In addition, the mind sees and lays hold of the unity of those objects in the thing (a fact it expresses to itself by constructing a proposition to which it assents, and that is the judgment). At this juncture, let us point out a fact which is, in our opinion, a kind of error of perspective in the otherwise very penetrating pages J. de Tonquedec has devoted to the judgment. When he insists on the analytic character of judgment, on its "first function" which would be "to decompose" "simple thought" (*op. cit.*, p. 186), he is really not speaking of the judgment itself but of the preparatory phase that pertains to simple apprehension (itself *in concreto* vitally ordered to judgment). Besides, he is not drawing enough of a distinction between simple apprehension and judicative apprehension (which is resolved either in the sense's experimental intuition or in the intellectual intuition of first principles).

64   Through simple apprehension, existence is grasped and presented to the mind not insofar as a subject has it or can have it (*existentia ut exercita*), but rather insofar as it can be conceived *per modum quidditatis*, as constituting a certam intelligible object, a certain quiddity (*existentia ut significata*). It is only in the mind's second operation (composition and division) and in the judgment, that existence is known *ut exercita*, as possessed (cf. Cajetan, *In Sum. Theol.*, I, 2, 1; 82, 3). Remember, the judgment does not rest content with a representation or apprehension of existence; it affirms it; it projects into it, as effected or able to be effected outside the mind, objects of concepts that have been apprehended by the mind. In other words, when the intellect judges, it sees in an intentional manner and through an act proper to it the very act of existing that the thing exercises or can exercise outside the mind. (It might even be said that in the judgment the transobjective

proceed in that way, it is necessary that every object set before the mind be set there as something able to exist outside the mind (or, if it is a matter of an *ens rationis*, as if it could exist outside the mind). In other words, our intuition or intellectual perception, far from putting us in the presence of a multitude of irreducible "simple natures," must necessarily put us in the presence of an object encountered on all sides and everywhere varied—being itself. In "being itself," all our notions are resolved without in any way impairing the irreducibility of essences. Judgment is possible on this condition; so, too, is a logical movement which makes its advances from one thing to the other in the very order of the purely rational (or, in modern language, the order of the *a priori*). The unity (of simple analogy or proportionality) of transcendental being, not "the unity of transcendental apperception," is the basis of the possibility of judgment.[65] Whether the judgment comes to bear on rational truths or on truths of fact, on the "ideal" or the "real" (actual), it is irreducibly realistic.[66]

And what does the mind want to scrutinize if not the thing, the transobjective subject in all its ontological wealth, in the infinity of its objectifiable resources? A pure object (if, indeed, such a notion were conceivable) would bring nothing with it but itself, and each time it would suffice without anything else—the mind would only have to leaf through the objective world as though it were a picture book. If Scheler's idea of a "perspectivism" of the world of essences is well founded, it is to the extent that this world arises from a world of things or subjects. In this world, whether they are considered each in its own essence or in the relations they have one with the other, new objects of thought are discoverable in endless supply in accordance with the successive directions to which the mind turns its attention.

---

subject is known as subject; I mean that in its role as subject, the transobjective subject is "lived intentionally" by the mind.)

That is the new factor in the intellectual order which is introduced in judgment, and it is an important factor concerning, as it does, the *esse rerum*. In virtue of it, the judgment is called by St. Thomas the completion of knowledge ("judicium est completivum cognitionis," *Sum. Theol.*, II–II, 173, 2). And that itself presupposes a reflection which is implicit rather than explicit, a reflection whereby the mind, when it judges, knows *in actu exercito* its own conformity with the thing. Cf. above, Ch. III, n. 45.

On the very important distinction between *existentia ut significata* and *existentia ut exercita*, see our *The Dream of Descartes*, pp. 130 ff.

65   "Quot modis praedicatio fit, tot modis ens dicitur," St. Thomas, *In Metaph.*, lib. V, lect. 9.

66   On the theory of judgment attention should be called to the work of Monsignor Charles Sentroul, *Kant et Aristote* (Paris, Alcan, 1913, new edition, revised and enlarged, of the 1905 thesis on *The Object of Metaphysics according to Kant and Aristotle*), which rightly insists on the fact that a true judgment is an identification in the mind that corresponds to an identity in the thing, or "the conformity of an identification with an identity." The same ideas are maintained in an article, "La verité et le progrès du savoir," *Revue Néo-scolastique de Philosophie*, May and August 1911.

14. The phenomenist notion of a pure object—a notion from which neither Russell's and Whitehead's realism nor German phenomenology has been successful in freeing itself—definitely appears as properly inconceivable. The unpardonable equivocation from which it suffers arises from the fact that, in order to think of such a notion, one has to place before himself being (from the moment one thinks: an object) and at the same time remove that self-same being (as soon as one thinks: a *pure* object). In fact, however, coming and going from one term of the contradiction to the other gives to the mind the illusion of conceiving that utterly imaginary notion. Victim in this of its own natural propensity for being, the apprehension of being helps the mind to feign that it is thinking of a thing which escapes that apprehension and all thought. Furthermore, by reduplicating its equivocation, being will come to give its name to the very pure object that abstracts from existence—as though being could abstract from existence—and the philosopher will be at great pains to carry on his meditations in the direction of an "ontology" without being. The moment a person understands that the notion of pure object demands that an abstraction be made from being or that *objici* is substituted for *esse*, he is delivered from these illusions.

Because being is the first thing given to the mind, it is impossible to think of a pure object separated from an ontological "stuff" possessing existence for itself or capable of so possessing it; it is impossible to think of a pure object separated from a *being for itself*, a being of which the object of sensation or understanding is but a determination or aspect. If such an object is not an aspect of a known thing, of a transobjective subject,[67] then it will have to become an aspect of the knowing thing: great idealistic doctrines have done everything to escape this alternative, and they have ended in failure. Husserl's phenomenology falls short in the very same way. It could be shown that when that phenomenology claims (through an ill-conducted abstraction that acts like a separation) to dispense with any extramental (metalogical) subject, it gives the lie to what it says by what it does. It can only use its "I-pole" and the various progressively constructed steps in its "objective world" by thinking in spite of itself of that world (and immediately challenging that thought) as a transobjective subject, and of the "I" as a cisobjective subject existing outside the mind's apprehension. And when it claims to reconstitute them both as subjects within the transcendental ego and the "universal consciousness of self,"[68] it only persuades itself that it has succeeded by having recourse to a conjuring trick which consists in using transcendental being, taken in its natural fullness, in such a way as to reduce it to a single one of its modalities (*being that is thought about*). In other words, this trick consists in drawing from extramental being (that has once and for all been put "in brackets") the reality

---

67   Or, in the case of a being of reason, a work of the mind made by means of such aspects of things.

68   Cf. E. Husserl, *Méditations cartésiennes*, Meditations 4 and 5.

and existence that are accorded to an ego and to other things, to which to have "real" and "existent" being is immediately denied, except in and by the intentional life of consciousness which is dependent upon transcendental subjectivity and inseparable from it.[69]

Let us make this point once more: realism and idealism are not transcended. There is no higher position that goes beyond and reconciles them. A choice must be made between the two, as between the true and false. Every realism that comes to terms with Descartes and Kant shall see one day that it belies its name.

Digression on Phenomenology[70] and the Cartesian Meditations

15. Strange as it seems, at the very outset of the phenomenological movement a kind of activation of post-Kantian philosophy took place by means of a contact with Aristotelian and Scholastic seeds, as transmitted by Brentano: the notions of *Wesenschau* and intentionality give clear indication of their origin. But, from the very outset, too, the whole thing went astray because reflexivity (though clearly recognized as such) was used as though it were primary. They set out from reflection to perceive, *a priori*, what is immediate— as though reflection could (by turning back upon direct operations and their object, which is grasped first) fashion for itself out of the latter an object that would be grasped before it and grasped more immediately (one, indeed, that would in the end substitute itself for it); as though reflection could lay bare evidences which, as "primary in themselves," should take precedence over "all other conceivable evidences;"[71] as though a reflective glance, whose proper function could only be purely critical, could be used in a constitutive and constructive role.[72] There lies the πρῶτον ψεῦδος of phenomenology.

---

69   "Every sense and every imaginable being, whether they be called immanent or transcendent, forms a part of the realm of transcendent subjectivity as constituting every meaning and every being" (E. Husserl, *op. cit.*, p. 71).

70   Phenomenology, considered in its Husserlian aspects, will be our present concern. In Germany, the phenomenological movement has been a very complex one and it would be a mistake to think that Edmund Husserl was its sole initiator. Even without mentioning the various tendencies that can be associated with the names Max Scheler and today, Nicolai Hartmann, Martin Heidegger, etc., there is a Munich school of phenomenology which does not follow Husserl in his neo-idealism; but the full importance of its teaching cannot be duly appreciated so long as Prof. Alexander Pfander's teaching has not been published in full (cf. A. Pfänder, *Logik*, Halle, 1929, 2nd ed.). Given the object of our studies, it is sufficient for us to consider phenomenology under the highly significant aspect (and the best known in France) it takes in E. Husserl. But let it be well understood that we are considering it here only under this aspect.

71   E. Husserl, *op. cit.*, p. 14.

72   Such concern for constituting and constructing right within the very heart of a reflexive process is revealed on almost every page of E. Husserl's Méditations cartésiennes (cf. especially pp. 6, 7, 12, 14, 15, 46–48, 53–58. 72–76, 88, 109, 111,

This basic misunderstanding is tied up with the phenomenological epoche[73] insofar as it "puts in brackets" the whole roster of extramental existence and in this way separates the object (the essence-phenomenon) from the thing. Of this epoche as of the Cartesian doubt, it must be said that it would be legitimate *ut significata*, as an eventuality that might be foreseen (and deemed impossible), but that it involves a contradiction *ut exercita*, i.e., as really lived and experienced. In demanding from the outset, by an imposed postulate whose conditions have not been critically examined, to wit, that this "putting out of play" of extramental being be lived, the possibility of stopping the mind at a pure phenomenon-object, that is to say, the possibility of *thinking of being while refusing to think of it as being*, is admitted in practice and by presupposition. They do not see that the Cartesian assertion, according to which, in order to build up a philosophy that is radically pure of "every preconception" not based on reason,[74] the mind has first to rid itself *in actu exercito* of every certitude bearing on extramental being, is itself a prejudice born of a naively materialistic conception of the life of the spirit, namely, that, in order to allow nothing to enter a material recipient that has not first been verified, that recipient must first be emptied of all content. But, because the power of self-knowledge and self-criticism, of a complete return upon self, is the mind's prerogative, the mind has no need of really emptying itself of its own certitudes in order to verify them critically. The mind can represent itself to itself ideally, as if doubting the very thing of which, *in actu exercito*, it is and remains really certain, in order thereby to find out whether such a doubt is possible. And it is only by such a signified, not lived, suspension of judgment that it can make a critical test of first truths. It is only because it is capable of a perfect

---

116–117, 122, 131: "A phenomenology that is developed in strict fashion constructs *a priori*, but with strict intuitive necessity and generality, the forms of imaginable worlds; it constructs them within the frameworks of all imaginable forms of being in general and of the system of its articulations. But it does so in an 'original' way, i.e., in correlation with the *a priori* of the structure of intentional functions that constitute them").

That is why Husserl looks upon phenomenology as philosophy itself, as replacing the old metaphysics and "naive ontology" (pp. 54, 61, 73, 74, 117, 132, 134). We, on the contrary, feel that what is to be retained of phenomenology (after decanting it), and of the "discoveries" in which it glories, belongs only to the reflexive and critical part of philosophy. The "transcendental experience" it disengages is, in what is authentic about it, only the mind's critical reflection upon itself, and it appears to be "novel" only to the extent that an impossible task of construction is imposed on such reflection. The first phase of phenomenology (the description of the *cogitata* as such) presents, from this point of view, much more of interest than does the second phase (the utterly artificial reconstituting of the "*a priori* structure" of universal reality).

73   "Suspension of judgment": this is the phrase used by Pyrrho and the ancient Sceptics, and here it is taken up once more in a methodical sense.

74   Cf. E. Husserl, *op. cit.*, p. 30.

return upon itself that it can undertake a description (reflexive) of its *cogitata as cogitata* without having any need of practicing Husserl's epoche to do so.

Also, they do not see that the intellect's first apodictic and absolutely irrefragable certitude has to do with possible extramental (metalogical) being of which it knows in an entirely and eternally certain and necessary way that insofar as it is, it is not nothing.[75] But because, misunderstanding the proper life of the intellect as such and confusing it with the life of sense, they take it for granted that this first certitude must bear on the actually given, they seek it in the pure *cogito*.[76] And they say: *ego cogito cogitatum* to assign the starting point for philosophy as a whole, while, if we would be faithful to our first intuitive evidence, we should say: *ego cogito ens*, to point out the starting point not of philosophy as a whole, but of that reflexive part of first philosophy which is critique.

16. The effect of this original deviation is that the very notion of intentionality, in passing from the hands of the great scholastic realists[77] to the hands of contemporary neo-Cartesians (as E. Husserl describes himself in his last work), has lost its effectiveness and value. And how could it be otherwise since its whole meaning first came to it from its opposition to the *esse entitativum* of the extramental thing? Intentionality is not only that property of my consciousness of being directed transparency, of aiming at objects in the depths of itself.

75   *Starting from that certainty*, it reflexively confirms for itself ("justifies" to itself) the veracity of sense and its own certitude of the existence of the sensible world. Thus, it is nonsense to posit (as is constantly done) the problem of the import of intellectual knowledge by bringing into question, as real being other than the *ego*, not, first of all, possible extramental being, but only existence or non-existence (in act) of the sensible world.

76   "My ego, given to me in an apodictic way—the only being I can posit as existing in an absolutely apodictic way...." (E. Husserl, *op. cit.*, p. 118). My own existence (grasped reflexively) is, indeed, the best founded and most irreducible of existences in act given to me. That is why in a very practical way it matters more to me than any other existence. But every actual existence which is not the existence of pure Act is contingent. And an *absolute necessity* (but in the order of possible existence or of essences) has to envelop the deepest and most irreducible of the data of *apodictic* knowledge or science. That is why the prime datum of speculative knowledge is the principle of identity and not the existence of the self. The ancients quite rightly thought that certainty regarding my own existence, absolute though it may be, is still not a certitude of science because it has to do with a contingent object and so, on the side of the object, they thought it did not have the necessity required to constitute a knowledge that would be unshakable on all counts.

77   *Cuique suum*. It is peculiar to see E. Husserl and many critics who write about the phenomenological movement paying honor to Brentano for the discovery of intentionality. That discovery was made, actually, more than seven centuries ago (nor was St. Thomas the one who invented it). The dependence certain characteristic aspects of phenomenology seem to have on Duns Scotus might also be noted, particularly his theory of ideas and *esse objectivum*.

Above all, intentionality is a property of thought, a prerogative of its immateriality, whereby being in itself, posited "outside it," i.e., being which is fully independent of the act of thought, becomes a thing existing within it, set up for it and integrated into its own act through which, from that moment, they both exist in thought with a single, self-same suprasubjective existence.

If a person does not go that far, if he refuses to the mind the power (which is only real if being itself is real) of "surmounting" being and rendering it inferior to itself, the pure transparency of intentionality is inevitably materialized by looking upon intentionality as a "constituent" of the object through its "structural rules,"[78] by requiring it to constitute *the other* and to confer its proper meaning upon it "beginning with my own being,"[79] whereas, on the contrary, intentionality brings the other into me "beginning with" its own otherness and makes me be the other. And even though, as it so often seems to happen to E. Husserl, he seems to be brushing the skirts of the true nature of knowledge, so to speak, in the final reckoning he always misses the great secret. He does not see that knowledge has no need to get outside itself to attain the thing that exists or can exist outside knowledge—the extramental thing which, because of this preconceived notion, must be got rid of. It is within thought itself that extramental being is grasped. The real or metalogical thing is touched and handled right within the concept; it is seized there; the mind

---

78   Cf. E. Husserl, *op. cit.*, pp. 46, 72, 131, etc. Husserl, an avowed foe of subjectivism (in the ordinary sense of the word), is known to oppose his own doctrine of transcendental subjectivity to the doctrine into which Kant fell by being inconsistent. This doctrine of Kant's encloses the mind within a subjectivity that might be termed entitative, and according to it the subject's activity, considered *secundum esse naturae*, would produce or engender the object of knowledge. For Husserl (cf. Gurvitch, *op. cit.*, p. 22) the object is not produced or engendered; the intentional synthesis constitutes the object by an act of attention or fixation, not by an act forming it. But in order that such a constituting synthesis take place in one way or another, the essential thing is that it be constituting with regard to the object (that is why Husserl, in his own way, admits Kant's "Copernican revolution"). To make that the proper function of intentionality is precisely to misconceive the most typical features of intentionality.

79   E. Husserl, *op. cit.*, p. 89. Cf. pp. 107, 111, 128: "After giving these explanations there is no mystery about my being able to constitute another self within myself or, to put it in an even more radical way, about my being able to constitute another monad within my monad and, after it is fashioned, to apprehend it precisely in its being other. But we can also understand a further fact, one inseparable from the first, namely, that I can identify the Nature constituted by me with the Nature constituted by the other (or, to speak with the precision the point demands, with a Nature fashioned within me as constituted by the other). . . . It goes without saying that it [transcendental intersubjectivity] is constituted an existent for me as arising from the well-springs of my intentionality. . . . Any apparent solipsism is removed, even though it still is true that everything that exists for me can only draw its existential meaning from within me, within the sphere of my consciousness."

feeds upon it in its own home, because the very glory of the immateriality of thought is not to be a thing in space exterior to another extended thing, but rather a life which is superior to the whole order of space. For the very glory of the immateriality of thought is to be a higher life which perfects itself by that which is not it, itself, even without going outside itself, by an intelligible reality whose fertile substance the mind grasps through the senses, that fertile substance drawn by the senses from actual, existing (material) things. The way to make the proper mystery of knowledge vanish is precisely to get rid of extramental being, to suppress those ontological (metalogical) "for them-selves," fully independent of my thought, and which my thought makes its own by making itself them.[80]

17. In spite of the important services phenomenology has rendered contem-porary thought (above all, perhaps, as Bergsonism as well has done, through its extra-philosophical influences—notably through the stimulation several scientific disciplines have received from it), and in spite of its primitive realistic impulse and its liberating virtue in respect to monism and mechanism, phe-nomenology ran the risk of equivocation from the very outset. Nothing is more instructive than the way phenomenology, after being finally vanquished by the false "radicalism" of Cartesian principles, ends up today by returning in a most decided fashion, proud of its rediscovered bonds, to the Kantian tradition and by declaring itself to be a new transcendental idealism different, it is true, from Kantian idealism, but chiefly in that it refuses to "leave open the possi-bility of a world of things-in-themselves, be they nothing more than concept-limits."[81] Whereas "naive metaphysics" worked "with absurd things-in-themselves,"[82] "for phenomenology," on the other hand, ". . . 'being' is a practical idea—the idea of an infinite task of theoretical determination,"[83] and the world, too, "is an infinite idea, referring to infinities of harmonious experiences."[84]

[Taking into account all the reservations required by the difference between the two cases, it could still be said that Husserl's position with reference to Kant is comparable to Berkeley's position with respect to Descartes. In his battle against the "thing," Berkeley also thought to vindicate intuition; by

---

80   These remarks apply not only to the idealism of Edouard Le Roy, Léon Brun-schvicg and so many others, or to Edmund Husserl's phenomenology, but also to Schuppe's solipsism and Rickert's general immanentism (concerning these last two doctrines see the work of André Krzesinski, *Une nouvelle philosophie de l'immanence*, Paris, Alcan, 1931).

81   E. Husserl, *op. cit.*, p. 72.

82   *Ibid.*, p. 133. We willingly grant the absurdity of the Kantian "thing-in-itself," unknowable and *separate* from the phenomenon (instead of being revealed through it). But Husserl is speaking here of everything capable of extramental or metalogical existence.

83   *Ibid.*, p. 74.

84   *Ibid.*, p. 53.

suppressing extramental "matter" he, too, believed he re-discovered the "meaning that the world (the objective world of realities) has for us all before any philosophy."[85] And, with a view to freeing transcendental idealism from "absurd things-in-themselves," Husserl reconstituted, by means of more and more artificial procedures, the whole universe of realism within the heart of the transcendental *ego* and "beginning with the well-springs of its own being."[86] And even though this "formidable" task be called the discovery of the aprioristic constitution of the real world and of all possible being through a complete explicitation of the transcendental *ego*, it is still, frankly, a reconstitution and, like every reconstitution, it presupposes some original: the world of naive realism from which phenomenological idealism is suspended like a parasite trying to suck its host into itself. It lives on that realism not only as regards the various layers or the different levels of objectivity it reconstitutes after having put them in brackets at the very outset, but also as regards its conceptual tools, the *Denkmitteln* it uses, tools that are borrowed by way of analogy from the conceptual roster of knowledge about things.

Nevertheless, an unexplained residue remains outside this universal science: the "naive" belief in extramental reality. Even if this belief is illusory, the reason for such a universal and irrepressible illusion still has to be given. But that would be to betray the method of phenomenology. But, if such a belief does not have to be explained because it, too, is finally reconstituted within the phenomenological epoche, then it is not an illusion and the thing in itself is not absurd. But then we put an end to phenomenology. The truth is that the belief in extramental reality is not reconstituted, but replaced by a substitute. We are, forsooth, dispensed from explaining it because a counterfeit of it, an idealist counterfeit, has been provided.

Thus, contradiction is at the very heart of the work. Extramental being, which we began by putting in brackets, by refusing to affirm or deny anything about it, is found (from the mere fact that, in order to build up a philosophy, the separation of object and thing is accepted *in actu exercito*) to be practically denied and, in the final analysis, abandoned (without ever having been criticized, and without our ever asking whether or not such a separation of object and thing were possible—a basic omission that should make us look upon transcendental neo-Cartesianism as a radically naive system). Although Husserl was much more logical than Descartes, understanding as he did (but only thereby to become more Cartesian than Descartes and sacrifice the notion of extramental being) that the Cartesian problem of passing from consciousness of thought to certitudes about the being of things (thanks to the divine veracity) is "nonsense,"[87] still, he undertook to build his whole philosophy without emerging from the phenomenological epoche. However, it just so

85   *Ibid.*, p. 129.
86   *Ibid.*, p. 116.
87   E. Husserl, *op. cit.*, p. 70

happens that in spite of himself he does emerge from it inasmuch as within the epoche he so completely reconstructs everything he has left outside and put in brackets that, in the end, everything that was in brackets will be found transferred within the transcendental ontology—everything, that is, except extramental subsistence and existence, and they have been cleared out of the bracket, through the other side of it, and cast into nothingness. But then there is no longer any bracket and there is no longer any epoche. By maintaining the epoche to the very end, the epoche is suppressed—and that is a glorious success for transcendental illusionism, but an undeniable lived contradiction as well.

The ambiguity in this final phase of phenomenology is such that it requires but a slip of the mind, a small mistake, to think of transcendental idealism, thus refurbished, in terms of realism. What has, in fact, been reconstituted within that "intentional consciousness" turned towards the *cogito* is the whole universe of Nature and Culture. And it is perfectly true that, insofar as it is known, it exists in the mind. But should one think involuntarily that this same universe is also (and primarily)—at least possibly—outside the mind in such fashion as to exist, then we have surreptitiously passed into the range of realism. We are not too sure but that it is not in virtue of such unnoticed slippings—nature's revenge—that idealistic philosophers can believe that they are thinking their own systems.]

Finally, it does seem that from the very outset phenomenology went along on a kind of unnatural cross-breeding between ontology and logic. It is a serious matter for a philosopher not to be able to distinguish between *ens reale* and *ens rationis*. He runs the risk, in spite of all his protests against constructionism, of setting about the task of "elucidating" a universe of fictions, and of leaving aside the proper task of a straightforward philosophy which is to assign the reasons for what is given to it and to gain an understanding of that datum. Other drawbacks, too, were bound to arise. In doing away with the transobjective subject, the proper effects of materiality are introduced into the very world of intelligible essences and of the *a priori*. It is vain to try not to treat this world in empiricist fashion,[88] as those do who misunderstand intelligible necessities and think with their eyes and treat of the world of sensible, concrete things with their hands. For if, in its own proper life, intellect is pure (I do not mean purified of what experience brings to it and whence it draws all its riches;

---

88   If phenomenology is presented as essentially an analysis or "eidetic" description, it is, so it seems, with a view to remedying this difficulty. But the remedy is still not adequate. By making the object of various intentional functions freely vary, by way of imagination, so as to keep only the *eidos* of those functions, a *de jure* necessity grasped in an essence is not thereby set free before the mind; only *de facto* necessity of intentional life is thereby stated, and it is but a substitute for true, intelligible necessity. Victor Delbos' remark, that phenomenology runs the risk of submitting the mind to sublogical indetermination, finds one of its verifying instances in this very fact.

I mean, rather, purified of all material co-action and of all empirical enslave-
ment), it is because whatever is contingent, potential and material, the whole
mass of inertia that can be defined through its resistance to intelligibility, forms
part of the world to which intellect is applied and which it knows. But that
world is located outside intelligence as is this world itself. On the other hand,
by the fact that the essences perceived by the mind are no longer grasped in
transobjective subjects existing outside the mind and themselves involved in
the flow of time, the extra-temporal objects of the intellect are, through an
unexpected return to Platonism, separated from real, temporal existence. And,
to regain that existence once more, there is nothing left to do but to invert the
intellect by giving time precedence over being, either by seeking to substitute
time for being with Mr. Bergson or by striving to rest being on time with Mr.
Heidegger. And that is to guarantee realism by destroying its primary foundation.

Concerning Idealism

18. From all the preceding considerations, it is quite clear that the problem of
thing and object[89] is the nub of the critical problem. Philosophers imbued with
Cartesian principles call every authentic realism a "naive realism." And although it is pointed out to them that when such a designation is applied to
Aristotelian-Thomistic realism it is itself childish, they will not be undeceived
because, as far as they are concerned, naiveté is to start with an act of
knowledge about things rather than with an act of knowledge about knowledge. Good! The mind does, indeed, have to choose its path right from the
start; an original decision is demanded of it, and it is a decision that will dictate
its entire fate. But the first act of reflection shows that the person who has made
his choice in keeping with nature, and without challenging the first light shed
upon his heart (I mean the first objective evidence), has chosen wisely. And it

---

89   Useful comments on this problem will be found in the work of J. de Tonquedec
       that has already been cited (on the notion of phenomenon, pp. 23–33), and in L.
       Noel's work (pp. 32–36, 125–154, 236–237). Cf. René Kremer, "Sur la notion de
       réalisme épistémologique," in *Philosophia Perennis*, t. II, p. 739.
           In the passages from *Réflexions sur l'intelligence* to which L. Noel so kindly refers
       (pp. 153–154), our discussion did not rule out reflexive observations and descrip-
       tions. It rather took them for granted. Observations which, moreover, are not
       mere empirical registrations but, rather, analyses of a special type capable of
       discerning the intelligible constituents and even the nature, as St. Thomas says,
       of the intellective act and of intellect. If, on the contrary, it is proper to make a
       distinction between what has to do with the object as object, and what has to do
       with the object as thing, then we do think there is no room for stopping between
       the first and second consideration in order to resolve certain epistemological
       questions (cf. *op. cit.*, p. 228), as though the notion of a pure object, one that would
       not be a thing and for which a thing would not be the basis, were thinkable even
       by abstraction.

indicates that the person who has made his choice against nature in demand-ing a second light before following the first one, has chosen absurdly: for he would fain start with what comes second.

One cannot think about a "thought thing" until after one has thought about a "thinkable thing"—a thing "good for existing," i.e., at least, a possible real. The first thing thought about is being independent of the mind. The *cogitatum* of the first *cogito* is not *cogitatum*, but *ens*. We do not eat what has been eaten; we eat bread. To separate object from thing, the objective *logos* from metalogi-cal being, is to violate the nature of intellect, to flee from the first evidence of direct intuition, and at the same time, to mutilate reflexive intuition (the very reflexive intuition on which we would make everything depend) in the very first of its immediate data. Idealism sets an original sin against the light at the beginning of the whole philosophical edifice.

19. Since Leibniz, the whole effort of idealism tends to suppress all material or subjective causality so as to leave only formal causalities. At the same time it tends to suppress every "thing," every cisobjective or transobjective subject so as to leave only pure objects. As long as the value of the thing or of the subject is not fully restored, it is useless to try to be a realist. Philosophy becomes more and more purely reflexive; it can no longer be called a philoso-phy of nature or metaphysics except in an equivocal manner. For where does the philosophy of nature have its proper object if not in a world of things subject to time and movement, things that are the same as those with which the experimental sciences work from another point of view? And where will metaphysics lead if not to a world of truths beyond time, truths realized in temporal existence, and to a supreme supratemporal reality which is all things supereminently? On the other hand, an exclusively reflexive philosophy judges not about what is, but about the idea of what is and the idea of the idea, and of the idea of the idea of the idea of what is. And it does so in a tone that is all the more superior, the more it fails to lay hands on the real and avoids the risk of scraping the skin off them; whereas the courage that properly belongs to the philosophy of nature, as well as to metaphysics, is to face up to extramental realities, to lay hands on things, to judge about what is. The humility that properly belongs to them is to submit it to be measured by things. Idealism wants nothing of that, at any price. Idealism is scandalized by the idea that an intellect be measured by a thing, by an ontological "for itself" that exists apart from it (with an existence less noble than knowing), a thing to which the intellect has to unite itself by an effort to submit to it, without ever being able to exhaust it. The scandal is in the fact that there exists an intellect which is not only created, but the lowest in the order of spirits. An angelic intellect is not the intellect; how much less, then, a human intellect! But, to tell the truth, the prerogatives of intellect do not suffer any loss in this, because, far from setting over against intellect I know not what purely material obstacle,

absolutely without relation to the intellect's nature, the being of things is a secret and as it were, dormant aptitude to be grasped by the mind. And when the intellect submits to be measured by things, our intellect, in the final analysis submits to be measured by intellect itself, intellect in pure act, by which things themselves are measured, and from which they derive their being and intelligibility. (On the other hand, even in our own case it is still the intellect—the intellect that illumines, a created participation in God's intellectual light—that makes things intelligible in act and which, by means of things and the senses, determines the intellect that knows;[90] and finally it is the intellect that completes the actualizing of its object within itself—under the self-same rays that are derived from the first Truth, and makes it so truly its own [that is the task of the mental word and its spiritual function] that, here below, it sees only what it itself expresses, transparent with its own transparency.[91]) The mystery of creation alone can allay the scruples of idealism. It is the asceticism proper to a created intellect that idealism rejects.

A hidden but powerful teleological motivation also intervenes at this point, to which idealism unconsciously obeys, so cheating at its own game. Idealism's concern is precisely that it be not led to a certain terminus; it aims to avoid a certain final conclusion. Now if, from the very start, things and the extramental stability whereby they regulate our thought are so carefully rejected, it is because of the fact, above all else, that owing to a secret instinct that is the more imperious in that it remains unconfessed, the mind does not want in the end to be forced to come face to face with a transcendent, supreme reality, an abyss of personality before which every heart lies open and which our thought has to adore. The bastions and fortresses of idealistic philosophy thus appear to be just so many vast defence-works against divine personality.

Nothing is more significant than those far-flung works. It is enough that things exist for God to be unavoidable. Let us but grant to a bit of moss or the smallest ant its due nature as an ontological reality, and we can no longer escape the terrifying hand that made us.

---

90   "Quae a nobis a materialibus conditionibus sunt abstracta, fiunt intelligibilia actu per lumen nostri intellectus agentis—(St. Thomas, *Comm. in de Sensu et Sensato*, lect. 1). Cf. below, Ch. III, n. 120.

91   Cf. below, Ch. III, § 27. We are speaking there, it goes without saying, of a perfectly inner, spiritual expression. The deeper the intellectual intuition, the more vital and intimate the spiritual expression in which it is completed—and the more inexhaustible it appears as regards oral and material expression. Cf. our *Philosophie bergsonienne*, preface to the second edition pp. xliii–xlv. On the other hand, we say by design: "It only sees what it itself expresses" for when the intellect knows without seeing an intelligible, when, for example, it divines or obscurely experiences, or joys in some beautiful thing, the fact is that it knows. I would not say it then knows without concepts, but, rather, it knows by using as its formal means something other than concepts—for example, affective connaturality or, as in aesthetic perception, the very intuition of the sense.

20. In this connection the definitions of the humblest grammarians take on a singularly deep meaning. "The first person is the one who speaks." It is thus that what we call the cisobjective subject is designated. That subject says "I"—not, indeed, in the sense of Husserl's pure I, which is stripped of all entitative subjectivity—but because a mysterious ontological or metalogical depth, a universe unto itself, a center of liberty, knows itself in that I.

Round about us is a vast multitude of transobjective subjects, and they are designated by the second person, the "one to whom we speak" and who speaks to us, each a center of mystery. The second person is also rich in a certain ontological or metalogical depth and is one who, in the relation of *I* to *Thou*, wants to be treated respectfully and lovingly. Thou spring, thou fish, thou sparrow; but let charity intervene supernaturally to complete our weak philosophical perception of the relations between things, and St. Francis will speak to his sister water, his brothers bird and fish. No attitude has a deeper metaphysical truth, and it is essentially realistic. For Mr. Brunschvicg there would obviously be no sense in calling upon a bird.

And what do all these things, that "I" address familiarly as "thee" and "thou," say to me? "The third person is the one of whom we speak." *He* is on every lip; all things speak of Him. And as long as I have not known Him for myself, I only hear the voice of creatures talking among themselves about him. But when I know Him for myself—without any intermediary other than the light and propositions of faith,—then it is *Thou*, yet more hidden, more mysterious and freer than anything that can be created and every person that can be created, it is *Thou* that I hear.

21. Things are opaque to us, and we are opaque to ourselves. Pure spirits see themselves and see all things transparently. And that is so because for pure spirits the object is the subject grasped in its entirety and from the inside, not by morcellated views as for us. But for pure spirits as well as for us the distinction between object and subject remains; their gaze does not exhaust the obediential potency that exists in them, nor all the predicates that will come to things with the advance of time. In God alone are subject and object identified in an absolute way, even as existence and understanding are identified. He knows Himself exhaustively and all things in Himself, because His act of knowledge is His very infinite essence.

Thus, the world of authentic realism is a world of things existing for itself, a world, a huge family, a *symposium* of individuals, persons and their interaction, just as the knowing thing is itself an individual or a person. And that knowing thing exists there in the midst of others so as to attract them in a certain fashion to its own bosom and nourish itself on what they precisely are.

"A thing can be perfect," says St. Thomas apropos of this point, "in two ways. In the first way, according to the perfection of its own being, which belongs to it in consequence of its proper species. But because the specific being of one thing is distinct from the specific being of another, the result is that amongst all created beings the perfection the one has falls as far short of absolute perfection as there is perfection likewise possessed by all other species: so that the perfection of every thing, taken in itself, is imperfect as apart of the total perfection of the universe which arises from the joining together of all those particular perfections gathered together.

"Thus, that there may be a remedy for such imperfection, another mode of perfection is encountered in created things, and according to that mode the perfection that is the property of one thing, is itself also encountered in another thing. Of that kind is the perfection of the knower as such, because insofar as the knower knows, the thing known exists within him in a certain way. . . . And as a consequence of that mode of perfection it is possible for the perfection of the whole universe to exist in a solitary particular thing."[92]

III
CONCERNING KNOWLEDGE ITSELF

22. This text of St. Thomas introduces us into the very mystery of knowledge. It is time we asked in what this mystery consists. What is the inner nature of that which we call knowing? It must be confessed that modern philosophers do not even begin to treat that question because they cannot make up their minds to ask it. Neither Descartes, nor Kant, nor the Neo-realists, nor even the phenomenologists (except, it seems, Nicolai Hartmann,[93] who has at least

---

92   *De Verit.*, II, 2.

93   Cf. Nicolai Hartmann, *Metaphysik der Erkenntnis* (2nd ed., Berlin, 1925). In a recent statement to the Kant-Gesellschaft (*Zum Problem der Realitaetsgegebenheit*, 1931, Heft 32), Nicolai Hartmann has insisted in the most remarkable way on the inadequacy of the point of view of ordinary phenomenology and upon the fact that knowledge implies a relation to a being independent of the mind, to a "transobjective" reality. With current conceptions of phenomenology "man vergisst die Hauptsache, die Beziehung auf des Seiende, dem die Erkenntnis gilt; ja man hat schon in der Problemstellung das Erkenntnisphaenomen verfehlt. So ergibtsich die paradoxe Sachlage, dass gerade diejenigen Theorien, die am meisten von Erkenntnissprechen, das eigentliche Erkenntnisproblem gar nicht kennen" (p. 9).

The return to a realistic attitude, evinced by many at this gathering of the Kant-Gesellschaft in May 1931, is a very significant fact. Unfortunately, the misunderstanding of the proper nature and the proper value of the object of understanding as such, as well as the misconception of the content of sense-intuition on the other hand, results in the fact that N. Hartmann proceeds to seek the given of reality in "transcendent emotional" facts (i.e., in facts wherein emotion itself implies and gives notice of the extramental reality of that which affects us). In so doing, Nicolai Hartmann forgets that the transobjective intelligible reality has to be sought in the possible real and also that the sense, on the other hand, grasps the extramental real as something existing and acting here

profoundly felt the antinomies with which it is pregnant) have faced it squarely. It is the peculiar merit of St. Thomas and his great commentators to have frankly formulated this problem, for it is he most important of all the problems of noetic, and one that can only be treated as it should by bringing into play the most delicately refined metaphysical equipment. And it is to their credit not only to have formulated the question, but to have given it its profoundest solution as well. Before tackling it, they warn us that we must raise our minds, because we are entering quite a different order of things, *et disces elevare ingenium, aliumque rerum ordinem ingredi.* Errors, that are so frequent in this realm, arise from the fact that too often we confuse a spiritual event, like knowledge, with the material events by which our ordinary experience is nurtured.

Permit us, *brevitatis studio*, to set forth at this juncture a very concise résumé in seven points of the Thomistic doctrine on the nature of knowledge. The advantage of condensations of this kind is to force one to a synthesis in which only what is essential is stated. [I]. There is a vigorous correspondence between knowledge and immateriality. A being is a knowing being to the extent that it is immaterial. [II]. Why is this so? Because, by an apparent scandal to the principle of identity, to know is to be in a certain way something other than what one is: it is to *become a thing other than the self*, "fieri aliud a se," to be or become the other as other, "esse seu fieri aliud in quantum aliud."[94] Now this presupposes, on the one hand, that the subject capable of knowing emerges above matter (which restricts or encloses things exclusively within their own being); and, on the other hand, that there is a kind of union, transcending every union of a material sort, between the knower and the known. For when matter receives a form, it is to constitute a third term with it, a *tertium quid*, i.e., informed matter. Thus, a material being can become other, i.e., it can itself change or be modified, but it cannot become the other. Whereas the knower,

---

and now. His work contains a brilliant analysis of all the facts of this (transcendental emotional) sort; and it is perfectly clear that concretely our life of knowledge and our emotional life do involve each other. But it is also clear that the facts in question and the feeling for the "hardness of the real" imply the primary value of certain facts of knowledge which are wrapped up in them; and by refusing to consider the proper order of knowledge apart—thanks to philosophical abstraction—and to treat the problem of thing and object within that order, N. Hartmann's realism only registers the testimony of consciousness. It is still unable to base a realism on reason and, by a truly critical analysis, defend and confirm the value of knowledge at its various levels—as is required of metaphysical wisdom.

94   Cf. *Réflexions sur l'intelligence*, p. 53. John of St. Thomas, translating Aristotle's, St. Thomas's and Cajetan's thought quite faithfully, does not say, as H. D. Simonin does in an article that is otherwise quite penetrating but not on this point (*Rev. des Sc. Phil. et Théol.*, May 1931): *to become the object's likeness*; John of St. Thomas says, *to become the other, to become* (immaterially and intentionally) *the object itself.*

even while maintaining his own nature intact, becomes the known itself and identifies himself with it, the knower being thus incomparably more one with the known than the matter with the form.[95] [III]. *To know* is to the sense and the intellect—taken as cognitive functions—as *to exist* is to the essence—to the quidditative function. It is a kind of existence that defines knowledge. To know does not consist in making anything nor in receiving anything, but in existing in a way better than by the simple fact of being set outside nothingness. Knowing is an active, immaterial superexistence whereby a subject not only exists with an existence limited to what that subject is as a thing enclosed within one genus—as a subject existing for itself—but with an unlimited existence in which by its own activity it is and becomes itself and other things.

That is why existence and knowledge in God, because He is infinite, are purely and absolutely the same thing. There is no distinction, not even a virtual[96] distinction, between *esse divinum* and *intelligere divinum*. His existence is His own very act of understanding.

Once we have arrived at this stage, we understand that the formula "to become the other as other" does, indeed, really define knowledge, but knowledge considered in what especially characterizes human knowledge, which is first turned to the other. An angel knows itself before knowing things; God knows Himself—He is the only object worthy of specifying His intellect, and He knows things—both possible or created—within His own essence. To give a definition of knowledge that is suited to its complete analogical amplitude, we would have to say that to know is to be or to become a thing—either oneself or other things—otherwise than by existence actuating a subject.[97] An angel, in knowing, is itself and other things otherwise than by its proper existence as a limited subject; by His knowledge, God is Himself and things otherwise than by an existence that would actuate a subject.

[IV]. The act of knowing is none of the actions we customarily observe round about us; it is not part of the category "action"—nor of the category "passion"—in Aristotle's table. Taken purely in itself, it does not consist in the production of anything, even within the knowing subject. To know is to advance oneself to an act of existing of supereminent perfection, and that, in itself, does not involve production.

In fact, there is a production of an image in sensitive knowledge[98] and of a mental word, or concept, in intellectual knowledge; but that inner production

---

95 Averroes, in III, *De Anima*, comm. V, *digressionis parte ultima*, q. 2.
96 Cf. R. Garrigou-Lagrange, *God: His Existence and Nature* (St. Louis, Herder, 1934), Vol. II, p. 63.
97 "Esse non per modum subjecti," Mr. Pierre Garin says in his thesis on *"L'Idée d'après les principaux thomistes"* (Paris, Desclée de Brouwer et Cie, 1932).
98 Not in the external sense, but in the internal sense (imagination, memory, etc.). The external sense "non format sibi aliquam formam sensibilem" (St. Thomas, *Quodlib.*, V, 9 ad 2).

is not formally the act itself of knowing. It is at once a condition and a means, and an expression of that act.[99]

That is why the ancients said the act of knowing is a properly immanent action, a perfectly vital action, belonging to the category "quality."

[V]. Wherever it is a matter of a knowing being other than God—for, by Himself, He is in supereminent fashion all things—we are forced, if we would conceive of knowledge without absurdity, to introduce the notion of a very special kind of existence, which the ancients called *esse intentionale*, intentional being, and which is opposed to *esse naturae*, i.e., to the being a thing possesses when it exists in its own nature. For after all, the scandals suffered by the principle of identity can only be apparent, and it is certain that, if it is proper to the knower to be another thing than what it is, we must needs, to avoid absurdity, distinguish two ways of having existence; we have to conceive of an *esse* that is not the proper act of existing of the subject as such or of its accidents.

In what manner is the knower the known? It cannot be what it is not in virtue of its own natural being.

How does the thing known exist in the knower? The tree or the stone does not exist in the mind, according to its natural being.

Another kind of existence must, then, be admitted; an existence according to which the known, will be in the knower and the knower will be the known an entirely tendential and immaterial existence, whose office is not to posit a thing outside nothingness for itself and as a subject, but, on the contrary, for another thing and as a relation. It is an existence that does not seal up the thing within the bounds of its nature, but sets it free from them. In virtue of that existence, the thing exists in the soul with an existence other than its own existence, and the soul is or becomes the thing with an existence other than its own existence. As Cajetan tells us, *intentional being* is there as a remedy for the imperfection essential to every created, knowing subject, to wit, the imperfection of possessing a limited natural being and of not being, of itself, everything else.[100]

In another order than that of knowledge, in the order of efficient activity, is it not equally necessary to admit an intentional manner of existing—the way, for instance, in which artistic power passes into the painter's hand and brush? For the whole picture is the work of the brush; there is nothing in the picture that is not really caused by the brush. And yet the beauty and intelligible brilliance, the spiritual values with which the picture is charged, far surpass everything of which the brush's proper causality, bound up as it is with the material universe, is capable. A causality higher than its own, a causality

---

99   Cf. *Réflexions sur l'intelligence*, pp. 58 and 106. On the production of the mental word by the act of intellection, immanent as such and virtually productive, see Cajetan, *In Sum. Theol.*, I, 27, 1; 34, 1, ad 2; John of St. Thomas, *Curs. Phil.*, *Phil. Nat.*, III P., q. 11, a. 1; *Curs. Theol.*, I P., q. 27, disp. 12, a. 5 (Vivès, T. IV).

100   *Réflexions sur l'intelligence*, p. 62.

superordered to it, must, then, pass through the brush. Examine everything "entitative" or existent in the brush, *secundum esse naturae*, and you will not find the painter's art; you will only find the substance and qualities of the brush whereby it is moved by the hand. Yet the art passes through it. Examine everything entitative about the medium that transmits sensible quality and you will only find the properties and movements—the wave movements and others—that the physicist sees in them. You will no more find quality there than you will find the soul under the scalpel. Yet quality passes through it, *secundum esse intentionale*, since the sense will perceive it when the wave or vibration reaches the organ. It is like a dream of a materialistic imagination to want, with Democritus, to have quality pass through the medium entitatively, or, since it is not there entitatively, to deny, with the votaries of modern "scientism," that it could pass through it at all. Even when *esse intentionale* has nothing to do with the world of knowledge, it is already a way for forms to escape from this entombment in matter. The scholastics often gave the name *esse spirituale* to this existence (which is not for itself), this tendency-existence whereby forms, other than their own, come upon things. We think it would be of great interest to philosophers to study the role that *esse intentionale* plays in the physical world itself, wherein there undoubtedly arises from such existing, that sort of universal animation whereby motion puts into bodies more than they are, and colors the whole of nature with a semblance of life and feeling undoubtedly derived from it.[101] However this may be, what is important for us at this moment is its role in knowing and in the material operations of knowing, the intentional presence of the object in the soul and the intentional transformation of the soul into the object, both a function of the immateriality—imperfect for sense, absolute for intellect—of the cognitive faculties.

[VI]. What is the means by which the union of the known and the knower is effected? What is the medium thanks to which the thing known exists intentionally in the knower and thanks to which the knower becomes intentionally the thing known? It is the whole world of intra-psychic immaterial forms that exist in the soul as vicars of the object. These the ancients called likenesses or *species*. The word "species" has no equivalent in our modern languages, and we feel that the most suitable expression to render it would be presentative or objectifying form.[102] For the philosophers, the notion of species

---

101   The motion of projectiles tbat caused so much difficulty for the ancients, could perhaps be explained by the fact that at the first instant of motion, and by reason of that motion, the qualitative state which, existing in the agent, is the immediate cause of the motion, passes into the mobile thing *secundum esse intentionale* (speaking in an ontological key; we are deliberately using terms that do not belong to the vocabulary of mechanics). With this point of view it would become possible to hold Galileo's principle of inertia to be valid not only from the point of view of physico-mathematical science (at least, according to Einstein's mechanics, for an ideally supposed space absolutely without curvature), but also from the point of view of the philosophy of nature.

is not, any more than the notion of *esse intentionale*, an explanatory factor already known and already clarified by some other means. Species are, as it were, the abutments upon which an analysis of the given leans for support, the reality of which the mind, by that very analysis, is compelled to recognize—with certainty, if the analysis itself has proceeded correctly and under the constant pressure of intelligible necessities. Some determination must, of necessity, actually supervene upon the knower, thanks to which a thing that is not the knower will exist in him *secundum esse intentionale* (not as an accident in a substance) and by which the thing will be able to exist with the very same active superexistence which is the existence of the knower that has become the thing known. The species is nothing but that internal determination.[103]

In the case of sensitive knowledge, the external sense, which is in a state of vital tension and has only "to open up" in order to know (everything is ready for it beforehand and, on that account, is like an already acquired intellectual *habitus*),[104] receives from the thing—acting upon the organ through its qualities and thereby offering itself to be sensed (we say: "sensible in act")—a *species impressa*, a presentative form impressed upon it—let us say a "received presentative form"—thanks to which it is specified as though by a seed that has entered into its very depths. The sense, having thus intentionally become the sensible thing in initial or "first" act (for the sense and the sensible thing are then but one and the same principle of operation), becomes it in terminal or "second" act in its immanent action itself, and exercises one and the same act with the sensed thing—not without at the same time producing an image of that sensed thing, a *species expressa* of the sensible order, in the imagination and memory.

---

102   The expression "presentative form" would be our preference, if the word "presentative" evoked the idea of *making present* rather than the idea of *presenting*, a meaning that is rather ill suited to the intelligible *species impressa* (it is the concept that presents the object to the mind). The expression "objectifying form" is better, but only on the condition that the thing itself is understood to be made object through that form (radically only, in the intelligible *species impressa*; expressly, in the concept). It is to be feared that habits of modern language lead to misunderstanding on this score.

103   Cf. St. Thomas Aquinas, *Cont. Gent.*, II, 98.

104   "τοῦ δ'αἰσθητικοῦ ἡ μὲν πρώτη μεταβολὴ γίνεται ὑπὸ τοῦ γεννῶντος, ὅταν δὲ γεννηθῇ, ἔχει ἤδη ὥσπερ ἐπιστήμην καὶ τὸ αἰσθάνεσθαι.   Καὶ τὸ κατ' ἐνέργειαν δὲ ὁλοίως λέγεται τῷ θεωρεῖς." Aristotle, *de Anima*, B, 5, 417b16–19. Cf. St. Thomas' commentary, lect. 12: "Quod nondum habet sensum et natum est habere est potentia ad sensum. Et quod jam habet sensum et nondum sentit est potentia sentiens, sicut circa scientiam dicebatur . . . Sensus autem naturaliter inest animali: unde sicut per generationem acquirit propriam naturam et speciem, ita acquirit sensum. Secus autem est de scientia, quae non inest homini per naturam, sed acquiritur per intentionem et disciplinam . . . Cum autem animal jam generatum est, *tunc hoc modo habet sensum, sicut aliquis habet scientiam, quando jam didicit*. Sed quando jam sentit secundum actum, tunc se habet sicut ille qui jam actu considerat."

The intellect, for its part, knows things by forming them in a fruit which it conceives in the bosom of its own immateriality. Following Aristotle, Thomists recognize in the intellect an active light (the "agent" or acting intellect) which, using sensible representations and setting free the intelligibility they contain in potency[105] (and this is possible only by leaving aside individuating characteristics vested in the sensible as such), specifies the intellect with the help of a *species impressa*, a "presentative form" abstracted from the sensible and "received" by it. Then the intellect is in initial or first act. Precisely as principle of action the intellect has intentionally become the object, which, through its species, is hidden in it as a fertilizing seed and co-principle of knowing (just as the intellect, the sufficient principle of its own action, already is, itself).[106] In this way, the intellect itself actuated by the *species impressa*, and then producing within itself a *species expressa* of the intelligible order, an "elaborated" or "uttered" "presentative form" in which it brings the object to the highest level of actuality and intelligible formation, becomes the object in final act. If the distinction between first and second act is thus once more encountered in knowledge, it is because knowledge, as we have already said, constitutes unto itself alone a whole metaphysical order apart, wherein meet in common both the distinction between essential form and existence in the line of being and the distinction between operative form and the operation in the line of action—now transposed on to one and the same line, the line of knowing. Is not knowing at once existence and (immanent) action? By its faculties of knowing the soul first (intentionally) becomes the object in first act so as to then become the object in second act, even as nature exists before acting.

[VII]. As regards the *species* or presentative forms, two roles or functions of quite different orders must be carefully distinguished. On the one hand, these immaterial forms, these species, are modifications of the soul, and by that title they determine the faculty in the same way as any form determines a subject; but these modifications of our proper natural being, these modifications of the entitative order, are only the prerequisite conditions for knowledge. In no way do they constitute knowledge.[107]

On the other hand, precisely as means of knowing, presentative forms are purely and formally vicars of the object, pure likenesses of the object (i.e., in the soul, they are the object itself divested of its proper existence and made

---

105   Material things are sensible in act, but are intelligible only in potency, and the whole process of human knowledge consists in progressively bringing them, first to intelligibility in act (in the *species intelligibilis impressa*), and then to a state of intellection in act (in the mental word and intellective operation).

106   "Intellectum et intelligens . . . ambo se habent ut unum agens" (St. Thomas, *De Verit.*, VIII, 6, ad 3). Cf. Cajetan, *In Sum. Theol.*, I, 14, 1: "Cum cognoscens debeat esse *sufficiens principium* suae propriae operationis, quae est cognoscere,—quia hoc omnibus perfectis naturis commune est,—oportet quod sit specificativum principium illius, quod est *esse cognitum*."

107   Cf. *Réflexions sur l'intelligence*, pp. 64–65.

present in an immaterial and intentional state). By this title they do not determine the faculty as a form determines a matter or a subject. They determine it according to a wholly immaterial and suprasubjective union in virtue of which one becomes the other intentionally, first in initial act and then in second act through its vital operation. This entirely immaterial informing, wherein the soul receives or submits only in order to exercise its own vital activity—only in order to bring itself in act to an existence that is not limited to itself alone—is that which constitutes knowing.

23. In short, knowing appears to us to be an immanent and vital operation that essentially consists, not in making, but in being; to be or become a thing—either itself or other things—in a way other than by an existence that actuates a subject. This implies a union quite superior to the union of matter and form which together comprise a *tertium quid*, and it supposes that the known object is intentionally made present to the faculty thanks to a *species*, a presentative form. Finally, intellectual[108] knowledge is accomplished thanks

---

108   It is not our intention to treat here of sensitive knowledge in any special way. (Concerning the proper mystery pertaining to that knowledge—a knowledge that implies immateriality while being the act of an organ, [cf. *Philosophie bergsonienne*, 2nd ed., pp. 268 and 276], a mystery that the philosopher can, in the final analysis, only explain by God's universal motion operating in everything that exists, a motion that is not only a general prerequisite for every action by a created being, but also, in a more particular way, for the objective influence of bodies on our senses, see R. Garrigou-Lagrange's remarkable pages in *Le réalisme du principe de finalité*, 1932; cf. Yves Simon, *Introduction à l'ontologie du connaître*, 1933, Ch. III, §§ 1, 2 and 3.) Let it only be noted that, whereas the object of intellectual knowledge is grasped—as we have already said (p. 116)—in the concept and mind, the object of external sense, on the contrary, is not grasped in a word or image, but just as it exists outside the mind, in the very extramental action of the thing on the sense: *sensus secundum actum sunt singularium quae sunt extra animam* (St. Thomas, *In de Anima*, lib. II, lect. 12), *sensatio terminatur ad res prout extra sunt* (John of St. Thomas, *Phil. Nat.*, III P., q. 6, a. 11 and 4; cf. *Réflexions*, pp. 31, 56). This is to say that, inasmuch as sensation is not a transient action, but an immanent action that is completed in the sense, the term of sensation just like the term of every immanent operation, a term that is contemplated or loved, but not produced, exists in the subject itself, *in ipso operante*. Sensible reality, on the other hand, is in the sense—by its transient action, *actio in passo*—just as it is outside the soul. Sensation, then, while terminating in the sense, terminates in the sensible thing as it exists outside, *prout est extra*, in the thing's very action upon the sense. And the actual existence, outside the knowing subject of the thing present in it through its action, is one of the constitutive conditions of the object of the sense as such. The entirely immanent act of sensation, at the beginning of which there is the *species impressa*, has a term, an object, which implies the actual existence of the thing within its own very objectivity—so much so that in the absence of a thing actually given through its action—(even if a star has ceased to exist at the moment the light reaches us, it is at that moment present by its action)—a sensation properly so called (I do not mean an imaginative perception

to a mentalword or concept, a presentative form uttered by the intellect within itself, and in that form the intellect intentionally becomes, in terminal act, the thing taken in this or that one of its intelligible determinations.

---

or an hallucination) is absolutely impossible. "Si organum sentiendi non moveatur a rebus extra, sed ex imaginatione vel aliis superioribus viribus, non erit vere sentire" (St. Thomas, *In IV Sent.*, dist. 44, q. 2, a. 1, sol. 3). "Cum sensus non sentiat nisi per hoc quod a sensibili patitur. . . sequitur quod homo non sentiat calorem ignis si per ignem agentem non sit similitudo caloris ejus in organo sentiendi. Si enim illa species caloris in organo ab alio agente fieret, tactus etsi sentiret calorem, non tamen sentiret calorem ignis nec sentiret ignem esse calidum, cum tamen hoc judicet sensus, cujus judicium in proprio sensibili non erat." (*De Potentia* 3, 7). Cf. *Sum. Theol.*, III, 76, 8, with J. de Tonquedec's very correct comments, *op. cit.*, p. 489. This resolving of the sense's knowledge into the thing itself and actual existence is, in the final reckoning, the primary basis for the veracity of our knowledge. Cf. John of St. Thomas, *Curs. Phil., Phil. Nat.*, III P., q. 6, a. 1.

By giving precision to the scholastic theory of sensation in this fashion, i.e., by admitting that the sense's intuition bears upon external reality itself, grasped not from the point of view of nature or essence (for that is the intellect's proper object, but *according as it actually acts* on the sense by its qualities or as it exists outside *in its action* upon the sense (an action that is something real but accomplished in the organ), there is little difficulty in replying to the main objections derived from "errors of the senses" (the broken stick in water, Doppler's effect, etc.). The sensible quality is perceived, in fact, *as it exists in the action* the body exercises through it and at the instant it reaches the sense after being transmitted through a medium (external or internal). The thoroughly realistic value of sense-perception and, at the same time, the *relativity* it entails—because of the materiality with which it is bound—are thus at one stroke safeguarded. (Cf. *Réflexions sur l'intelligence*, p. 31, no. 1.)

To sketch, in a simple diagram, the diverse moments in sensitive knowledge and intellectual knowledge, one might try it like this:

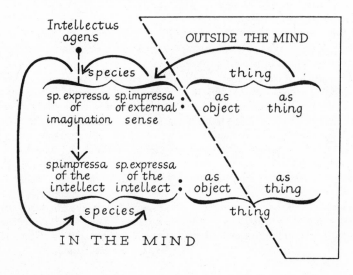

The Concept[109]

24. Thomists distinguish between two kinds of essentially different signs: what they call instrumental sign, and what they call formal sign. An instrumental sign is anything that, being itself first known, makes some other thing known consecutively: a streak of smoke we see rising into the sky, a portrait painted on canvas that we see in a gallery—both are objects upon which our knowledge first bears, only to pass from thence to other objects that are known thanks to them—to the fire of which the smoke is the effect, to the sitter of whom the portrait is the image and the sign.

A formal sign is a sign whose whole essence is to signify. It is not an object which, having, first, its proper value for us as an object, is found, besides, to signify another object. Rather, it is anything that makes known, before being itself a known object. More exactly, let us say it is something that, before being known as object by a reflective act, is known only by the very knowledge that brings the mind to the object through its mediation. In other words, it is not known by "appearing" as object but by "disappearing" in face of the object, for its very essence is to bear the mind to something other than itself.[110] All that we have established up to this point enables us to understand that the species expressae, or the elaborated presentative forms which intervene in knowing, are formal signs, not instrumental signs. A remembrance, or presentative form retained in memory and used by the memory *hic et nunc*, is not *that which* is known when we remember. It is the means by which we know. And what we know by that means is the past itself, the thing or event woven into the web of our past.[111] The concept or mental word is not that which is known when our intellect is at work; it is the means whereby intellection takes place. And what we know by that means is the very nature or intelligible determination of an actually or possibly existing thing. Presentative (elaborated)[112]

---

109   For more detailed explanations, we refer the reader to the pages that treat the same subject in Réflexions sur l'intelligence, Chs. I and II (cf. Philosophie bergsonienne, preface to the second edition, and Part II, Ch. II). This paragraph, like the foregoing paragraphs, presupposes and completes these explanations.

110   See below, §§ 25 and 26, and Appendix I.

111   Cf. our work *Philosophie bergsonienne*, 2nd ed., pp. 273–280.

112   Received presentative forms (*species impressae*) are not called formal signs by the scholastics because they are at the beginning, not at the end, of the act of knowing and, hence, are not themselves known (*in actu exercito*) by the same knowledge that grasps the object. See below, Appendix I, § 4. They are part of the preconscious equipment of knowledge: if consciousness can grasp these forms (cf. *Sum. Theol.*, I, 85, 2; *Cont. Gent.*, II, 75; *Comp. Theol.*, cap. 85), it is by means of the mind's reflection upon its own acts ("secundum eandem reflexion em intelligis et suum intelligere et speciem qua intelligit," *Sum. Theol.*, *ibid.*), and only insofar as it is conscious of the knowledge of the object of which it is the species ("intellectus cognoscit speciem intelligibilem non per essentiam suam, neque per aliquam speciem, sed cognoscendo objectum cujus est species, per quamdam reflexion em." *De Verit.*, X, 9, ad 10). When the intellect is actualized by understanding the

forms are the only realities that correspond to the notion of "formal sign." This notion has been "made to measure" according to the exigencies of an analysis that respects the proper nature of knowledge. It belongs there and there only. All other signs of which we have experience are instrumental signs. That is why, the moment one neglects or forgets their reducible originality of matters affecting knowledge, presentative signs are so easily confused with instrumental signs, just as the immanent activity of sensation and intellection are confused with the transient activity proper to the world of bodies. And, at once, knowledge is destroyed.

St. Thomas, refuting beforehand certain idealistic positions, takes great pains to warn us that the *species* or presentative forms are not the object we know, but pure means of our knowing. They only become the object of knowledge reflexively, and thanks to the production of a new concept. If our knowledge, he explains,[113] stopped at those forms, if it were our representations that we know, then, on the one hand, all the sciences would be absorbed into a single science—and it would be psychology—and, on the other, contradictories would be true—since a true judgment would then be a judgment in conformity with our representations; a person judging that 2 + 2 equals 4 and one judging that 2 + 2 does not equal 4, would be equally right, since each is expressing his respective representations. Thus, presentative forms, concepts in particular, are pure means of knowing; scholastics called them *objectum quo*, mental objects by which knowledge takes place. What is known through these immaterial *species*, they called *objectum* quod, the object *which* is known.

25. If we should group together in a synoptic chart the various elements that concur in an act of intellectual knowledge, we get a schema whose

---

object, it becomes (but only insofar as it is thus actualized and as it perceives the object) intelligible in act to itself (for nothing is intelligible except as it is in act). And it is by its very reflection upon its own *intelligere* extending itself further and further, by its very awareness of knowing the object, and by that alone, that the intellect becomes conscious of the *species impressa*, the *habitus* and the power, both in regard to their existence and in regard to their nature (inasmuch as it knows them as the principles of that act—which, in fact, they are by their very essence), and also of the soul itself, but only as regards its existence (for the soul "non est principium actuum per suam essentiam, sed per vires suas." *De Verit.*, X, 9. Cf. above, Ch. III, n. 45, and below, Appendix V, § 2). This is a concrete and individual awareness, quite different from abstract and universal (and also reflexive) scientific knowledge of the nature of *species, habitus*, power, and soul.
. . .

At this point we are bound to rectify a mistake: through inadvertency the *species impressa* was called a "formal sign" in various passages in *Réflexions sur l'intelligence*. These passages should be corrected, and they should read that it is "a pure means [*quo*]."

113   *Sum. Theol.*, I, 85, 2

scholarly aspect demands an apology but which, none the less, will help us to clarify distinctions that are, in our opinion, of capital importance.

We have distinguished two features in the concept: an entitative function, by which the concept is a modification or accident of the soul, and an intentional function, by which it is a formal sign of the thing and in which the object is grasped by the mind. That object grasped by the mind by and in the concept is the thing itself, taken under this or that one of its determinations, for that thing has been transported—though stripped of its own existence—within the mind, first by means of sensation and then by abstraction. For the first three terms of this chart are all within thought: it is in the bosom of thought that the object is attained;[114] it is known in the core of the intellect. (That is why the ancients often called it *conceptus objectivus*.) Only the thing, taken in its own proper existence (either actual or possible), is extramental or metalogical. But what is capital in this regard is that while existing in two different states (1. in the concept, in a state of abstraction and universality which allows it to be handled, divided, compared by the mind, and to enter into the concatenations of discourse; 2. in the thing, in a state of individuality and concreteness), nevertheless the *object* and the *thing* do not constitute two known terms, two *quod*'s, but only one. One and the same term of knowledge, one and the same *quod*, exists for itself as thing, and is attained by the mind as object.

The *thing* may be Peter, for example. He exists outside the mind in a certain place; he is not only man but also animal, substance, etc., philosopher or musician, well or ill. The object may, for instance, be the object-of-thought "man," which in Peter, and outside the mind, has a natural existence, and in the concept and within the mind, an intentional existence (and as known, or placed before the mind, it has only an ideal existence or existence of reason).[115]

114   "Objectum quod intelligitur debet esse intra intellectum et intra ipsum attingi" (John of St. Thomas, *Curs. Theol.*, I P., q. 27, disp. 12, a. 7, n. 4). (Vivès, t. IV, p. 142.) "Intellectus non intelligit nisi trahendo res ad se, et intra se considerando, non extra se inspiciendo. Et D. Thomas docet rem intellectum non posse esse rem ut ad extra, sed ut intra, et ut est unum cum intellectu, ut q. 9 *De Potentia*, a. 5, et q. 8, a. 1, et locis infra citandis." *Ibid.*, a. 5, n. 5 (p. 94). Cf. *De Verit.*, IV, 2, ad 7.

115   Thus, three *esse*'s of the thing should be distinguished: 1. the *esse naturae*, according to which the thing existing outside of thought is of itself singular and concrete: entitative existence or the existence of thing; 2. the *esse intentionale*, whereby the thing existing in thought, in order to be known, is of itself abstract and universal: representative existence or the existence of sign; 3. likewise abstract and universal, the *esse cognitum seu objectivum*, whereby the thing existing by and for thought, precisely as known, is purely ideal and brings no real determination either to the thing or to the mind (except by presupposition, insofar as the object's being-thought supposes the mind's thinking). It is ideal existence, or the existence of the signified *reduplicative ut sic*. (Moreover, such existence is of interest only to the mind's logical reflection upon itself, that is why we have not treated it here. On the *esse cognitum*, cf. John of St. Thomas, *Curs. Theol.*, I P., q. 12, disp. 15, a. 3; R. Dalbiez, "Les sources scolastiques de la théorie cartésienne de l'être objectif," *Rev. d'Hist. de la Philos.*, Oct.–Dec. 1929.)

	IN THE MIND			OUTSIDE THE MIND
	concept (QUO)		thing (QUOD)	
Saint Thomas Aquinas	as modification of the subject	as species (formal sign)	as object (formal object)	as thing (material object)
		here ← possessing → there an intentional existence		an existence of nature
	idea (QUOD)			ideated (QUOD)
Descartes	"formal" reality of the idea		"objective" reality of the idea	thing which the idea resembles
		[the intentional disappears]		
Berkeley			idea-thing	no thing
Kant			constructed phenomena	unknowable thing-in-itself
Hegel	IN ABSOLUTE THOUGHT			no thing-in-itself except thought itself
		[productive spontaneity]	the mind's self-objectivation	
Phenomenologists and Critical Realists	IN INTENTIONAL AWARENESS			no thing-in itself
		[the intentional reappears]	object-essence	
American Neo-Realists	IN KNOWLEDGE			thing immanent to thought qua thing

It is essential to the concept to be abstract and universal.[116] It is essential to the extramental thing to be singular and concrete. The object, on the contrary, existing as it does in the thing with an existence of nature (singular and concrete, and proper to the thing), and also existing in the concept with intentional existence (abstract and universal, and proper to the concept), is in itself indifferent to one state or the other.[117] It is posited before the mind in a state of abstraction and universality that comes to it from its existence within the concept, wherein it is grasped by the mind; that state, however, is not essential to it, since in a judgment—for example, when we say "Peter is man"—I identify the individual Peter and the object of thought, man.

26. As concerns the concept or mental word which I have in mind when I think "man," it is said to be a sign of the thing, a likeness or vicar of the object, an interior term wherein the object is perceived intellectually (*terminus in quo*). But in this connection, let us be on our guard against that sort of materialization or spatialization which language brings with it, unless we are on the watch for it. The object does not in any way exist in the concept as a material content exists in a material container; the concept is emphatically not a material thing enveloping another material thing. It is an immaterial "word," an utterance of the mind expressing the object. For the concept "to contain" is purely and simply to know. The object exists in the concept and is grasped in it in the sense that by the very fact of emitting the concept, and fulfilling itself in this spiritual production, the immanent act of understanding immediately attains the object and attains it, clad in the conditions of the concept. And that itself is possible

---

On the contrary, the other two kinds of existence belong to the real or "physical" order (in the scholastic sense of the word "physical"). The first posits the thing in nature outside nothingness; the second posits the presentative form of the thing in the mind and leads the mind to the thing—and it is also the very existence whereby the mind is the thing. Intentional existence is an immaterial and non-entitative existence, not-for-itself, but real, and it has this formal effect, to wit, not that the thing exists (except in the mind through its presentative form), but rather that the mind is the thing, that it knows. Intentional existence really and physically affects the species which makes known and the mind that knows. It brings a tension, a stimulation, a fullness to the mind; it fertilizes it (in the *species impressa*), or proceeds from the mind according as the mind perfects itself (in the *species expressa*).

116 Yet this does not prevent there being, let us note in passing, a proper and distinct reflex concept of the singular (by turning to the images). Cf. John of St. Thomas, *Curs. Phil., Phil. Nat.*, III P., q. 10, a. 4, *dico secundo*.

117 When nature is considered in this way *secundum se, seu in statu solitudinis*, it is neither singular nor universal; considered *secundum esse quod habet in rebus (esse naturae)*, it is, in fact, singular; seen *secundum esse quod habet in abstractione intellectus (esse intentionale* and *esse cognitum seu objectivum)*, it is, in fact, universal. This whole doctrine presupposes the real distinction (in everything that is not God) between nature and *esse*. Cf. St. Thomas Aquinas, *De Ente et Essentia*, cap. IV; John of St. Thomas, *Curs. Phil., Log.*, II P., q. 3, a. n. 1.

only because the concept is a sign, vicar or likeness of the object only insofar as it is a formal sign, as we have pointed out above.

And what does this mean if not that the notions "vicar" or "likeness" or "image" must in this case be purified of everything that would make of them things that first come before the mind's eye, like a portrait falling under the gaze of the eyes of the body. But then, if the concept is not a thing that resembles the object, what is left for it? As something existing intentionally in the soul and bringing the object to the ultimate level of spirituality there in the soul, as something making known, it remains for it to be what the thing or object is as it is known. The concept and thing make two from the point of view of entity; but as formal sign, and in the pure line of knowing rather than being, we must say that it and the object do not make two. The fruit of understanding in act, it has as its intelligible content the object itself. But this intelligible content set, as object, before the mind, is vitally expressed as concept by the mind and has, as its proper existence, the act of intellection itself. As for its intelligible constitution, the concept is therefore identical with the object—not, certainly, as if it were that which is known: that is not what I mean; rather I mean precisely this: it is identical insofar as it is the inner sign and term by which the intellect becomes, in ultimate act, what it knows. A moment ago we said the formal sign is not something that is first known and afterwards makes known another thing. We now understand that it is something known precisely insofar as it makes known, and in the very act of making known. The immanent reason of the presentation of the object to the intellect in act, the concept or mental word is steeped in intellectuality in act; to be thought in act, to terminate understanding in act, is, for the concept, an intrinsic denomination, since it is in the concept that the object, like the intellect, is in the ultimate act of intellectuality. But it is not as object that it is thought and known; it is not as term signified that it is *intellectum in actu*, grasped and shot through with actual understanding. It is a signifying term.[118]

27. Finally, the concept in its entitative role and as modification of the subject, and the concept in its intentional role and as formal sign, are not two distinct things (indeed, intentionality is not exactly a thing-in-itself but, rather, a mode). These are two formal aspects or two distinct formal values of the same thing, the intentional role being of importance only to knowing, the entitative function, to the being of nature (in this case, of the soul itself). Just as the divine essence, being understanding in pure act, has itself the value of

---

118 Verbum est "quiddam mente conceptum quo homo exprimit mentaliter *ea* de quibus cogitat" (St. Thomas, *Sum. Theol.*, I–II, 93, 1, ad 2). Concerning the nature of the concept and its identity—in respect of its intelligible constitution—with the object, see the long discussion contained in Appendix I, regarding Fr. D. Roland-Gosselin's criticisms. We are pleased that J. de Tonquedec has graciously called attention to his own agreement with our views on this important question (cf. *op. cit.*, pp. 145–146).

species impressa and *species expressa* for the intellect of the blessed, and just as the angel's substance is itself *species impressa* for the angel's intellect, so the entity of the concept is itself, in us, the formal sign of the object. As thing or entity, the concept is an accident, a quality or modification of the soul;[119] but arising, as it does, within the soul as a fruit and an expression of an intellect already formed by the *species impressa*, already "perfect,"[120] and under the

119　The scholastics classified it among qualities of the first class (dispositions and habits), because it suitably disposes nature insofar as it is knowing nature (cf. John of St. Thomas *Log.*, II P., q. 18, a. 2. Reiser, I, p. 613). But, differing from habit in the ordinary sense of the word—which is from the side of the subject and its dynamism—the concept is on the side of the object which the concept presents to the mind.

120　Once the intellect is actuated into first act by the *species impressa*, it is a sufficient principle of its own operation. That is why Aristotle and St. Thomas call intellective action *actus perfecti*, the act of a thing that is already in act. "Hujusmodi autem actio [sc. quae est perfectio ipsius agentis] est actus perfecti, id est existentis in actu, ut dicitur in 3 *de Anima* (lect. 12)." (*Sum. Theol.*, I, 18, 3, ad 1.) On that score, the little apocryphal work *De Natura verbi* contains a precious word, but one that has to be understood properly: "Prima actio ejus [sc. intellectus] per speciem at formatio sui objecti, quo formato intelligit, simul tamen tempore ipse format et formatum est, et simul intelligit, quia ista non sunt motus de potentia ad actum, quia jam factus est intellectus in actu per speciem, sed *processus perfectus de actu in actum*, ubi non requiritur aliqua species motus." And, on his side, John of St. Thomas writes: "Ex quibus patet pertinere ad ipsum intellectum, suo actu qui est intelligere, formare sibi objectum in aliqua similitudine repraesentante, et intra se ponere, ibique unire per modum termini seu objecti ad quod intelligere terminatur, sicut per speciem impressam unitur ut principium determinans intellectum ad pariendum notitiam. Ille autem actus quo formatur objectum est cognitio: cognoscendo enim format objectum, et, formando intelligit, quia simul format, et formatum est, et intelligit . . ." (*Curs. Theol.*, I P., q. 27, disp. 12, a. 5, n. 5, Vivès, t. IV, p. 95). The actuating of the intellect, insofar as the object is not formed in the word, still remains imperfect on the side of its term, and that is why this *processus de actu in actum*, which is "perfect" as regards its principle of intellection and as the *species impressa* has formed and actuated the intellect, at the same time constitutes a *fieri* for understanding wherein, in the very instant it takes place, it *perfects* the actuating of the intellect, as regards its term, by producing the word and forming the object in it. Moreover, the word itself is not perfect within us at the first stroke; on the contrary, it is constantly taken up once more, elaborated step by step and matured in the course of discursive activity (cf. St. Thomas, *In Joann.* I, 1.) "[Verbum] debet exprimere rem ut vitaliter attractam ab ipsa cognitione, ergo non solum est intelligibilem in actu primo, sed ut intellectam in actu secundo. . . [Aliquando procedit verbum] ex necessitate et indigentia, quia objectum ipsum non est sufficienter explicatum, et evolutum, et ita proceditur ab imperfecto ad perfectum, sicut in nobis fit per discursum et cogitationem, et sic praecedit verbum intelligere perfectum, sed procedit ab intelligere imperfecto, et in fieri: et generaliter quandocumque formatur verbum, ipsum fieri verbi etiam est intelligere in fieri. Aliquando vero procedit verbum ex abundantia intelligendi. . . ." (John of St. Thomas, *Curs. Phil.*, *de Anima*, q. 11, a. 1, *dico tertio*, Vivès, t. III, p. 494).

der the influence of that created participation in the divine intellectual power, that focus of ever-actual immateriality, the highest point of spiritual tension naturally present within us—which must be called the active intellect (*intellectus agens*) and from which the intellect which knows derives all its formative energy[121]—this quality, this modification of the soul which is the concept, has (as all objectifying forms do) the privilege of transcending the entitative, informing activity it exercises and of being present in the faculty after the manner of a spirit. It is from the intellect itself, from the intellect in vital act,

---

Causae ad invicem sunt causae in diverso genere. Without there being the slightest priority in time of one over the other, the concept is at once produced by understanding in act and the condition of that act (on the side of the object); the intellect itself is actualized in final act in forming the concept.

121   It would, indeed, be a mistake to think the role of the agent intellect ceases with the formation of the *species impressa*. St. Thomas has a much loftier idea of it, and the metaphysical importance of his view is often misunderstood. The agent intellect is the stamp of the divine light upon us. Whereas in the angel the strength or light of the intellect and the angel's own vitality are absolutely one and the same, in us there is a division into two: the intellect that knows and is originally devoid of any form, has by itself a vitality characteristic of knowledge, is capable by itself of becoming the object in a living manner, yet the power it thus has is only actualized through the efficiency of an ever-actual intellectuality that alone can provide the reason for the process of immaterializing and understanding of which we are the authors and which already exists by itself at the highest level of actuality, but without an object, and in order to illumine, not to become. Thus, the agent intellect is the activator of intelligence, its light, the focus of all its force: "principium activum proprium, per quod efficiamur intelligentes in actu . . . Philosophus dicit, quod intellectus agens est ut habitus quidem et lumen (III *De Anima*, c. V); et in Psalmis dicitur: signatum est super nos lumen vultus tui." (St. Thomas, *Q. Disp* , a. 5. Cf. *ibid.*, a. 4, ad 6; a. 15, ad 3; ad 19; a. 18; *De Verit.*, X, 6.) St. Thomas also says (*Q. disp. de Anima*, a. 15, ad 9): "cum erit anima a corpore separata, per intellectum possibilem recipiet species effluentes a substantiis superioribus, et *per intellectum agentem habebit virtutem ad intelligendum*"; and *Cont. Gent.*, III, 15: "Cum anima a corpore tali fuerit separata, intellectus possibilis intelligere poterit ea quae sunt secundum se intelligibilia, scilicet substantias separatas, *per lumen intellectus agentis*, quod est similitudo in anima intellectualis luminis quod est in substantiis separatis." Cf. also Cajetan, *In*, III, 9, 4. Let us conclude, then, that, in the state of union with the body, it is through the activation of the agent intellect that the knowing intellect, after having been fecundated by the agent intellect by means of phantasms and formed *in actu primo* by the *species impressa*, produces within itself the *species expressa* and actuates itself in ultimate act.

In the (apocryphal) opusculum *De Natura verbi*, wherein we do not find the balance of language proper to St. Thomas but where from time to time vivid and penetrating flashes are sometimes found, we read: "Idem lumen quod intellectus possibilis recipit cum specie ab intellectu agente, per actionem intellectus informati tali specie diffunditur cum objectum formatur, et manet cum objecto formato, et hoc habet plenam rationem verbi, cum in eo quidditas rei intelligatur."

that that quality holds this privilege, as though the intellect gathered together its own spirituality into this active point, there to bring it to a maximum. Thus, the concept exists in the intellect not only in an entitative manner and as an informing form, but also as a spiritual form, not absorbed in actuating a subject so as to form a *tertium quid* with it, and therefore actuating, on the contrary, or rather, terminating, the intellect intentionally and in the line of knowing, in that it expresses the object and renders it transparent.

On the other hand, the form that the intellect, once it has been placed in first act by the *species impressa*, engenders within itself, under the uninterrupted irradiation of the agent intellect, is truly, as we have said, the object's pure likeness, spiritually on fire, or rather the object itself now made spirit[122] and intentionally present (not as object but as sign): because its entire specification comes from the object. The intellect that illumines and the intellect that knows are by themselves equally undetermined. Thus, the concept (in its intentional role) and object are indistinguishable, save that one makes known and the other is known, one is sign and the other is signified, one exists only in the mind and the other exists at the same time in the mind and in the thing.

Thus, we see that the intuitivity proper to the intellect consists (at the lowest stage) in the abstractive perception performed by means of the concept,[123] and that, for the things that fall, in the very first place, within the grasp of our intellect, that perception is absolutely infallible. It delivers to us those first principles which are known of themselves and command the whole development of knowledge. And yet, since our intellect has thus to form its own objects for itself and, in proportion as it advances in knowledge, actively draw, from the same presentative form (*species impressa*) it has received, various concepts that set forth the various aspects of the same intelligible nucleus according to the various directions of attention that prevail within the mind—(for things

---

122   If it is better to know than to love things below man (*Sum. Theol.*, I, 82, 3), it is because they exist in the mind in a better mode of being than in themselves. That is why "in a general way, material realities are more effectively known *per similitudinem* than they would be *per essentiam*" (Fr. D. Roland-Gosselin, *art. cit.* from *Philosophia Perennis*, t. II, p. 719). Cf. *De Verit.*, III, 1, ad 1 and ad 2; *De Potentia*, 7, 7, ad 5. These passages from the *De Veritate* and the *De Potentia* (they occur in connection with God's knowledge of things in His essence) should be understood in a very formal sense; it is from the point of view of the immateriality of the *esse* that material things are better known *per speciem* than they would be through their essence—supposing that, in spite of its materiality, that essence could be a medium of knowledge. It is quite clear that from other points of view we know much less about things in knowing them *per speciem* than if we could know them through their essence. God's essence is *"supereminens similitudo rerum."*

123   Cf. J. de Tonquedec, *La critique de la connaissance*, p. 144. The author points out that, in this connection, Aristotle uses the term ὄψις, view," *Eth. Nic.*, I, c. VI (alias IV), n. 12, 1096; *In de Anima*, III, c. IV, n. 2, 429 a 14. See also *Réflexions sur l'intelligence*, pp. 74–77.

are not merely brought to actual intelligibility in the *species impressa*; within the bosom of the intellect an inventory of them is taken and they are sorted out in many ways in order to be brought to the final degree of actual intellection in the concept); we also see that the conceptual task is highly complicated and slow moving; we see that it proceeds from the indeterminate and generic to the determined; we see that it admits of a large measure of construction and artifice; we see that it makes us take very indirect or "confused or partial or derivative or negative" views of things, and finally that it runs the risk of error in proportion as it advances—not only from the fact of judgment and reasoning but from the fact of abstractive perception as well, because when our intellect is already busied with forms, the new concepts it engenders (whose formation no longer depends on the thing alone, but on objects already possessed and in virtue of which the new object is placed before the mind) can be formed awry. Undoubtedly, they always present to the mind some aspect of the real—or some being of reason based on the real—when they are not pseudo-concepts giving the mind a complex of contradictory elements (such as the greatest whole number or the most perfect world); yet they may be capable of being cut up or recast in such arbitrary fashion that the gain will be very slight, if not illusory. Thus, we witness that certain concepts used by science, oftentimes for quite a long while—and, indeed, not absurdly—disappear forever and leave no trace; the ancient chemistry had its phlogiston,[124] and in the sociology that came from Auguste Comte, as well as in our modern psychology, concepts that are quite as perishable are to be found.

Idealistic Positions and Attempts at Reaction

28. Well, after that, if we come back once more to our diagram, we can easily discern for ourselves the classical moments in modern idealism. The latter is characterized, truth to tell, by a radical misunderstanding of the true nature of the idea and of the intentional function of knowledge, thenceforth conceived upon the pattern of events in the material order. Descartes clearly saw that the known object is known within thought; his capital error was to have separated the object from the thing, believing as he did that the object is in thought, not as an intelligible entity rendered present to the mind through an immaterial form—and with which the mind is intentionally identified—but as an imprint stamped on wax. Henceforth, the intentional function disappears; the known object becomes something of thought, an imprint or portrait born within it; understanding stops at the idea (looked upon as instrumental sign). This idea-portrait, this idea-thing, has as its double a thing to which it bears a resemblance but which is itself not attained by the act of understanding. They are two separate *quod*'s, and the divine veracity is needed to assure us that

---

124   On this point some interesting remarks will be found in Vol. II of E. Meyerson's work, *De l'explication dans les sciences*.

behind the *idea-quod* (which we attain), there is a *thing-quod* corresponding to it. Of itself thought attains nothing but itself.[125]

Thenceforth, the idea becomes—as, later, Locke will say—the immediate object of thought.

Berkeley will see, not unreasonably, that under these conditions there is no legitimate reason for keeping the thing as a double of the idea, and he will believe he is returning to the evidence of common sense in affirming that we immediately perceive objects, but that those objects are themselves our ideas. Finally, Kant will once more admit, with Descartes, a thing (*das Ding an sich*) hidden behind the *object*. But because he looks upon the object as something constructed by the mind's activity in accordance with its *a priori* laws, will arrest our knowledge at the phenomenon that is thus constructed, the thing in itself remaining unknowable.

All these philosophers equally disregard the proper nature of knowledge. They envisage the operation of knowing after the pattern of material operations; they regard an activity which is essentially immanent, as an activity *ad extra*. For Cartesian innatism, thought is essentially passive; it is a certain matter that has received an imprint. The same is true for the empiricists who will look upon that imprint as caused in thought not by God but by things. Kant sought to restore the activity of thought, but always according to the same type of a transient or productive activity imposing a form on matter. This time, however, the form belongs on the side of the mind; concepts are empty forms and it is sensible matter that is subsumed and organized by those forms. The inexhaustibility of the thing as a subject to be known will pass, by virtue of the "Copernican principle," to thought as generative of the object, and thought itself will appear to be an indefinite process of fabricating the object.

Indeed, once the intentional function disappeared, knowledge became perfectly unintelligible. For in the entitative order it is clear that a thing cannot

---

125 Various scholastic deviations (for example, Vasquez's notion of the *conceptus objectivus* pointed out in Fr. Geny's *Critica* and in our *Réflexions sur l'intelligence*, and the Scotist notion of *esse objectivum* pointed out by Roland Dalbiez, *art. cit.* Ch. III, n. 114) have prepared the way for this great Cartesian mistake. That mistake is lustily attacked by L. Noel (*op. cit.*, pp. 11–17, 31–36, 71–76, 84, etc.). And, on his own account, R. Kremer writes, "Few, if any, scholastics would want to defend the view that what we directly know is but a copy, a subjective transfer of the object. For St. Thomas and the ancients in every case there is no question but that we do not know representations of things but, rather, things themselves (see, for example, *Sum. Theol.*, I, 85, a. 2). Now to know is to have that object as the normal term of intentional activity; the subjective intermediary used to know things is not known to us in the first instance; its existence is revealed dependently upon that first direct knowledge. And that, we feel, is the essential thesis of "immediate" or "direct realism" (*art. cit.*, *Philosophia Perennis*, t. II, p. 736). Cf. concerning Descartes and the scholastics, E. Gilson, Etudes sur le rôle de la pensée médiévale dans la formation du système cartesien (Paris, Vrin, 1930); and our *The Dream of Descartes* (New York, Philosophical Library, 1944).

be something other than what it is. Thus, our idealists deem it absurd to look for an *outside* of thought, as they say. Everything is absorbed within thought, and, for thought, to know is henceforth to develop itself as a plant or an animal, a lichen or a polyp vegetates and grows.

As to present-day reactions against idealism, reactions that seem to us seriously incomplete, they appear under two main aspects. On the one hand, the Neo-realist[126] school, by insisting on the thing's immanence within knowledge, seems to disregard any distinction at all between thing and object, and encloses the extramental thing itself within the mind. And that has every appearance of being a contradiction.

On the other hand, a much more important group—and in spite of their differences we might at once attach to this group such thinkers as Russell and Whitehead, along with those who have chosen the name "Critical Realists,"[127] as well as the Phenomenologists in Germany—stops knowledge short at an *object* which is no longer a product of the mind, as it is for the idealists, but rather an *essence*, an *irreducible datum*, an intelligible entity independent of the mind, or at least exhibited to it in an intuition. But such an object-essence remains for them, as it did for Kant and for the whole modern tradition, still separate from the transobjective subject or the extra-mental thing. The latter is only hypothetical or problematical and, indeed, it would be better—in virtue of the principle of economy and Ockham's razor—to do without it. Or else that extramental thing will be held by others to be "absurd";[128] and they, remaining, without realizing it, to a certain extent dependent upon Hegel— while still vigorously reacting against his pan-logism (yet it was from him they learned to confuse logic with ontology)—will be forced, as Hegel was, to resorb the thing into idea. And they will attribute to the object, taken as separated from any transobjective subject, characteristics that can, in reality, come to it only from that subject. And when I say "in reality," I do not mean that reality for itself which Hegel granted to the Idea, but rather the characteristic of not being producible by the mind, the irreducible consistency of essence.

All this makes the object to be something absolutely irrational, for the object is neither an aspect of a thing nor a modification of the mind; and it also makes knowledge to be a completely unintelligible process, neither vitally immanent nor productive. Moreover, even though it be not productive or transformative, as Kant would have it be, that process still remains, properly speaking, without a term: not "without a term" in the very true sense that knowledge continues to go on penetrating things by adding truth to truth, but in the sense that, in not laying hold of any thing that regulates it, it can—in spite of the ephemeral constructions reared by the theoricians of this idealism redivivus—only over-

---

126   Messrs. Perry, Spaulding, Marvin, Montague . . .
127   Messrs. Strong, Sellers, Santayana . . .
128   See above, Ch. III, n. 81.

reach itself endlessly by substituting one truth for another and forever attain nothing.

The Universe of Existence and the Universe of Intelligibility

29. Everything we have said of the concept presupposes the Aristotelian theory of abstraction according to which the intellect actively draws from sensible data, from things as the sense first lays hold of them, this or that content which is potentially intelligible in those data—an operation which is possible only if individuating notes, invested in the sensible as such, are left aside. It is this intelligible content which the intellect actualizes and expresses in the concept—and which is the object known by it. If, with Aristotle and St. Thomas, *thing* and *object* are distinguished in this fashion but not separated, and if, while maintaining their unity, allowance is made for what comes from the thing and for what comes from the mind in knowing, then it is clear that from the things which exist outside our mind and constitute what may be called the universe of existence, the mind draws forth a world of objects composed of abstract and universal concepts which we may term the universe of intelligibility or of human knowledge. And that universe is, on the one hand, detached from the universe of existence, in order that it may be known. It is, on the other hand, identified with it, in order that it may itself subsist. Thus, we really do attain the things of the world of existence when we attain the world of intelligibility, but we do not attain them in their singularity nor in the contingency proper to the flux of their singular occurrences. Our senses attain them in that way; our scientific knowledge attains them directly only in the universal natures and universal determinations which are the scene of intelligible necessities. And, as Cajetan says in a text we have cited above,[129] it is by turning back, with the aid of the senses, to the singular and contingent things wherein the universal is realized, it is by reintegrating the intelligible in the thing that exists—whether it be a sensible existent or a spiritual one—that the intellect completes its grasping of the real.[130] (One of these, the sensible existent, is at the root of all our knowledge. The other, the spiritual existent, is known—whether it be reflexively experienced, when the soul knows itself through its own acts, or attained through reasoning, when it knows God and spirits—by analogy with sensible existents, to which our mind has to refer in some way or other even in its knowledge of the suprasensible.)

129   Cajetan, *In Anal. Pos.*, I, 1, c. 8. See above, Ch. II, § 5.
130   Even in mathematics, which abstracts from the order of existence, there must be a return to an imaginable existent, I mean to constructibility within imaginative intuition—at least by an indirect or analogical way and in relation to entities that can be directly constructed. Thus, for example, non-Euclidian geometries, in the final analysis, derive their complete logical validity from the possibility of our constructing Euclidian models of them, and the intrinsic coherence (free from internal contradictions) of Euclidian entities is itself guaranteed by their existing for the imagination.

30. Let us not, indeed, forget that even though the singular as such is not the object of science and cannot be directly grasped by the human intellect, it can still be grasped by it indirectly in reflex concepts; and also that science comes to its term in the singular (as transobjective subject), thus completing the circle of its intelligible movement. That is why we need the sense not only in order to derive our ideas from things, but also to resolve our judgment, for in one way or another judgment (even when it does not have to be verified in the sensible)[131] has to be made in the senses, *sicut extremo et ultimo, ad quod resolutio fiat*,[132] because judgment has to do with existence (actual or possible), and the "sensible and visible thing" is for us the paradigm of the existent.

For St. Thomas, a science of nature that would not return to the singular, real entity would not be a science but a dream. And, analogically, the same thing is true of metaphysics—which also goes back to the singular—and mathematics, insofar, at least, as it comes back to a singular that can be intuitively constructed and in which their basic entities have an imaginable existence.[133] Indeed, "the term in which the knowledge of nature is completed, is the thing attained by the senses, and especially by sight. Just as the cutler seeks a knowledge of 'knife' only for the work he has to do—I mean in order to make this particular knife—so, too, the scientist seeks to know the nature of 'stone' or 'horse' only in order to know the reasons of the things that fall under the senses. And as the craftsman's judgment about the knife would be faulty if he did not know the work it was to do, so also would the scientist's judgment about the things of nature, if that which falls under his senses were unknown. Moreover, everything our intellect knows [even mathematical beings and metaphysical realities] in the present state of union with the body, it knows by referring it in some way to the sensible things of nature. Moreover, it is impossible for the judgment of the intellect not to be faulty in us when the external senses are fettered by sleep.[134]

---

131   See above, Ch. II, § 22.
132   St. Thomas Aquinas, *De Verit.*, XII, 3, ad 3. It is worth noting that judgment, the intuition of the senses, and appetite have all three a relation to the *esse rerum*, even though in three quite different ways: judgment, with a view to stating how the thing, which is attained in our notions, behaves in this *esse* (actual or possible); the intuition of the senses, in order to attain in esse the sensible thing which exists in act; appetite, in order to bring the subject to the thing as it exists in act.
133   See above, Ch. III, n. 129.
134   *Sum. Theol.*, I, 84, 8. Cf. *De Verit.*, XII, 3, ad 2: "Ad secundum dicendum, quod judicium non dependet tantum a receptione speciei, sed ex hoc quod ea de quibus judicatur, examinantur ad aliquod principium cognitionis, sicut de conclusionibus judicamus eas in principia resolvendo. In somno igitur ligatis exterioribus sensibus, interiores vires quasi quietate ab exteriorum sensuum tumultibus magis percipere possunt interiores impressiones factas in intellectu vel imaginatione ex illustratione divina vel evangelica, vel ex virtute caelestium corporum, aut quorumcumque; sicut tenui phlegmate decurrente ad linguam videtur dormienti quod dulcia comedat. Sed quia primum principium nostrae cognitionis

31. Indeed, we do not derive a single world of intelligibility by abstracting from the world of existence; there are as many universes of intelligibility as there are degrees of immateriality or immaterialization of the object.

Being of Reason

32. Our mind not only draws out of the sensible such and such intelligible natures realized in the world of existence; it not only sets before itself those natures whose notion is born to it from the consideration of those natures, and which can all exist; in short, it does not conceive only real beings, i.e. beings capable of existing. It can also construct in the image of these natures, *ad instar entis*, objects of thought that are incapable of existing outside the mind (for example, genus and species, subject, predicate, etc.), which the ancients called beings of reason, *entia rationis*.

Our mind does not create these objects of thought—which do not deserve the name essence, since essence is the capacity for existing (*esse*)[135]—out of whole cloth. It makes them out of elements that are essences or intelligible aspects first grasped in things: for example, it makes the object of thought "nothing," from "being," to which it adds negation. In themselves they are never anything but simple non-essences (negations or privations)—a chimera is a non-being conceived in the likeness of an animal—or relations which, even though they cannot exist outside the mind, still have the same intelligible content and the same definition πρὸς τί as real relations. Such objects are not things, and yet they are not *pure objects* separated from any transobjective subject as the "phenomena" of the moderns[136] are, for they are conceived in

est sensus, oportet ad sensum quodammodo resolvere omnia de quibus judicamus; unde Philosophus dicit in III Caeli et Mundi, quod complementum artis et naturae est res sensibilis visibilis, ex qua debemus de aliis judicare, et similiter dicit in VI Ethic. (cap. VII, in fin.) quod *sensus sunt extremi sicut intellectus principiorum*; extrema appellans illa in quae fit resolutio judicantis. Quia igitur in somno ligati sunt sensus; non potest esse perfectum judicium nisi quantum ad aliquid, cum homo decipiatur intendens rerum similitudinibus tanquam rebus ipsis; quamvis quandoque dormiens cognoscat de aliquibus quod non sunt res, sed similitudines rerum."

135   "Essentia dicitur secundum quod per eam et in ea res habet esse" (St. Thomas Aquinas, *De Ente et Essentia*, cap. 1). "Non habet [ens rationis] essentiam aliquam" (Cajetan, *In de Ente et Essentia*, cap. 1, q. 1).

136   Let it be added that they are made by the mind before being known to it as beings of reason. I employ the idea of blindness or of death to signify that a man is deprived of sight or has ceased to live, long before I know these beings of reason as such, long before I perceive that I am thinking "death" and "blindness" as if they were things. From this point of view, the dictum *"esse est percipi seu intelligi"* is not true even of beings of reason: they exist in the mind before they are known. No doubt (and it is here that the idealistic formula applies to beings of reason) that existence in the mind itself is no more than an *esse objectum seu cognitum* but it refers to the *"cognosci"* of the real elements out of which the being of reason

the image of those subjects (of which they presuppose a previous knowledge) and are constructed with elements borrowed from the real. Far from being separated from what is real, they are bound to it on these two counts. The real (actual or possible) remains their root or their occasion. They derive all the objective consistence they have from the real. If we can make judgments about them, it is because we treat them as though they were things: "ratio de eis non entibus negotiatur quasi de quibusdam entibus, dum de eis affirmat vel negat aliquid";[137] and if the mind can be true or false in respect to them, it is by indirectly referring to the real which served as their occasion or basis. Do away with the nature of the circle and of the square, and you can no longer say a square circle is unthinkable; get rid of every nature that is knowable in various degrees of determination, and you can no longer say that a species is part of genus.

If, as the critical realism of Aristotle and St. Thomas teaches, intelligible, extramental being is the first object of our intellect, and if the real existent is first given to us by the senses—whence our intellect draws its ideas—then we are assured that our first intellectual apprehensions do not bear upon beings of reason. *Ab actu ad posse valet consecutio*: since there are ants, the ant is possible. And as for the possibility of being in general, it is certified for us—even independently (*de jure*) of any perception of actual existence[138]—by the very first judicative intuition of our intellect, for it affirms precisely that being is not non-being.[139] But in a philosophy which starts only with thought, a philosophy according to which the mind attains at first only itself, how can we be sure that all our objects of thought are not beings of reason? That is where the Evil Genius plants his barb. That problem was crucial for Descartes

has been constructed and of the realities in the likeness of which it has been conceived and not to the *cognosci* of the being of reason as such. It is only of the mental concept that one may say purely and simply "*esse est intelligi* (ipsum intelligi intrinsecum)." See below, Appendix I, § 4, IX. "Cognitio formans ens rationis non est reflexa respiciens ipsum tamquam rem cogitam ut quod, sed illa cognitio directa, quae *ipsum non ens reale, vel quae realiter non est*, denominat cognitum ad instar entis vel relationis realis . . . Non . . . cognitio reflexa qua praecise ens rationis denominatur cognitum ut quod, sed cognitio directa quae denominatur cognitum ad instar entis id quod non est, formaliter et per se primo format ens rationis" (John of St. Thomas, *Log.*, II P., q. 2, a. 4, *dico ultimo*; Reiser, t. I, p. 304).

137 St. Thomas, *In Metaph.* lib. IV, lect. 1, n. 540.

138 Cf. above, Ch. III, n. 49.

139 Thus, "we see at once that it is not only inconceivable, but really impossible, for a thing at once to be and not be. And we thus affirm already the objective and ontological value of the principle of contradiction *before any judgment of existence*, before reflecting that this primary affirmation presupposes ideas, and before verifying the fact that these ideas come to us, by abstraction, from sensible things grasped by our senses" (R. Garrigou-Lagrange, *art. cit., Rev. de Phil.*, Jan.–Feb. and March–April, 1931, p. 18 of the offprint). (Cf. *Existence and the Existent*, pp. 26 ff., n. 13. Tr.)

(and for Leibniz, too). By the force of that violent splitting in two, that lived contradiction which is at the heart of idealism, must we not at last ask ourselves if being itself—in the likeness of which being of reason is thought and which is, in fact, conceived at first blush as a (possible) reality—must we not ask ourselves, I say, whether being itself is not a being of reason?

33. God does not make beings of reason. It is a mark of the weakness of our abstractive intellect that it is not able, in many cases, to conform itself to the real except by forming beings of reason. We can lay hold of defects in being only by conceiving them in the likeness of being.[140] "Tunc efficitur ens rationis, quando intellectus nititur apprehendere quod non est, et ideo fingit illud, ac si ens esset."[141] At this point, let us note that if there are beings of reason (like the square circle, the largest whole number, a chimera, the best possible world), which cannot exist because they are intrinsically contradictory—these are the thieves and forgers among beings of reason—there are, on the other hand, many others, the honest beings of reason, which cannot exist either, not because they themselves are composed of incompossible characteristics, but only because to posit them in existence would be incompatible with one of their objective notes. The notion "predicate" is not an absurd one, but it would be absurd to attribute existence outside the mind to a predicate, for it is defined by a certain function which a thing has precisely inasmuch as it is known.

Since these beings of reason imply in their very notion a relation to something real which is attained by the mind, they are said to be *founded on reality*. It thus happens that a being of reason, which cannot exist outside the mind as it itself is presented to the mind, i.e., as a being, does make manifest, by reason of its foundation in the real, that which exists outside the mind, and it has not even been constructed except for that purpose. To say that Neptune is observed by an astronomer is to put a relation of reason in Neptune, but it is a

---

140   And we can perceive relations only by forming a separate concept of them, abstracting from the subject in which they have or do not have their basis. Since relation is only a "between-two," a "between-things," if we can talk that way, implying in its notion neither a demand to exist in itself nor a demand to exist in something else but purely a reference of this to that, it (i.e., relation) is an intelligible object which does not necessarily and of itself imply any ontological stuff, and is real only by reason of the basis it has in its subject. "Quia ex proprio conceptu est *ad aliud*," John of St. Thomas says, with deep insight, "requirit fundamentum, non solum ut existet, sed etiam *ut sit capax existendi, id est ut sit entitas realis*" (*Log.*, II P., q. 17, a. 2). Thus, an abstractive understanding will conceive this object of thought just the same when it has a real foundation in a subject referred to a term (and then the relation is real; thus the boat really does leave the river-bank), and when it does not have a real foundation in that subject (if it has a real foundation elsewhere, then we have a relation of reason based on the real, as when the river-bank is said to withdraw from the ship). Concerning the conditions required for a relation to be real, see the article of John of St. Thomas just cited.

141   Opusc. (apocr.) *De natura generis*, cap. 3.

real fact that the astronomer does observe Neptune. Evil is a being of reason in the sense that to think of the lack of a good that should be in a subject, I am compelled to conceive that lack as if it were something. But evil does exist in a very real and very positive way, in the sense that the subject in question is indeed deprived or despoiled of a good that should exist in it. The physician does not find deafness in the ear and he does not seek to destroy it as he strives to destroy a colony of bacteria. Yet to be deprived of the sense of hearing is actually something real; the being of reason "deafness" is based on a very real disturbance in the inner organization of the ear.

Moreover, such and such objects of thought can be affected by the mark of unreality characteristic of a being of reason in very different degrees. Evil and deafness, while referring to the very real fact that a subject is deprived of some good due it, are non-beings as objects posited before the mind in the manner of substance or a quality. A geometric surface is a possible being (if it is a Euclidian surface) affected by a condition of reason that prevents it from existing in nature with the absolute lack of thickness its definition implies. Motion is the reality par excellence of sensible nature; but we can only conceive it by retaining in memory that part of it that has already flowed by, so that "if the soul did not exist," time and motion would not exist,[142] meaning they would not exist with that unreal consistence (a condition of reason) which our apprehension bestows upon them.[143] As we shall see in the next chapter, it is very important to consider the role played in our knowledge by beings of reason, founded *in re*.

---

142 "Ἀδύνατον εἶναι χρόνον ψυχῆς μὴ οὔσης . . ." (Aristotle, *Physics*, IV, 14, 223a26). On this point, see our *Philosophie bergsonienne*, 2nd ed., pp. 193–195, and xxvii–xxviii, n. 2; *Theonas*, 2nd ed., Ch. VI.

143 In these last two cases the mind has "completed" the real by some element that cannot be realized, and it is only on this account (*completive*) that the object conceived by the mind is an *ens rationis*. Cf. Cajetan, *in I*, 28, 1, *Ad primum vero dubium*; St. Thomas, *In I Sent.*, dist. 19, q. 5, a. 1.

CHAPTER IV

KNOWLEDGE OF SENSIBLE NATURE

I
THE MAIN TYPES OF KNOWING

1. WE HAVE POINTED OUT THAT SCIENCE in the precise though very general sense of knowledge perfect in its mode, and irrefragable—attains intelligible universes which are immanent in the universe of existence, but which science considers apart in order in some fashion to whip them into line with the universe of existence. These realms of knowledge are universes of abstract natures (grasped in themselves or in substitutes), universes of laws and of necessary relations. The universe of existence, on the other hand, is a universe of individuals and of events. In the latter universe there is contingency and chance; there is the irreversible flux of interacting singular formations, none of which will ever recur in exactly the same way; there is liberty. This is the universe in which we act in the midst of particular and contingent circumstances. It would be foolish to imagine that this universe could be completely reclaimed by human science. For the things we have just listed are not as such the objects of science in the strict sense.

From the speculative point of view, knowledge of the world of existence, taken precisely as concrete and existent, belongs to the realm of experience and history, of factual observation, of certitudes of perception and memory, as well as of conjecture and of well-founded opinion. In short, it belongs to the realm of the work of the intellect as immersed in the activity of the senses. From the practical point of view, it belongs to the realm of art, of prudence and of knowledge by connaturality.

Science, knowledge in the strict sense of the word, considers only the intelligible necessities immersed in the reality of this world of existence. Each of our typical knowledges considers in it one, and only one, universe of intelligible necessities, while if there is a supreme knowledge, a knowledge-in-chief, a knowledge of first principles, it will consider all these different universes together, not in such a way as to replace the particular knowledge that concerns itself with each of them, but in order to know that knowledge itself, to defend and justify its principles, and thus to establish unity. What are, then, at least in their most general types, these diverse universes of intelligibility which our intellect brings into focus when it works while, disengaged from the activity of the senses? As we have already recalled,[1] the Aristotelian tradition recognizes three principal universes, which correspond to what Thomists call the three degrees or orders of abstraction. They are:the universe of the principles and laws of sensible and mobile nature, or the world of *Physica*; the universe of quantity as such, or the world of *Mathematica*; the universe of being and of the intelligible objects which of themselves do not require matter as a condition of their real existence, or the world of *Metaphysica*.

Shall we give to these three degrees of abstraction names more in conformity with the usages of modern didactic language? Along the lines of the terminology proposed above,[2] we might say that if the whole complex that the knowing subject can attain in the transobjective subjects submitted to its intelligible grasps (that is to say, all the elements of the whole complex presented to the intellect as objectifiable),[3] constitute in general *the transobjective intelligible*,[4] then the first zone with which the human intellect is in contact in that vast whole, is a universe of objects which can be realized only in sensible or empirical existence. And so let us call it the universe of the *sensible real*.

How can the human intellect get beyond that universe? It may side-step the real by ceasing to order its knowledge to that supreme value which is existence outside the mind, I mean by busying itself with objects which can be realized (if they are realizable) only in sensible existence but which are conceived without order to existence. We have, then, the second zone of the transobjective intelligible, the universe of the *praeter-real*, the universe of the mathematician. Or it may extend beyond the sensible by busying itself with objects which are conceived as ordered to that supreme value which is extra-mental existence but which can be realized in a non-sensible, non-empirical existence. This is the third zone of the transobjective intelligible, the universe of the *trans-sensible*—the universe of the metaphysician, which opens out into the transintelligible (for us) which can be known only by analogy.

2. These three general types of knowing belong to the order of speculative knowledge. When it is a question of the order of practical knowledge, then the mind turns back from the heights of metaphysical knowledge towards the world of existence as such, and through the degrees of moral philosophy, the practical sciences which continue it and finally, prudence, reaches down to immediate contact with the singular action to be regulated. We are not concerned with this practical order at the moment.[5]

The supreme knowledge in the speculative order, the knowledge-in-chief

---

1   Cf. Ch. II, § 12.
2   See Ch. III, § 11 above.
3   These subjects, proportioned (connatural) to the human intellect, are corporeal or sensible things.
4   In the didactic term here proposed "intelligible" is taken in the sense of intelligible *for us*.
5   We will treat it in Ch. VIII and Appendix VII.

which we just mentioned, is metaphysics. We might ask ourselves with Kant whether metaphysics is possible as scientific knowledge (and our answer would be in the affirmative). We might ask ourselves with Maine de Biran and Bergson whether metaphysics itself, and by its very nature, is an experimental science (and our answer would be in the negative). In any case, no other knowledge, and particularly none of the experimental sciences, share with metaphysics the universe of the trans-sensible or of the third degree of abstraction. Inversely, there is no philosophy or ontological knowledge which shares with mathematics the universe of the praeter-real, or of the second degree of abstraction.

But on the first degree of abstraction we find two different knowledges which share the universe of the mobile or sensible real: a knowledge of the ontological order, the *philosophy of nature*, and a knowledge of the empiriological order, the experimental sciences (κατ' ἐξοχήν "Science" in modern language). It is also on this first degree that the problem, or should we say the conflict, of philosophy and science arises in its most significant fashion. We have already examined this problem as it appears from the very outset to reflexive knowledge, I mean from the methodological point of view of the theoretician of the sciences. We would like to try to go into it more deeply here from the point of view of critical philosophy. To that end, we shall return to physico-mathematical science in order to examine once again the nature of that queen and goddess of the experimental sciences.

Modern Physics Considered in its General Epistemological Type

3. As we have already seen,[6] physico-mathematical science appears from the outset as a mathematization of the sensible. From induction it requires a well-established empirical fact, but only in order to submit it to the deductive form and rule of explanation of the mathematical order. So it corresponds to the epistemological type which the ancients called "intermediary sciences" (*scientiae mediae*), sciences which straddle the physical order and the mathematical order. They are materially physical and formally mathematical. Thus, they have more affinity with mathematics than with physics as to their rule of explanation and yet at the same time are more physical than mathematical as to the terminus in which their judgments are verified.[7]

A first point, which furnished one of the themes of the chapter devoted to scientific experience, must be clarified. Physico-mathematical science does not search into the nature, itself, of physical causes. It works on the physical real but for the purpose of envisioning it from the formal point of view of mathematics, and of the mathematical laws or prescriptions which link together the measurements gathered from nature by our instruments. It resolves all its concepts into the measurable. And the deductive synthesis which it constructs

6   Cf. Ch. II, §§ 4 and 29.
7   Cf. above Ch. II, § 4.

is verified only by the coincidence of the numerical results of that synthesis with effectively discovered measurements. Thus, it does not follow that the mathematical beings which play a part in this synthesis actually represent real causes and entities which are the ontological articulations of the world of sensible nature.[8] It is only *en bloc* that the physical theory is verified by means of the correspondence established between the system of signs that it employs and experimentally known measurable events.

4. But a second point must also be emphasized, one which derives from the preceding observation that physico-mathematical knowledge remains more physical than mathematical as to its terminus even though it belongs to the mathematical order by its formal texture. Ontological preoccupations will intervene obliquely in this science. Although it will not constitute a science of physical being as such, nevertheless it will obliquely carry along with it ontological values.

The network of mathematical relations which it seeks to establish between sensible phenomena, and which constitute its most formal object, can neither satisfy by itself alone nor sufficiently stimulate the mind of the scientist. The scientist is attached to the physical real. By reason of the very reality on which his science is founded and in which it terminates, the invincible ontological tendency of the human reason as well as the pressure exercised on it in spite of everything by the principle of causality must necessarily influence him in some way. He will be led necessarily to integrate into his mathematical deduction—I am saying into the domain of the science itself—to integrate into the formally mathematical explanation of observable appearances a system of principles and causes of the physical (ontological) order which he will have reconstructed for this purpose. (Thus the intuition of a physically conceivable explicative entity will often be found at the initial conception of a new theory.)[9] And so such a science will bear within it a relation to real being considered not

---

8   *Ibid.*, § 29.
9   The mathematical manipulation, however, will involve certain consequences to which M. Emile Picard has rightly called attention. "If we ask on what Fresnel's theory of waves is based, we must reply—and here we are touching on a capital point of scientific philosophy—on a system of *differential equations*. But, and this fact is sometimes forgotten, these equations were only able to be constructed by starting from a molecular conception of ether as medium, making numerous hypotheses on the relations of this ether with ponderable matter, and passing from the discontinuous to the continuous in a way to obtain the differential equations, reduced moreover, in order to avoid inextricable analytical difficulties, to the linear form, as in so many physico-mathematical questions. More or less analogous circumstances are found everywhere, and, under these conditions, we can see how difficult it is to definitely condemn the initial conception of any theory" (Emile Picard, *Un coup d'oeil sur l'histoire des sciences et des théories physiques. Lecture faite le 16 décembre 1929 à l'Académie des Sciences*, p. 34).

only as an inexhaustible source of effectuable measurements but also as the basis of the reconstructions of which I have just been speaking.

It is important to observe immediately that this science is completely indifferent as to whether these explicative entities so constructed are real beings or whether they are beings of reason. It is for the philosopher, if he can, to make this distinction among the diverse entities used by the physicist. The physicist himself does not bother about that, since all that matters for him is the explicative value of these entities in function of the network of equations of the physical theory. And so his ontological appetite will be as well, if not better, satisfied by beings of reason as by real beings.

It may happen that the scientist will be shocked at hearing the philosopher talking in this vein. Much misunderstanding arises from the fact that the two of them attach a different meaning to the word "real." The philosopher opposes real being to being of reason in the logical and critical sense that we have made precise here, and it is very important for him to seek to which of these two classes the entities he deals with belong. That opposition and that investigation have no interest for the physicist as such; he is even unaware that they exist. He maintains that as long as they are defined by at least theoretically realizable operations of measurement, the entities he uses are real, that is to say, they express in an authentically physical fashion the real behavior of nature. Doubtless, replies the philosopher. That is what they are made for, even those among them which are most obviously *entia rationis*. And not to be outdone by his colleague, the physicist will immediately add that these real entities are "shadows" or allusions from which it would be silly to expect anything concerning the intimate nature of matter. . . .

Real Being and Being of Reason in Physico-Mathematical Knowledge

5. We may verify here in a typical case the importance, which we pointed out at the end of the preceding chapter, of the role of beings of reason in human knowledge. Since a being of reason—the order existing among the objects of our concepts taken precisely as known, that is to say, according to the life they lead in our mind—since a being of reason constitutes the specifying object of Logic (that is the privilege of this science), we might be tempted to think that *entia rationis* play a role only in Logic. That would be a grave mistake. Even common knowledge continually makes use of beings of reason. For example, such is the case when we say *"evil* has triumphed in his soul," or "this man was the victim of *his own deafness*," or "the sun *rises*," for *evil* and *deafness* are privations, not essences capable of subsisting, and the sun does not really climb in the sky. Mathematics constantly forms beings of reason, such as irrational number, imaginary number, transfinite number,[10] the species of

---

10 We think that transfinite number is a *possible real* entity (absolutely speaking) as to the transcendental multitude, infinite in act, implied in its very notion, but that it is *of reason* as to the *unity of the whole* which completes this notion (and

configurations, etc. And it is clear that a knowledge of the physical real which does not examine the essence and the causes of it in themselves, in their properly physical or ontological reality, but which reconstructs it from the pure point of view of the relations of measurement involved in it and according to the exigencies of a mathematical deduction as general as possible, will necessarily make use of many beings of reason as indispensable auxiliaries. There will be, moreover, beings of every degree among the entities which enable the physicist to think his numerical registers in function of the actual state of physical knowledge. Thus, there will be in the first place a multitude of entia rationis more-or-less elaborated which merely correspond to experimental observations and conceptually translate observable causations[11] and observable structures of the real. Then, there will be entities like the atom and electron which appear, in answer to the question an sit, to be realities (something exists which the words electron and atom circumscribe determinately), and, in answer to the question *quid sit*, to be not only approximative but symbolic images of the primordial parts of the spatio-temporal organization of matter (let us say they[12] are symbolically reconstructed real beings). Finally, there will be entities of which Einsteinian "times" afford the best-known examples today, and which are completely beings of reason, substitutes for certain realities whose ontological value is of no interest to science. We are speaking, naturally, of beings of reason founded on the real, since they are founded on the real behavior of nature, on measurements and facts really culled from nature—for example, on the findings of Michelson—but which remain beings of reason, entities incapable of existing as such, and which have no more intrinsic and direct ontological value than the material models constructed in space by Lord Kelvin.

6. How are we to understand this formation of explicative entities which appear to be *entia rationis* of various degrees and are nevertheless always founded on reality? An answer is possible only by holding to an exact doctrine concerning quantity.

When we consider things from the point of view of the philosopher and not

---

which is only a unity of apprehension), and this permits the return, so to speak, and the analogical reimposition of the mathematical order and of mathematical considerations of equality, inequality, etc., on the purely metaphysical order to which transcendental multitude taken simply as such belongs. "God made whole numbers," said Kronecker, "all the rest are the work of man."

11   See below, Ch. IV, n. 39.

12   M. Wolfers rightly complains that "many researchers have adopted the habit of reasoning about electrons, protons, photons and atoms like pawns in a game of chess, forgetting that these terms still conceal hypotheses, obscurities and subjective ideas" (*Transmutation des éléments*, Paris, Soc. d'édit. scientif., 1929, p. 19). On the physical significance of wave-mechanics, cf. André George, *L' oeuvre de Louis de Broglie et la physique d'aujourd'hui*, par. III (Paris, 1931). "The attempts at physical representation by more or less traditional means have not succeeded."

of the physicist, and speak the former's language, then quantity, that is to say the extension of substance and of its metaphysical unity into diverse parts according to position, is a real property of bodies. There are in nature real dimensions, numbers and measurements,[13] a real space,[14] a real time.[15] It is

---

13   Cf. R. Dalbiez, "Dimensions absolues et mésures absolues," *Revue Thomiste*, March–April 1925. And we might make more precise here what we wrote in *Théonas* (2nd ed., Ch. VI and nn. 21 and 23). On the basis of the Aristotelian doctrine of the three kinds of predicamental relations (*In Metaph.*, Bk. V, Ch. 15, lect. 17 of St. Thomas; cf. John of St. Thomas, *Curs. Phil., Log.*, II P., q. 17), we must distinguish the measure of specification, which is the basis of relations of the third kind and which rules the thing measured *secundum comensurationem esse et veritatis* (this measure is as such of another order than what is measured), and the measure *of comparison*, which is the basis for relations of the first kind, and which compares in particular a number with a unity, a size with a standard (mathematical measure).

Our physical measures imply a *transcendental relation* (or *secundum dici*) of our unities and our instruments to the reality to be measured; a real (predicamental) relation *secundum esse* of the *first* kind referring the quantity measured to our unities (measure of comparison); and a relation *secundum esse* of relation of reason of the third kind making the way in which we conceive the being of the things measured depend on our mensurations (measure of specification).

Besides the real (ontological) measures of specification, which can even be concerned with quality (for we believe that it is to this category of measures that must be related the *mensura intrinseca* "quae est in mensurato sicut accidens in subjecto" [St. Thomas, *In II. Sent.*, dist. 2, q. 1, a. 2, ad 1]; so that a body is intrinsically "measured" by its own dimensions, ontologically determined), there are in nature real measures of comparison, which are ontological measures, according to which things, and in particular their dimensions, are extrinsically determined and linked to one another in a unity of coordination or of subordination ("unumquodque mensuratur simplicissimo sui generis" [*Sum. Theol.*, I, 10, 6]; cf. *In Metaph.*, lib. X, lect. 2), and which the philosopher can call numbers (in the sense in which, according to St. Thomas, as we recall below, number exists *a parte rei* and a numerable before being numbered), but which has nothing to do with the numbers found by an observer (the physicist's numbers). This is, for example, how the times linked to the most fundamental motion (which the ancients sought on the side of sidereal motions, and that are sought today rather on the side of intra-atomic motions or of the motion of light) measures the other times of the material universe. (Similarly, St. Thomas will say that there is only one *aevum*, measured by the duration of the first angel, since the concept of measure can be used analogically.) But the measure or standard of nature is unknown to us, since in reality there is here no measure or standard to be applied to a quantity, but only the ontological foundation of such an application. If there are measures and standards, they are only those which the Creative Intelligence has had in mind.

St. Thomas explains (*In Phys. Arist.*, lib. IV, lect. 23) that without a numerating mind there cannot be any numeration but there can be number: "Sicuti possunt esse sensibilia sensu non existente, ita possunt esse numerabilia et numerus non existente numerante." In other words, this number is not numbered (in act). It can be called "numbered number" only because it offers itself for numeration;

precisely under the conditions and modalities of this real quantity, or, to put it in another way, it is as quantitatively measured and regulated, that the interacting causes in nature develop their qualitative activities. *In mensura, pondere et numero.* Physical reality abounds with entitative riches that are irreducible to quantity. But, by reason of its materiality, and from the fact that it emanates from corporeal substance through the intermediary of quantity, this world of qualities is subjected intrinsically to quantitative determinations (and that is why it is accessible to our extrinsic and artificial mensurations). Quantity thus considered ontologically as the first accident of corporeal substances and as the matrix of cosmic activities is an object of the philosopher-of-nature's consideration. And yet he is not able to pass from such consideration to a knowledge of the quantitative determinations to which the things of the physical world are subject, nor to discover for human use the measures and standards of nature.

But quantity can be considered in an entirely different way. It can be disengaged from its subject by an *abstractio formalis*, and held before the mind for itself alone, thus constituting by itself alone a separated universe of knowledge (the universe of the praeter-real). It is then considered no longer ontologically, or from the point of view of being, but quantitatively, or from the point of view of the very relations of order and measurement which the objects of thought discernible in it, as forms or essences proper to it, maintain among themselves. Quantity so considered is the object of the mathematician. I am quite well aware that for many modern theorists of pure mathematics, the latter has no object other than purely formal logical relations, so that according to the celebrated definition of Bertrand Russell, it is reduced to "a study in which one does not know what he is talking about or whether or not what he says is true," to a discipline without content, and to which a definite objective content may only be supplied by physics. But I think that this nominalist tendency has prevailed in mathematics only because an unjustifiable abandonment of intuition has been foisted upon the valuable rational discoveries represented by the development of axiomatics.[16]

"numerus numeratus dicitur . . . id quod numeratur actu, vel quod est numerabile" (*ibid.*, lect. 17).

14   See below, §§ 18 and 19.

15   Cf. *Théonas, loc. cit.*, and nn. 9, 14, 15, 16, 17.

16   As M. René Poirier observes correctly (*Essai*, pp. 126–127), "any theory can be called axiomatic if its postulates and indefinables are plainly set forth. Every rigorously formal science is then axiomatic. But this term can also designate, in opposition to another theory in which an attempt is made to preserve the customary comprehension of the primitive notions the ones in which no meaning whatsoever is attributed to the primitive notions and in which the latter are viewed as simple terms whose whole significance consists in being used according to some or other particular formal conventions. In this sense current intuitive geometry is not axiomatic, whereas Hilbert's geometry is almost perfectly so. The ambiguity is apparent in formulae like the following, which everybody

The intuition of which we are speaking here is not an intelligible intuition (nor a pure intuition in the Kantian sense), as the geometricians believed for a long time when they thought that their proper object was a world of Platonic models delineated in an amorphous milieu which pre-existed the figures that specified it (an eternal container conditioning the universe) and which would be "space." Nor is it an experimental intuition belonging to external perception, with the observations and measurements we effect by means of our senses and our instruments. It is an imaginative intuition, an intuition of the "internal sense" which depends on external perception only as a presupposition, as does the imagination itself.

We can clearly grasp this role of the imagination from the fact that quantity, which is the first accident of corporeal substance, precedes (by a priority of nature) the whole qualitative (energetic and physical) order and therefore the whole sensible order, and yet is itself known to the senses by means of sensible qualities, though not without the whole synergic elaboration of perception (for it is a "common sensible"). Thus, the imagination at the service of the intellect can penetrate into the world of pure quantity, detached by abstraction from sensible matter. It can do this, moreover, precisely insofar as the imagination, though it presupposes the external sense, is free from it (by which I mean its objects are not subject to the conditions of relativity which affect *hic et nunc* those of perception and which derive from actual dependence on external physical circumstances). And so it is that the intuitive schemes of the imagination—which are not at all the object itself of mathematics but only the sensible symbol or illustration of that object—manifest to us in a sensible way, though independent of every experimental condition, essences and properties which of themselves precede the sensible order and are independent of it. Moreover, though this role of the imagination does not at all dispense from

accepts without understanding them in the same way: every theoretical science should tend towards the axiomatic form. If we adopted the first of the two senses just enunciated, this simply means that such a science ought to be expounded in a rigorous hypothetico-deductive fashion. If we adopt the second sense we reach a more seditious conclusion, namely, every pure science consists in the invention of an algorithm and set up in such a way that the judgments about its subject correspond to judgments of experience in a purely symbolic and verbal manner. In other words, a truly abstract theory of phenomena is made of symbols deprived of meaning." Contrary to M. Poirier, we do not think that the first thesis implies the second.

On the other hand, we may indeed suspect that it has been the development of physico-mathematical science alongside that of axiomatics that has been at least partially the occasion of the epistemological perturbation by which those moderns who misconceive one of the basic hierarchies of knowing tend to integrate mathematics—to the extent that it is given a content—with physics. A correct critical appreciation of physico-mathematical science as *scientia media* by the very fact that it requires an exact notion of the pure epistemological types which come together in it would, on the contrary, restore to mathematics its independent content and superior rank.

the strict and meticulous rationality of the logical verifications as the intuitionists too often have seemed to believe, nevertheless it is indispensable, since the object is not here purely intelligible as in the case of metaphysics. And so it is necessary that constructibility in imaginative intuition manifest *ad sensum* the intrinsic possibility of the entities considered by the mind, especially the indefinables which are at the origin of the science, and so assure us that far from involving any secret incompossibility, they are veritable essences (on the basis of which beings of reason capable of ideal existence can, in their turn, be constructed).

When the entities constructed or reconstructed by the axiomatic method are not directly figurable in intuition, they at least fall indirectly and by analogy within the field of the imaginable. The latter is the case with non-Euclidian multiplicities whose legitimacy was imposed on all geometricians on the day when, following Beltrami, it was seen that an Euclidian translation of them was possible. But, in any case, such entities appear, by this very attachment to the intuitive sources of mathematics, to constitute for the latter a content, a proper field of truth and of intelligibility. And this field is absolutely independent in itself (if not in the prescientific ways which lead our mind to it) of physical observations and experimentable existences. Thus the confusion of mathematics and logic comes from a fundamental ignorance of the true nature of logic. For a non-reflexive science, which does not, like Logic, find its proper object in the objects of the other sciences insofar as they are considered in the mind ("insofar as they are known"), has necessarily its own domain of knowable natures, a proper and direct objective content.

Though an entirely new synthesis must be built on their principles, nevertheless the ancients saw that the objective content of mathematical knowing is indeed the beings of quantity taken as such, their proper forms and "qualities,"[17] the relational structures and properties of order and measure decipherable in continuous and in discrete quantity. On the one hand, the unceasing conquests of modern mathematics compel us to deepen, as by successive logical soundings, to revise and refine, many notions formerly accepted concerning these beings. On the other hand, by a sort of attempt at the absolute spiritualization of all mathematical knowledge, for some three centuries number has tended to reduce and absorb the irremediably potential domain of the continuous, and at the same time to escape, if such were indeed possible, from quantity and spatiality in order to extend its empire over transcendental multitude. However this may be, these mathematical beings, as we have already pointed out, abstract not only from existence but even from any order to existence and so, though they remain legitimate objects of science, they can be *indifferently*, either *real* (in the philosopher's sense)[18] or *of reason*. And it is

17   See above, Ch. II, n. 26.
18   It goes without saying that the word "real" is not taken here in the sense in which the mathematician distinguishes real numbers from imaginary numbers. Irra-

precisely by entering so decidedly into the field of the being of reason and of pure ideality that modern mathematics has made so many admirable discoveries.

7. Now, since quantity, which is the first accident of bodies, is grasped by mathematical knowledge at a higher degree of abstraction and of immateriality than the physical degree,[19] it is possible to have a mathematical exegesis of the physical real. Nor is it difficult to grasp the fact, therefore, that the physico-mathematician will be as indifferent as the pure mathematician to the *real being* or *being of reason* characteristic of the entities he employs. He may even be led, moreover, to make use of entities presented to him by mathematics and most certainly inapt for extramental existence to explain the extramental real, as is only too evident in our day. Consequently, the universe that he constructs will become as unfigurable as the mathematical beings of reason which he employs in its construction, beings of reason which are no longer directly representable in imaginative intuition as are the *entia realia* of Euclidian geometry and of the arithmetic of whole numbers.

It is still true, however, that mathematical beings of reason are founded on mathematical real beings, and that the latter have been disengaged by mathematical abstraction from experience of the real world, apprehended in the heart of that same real quantity which the philosopher considers ontologically. Real quantity is there, and that is what gives definitively and in the most

---

tional numbers are real numbers in the mathematical sense—and the philosopher must hold them as beings of reason, as imaginary numbers. Imaginary number is so called because it does not correspond truly to the notion of number, it is an analytical expression.

19   "Mathematica dicuntur per abstractionem a naturalibus; naturalia autem se habent per appositionem ad mathematica; superaddunt enim mathematicis naturam sensibilem et motum, a quibus mathematicalia abstrahunt: et sic patet quod ea quae sunt de ratione mathematicalium salvantur in naturalibus, et non e converso" (St. Thomas Aquinas, *In de Coelo et Mundo*, lib. III, lect. 3). That is why anyone studying nature can use mathematical principles in his demonstrations: "Magnitudo addit positionem supra numerum; unde punctus dicitur esse unitas posita. Similiter autem corpus naturale addit materiam sensibilem super magnitudinem mathematicam: et ideo non est inconveniens si naturalis in demonstrationibus utatur principiis mathematicis" (*ibid.*, lib. 1, lect. 3. Cf. above, Ch. II, n. 30).

This use of mathematical principles in the knowledge of nature can remain accidental and represent a borrowing by the *naturalis* from mathematics, or it may be essential to the science considered, which is then properly a *scientia media*; and obviously diverse degrees of accidental "mathematization" must lead progressively from purely physical science to *scientia media*. The physico-mathematics of the moderns realizes perfectly the type of *scientia media*. But we do not believe that the use of mathematics in biology, for example, or psychology will ever succeed in subordinating these disciplines in this typical fashion to the rules of mathematical explanation.

radical fashion a basis in the real for the entities constructed by the physicist and enables him to return from such mathematical constellations to the earth of nature from which he derives measurements effected with the aid of conventional standards and from which he rises to those mathematical skies. It is this unlimited circulation that assures the perpetual growth of physico-mathematical science.

Finally, by this very growth this science, though not itself concerned with the ontological as such, will pile up physical facts. And these latter, however wrapped up in theories, however difficult it may be to formulate them apart, have, nevertheless, their own proper and independent value. Among the entities constructed by this science those which more directly (I mean with less theoretical interpositions) correspond to experimental data will have the stronger index of reality and will involve less completely the conditions of reason. Moreover, the progress that theoretical physics—the more speculative part of physico-mathematics—achieves by the ever greater use of mathematical ideality, should not blind us to the immense treasury of purely physical results, of observable facts and causations, in short of *entia realia*, accumulated by laboratory physics—the more experimental part of physico-mathematics— even though they be of a more particular nature and, so, less interesting for the philosopher.

Ontological Explanation and Empiriological Explanation and Some Recastings of the Notion of Causality

8. By submitting completely to the attraction of mathematical explanation and becoming informed by mathematics, physics has achieved its autonomy with regard to philosophy. That is the great scientific revolution wrought by da Vinci, Galileo and Descartes. The other experimental sciences have followed the example of physics more-or-less completely and more-or-less rapidly. For three centuries we have witnessed, and we still continue to witness, a general enfranchisement of the sciences of phenomena. If we seek to characterize the way in which this enfranchisement has been brought about, we may say that alongside the conceptual lexicon of philosophy, which is of the ontological order, there has been established an entirely different conceptual lexicon of the empiriological order.

When we observe a material object which is, so to speak, the meeting place of two knowledges, sensible and intellectual, we are in the presence of a sort of sensible flux stabilized by an idea, or to put it the other way around, an ontological or thinkable core manifested by an ensemble of qualities perceived hic et nunc. (On a botanical excursion I encounter a plant previously unknown to me. It is a being of a certain species—and one which my sense of sight, smell and touch eagerly explore in order to discern its characteristic notes. With regard to it I may wonder: What is a vegetative living thing? I may wonder: How will I classify it in my catalogue of herbs?) In such cases there are, consequently, two ways in which our concepts may be resolved. There can be a resolution ascending towards intelligible being, in which the sensible remains, but indirectly and at the service of intelligible being, as connoted by it. And there can be a resolution descending towards the sensible and observable as such,[20] in which, no doubt we do not absolutely renounce being (for without being there would be no thought), but in which being passes into the service of the sensible itself, and especially of the measurable, and is but an unknown which assures the constancy of certain sensible determinations and certain measures, and permits the delineation of stable limits circumscribing the object of the senses. This is, indeed, the law of the resolution of concepts in the experimental sciences. We may designate these two types of resolution of concepts, or of explanation, as *ontological* (in the most general sense of the word)[21] and *empiriological* or spatio-temporal, respectively.

Needless to say, in "ontological" explanation, being is still considered (as long as it is confined, as in the present chapter, to the first degree of abstraction) in the order of sensible and observable data. But the mind enters that order in the search for their intimate nature and intelligible reasons. That is why, in following this path, it arrives at notions like corporeal substance, quality, operative potency, material or formal cause, etc.—notions which, while they bear reference to the observable world, do not designate objects which are themselves representable to the senses and expressible in an image or a spatio-temporal scheme. Such objects are not defined by observations or measurements to be effected in a given way.

On the other hand, in "empiriological" explanations, as we noted a moment ago, ontology is still present, since it is a question of intellectual knowledge and we do not become animals without reason in order to construct experimental science. In this sense, the scientist, like any other man, remains firmly fixed to ontology. But ontology is present in empiriological explanation only indirectly and obliquely. Ontology is never disengaged, there, for its own sake. It exists there only as a foundation for empirical representations and definitions or physico-mathematical entities. The mind, then, goes out to its object as to the source of certain constant registers, as to a complex which can be designated, by its encounter in a given way with our senses and our instru-

---

20   Cf. above, Ch. II, § 13.

21   This use of the word "ontological" extends beyond the field of that part of philosophy that is general ontology or metaphysics. It designates a characteristic common to all the philosophical disciplines. To prevent any misunderstanding we should add that *ontology* so understood does not at all corner the claims and demands of reality. While these are manifested in a different way in empiriological knowledge, they are no less pressing here than in ontological knowledge. So it would be a mistake to consider our position to be in opposition to that of E. Meyerson on this point. When physics constructs beings of reason, it is only in order the better to grasp observable reality—according to its own mode of conceptualization and explanation.

ments. Thus the type, or the essential conditions, of the *observability* of the object plays a determining role with regard to scientific explanation. All the derivative notions introduced by science in order to "improve" description in such wise that "the trees do not hide the forest," are constructed only to condense the observable or the measurable. And if the analysis leads to terms not themselves attainable by the senses (or if it is a question of psychology, by introspection, since all experimental psychology is not necessarily behavioristic), those terms are still conceived in relation to imaginary registers and perceptions (even impossible in fact, as in the case of ether for example), as hidden observables indirectly attained by means of the patent observables which demand them. Thus, all the notions employed belong strictly to the order of what falls, or might have fallen, or should be able to fall within the experience of the senses.[22] In this sense, and to speak succinctly, we may say that empiriological explanation has no ontological value, that is, *directly* ontological. It attains the being of things only obliquely and as an indirect foundation, without making it known in itself. What it works on are the natures or essences of the corporeal world, but these are not as such its proper object.

9. In this very empiriological category two clearly different types of explanation can be distinguished. The empirical content (in this case the measurable) may receive its form and its rule of explanation from mathematics. Then we have an "empiriometric" type of explanation characteristic of physico-mathematical science. Or, the empirical content (in this case the observable in general) may call for a purely experimental form and rule of explanation. Then we have an "empirioschematic"[23] type of explanation characteristic of the non-mathematical, or at least non-mathematicized, sciences of observation. We shall come back to this distinction later. For the moment we wish merely to note that in both cases the empiriological terminology proper to the sciences of phenomena tends to be established in a more and more perfect independence from the ontological terminology of philosophy.[24]

This sort of purification is particularly far advanced in physics. Either by the elaboration of new concepts or the recasting of definitions, or by a new use of common concepts (of a philosophical or pre-philosophical origin), applied exclusively to sensible verifications, sciences like biology and experimental psychology, which can be put under the empirioschematic type—we shall say

---

22   It is precisely this which, in the working of the sciences of nature, founds the Kantian notion of phenomenon (abstracting from the philosophical system in which that notion is rooted).

23   By this we mean that experience itself is not thought or rationalized according to the law of mathematical conceptualization, but according to the experimental schemas themselves discovered by reason in the phenomena.

24   That is what an eminent scientist calls "an assertion of freedom for autonomous development" (A. S. Eddington, *The Nature of the Physical World*, p. xvii).

in a moment under what conditions and with what reservations—also tend to establish a more and more autonomous notional terminology. Since they abide in a much less precarious continuity with philosophy, it is more difficult for them than for physics to isolate this terminology and to prevent its being invaded by philosophical concepts which, in this domain, would give rise to pseudo-explanations. They persevere in the attempt, however, and often seem even to prefer rudimentary conceptual tools (like the system of psychological notions employed by the Freudian school)[25] on condition that it assures this independence.

Thus, in a general fashion, within the whole empiriological register the resolution of concepts is made in an infra-philosophical direction. *What* things are *in themselves* does not interest them. What is important are the possibilities of empirical observation and measurement which those things represent, as well as the possibility of linking together according to stable laws the data furnished by these observations and measurements. Every definition should be given, not now "by means of the proximate genus and specific difference," but by well-determined observable and measurable properties, with the means of rediscovery and practical verification being stated in each case.

So, for such knowledge, the possibility of observation and measurement replaces the essence or quiddity which philosophy seeks in things.

Similarly the register of conditionality (which keeps the mind in the order of the sensible and imaginable) tends to substitute itself for that of causality, which, when pure, leads immediately to beings of reason, not representable to the senses.

10. At least such is the *ideal* towards which empiriological knowledge tends. In fact its notional materials are far from being homogeneous. If a cross-section were made, what we would find, even for a single notional function, would be a series of layers of conceptualization exhibiting different intelligible densities and, so to speak, different indices of refraction. For example, not only is the existence of stable natures or essences in the corporeal world a postulate of the scientist's prephilosophy, but in the very practice of science the natural notion of this ontological core furnished by common sense continues to play a role on certain planes, while on others it will be replaced by the scientifically recast notion of the possibility of measurement. In a similar fashion there are different notions of causality that a scientist will use all at once on different planes of conceptualization. There is the ontological notion of "cause" as activity productive of being, furnished in a confused state by common sense and incarnate, for it, in an observable or measurable relation. Then there is the vulgar (and, to tell the truth, intrinsically ambiguous) empirio-ontological

---

25   We should not forget that in spite of the value of the psychoanalytic method of investigation the (empiriological) psychology of Freud is itself contaminated by a general philosophy which is fundamentally erroneous.

notion of "cause" as a phenomenon productive of another phenomenon. There is also the scientific empirio-ontological (philosophical and mechanistic) notion of "cause" as a phenomenon to which another phenomenon is linked in a necessarily universal concatenation in which a "law" of the world is expressed. Finally, there is the pure empiriological notion of "cause" (from which any trace of philosophical content has been eliminated) as the spatio-temporal conditions of a phenomenon, or the constellation of observable and measurable determinations to which a phenomenon is linked. This last notion of "cause" finds its perfect expression in the formulation of physical connections with the aid of mathematical relations like those furnished by differential or tensorial calculus. On this plane of conditionality, the idea of transitive action, constantly changing under the diverse masks of causality which we have indicated briefly here, is completely molded into the idea of phenomenal co-determination.

At the same time, science reaches a sort of critical point in this regard, as we see today. As it progresses in its own line, it sees some of its laws take on the form of statistical laws thrusting causal determinations into the background. Other laws are transformed into so-called identity-laws or "truisms," which explain the behavior of things by the behavior itself, changed, thanks to a few mathematical disguises, into a property of the structure of a world fabricated on purpose by the mind (that is what has happened particularly in the geometrical recasting of certain chapters of physics, as that concerning gravitation).

But above all, once it had crossed the threshold of the atomic world, it discovered that mechanics cannot account for the movement of a particle in a manner completely determined at each instant. Wave-mechanics teaches us that it is impossible to assign a determined trajectory to a particle associated with a group of waves. The latter allows only the probability of the presence of this particle in a more-or-less extensive area to be known, and the particle can never have a perfectly defined position and a perfectly defined energy at the same time. The quantum mechanics of Heisenberg and Born, which is in agreement with the wave-mechanics of Louis de Broglie and Schroedinger, although it points out that the principles of that mechanics must be given a statistical significance and views the associated wave as a pure mathematical symbol, likewise abandons the possibility of following the movement of each particle. So science reaches the "principle of indetermination" or Heisenberg's "relations of uncertainty." It is possible to determine the speed of a particle only by leaving its position undetermined at the same instant, or to determine its position only by leaving its speed undetermined at the same instant.[26] The reason for this is that in order to observe the position of an electron with

---

26   More precisely: the product of the error concerning the position times the error
      concerning the state of movement is always at least equal to Planck's constant
      (h).

precision its speed must be disturbed (by illuminating it with a light of short wavelength of low quantum). "The traditional idea which attributes a completely determined position, speed and trajectory to a corpuscle" must be abandoned definitively. We can no longer attribute "a well-defined energy to a corpuscle, but only speak of the probability that it will show up with a certain energy."[27] Henceforth the series of waves is, in Heisenberg's words, only a *parcel of probabilities.*

So we see science obliged to abandon determinism precisely under the form in which determinism is "scientific," and signifies not that the course of natural events excludes all contingency, but simply that, on the hypothesis that certain circumstances are given at a certain instant, the laws of nature permit us to determine strictly the way in which a certain material phenomenon will offer itself for observation and measurement as a subsequent instant.[28] So we see what has happened to the principle of causality, precisely under the form of

---

27   Louis de Broglie, *Introduction à l'étude de la méchanique ondulatoire* (Paris, 1930, p. 150).

28   Here it is important to point out an equivocation which victimizes the public all too often (and sometimes scientists themselves), and which, to tell the truth, constitutes a gross sophism.

The philosophical principle *natura determinatur ad unum* which was discussed above (Ch. II, §§ 3 and 4) is translated on the empiriological plane for the scientist by the following formula. "The initial state of a (material) system shielded from any external action completely determines its subsequent states." Or again, "If the state of a universe (composed, by hypothesis, of purely material agents) be given at a certain instant, the state of that universe at any subsequent instant is completely determined." This is simply the statement of scientific determinism.

But the very statement of that formula presupposes, implicitly and explicitly, that the speaker is confronted by purely material systems, by purely material agents and phenomena (in the philosophical sense of this word, i.e., the behavior of which depends entirely on the natures in interaction) for which the law of causality takes precisely this form. Scientific determinism is thus a *conditional* determinism (that we "suppose that there are only purely material agents"). It is not at all an absolute determinism, determinism as a philosophical doctrine, which denies the possibility of free will. It is a simple piece of trickery to draw from this formula an argument in favor of philosophical determinism, and conclude that there can be no spiritual and free agents. For by definition their behavior, insofar as it is free, escapes the domain of the sciences of matter; and their action, without changing the laws proper to matter, prevents, by the introduction of a new (non-material) factor, the initial state of a system in which they are found from completely determining the subsequent states.

Similarly, the formula of scientific determinism presupposes that all the conditions of the initial state (or of a state considered at a given instant) be given, and thence it follows that a subsequent state is determined. But it in no wise states that certain of these conditions cannot be simple positions of fact (depending, for example, on the intersection of causal lines, or, if it be a question of the absolutely initial state, of an arbitrary decision). That is why, as was shown in Ch. II, scientific determinism does not exclude contingency in the philosophical sense of the word.

phenomenal co-determination to which science had reduced it! It is exposed to exceptions, riddled with lacunae, deprived of its universal value. And, indeed, the abandonment of the properly ontological (philosophical) point of view does not allow any protest against this result. It is obvious that it had to come to this point with a science deliberately dedicated to pure empiriology or empiriometry and more and more captured by mathematical being of reason. (We are indebted to the New Physics for having brought this feature out into the open.) But scientists do not seem to be yet prepared to resign themselves to this, for their work of research derives its inspiration from the common belief in the principle of causality. So, as did Einstein, they look for the day when "strict causality" will regain its sovereignty in physics. Einstein expressed this wish in 1927.[29] Since then micro-physics seems, on the contrary, to have increased its "indeterminist" tendency.[30] Whatever form it may take in the future, even if it could return to the methods or merely to the idea[31] of

29   "It is only in the theory of quanta that the differential method of Newton becomes inadequate, and strict causality is effectively lacking to us. But the last word has not been said. May the spirit of the method of Newton enable us to re-establish the accord between physical reality and the most profound characteristic feature of Newton's teaching, strict causality" (Message on the occasion of Newton's centenary, *Nature*, March 26, 1927, p. 467).

30   Contrary to Einstein, Dirac considers the possibility of a return to "strict causality" as definitively excluded. "Since physics is concerned with observable magnitudes, the classical determinist theory is indefensible. . . . In the theory of quanta also, we begin with certain numbers and deduce other numbers. Let us try to penetrate the physical essence with these two series of numbers. The disturbances that an observer inflicts on a system in order to observe it are directly subject to his control and are acts of his free will. Only the numbers which describe these acts of free choice can be taken as the initial numbers for calculation in the theory of quanta. . . ." (*Mémoire au Congrès Solvay de 1927*). Thus, by the rigorous application of the principle that "Physics is only concerned with observable magnitudes," the physicist becomes aware of the inalienable part that he and "his acts of free choice" take in his calculation of phenomena. It cannot be otherwise since he can only observe with the aid of material means, and not as a pure spirit (cf. below, Ch. IV, § 33).

31   As a matter of fact, M. Paul Langevin, in the process of renovating physical representation, wa s compelled to realize Einstein's wish and surmount the indeterminist crisis. (Cf. André George, *L'oeuvre de Louis de Broglie et la physique d'aujourd'hui*, Paris, ed. by de Cerf, 1931; the author refers to a lecture of Langevin at the College de France and to conferences given by him at the Union Rationaliste in 1930 still unpublished at the time of this writing.) Langevin points out that the question: Is it possible to follow the movement of a particle by determining its speed and position at each instant? only arises if one first admits the notion of an individual particle. But if there is no individual, the question of the application of the law of causality to its behavior does not arise. He proposes, therefore, to sacrifice corpuscular individuality to save determinism.

    Langevin's attempt seems to proceed, not only from purely scientific preoccupations, but also from philosophical conceptions which to our mind are inaccurate. For example, according to him it is in virtue of an anthropomorphic

strict determination, what is important for the philosopher and throws a singular light on the nature of empirio-logical knowledge (and, incidentally, justifies this digression) is the fact that science one day came to find itself in such a characteristic state with regard to causality as that in which we actually see it.

11. Now, to resume the theme with which we began, the heterogeneity of materials of the same notional line used by science is evident. A vast field of critical analysis is thereby opened up which we have wished merely to indicate in passing. The essential thing to understand is that it would be a serious mistake to conceive science in a static fashion as something achieved, "completely made." And this is true not only from the point of view of its extension and of the objects it has to know, which is obvious, but also from the point of view of its internal noetic morphology and of its intension with regard to its typical forms. By the very fact that it leaves behind its pre-scientific basis in common sense in order to attain more and more purely the state of science, its progressive extensive growth is accompanied by a progressive intrinsic formation which brings it into line with certain determined epistemological types which it has as yet only realized partially and to diverse degrees. But though a total and homogeneous realization of these ideal types must be regarded as an asymptotic limit, it is remarkable how science, encroaching, so to speak, on future possibilities and undergoing especially the exigencies of its ideal form, uses only materially, and as though without recognizing them or rendering them competent, notions which belong to less evolved strata of conceptualization. The formal element of scientific intelligibility is current especially in the higher strata, in notions which are most typically pure. That is why in the kind of knowing with which we are at present concerned, the sciences of

extrapolation that the notion of individual is applied to the atomic world, "the portion of matter that we label and can follow is a projection of our individual consciousness," which amounts to a denial of any ontological value to the notion of individuality. On the other hand, in seeking to save scientific determinism, it seems that he also pretends to save the philosophically determinist conception of the principle of causality, not making any distinction between the two realms. But nothing prevents us from supposing that on the empiriological plane science may find it decidedly to its advantage to be rid of the idea of corpuscular individuality as it rid itself of the notion of absolute time. Since in the new dynamics physical masses are represented by pure mathematical symbols (*operative factors*), it is conceivable that a being of reason taking the place of a corpuscle can be constructed from which the note of individuality would be excluded. It should be noted, however, that in the actual state of science Langevin's solution encounters serious difficulties. Louis de Broglie does not seem disposed to rally to it. Cf. A. George, *op. cit.*, pp. 42–44: the author remarks that the abandonment of the individual corpuscle is not easily reconciled with atomic conceptions which have become fundamental in modern physics, nor with many experiments concerning photons and electrons (the method of C. T. R. Hilson, the Compton effect, photo-electric effect . . .).

phenomena, the formally activating value is linked up with the elimination of the ontological and the philosophical, to the profit of a wholly empiriometric or empirioschematic explanation.

It is understandable that, for a mind limited by professional habits to the intelligibility of this degree, philosophical notions can lose all significance. It is likewise understandable that the experimental sciences have in a certain sense made progress by warring on the intellect. For the intellect has a natural tendency to introduce into the conceptual register proper to the sciences, meanings which derive from another register, the philosophical register, and which consequently disturb or retard experimental knowledge as such, and prevent it from achieving its pure type.

Definitively, it may be said that the sciences of nature are bound to ontology in an implicit, obscure, ungracious and unavowed fashion, and that for a two-fold reason: first, to the extent that these sciences necessarily presuppose a philosophy or pre-philosophy, a latent substructure which may be rudimentary, unformulated, unconscious, but which is none the less real, and for which the existence of things distinct from thought, and the possibility of attaining these things more-or-less completely by knowledge, are indisputable postulates; and then, to the extent that the science itself refers obliquely to the being of things as the foundation for the explicative representations that it elaborates.[32] Simply from the fact that for science, everything rests on observation, and therefore on the intuition of the senses (whose testimony the scientific use of measuring apparatus and precision instruments dissolves, so to speak, into a multiplicity of points of perception, I mean into simple graduated readings, but which always remains presupposed by this very practice), does it not, like sense intuition itself, implicitly declare the existence of hidden ontological structures in the exterior world, the investigation of which in themselves, moreover, does not belong to it any more than it does to the senses?

But except for this double implicit and indirect relation to the ontological, the sciences of nature, in their very structure, tend to free the observable as much as possible from the ontological.

The New Physics

12. We were speaking above of physico-mathematical knowledge in general. In our day, this knowledge is undergoing a marvelous renewal the

---

32   It seems to us that in the very suggestive pages of *L'Explication dans les sciences*, M. Meyerson has not sufficiently noted the difference between the two orders of epistemological facts which we are distinguishing here. In both cases it is a question of references to ontology to which the scientist gives evidence, in fact, that he is obliged to do so as a scientist. But in the second case these references to ontology intervene *in the very structure of experimental science*. In the first case, on the contrary, they remain subjacent to the science, and constitute so to speak the (inchoative) philosophy of the scientist as such.

importance of which cannot be exaggerated. With extraordinary rapidity science is revising and readjusting its basic concepts, the pillars of the Newtonian sky are shaken, and the theorists of science, quite rightly it seems, attribute to the work of an Einstein or a Planck a magnificence of the same order as that of the great initiators of the classical age. Few spectacles are as beautiful and moving for the mind as that of physics thus advancing towards its destiny like a huge throbbing ship. It is fitting that our reflection should linger a moment over the New Physics, not to indulge in any rash prophecies on the future of its theories, but to see whether its scientific progress confirms or invalidates the epistemological principles we have been trying to establish up to this point.

From the epistemological point of view, the New Physics seems from the very outset to be an effort to free the knowledge of nature from the domination of a certain number of preconceived mathematical ideas, and, to put it in a nutshell, it seems to be the reaction of the physicist as such (the theoretical-physicist) against frameworks imposed beforehand on physics by rational mechanics which is itself held to be a purely mathematical science. (Henceforth mechanics must become a department of physics itself; and that will rejoice the heart of any Aristotelian, for in good Peripatetic doctrine, movement of its very nature is a physical not a mathematical thing. What the mathematician retains of it—the variation of the distances of a point to the axes of the co-ordinates, a variation obviously "reciprocal," as Descartes said, and which by itself posits no more of reality in the point than in the axes or vice-versa—is not movement itself but its effect and its translation into the register of ideal quantity. Of itself mathematics abstracts from movement. That is why mechanism, taken as the metaphysical universalization of mechanics in the classical sense, while pretending to explain nature in its entirety by extension and movement, is in reality the voiding of reality of all movement, which then becomes wholly ideal.) The New Physics declines to attribute the character *absolute* to any of the elements of the scientific tableau of nature. By *absolute* we mean the possession of unvarying quantitative properties or determinations which belong to elements of the same name when they are considered in themselves or in their essence by the mathematician independently of any physical means of observation and measurement. (Classical Physics attributed this character to them because it placed its tableau of nature in a framework, not only mathematical—which was normal—but also thought of and pre-established, according to a mode of conceptualization and determination proper to the mathematician as such, not to the physicist.) It gives up absolute dimensions of bodies, absolute bearings in space and absolute bearings in time (even the existence of ether), the absolute character of mass, any system of privileged axes, whether it be a question, as in restricted relativity, of Galilean systems of reference in uniform motion in relation to one another, or, as in generalized relativity, of systems of reference having any movement whatsoever in relation to one another. On the other hand, quanta theories, and the growing importance given to the discontinuous in new scientific conceptions, may be regarded as the revenge of physics for the privileges that mathematical analysis and recourse to differential equations for expressing the laws of nature tended to accord to the conditions of continuity.

The claims to a sort of realism on the part of the physicist as such—by which I mean the resolution of the primordial concepts of the science into complexes of elements exclusively determined by physical measurements really or imaginatively feasible—thus succeed in shattering an image of the physical world that the classical age had made conformable to the supra-physical, ideal privileges of the mathematical world. By the same stroke the physicist rediscovers in their original strength the urge and desire immanent in his *habitus* which make him eager to uncover the ways and secrets of nature, the proper mystery of the world of bodies. (*Rerum cognoscere causas*, from this point of view things have not changed since the time of Lucretius and Virgil, and the decisive developments which have renewed our science of matter are rightly attributed to the faculty of intuition of the physical real amid the most abstract mathematical symbols.)[33] Moreover, without such a desire to penetrate that which is, what would be the *primum movens* of the physicist, even one most addicted to positivist macerations? They claim, therefore, to possess mathematics and not to be possessed by it, to make use of it as of a simple language and a simple instrument in order to investigate the nature of matter.

13. But how do they set to work to realize this plan? What, as a matter of fact, do we observe? We see the New Physics expressly tending towards a complete geometrization. It is by becoming more profoundly aware of this exigency, inscribed in the nature of modern physics, that it has established itself and won all its victories. But it can progress in this way only by giving up, more perfectly than Classical Physics, any ontological pretension, and, on the other hand, by multiplying more confidently than ever, and with all the advantages of complete awareness, physico-mathematical beings of reason.

It is often remarked—and it is pertinent in passing to determine the import of this remark—that the Einsteinian theory of relativity truly proceeds from an absolute concern and a far-reaching effort to bring science to a superior degree of independence in regard to the particular points of view of diverse observers. In thus proceeding, the very spirit and ideal of physical theory has

---

33   "For him [Einstein] the veil of the symbol never masks the reality. There are many minds for whom the sign often hides the thing signified; Einstein moves with ease in the world of symbols, but they have never concealed the physical aspect of things from him" (P. Langevin, "L'oeuvre d'Einstein et l'astronomie," *L'Astronomie*, July 1931). Thus, there is at the basis of the New Physics a sort of Pascalian tendency. Its greatest achievement is to finally reconcile this tendency (but at the expense of mechanism and Cartesian clear ideas) with the Cartesian tendency to universal mathematicization.

evolved and progressed. In the new synthesis the laws of nature are presented in the same fashion,[34] and the magnitude par excellence, which is like the sovereign of physical world—the speed of light (a speed at which lengths become zero and the mass of matter infinite)—is measured by the same number for observers of no matter what system of reference, whatever be the movement of the systems in question in relation to one another. The image of things themselves and the connections between events consequently vary. We have already had occasion to emphasize the importance of the distinction that should be drawn between the laws of nature and the concrete course of events. Let us say that if the New Physics smites the course of events with relativity (not as to the events themselves produced *hic et nunc*, but as to the displaying of their relations in space and time), it is in order to assure, at their expense, universally absolute character to the form of the laws.

But it is outside of things, so to speak, in the formal texture of its deductive system it constructs, that physico-mathematical science reaches this absolute "plus," this expansion into the unconditioned, to which everything that is spiritual tends of itself. It is not by discovering the absolute in things themselves. Quite the contrary, it is by turning aside from the ontological, by declining to integrate into the scientific tableau of nature the absolute elements that philosophy and common sense recognize in the real and by replacing these elements with beings of reason elaborated according to the exigencies of the deductive system to be constructed. The philosopher knows that bodies have absolute dimensions, that there are absolute movements in the world, an absolute time, absolute simultaneities for events as far apart as you wish in space. Here *absolute* signifies entirely determined in itself independently of any observer. The philosopher does not try to know what they are, i.e., to discern these dimensions, these movements, these times, these absolute simultaneities (at a distance), with the aid of our means of observation and of measurement. He willingly concedes that that is not possible.[35] It is sufficient for him that

---

34   That is to say that a Universe being a multiplicity of four dimensions, and its properties depending "on the coefficients in quadratic form of the differentials of the four coordinates corresponding to an event," the laws of nature are expressed "by relations preserving in relation to this quadratic form an unvarying character for any transformation whatever of the coordinates" (Emile Picard, *op. cit.*, p. 40).

     Many judicious remark will be found in the already cited thesis of M. Rene Poirier (*Essai sur quelques caractères des notions d'espace et de temps*, Pans, Vrin, 1931) concerning the question of the unvarying form of the laws of nature in the New Physics, the notion of geometric explanation, the dissymmetry that generalized Relativity introduces from the point of view of the geometrization itself between the domain of gravitation and the electromagnetic domain. The examination of the strength and weakness of relativistic theories (§ III, Chs. II and III) is conducted in a particularly happy fashion.

35   On the *relational* character of physics see the article of Roland Dalbiez, already cited (Ch. IV, n. 13), "Dimensions absolues et mesures absolues," *Revue Thomiste*,

they be discernible by pure spirits, who know, without observing from a point of space or at a moment of time. The physicist makes a like renunciation and with good reason. But for him, who does not philosophize, and who is concerned with what he can measure and to the extent that he can measure it, the existence of these absolutes does not count and in their place he knows and handles only relative entities reconstructed by means of measurable determinations: *entia rationis cum fundamento in re.*

14. Could the distinctive traits of the "realism" of the New Physics lead to any other result? Making "the whole object of the exact sciences" consist" in pointer readings and similar indications" and rejecting from physics every notion which cannot be resolved into physically effectable measurements frees physics from all ideal supports coming down from the heaven of pure mathematics and making one flesh with it. But it also frees it much more radically than ever before from any ontological notion, from any mode of ontological conceptualization (be it either the naive ontology of every-day observation or philosophical ontology).

The improvements brought about in the vocabulary of physics by the theory of relativity are very significant from this point of view. Listening to Mr. Einstein lecturing on simultaneity, it was very remarkable to hear him constantly returning to the question: what does the word "simultaneity" mean for me, a physicist? And he always replied in conformity with the methodological theme, the fundamental importance of which we have emphasized

---

March–April 1925. The author recalls the words of Jules Tannery: "The idea of determination is independent of the possibility of formulating in what this determination consists," and writes quite correctly: "quantity is not identical with relation, and a quantitative being is provided with a quantity which is proper to it before any comparison with a standard. . . . We know that bodies have an absolute figure, but we do not know what this absolute figure is. . . . Our physical knowledge bears only on relations. We are certain that objects have absolute dimensions, but we cannot know whether these absolute dimensions are kept intact."

In our *Réflexions sur l'intelligence* (pp. 235–241) we have shown how these principles apply to the question of the speed of a moving object, particularly to the speed of light. The "real" speed (ontologically determined, and which a pure spirit could know in relation to an absolutely immobile point of reference—ideal of necessity) with which the philosopher is concerned is not at all the "real" speed, that is to say really measured by an observer, with which the physicist is concerned, a speed relative to our frames of reference and which alone is discernible to our human knowledge.

The ancients well knew the distinction enunciated by Jules Tannery and which goes back to the distinction of the *quid est* and the *quia est*. If they did not make it with regard to the numbers of nature and the dimensions of bodies, they did make it with regard to the angel and their differentiations (at once specific and individual): "Novimus, inquam, differentiam esse in illis, sed quae sint illae, latet" (Cajetan, *In de Ente et Essentia*, cap. 6, q. 14).

above: Give me a definition that will tell me by what ensemble of measurements, concretely realizable in each case, I can verify that two events deserve to be called simultaneous or not; only then will I have a definition of simultaneity which can be handled by a physicist and have value for him.[36]

There is, therefore, no question here of the essence of simultaneity, of what it is in itself. For the physicist time, simultaneity, space—concepts entirely recast and freed from any philosophical undertone—take on a purely empiriometrical significance. One would have to be very naive to attribute any directly ontological value to that significance. Thus, physics is freed as perfectly as possible from philosophy. And, by the same stroke, it tends to be freed from common sense, not only from the imagery of common sense of which it was a question at the beginning of the preceding chapter, but also from the implicit philosophy of common sense, from the natural principles and natural data of the intelligence, except in what concerns the principles of mathematical interpretation itself and the ontological postulates implied by the rules of observation. This liberation from common sense is legitimate from the moment that it is accompanied by an equally broad renunciation of ontology.

15. From these considerations it follows that the idea of discovering in itself the nature of matter and of corporeal things must appear decidedly as a pure archaism for the New Physics, much more decidedly than for the physics of yesterday and the day before. "The scientist of today cannot indicate the essence of the real. It is precisely this which distinguishes his attitude from that of his materialistic predecessor, and still more from that of the medieval physicist. He no longer asserts that he truly attains real being, which, on the contrary, appears to him as enveloped in a profound mystery."[37] It is remarkable that quanta theories, at the same time that they declare the infigurable character of the universe of science, deepen the rupture between this universe and knowledge of the ontological type. It is understandable that when a scientist of today reflects on his science he discovers in it only a world of

---

36   The vocabulary of the physicist contains a certain number of words such as length, angle, speed, force, potential, current, etc., all of which we call "physical quantities." Now it should be stated that it is essential that these quantities be *defined* according to the way in which we really recognize them when confronted by them and not by the metaphysical meaning we could have attributed to them by anticipation. In the old manuals mass was defined by "quantity of matter"; but when it came to determining it an experimental method emerged which was not based on this definition. To believe that the quantity established by this method duly represented the quantity of matter contained in the object was a "pious opinion." Actually, to say that the quantity of matter contained in a kilogram of lead is equal to that in a kilogram of sugar doesn't make sense. The theory of Einstein sweeps away these "pious opinions" and insists on the fact that every physical quantity must be defined as the result of certain operations of measurement and calculation" (A. S. Eddington, *op. cit.*, p. 257).

37   E. Meyerson, "Le Physicien et le Réel," in *Le Mois*, June 1931.

symbols. "We have suffered," says Mr. Eddington, "and we still suffer from expectations that electrons and quanta must be in some fundamental respects like materials or forces familiar in the workshop—that all we have to do is imagine the usual kind of thing on an infinitely smaller scale. It must be our aim to avoid such prejudgments, which are surely illogical; and since we must cease to employ familiar concepts, symbols have become the only possible alternative. . . . If then only pointer readings or their equivalents are put into the machine of scientific calculations, how can we grind out anything but pointer readings? . . . Whenever we state the properties of a body in terms of physical quantities we are imparting knowledge as to the response of various metrical indicators and *nothing more*. After all, knowledge of this kind is fairly comprehensive. A knowledge of the response of all kinds of objects—weighing machines and other indicators—would determine completely its relation to its environment, leaving only its un-get-able nature undetermined. . . . The Victorian physicist felt that he knew just what he was talking about when he used terms such as *matter* and *atoms*; atoms were tiny billiard balls, a crisp statement that was supposed to tell you all about their nature. . . . But now we realize that science has nothing to say as to the intrinsic nature of the atom. The physical atom is, like everything else in physics, a schedule of pointer readings. . . . Scientific investigation does not lead to a knowledge of the intrinsic nature of things. . . . The external world of physics has become a world of shadows."[38]

"Out of the numbers proceeds that harmony of natural law which it is the aim of science to disclose. We can grasp the tune but not the player" (*ibid.*, pp. 291–292).

Mr. Eddington seems to forget here that the measurements gathered from nature by our apparatus deliver to us something of the real. (This may seem a "shadow" in regard to the universe with which we are familiar, but the philosopher knows that they are so many points of emergence through which an aspect of things existing in themselves appear to us.) Still more, he seems to forget that the first degree or first moment of conceptualization, sometimes very elaborated, at which we disengage from these measurements a descrip-

---

38   A. S. Eddington, *op. cit.*, pp. 248–249, 252, 257, 259, 303, xvi (the italics are the author's). Let us cite again the following passage which is so highly characteristic: "*Something unknown is doing we know not what*—that is what our theory amounts to. . . . There is the same indefiniteness as to the nature of the activity and of what is acting. And yet from so unpromising a beginning we really get somewhere. We bring into order a host of apparently unrelated phenomena; we make predictions, and our predictions come off. The reason—the sole reason —for this progress is that our description is not limited to unknown agents executing unknown activities, but *numbers* are scattered freely in the description. To contemplate electrons circulating in the atoms carries us no further; but by contemplating eight circulating electrons in one atom and seven circulating electrons in another we begin to realize the difference between oxygen and nitrogen. . . .

tion of the observable behavior of things, also puts us in the presence of realities—I mean observable and measurable, and grasped precisely as such—introduces us into a world of facts, of observable causations[39] and of observable structures that the theoretical physicist has the tendency to take as simple matter offered to his constructive genius, but concerning which the laboratory physicist is not disposed to permit any misapprehension about their being already authentically a part of physical science itself. These facts may be established in a more-or-less certain or more-or-less hypothetical fashion, they may imply to one degree or another an ideal completion of the real by reason;[40] nevertheless, they pertain to the order of real being. Such notions as the constitution of gas by individual molecules in endless agitation, or of the reticular structure of crystals, and a multitude of similar notions, must be taken as something other than mere symbols. I mean to say precisely insofar as they are translations of the measurable and of the observable, and before theoretical effort, in striving to deepen their significance and to discover in a complete explanation what they tell us about, enables us to understand that in the last analysis we know only symbolically what they speak to us about. But it is precisely this second degree or this second moment[41] of scientific conceptualization that Mr.Eddington had in view; and there it would be rash to reject his testimony.

16. The two traits that we have just pointed out in the New Physics seem at first glance strongly contradictory: on the one hand, an impulse of the mind towards the physical itself and the proper mysteries of its behavior, a desire for physical realism; on the other hand, the construction of a world of symbols,

---

39   A causation is not *observable* as such or insofar as it is an intelligible relation. However we use this word to designate causations which belong to the field of observation, and especially by pointer readings, if not immediately, at least proximately. Thus, the experiment of Puy de Dome shows in a very proximate if not immediate fashion that atmospheric pressure is the cause of the height of liquids in barometric tubes. Likewise, observation shows (in an already much less proximate fashion) the—hypothetical—fact that the dissociation of molecules into ions is the cause of the phenomena of electrolysis. This example can serve as a transition for passing to another class of causations that may be called *theoretical* causations, and which are shown by observation only in a very distant fashion, by the intermediary of a whole physico-mathematical construction of which experiment does no more than verify its points of incidence with the real. It is to these theoretical causations that belong the causal explanations elaborated by physical theory at the second degree or second moment of conceptualization of which it is a question here, for example in the Einsteinian theory of gravitation in which the presence of matter is the cause of the curvature of space.

40   See above, Ch. III, § 33.

41   Needless to say, when we speak of two moments we are not pretending there is any question of two successive phases; these two moments are constantly joined in the course of elaboration of physico-mathematical knowledge, and it is only by abstraction that they can be separated.

and a recourse more decided than ever to mathematical and geometrical beings of reason. This contradiction is purely apparent. The paradox is explained by what was said above about physico-mathematical knowledge in general, and gives us the best illustration of the theory of *scientiae mediae*. In its opposition to Newtonianism the New Physics reminds us that physico-mathematical knowledge is more physical; and at the same time if it goes beyond Newtonianism, it is by revealing much more strikingly the formally mathematical character of this knowledge. The physicist *regards* mathematics as a simple instrument, a simple language; but it *is* not for him a *simple* language and a *simple* instrument. He derives from this means and this language the very rule of analysis, of conceptualization and of explanation which gives to his knowledge its proper form of science. We said he wishes to know the nature of corporeal things and their physical causes; did we say that he wishes to know this nature *in itself* and these causes *in themselves*? We said that he does not attempt to know in themselves the nature of things and their physical causes (and reduced to their essential meaning, the phrases which we have just quoted from Mr. Eddington signify nothing else); did we say that he abandons all attempt to know them in any way? The impulse that spurs him towards the physical real can attain this real only in its measurable aspects themselves, in its measurable structure as such, that is, by mathematicizing it, and finally by constructing something in its place. The physicist wishes to penetrate the secrets of matter; but the very type of knowledge to which he is bound prohibits him from attaining the nature of matter in itself. He attains it in the observable and measurable, and thereby real, determinations which are for him the substitutes for the essence, and he scrutinizes it and fathoms it to the very degree that he mathematically symbolizes it.

Let us say that his knowledge is not a knowledge of the real (the given real) by the real (by a more profound real), but a knowledge of the real by the mathematical praeter-real. It is a knowledge of the physical real which becomes symbolic to the extent that its mathematical regulation obliges it to attempt a complete explanation of the real wherein things, the form and formation of which belong to a world of qualities, will be formulated in a wholly quantitative fashion. Or again, if it is permissible to use an old Platonic word, more expressive perhaps than the modern word, symbol,[42] it is—at least

---

42   It is customary among the scientists themselves to use the word "symbol" in a more limited sense. They say, for example, that the "associated wave" of wave-mechanics is a pure mathematical symbol, "a simple symbolic representation of probability." And the reason is that no imaginable spatio-temporal representation, no physical image of this wave, is itself possible. Or, in other words, it is impossible to define it as an immediate object of a certain sequence of operations of physical measurements that are at least theoretically feasible. It is unnecessary to point out that the philosopher (or the scientist when he uses the language of epistemology) understands the word symbol in a much broader sense. It is in this broader sense that it must be understood in the present study.

as to the second moment of theoretical elaboration of which we were just speaking—a knowledge of the physical real by way of myths,[43] I mean verified myths; that is to say, myths which agree with the measurable "appearances" and which "save" the latter: a science or knowledge of the physical real at once *experimental* and *mytho-poetical*. That is what gives to theoretical physics and to its most inspired discoveries such striking kinship with artistic creation. But it is a question (and this is the marvel) of a speculative art, of an art *for the sake of knowing*, in which the imagination is inventive only in submission to the constraints of a world of rigorous determinations, of laws established by the strictest exactitude. In a previous chapter,[44] we noted that Plato perceived in a very clear fashion the proper method of the mathematical knowledge of nature. He likewise saw, and with equal profundity, that the creation of scientific myths—the noblest species of beings of reason founded *in re*—is a necessary consequence of this method. The myths of the *Timaeus* have grown old. But it was not as a confession of impotence or as an escape into poetry that the *Timaeus* used myths. It was in virtue of an admirable intuition of the proper conditions of physico-mathematical knowledge and of what are called the exact sciences, when ceasing to be purely mathematical, that they undertake to explain the world of experience. Aristotle was engaged in a different task, a task which Plato had not seen. He founded the philosophy of sensible nature. And to do that he had to attack the Platonic metaphysics and the theory of Ideas. But although he recognized the existence of *scientiae mediae*, and with the theory of homocentric spheres, had himself constructed a first-rate physico-mathematical myth, he seems to have accorded to these spheres a full ontological value, a reality not only fundamental (as to their foundation in the nature of things) but formal and entire (as to their formality, to their thinkable constituent itself). Because the point of view of the philosopher of nature predominated in him he did not see as well as Plato did the aspect of ideality necessarily embodied in the mathematical knowledge of the phenomena of nature precisely as exact science.

17. Let us suppose that a scientist, who is sealed in a room of ground glass and receives by radio the experimental information on which he works, learns one day about a certain machine capable of hurling its own weight to a height three hundred times its own. He will not have much difficulty in roughly imagining this machine, unknown in itself, as a sort of catapult constructed according to the furnished data. He will correct and make the image more precise as new information reaches him. Suppose he learns that this machine manifests the properties of what men call memory. That is to say it modifies,

---

43   We do not mean that all the entities of the physicist are "myths." For us, this word designates the beings of reason that he utilizes, especially those he utilizes at the term of his theoretical elaboration and of his reconstruction of the real, precisely when he penetrates the farthest into the secrets of matter.

44   Cf. above, Ch. II, n. 51.

in proportion as it functions, its very manner of functioning and of reacting to stimuli, a thing which his reconstructed apparatus does not do. Perhaps he will solve the difficulty by endowing the space occupied by this apparatus with some new dimension according to which the past of the machine would be preserved and would modify in an invisible manner its very structure. We who walk the streets and put up at inns can know that the machine in question is called a flea. The scientist will not know this but the construction that he ceaselessly alters (turns upside down, if necessary, to meet a "crisis") will present at each instant the sum of all the measurable properties found in the flea and actually known by him. Obviously, in creating such a construction which is fictitious but founded on the real and always exactly and rigorously determined, in that way he will acquire ever more and more profound knowledge about the nature of the flea, but always by way of myth and of symbol. It would be inaccurate to say that he does not know this nature. He does not know it ontologically or *in itself*.

Let the simplicity of this metaphor be excused. It translates into sense language the way in which symbolism and realism are indissolubly united in the most highly conceptualized parts of theoretical physics. Here it would be an error to separate and oppose them. In this particular domain they constitute the warp and the woof of the same cloth. It is by creating its most audacious myths that physical theory scrutinizes material reality most profoundly—in its own way, of course, which is not the way of philosophy. It is by connaturalizing the intellect with material reality—not grasped in itself—that it constructs upon it, and in place of it, a universe of verified symbols or myths. The closer it approaches physical reality, the more it constructs beings of reason remote from our common experience. Just as in the finite world of Einstein, by dint of receding from a point one ends up by rejoining it, so the farther physical theory transports us from the nature of the atom or electron considered in itself, the closer it approaches that nature.

Let us hasten to add that physical theory is not symbolic as such. It is, as we noted above, *indifferent* in its use of real entities disclosed in the measurable behavior of things or of symbols and beings of reason founded on that same measurable behavior. As a matter of fact, we observe today that it becomes more symbolic in proportion as its conceptualization rises to higher degrees and the explanations elaborated by it become at once both more universal and more pure (as to its epistemological type). The epistemological complexity of the *scientiae mediae* may offend the taste for simplification and facile classification to which philosophers sometimes yield. To tell the truth, they only have to accept it as it is.

Finally, the interpretation of physical theory here proposed is more realist than that of some physicist philosophers, notably Mr. Eddington. It places more emphasis upon the epistemological importance of the real entities, simple, observable data or conceptualizations more or less proximate to them, which are also a part of physics and are utilized by theory. Moreover, while recognizing all the ideality inevitably involved in the geometrization of physics, it nevertheless affirms its value as a knowledge of the real. For one may know by another way, to wit, precisely as a philosopher, the existence of corporeal substances and of their natures, which physics attains not in themselves, but which it nevertheless does attain in the substitutes which it elaborates for that purpose and which it founds on those natures. These are so much the better the less they pretend to pass themselves off as ontological articulations of reality. Indeed, though Mr. Eddington seems to incline towards a sort of idealism or pure symbolism when he reflects on physics (since for him, as it would seem, sensorial perception is itself already symbolic—that involves a whole metaphysics), he certainly adopts a much more realist attitude when he speaks as a physicist.

Did not he himself write: "The physicist, so long as he thinks as a physicist, has a definite belief in a real world outside him. For instance, he believes that atoms and molecules really exist; they are not mere inventions that enable him to grasp certain laws of chemical combination. . . ."[45] To tell the truth, there is no mental attitude more contrary to idealism than that of the scientist who, confronted by nature, feels the inexhaustible ontological richness with which it is charged, yet declines to penetrate it except by necessarily inadequate means, and, as it were, by donning a mathematical diving-suit. He has "the feeling of being in the presence of an enigma at once admirable and disturbing. He contemplates it with a respect that is almost fearful and perhaps not without some analogy with that which the believer experiences in the face of the mysteries of his faith."[46]

A Digression on the Question of "Real Space"

18. There is no word clearer than the word "reality." It signifies *that which is*. But its use requires many distinctions, and a critical labor that is sometimes difficult. In order to apply our considerations concerning the New Physics to a particular case, let us try to examine the question of "real space." What is meant by such questions as the following: Is real space Euclidian or non-Euclidian? Is the space postulated by the Einsteinian theory of gravitation real or not? Or by such a declaration as this: Thanks to the New Physics, one of whose characteristics is, however, to reach to a degree never before attained, the identification of geometry and physics, "are we gradually reducing the distinction between physical space and geometric space?"[47] We hold this distinction as fundamental, yet it must be understood in its true sense.

The word "real" has not the same meaning for the philosopher, for the

45   A. S. Eddington, *Space, Time and Gravitation* (1920, p. 180).
46   E. Meyerson, *Le Mois*, June 1931.
47   W. Vernadsky, "L'étude de la vie et la nouvelle Physique," *Revue Générale des Sciences*, December 1930, p. 701.

mathematician and for the physicist. If we are aware from the outset of this diversity, the question here posed is nothing more than a nest of equivocations.

For the geometrician, a space is "real" when it is capable of mathematical existence, that is to say when it implies no internal contradiction, and duly corresponds to the mathematical notion of space, that is, duly constitutes a system of objects of thought verifying the axioms of a geometry. It is clear that from this point of view, in virtue of what may be called the circumincession of the diverse geometrical systems—the latter being translatable into one another and including one another, so that the non-Euclidian geometries contain the Euclidian as a particular case, and can themselves, however, be constructed with the aid of Euclidian materials[48]—all these geometries, and all the more "general" geometries that may be invented, are equally true, and therefore all their spaces equally "real." Euclidian space enjoys no privilege here, except for the fact that the constructibility of Euclidian entities in imaginative intuition is the fundamental guarantee of the notonal coherence (absence of internal contradiction) of geometrical entities, Euclidian and non-Euclidian (since these latter can always be "translated" into a Euclidian multiplicity), or to put it differently of the compatibility of both Euclidian and non-Euclidian axioms.[49]

For the physicist, a space is "real" when the geometry to which it corresponds permits the construction of a physico-mathematical universe in which all our pointer-readings are "explained," and which at the same time symbolizes physical phenomena in a coherent and complete fashion. It is clear that from this point of view there is no privileged space. For a long time Euclidian space sufficed for the interpretations of physics. In order to build up a satisfying image of observable phenomena, it postulated for the universe, as common

---

48   F. Gonseth, *Les fondements des mathématiques*, p. 15. In a general fashion, it is possible to enclose a non-Euclidian multiplicity of *n* dimensions in a Euclidian space of (n[n + 1])/2 dimensions. Gonseth wrote: "We have emphasized again and again that the non-Euclidian geometries can be realized with the aid of Euclidian materials. The conclusion could therefore be drawn that these geometries have only a domain of validity inferior, or should we say *interior*, to that of Euclidian geometry. On the other hand, we have seen that this latter geometry is a limiting case between hyperbolic geometry and elliptical geometry: and from this point of view it seems to have a restricted field of validity. To make the paradox more apparent, Euclidian geometry could easily be constructed with the aid of materials borrowed from the geometry of Lobatchevsky, for example. . . . The paradox is perfectly symmetrical: of any two geometries whatever, each appears in turn to be contained in the other, or to contain it." Thus "every affirmation of a non-Euclidian geometry is also an affirmation of Euclidian geometry" (*ibid.*, pp. 92–93). The same author gives (p. 37) a Euclidian model of a non-Archimedean straight line.

49   In this way, the methodological exigency formulated by St. Thomas still persists, even for modern mathematics, and must be understood: "In mathematicis ad imaginationem, et non ad sensum, debemus deduci." See above, Ch. II, n. 42.

sense invited it to do, Euclidian geometrical properties,and attributed to the presence of factors of another order (physical) everything that could not be predicted by these properties. Today it has abandoned this division. To interpret the measurements it gathers from nature within a synthesis in which geometry and physics are as far as possible amalgamated, it has recourse to spherical or elliptical spaces. These are, therefore, what it holds to be "real" in the sense we have just noted. Tomorrow it may be others.

But for us, the problem presents itself neither from the point of view of the physicist nor from that of the mathematician. For us, it is a question of knowing what is real space in the philosophical sense of the word, that is to say, in the sense that "real" entity is opposed to entity "of reason" and designates an object of thought capable of extramental existence, surely not indeed according to the mode in which it exists in thought, but according to the ensemble of objective characteristics themselves which integrate its notion or definition. Taking into account the peculiar conditions of mathematical beings, and the condition of reason (ideal purification) which always affects their very definition, we can say that a mathematical entity is real (in the philosophical sense of the word) when it can exist outside the mind, not, doubtless, under the conditions proper to mathematical abstraction, but insofar as its definition reveals in a pure state or according to its ideal perfection such or such characteristics (pertaining to the accident quantity) which exist or can exist in the world of bodies. (Although there is in nature no point without extension or line without thickness, nor any abstract number; yet point, line, whole number are real beings.) In order to be thus an *ens reale* such an entity does not cease to be mathematical, though it cannot have actual and sensible existence except by losing its mathematical purity. Taken as existing in a thing, it is a characteristic of the latter which can be scientifically known only as disengaged by mathematical abstraction. The latter leaves aside all properties concerned with the activity of bodies, their movement, their qualitative diversities, their sensible characteristics, and retains only what remains after the removal of the physical.

Let us add that though Euclidian, Riemannian, etc., geometrical entities are "translatable" from one system to another, and that consequently all these geometries are equally true, they cannot, however, be equally real in the philosophical sense of the word. The straight line of an elliptical plane, for example, and the figure which corresponds to it in a Euclidian model are not different expressions of the same thing. (In the order of the mathematical praeter-real there is no other "thing" than the object of thought itself constructed according to such or such a system of axioms.) They are intrinsically different entities[50] belonging to intrinsically different worlds, and from one of

50   The expression Euclidian or non-Euclidian "supposes successively an alignment and a metrical organization of multiplicity, which are independent. The epithet given to space is only a way of designating by abstraction the conventional properties of figures. There is therefore no contradiction between the diverse

these worlds to the other they correspond analogically. To affirm the reality of one space is therefore not to affirm at the same time the reality of all the others, but their unreality. No entity of these latter figures in the former.

19. Now, how can we know if a mathematical being—and especially that system of geometrical entities that is called a space—is or is not real in the philosophical sense of the word? Mathematical intelligibility by itself alone tells us nothing. It is just as concerned with beings of reason as it is with real entities. Nor will the verifications of our senses and of our measuring instruments tell us anything, since with them we quit the mathematical order for the physical order, and since they presuppose a mathematical core or model which serves them as a "nucleus of condensation,"[51] a model which we have taken into account in order to construct our instruments and in respect to which we correct and interpret the ensemble of measurements taken, while indicating the role of the accessory variations due to diverse physical circumstances.

In our search for a criterion two ways, and two ways only, lie open. We may either analyze the genesis of the notions in order to see if the entity in question, without involving any internal contradiction or incompossibility in its constitutive notes (in which case it would have no mathematical existence), does not imply a condition incompossible with existence outside the mind. (Thus a logical entity, such as Predicate or copula, is certainly not intrinsically contradictory, but it would be a contradiction to suppose it existing outside the mind.) Or we may consider a condition to which the philosopher knows that the reality of mathematical entities is subject. (He knows that for these entities to exist outside the mind means to exist with sensible existence, and that whatever cannot be constructed in imaginative intuition, which represents freely and in a pure fashion whatever belongs to quantity, has *a fortiori* no

---

geometries, since *they deal with different objects*" (R. Pouier, *op. cit.*, p. 192). Though starting from the point of view of a philosophy, which to our mind is erroneous (he was a disciple of Bertrand Russell), Jean Nicod made, in relation to a similar question, certain remarks which could be put to good use (*La géometrie dans le monde sensible*, Paris, Alcan, 1924 pp. 27–28).

51   F. Gonseth, *op. cit.*, I, 104. Doubtless, the space of perception, of our gross perceptions, appears to be Euclidian. In other words the physical measurements made by us, on the scale of our senses, in the region we occupy, are interpreted in the most simple and perfectly satisfying fashion with the aid of a Euclidian model. But the conclusions drawn from physical measurements can have, as such, only an approximative value, and in its symbolic constructions Physics can use non-Euclidian spaces as much as it wishes, as long as it chooses them tangent to Euclidian space. But "a hyperbolic model can always be found, the metric of which varies, in whatever of its parts one chooses as little as one requires from Euclidian metric" (*ibid.*, p. 114). It follows from these considerations that "it is impossible to prove experimentally that space is Euclidian" or non-Euclidian, because to tell the truth "experimental science does not know space, it knows only the phenomena, that space binds together" (*ibid.*, p. 103).

possibility of being posited in sensible existence.) This condition is direct constructibility in intuition.

Now among the systems of geometrical entities that are called Euclidian, Riemannian, etc., spaces, only tri-dimensional Euclidian space is directly constructible in intuition. It is only by the intermediary of this space that others can satisfy the condition posited.[52] The model of the thermic universe invented by Poincaré, and in which we would be born with the geometry of Lobatchevsky, and that sequence of very simplified sensations that Jean Nicod has thought up and which would give to a fictitious subject the idea of the most diverse geometries, confirm by a sort of counter-proof this privilege of Euclidian space. To represent as natural to a thinking subject another geometry than that of Euclid, it is necessary to imagine a universe which is itself a being of reason as chimerical as an *animal rationale alatum*. Finally, if intuition assures us, as we have already remarked, that Euclidian entities (and hence the others) are exempt from internal contradiction, it is because it began by assuring us that, to the exclusion of the others, they are apt to exist outside the mind, in the nature of things.

On the other hand, it could be shown that if it is possible to pass by mathematical transformations, from non-Euclidian spaces to Euclidian space, and inversely, it is because, in truth, the non-Euclidian geometries presuppose notions of Euclidian geometry, not indeed in their own structure and their own logical development, but as the foundation of the logical coherence of the entities they may construct and as the psychological basis of conceptualization. The process of generalization which gets its support from Euclidian

---

52   As we wrote in *Réflexions sur l'intelligence* (p. 257, note), "all the attempts that have been made to obtain an intuitive representation of non-Euclidian geometries, by Einstein for example in his opusculum on geometry and experience, show precisely that these geometries can be rendered imaginable only by reduction to Euclidian geometry. Obviously, as Mr. Eddington tells us, in order 'to perceive non-Euclidian space' I have 'only to look at the reflection of this room in a polished doorknob and imagine myself one of the actors in what I see going on there' (*Space, Time and Gravitation*, p. 14): the image of my room in a doorknob is a duly Euclidian model traced on a certain determined surface of Euclidian space."

"Shall we say that the explanation of gravitation by the curvature of space-time has an exceptional intuitive value? Evidently not: this space-time is doubly unrepresentable. First because time is joined to pace in a purely allegorical fashion; then because the curvature of a multiplicity has intuitive sense only if it is plunged in a space of a higher order. All that we can do is to represent to ourselves a surface in Euclidian space. If we wish to go further, we are obliged to have recourse to the image of a metric established on a Euclidian multiplicity, to have recourse to a Caylean point of view. That is what M. Einstein does at the end of his little book where he attempts to put his ideas within reach of a reader who is not a geometrician. Practically, we will imagine foreshortened meters, clocks which run slow for no perceptible physical cause. The geometrical rational will be presented as a physical irrational" (R. Poirier, *op. cit.*, p. 338).

geometry results in truth, not in more extensive *generic* concepts, of which Euclidian, non-Euclidian, non-Archimedean, etc., would be the determinations, but in *analogical* concepts which are included in one another and of which the Euclidian concepts represent the principal analogate. From this point of view it must be said, with Hamelin, that "non-Euclidian geometry, basically, is not self-sufficient,"[53] and that non-Euclidian, non-Archimedean, etc., entities have as the foundation of their logical existence Euclidian entities. Non-Euclidian spaces can therefore without the least intrinsic contradiction be the object of the mind's consideration, but it would be a contradiction to suppose them existing outside the mind, and by that same fact to suppress from existence, to their advantage, the foundation which supports their notion.

In both ways we are thus led to admit that non-Euclidian spaces are beings of reason in spite of the use that astronomy makes of them, and that the geometric properties of existing bodies, the properties that the mind recognizes in them when everything physical is voided, are those which characterize Euclidian space. It is Euclidian space which appears to the philosopher to be an *ens geometricum reale.*[54]

20. But by the same words, "real space," we can understand something else again. We can designate space precisely as filled with physical existences and actions, and composed by the properties of bodies (no longer geometric but physical), their activity and their causality, into a network of tensions or of heterogeneous qualitative intensities. Then, precisely, space is no longer considered as mathematical or geometrical, but as "physical." It is a qualified space, and the determinations that it admits are due *to that which is* in space, to that which fills it.[55] Thus the philosopher distinguishes—and it is a classical

---

53   O. Hamelin, *Essai sur les eléments principaux de la représentation* (2nd ed., p. 100). In this matter, Hamelin insisted on the condition of homogeneity required by the comparability of figures (an argument which is valid only if we suppose the irreducibility of geometry to arithmetic, and at the same time the impossibility of separating geometry from its intuitive origins). It is also in the name of the homogeneity of space that Mr. Whitehead, from an entirely different point of view, seeks to maintain the Euclidian character of the geometric structure of our universe.

54   For the Philosophy of Nature elaborated by the scholastics (as also, but in a very different sense, for the New Physics), this real geometric space is finite, that is to say actually existing space is co-extensive with the amplitude of the world. Infinite geometric space is a being of reason ("imaginary space").

55   It is in this sense, it seems, that Pierre Curie at bottom envisaged symmetry as the state of space, that is as the structure of physical space. (W. Vernadsky, "L'étude de la vie et la nouvelle physique," *Revue Générale des Sciences*, December 3, 1930, p. 705), and that one can also say with W. Vernadsky that: "the space of life has a particular symmetrical state, unique in nature" (*ibid.*, p. 712).

The metrical properties of bodies, insofar as they are physically measured, pertain to real physical space. And so it is quite true that "only the ensemble of geometry and physics is susceptible of empirical verification" (H. Weyl, *Espace, temps et matière*, p. 80). And without thereby abandoning the reality (though not

distinction—physical space from geometrical space, and can foresee that, understood in this sense, as *physical* space, real space is not Euclidian (neither homogeneous, nor isotropic), since Euclidian space is precisely that space (purely mathematical) which the mind considers after the voiding of all physical content.

It is important always to keep in mind that when a philosopher so speaks— from the very fact that he opposes the physical and the geometrical as two irreducible orders—he understands things in an entirely different way than the New Physics. Faithful to the essential spirit of modern science, the latter tends, however far it falls short of it, to be transformed completely into geometry. Thereby and for that very reason it abandons the absolute discrimination between the physical and the geometrical as well as the search for physical causes considered in themselves or in their qualitative reality. In order to advance freely in this way, Einstein's stroke of genius was to have bent geometry itself to the needs of physics,[56] and to have conceived a space which by its *geometric* properties renders account of all the phenomena of gravitation.[57] The continuum according to which the universe is extended becomes, then, a non-Euclidian and four-dimensional continuum in which time and space are no longer measured in an independent manner but form an indissoluble complex. The geometric properties of the space-time thus conceived are themselves modified by the matter which occupies it (that is to say by what is capable of putting the measuring-instruments with which we explore it off: clocks, graduated scales, light-rays, compasses, electro-scopes, etc.). The movement of the stars follows natural paths which are the geodesic curves of his space-time, curves that are accentuated in the presence of material mass so that the planets turn as in a sort of basin, owing to the curvature of space in the vicinity of the sun.

Newtonian physicists reproach this synthesis raised on the foundation of a vast ensemble of measurements gathered from nature, and confirmed by many verified predictions, with being a "put-up job." They complain that the search for physical forces which ought to account for the phenomena of nature is abandoned. Just as the Cartesian physicists saw in the substitution of attraction at a distance for vortex motions an avowal of impotence, they, in

experimentally verifiable) of Euclidian space, the philosopher can add, in another sense than the physicist, that the metrical structure insofar as it is physically measurable is not given *a priori* in a rigid way, but "constitutes a *state field* of physical reality, which is in causal dependence on the state of matter. . . . Like the snail, matter itself constructs and forms its own house" (Idem, *Mathematische Analyze des Raumsproblemes*, Berlin, 1923, p. 44; quoted from Meyerson, *La déduction rélativiste*, p. 93, note).

56   "The metric field depends on the material realities which fill the universe" (H. Weyl, *Espace, temps et matière*, p. 193).

57   "Gravitation will appear to us as an emanation of the metric field" (*ibid.*, p. 198). Thus, "geometry, mechanics and physics form . . . an indissoluble theoretical unity, that must be viewed *en bloc*" (*ibid.*, p. 57).

their turn, will see an avowal of impotence in the substitution of the geometric curve for mechanical force. They forget that it was along this line that modern physics committed itself from the beginning. It was by avowing, not explicitly indeed (since in the beginning it was thought to be a philosophy of nature), but practically, its impotence with regard to physical causes considered in themselves or in their essence, that it began to compose a mathematical myth of the physical world which delivers to it in enigma the secrets of that world. The "forces" of classical physics appear from this point of view as a precarious compromise between the "causes" of philosophy and the purely empiriometric entities of an evolved science of phenomena. And it must be said that the New Physics has accomplished a progress of the first importance in the scientific conception of the universe by manifesting, this time, in a radical and explicit fashion, the renunciation by physico-mathematical knowledge of the search for physical causes taken in themselves, and the profound tendency of the latter to free itself completely from philosophy.

21. But let not this liberation from philosophy be taken as a new philosophy! There are two possible ways of interpreting the conceptions of the new physics philosophically. The one transports them literally, just as they are, on to the philosophical plane, and thereby throws the mind into a zone of metaphysical confusion. The other discerns their spirit and their noetic value, in an effort to determine their proper import.

In the first case, it will be said, not only in the language and from the point of view of the physicist as was accurately described above,[58] which would be quite legitimate, but also in a philosophical sense, that the space postulated by the New Physics is *real geometric* space, and manifests the *real geometric* properties of the corporeal world. Hence, the latter becomes (in the measure in which the New Physics has or will achieve the explanation of the universe by the geometric properties of the space invented for this purpose) amenable in itself to a purely geometric exegesis. To distinguish physical space from geometric space will then be to distinguish one geometric space from another geometric space,[59] to distinguish the properties of *real geometric* space, when there is matter in it, from the properties of this same *real geometric* space, when it is void of matter (mass or energy, quantity of movement, pressures . . .)[60] and occupied solely by something like that "immaterial" ether without which we

---

58   See above, Ch. IV, § 18.

59   In this sense, one is dealing not with a distinction but with a fusion. As E. Meyerson has noted, "the confusion between physical space and mathematical space—it is hardly necessary to point out that we are using the term confusion without giving it any pejorative sense—constitutes a peculiarity of recent conceptions and clearly distinguishes them from preceding ones" (*La déduction rélativiste*, p. 93).

60   It will also be to distinguish *real geometric* space (void of matter or obstruction) from the diverse spaces abstractly conceivable by pure geometry.

have not yet succeeded in getting along.[61] At the same time, the proper object of geometry, as well as its superior level of abstraction and epistemological independence, is misunderstood. To the extent that it is not a "pure" empty form, it is regarded as an "experimental science,"[62] which only gets an objective content rendering it "true," from physical entities and physical measurements thanks to which the mind chooses as "real space" the one, from among the diverse formal spaces that it pleases to imagine, which permits the greatest and most perfect geometrization of physics. Under the pretext that space is a network of distances (but which the geometrician "measures" ideally and deductively), one will pretend to give to geometry (as a "natural-science") as object a network of distances materially and empirically measured with the aid of physical apparatus.

In the other case, the space of the New Physics ("empty" or filled with matter) will be recognized as a physico-mathematical being of reason ex-

---

61   See below, Ch. IV, n. 80.
62   A. S. Eddington, *The Nature of the Physical World*, pp. 161–162. Cf. Albert Einstein, La géometrie et l' expérience (Paris, Gauthier-Villars, 1921); and our *Réflexions sur l'intelligence*, p. 255, n. 1. M. Hermann Weyl thinks likewise that "the existence of a geometry independent of physics is definitively compromised" (*Espace, temps et matière*, p. 290). As Roland Dalbiez wrote (*art. cit.*, pp. 152, 153), "the metaphysician can only see in this a manifestation of the old empiricist and nominalist spirit which recognizes truth only in existential propositions. That is the basis of the debate. On the hypothesis that no body existed, could one still speak of geometric truth or not? . . . For any philosophy which goes beyond pure empiricism, mathematical propositions do not require the existence of material objects in order to be true, which does not mean however that we are able to acquire the knowledge of these propositions independently of sensible experience. Mathematical truths are of the purely essential order; when anyone wishes to formulate a physical law mathematically, he is obliged to effect a passage from the essential order to the existential order."
   Is it necessary to point out here that the etymology of words is a mediocre means of teaching us about the essences of the things signified by them, and that if a geometrician is etymologically a land-surveyor, geometry began to constitute itself as science only when it became aware that it was something distinct from land-surveying? The new school methods of the "concrete" teaching of geometry have doubtless great pedagogical advantages as a method of *initiation*, precisely because they take the child where he is, not yet on the threshold of geometry, in order to raise him little by little up to this science and to its proper degree of abstraction. But if such methods were taken as the methods of geometric *knowledge* itself, they would bring about its reversion to a state of pre-Pythagorean infancy. It must be confessed moreover that the question of the nature of geometry does not seem to be very clearly elucidated by the theorists of the New Physics, who pass over it all the more quickly as they fed it to be more thorny. They have not yet explained to us how it is that if geometry is "properly speaking, an experimental science" it can nevertheless and with advantage have" an unfettered development as a purely mathematical subject" (A. S. Eddington, *op. cit.*, p. 162).

pressly constructed in such a way as to save all the known appearances and which will be modified in proportion to any deviations that will be observed between the construction already established by reason and new data of experience.[63] This being of reason then appears as a *geometric symbol* of *real physical* space (understanding "physical" space in the sense given to this word by the philosopher of whom we were speaking above). It appears as the geometric or meta-geometric symbol which best translates the reality of physical interactivities, the ontological investigation of the nature of which is abandoned for the sake of a better mathematical analysis. So the double irreducibility (a sort of sacred good for the intellect) of the physical (ontologically considered in its essence) to the mathematical, and of the geometrical to the experimental, is safeguarded. At the same time, it is understood that the geometrization of physics can be accomplished only by means of the introduction of a physics mathematically recast into the very heart of geometry itself. It will abound all the more richly in beings of reason and in proportion as it is asked to absorb into its symbols and to mathematicize real *physical being*, it will leave behind the more decidedly, real *geometric* being.

22. The same considerations hold, *mutatis mutandis*, for the mathematicization that the Quantum Theory accomplishes on the physical real in other ways than that of Relativity. They hold particularly for the structure that the New Physics attributes to the atom, or better, the continuously varying structure of the atom demanded by it for some years now. It sees that science tends to form a pure abstract mathematical equivalent of this structure—which thereby becomes unrepresentable to the imagination, and at the same time divested of any ontological meaning. This equivalent tends to become a more and more fictitious and more and more perfect symbol of the real nature, unknown in itself, of that existing something or other to which determinatively corresponds the name atom. Thus, it knows this nature more and more profoundly, yet more and more enigmatically, and metaphorically, to put it bluntly, in the measure that it constructs the myth—a being of reason founded *in re*—which takes its place.

II
THE PHILOSOPHY OF NATURE

23. According to a remark of Mr. Eddington, the physicist of today who

---

63　"That which concerns the deviation of light, leaves the way open for an evolution of the theory of generalized relativity: the explanations of gravitation by non-Riemannian geometry are being developed, and perhaps the new geometries will have as a result the achieving of the synthesis of electromagnetism and consequently of Physics and gravitation" (P. Langevin, *L'oeuvre d'Einstein et l'astronomie, art. cit.*, p. 294).

knows "that our knowledge of objects treated in physics consists solely in readings of pointers and other indicators," and who knows likewise that "this schedule of pointer readings is attached to some unknown background,"[64] is much less tempted than the physicist "of the time of Queen Victoria" to admit that nothing is true except what an engineer can reconstruct,[65] and to believe that physics is everything. On the contrary, he is disposed to think "that a just appreciation of the physical world as it is understood today carries with it a feeling of open-mindedness towards a wider significance transcending scientific measurement,"[66] although he feels all too ill equipped to discover whither this feeling ought to lead.

That is true not only of physics, but of empiriological knowledge in general. Obviously, such knowledge remains by essence insufficiently explicative. The mind cannot rest content with it. Those philosophical or pre-philosophical substructures without which the scientist cannot get along are a sure sign of it. It is a knowledge of being itself that is needed; I mean a knowledge of corporeal, sensible and mobile being, of the being immanent in those realities of nature in which the sciences of phenomena reach their terminus and find their verification, those realities which constitute the basis of all their conceptual constructions, and over which these constructions give us practical mastery. Evidently, such a knowledge must have another object and other characteristics. It must be set up on another noetic plane than that which modern language calls science. Its office could not consist in extending science on its own plane (on that score, as M. Bergson once said, "beyond science there is only ignorance"), nor in decorating the results of science with noble but vague meditations. Although its rules of explanation are not those of science in the modern sense of the word, nevertheless, it will better deserve the name science in the qualitatively more profound and more authentic sense than that the ancients gave to this word; and under that rubric it is possible. For the sciences of nature not only lead the mind to desire it. They themselves by witnessing that, on the one hand, nature is knowable but, on the other hand, that they know it only in an essentially unsatisfying manner, thereby witness that a knowledge is possible in which the intellect, actualizing the mysterious intelligibility of things on a deeper level, discovers in them the being to which

---

64   A. S. Eddington, *op. cit.*, pp. 258, 259.

65   The fact cannot be concealed that: "The physicist now regards his own external world in a way which I can only describe as more mystical, though not less exact and practical than that which prevailed some years ago, when it was taken for granted that nothing could be true unless an engineer could make a model of it. There was a time when the whole combination of self and environment which makes up experience seemed likely to pass under the dominion of a physics much more ironbound than it is now. That overwhelming phase when it was almost necessary to ask the permission of physics to call one's soul one's own is past" (*ibid.*, p. 344).

66   *Ibid.*, p. xviii.

it aspires as to its natural object. It *is* possible, on condition that the intellect resign itself to the asceticism and restrictions it demands and understand that to grasp a little of the being of things, it must refuse to utilize such knowledge (which though nobler is quantitatively poorer) for any speculative or practical exploitation of their phenomenal riches.

A knowledge which is a wisdom, even though only in a certain respect, and in a given order (in the order of sensible nature), is a thing for "enjoyment," not for "use." And all wisdom must, in one way or another, pass through the eye of a needle.

Knowledge of sensible nature began in the search for philosophical knowledge of this kind; but it took a long time to learn the spirit of poverty. The ancients thought their philosophy of nature was a science of the phenomena of nature. That was their misfortune. Let us still call the philosophical knowledge which we are now trying to define, the Philosophy of Nature. That is its proper name. But let us realize that it must give up any pretension to transgress the limits of its own essence and of conquering the world. For our part, we subscribe to that Philosophy of Nature which, in our opinion, is the best founded, and has the privilege of being in continuity with the purest metaphysics, namely, the Philosophy of Nature conceived according to the principles of Aristotle and St. Thomas Aquinas. But we are fully aware that it is indispensable (and certainly less troublesome than is usually imagined) to separate these principles from the applications and illustrations current for so long a time in the scientific conceptions of the ancients, and to see clearly that this knowledge of wisdom, this philosophy of being essentially subject to change, is in itself entirely free from an astronomy and a physics forever in ruins.

24. We must now take up, however, the epistemological conditions and characteristics of the Philosophy of Nature. It is in intelligible being itself, however obscured by sensible matter, that knowledge of this sort resolves its concepts. It belongs to an ontological type of explanation, wherein the natural movement of the speculative intellect finds full play. It does not cling to empirical conditions, but to reasons of being and to causes properly so called. It aims to discover the essence of things. Proceeding, as all philosophy does, according to an analytico-synthetic method, it depends on experience much more stringently than Metaphysics and must be able to carry its judgments right down to sense verification. Nevertheless, it is a deductive science, assigning reasons and intelligible necessities in proportion as it ascertains the intrinsic constitutive or the "quiddity" of its objects. For example, it belongs to the Philosophy of Nature to instruct us about the nature of the continuum and of number, of quantity, of space, of motion, of time, of corporeal substance, of transitive action, of vegetative and sensitive life, of the soul and its operative powers, etc. It is also its role to consider the ontological disposition of this

universe, even—as Aristotle did at the end of the *Physics*—its relation to the First Cause, and the balance between the necessary, the contingent, and the fortuitous in the course of events.

If we want to define the Philosophy of Nature, we shall have to say that it is a knowledge whose object, present in all things of corporeal nature, is mobile being as such and the ontological principles which account for its mutability. For it is essentially a philosophy of mutability. This knowledge came into existence with Aristotle when he showed that an ontology of the sensible world is possible, not precisely insofar as it is sensible, but insofar as it is the very world *changing being*, and that it implies in its structure intelligible invariants depending upon specifying forms.[67]

Whereas metaphysics embraces the whole domain of intelligibility not of itself immersed in the sensible, physics in the Aristotelian sense embraces the whole domain of intelligibility of itself immersed in the sensible. In the conception of the ancients, all the sciences of the material world were part of this knowledge. This stamped it with a singular optimism and a candid philosophical imperialism. Since they kept their eyes, above all, on philosophy they tended to absorb all the sciences of nature into it. Nevertheless, in certain domains even among the ancients these sciences had already become aware of their own methods and of their autonomy, but that was in the special case of the *scientiae mediae* envisaged as treating questions of Natural Philosophy mathematically. Moreover, to the extent that the Philosophy of Nature took the place of a scientific investigation and systematization of phenomena in detail, it too frequently gave rise to explanations of an extreme analytic insufficiency, sometimes merely verbal.

As we had occasion to note in a previous chapter, it is important to remember, as St. Thomas often sad,[68] that, in general, the essence of sensible

---

67   Apropos of the definition of the Philosophy of Nature, as it is proposed here, it behooves us to mention that in his opusculum *De Subjecto Naturalis Philosophiae*, Cajetan clearly shows that *being*, taken under the formal aspect of its mutability, which restricts being but does not rob it of its analogical character, must be designated as the proper object of the philosophy of nature. He also shows why the expression *ens sensibile*, however legitimate it may be, is, nevertheless, less formal and less philosophical than the expression *ens mobile*, for the latter "liberates at the outset the philosophy of nature from the undertakings of Parmenides and Melissus."

68   Cf. *In II Sent.*, dist. 35, q. 1, a. 2, ad 3: "Sicut aliquando utimur non veris differentiis loco verarum, propter earum occultationem, ut in *I Post.*, text. 35 dicitur, ita etiam loco veri generis potest poni aliquid per quod genus magis innotescat."
De Verit., IV, 1, ad 8 (text quoted below, Ch. V, n. 5).
Cont. Gent., I, 3: "Rerum sensibilium plurimas proprietates ignoramus, earumque proprietatum, quas sensu apprehendimus, rationem perfecte in pluribus invenire non possumus."
In Metaph., lib. VII, lect. 12: "Quandoque aliquis dividens . . . dividat per ea quae sunt secundum accidens, propter hoc quod non potest invenire proprias et per se differentias. Aliquando enim necessitas cogit ut utamur, loco per se

things remains hidden from us because of the matter in which it is, as it were, buried. It is only in the mathematical order that we can openly consider a world of essences. That is why mathematics is the most imperious and the most luxurious type of human science. In the physical order it is possible to attain to essential and specific definitions which are certain concerning man and the things of man (his powers, habitus, etc.), but below man, for the most part, the element of resistance to intelligibility introduced by matter rendering corporeal essences opaque to our view, knowable by signs rather than by properties in the ontological sense, keeps the essences hidden from us *in their specificity.* From these observations it follows that the Philosophy of Nature cannot reach down to the ultimate specific diversities of corporeal nature. And this implies a graver restriction on the philosophical optimism of the ancients.

When it is a question of the distinction between certain vast domains—between non-living and living bodies, between animals and plants, between man and irrational animals—the Philosophy of Nature does indeed grasp the essential differences. There we are in a region accessible to the philosopher's view and we can attain properly philosophical certitudes in the very order of typological discrimination. In other words, we know that there is an essential difference between plant irritability and animal sensibility, we know that the immanent action by which the living organism constructs itself, the activities of sensation, and intellection, all disclose quidditative principles which enable us to penetrate into the intimate structure of the beings we are considering. We know that a body as such is constituted by two complementary ontological principles, one purely potential and determinable, the other specifying and determining, which we call "prime matter" and "substantial form."

differentiarum, differentiis per accidens, in quantum sunt signa quaedam differentiarum essentialium nobis ignotarum." See below, Ch. V, n. 8.

"Here below," wrote R. Garrigou-Lagrange, "man is the only being whose specific difference belongs to the purely intelligible world and not to the sensible world; that is what permits the deduction of his different properties from it. Inferior beings become truly intelligible for us only in their transcendental (common to all beings) and generic notes.

"We know for example that mercury is a corporeal substance, a liquid metal, but we do not know its specific difference. When it is necessary to specify the generic notion, we have only an empirical, descriptive definition, which does not succeed in rendering intelligible the properties of this body. We are content to say: mercury is at ordinary temperature a liquid metal, silvery in color, which solidifies at -40°, boils at 360°, is very heavy; its salts are very active antiseptics, but also very toxic. We observe the facts but cannot know the why. Similarly for the plant, the animal. Who will assign the specific difference of a certain species so as to be able to deduce its properties? If it is a question of man, on the contrary, then among all the notes common to all men: rationality, liberty, morality, sociability, speech, religion, etc., one of them, rationality, appears as the *raison d'être* of all the others. . . . All these notes can be rendered intelligible, that is re-united with being by the intermediary of rationality" (*Le sens commun, la philosophie de l'être et les formules dogmatiques,* 3rd ed., pp. 104–105).

Nevertheless, the Philosophy of Nature has to be satisfied in such matters with certitudes of very lofty universality. It must abandon all the specific diversities and peculiarities of the world of bodies, all the detail of the operations of sensible nature, to what Leibniz called "symbolic" or "blind" knowledge, and we propose to call empiriological knowledge. Indeed, this latter knowledge does descend to detail, but the essence escapes it. When there is question of deciphering the intricacies of becoming, and the interactions which comprise the marvelously multiform and compact play of nature, the Philosophy of Nature can doubtless have, indirectly, a heuristic value, by reason of the stimulations it is capable of giving to the minds of scientists (especially in the case of the sciences we have called empirio-schematic). But in itself, and within its own domain, it has no pretension in this regard. There is no other science of the phenomena of nature than empiriological science, and this science is not a philosophy.

25. Now let us note that there is perfect knowledge only when we know things, not in a more-or-less indistinct fashion by stopping at generic determinations, but by coming right down to ultimate specific determinations. If metaphysics is a perfect knowledge (we shall return to this point later), it is because its specifying object (being, disengaged precisely as being by *abstractio formalis*) is not a genus, but a transcendental, which, taken as such, stands at the ultimate degree of logical determination. What, then, is the case for the Philosophy of Nature? Its object is not *ens inquantum ens*, the object of the metaphysician.

Nor, as we have just seen, are the specific natures of the world of bodies its proper object. These natures *would be* the specifying object of the sciences of nature, if these sciences could attain them. But they cannot; they stop at an empiriological knowledge of nature. However, the Philosophy of Nature does not deal with simple generic determinations, no more than metaphysics does. In reality it considers corporeal and mobile things from the point of view of the transcendental being incarnate in them. Hence, it participates in some way in the light of metaphysics, even as our soul participates in some way in the nature of pure spirits. The specifying object of the Philosophy of Nature is the ontological mutability and the formalities in which the mind can discern a difference of being (corporeity, quantity, motion, life, animality, etc.) within corporeal natures taken as such. And this suffices to assure its distinction and autonomy in regard to the experimental sciences.

On the other hand, however, sensible or mobile being is itself complete, that is to say it has the integrity of its determinations, only in specific natures. Hence, it follows that the Philosophy of Nature is not a *complete* knowledge without the sciences of nature. Experimental Science and Philosophy of Nature are two distinct but incomplete knowledges, subject to different controls, the one above all of the intelligible, the other above all of the observable, which complete each other as best they can. They both, thereby, belong to the same degree of abstraction, though from another point of view the Philosophy of Nature, as we have seen, is essentially different[69] from the Sciences of Nature.

26. I would have no objection to comparing the relation of the Philosophy of Nature with the Sciences of Nature to the relation of the rational soul with the body.[70] In itself the first is independent of the state of development of the second and of their hypotheses. It relies on "philosophical facts" which are much more simple and fundamental than "scientific facts."

However, to insist too exclusively on this independence, as a philosopher might be inclined to do, would be to risk losing sight of the intimate and substantial union that ought to prevail between these two parts of the knowledge of the sensible world. For some three centuries during which the fascination of a mechanistic metaphysics was imposed on the sciences of nature, the authentic Philosophy of Nature was like a separated soul. During that time it got rid of many impurities. Today it is re-establishing contact with Experimental Science. That contact is natural and necessary.

It is true that the philosophical facts on which the Philosophy of Nature is based (for example, that there are real specific diversities in the world of

---

69   This difference must be regarded as appertaining to the essential and specifying order, if it is true that it is the degree of immaterialization of the object constituting the *terminus ad quem* of the abstractive operation, and manifested by the *mode of defining*, which introduces specific differentiations between sciences situated on the same generic degree of abstraction (cf. above, Ch. II, n. 26). It is obvious that empiriological definition, by resolution into the observable as such, is essentially different from definition of the ontological type, by resolution into intelligible being. The difference between the Philosophy of Nature and the sciences of phenomena, whether of the empiriometric or empirioschematic type, is much more marked than the difference between arithmetic and geometry, which were for the scholastics two specifically distinct sciences. This is the way in which John of St. Thomas distinguishes Natural Philosophy and Medicine ("quia licet utraque abstrahat a materia singulari, tamen magis concernit materiam corpus ut sanandum quam corpus mobile ut sic," *Log.*, II P., q. 27, a. 1, Reiser, t. I, p. 825; cf. *Phil. Nat.*, I P., q. I, a. 2, Vivès, t. II, p. 16). And, if St. Thomas seems to place the Philosophy of Nature and the Sciences of Nature in the same specific class in which the diverse degrees of concretion of the object involve only differences of more or less of the same (cf. *Comm. in de Sensu et Sensato*, lect. I), it is precisely because in his epoch the Sciences of Nature, except in certain already mathematicized domains such as astronomy and optics, had not yet won their methodological autonomy and still constructed their definitions according to the same typical model as the Philosophy of Nature.

70   The soul and the body constitute a complete substantial whole *ratione speciei*. In this respect the comparison of the relation between the Philosophy of Nature and the sciences on the one hand, and the relation of the soul and the body on the other, is defective. It is from the point of view of the integrity of the reality to be known by the Philosophy of Nature and by the sciences that the comparison is valid.

bodies, there are substantial changes, living organisms are endowed with activities which issue from the self and revert to the self, etc.) can be established starting from common observation (philosophically criticized). Nevertheless, it is fitting that in proportion to the development of the positive sciences these facts be also clarified starting from scientific facts themselves, to the extent that they can be disengaged from the theories. Scientific facts all by themselves cannot furnish the least philosophical decision. But the proper light of philosophical objects and principles, like the light of the agent intellect illuminating phantasms, causes the philosophical content with which they are pregnant to issue forth from them.[71] Perdurable in its essential determinations, the Philosophy of Nature must, therefore, accept the law of ageing and rejuvenation, of molting and renewal imposed on the fleshly garments it receives from the experimental sciences, and thanks to which its factual material is marvelously increased and by which it is, at the same time, freed from that imagery (not philosophical, but common or "vulgar") which it takes from prescientific interpretations running through the familiar world of the senses.[72]

The hylomorphic doctrine, for example, is as true today as it was in the time of Aristotle. Its vocabulary and exemplifications have grown old, but not its substance. The four elements of former times are replaced by the ninety-two elements of Mendelejeff's Table. They correspond to a very different scientific notion. We have a much more rigorous knowledge of this family of elements than did the chemists of a hundred years ago. We hold as probable that they

---

71   Cf. the very wise views indicated by the lamented P. Gény in his article "Metafisica ed esperienza nella cosmologia," *Gregorianum*, 1920, Vol. I, fasc. 1.

72   Thus many ideas admitted by the Natural Philosophy of the ancients concerning the continuity of matter have had, since the invention of the microscope, and will have still more, with the progress of the theories of corpuscular physics, to be submitted to serious revisions, both in the case of bodies that only apparently manifest the character of substantial individuality and in the case of bodies that really manifest that character. The problem arises whether the substantial unity of a corporeal individual (for example, like a molecule of a gas, or a living organism) necessarily requires continuity in extension, as the ancients believed. In other words, cannot a substantial form inform a whole of discontinuous parts, whether contiguous (as blood plasma is contiguous to the walls of the blood vessels) or, on the atomic scale, separated by inter-atomic or intermolecular interstices (in the case that, contrary to the hypothesis of Gredt, these interstices would not themselves be informed by the substantial form of the individual whole). In my opinion, such a structural discontinuity is compatible with the substantial unity of the individual whole, and I think that, in that case, the Thomistic theory of individuation by *materia signata quantitate* is verified without special difficulty. The transcendental relation of matter to quantity would then mean, a transcendental relation to a constellation of positions.

On the other side, it would appear that "organization" must no longer be regarded as the privilege of living matter. The atom also is "organized"—but without the progressive equilibrium and *self-perfecting* activity (*actio immanens*) characteristic of life.

all derive from the atom of hydrogen by a series of changes which a philosopher must needs regard as substantial mutations. The phenomena of radioactivity offer the spectacle of such changes *of nature* in the world of bodies. This is not a pure and simple scientific verification. (It belongs to philosophy, not to science, to establish a fact, whose formulation implies notions of substance, nature, species, etc., metaphysically understood.) But it is a remarkable empiriological indication or "sign" which the philosopher can prudently point to as such. The existence of the microstructure of matter is a definitively acquired fact. (It leaves open the properly ontological question of the essence of matter.)[73] When science incessantly renews its conceptions concerning the spatio-temporal organization and the properties of the atom, it affirms, to that extent, the existence of the primitive complex it so names. Indeed, this ensemble of empiriological knowledges lends itself better to the ontology of Aristotle than to that of Democritus or of Descartes (and, may I add, better, no doubt, than the experimental conceptions in favor among the alchemists of the Middle Ages).

Complementary Elucidations

27. Yes! But doesn't Mr. Eddington, in his rich imagery, tell us that a body is a "tube of the four-dimensional universe, separated from the rest of space-time by a more-or-less sharp limit"? Surely we are far from the universe of Aristotle.

We are certainly far from the scientific ideas of Aristotle. But we are talking about his philosophy. Whether an elephant be an isolated tube of a four-dimensional universe, or a lump of flesh and bones composed of four elements and four primary qualities, in either case there is no resemblance between the idea that science or common-sense forms of this animal (an idea that can be expressed in an image, or in a spatio-temporal scheme, which is at least *reductively* imaginable),[74] and the essentially unimaginable, and purely onto-

---

73   Although the actual state of microphysical theories and the epistemological structure of physico-mathematical knowledge are clearly contrary to such a hope, we may imagine, *per impossibile*, that one day the configuration of matter, the network of the distribution in space of its structural parts—not only of the particles, molecules, ions or atoms into which the mind decomposes a material mass of great dimensions, but of the constitutive parts of the atom itself—would become the object of a knowledge from which all symbolism had been eliminated. The supposition that such a knowledge of the *configuration* of matter had been perfected would always leave open the question of the essence of matter. As to its configuration, a body may be composed of a swarm of electrons and atoms; as to its essence it is a substantial composite of potency and act.

74   Such an idea may be (cf. above, Ch. II, § 15) *unimaginable by default*, by reason of the very conditions of the observability of the object, it may also, by reason of the mathematization of physics, be representable to physical imagination only metaphorically, or even be only representable to mathematical imagination (and

logical, conception which philosophy reaches from the first principles of which the substance of the same animal is constituted.

Prime matter and substantial form belong to another noematic universe than this lump or tube. Neither favors the hylomorphic theory more than the other. It rests on something other than these images. Whether it be a tridimensional lump or a quadridimensional tube, an elephant still has to perform that operation which both the ordinary man and the scientist call "eating," although they may form very diverse images of it; and it still has to end with the phenomena that both call "dying." The philosopher knowing that the elephant in question is an individual substance, "one in itself," specifically different from the plant that it assimilates by nutrition and the inorganic materials into which its corpse will decompose, is forced to seek the subject of these substantial mutations in a radical potentiality which, following Aristotle, he will call prime matter (though one could wish for a better name). Naturally, he is unable to describe what figure prime matter has either in three-dimensional or four-dimensional space (because it doesn't have any figure). Nor can he say how, once it is informed or transcendentally determined by the specifying "form" which composes with it a single substantial being, it is clothed with "accidents" and becomes accessible to the calculations of a scientist and to the observations of an ordinary man under the appearance of either a compact, tangible, visible mass, or a huge—and unrepresentable[75]—swarm of protons and electrons, i.e., of "vague particles" and waves propagated in configuration space, and which are only statistical symbols. An impassable gap will always attest the difference of order which distinguishes philosophical from scientific explanation, both of which are legitimate and necessary. By way of parenthesis, it may be remarked that were eminent scientists sufficiently attentive to this fact they would be saved from confusing "substance," in the philosophical sense, with "substance" in the popular sense, viz., as it is imagined by that first attempt at science which is common knowledge, thanks to which it explains to itself that a table is not penetrated by the paper placed upon it. . . .

28. Still, according to our principles, the Einsteinian universe of four dimensions and its curvature, as well as the electron or proton of today, must be regarded as pure physico-mathematical beings of reason founded on the real. The question then arises as to what relation the Philosophy of Nature can have, not, now, with the facts, or with *entia realia* more-or-less completed by reason, but with pure *entia rationis* and the well-founded myths of science. Let us complete what we were saying above.[76] We believe that the Philosophy of

---

even to it only indirectly and by analogy), as is the case for the waves of wave-mechanics. It does not cease to belong, at least reductively, to the order of the imaginable and the figurable, in the same way that the point, though unextended, still belongs, *reductively*, to the order of the extended.

75   See the preceding note.

Nature ought to take over the *entire* material supplied by the Experimental Sciences. But although it can base itself on facts established by these sciences, as upon foreign material that it appropriates, it clearly cannot require from a physico-mathematical being of reason the means of elucidating the nature of things in itself and ontologically. It ought to make use of such beings of reason, but in another way, namely, inasmuch as the latter is one of the elements in the image of the universe established by science. For the Philosophy of Nature cannot do without a scientific imagery. It needs the image (Can this word still be used? It has become *unimaginable.*[77]) or the symbol that the science of its day fashions of the world. It knows, moreover, that some of the most impressive entities that science constructs are myths that present to the mind the real—though in disguise. It should be grateful to science for rendering these myths—because of the mathematical beings of reason that enter into their construction—more and more unrepresentable to the imagination. For, it is thereby delivered, by an heroic remedy, from the temptation to represent, in the fashion of a Democritus or a Descartes, the secret fibers of nature after the gross pattern of forms that our eyes and hands can grasp. Science here gives philosophy an important lesson. For although science moves in the domain of the sensible and the imaginable, it is led by its very progress, not to transcend, but rather to dissolve the whole domain of the sensible and imaginable and to move onward to what belongs only reductively to the figurable. Should the philosopher not have understood for himself that from the very fact that the primary spatio-temporal elements of the world of bodies *make up* the complexes which naturally fall under our senses, they cannot *resemble* those complexes? The world which they constitute must not resemble in the least the world our senses know. To penetrate into it, it is necessary to cross a threshold of shadow and confusion for the imagination. And in the lack of a more perfect knowledge, the unrepresentable myths of science have at least the merit of reminding us of this fact.

Meanwhile, what can the philosopher himself make of a myth? Obviously, only another myth—this time, a philosophical one. There is no other way for the Philosophy of Nature to take up into its own order the well-founded myths of physico-mathematical knowledge than to become a fabricator of myths in its turn. Do we not know that the philosopher is in a certain way a "lover of myths"? *Philosophus est aliqualiter philomythes?*[78]

A vast field is thus opened to the creative imagination of the philosopher when, for example, he aims to interpret in the light of an otherwise well-established philosophical doctrine, like the hylomorphic doctrine, the provi-

76   See above, Ch. II, §§ 29 and 30.
77   See above, Ch. IV, n. 74.
78   St. Thomas Aquinas, *In Metaph.* lib. I, lect. 2. As a matter of fact, Aristotle did not say that a philosopher is in a certain way a mythophile, but that a mythophile is in a certain way a philosopher: "ὁ φιλόμυθος φιλόσοφος πώς ἐστιν" (*Metaph.*, A, 2, 982 b 18).

sional image which science fashions of the microstructure of the atom. Hardly will he have invented a sufficiently probable hypothesis—admitted, for example, that the substantial form informs the intra-atomic ether as well as the central nucleus and the electrons that encircle it[79]—than the schema of Rutherford and Bohr, to which this interpretation is related, will be already on the way to bankruptcy. He will have to readapt it or invent another. The philosopher might also busy himself with the four-dimensional universe, or with the ether that present-day physicists "try not to talk about,"[80] though, it seems, they still have difficulty in doing without it. But if he thought that this was engaging in the work of philosophical knowledge properly so called, one could only regret his courage.

Perhaps it is fitting, then, that the Philosophy of Nature add to its philosophical knowledge, properly so called, a region of philosophical myths destined to harmonize it with the well-established myths involved in physico-mathematical theories. In this way it may complete its union with the experimental body that the sciences construct for it. And so, though there can be no continuity as to the rational explanation and the understanding of things between physico-mathematical theories and the Philosophy of Nature, a secondary continuity may be established through their common ground of imagery.

29. It is certainly remarkable that only in the world of sensible Nature do we find our knowledge shared by a philosophy and an experimental science related to each other as the soul to the body. No such duality is found in the other universes of intelligibility. Mathematics has no ontological soul; it has

---

79 J. Gredt, *Die Lehre von Materie u. Form u. die Elektromentheorie*. Cf. M. de Munnynck, *Commun. au congrès thom. de Rome* (1925); articles of the *Revue Thomiste* (1900) and of *Divus Thomas* (Fribourg, 1928); Leslie J. Walker, article in *Philos. Perennis*, t. II, pp. 831–842; and the *Essai* of P. Descoqs, which, in our opinion, is very questionable.

80 "I remember a conversation that I had some twenty years ago with P. N. Lebedoff, the eminent Russian physicist, who told me that he felt secure only when speaking about the ether. That was at the time when the notion of the electron began to enter Physics. Today physicists try not to speak about ether and some doubt its existence" (W. Vernadsky, *art. cit.*, *L'Etude de la Vie et la Novelle Physique*, p. 700). "Ether," proclaimed Lord Kelvin, "is not an imaginary creation of speculative philosophy; it is as essential for us as the air we breathe" (Emile Picard, *Un coup d'oeil sur l'histoire des sciences* . . . p. 34). "It is admitted today that ether is not a form of matter. . . . That doesn't mean that ether is suppressed. We need ether. We cannot decompose the physical world into molecules of matter or of electricity with an inter-space between them deprived of any characteristic . . ." (A. S. Eddington, *op. cit.*, p. 48). Einstein likewise thought that we cannot eliminate the notion of a "milieu deprived of all mechanical and kinetic properties, but which determines mechanical and electromagnetic phenomena" (E. Picard, *op. cit.*, p. 41).

only an abstract and ideal body. Metaphysics has no empiriological body; it is only spirit.

III

MECHANISM

30. If the preceding analyses are correct, we can see that the central error of modern philosophy in the domain of the knowledge of nature has been to give the value of an ontological explanation to the type of mechanist attraction immanent in physico-mathematical knowledge, and to take the latter for a philosophy of nature. It is not a philosophy of nature. It is an empiriological-analysis of nature, mathematical in form and control (an "empirio-metric" analysis). If it is true that an analysis of this type must inevitably construct a world of explicative entities destined to sustain mathematical deduction, it is clear, on the one hand, that this world will be, as we have seen, a pseudo-ontological world in which beings of reason will abound, and, on the other, that it will be oriented towards mechanism as to its ideal limit (never achieved, however, since all the "irrationals" which science is bound to admit are opposed to an effective mechanistic reduction). Mechanistic representations are in fact the sole residue of ontological explanations capable of entering into the physico-mathematical texture itself. And so it is that the physicist will be forced to construct with them the principles and the reasons of being of the physical or geometrical order which he needs. That, however, is a question of provisory representations whose whole value derives, not from the essence of the real envisaged in itself, but from the mathematical relations they sustain; a question not of a philosophical mechanism, but of a methodological mechanism, at once problematic and auxiliary. Philosophy might well retain the approximative spatio-temporal image, the well-founded myth it may have contributed to build up forming the structure of this universe and these elements; but it ought not to confer on it an ontologically explicative value.

To what extent does the present "crisis" in physics here introduce new points of view?

It seems from the outset that the New Physics has turned its back on mechanism. That is true if the word "mechanism" be taken in the strict sense, and Descartes' motto "my whole physics is nothing but geometry" be understood as referring to classical geometry. But the deepest lair of mechanism is mathematicism, not geometrism, and, on the other hand, as geometry itself becomes more abstract it tends to become co-extensive with mathematics. Let us say that the new scientific conceptions only manifest more daringly the intent of transmuting physics into a universalized mathematics. We have already pointed out that in the new scientific conceptions, the geometrization of physics is accomplished by a recasting of geometry under the influence of the physical itself (and that geometry will the more easily reduce itself to the physical in proportion as pains are taken to introduce the physical into it). But that matters little to the over-all result. Crises or transformations of the mechanistic ideal should certainly not be taken for the death of that ideal. The physicist will always remain attracted by the ideal of a "unification of all the knowledges concerning the physical world in a single science expressed . . . in geometric or quasi-geometric terms," and since he is not thereby tending to a philosophical geometrism, he will accept without difficulty, in order to more closely approximate this ideal, all the revisions that the apprehension and symbolization of the physical real impose on mechanics and geometry themselves.

31. It is here that the epistemological superiority of the New Physics becomes patent to the eyes of the philosopher. It manifests much more clearly than classical physics, makes obvious to all the purely methodological and auxiliary character of the mechanism or Pythagoreanism of the scientist. On the one hand, it has rehabilitated the reality of motion which strict mechanism had destroyed (it is the awareness of this irreducible reality that is present, it seems—at least to the eyes of a philosopher—at the very beginning of the theory of relativity), but then, in order to safeguard the geometrization of physics, it had to *mobilize* the measured magnitudes, the pointer-readings effected by observers from diverse systems of reference, to abandon the unique and absolutely immobile spatial frame which the mechanist philosopher took over from mathematics as a lodging for his cosmos and within which the mechanistic philosopher saw all the motions of the universe as variations of a pure ideal spectacle, because, giving an ontological value to geometrism, he had no means of philosophically conceiving motion as real. Neither does the New Physics philosophically consider the reality of motion (that is not its business). It makes room perforce (and with the aid of many beings of reason) for that reality in the physico-mathematical synthesis. And by that very fact it attests that the mathematicism to which it tends has no ontological pretensions whatsoever.

On the other hand, the New Physics has had to recognize a certain disparity between the notions and principles applicable to phenomena on our scale of large dimension, and the notions and principles applicable on the atomic scale. This is so because, as was noted above, on the atomic scale material particles taken individually cannot be subjected to continuous observation and determination. But, if it is true that in empiriological knowledge the resolution of concepts is made exclusively into the observable and measurable, and that consequently in this kind of knowledge a concept has no meaning except in relation to the experimental method and circumstances which serve to define it,[81] it follows that on the atomic scale the very notion of the empiriological

---

81   "Our knowledge of the exterior world cannot be divorced from the nature of the

object is modified. It always designates something observable and measurable, a possibility of observation and mensuration, but this observability and measurability are themselves fundamentally different.

Hence, it is not surprising that the whole organism of scientific explanation should differ in the two cases, and that it should admit, for example, two incompatible exigencies for the law of causality in the one and in the other case, respectively. This supremely interesting result manifests clearly that mathematicism (especially in its statistical, and, in the case of microphysics, indeterministic, form) and the geometrization of physics have here lost all philosophical pretension, all pretension of delivering to us the nature of material things in itself. Otherwise, physics would not allow itself to propose, concerning the same world considered on two different scales, not only two different images—that goes without saying—but two heterogeneous rational conceptions between which mathematical formalism alone assures continuity.[82]

Dangerous Liaisons

32. This is not the place to enumerate the resources that the New Physics offers to philosophy, either in the order of facts or in that of apt apologetic opportunities, so to speak, that it presents in regard to philosophy. We shall only offer some brief suggestions on this subject.

Can the principle of Carnot, about which Mr. Eddington has written such charming pages (which is not itself an acquisition of the New Physics, but which stands unshaken within it, at least on the macroscopic scale), throw any light on the problems concerning the origin of the world? The disappointments that have resulted from certain philosophical attempts, even the diversity of opinion among scientists concerning the degree of respect due to this principle, call for the greatest reserve in this matter.[83]

---

appliances with which we have obtained the knowledge" (A. S. Eddington, *op. cit.*, p. 163).

82 Supposing the physics of the future gives up, with P. Langevin, the notion of corpuscular individuality, in order to save scientific determinism, the two tableaux of which we are speaking would remain none the less heterogeneous, as is evidenced precisely, in this case, by the abandonment of the notion of the individual on the atomic scale.

83 In any case, by itself alone, this principle can give us no "scientific" elucidations on the problem of creation, even if it be granted that it obliges us to suppose at the starting point of the history of the cosmos a maximum degree of organization of energy, an organization which "is, by hypothesis, the antithesis of the probable, something which cannot happen by chance." To conclude from that to a divine intervention at the origin of the world would be for science to go beyond the sphere of its competence, μεταβαίνειν εἰς ἄλλο γένος. To establish such a philosophical conclusion, it is necessary to proceed philosophically. This supposes the bringing into play of philosophically elucidated notions (which the physicist as such does not know) such as ontological causality, analogy of being,

The second principle of thermodynamics offers still other resources to the Philosophy of Nature especially in regard to the philosophy of the living organism. Is it not one of the marks of the irreducible specificity of living things that, without violating this principle but rather using it for its own advantages, they profit by the universal process of the degradation of energy variously to reconstruct order and organization, to raise for a time the degree of being (I do not mean as to the quality of the energy, for life does not release a special form of energy, but as to perfections of a higher order, properly biological or psychic)? Life—material life—is a constructive fire which feeds upon decay.

On the other hand, certain agreements seem to create zones, as it were, of affinity between the Philosophy of Nature and the image of the universe elaborated by the New Physics. The hope of deducing physical diversity and the world of experience from a minimum of primary notions (and with a gratuitousness which metaphysics can never know), the idea of a finite universe, which is nevertheless without limits because of the curvature of space, and which, according to the most recent hypotheses, is expanding, and also the ideal of the discontinuity of energy and the variability of mass find, if one abstracts from their proper and scientific value, certain apriori complicities so to speak in the philosopher of nature (I do not speak necessarily of a Cartesian philosopher).[84] Sometimes he even fancies he discerns in certain conceptions

potency and act, order, finality, etc., and that the notion of entropy itself had taken on a philosophical as well as a physico-mathematical sense.

True, to rise thus to a higher plane of intelligibility is perhaps possible in the light of philosophical principles. If it be admitted that the second principle of thermodynamics is applicable to the universe considered as a whole, and if what Mr. Eddington thinks of the notion of entropy (cf. *op. cit.*, pp. 117–118) be granted, it seems that such an extrapolation would be permissible, by reason of the very singularity of this notion. In this way, observing that as time advances, the more a certain internal order immanent in the activities of the material world is irreparably dispersed (the empiriometrical sign of which is "the growth of entropy"), the Philosophy of Nature, before yielding ground to metaphysics, could already rise to a consideration of the first cause from which the order in question proceeds.

Such a way to the first cause would nevertheless remain less perfect than those of metaphysics, because it shows in any case the necessity of divine operation only at the *beginning in time* of the evolution of the cosmos (or of the evolutions of the cosmos, since we do not know whether another state had not preceded this one). Is it necessary to add that a philosopher, precisely because he proceeds philosophically, and knows that divine causality is always exercised, would not think that "some billions of years ago God wound up the material universe and has left it to chance ever since"? Throughout all time the course of events in the universe, and chance itself, are subject to divine causality and divine government.

84   Even more than the philosopher, the physicist, who has a concern for metaphysical problems, will be sensitive to these accidental philosophical connections of the New Physics. For example, he will find that the theory of relativity assists him in understanding the relation of the time of creatures to the eternity of God.

of the New Physics some kind of kinship of style (not indeed the slightest substantial likeness) with certain antique accessories in the Peripatetic shop, such as *natural place* and *condensation and rarefaction* or that difference of nature between the matter of the celestial bodies and that of corruptible bodies, of which the distinction, very much more clear-cut, between the "matter" of the physicist and his "non-material" ether (to the extent that he grants ether) seems to be a sort of modern replica.

The philosopher notices, moreover, that one of the effects of the revolution occurring in physics is broadening its scope to embrace living phenomena, as M. Vernadsky indicated in a remarkable address to the Societies of Naturalists of Moscow and Leningrad.[85] This expansion shows that the planetary importance of such phenomena may henceforth be more easily recognized. Besides, as the typical traits of their physico-chemical behavior (irreversibility for example or again dissymmetry) now extend into the inorganic universe where they had been neglected, the vital will perhaps furnish science with new ways of conceiving the physical.

Finally, how could the imagination of the philosopher (or of the poet) not be enchanted by those light atoms that condense and transform themselves into heavy ones in order to radiate light and heat, by that matter whose mass has its internal energy as measure, by those stars which by ceaselessly reducing their erstwhile enormous mass and that will go out completely after thousands of billions of years, meanwhile pour energy into the universe.[86] How could he

---

(Cf. K. F. Herzfeld, "The Frontiers of Modern Physics and Philosophy," *Proc. of the American Cath. Phil. Assoc.* (Chicago, Loyola Univ., Dec. 29, 1930); "Scientific Research and Religion," *The Commonweal*, Mar. 20, 1929; "Einstein as a Physicist," *ibid.*, Feb. 4 and 11, 1931.) And that is certainly legitimate so long as it is understood that these are so many comparisons and metaphors that can assist the mind in grasping a truth (in this case a philosophical truth) without, for that reason, being themselves necessarily true (I mean, as far as the theory of relativity is concerned, ontologically or philosophically true).

85   *Art. cit., Revue Générale des Sciences*, December 31, 1930. The author insists on the importance of the actual scientific crisis to which he accords the value of one of the great "recurring crises" of thought. He points out that while effecting the reintegration of life in the "scientific tableau of the universe," it will tend to dissipate the striking contradiction constantly emphasized in the course of the classical period, between the objective tableau of the scientific universe (where mechanics and physico-chemistry alone had rights, and everything living and human was made to appear "fragile" and "nil") and the work of science itself as a "world-wide social formation," "constituted by living personalities" of whom more than nine-tenths are studying domains "without any relation to the tableau of the cosmos falsely considered as the result of over-all scientific work." These remarks on science, sociologically considered, are of great interest.

86   "We are therefore obliged to admit that, in the course of its complete evolution a star diminishes in mass at least in the proportion of 1000 to 1.

"It must be admitted that this loss of mass is linked to radiation since there is no loss of matter; these enormous stars do not let go of the atoms they contain."

not see in these things huge symbols of the very mysteries of the life of the spirit?

33. May it never be forgotten what an error it would be to try to build a Philosophy of Nature, and *a fortiori* a metaphysics, on the theoretical conclusions of modern physics and its explanations of the world, taken as ontological foundations, as if those conclusions and explanations could be utilized as such by the philosopher and without a previous rigid critique. That was the error committed by Spinoza with the physics of his day. It seems to us that in our own day, from very different standpoints, M. Bergson, and, if we have rightly understood his thought, Mr. Alexander, leave themselves open to a similar reproach. The former seeks to set free a so-called creative *durée*, immanent in the world of the physicist but which the physicist misunderstands; the latter makes of the world of the physicist a sort of matrix from which emerge worlds of ever more qualified and ever more compact realities. It would be a similar mistake should anyone, misled by the diverse advantages of which we have just been speaking, claim to draw a Philosophy of Nature out of the new physical theories, or demand from the indeterministic conceptions of contemporary physics any argument whatsoever against philosophical determinism. The latter can only be philosophically refuted. However important and significant the ideas of Heisenberg may be for the theoretician of the sciences, they have absolutely nothing to do with the problem of liberty. To be sure, they can contribute to the discrediting of various popular scientific notions. But if one were so foolish as to try to use them directly for the vindication of free will, they would have no more value in that domain than the *clinamen* of Epicurus and Lucretius.

To say this is not to deprecate the important bearing that the reversal of values provoked by the conceptions of the New Physics has had upon not only what concerns science itself and its own interests, but also the general intellectual regimen of the human subject, the social interests of the economy of the intellect. From this, so to speak, epistemo-sociological point of view, science is no longer considered *in itself*, that is, in respect to what is true or what is false, nor in respect to the determinations which necessarily result from the exigencies of science in the knowledge of things. Rather, it interests us as a collective

---

Consequently, we are led to admit that the loss of mass corresponds to a complete destruction of matter, to a profound neutralization of the electron by the proton, with, like a swan-song, a grand production of light, two photons resulting from the reciprocal neutralization of a proton and an electron.

"The complete destruction of matter in order to produce light probably requires, for its production in a significant degree, conditions of temperature and pressure in the depths of the stars which are profoundly different from any which we know how to realize. M. Eddington calculated the central temperature of most of the stars to be forty million degrees and the pressure would have to be figured in billions of atmospheres" (P. Langevin, *art. cit.*, p. 290).

attitude or spirit engendered *hic et nunc* in the mind of men. So considered, it influences the evolution of the mind as a ferment or a center of organization of various activities belonging to an associative, rather than a rational, order and accidental in relation to the essence of science itself.

Thus did classical physics—*per accidens*—lend wings to the illusion of an integral mechanistic explanation of the universe. A so-called scientific tableau of the cosmos hovered, like a mirage in the sky, over the minds of searchers, who believed it impossible to begin their research without offering libations to it. In it everything involving consciousness and life was to be reduced to physico-chemical processes, and the latter, to mechanical processes. In it, thanks to a single formula like that of Laplace's dreams, the calculation of the movement of material points according to the Newtonian laws of attraction would permit, in right if not in fact, the prediction of all events and of the whole history not only of the world of raw matter, but also of the organic world and the human world, and even the development of thought, the quivering of a reed as well as the movement of the stars.[87]

By abandoning classical mechanics, and even more, by proclaiming the principle of indetermination for phenomena of the atomic scale, and by affirming that it is contradictory to suppose that science can follow and determine the behavior of an individual corpuscle at each instant, or in other words know its past completely and with the aid of the past foresee, apriori, its future, the New Physics eliminates even the occasion for all this pseudo-philosophy, which regarded the spirit and free will as a scandal for science. That is a considerable result from the point of view of the sociology of the intellect. "Physics no longer creates any moral opposition to free will." But this result of itself has no formal and intrinsically philosophical value. For it was quite untrue that the classical mechanics and physics necessarily entailed the negation of free will.[88] It was also quite untrue that the mechanistic postulate

---

87   "An intelligence that, for a given instant, knew all the forces animating nature, and the respective position of all the beings that compose it, if, moreover, it were comprehensive enough to submit these data to analysis, would embrace in the same formula the movements of the greatest bodies in the universe and those of the least atom; nothing would be uncertain for it, and both the future and the past would be present to its eyes" (Laplace, *Essai philosophique sur les probabilités*, 1814). Similarly, Taine spoke of the "supreme law" in which are found inscribed "the eternal torrent of events and the infinite sea of things."

These famous pronouncements are doubly erroneous. They admit that contingent non-free events depending on universal interaction can be calculated in advance and foreseen with certitude, which is not exact: for to calculate in advance such events would require an infinite intelligence, (but such an intelligence does not need to foresee, it sees. Cf. our *Philosophie bergsonienne*, 2nd ed., Preface, pp. lxix–lc). They also deny the possibility of *contingent free* events, depending on the will of intelligent agents removed, in the measure in which they are spiritual, from the domain of the sciences of matter. (Cf. above, Ch. IV, n. 28.)

of the possibility of expressing everything by the laws of motion (or, to put it differently, of reducing everything to the displacement of corpuscles) involved any metaphysical conception whatsoever. The debate between "determinist" mechanics and "indeterminist" mechanics is quite outside the field of philosophical problems. The same is true of the indeterminism of the new corpuscular mechanics. It could be given philosophical significance only by binding it to a metaphysical error. In that case, one would have to imagine that this indeterminism invalidated the axiomatic value of the principle of causality (philosophically understood). We pointed out above that the principle of indetermination introduces gaps in the field of scientific causality,[89] or more exactly in the field of those substitutes for causality which physico-mathematical knowledge reaches by recasting the concept of cause. But if such can be the case, it is only to the precise extent that science abandons any ontological point of view, and gives up thinking phenomena *sub ratione entis*. "We have abandoned strict causality in the external world," wrote one of the most esteemed theorists of the New Physics.[90] Instead of the pronoun "we," it would be better to read: "empiriometric knowledge"—that knowledge which resolves its concepts not in being, but exclusively in the measurable, and which now perceives that everything in the physical world cannot be strictly measured. To give philosophical value to this abandonment, which makes sense only in the empiriological domain, would be a grave mistake. It is impossible for human science to know determinately the behavior of a corpuscle at each instant. For it observes and measures things with the aid of material instruments and in virtue of physical activities, and can only see an electron by jogging it with light. But suppose a pure spirit, who knows *without material means* (and so, no longer by means of empiriological concepts) the behavior of this corpuscle[91] at each instant, it would see that the principle of causality applies strictly and in its full ontological sense. The hypothesis of a pure spirit has no meaning for the physicist. But if it had no meaning for a metaphysician, there would be no metaphysics.

In spite of the validity of their distinctions, we may hardly expect that the social behavior of the scientific and philosophical intellect will be more sensitive to them in the future than in the past. The New Physics will influence the common intellect in the same irrational fashion as classical physics did. Through some sort of associative influence or sub-intellectual induction, it will

88   See above, Ch. IV, § 10.
89   See above, Ch. IV, § 10.
90   A. S. Eddington, *op cit.*, p. 328.
91   We called attention above (Ch. IV, n. 31) to the hypothesis of P. Langevin, who abandons the notion of the individual corpuscle. Whatever be the scientific destinies of this hypothesis, the philosopher, even if he does not know what are the ultimate individuals of the atomic world, at least knows that the concept of individual is valid (I mean in the ontological sense given to it by the Philosophy of Nature) in this world as well as in the world of large dimensions.

probably give birth in its turn to an inchoate philosophy, a new "scientific tableau of the cosmos," which will save us from the former errors only at the price of illusions of another type. Doubtless public opinion will be stirred up by a prejudice in favor of contingency and liberty only by casting doubt on the substantiality of matter and the principle of causality.

As for us, we know that physico-mathematical explanation can have no continuity with philosophical explanation.[92] From this point of view they are right indeed who think it would be prudent to forbid philosophers to trespass on the work-yards of the new theory of quanta. To tell the truth, the physico-mathematical universe constitutes a closed world, in which geometrism (understanding that word in the broadest sense, insofar as it conforms to the ideal of the New Physics as well as to that of classical physics), or mathematicism, introduces a pseudo-ontology, a substitute for the Philosophy of Nature and metaphysics. This pseudo-ontology has only a methodological and auxiliary role, but it is really present, and, thanks to its beings of reason founded on the real, it constructs a system of total explanation that makes of this universe of intelligibility a whole closed within itself. The philosopher may explain how this physicist's universe is constructed. He may borrow material from it. From it also, as we have said, he may seek his image of the physical world, in accordance with which he can, in his turn, create myths, in the Platonic sense of the word. But he will have to superimpose on this universe an utterly different one.

Ontology and Empiriology in the Study of the Living Organism

34. The case is different for other experimental sciences—especially biology and Experimental Psychology—which are not essentially mathematizations of the sensible, and in which the mode of resolution of concepts and of explanation belong rather to the epistemological type which we have called "empirio-schematic." In so speaking we certainly do not mean that these sciences reject all mathematical treatment of observable data. Far from that! If such treatment finds its pre-eminent field in physics, from the fact that corporeity as such bathes ontologically in the quantitative, it should be able, nevertheless, to penetrate every region to which the shadow of quantity, and ultimately of matter, extends. And this shadow extends even to the things of the soul. However, as one rises above the world proper to physics, and as the object gains in ontological richness and perfection, the quantitative aspect of the behavior under consideration becomes, not less real, but less significant and more subordinate, and the science in question less reducible to an interpretation which looks solely to mathematics for its form and laws.

It would certainly be foolish to ignore the role already played by physico-chemical analysis (and hence calculation) in biology, a role which is destined

---

92   See above, Ch. II, §§ 29 and 30.

to increase daily.[93] In a field as irreducibly biological, as strictly governed by the concepts of form and organic totality as experimental embryology, Brachet could write: "The physico-chemical period is in its first tentative stages here, but without any doubt the future belongs to it."[94] As a matter of fact what is so studied is the material conditioning, the material means of life. And, since everything within the living organism is effected by physico-chemical means, this analysis can and should progress indefinitely.

Does this mean that some day it will exhaust biological reality? By no means. For if within the living thing everything is effected by physico-chemical means, everything is also effected by the soul (and its vegetative powers) as first principle. Rooted in a substance endowed with immanent activity, physico-chemical energies produce in it, as *instruments* of the soul and the vegetative faculties, and without violating the laws of inanimate matter, effects which surpass what they could do by themselves alone, in this sense, namely, that they actuate and ontologically elevate the subject itself. Doubtless, an experimental biology could be conceived which, consenting to a sort of amputation, would turn exclusively to an energetic and physico-chemical analysis of living phenomena and thus be oriented towards the mathematicist and mechanist ideal, leaving everything else to the Philosophy of Nature.

In our own day modern biology manifests a very strong anti-mechanistic reaction. But whatever orientation it may in fact take, we hold, nevertheless,

93 We do not subscribe to the judgment of M. Bergson: "In the domain of life calculation touches, at most, certain phenomena of organic *destruction*. Organic *creation*, on the contrary, the evolutionary phenomena which properly constitute life, we cannot in any way subject to a mathematical treatment" (*L'evolution creatrice*, p. 21). Nor do we subscribe to mechanistic pretensions. We think that mathematical treatment applied to living phenomena is capable of continual progress in this field. Nevertheless, it will normally remain subordinate to another treatment of the same phenomena which is properly biological. In this way (to use Buytendijk's term) the scientist will endeavor to "comprehend" truly and not merely materially explain these phenomena. On the question of physico-mathematical analysis in biology, cf. W. R. Thompson, "A contribution to the study of Morphogenesis in the Muscoid Diptera," Ch. III (*Transactions of Entomological Society of London*, December 31, 1929).

94 A Brachet, *La vie créatrice des formes* (Paris, 1927, p.99). The same is true in physiology. If, for example, muscle must be considered, according to the studies of Hill and Meyerhof, as an absolutely special moving power (chemico-colloidal) of a type unknown in mechanics, that doesn't prevent the appearance of mechanism. "The mechanism appears (apart from certain secondary lacunae) as entirely physico-chemical, involving no reaction, no force that has not been met in inanimate matter, and rigorously subject to the law of the conservation of energy" (Louis Lapicque, in the collective volume *L'orientation actuelle des sciences*, 1930). What is here "entirely physico-chemical" is the ensemble of energetic and material means of the phenomenon. *Materially* physico-chemical, the phenomenon itself is formally vital, it is an *auto-actuation of the subject*, and it implies that the physico-chemical energies in play are precisely means, instruments of a radical principle of immanent activity.

as certain that an empiriological analysis is both possible and necessary in the experimental domain, but it aims at penetrating living phenomena *as such*. This analysis, while remaining clearly distinct from the Philosophy of Nature, must make use of experimental (concepts like *prospektive Bedeutung* and *prospektive Potenz*,[95] centers of organization, specificity of plasmas,[96] etc.) which are strictly and irreducibly biological and super-ordinate to physical and chemical energetic concepts. Thus, for example, while the ontological concept of finality has its place among the explicative concepts of the Philosophy of Nature, the facts of biological finality represent for physico-chemical analysis only an irrational that must be reduced as much as possible. And, for the properly biological experimental analysis of which we have been speaking, those facts come under an empiriological concept that may be designated by the same name of finality,[97] but which should be completely recast, and emptied of its philosophical significance. Here, leaving aside any use of finality as a causal explanation, it will merely express that general pre-explicative[98] condition that the functions of the living thing, and the use it makes

---

95   These notions introduced by Hans Driesch are admitted today into the current terminology of science under the name, somewhat less happily chosen, of "real potentiality" and "total potentiality." Brachet has called attention to their fecundity.

96   "We see emerging again the very biological notion which Emil Rohde has expressed in striking terms: there are as many species of plasma as there are species of animals and plants; still more each living individual possesses its own 'specific' plasma, so that there are as many individual plasmas as there are individuals on the Globe" (Remy Collin, "La théorie cellulaire et la vie," *La Biologie Médicale*, 1929, n. 4). In a general way, the strictly biological experimental concepts of which we are speaking here belong to what H. André calls the "typological laws," or "laws of specification" of life. (H. Andre, "La typologie des plantes," *2e Cahier Philos. de la Nature*, Paris, Vrin, 1929.)

97   Cf. Eugenio Rignano, *Qu'est-ce que la vie?* (Paris, Alcan, 1926).

98   By this we understand a condition of simple observation presupposed by the explanation and which itself plays no explicative role. Such a "pre-explicative" condition is quite different from the sort of condition, of which we spoke above (Ch. IV, § 9), which is a substitute for causality and which does play essentially an explicative role. The latter is regulative and determining in regard to the phenomenon (it might be called a conditioning condition). The other is a simple factual state recognized in the object as linked to its existence (it could be called a conditioned condition). This notion links up with that of the Meyersonian "irrational," with this slight difference—that the word irrational evokes a resistance that reason is forced to reduce, whereas here it is simply a question of a datum which is not explicative, but which empiriological analysis accepts once for all and leaves to philosophy the task of establishing its ontological value.

On this question of finality in biology, see our discussion with Elie Gagnebin (Elie Gagnebin and Jacques Maritain, "*La finalité en biologie*," in the collection *Questions Disputées*). Lectures on hylomorphism and on animism are also in preparation, in which we hope to treat more profoundly the philosophy of the living thing.

of its own structures, serve for the continuance of life. As for concepts of the soul and of vegetative powers, they play an indispensable role in the Philosophy of Nature, but remain outside the domain of properly biological experimental analysis as well as of the physico-chemical analysis of the phenomena of life.

35. From this it should be clear what we meant by saying that the essence of biology does not consist in a mathematization of the sensible. However great use biology may make of mathematics in progressing, as it ought, towards the material analysis of life, the mathematical instrument remains for it a simple instrument. It is not obliged to substitute quantitatively reconstructed entities for the sensible and qualitatively determined objects with which observation supplies it. In relation to mathematical rules of explanation, it remains an autonomous science, borrowing the mathematical method when it wishes. It does not set itself up as a mathematics of the phenomena of life. Sciences like Experimental Biology and Experimental Psychology normally apply themselves to the acquisition of a knowledge of vegetative life or of affective and cognitive life, the ontological index of which is indeed very weak. For in such knowledge, being is taken into account merely as the support of the observable, and the typical law of knowing remains: *to save sensible appearances.*[99] On the other hand, it does not recompose its object in the field of mathematical ideality by removing it as much as possible from its proper reality and the world of sensible nature. Hence, it can enter into a certain theoretical continuity with philosophical explanation. Should these sciences form explicative beings of reason, this would not, in any case, be for the purpose of constructing a universe of deduction to be substituted for the universe of real beings. They remain imperfectly deductive. Instead of forming, like the physico-mathematical sciences, a closed universe on which is superimposed the universe of the Philosophy of Nature, they rather constitute with the Philosophy of Nature two distinct levels of the same universe.

To the extent that they approach the purity of their type, they tend, as we

---

99   It is clear from this that Duhem's theory was much too narrow, for it identified the σώζειν τὰ φαινόμενα with the pure translation of physical data into a system of mathematical equations, abstracting from any search for "causal explanation." In the sciences of which we are speaking, the mathematical translation of phenomena, however important it may been joys an entirely instrumental, not a formal role, and the search for empiriological "causal" explanations remains preponderant (understanding the word "causal" according to the recastings of the concept of cause of which there was question above, see § 10). And yet they also have as their typical law the σώζειν τὰ φαινόμενα. This law rules the whole empiriological domain whether it be empirioschematic or empiriometric. And within empiriometric knowledge itself it applies, as we have seen, to a rational process which is at once a mathematical translation of physical data and a search for "causal explanations" (proliferating in physico-mathematical beings of reason). Cf. Ch. II, n. 51.

have said, to create an autonomous empiriological terminology. Now this system of notions will not admit into its formal texture any ontological or philosophical concept. It will not be properly "subalternated" to philosophy, nor will it borrow its principles from it. But it will demand that the latter furnish, as its climate, so to speak, and the conditions of its milieu, those preconceptions of a general order and that feeling of its proper significance in the universe of thought which every science needs. It will likewise demand from it those stimulations of the heuristic order thanks to which it may progress *in via inventionis*. Thus, far from being linked with a mechanistic pseudo-ontology, it will be in a sort of dynamic continuity with the specifically different system of ontological notions belonging to the Philosophy of Nature. Truth to tell, it will only be able to achieve its autonomy in a truly scientific fashion and escape from the disorder, arbitrariness and conceptual muddle which still afflict the sciences of living nature, and especially Experimental Psychology, if there be a strong, logical and critical, philosophical discipline in the mind of those who work in it. In brief, the sciences of which we are speaking do not submit *de jure* to the attraction of mathematics, but to that of philosophy. And so it is that biology is today becoming aware of the fact that, while it gives ever greater place to the physico-chemical and energetic analysis of the phenomena of life, it will truly progress only by explicitly breaking with mechanism.

The Anti-Mechanist Reaction in Biology

36. From this point of view, the works of Hans Driesch devoted to *Entwicklungsphysiologie* have considerable historical importance.[100] Following Driesch, and under the influence of either Bergson, or of Scheler and the phenomenological school, or of Aristotelian-Thomistic philosophy, biologists renowned for their experimental research have undertaken to rehabilitate concepts such as "organic," "life," "immanent activity," even "soul," that the science of the last century considered its duty chastely to discard. They are not afraid to philosophize, to insist with August Krogh and Rémy Collin on the necessity of "the exercise of the spirit"[101] in science, to note the agreement of their conceptions with one philosopher or another and even with the intuitions of a poet of genius like Claudel.[102] If Claudel, with regard to the autodetermi-

100   We have already pointed out the importance of these works in a study published in 1910 "Néovitalisme en Allemagne et le darwinisme" (Révue de Philosophie, Oct. 1, 1910) and in the preface of the French translation of *La philosophie de l'organisme* (Paris, Riviere, 1921).

101   August Krogh, "The Progress of Physiology," address delivered at the opening of the 13th International Physiological Congress, Boston, August 19, 1929 (*The American Journal of Physiology*, Oct. 1929, p. 248).

102   See in particular the study of F.J.J. Buytendijk and Hans Andre on "La valeur biologique de l'*Art Poétique* de Claudel" in the 4th *Cahier de Philosophie de la Nature* (*Vues sur la psychologie animale*, Pari, Vrin, 1930).

nation of living forms, speaks of "notes, which play themselves by extending fingers on all sides," Uexkuell writes in similar vein: "Every organism is a self-singing melody." Buytendijk opposes *erklaren* and *verstehen*, analytical and mechanistic reduction and synthetic intellection of the things of life, material explanation and comprehension. He vivifies his experimental researches by contact with certain ideas that belong properly to the Philosophy of Nature, for example the phenomenological intuition of the "organic," and the conception (independently reached by Claudel, on the one hand, and Wasmann, Erick Becher, Vialleton, on the other) of biological finality as going beyond strictly useful structure, in virtue of a superabundance and, as it were, entitative ostentation.

This reaction against the scientific conceptions prevailing in the nineteenth century is significant. It stands, perhaps, at the beginning of an important renewal. But it will be lasting and efficacious only if it maintains the essential distinctions between objective fields, which cannot be confused without injury to the mind and if a sort of irrationalism which everywhere irrupts and proliferates, as soon as there is any relaxation of the intellectual disciplines, does not produce some day a regrettable inhuman stoicism of a psychology without a soul and a biology without life, "purifications and macerations" in the name of which that sort of science would demand of its initiates the sacrifice of "a part of their intellectual and moral goods."[103] The great fault of this science has been to try to protect itself against the intellect;by dint of creating a vacuum it itself risks asphyxiation. But the re-entry of intellect into science is an event which is not without danger.

It is clear that only the intellect itself can ward off that danger. Only good philosophy can oust bad philosophy. (And yet good philosophy is more difficult than bad.)

37. From this point of view, the insufficiency of the phenomenological method, as well as Bergsonian irrationalism, is to be feared. Phenomenological intuition, in contrast to Bergsonian intuition, is of the intellectual order. But it takes its position from the start in a reflexive thought which does not admit the thing (the transobjective subject). Hence, it is devoted to a pure description of essence-phenomena which it isolates (contrary to their nature) from extra-mental being. And so it is locked up in a noetic atomism comparable to the Cartesian pluralism of "simple natures" (atoms of evidence). Since it refuses to recognize the primary value of transcendental being in which all our notions are resolved and on which are founded truths known per se, phenomenological intuition sticks half way. It does not succeed in surmounting an empiricism of the intelligible which, though aprioristic, remains none the less radical, nor in constituting a veritable ontology,[104] a metaphysics or a Philosophy of

103 Rémy Collin, Foreword to the 4th *Cahier de Philosophie de la Nature* (quoted above).
104 The word "ontologie" employed by Husserl in his recent publications (notably

Nature. In the absence of such a knowledge and of a rational resolution into the principles of a philosophical knowledge of being, this intuition can be of real use only in the sciences of phenomena. (It is from the point of view of its invasion of the practice of scientists that it interests us here.) Although in these sciences it in fact recaptures an interest in the extramental thing, a realist value, an efficiency that it did not have in the philosopher himself, it remains without adequate control and exposed to arbitrariness, such as the analogical (metaphorical) procedure to which it soon gave birth and which proliferates endlessly.

Fruitful for invention, capable of liberating the intelligence and nourishing it, a precious instrument of renewal and discovery, it is *in via judicii* that the method is deficient. Where there is no "autonomous" ontology, no Philosophy of Nature existing for itself, there can be no clear distinction between ontology and empiriology, between the Philosophy of Nature and Experimental Science. And so the phenomenological method, while delivering biology from the mechanistic tyranny, runs the risk of introducing into it concepts valid of themselves for the Philosophy of Nature but without value for science, and sometimes even no longer valid for the Philosophy of Nature. Finally, even the deliverance of which we have just spoken runs the risk of being illusory. If the whole of empiriological knowledge is abandoned to physico-chemical analysis, everything which belongs to properly biological apperception finds itself *de facto* transferred to a Philosophy of Nature encroaching on science. Meanwhile this philosophy, in its turn, runs the risk of yielding to an intemperate vitalism, counterfeiting an authentic ontology of the living thing, and to an irrational metaphysics which has already given *Naturphilosophie* a bad name.

It is normal that, as a matter of fact, the initiators who have restored to biology the value of its proper objects, should have, like Driesch and like Buytendijk, the preoccupations of philosophers of nature along with those of scientists. We know that these preoccupations ended by drawing Driesch into philosophy alone. But this union of two "formalities" in a same thinking "subject" should not make us forget their distinction, a distinction of fundamental importance for the interests of philosophy as well as for those of science. That is why we have insisted on the existence (required at least *de jure*) of an "autonomous" Experimental Biology distinct from the philosophy of the living organism; in other words, on the existence of an empiriological analysis, not only physico-chemical, but also properly and irreducibly biological, of the

---

in his *Formale und transzendentale Logik* and in his *Méditations Cartésiennes*) is purely equivocal. This apriori "discovery" of the universe of the sciences beginning with the "egologie solipsiste" is not a science of being which could be distinguished from empiriological analysis as a different and more profound scrutiny of the same reality. And in spite of all the philosopher's efforts, in spite of the realist tendency which gave birth to phenomenology, it remains radically incapable of furnishing anything but an illusory idealistic substitute of the real. (Cf. above, Ch. III, § 14.)

world of living bodies, which cannot be confused with the ontological investigation proper to the Philosophy of Nature. This double empiriological analysis, physico-chemical and strictly biological (the former subordinated to the latter), constitutes "Experimental Biology" in opposition to the "Philosophy of Nature" (here, of living nature) with which it is nevertheless in continuity. Moreover, the works of scientists like Heidenhain, Brachet, Cuenot, Rémy Collin, H. André,[105] Emil Rohde attest that the existence of an analysis at once rigorously empiriological and strictly biological is not merely possible.

Specifically distinct from such an analysis, the ontological and philosophical knowledge of the living thing appears as its rational justification. In fact, it is part of its task to root out the double illusion of mechanism and vitalism, understanding the latter word in the pejorative sense that the history of medical and biological sciences compels us to attach to it. As a matter of fact, classical medical vitalism is linked to a conception of life which is the strict counterpart of mechanism. It has on the one hand, from the philosophical point of view, all the disadvantages of a dualism. According to this conception an organism is a corporeal substance already constituted and existing, in which resides in addition, an alien principle, a vital spirit or vital energy. On the other hand, it resists the exigencies proper to scientific analysis, in the sense that it juxtaposes to the physico-chemical means of life other principles of a specifically vital order which run counter to physico-chemical laws and dispute the ground with them. In such a conception the vital would have as its own only what is taken away from the physico-chemical. And so its field is the more reduced as the physico-chemical study of the phenomena of life progresses.

The authentic conception of the organism, the "animist" or "hylomorphist" conception, is opposed to vitalism, so understood, no less than to mechanism. According to it, the principle of life is the formal principle itself, in the Aristotelian sense of the word, the substantial "act" or entelechy of the living body. Thus, the energetic and the psychic, matter and the soul, make but one and the same single being, which exists, with all its constitutive determinations and its structures, physico-chemical and vegetative, or sensitive, or intellective, only by virtue of the soul. Thus, the vital is not juxtaposed, but rather *superordinate* to the physico-chemical; and a properly biological experimental analysis is all the more required as the physico-chemical analysis of the phenomena of life progresses.

---

105   Let us call attention to the important volume of Hans André, *Urbild und Ursache in der Biologie* (Munich and Berlin, Oldenbourg, 1931.) He treats in a profound manner, particularly in the second and third chapter (*"Der Kampf der Mathematisierenden und der Biolog. Naturanschauungen"*; "Der Ausgang dieses Kampfes in der Gegenwart"), some of the problems touched on here. The fourth chapter draws certain confirmations of the greatest interest from the actual state of vegetative biology.

Concerning the True and the False Philosophy of the Progress of the Sciences in Modern Times

38. From these considerations it follows that while the Philosophy of Nature takes the Experimental Sciences as an empiriological body, as we noted above, it does so in one way in the case of sciences of the type of physics and in another way in the case of sciences of the type of biology. In the first case, the resolution of concepts is of the empiriometric order. Here it must separate as much as possible, within the results of the science, what belongs to the formally mathematical deductive explanation from what belongs to established facts. It can enter into continuity with established facts in the line of knowledge properly so called. But with the beings of reason constructed by physico-mathematical theory it can realize only a secondary continuity, in the line of image and of myth. In the second case, the resolution of the concepts is of the empirio-schematic order. By interpreting these concepts in its own light, the Philosophy of Nature can base itself on the sum-total of the results of experimental science.

We believe, furthermore, that a particularly important truth emerges from the critical analysis of the empiriology and the ontology of the sensible to which this chapter has been devoted, to wit, that the ever clearer differentiation between knowledge of the ontological type and knowledge of the physico-mathematical type is not a simple contingent fact due to particular historical circumstances but corresponds to a necessary law of the growth of speculative thought. It constitutes one of the most authentic advances, in the order of the morphology of knowledge, that thought has accomplished in the course of modern times and of which reflexive and critical philosophy has become aware.

We have noted that although the ancients clearly understood the method of the *scientiae mediae* in certain privileged fields, nevertheless they tended in fact to submit the whole knowledge of nature to the law of ontological or philosophical knowledge. There is an inverse and symmetrical fault (more serious since it stems not from a *de facto* lack but from a *de jure* error) which consists in admitting as legitimate knowledge, at least in the field of the knowledge of nature, only empiriological knowledge dressed up under some other name. This has been the positivists' error. They have made this knowledge co-extensive with the universe of thought. In a quite different fashion, that error is repeated by certain philosophers, this time in the name of metaphysics. Of the scientific knowledge of nature they retain only empiriometric explanation and hold for nought the sciences of life. They wish to find in mathematical and physico-mathematical knowledge the unique type of all rational activity (when it is not purely reflexive) truly worthy of the name.

39. The attitude of these philosophers must be designated as retrograde and, to tell the truth, pre-Copernican. The arbitrary precept of a metaphysics which

is constituted by a "total and sweet renunciation" of being and object obliges them to return to the positions of a most naive epistemological monism, proclaimed this time for the benefit of a type of knowledge which is farthest removed from any grasping of the real in itself. This false philosophy of scientific progress is thus prevented from discerning the profound sense of the Copernican revolution. It fails to understand the admirable organic diversity in the play of the intellect, which has been manifested by four centuries of scientific development, both within science itself and in the distinction of science and philosophy.

All that is left of reason in this philosophy is reduced to the mathematical use, and to what we have here called the empiriometric use, of the intellect.[106] Here we have, if we may dare so to speak, a rationalism retired from business that tries to live like a gentleman of means but can only maintain itself by drawing on the capital of ancient reason. But we wish to make clear that the principles of a realistic noetic, as expounded in the present work, provide a place within the system of knowledge, for the methods and claims proper to the "reason" of this nominalist rationalism, granting their validity in certain defined limits, but noting at the same time that they cannot be the whole of thought.

The capacity of a doctrine to integrate whatever is positive in systems which invoke different principles might perhaps be taken as an indication of its truth. In any case, it seems that a true philosophy of the progress of the physical and mathematical sciences in the course of modern times, precisely because it is its duty to set forth by critical reflexion the spiritual values with which that progress is pregnant, must recognize in it the sign, not of a restriction and impoverishment, but of an improvement and growth within the organic structure and differentiation of thought. It must therefore, on the one hand, reveal the essential compatibility of this mathematical and empiriometrical progress with the knowledge of the ontological type which is proper to philosophy. On the other hand, it must respect the nature of the Experimental Sciences, which of themselves escape from complete mathematization, and it must render justice to their working methods, which will extend to ever larger sections of the scientific domain the more they assert their autonomy. In effect, it would be completely arbitrary to refuse to biology, and other sciences of the

---

106   It could be shown that this was the necessary logical outcome of an intellectualist nominalism, which endeavored to mask by an extreme idealism the residue of sensualism which its refusal to grant to the intellect an original power to perceive intelligible natures or essences, and even more generally any objects whatsoever which correspond to its proper conditions of spirituality, inevitably leaves at the basis of thought. That residue of sensualism remains no matter what is done. And that is why the only knowledge that can be recognized outside mathematical knowledge is the knowledge that we have called empiriometric. This designation is certainly less noble but more exact than that which brings about a betrayal of the name of "reason."

same epistemological type, the rank of authentic knowledge. This type of knowledge merits the attention of the philosopher and it is playing an ever more important, perhaps one day preponderant, role in the progress of speculative thought.

CHAPTER V

METAPHYSICAL KNOWLEDGE

To Raïssa Maritain

I
DIANOETIC INTELLECTION AND PERINOETIC INTELLECTION

1. WE HAVE TREATED THE QUESTION of the Philosophy of Nature in its relations with the sciences at such length because the restoration of the Philosophy of Nature seems to us to be in accordance with a profound desire of the contemporary mind. Moreover, it seems to us that only the critical realism of St. Thomas is in a position to fulfil this desire without detriment to the Experimental Sciences and their methods, but rather with great benefit to them.

The theory of intellectual knowledge outlined in Chapter III shows how, according to the principles of Thomas Aquinas, there can be two complementary knowledges of one and the same reality which is the world of sensible nature and of movement: the Sciences of Nature and the Philosophy of Nature.

Likewise, it shows how metaphysical knowledge can and should rise above the Philosophy of Nature.

According to the terminology that it has seemed to us opportune to adopt, the cisobjective subject attains, in order to become them intentionally, things themselves, or transobjective subjects posited in extramental existence. It does so by constituting them its objects, or by positing them for itself—by means of the concept or of the uttered presentative form—in "known" existence, *in esse objectivo seu cognito*. This cisobjective subject is at once spiritual and corporeal—it has senses and an intellect.

We have called the transobjective intelligible the infinite (transfinite) ensemble of subjects which it can subject to its intelligible grasps, or which can be delivered to it as objects. To be very precise, we mean by these subjects those whose essence or first intelligible constitutive can itself (even though only in its most universal notes) become object for it in a concept. Let us say they are by definition subjects which are knowable to it in some degree "in themselves" or by dianoetic intellection.[1] They are corporeal things which, since they can

---

1 By this we mean (in opposition to "ananoetic" knowledge or knowledge by analogy on the one hand and on the other "perinoetic" knowledge or knowledge by substitute-signs) that mode of intellection in which the intelligible constitutive

fall under the sense, can fall also under the light of the agent intellect, and so deliver their essence to grasps of abstraction, at least to the extent that there appears in its intelligibility some determination of being.

It is fitting that for an intelligence that makes use of senses there correspond, as naturally proportionate, object-essences immersed in the sensible. That is why the scholastics said that the essences of corporeal things are the connatural object of our power of intellection. Plunged into the ocean of the transobjective intelligible our intelligence illumines material things in order to reveal the hidden structure, and to actualize as much as it can the intelligibility detained in them in potency. And by discourse it continually accomplishes new actuations of intelligibility.

From the very fact that it emerges from sense knowledge, dianoetic intellection does not know, in any case, the essences of corporeal things "by themselves" and immediately. It is not a vision of essences, a knowledge which penetrates at the first glance to the inside, to the heart of being, like the non-discursive knowledge of the Angels or the perfectly immutable knowledge of God (or like the knowledge Descartes believed he received from the clear and distinct ideas of thought and extension). Let us say that it is not a "central" knowledge but a "radial" knowledge that goes from the outside in, that attains the center only by starting from the circumference. It attains the essence, but by the signs, as St. Thomas says,[2] which manifest it, and which are the properties. The hunt for definitions passes through the thickets of experience. It is after having experienced in ourselves what reason is and having recognized in the possession of this faculty the *principalissima* property of the human being, that we discern and can express in a definition the nature of this being. And without that we would never succeed in discovering and dividing the virtualities enfolded in this definition.

2. It is fitting, moreover, to distinguish two modes of dianoetic intellection, according as it bears on substantial natures and on the realities which are the object of philosophy, or on mathematical entities (which, considered ontologically, and inasmuch as they are *entia realia*, are accidents). In the first case, as was just recalled, the essence is known by the accidents. In the second, it is known, so to speak straight away, by its very intelligible constitution, at least insofar as the latter is manifested by means of signs which can be constructed in some way in imaginative intuition. Right here arises, with all its difficulties, the problem of mathematical intellection. Mathematical essences are not

---

of the thing is objectivized in itself (if not by itself at least by a sign which manifests it, by a property in the strict sense of the word). We have chosen the word "dianoetic" not at all in order to evoke διάνοια (the faculty of reasoning), but in order to designate an intellection which through the sensible attains the nature or essence itself.

2   St. Thomas says that the properties are signs of the essential form. Cf. *In II Analyt.*, lib. II, cap. XII, lect. 13, n. 7, and the commentary of Zigliara.

grasped intuitively from within. That would be proper to angelic and not human mathematics. Nor are they perceived from the outside, which would be by accidents emanating from them, as an operation emanates from an active potency and from a substance. Nor are they created by the human mind, of which they would simply translate the nature and laws. We say that they are recognized and deciphered so to speak, by means of a construction beginning with primary elements abstractively disengaged from experience. This very construction of the intelligible constitutive requires or presupposes a construction in imaginative intuition in some way or other.[3] It is a *reconstruction* with regard to those mathematical entities which are essences properly so called (possible real beings), and a *construction* with regard to those which are beings of reason founded on these essences. Thus, the mind is confronted by an objective world which has its own consistency, independent of the mind and founded ultimately on the divine Intellection and Essence themselves, and which it nevertheless deciphers deductively and as it were a priori. Such an intellection is still "dianoetic" (and not comprehensive, or exhaustive) in this sense that the essence is not grasped *intuitively* by itself (by means of a non-abstractive intuition which would exhaust it at a glance) but indeed *constructively* by itself (thanks to a construction of notions that is on the other hand at least indirectly imaginable and remains as it were an "outside" by which the essence is attained). Thus, however full of mystery and surprise the mathematical world may be for the mind, it is nevertheless true that, with the reservations we have just indicated, its entities are conceived (constructively) by themselves or by their intelligible constitutive itself. Hence, it is clear that if one takes mathematical intelligence as the type and rule of all intelligence one ends inevitably in Spinozism, especially in a Spinozist conception of substance which will be then thought to be known or manifested by its very essence (not by its accidents), or "conceived by itself."

As far as substantial essences are concerned, J. de Tonquédec was certainly right in noting against Rousselot that "when it is a question of thinking substance, even in the most imperfect fashion, the mind never 'stops short at the accidents.' That would be contradictory. It always regards something beyond them. But on the other hand, a moment is never reached when the mind, having left the accidents behind, 'passes beyond' and 'discovers' the bare substance. It is by remaining attached to the accident that it finds the means of seeing beyond. . . . The mind always goes beyond the accidents, but by continually relying on them."[4]

On the other hand, we would fall into the opposite excess were we to conclude from this that we "do not attain" substantial natures. On the contrary, by virtue of this very doctrine, it must be said that by dianoetic intellection— where it is possible and to the extent that it is possible—we attain substantial

---

3   Cf. above, Ch. IV, § 6.
4   J. de Tonquédec, *La critique de la connaissance*, p. 538.

natures "in function of and through their very manifestations, which are the accidents." How would they be not "attained" when they are "manifested"? How would they be not "seen" when "by remaining attached to the accident," the mind "finds the means of seeing beyond"? By the properties these natures are attained *in* themselves, that is to say, in their formal constitutive, in their intelligible constitution itself. And in such a case the accidental forms are also known in themselves, by their proper effects.

3. However laborious it may be, this knowledge of things, not by their essence, but in their essence, this dianoetic intellection is not always granted us and normally stops, except in the world of human things, at the more universal notes rather than specific notes. In the universe of the sensible real, as we have seen, below the level of the Philosophy of Nature we have to be content with a knowledge by signs. And in this case it is not knowledge by signs which manifest essential differences, but by signs which are substitutes for those differences and are known in place of them.[5] This knowledge, to be sure, bears on the essence, grips it from the outside, but as it were blindly, without being able to discern the essence itself or the properties in the onto-logical sense of this word. This is peripheral or "circumferential" knowledge which may be named *perinoetic*, and an example of which is what we have

---

5   Of such *substitutes* of the essential differences, purely descriptive signs or em-piriological "properties," we find a curious example in the following text, which at first sight might be badly understood: "Secundum quod natura alicujus rei ex ejus proprietatibus et effectibus cognoscere possumus, sic eam nomine possu-mus significare. Unde, quia substantiam lapidis ex ejus proprietate cognoscere possumus secundum seipsam, sciendo quid est lapis, hoc nomen, lapis, ipsam lapidis naturam, secundum quod in se est, significat: significat enim defini-tionem lapidis, per quam scimus quid est lapidis" (*Sum. Theol.*, I, 13, 8, ad 2). St. Thomas does not mean here that we are in possession of a quidditative definition of stone. And the proof of this is that the "property" of which he is speaking is (cf. the body of the article) *laedens pedem*. Supposing this etymology is valid, that is, in any case, a wholly descriptive property, a wholly empirical sign, which is of value only for a nominal definition. Cf. *De Verit.*, IV, 1, ad 8: "Quia differentiae essentiales sunt nobis ignotae, quandoque utimur accidentibus vel effectibus loco earum, ut VIII *Metaph.* (VII, lect. 12) dicitur; et secundum hoc nominamus rem; et sic illud quod loco differentiae essentialis sumitur, est a quo imponitur nomen ex parte imponentis, sicut lapis imponitur ab effectu, qui est laedere pedem; et hoc non oportet esse principaliter significatum per nomen, sed illud loco cujus hoc ponitur." This text of the *De Veritate* defines very exactly what we are calling here perinoetic knowledge. If, moreover, even after scientific investi-gation, the *quod quid est* of the stone is not discovered by us, it is not because it transcends our power of knowing; it is rather because it does not come up to its level. We can then circumscribe it thanks to signs of the same sort as the "property" in question, but better chosen. The name of stone signifies to be sure the nature of the stone according as it is in itself, but without this nature being discovered by us. It signifies it as a thing to be known, not as a thing known.

called the empiriometric analysis and the empirio-schematic analysis of observable realities. Mineral, vegetable, or animal, the immense variety of corporeal natures inferior to human nature refuse to deliver to us openly their ultimate specific determinations.

Scholastic Digression

4. Thus, a capital distinction is imposed on the mind between two knowledges (though in order to be concise the expression "knowledge by signs" is used in both cases). There is, on the one hand, the knowledge of essences (substantial) by "signs" or accidents (properties) which manifest them, at least in their most universal notes (*dianoetic intellection*). On the other hand, there is the knowledge of essences by the "signs" of which it will be a question below and which are known *in place of* the natures themselves, which in this case remain inaccessible in their formal constitutive (*perinoetic intellection*).[6]

There, to tell the truth, lies an important problem, to which it would be desirable that some modern works should be devoted, similar to what the ancients called the hierarchy of accidental forms, and elucidating metaphysically the distinction (which would no longer remain in these metaphorical terms) between accidents more-or-less "profound" or "intimate," "exterior" or "superficial."

It is clear that in the one case we are in the presence of characters of explicative fecundity (from *rationale* can be deduced *docibile*, *risibile*, etc.); in the other, sterile characters, which cannot be used to render the reason of something else. But this is only a sign of the hidden difference. It is the theory of the proper accident and of the common accident which is, according to us, at the core of the difficulty. When the mind holds a property in the strict and philosophical (ontological) sense of this word, a difference of being is attained, an accidental form is seized in its intelligibility, and, by it, the essence (as human nature by rationality, or animal nature by sensitivity). That is what happens in dianoetic intellection. But in the other case the properties in the

---

6   The definition of man as *animal rationale* and that of horse as *animal hinnibile* (or as perissodactyl ungulate mammal having a single complete toe on each foot), of dog as *animal latrans* (or as canidae carnivorous mammal, etc.), of lion as *animal habens abundantiam audaciae* (or as a digitigrade carnivorous mammal with retractile claws, etc.), have the same logical structure. They conceal, from the critical or noetic point of view, an essential diversity. And this is far from being explained solely by the fact that *hinnibile*, *latrans*, etc., are situated on the specific degree, *rationale* and *irrationale* on the generic degree on the ladder of differences. For 1. *irrationale* is indeed a generic difference, but *rationale* is a specific difference, which joined to *animal* constitutes a *species atoma*; 2. definitions can be given of man himself (for example *animal gressibile bipes*) which differ as much from a quidditative definition as *animal hinnibile*, etc.; 3. differences situated on the generic degree (*gressibile* for example, or "ungulate," etc.) can as little reveal the formal constitutive of the quiddity as *hinnibile*, etc. Cf. further, Ch. V, n. 9.

strict sense of the word remain inaccessible. Clusters of sensible accidents (common accidents), grasped exclusively as observable or measurable, are taken *in their place* (like the descriptive "properties," density, atomic weight, melting point, boiling point, spectrum of high frequency, etc., which serve to distinguish bodies in chemistry). These descriptive characters are given the name "properties," but the import of the name is here quite different and no more philosophical (ontological) than that of the word "substance" in the usage of chemists. They are at once exterior signs and masks of the veritable (ontological) properties. They are empiriological properties, substitutes for properties properly so called. The mind cannot decipher the intelligible in the sensible, it makes use of the sensible itself in order to circumscribe an intelligible core that escapes it. It is then that we say that the form is too immersed in matter to fall within the grasp of our intelligence. It is impossible by such properties to attain in any degree whatever the substantial nature in itself or in its formal constitutive. It is known not by signs which manifest it, but by signs which hide it. That is what happens in perinoetic intellection.

5. It may be said definitively that every (instrumental) sign manifests by hiding and hides by manifesting. Dianoetic intellection is a case in which the signs manifest more than hide. Perinoetic intellection is a case in which the signs hide more than manifest.

To fix our terminology, let us say that in dianoetic intellection substantial natures are to some degree known *in themselves*, *by signs* which are proper accidents, properties in the philosophical sense of the word. (As for these properties themselves, they are known by other accidents which are the operations.) In perinoetic intellection substances and their properties are known *by signs and in signs.*

By a latitude which the indigence of human language authorizes, and if every danger of a false Cartesian or Spinozist interpretation is removed, we believe it is licit[7] to say that in dianoetic intellection substantial essences are to some degree "discovered" by the mind, neither "bared" certainly, nor from within (that was the error of the absolute intellectualism of Descartes), but discovered *by their outsides* (the accidents, in turn, not being known by the inside, which would be to know them in derivation from the substance, but by the operations). In saying that in dianoetic intellection essences are attained "openly," we do not mean in any sense to say that they are attained "naked" or by the attributes which would be the constitutives themselves of the substance, but indeed that they are manifested by their proper accidents. We are aware of the imperfection of this terminology (and of all terminology). But we are certain that the distinctions that it expresses are founded on reason, and rendered absolutely necessary by the modern development of the Experimen-

---

7   Cf. above, Ch. II, §§ 9 and 10.

tal Sciences, of which the mode of conceiving differs essentially from the philosophical mode of conceiving.[8]

The Human Intelligence and Corporeal Natures

6. Is it not scandalous that though our intelligence has as its connatural object the essences of corporeal things, in face of them it meets such serious impediments that it has to be content, in a vast sector of its knowledge of nature, with the imperfect intellection that we call "perinoetic"? If we reflect on this paradox, we are led to understand, first of all, that for a human intelligence taken in the state of nature, or rather of primitive culture, the natural ordination of which we are speaking is verified on an entirely different plane than that of didactic thought, to which the philosopher, by a sort of professional habit, is always tempted to return. The behavior of primitive men

---

8   As for the texts of St. Thomas that can be cited on this question, most of them affirm the general principle that the substantial essences of things and their proper differences are hidden from us, and that in order to attain the essence we must use differences taken from the accidents. ("In rebus enim sensibilibus etiam ipsae differentiae essentiales nobis ignotae sunt, unde significantur per differentias accidentales, quae ex essentialibus oriuntur, sicut causa significatur per suum effectum" [*De Ente et Essentia*, cap. 6]. "Formae substantiales per seipsas sunt ignotae; sed innotescunt nobis per accidentia propria. Frequenter enim differentiae substantiales ab accidentibus sumuntur, loco formarum substantialium quae per huiusmodi accidentia innotescunt; sicut bipes et gressibile et hujusmodi; et sic etiam sensibile et rationale ponuntur differentiae substantiales." [*De Spirit. Creaturis*, a. 11, ad 3]. Cf. *Sum. Theol.*, I, 29, 1 ad 3, etc.) Writing at an epoch when the Experimental Sciences were not yet differentiated from the Philosophy of Nature it is understandable that St. Thomas should stick to these very general statements.

However, other texts can be classified in two different lines, according as they refer rather to accidental differences which leave the essential differences hidden (see the texts cited above, Ch. IV, n. 68, Ch. V, n. 5, in particular that of the *Commentary on the Metaphysics*, lib. VII, lect. 12, in which St. Thomas contrasts these differences *per accidens* with differences per se) or according as they refer rather to differences which, while stemming from the accidental (predicamental), are an intelligible manifestation of essential differences, and lead the mind to a knowledge of the latter: "Quia principia essentialia rerum sunt nobis ignota, ideo oportet quod utamur differentiis accidentalibus in designatione essentialium; bipes enim non est essentiale, sed ponitur in designatione essentialis. *Et per eas, scilicet per differentias accidentales, devinimus in cognitionem essentialium.*" (*In de Anima*, lib. I, lect. 1). "Quia substantiales rerum differentiae sunt nobis ignotae, loco earum interdum definientes accidentalibus utuntur, secundum quod ipsa *designant vel notificant essentiam, ut proprii effectus notificant causam;* unde sensibile, secundum quod est differentia constitutiva animalis, non sumitur a sensu prout nominat potentiam, sed prout nominat ipsam animae essentiam, a qua talis potentias fluit; et similiter est de ratione, vel de eo quod est habens mentem." (*De Verit.*, X, 1, ad 6). Cf. *De Potentia*, 9, 2, ad 5; *In II Sent.*, dist. 3, q. 1, a. 6; *Sum. Theol.*, I, 77, 1, ad 7; I–II, 49, 2, ad 3.

with regard to a river, a forest, animals to be hunted or avoided, their differential knowledge which is extraordinarily developed from concrete features, implies an intellectual discernment which is wholly practical and wrapped up in the exercise of the senses, but very precise and very exact, of "what are" the beings of nature with which they have to deal. That is the humble, entirely pre-scientific, fashion in which the human intelligence is primitively brought to the nature of corporeal things, and no matter how weakened it may be in civilized life it remains always primary and fundamental. We find a significant equivalent of this in the knowledge that a peasant has of the ways of the land, the skilled worker of those of his art or his machine.

To employ an important distinction of Cajetan, to know "a quiddity" is in general quite a different thing than to know it "quidditatively." Thomists teach that the human intelligence has as its connatural object the essence or quiddity of corporeal things, they have never taught that it must always know this object "quidditatively." That is a perfection of knowledge that can be realized and is *de facto* realized only within certain very narrow limits. The most lowly human knowledge, the knowledge quite common and patrimonial implied in language and nominal definitions,[9] grasps quiddities, but in the most imperfect and least quidditative fashion, like a needle in a bundle of straw.

When there is question of the human intelligence cultivated and formed by the intellectual virtues, then it is to the knowing of the corporeal essences scientifically that, exploiting progressively the possibilities of dianoetic intellection, it is borne by the very impulse of its nature, as radical principle, and of the habitus, which perfect it, as proximate principle. But if, as we have said, it must fall back on empiriological substitutes for the specific detail of the infrahuman world, it is because, to tell the truth, it is man himself and the proper world he represents which is its most exactly proportionate object in the world of the sensible real. Spirit tends to spirit; pure spirit to pure spirit; spirit involved in the senses to spirit which is the form of a body. We should understand that our intelligence, which from the fact of its union with the body is naturally turned outwards and towards natures here below, must complete the great periphery of the knowledge of the world, precious, robust, admirable—ultimately delusive, whether it be philosophical or experimental—to arrive at man and the soul. Then by a double movement, it will penetrate

---

9   It is in relation to the common intelligence of humanity, not in relation to that of scientists, that St. Thomas in exemplifying his Logic presents the quiddity of stone as designated by the property *laedere pedem*, or that of dog by the property of barking. One who would reprove him for that would be simply mistaken and guilty of pedantry. It is a question of a wholly extrinsic designation of a quiddity which is not attained in itself. These nominal definitions precede science and are prerequisites of the movement of intellectual inquiry. But it is both more certain and more humble to choose them as illustrations for a lecture in Logic rather than quidditative definitions which are more perfect but can have the disadvantage of not existing.

within to take cognizance of the things of the soul and to know the works of man, by reflexive philosophy and by practical philosophy, ethical, cultural, aesthetical; and it will rise above itself to perceive the things of God, to pass on to metaphysics. Such is its natural itinerary, by reason of which the figure of Socrates stands for ever at the human crossroads.

7. But let us return to the natures of corporeal things. The universe of the sensible real, with its double valency, ontological and empiriological, is, we know, but the first degree of the knowledge we get of these natures, or the area of the lowest abstraction. A second area of intelligibility is that of the mathematic praeter-real. Here the mind escapes into a world of entities which were first grasped in the bodies of nature but immediately purified and reconstructed, and on which other entities, which are indifferently real or "of reason," will be endlessly constructed. This world frees us from the sensible real but only because in it we sacrifice any order to existence. That is why philosophies, into which geometry provides the only entry, are doomed to idealism.

But there is a third area of intelligibility which makes us pass beyond the sensible without giving up the order to existence, and so it introduces us into the *more real* than the sensible real, or into what funds the very reality of the

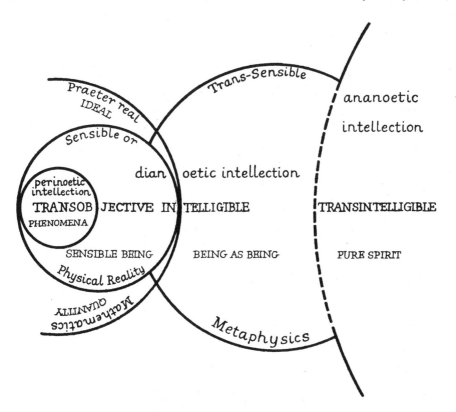

latter. This is the area of the trans-sensible or of metaphysics, which follows immediately the area of the sensible real.

II
THE METAPHYSICAL INTELLIGIBLE

8. When things become the object of our intelligence, they do not merely deliver to us their determinate specific or generic nature, whether in itself or in an empiriological substitute. Before knowing that Peter is a man, I have already attained him as something, as a being. And this intelligible object "being" is not the privilege of one of the classes of things that the Logician calls species, genus, or category. It is universally communicable. I find it everywhere, everywhere itself and everywhere varied. I cannot think anything without positing it before my mind. It imbues everything. It is what the scholastics called a transcendental object of thought. In the first article of the *De Veritate* St. Thomas has briefly described the double movement of resorption and transgression proper to being as object of concept. It is opposed as much to a pure monism like that of Hegel as to a pure pluralism like that of Descartes. For being is a primordial and common object of concept (in contrast to the Cartesian simple natures) which (in contrast to the hypostasized idea of Hegel) is itself and right from the start essentially diverse in the diverse subjects in which the mind meets it. It is being which is first known and into which every object of thought is resolved for the intellect. But nothing can be added to it from outside in order to differentiate it. Everything which differentiates it comes from within it, as one of its modes, presented to the mind by another concept. Sometimes it is a special mode of being which is opposed to another mode of being, that one subject has and another has not, and by which is manifested the infinite multiplicity of essences which divide being. (Thus, in the movement of our thought, the object of concept "being" resorbs in itself the genera and species.) Sometimes it is a mode co-extensive with being, which every subject has which has being, and which therefore constitutes an object of thought that is transcendental like itself.[10] These are the functions of being

---

10   Cf. *De Verit*. I, 1: "Sicut in demonstrabilibus oportet fieri reductionem in aliqua principia per se intellectui nota, ita investigando quid est unumquodque; alias utrobique in infinitum iretur, et sic periret omnino scientia et cognitio rerum.

"Illud autem quod primo intellectus concipit quasi notissimum, et in quo omnes conceptiones resolvit, est ens, ut Avicenna dicit in principio *Metaphysicae* suae (lib. I, c. ix). Unde oportet quod omnes aliae conceptiones intellectus accipiantur ex additione ad ens.

"Sed enti non potest addi aliquid quasi extranea natura per modum quo differentia additur generi, vel accidens subjecto, quia quaelibet natura essentialiter est ens; unde etiam probat Philosophus in III *Metaphys*. (com. 1), quod ens non potest esse genus, sed secundum hoc aliqua dicuntur addere supra ens, in

as such, *passiones entis*. (Thus, being transgresses itself in the transcendentals.) Among these transcendentals a trinity stands out: being itself; then, in relation to mind, which alone can confront being with equal amplitude: the true (ontological), that is to say being as the expression of a thought from which it emanates, and as intelligible in itself to the extent that it is; and the good (metaphysical), that is to say being as the term in which love can delight, and as apt to move desire by the very reason that it is. From this we see, at once, the value and the imperfection of our knowledge, and above all, of the idea of being itself in relation to that which is. The first intelligible "formality" by which that which is becomes object, and which is attained in the concept of being, imbues everything real, is capable of everything that is. And yet it is attained in the concept of being as already distinct (by a distinction of reason) from the transcendental formalities (attained by the idea of the one, the true, the good, etc.), which in that which is are identical with it.

Aristotle compared specific essences to whole numbers. Just as an added unity constitutes a new number, every specific difference constitutes a new essence. The transcendentals might be compared to transfinite groups of the

---

quantum exprimunt ipsius modum, qui nomine ipsius entis non exprimitur.

"Quod dupliciter contingit: uno modo ut modus expressus sit aliquis *specialis* modus entis, sunt enim diversi gradus entitatis, secundum quos accipiuntur diversi modi essendi, et juxta hos modos accipiuntur diversa rerum *genera*; substantia enim non addit supra ens aliquam differentiam, quae significet aliquam naturam superadditam enti, sed nomine substantiae exprimitur quidem specialis modus essendi, scilicet per se ens; et ita est in aliis generibus.

"Alio modo ita quod modus expressus sit modus *generaliter consequens omne ens*; et hic modus dupliciter accipi potest: uno modo secundum quod consequitur omne ens in se; alio modo, secundum quod consequitur unumquodque ens in ordine ad aliud.

"Si primo modo, hoc dicitur, quia exprimit in ente aliquid affirmative vel negative. Non autem invenitur aliquid affirmative dictum absolute quod possit accipi in omni ente, nisi essentia ejus, secundum quam esse dicitur; et sic imponitur hoc nomen *res*, quod in hoc differt ab *ente*, secundum Avicennam in principio *Metaphys.*, quod *ens* sumitur ab actu essendi, sed nomen *rei* exprimit quidditatem sive essentiam entis. Negatio autem, quae est consequens omme ens absolute, est indivisio; et hanc exprimit hoc nomen unum; nihil enim est aliud *unum* quam ens indivisum.

"Si autem modus entis accipiatur secundo modo, scilicet secundum ordinem unius ad alterum, hoc potest esse dupliciter. Uno modo secundum divisionem unius ab altero; et hoc exprimit hoc nomen *aliquid*, dicitur enim aliquid quasi aliud quid; unde sicut ens dicitur unum, in quantum est indivisum in se, ita dicitur aliquid, in quantum est ab aliis divisum. Alio modo secundum convenientiam unius entis ad aliud; et hoc quidem non potest esse nisi accipiatur aliquid quod natum sit convenire cum omni ente. Hoc autem est anima, quae quodammodo est omnia, sicut dicitur in III *De Anima* (text. 37). In anima autem est vis cognitiva et appetitiva. Convenientiam ergo entis ad appetitum exprimit hoc nomen *bonum*, ut in principio *Ethic.* dicitur: *Bonum est quod omnia appetunt*. Convenientiam vero entis ad intellectum exprimit hoc nomen *verum*."**insert1**

same power. The transfinite group of even numbers has the same power as the transfinite group of whole numbers; the being, or the true, or the good has as much amplitude alone as all three together.

Even by the perception of the generic or specific nature the intellect attains in the individual more than the individual itself. It attains a universal object of concept communicable to all the individuals of the same species or of the same genus. And this is called *univocal*, since, presented to the mind by a plurality of transobjective subjects and restored to them in judgments, it is purely and simply one and the same in the mind. *Unum in multis*, it is an invariant without actual multiplicity, realized in several, and by that very fact positing among them a community of essence. But in the perception of the transcendentals, we attain in a nature more than itself, an object of concept not only transindividual, but trans-specific, transgeneric, trans-categorical, as if in opening a blade of grass one startled a bird greater than the world. Let us call such an object of concept *superuniversal*. The scholastics call it *analogous*, that is to say realized in diverse ways but according to similar proportions in the diverse subjects in which it is found.[11] It differs essentially, even as object of concept, from the universals, not only because it has a greater amplitude, but also and primarily—and this is what is most important, because it is not like them purely and simply one and the same in the mind (let us say monovalent)—it is polyvalent, it envelops an actual multiplicity; the bird we spoke of a moment ago is at the same time a flock.

9. Let us try to grasp the proper mystery of these transcendental objects. When I look at a man and think: "This is a being," or "He exists," I grasp a certain determinate being, finite, perishable, fleshly and spiritual, subject to time and (M. Heidegger would say) to anguish, and a certain existence similarly qualified. But the analogous object "being," "existence," thus thought by me outreaches this analogate[12] in such a way that it will be found also, intrinsically and properly, in analogates *which differ from man by their very being and their very mode of existing*. Everything that differentiates a stone from a man is a difference of being, just as everything that differentiates a man from a stone. If there are electrons, an electron is a being, finite, corporeal and imperishable, subject to time but not to anguish. If there are angels, an angel is a being, finite, incorporeal and superior to time. Everything which divides these beings from one another is the same being which I find in each of them—varied. I simply have to fix my attention on it to see that it is at once one and multiple. It *would be* purely and simply one if its differentiations were not still itself, or to put it otherwise, if the analogue presented to the mind

---

11   See below, Appendix II.
12   For clarity of expression we reserve in this whole discussion the word *analogue* for what the scholastics called *analogum analogans*, and we designate simply by the word analogate what they called *analogum analogatum*.

made complete abstraction from its analogates; if I could think being without thereby rendering present to my mind (whether I am *de facto* explicitly aware of this or not is quite accidental) in essentially different ways some of the others in which this object of concept is realizable outside the mind. It *would be* purely and simply multiple if it did not transcend its differentiations, or, to put it otherwise, if the analogue presented to the mind made no abstraction from its analogates: in which case the word "being" would be purely equivocal and my thought would fly to pieces; I could no longer think: Peter is man and this color is green, but only ah, ah.

The concept of being (and it is the same with all transcendental concepts, essentially superuniversal or analogous, with that analogy that the scholastics call "analogy of proper proportionality," and which alone interests us here)— the concept of being is therefore *implicitly and actually multiple*. This is so because it only makes incomplete abstraction from its analogates, and in contrast to universal concepts it envelops a diversity which can be essential, and admit infinite hiatus, abysmal distinctions, in the way in which it is realized in things. And it is *one in a certain respect*, insofar as it does make incomplete abstraction from its analogates, and is disengaged from them without being conceivable apart from them, as attracted towards, without attaining, a pure and simple unity, which could alone be present to the mind if it were able to see in itself—and without concept—a reality which would be at once itself and all things. (Let us say the concept of being demands[13] to be replaced by God clearly seen, to disappear in the face of the beatific vision.) It is said to have a unity of proportionality; the being, man, stands to its man-existence as the being, stone, to its stone-existence, and as the being, angel, to its angel-existence. It signifies, therefore, not precisely one object, but a plurality of objects of which one cannot be posited before the mind without dragging the others along with it implicitly because they are all linked together in a certain community by the likeness of relations they sustain with diverse terms.

"Superuniversal" or "polyvalent," a transcendental object of concept is *unum in multis* only as a variable enveloping an actual multiplicity, and realized in several without thereby positing a community of essence among

---

13   It goes without saying that we are here speaking of an inefficacious desire. John of St. Thomas explains (*Curs. Theol.*, I P., q. 12, disp. 12, a. 2) that the adequate object of the created intellect envelops in its amplitude God Himself seen by His essence, *Deus visus continetur intra latitudinem objecti adaequati intellectus creati*. But God clearly seen—a wholly supernatural object with regard to which a created intelligence is only in obediential potency—is above everything that the created intelligence can attain by its natural powers alone and by the concept of being. It is seen without concept. The amplitude of the "adequate object" of the created intelligence, that is to say of being itself, surpasses the resources that the use of the concept of being, the instrument of our natural knowledge, offers to the intellect. This concept will be "evacuated" in Vision.

them. It is not analogous after the fashion of an originally univocal concept that a metaphor attributes afterwards, but in an extrinsic and improper way, to other transobjective subjects than those in which it was first grasped. It belongs intrinsically and properly to all the subjects to which it is attributable because it is analogous from the very start and by its essence. From the first instant in which it is grasped by the mind in a subject, it bears within itself the possibility of being realized according to its proper significance (*formaliter*, the scholastics would say) in subjects which by their essence differ totally and absolutely from that one.

10. Such objects are trans-sensible. For, though they are realized in the sensible in which we first grasp them, they are offered to the mind as transcending every genus and every category, and as able to be realized in subjects of a wholly other essence than those in which they are apprehended. It is extremely remarkable that being, the first object attained by our mind in things—which cannot deceive us since being the first, it cannot involve any construction effected by the mind nor, therefore, the possibility of faulty composition—bears within itself the sign that beings of another order than the sensible are thinkable and possible.

I am quite aware that here it is a question only of an entirely undetermined possibility. Is such and such a particular determined incorporeal subject positively possible? We can know that only if we know that it exists, thus concluding *ab actu ad posse*. Do certain incorporeal subjects exist? Human souls, created pure spirits, Uncreated Self-subsistent Being? It is by reasoning from the data actually given to us in sensible existence that we can know this.

As the first object grasped by the intellect, it is clear that being is not known in the mirror of some other previously known object. It is attained in sensible things by dianoetic intellection. Just as a generic or specific nature is known in itself by the property which reveals its essential difference, so an analogue (*analogum analogans*) is known in itself by that one of its analogates (*analogum analogata*) which first falls under the senses. Our power of abstractive perception goes beyond this analogate itself which serves it as a means, to grasp in its transcendence the analogue of which it is only one of the possible realizations. There is, therefore, an intellectual perception of being which, being involved in every act of our intelligence, in fact rules all our thought from the very beginning. And when this is disengaged for itself by the abstraction of the trans-sensible, it constitutes our primordial philosophical intuition without which we can no more acquire the science of metaphysical realities than a man born blind acquires the science of colors. In this metaphysical intuition the principle of identity: "being is not non-being," "every being is what it is," is not known merely *in actu exercito* and as an inescapable necessity for thought. Its ontological necessity is itself seen. (For this is not a logical principle, it is an ontological [metaphysical] principle, the first law of being. And that is why when it is transferred into the logical order, where it becomes the principle of non-contradiction: *non est affirmare et negare simul*, it is also the first law of thought.) From similar intuitions bearing on the primary aspects of being (and provoked in the mind by some sensible example) proceed the other metaphysical axioms, truths known of themselves by all or at least by the wise. It is true that many of those who profess to be philosophers preen themselves on putting these axioms in doubt, blissfully unaware that they are cutting off the limb on which they are sitting. They only prove that such intuitions are irreplaceable: either you have them or you don't. Reasoning presupposes them. It can lead to them by clarifying the sense of the terms. It cannot substitute for them.

First principles are seen intellectually. Quite otherwise than by empirical observation. I do not see a subject-thing in which a predicate-thing would be contained as in a box. I see that the intelligible constitution of one of these objects of thought cannot subsist if the other is not posited as implying it or as implied by it. This is not a simple observation as of a fact known by the senses; it is the intellection of a necessity. Besides, first principles impose themselves absolutely, in virtue of the notion of being itself. Their authority is so independent and so rooted in the pure intelligible, they are so far from being the result of a simple inductive generalization, or of apriori forms destined to subsume the sensible, that sensible appearances are in some way disconcerted by them and lend themselves only with ill grace to illustrate the fashion in which they rule things. I affirm the principle of identity and I look at my face in a mirror; already it has aged; it is no longer the same.

Finally these principles are analogous like being itself. Every contingent being has a cause. But the object of thought "cause" is polyvalent like the object of thought "being." Just as there are essentially and absolutely different ways of being, so there are essentially and absolutely different ways of causing. . . . To understand the word "cause" of only mechanical causes for example, either in order to submit all things to universal determinism, or in order on the contrary to deny the value of the principle of causality, is not to recognize this analogy and to cut oneself off from the possibility of thinking metaphysically. By virtue of the essentially and primitively analogous character of the super-universal object on which it bears, the axiom of identity is at the same time the axiom of the irreducible diversities of being. If each being is what it is, it is not what the others are. This is what is not seen by those philosophers who, following Parmenides, demand that this principle reduce everything to absolute unity. Far from reducing everything to identity, it is the guardian and the protector in our mind of universal multiplicity since it maintains the identity of each. And if it compels the intellect to affirm a transcendent One, that is because this very multiplicity demands such a One in order to save its own existence.

11. In one sense, there is nothing poorer than being as being. In order to perceive it, it is necessary to discard everything sensible and particular that cloaks it. In another sense, it is the most consistent and most steadfast notion. There is nothing in all that we can know which does not stem from it. It is this steadfastness which escapes those who consider being to be univocal and make of it a genus, the vastest and most naked of all.[14] It would then be, as Hegel saw, at the confines of nothingness, and even indiscernible from nothingness. Because it is, on the contrary, analogous, it is a consistent and differentiated object of thought with which a science can deal without by that very fact becoming hypertrophied in a panlogism destructive of essences.

Still, being as being is a manna of little savor for minds obsessed with the flesh-pots of experience. Descartes had already judged that it was sufficient to have considered once in his life the first truths on which physics is founded, and to devote a few hours each year to metaphysics, which was thus already reduced to a justification of science. After Hume and Kant, a great many philosophers have refused all proper intelligibility to existence, seeing in it only an empty concept, or a pure sensible position, or a pragmatic feeling. It is difficult to come across a more radical error, or one more offensive to the intellect. In the first place, the notion of existence (and that of being, since being is that which exists or can exist) has an absolutely primordial intelligible content. If existence as exercised does not offer to the mind any other content to be apprehended than existence as signified or represented (so that, although the notion of an All-Perfect necessarily has existence among the number of its perfections, I cannot conclude from that that this All-Perfect must effectively exist), on the other hand, existence as represented is quite another thing for the mind than non-existence. There is much more in a hundred existing dollars than in a hundred possible dollars. But still more, existence is perfection par excellence, and, as it were, the seal of every other perfection, if it is true that an existing half-dollar is worth more than a hundred simply possible dollars and a living dog more than a dead lion. Doubtless of itself it says only *positio extra nihil*, but it is the positing *extra nihil* of *this* or of *that*. And to posit outside nothingness a glance or a rose, a man or an angel is something essentially diverse, since it is the very actuation of all the perfection of each of these essentially diverse subjects. Existence is itself varied and admits all the degrees of ontological intensity according to the essences which receive it. If anywhere it is found in the pure state, without an essence which receives it—in other words, if there exists a being whose essence is to exist—existence must there be identical with an absolutely infinite abyss of reality and perfection.

---

14   Being as being, the object of the metaphysician, who seizes it, by virtue of an *abstractio formalis*, with the essentially varied intelligible consistency of its analogical comprehension must indeed be distinguished from being seized by a simple *abstractio totalis* as the most universal of our logical classes.

12. Being, disengaged as such by *abstractio formalis*, being, with its transcendental properties and the cleavages it presents throughout the whole extent of things, [15] constitutes the proper object of metaphysics. We have not here those supreme genera, like the categories, in which the mind attains only the first outlines of objects of knowledge (the natures of things) which are complete only at the specific degree, and hence remain at the level of a quite incomplete knowledge, insofar as it is a knowledge of the real. The object of metaphysics is not in the least the world of the universal known in the most general and therefore least determined fashion. In other words, it is not the generic classes of the things of nature. It is an entirely other world, the world of the superuniversal, the world of transcendental objects which, disengaged as such, do not demand, as genera do, to be completed by progressive differentiations coming as from outside, but offer a field of intelligibility which has in itself its own ultimate determinations. And those objects can be realized outside the mind in individual subjects which do not fall under the senses and so are outside the whole order of the genera and differentiations of the world of experience. That is why metaphysics is a perfect knowledge, a true science. Not without reason did Aristotle study the categories in logic. For knowledge of the categories furnishes the first instruments of knowledge, *introduces* the mind to the science of things. If metaphysics studies substance, quality, relation, etc., if the Philosophy of Nature studies corporeal substance, quantity, action and passion, etc., it is from another point of view insofar as these are determinations either of being as being or of mobile and sensible being. (In the latter case, as we have seen, the knowledge is complete in its own order only if to the philosophical knowledge there is added that of the experimental sciences.) The human soul, insofar as it is a spirit, and is capable of activities that are wholly immaterial in themselves, as well as of a wholly immaterial subsistence, is an object of metaphysics. Thus, anthropology is on the border-line of the Philosophy of Nature and metaphysics.[16] By it the Philosophy of Nature is crowned with metaphysics. The field of metaphysical wisdom itself comprises the reflexive knowledge of the relation of thought to being (critique), the knowledge of being as being (ontology in the strict sense), the knowledge of pure spirits and the knowledge of God according as these knowledges are accessible to reason alone (pneumatology and natural theology).

Like mathematics, metaphysics emerges above time. It causes a universe of intelligibility other than that of the experimental sciences (and of the Philosophy of Nature) to stand out in things and thereby grasps a world of eternal truths, valid not for a particular moment of contingent realization, but for all

15   "Illa scientia est maxime intellectualis, quae circa principia maxime universalia versatur. Quae quidem sunt ens, et ea quae consequuntur ens, ut unum et multa, potentia et actus." (St. Thomas Aquinas, *In Metaph.*, proemium).
16   We do not mean that it is astride the Philosophy of Nature and metaphysics, but that it is the highest part of the Philosophy of Nature, by which the latter communicates with metaphysics.

possible existence. Unlike the Philosophy of Nature, it has no need to find its terminus in the verifications of the sense in order to establish these truths which are superior to time. But, unlike mathematics, it always looks, in establishing these truths, to subjects which exist or can exist. In short, it does not abstract from the order to existence. The mathematical praeter-real does not imply matter in its notion or definition, but, enclosed in a genus, it can (when it can exist) exist only in matter. The metaphysical trans-sensible, since it is transcendental and polyvalent (analogous), is not only free from matter in its notion and definition but can also exist without it. That is why the order to existence is embowelled in the objects of metaphysics. To admit beings of reason as object would be unworthy of the science of being as being. If moreover, as we remarked above,[17] metaphysics descends to the actual existence of things in time, and rises to the actual existence of things outside time, it is not only because actual existence is the sign par excellence of the intrinsic possibility of existence, but also and especially because existence itself is, as we have said, the seal of all perfection, and cannot remain outside the field of the highest knowledge of being.

The Metaphysical Transintelligible and Ananoetic Intellection

13. If an intelligible analogue is the object of dianoetic intellection, it is not the same for those of its analogates which do not fall at first within our grasp but which are known by the intermediary of the primordially apprehended analogate. They are known in the latter as in a mirror, in virtue of the likeness it has with them. This is specular knowledge or knowledge *by analogy*. Let us call it "ananoetic intellection." Strictly speaking, the transobjective subjects in which they are realized are not *subject* to our intelligible grasps, do not *give themselves up* to us as objects. It is not their essence or their first intelligible constitutive which is objectivized for us by means of our presentative forms and of our concepts. They are known, however, intrinsically and properly designated, constituted as objects of intellection, but as it were at a distance and not "in themselves." The ray of the intellect that attains them has been refracted or reflected, and they always remain above the knowledge we have of them, superior to the grasps that reach up to them, separated from our mind in the very act which unites it to them. This paradox is due to the fact that they are attained in an object that another subject has rendered present to our intelligence, and which being itself one of the analogates, one of the valences of an analogue, causes us to pass by the latter[18] to those other analogates that we do not attain in themselves. Thus, the divine perfections are attained by us

---

17   See Ch. II, § 25.

18   *By the latter*: It is by means of the abstraction of the transcendental *analogue* that the transintelligible analogate is known in the analogate proportionate to our intelligence. On this point see the very correct remarks of T. L. Penido, *Le rôle de l'analogie en théologie dogmatique* (Paris, Vrin, 1931, p. 189.)

in the perfections of created being, which by the analogy of being makes us pass to uncreated Being, which no created mind can naturally attain in Itself. This universe on which metaphysics opens out,[19] and the knowledge of which requires that it have recourse to a whole art of deciphering the invisible in the visible, we are calling *transintelligible*. We do so not, certainly, because it is *unintelligible* in itself (on the contrary, it is the domain of absolute intelligibility), nor because it is *unintelligible* for us, but because it is disproportionate to our human intellect. It is not intelligible for us in an experimental nor in a dianoetic way. In other words, it is not connatural to our power of knowing. It is intelligible to us only by analogy. Our bat's eyes can discern nothing in this too pure light except by the interposition of obscure things from here below. To penetrate into this transintelligible is the deepest desire of our intellect. From the outset it knows instinctively that only there will it find its repose. And according to the saying of Aristotle, it is a more precious joy for it to glimpse anything of that world obscurely and in the poorest fashion than to possess clearly and in the most perfect fashion that which is proportionate to us. It aspires to things divine. Descartes can never be forgiven for having preferred to this effort and to this stripping a comfortable and rich establishment in a world of clear ideas. He preferred thereby the comforts of the understanding to the dignity of the object (and to the spiritual perfection of the same understanding).

The intellection that we have called dianoetic now appears to us to be held between an intellection that is imperfect by reason of the ontological imperfection itself and the subintelligibility of the realities with which it is concerned (perinoetic intellection), and an intellection that is imperfect by reason of the too great ontological perfection and the superintelligibility of the realities that

---

19   The *subject* of metaphysics is the analogue, being, considered in the inferior analogates in which we apprehend it *de facto*; created and material being common to the ten predicaments. (It is in created and material being that being appears to us with the notes of unity and multiplicity, of potency and act, etc., being attained by dianoetic intellection.) This is what we are calling in the present study the "trans-sensible intelligible." But the same science that has such sort of things as *subject* deals also with the *causes* of this sort of things. That is why metaphysics opens out on what we are here calling the transintelligible (for us), that is to say, on the superior analogates of being. "Unde oportet quod ad eamdem scientiam pertineat considerare substantias separatas et ens commune. . . . Ista scientia . . . considerat ut subjectum . . . ipsum solum ens commune. Hoc enim est subjectum in scientia, cujus causas et passiones quaerimus, non autem ipsae causae alicujus generis quaesiti. Nam cognitio causarum alicujus generis, est finis ad quem consideratio scientiae pertingit. Quamvis autem subjectum hujus scientiae sit ens commune, dicitur tamen tota de his quae sunt separata a materia secundum esse et rationem. Quia secundum esse et rationem separari dicuntur, non solum illa quae nunquam in materia esse possunt, sicut Deus et intellectuales substantiae, sed etiam illa quae possunt sine materia esse, sicut ens commune. Hoc tamen non contingeret, si a materia secundum esse dependerent." (St. Thomas, *In Metaph.*, proemium).

it knows (ananoetic intellection). These two imperfections correspond in a certain way with each other on either side of the dianoetic register, but their proper condition, their style, is quite different. Perinoetic intellection stops at the surface, at substitutes for the essence. Yet it makes use of rich means which give to the understanding the maximum of self-satisfaction (not without some bitterness in the end). Thanks to the ever-growing technical perfection of its means, perinoetic intellection makes the understanding advance endlessly in a more and more detailed knowledge of the behavior of essences which it does not grasp in themselves but only attains in a "blind" fashion and which remain a connatural object for it. Ananoetic intellection makes use of poor means, which give to the understanding little self-satisfaction (it is from the object that its enjoyment is derived) and which makes the understanding, as its knowledge improves, ever more aware of its disproportion with regard to what it knows. Nevertheless, thanks to the analogy of being and of the transcendentals which serve as its instruments, this intellection, however imperfect and precarious be its mode, still reaches the essence of its object, though that essence is attained enigmatically in other natures which reflect it and without anything of it being known in itself. We may add that it is very remarkable that what the moderns call by a privileged title science, succeeds (in dianoetic fashion in mathematics, in perinoetic fashion in physico-mathematical knowledge) in achieving its highest degree of rationality only by causing, as we saw above, ideal constructions and beings of reason to proliferate. Meanwhile philosophy is wholly occupied with real being, and is constrained to have recourse to artifices of ideality (above all, under the form of distinctions of reason founded *in re*) only in the ananoetic part of metaphysics (in the area of the transintelligible).

14. Three degrees in the ananoetic intellection of things superior to man can be distinguished. Only the first two belong to metaphysics; the third is supernatural.

It is impossible to say that the possible existence of pure spirits implies any contradiction. For the notions of spirit, knowledge, love, far from implying existence in matter, of themselves imply immateriality. That pure spirits do exist in fact, we have (abstracting from certitudes furnished by revelation) some well-founded indications of the natural order. We are spirits. Substantially united to matter, we experience the life of the spirit in ourselves and that in us it is only at an inferior and wretched degree of spirituality. What is more reasonable than to think that such a life, which cannot arise from the energies of the visible world, knows, in an invisible world, superior degrees more in conformity with the consistency and vigor connoted by the idea of spirit? Since the course of terrestrial events is subject to a providential government which can modify it at each instant (I am talking about the natural order itself, leaving aside the case of miracles) in such a way that the constellation of causes preparing the death of a certain invalid may be little by little diverted by the prayer of a free creature, is it not fitting to think that the world of sensible causalities is not closed in itself, but open to the action of invisible assistants to whom the free decrees of immobile eternity are perceptible as time unrolls? These suitabilities of a philosophical order give, in regard to the natural reason alone, a high theoretical probability to the existence of "separated forms." On the other hand, certain sensible facts which are open to investigation, in spite of their relative rarity, in the biographies of saints, in treatises on demonology, in the annals of spiritism, of clairvoyance, etc., appear as the vestige of this existence in the empirical world, which is as irrecusable as it is disconcerting.

But even if this existence be taken as simply possible, metaphysics is not dispensed from considering its discoverable laws. He who has not meditated on the angels will never be a perfect metaphysician. The Tract on the Angels is a theological treatise in which St. Thomas depends on revealed enlightenment. But it virtually contains a purely metaphysical treatise concerning the ontological structure of immaterial subsistents, and the natural life of a spirit detached from the constraints of our empirical world.

The knowledge we can thus acquire of created pure spirits belongs to the first degree of ananoetic intellection or intellection by analogy. The trans-objective subject dominates the knowledge that we have of it and becomes object for us only in the objectivation of other subjects which are subject to our grasp and are considered transcendentally.[20] Nevertheless, the superior analogate does not overrun the analogous concept that apprehends it. The transcendental amplitude of the concept of spirit is sufficient to embrace created pure spirit. Not only are such notions as substance, essence, existence, knowledge, appetition, etc., realized in the angel formally or according to what they properly signify (although eminently or in a fashion that transcends their mode of signification), but the reality they signify, being finite, is contained,[21] described or circumscribed by them in the angel as in man. (Thus we know, for example,

---

20   In scholastic terms its quiddity escapes us, *de forma separata non scitur quid est.* See Ch. V, §§ 18 and 19; Ch. V., n. 53; and Appendix III.

21   It is not contained by these notions as something that they would make known in itself, nor (*a fortiori*) as something which could be "comprehended" by us, in the sense in which "to comprehend" implies exhaustion, or full adequation between knowledge and the known. (cf. *Sum. Theol.*, I, 12, 7). It is contained by these notions as something which they make known *analogically,* and (*a fortiori*) without our being able to "comprehend" it in the exhaustive sense of the word, but which does not overrun the analogical concept we form of it. In this absolutely strong sense, moreover, there is nothing which we can veritably "comprehend" here below. We comprehend that 2 and 2 are 4, but we do not exhaust the intelligibility of this property of numbers. Let us add that this is so because of the weakness of our discursive intellect—even with regard to things lowest in intelligibility. On the contrary, the incomprehensibility of God comes from the infinite elevation of the object in relation to any created intellect, even placed in the conditions of the beatific vision (cf. *Sum. Theol., ibid.*).

that essence and existence, substance and powers, intelligence and will are really distinct in it.) We shall say that the analogy we use here is an embracing or circumscriptive analogy.[22]

15. The same is not true in the case of our knowledge of God.

How does the rational movement—an instinctive uprush in common-sense knowledge, an explicit demonstration in the case of metaphysical knowledge—proceed by which the existence of God is imposed on our intellect with complete certitude? Even in the knowledge by which our mind knows *that God is* it submits to the absolute transcendence of a reality which ananoetic intellection attains only in recognizing itself surpassed on every side by it. Let us try to follow this movement of the reason along one of the typical paths it may take. A philosopher thinks and grasps reflexively his own act of thought. Here is a reality that has a certain ontological quality or value and the existence of which *hic et nunc* is indubitable to him. Even if he had not read Pascal, he would know that millions of solar systems are *less* than the least thought that knows a blade of grass and that knows itself. I say less without presuming thereby a common measure between the two terms compared. On the contrary, there is question here of two incommensurable orders. But orders without a common (univocal) measure can be compared with one another according to their (analogical) participation in being.

Moreover, this philosopher knows that his thought which is a mystery of vitality to the world of bodies is at the same time a mystery of debility in itself. For it is subject to error and to time, to forgetfulness and to sleep, to distractions and to apathies. More still, in its very structure it suffers conditions of servitude hardly worthy of thought. It is not transparent to itself. It beats against objects that remain obscure to it. It must needs divide, compose, construct, logically elaborate data that are not logical but real. (What need has an eye for logic? It only needs to be opened!)

Finally, by his very awareness of this servitude, our philosopher knows that thought taken in itself and in its pure formal line has exigencies of a transcendent order the ultimate term of which he is able to determine. He has learned the true lesson of modern idealism. He has understood that the latter, born as it was of the scandal that man's thought is not pure thought, remains a marvelous witness to the privileges of pure thought.[23] Absolutely pure

---

22   We believe that, though presented in a different terminology, these precisions on our analogical knowledge of created pure spirits are in conformity with the doctrine expounded by Cajetan (*In de Ente et Essentia*, cap. VI, q. 15) (*Num intelligentiae sint a nobis quidditative cognoscibiles in hac vita*).

23   It is a very remarkable thing that the progress of modern idealism should thus be exactly inverse and symmetrical with that of anthropomorphism: a "Theomorphism" of thought. So it is that some philosophers, while recognizing the existence of God, have, according to an imaginative mode of thinking, attributed to Him the perfections of creatures carried to a maximum in their very line of

thought is, for itself, its own object. It is absolute spontaneity, it is absolutely self-sufficient. For it to exist is but to think, and to think, not a thing, but the very act of thinking. If, for it, there are things, it receives nothing from them; it makes them.

And so it is clear to our philosopher that he himself is not thought. He *is* not thought; he *has* thought. But if he has it without being it, does he derive it from something other than himself; from a cause? The principle of causality does not arise from a parcelling out of the sensible, but from necessities intuitively grasped in being. From the moment that there are diverse things, no one suffices unto itself to exist; otherwise it would be the all; it is necessary, therefore (even though we have never seen one billiard ball bumping another, or become conscious of muscular effort, etc.), that it depend on another without which it would not be, and in which it finds its own sufficiency.[24] In the case at hand, the philosopher may be said to experience the non-sufficiency of his own thought unto itself. Of course, he does not experience the "insertion" into it of the creative activity on which it depends. But he cannot think this non-sufficiency unto itself of his own thought without knowing that his thought depends on another. It depends, that is to say, not only on the material conditions that limit it from below, but on a certain unknown from which it holds its very actuality and its being as thought, and which is itself, consequently, thought or suprathought. In me, with me, it causes my act of thought insofar as my thought has being. Thought of which my thought (and would it remain *my* thought?) would be but a moment? Then it would share in the weakness of my thought, and its multiplicity, and it would have to be said that it has not its sufficiency in itself, that it is caused. Itself an effect of another thought? I do not know if such an assumption has any meaning. But in any

created perfections. They anthropomorphize God because they have not risen to the degree of abstraction required by true analogy. Meanwhile, idealists rise (without knowing that they do so) to this degree of abstraction. And it is the *analogous perfection* of thought (analogically common to uncreated and created thought) that they carry to the pure state when considering "Thought" in general (and *de facto* human thought) without realizing that in reality they are talking about the thought of God the Creator. And so they end up with a notion of thought which (if we abstract from all the jumbling which inevitably results in such conditions) belongs only to divine thought, while they do not recognize the true God; they "theomorphize" thought in general.

24 The "cause," the (ontological) concept of which is thus imposed on us, so little derives from an anthropomorphic schematization of experience that it is difficult to discover its notion in the "causes" of common experience, and then only at the price of a considerable *diminution*. As for the "causes" of scientific experience (and of the philosophy springing from mechanism), they are reduced to the spatio-temporal conditioning of a phenomenon, or to the network of determinations with which a phenomenon is bound up. That is an analogate of the concept of cause so profoundly reconstructed that the word has become almost equivocal. (See above, Ch. IV, § 10.) Obviously, it is not cause so understood that is in question here, but rather cause in the full ontological sense of the word.

case, though an infinite series is certainly not impossible of itself, a regression to infinity is not possible *here*. For we are looking for a reason of being. And to say "an infinite series" is to say precisely "no reason of being" (each term going back to another endlessly in postulating this reason of being).[25] There must, therefore, be a thought which is thought, and which is the first cause of my thought. From it must be excluded absolutely any relation as a stuff or any material causality whatever with regard to my thought. It is a cause which compenetrates with its pure efficiency the whole being of my thought, and is absolutely separated in its essence from that same thought (which thus remains really my thought). It is the absolutely uncaused Thought itself which causes in me and with me my act of thought. I already glimpsed the proper conditions of such thought which has itself as its existence and as its object. Now I know these privileges are those of an existent real. Absolutely self-sufficient for existing, it is pure act, and therefore infinitely perfect; knowing that it exists, I deduce its infinite perfection from its aseity. It is by a palpable sophism that Kant claims that such a deduction depends implicitly on the ontological argument of Descartes and St. Anselm and lies in ruins with it. The ontological argument does not at all consist in the identification of existence *a se* and total-perfection. It consists in the claim to deduce from the simple idea of the All-perfect its real existence. If I know first of all and in another way (starting from such a fact as the existence of my thought) that being *a se* exists, I am obviously justified in concluding, without the least recourse to the ontological argument, that since the notion of aseity involves that of total-perfection (and vice-versa) this being *a se* which exists is effectively all-perfect.

16. Now just what has been effected by such reasoning? It has necessarily involved raising to the pure state the analogous and polyvalent object of

---

25   Whatever be the way pursued, the consideration of intermediary causes plays an entirely different role with St. Thomas than it does with Aristotle. In Aristotle's system the series of subordinate causes enters into the reasoning to lead to the Prime Mover by a hierarchy of cosmic degrees the structure of which affects the metaphysical picture of the real. In St.Thomas' ways this series intervenes in truth only as an auxiliary means used to show that in any case a process to infinity cannot be involved, and so the structure of this causal series is of no concern to metaphysics, for in fact the Pure Act to which these ways lead will be explicitly known as Creator, and the creation of things does not admit any intermediary (*Sum. Theol.*, I, 45, 5). Hence, although the physical image of the universe was the same for St.Thomas as for Aristotle, his metaphysics, nevertheless, is from the outset free of that image. The hierarchy of intermediary spheres plays no role whatever in regard to creative causality. All things are equally bared to that causality. (Cf. E. Gilson, *The Spirit of Medieval Philosophy*, Ch. IV.) With regard to the *conservation* of things, where created causalities do have their part, our image of the physical universe accords as well and even better than that of Aristotle with the metaphysical doctrine St. Thomas gives concerning it (*Sum. Theol.*, I, 104, 2).

concept: thought. And the superior analogate thus attained as absolute Thought infinitely surpasses the concept of thought, since it is not only thought, but being per se, and every perfection belonging to the transcendental order; and since it is all that in absolute simplicity and unity. It is what the analogous concept, thought, signifies; that and infinitely more.

St. Thomas' ways do not terminate at a first of an univocal series, at a first cause which would be a thing like other things, a cause like other causes, a being like other beings: greater, higher, more perfect yet circumscribed as they are by the concept of being. That is why the criticism of them formulated by M. Edouard Le Roy is a veritable *ignoratio elenchi*. They lead to a first without any common measure with the second and with the whole subsequent series; to a first separated, isolated in infinite transcendence. Ananoetic intellection crosses the infinite abyss which separates it from everything; but the analogous concepts it uses avow at the same time their impotence to enclose or delimit the reality they then designate. *Ut omne genuflectatur.* They make God known only by kneeling before Him.

May we be permitted to point out what delicacy, what filial fear is apparent in the very word, *ways*, used by St. Thomas. These ways are proofs, demonstrations.[26] But when we are dealing with things proportionate with, or connatural to, our intelligence, demonstration, while all the while submitting to the object, also, in a certain way, subjects the object to our grasps, to our means of verification which measure it, delimit it, define it. It seizes the object, touches it, manipulates it, judges it. This is all the more obvious the more material are the procedures used. And perhaps scholastics, who have inherited a high notion of a chaste science, whose very rigor and strict intellectuality derive from a religious respect and an exigency for purity in the face of being (and it is their mission to maintain this notion as a sacred good), perhaps they sometimes forget how charged with materiality have become the words: "science," "demonstration," "proof," in the usage of the moderns, ever since thought turned above all to the domination of sensible nature, and since "to verify" evokes for modern thought only methods of measurement and laboratory apparatus. When they decline, as they ought, to accept a degraded vocabulary, they run the risk of insufficiently explaining their own terminology. But in any case, they know that to demonstrate the existence of God is neither to subject Him to our grasp, nor to define Him, nor to seize Him, nor to manipulate anything except ideas which are inadequate to such an object, nor to judge anything except our own proper and radical dependence. The procedure by which reason demonstrates that God exists, puts reason itself in an attitude of natural adoration and of intellectual admiration.

Everything has changed since the Cartesian clear ideas, which dissipated into thin air any ananoetic intellection and any knowledge by analogy. Since then, to enter into mystery by the intellect has become a contradiction in terms.

---

26   Cf. *Sum. Theol.*, I, 2, 2; *De Potentia*, 7, 3; *Cont. Gent.*, I, 12; III, 39.

If the Cartesian reason, wholly suspended from God, does not wish to treat God as a thing subject to it, it must submit to Him with closed eyes and only open them when it turns to the created and the finite. It is in this sense that Descartes "never treated of the infinite except to submit to it." Hence, that great movement of "holy" flight, which precipitated him towards things below. After him, Malebranche and Leibniz will apply that same reason—which knows only by judging according to its own measure—to the justification of God. What had been called *natural theology* will henceforth be called *theodicy*, and, setting out to comprehend the divine ways in order to render them acceptable, will religiously prepare the way for atheism. All that He has done is well done because it is He who hath done it, said Christian reason. It is He who has done all, since it is well done and since I know why, and besides, He is bound to do the best, says Leibnizian optimism—a materialized and corrupted scholasticism which would not only have seemed impious but absurd to a Thomas Aquinas.

III
THE DIVINE NAMES

17. Our knowledge of God does not proceed merely by ananoetic intellection or intellection by analogy. It is necessary to add that this analogy is uncontaining, *uncircumscriptive*.

In what we have called the transintelligible, the deity (let us designate by that name the Divine Essence considered in itself, the ipseity of God) is infinitely more above the angels than is the angelic essence above bodies. Concepts and names which designate perfections belonging to the transcendental order belong to Him intrinsically and in their proper sense, they do not fade away, they do not fly to pieces, they retain their proper significance when applied to God. But while they are realized in God better than in things, they do not enclose or delimit the Divine Reality; they leave it uncontained and uncircumscribed.[27] Because we receive these intelligible analogues from creatures (their inferior analogates), we cannot think them without thinking, at the same time as we think what they signify, the distinct contours that they have

---

27   "Sic igitur, cum aliquod nomen ad perfectionem pertinens de creatura dicitur, significat illam perfectionem ut distinctam secundum rationem distinctionis ab aliis: puta cum hoc nomen sapiens de homine dicitur, significamus aliquam perfectionem distinctam ab essentia hominis, et a potentia et ab esse ipsius, et ab omnibus hujusmodi. Sed cum hoc nomen de Deo dicimus, non intendimus significare aliquid distinctum ab essentia vel potentia vel esse ipsius. Et sic, cum hoc nomen sapiens de homine dicitur, quodammodo circumscribit et comprehendit rem significatam: non autem cum dicitur de Deo, sed reliquit rem significatam ut incomprehensam et excedentem nominis significationem." (*Sum. Theol.*, I, 13, 5).

in the things in which we first grasp them. We can think being only by thinking it as distinct from knowing; knowing, only by thinking it as distinct from loving. But, if we have understood the nature of ananoetic intellection, we know very well that in it there are two things, inseparable for us, distinct in themselves: *what is signified* by the analogous and polyvalent concept; and the *mode of our conception*, limited to the inferior, material and created analogate. What is signified belongs to the divine analogate. It belongs to Him even before belonging to creatures, and more properly than to them. Of itself the name "being" belongs to God before pertaining to things. The mode of signification in no way pertains to Him.[28] This is so not only, as in the case of the angels, because this mode pertains exclusively to a material analogate, while the superior analogate is spiritual, but in a much more general and much more radical fashion, because that mode pertains exclusively to a created analogate, while the superior analogate is uncreated. The way in which I conceive being is absolutely deficient in relation to God.

All this amounts to saying that we can conceive of nothing except as delimited (that goes for being itself, insofar as it is distinguished from its determinations). But sometimes the limitation belongs to what is signified itself. Such is the case with notions like those of body, movement, etc., which can be said of God only metaphorically (the perfections of these things are in God *virtualiter-eminenter*). Sometimes the limitation belongs only to our mode of conceiving. Such is the case with notions which belong to the transcendental order, and which may be said properly of God.[29] Being, knowledge, goodness are in God *formaliter-eminenter*, i.e., according to what is signified by these concepts (which remains and does not perish), but in a mode not only—as when they are said of an angel—superior to that in which being, knowledge, goodness are in the things in which I grasp them, but so much superior that these intelligibles lose there the delimitations which distinguish them and without which I, myself, cannot conceive them (but without which they can exist because they are analogous, and because these delimitations are proper to their created analogates). All the divine perfections are strictly identified in God. When I say being of God, the word continues to signify being and does not signify, does not present to my mind, goodness or knowledge,[30] and yet

28   "In nominibus vero quae Deo attribuimus, duo est considerare: scilicet ipsas perfectiones significatas, ut bonitatem, vitam et huiusmodi; et modum significandi. Quantum igitur ad id quod significant hujusmodi nomina, proprie competunt Deo, et magis proprie quam ipsis creaturis, et per prius de eo dicuntur. Quantum vero ad modum significandi, non proprie dicuntur de Deo: habent enim modum significandi hunc qui creaturis competit" (*Sum. Theol.*, I, 13, 3). This distinction of the *significatum* and the *modus significandi* dominates the whole Thomist doctrine of the divine names, it is always present in St. Thomas. Cf. *In I Sent.*, dist. 2, q. I, a. I, and especially a. 2; *Cont. Gent.*, I, 30; *De Potentia*, 7, 5; *In de Ente et Essentia*, cap. VI (and q. 13 of Cajetan's commentary), etc.

29   Cf. *Sum. Theol.*, I, 13, 3, ad 1 and ad 3.

30   *Ibid.*, 13, 4: "Hujusmodi nomina dicta de Deo, non sunt synonyma."

the being of God is His knowledge and His goodness, His mercy and His justice.

18. Thus, the deity is above what circumscribes the concept of being[31]; if the idea of being existed apart like a Platonic archetype, it would remain indefinitely inferior to God. And yet God is Being itself subsisting *per se, ipsum Esse per se subsistens.* The name, *He who is,* is His proper name par excellence. The concept being passes to God with its proper intelligibility, and the law of being as being, the principle of identity, continues to be verified in God, or rather begins by being verified in Him:[32] not that God would be subject to the

---

31   Cf. Cajetan, *In I,* 39, 1, n. 7: "Res divina prior est ente et omnibus differentiis ejus, est enim super ens et super unum. . . ." St. Thomas wrote against the Platonists (*In lib. de Causis,*lect. 6): "Causa prima at supra ens, inquantum est esse infinitum"; that is because *esse infinitum* itself infinitely transcends what the idea of being would be if, *per impossibile,* it subsisted in a Platonic fashion.

32   In the treatise on the Trinity, St. Thomas shows that in the very depths of the mystery the principle of identity is never in default. Let us remember that this principle in no wise consists in a simple reiteration of the same logical term. Rather, it expresses the extramental coherence of being with all its analogical degrees. In God it refers to a transcendent and infinite *esse,* to the deity itself, whose plenitude necessitates *a parte rei* our distinctions of reason and which contains *eminentissime et formaliter* everything which pertains to absolute perfection and everything which pertains to the triune relations (Cajetan, *In I,* 39, 1). Since the Divine Essence is thus "virtually multiple," a real distinction can intervene, from the fact of relative opposition, between hypostases which from the point of view of absolute perfections differ from the essence only by a distinction of reason. Cf. *Sum. Theol.,* I, 28, 3 ad 1 (and John of St. Thomas, *Curs. Theol.,* on the same article, disp. 12, a. 3): in God the subsistent relations are really identical with the Divine Essence from which they differ only by a distinction of reason, and yet they differ really from one another, that is because "as the Philosopher says in the Third Book of the Physics, two things identical to a third thing are necessarily identical to each other, when their identity to this third belongs at once to the real order and to the notional order, but not when it is accompanied by a difference in the notions (in his quae sunt idem re et ratione, sicut tunica et indumentum; non autem in his quae differunt ratione)." St. Thomas does not mean here, as it might seem at first sight, that no difference as to the notion must exist between the third term and each of the other two; one could then object, reviving Auriol's argument, that this would destroy the whole theory of the syllogism, since in every proposition the subject and the predicate differ notionally. As Cajetan points out, he means that the two extremes must be identical with each other only in what makes their notion identical with that of the mean, or to put it otherwise according to the very reason of their identification with the mean. "Non oportet eadem medio identificari inter se, secundum id in quo non identificatur medio; id est quod non est ratio identificationis ipsi medio." The Divine Persons are really distinct from one another by reason of their relative opposition but by reason of absolute reality each is really identical with the Divine Essence, they are each the same absolute reality, and by reason of the absolute reality there are no distinctions between them.

principle of identity "as to Styx or the fates."[33] But if this principle is a law of being as such, to which all created and creatable things are subject, it is (in the ontological order, *in via judicii*) because first of all God exists, in whose very essence and thought this axiom has, as all the eternal truths, its root and foundation. Our knowledge of God is subject to it; God is not subject to it. God renders it necessary with His own necessity; so that to annihilate the truth and the necessity of the principle of identity, it would be necessary to annihilate first the Divine Essence. For our knowledge, which sets out from below, the Divine Being is one of the analogates of the concept of being which precedes it. In itself it is the Divine Being which is first, giving a basis to the intelligibility of analogous being, an infinitely transcending all created or creatable being.

The Divine Essence, constituted as object for us not in itself but by means of the objectification of created subjects (considered in those of their perfections which belong to the transcendental order), is attained and known in things which at the same time resemble and infinitely differ from it.[34] Even as they make the Divine Essence known to us, our concepts, while remaining themselves in it, are absorbed in its abyss. In God, what they signify escapes, without our being able to know how, our mode of conceiving. The Divine Essence is, therefore, really attained by our metaphysical knowledge, but without delivering itself; it is known, but its mystery remains intact, unpenetrated. To the very degree that we know it, it escapes our grasp, infinitely surpasses our knowledge. "Quamcumque formam intellectus concipiat, Deus subterfugit illam per suam eminentiam," said St. Thomas,[35] echoing St. Augustine and Boethius.

The very Doctor who asked: "What is God?" at the first awakening of his intelligence, who never ceased explaining and detailing the Divine Perfections, and whose proper task was to lead the human soul to some under-

---

33 "To say that these truths are independent of Him is, in effect, to talk of God as of a Jupiter or Saturn and to subject Him to Styx and the fates." (Descartes, *Letters to Mersenne*, April 15, 1530, A.-T., I, 145). They are not independent of Him, but it is on His essence as exhausted by His intellection that they depend, not on His free will, His creative will, Cf. our *The Dream of Descartes*, Ch. IV.

34 "Unde similitudines rerum sensibilium ad substantias immateriales translatas vocat Dionysius, II *Cael. Hier.*, dissimiles similationes" (St. Thomas, *In Boet. de Trin.*, q. 6, a. 3.

35 *In I Sent.*, dist. 22, q. 1. "Sicut Deum imperfecte cognoscimus, ita etiam imperfecte nominamus, quasi balbutiendo, ut dicit Gregorius" (*ibid.*). St. Thomas will take up again and explain the same formula in the *De Potentia*, 7, 5 ad 13: "Deus subterfugit formam intellectus nostri quasi omnem formam intellectus nostri excedens; non autem ita quo intellectus noster secundum nullam formam intelligibilem Deo assimiletur. . . ."

"Deus est potior omni nostra locutione et omni cognitione et non solum excedit nostram cognitionem et locutionem, sed universaliter collocatur super omnem mentem etiam angelicam et super omnem substantiam," St. Thomas says again (*In Div. Nom.*, c. 1. lect. 3).

standing of the mysteries of the deity, affirms that here below we cannot know of God what He is in Himself, *nos non scimus de Deo quid est*, and know Him only with the same knowledge which assures us of His existence; *quamvis maneat ignotum quid est, scitur tamen quia est.*

Previous reflections have given us in advance the meaning of these formulas in which it would be vain to seek a shadow of agnosticism or of semi-agnosticism. The first does not signify: "We do not know what God is" in the sense that we would not know what predicates should be attributed to God intrinsically and in their proper sense. For we know with certain knowledge, more certain than mathematical knowledge, that God is simple, one, good, omniscient, all-powerful, free .. , we are more certain of the Divine Perfections than of our own heart. This formula signifies: "We do not know of God what he is" in the sense that we do not attain in itself the quiddity of God, we do not know in what the deity itself consists. For when we attribute to God one or another predicate, it is not His essence formally seized as such that we attribute to Him; it is a perfection which is certainly contained in that essence, but which we can only conceive as it exists elsewhere. Indeed that a predicate be attributed to God is itself a result of our inadequate way of conceiving.[36] In him there is no duality of subject and predicate. To know Him as He is could only consist in an absolutely simple vision.

19. Indeed, the very formal language of St. Thomas has here the precise technical sense it enjoys in the Peripatetic School. It would be a total misunderstanding to think that *scire de aliquo an sit* or *quia est* consists exclusively in proffering judgments concerning existence without knowing anything about what the thing is. To translate *scire quia est* and *scire quid est* accurately into modern terms, it is necessary to say, in the first case, to know in the order or the perspective of a simple certitude of fact, in the second, to know in the order or the perspective of the reason of being, or of explanation.[37] All knowledge which does not attain the essence *in itself* belongs to *scire quia est*. In knowing a thing not by its essence in itself, but in what concerns its existence, in knowing it not in the perspective of the reason of being, but only in that of fact, it always attains in an imperfect way what the thing is (if not it would not know of what it was positing the existence); it includes a certain diminished knowledge of the essence, known not in itself as in the case of dianoetic intellection, but in another thing.

Thus, in a nominal definition, it is already the thing that is signified, though in a confused and imperfect fashion. Thus, in empiriological knowledge it is the essence of corporeal things that is attained, but blindly, in the signs which are its substitutes. All the more so when we know God by means of created

---

36   Cf. *Sum. Theol.*, I, 13, 12 ad 2; *De Potentia*, 7, 4.
37   See R. Garrigou-Lagrange, *Dieu, son existence et sa nature*, 5th ed., p. 512; see also below, Appendix III.

perfections, which, in their very essence, by that which is most profound and basic in them, stamp a likeness to God in the very heart of things, we know the Divine Essence, not, to be sure, in itself, *sicuti est*, nor by a real definition which is indeed impossible, but very truly and very certainly, in virtue of an analogy which, though wholly uncircumscriptive, attains what is found properly and intrinsically in that same essence. And so it enables us to assign—in place of an impossible real definition—what is, according to our mode of conceiving, the formal constitutive of the Divine Essence. The inviolable secret of the deity does not, then, prevent the Divine Essence being known by us, not in itself, but because it communicates a created participation of itself to what is not itself—that word "participation" expresses in the ontological order the same thing expressed by the word "analogy" in the noetic order. And the more rigorous the knowledge, the more it witnesses to the transcendence. A formula of endothermic reaction that a chemist writes on paper and handles with his pen enunciates a vertiginous conflagration; in saying "Subsistent Being itself," or "in Him there is no real distinction between essence and existence," the metaphysician designates, without seeing it, the sacred abyss which makes the angels tremble with love and with awe.

The Divine Nature remains veiled, not revealed, to our metaphysical gaze. It is not objectivized according to what it is in itself. It is attained in things; it is untouched in itself. And yet, thanks to ananoetic intellection, it is constituted the object of an absolutely stable knowledge, of a science which contemplates, and delineates in it, determinations which imply negation only in our mode of conceiving. Certain of leaving intact the absolute Simplicity and precisely because we are certain of not misunderstanding it, we introduce into the Divine Nature all our distinctions of reason: one perfection after another, science of simple intelligence and science of vision, antecedent and consequent will, determining and permissive decrees. . . . The multiplicity of these distinctions of reason, demanded by the very eminence of the reality to be known, attests nothing except the humility of such a knowledge. It is not the Divine Simplicity that we divide; it is our concepts that we adapt and work over in order to submit our intellect to it and to know the Almighty according to the mode of our poverty.

The Name of Person

20. A person is a center of liberty; a person confronts things, the universe, God; talks with another person, communicates with him by understanding and affection. The notion of personality, however complex it may be, belongs primarily to the ontological order. It is a metaphysical and substantial perfection which unfolds in the operative order in psychological and moral values.

The first metaphysical root of personality is what is called subsistence. Subsistence presupposes a (substantial) nature that is individual or singular (i.e., having the ultimate of actuation and determination in the very line of nature or essence). What it properly signifies, insofar as it gives the final completion to the order of created things,[38] is that this nature, from the fact that it is endowed with subsistence, cannot communicate with any other substantial nature in the very act of existing, it is, so to speak, absolutely enclosed in itself with regard to existence. My person exists before acting; and it possesses its existence, as it possesses its nature, in a way absolutely proper to it and incommunicable. Not only is its nature singular, it owns so completely the existence which actuates it that it desires to keep it to itself alone; it can share this existence with no other.

If, in all that is not God, the essence is really distinct from existence, and related as potency to act, it is nevertheless clear that the act of existing does not complete the essence in the very line of essence, for it belongs to another order (it declares the position *extra nihil* of the essence entirely constituted in its own line). In order that the existence it receives be its own existence, actuate it as belonging to it alone and unable at the same time to actuate another, it is necessary that the nature first receive another kind of completion or termination, a metaphysical mode, thanks to which it confronts existence as a closed whole, as a subject which appropriates to itself alone the act of existing that it receives. This is that subsistence about which there has been so much dispute and the notion of which imposes itself the moment one grasps the import of the intuition of genius by which St. Thomas saw in the essence itself with all its intelligible determinations a potency with regard to the act of existing.[39]

Subsistence is for the nature an ontological seal, as it were, of its unity. When this nature is complete (a separated soul is not a person) and above all when it is capable of possessing itself, of taking itself in hand by the intellect and the will, in short, when it belongs to the spiritual order, then the subsistence of such a nature is called personality.

Such, in the terminology of the Schoolmen, is the metaphysical notion of personality. This is the notion we all use (as M. Jourdain, prose) when we say that every man has a personality, is a person, endowed with free will. But for subjects that are corporeal as well as spiritual and who share the same specific nature so that the personality of each supposes its individuation by matter, and who are obscure to themselves, and for whom change is the proper

---

38 The created and finite subsistence of Peter signifies that no other substantial nature can communicate with him in the act of existing. If we pass to the uncreated order, the uncreated and infinite subsistence of the Divine Nature signifies that it cannot communicate in the act of existing with anything which is not itself, or which it itself is not already. Each Divine Person is God, and thus each exists with the same common existence which is the uncreated essence itself. God is eminently all things, and thus the uncreated subsistence of the Word, since it is infinite, can "terminate" and cause to exist with Divine Existence a finite nature (without its own subsistence) hypostatically assumed. See Appendix IV.

39 See Appendix IV.

condition, this metaphysical root, hidden in the depth of being, is only manifested by a progressive conquest of the self by the self accomplished in time. Man must win his personality as he wins his liberty; he pays dearly for it. He is a person in the order of acting, he is *causa sui* only if rational energies and virtues, and love—and the Spirit of God—gather his soul into their hands— *anima mea in manibus meis semper*—and into the hands of God, and give a face to the turbulent multiplicity that dwells within him, freely seal it with the seal of his radical ontological unity. In this sense, one knows true personality and true liberty; another knows them not. Personality, while metaphysically inalienable, suffers many a check in the psychological and moral register. There it runs the risk of contamination by the miseries of material individuality, by its meannesses, its vanities, its bad habits, its narrownesses, its hereditary predispositions, by its natural regime of rivalry and opposition. For that same man who is a person, and subsists in his entirety with the subsistence of his soul, is also an individual in a species and dust before the wind.

21. Great truths weigh heavily on the shoulders of men. One could say that India has been unable to sustain the idea of Divine Transcendence, as though a burning sense of the solitude of God had led her to an a-cosmic metaphysics which, by a hopeless circle, risked ruining in its turn that same transcendence. For having felt too keenly, on the contrary, that there is nothing, so to speak, so widespread as divinity (for we cannot take a step without stumbling on a manifestation of an attribute of the Creator), so that the universe is nothing profane, but sacred, and abounds with signs of the Divine, the Greco-Roman world fell into the adoration of creatures and into Stoic or neo-Platonic pantheism.

In the one as in the other the personality of the true God is destroyed. Clearly the god of immanence, be it the naive immanence of the old pantheists or the rehashed and senile immanence of modern idealism, cannot be a personal God, lost as he is either in things or in the thought of philosophers and scholars. On the other hand, the idea of Divine Transcendence, if too humanly understood, and insufficiently transcendent, seems at first sight equally incompatible with personality. How could an immense God, high above all things and all the concepts we use to name Him, be a person, one who says "I" as we do? In speaking so, we have forgotten at once the true import of ananoetic intellection and the true meaning of personality; we cling to images both to represent the Divine Eminence to ourselves and to think of person.

All that the current use of the word "personality" implies of the laborious and the limited, of the indigent and the complicated together, of the return to a wretched center and to wretched designs, the whole anthropomorphic charge with which this word is burdened (And is it surprising? It designates in man the fullness of the human.) stems uniquely from the union in us of personality with individuation, and therefore from our material condition. We must free the notion of personality from this dross in order to grasp it in its transcendental value and in its ananoetic force. There remain the great ontological notes to which we have called attention: individuality (I do not say individuation: individuation by matter is a condition exclusively proper to corporeal things), unity and integrity, subsistence, intellect, will, liberty, the possession of the self by the self. "The notion of person," says St. Thomas, "signifies what is most perfect in all nature."[40] Think of what an angelic Person must be. Such a one is still a created subject, but each exhausts by himself alone a whole specific essence. Finite in relation to God, he is infinite in relation to us. He subsists immutably above time, a mirror of God and of the universe. He is a person transparent to himself, who grasps himself completely in one word which expresses his very substance. He knows all things in the depth of his self-knowledge. His liberty knows only forever definite acts. It is among the myriads of pure spirits, humming from the top-most to the lowest with intelligible communications and conversations with soundless words, that the concept of person begins to reveal itself in the amplitude and purity of its transintelligible analogates.

In reality, as soon as one leaves images behind in order to think of the Divine Transcendence, it is clear that it demands personality absolutely and necessarily. Personality is the seal of that transcendence. Without it, the ocean of infinite perfections, however high above all thought they may be recognized to be, would not achieve separate existence. The transcendence would yield to that call for endless surpassing, for a passing beyond the already experienced, that the modernists substitute for it, and which only attests the inexhaustibility of our own nature or the indefiniteness of spiritual becoming in us. If God does not possess personality, the Divine Attributes, everywhere participated, will never be united in an absolute sufficing unto itself without things, the resplendent threads of divinity will never be tied together. O the treachery of metaphor! That personality be a knot, a synthesis of the diverse, is its proper condition in the created, but in its uncreated analogate it is nothing but pure simplicity.

In Pure Act there is absolute unity, absolute integrity of nature, absolute individuality (i.e., perfection of nature to the ultimate degree). There subsistence is identical with essence; since subsistence enables an essence to appropriate existence to itself, and since the Divine Essence is precisely its own existence, these three terms are absolutely identical in God. In Him thought exists in the pure state, and what necessarily follows on thought: love, liberty. There is possession of the self by the self in the pure state, since His existence is His very intellection and His love. Thus He not only exists and grasps Himself by intelligence and love, as do created minds. Uncreated Spirit, to exist is for Him so to grasp Himself.

---

40   *Sum. Theol.*, I, 27, 3.

22. Metaphysics, therefore, knows demonstratively that the Divine Essence subsists in itself as infinite personality. (And faith holds from revelation that it subsists in three relative Subsistences or relative Personalities, really distinct from one another but not from the Divine Essence itself. And so in the deity there is, all at once, a trinity of persons and perfect community and without any sharing of the same individual nature, because there is perfect personality without shadow of individuation, not even, as in the case of the angels, by the reception of existence in essences distinct from it.) We know that the Divine Transcendence is that of an absolute subject[41] (provided we eradicate from the notion of subject all passivity or receptivity and retain only the significance of a reality in itself and for itself. The transobjective profundity of this subject is so immense that even the blessed spirits who *see* it will never *comprehend* it). It is subject par excellence, separated absolutely by its very infinity from all others, created or creatable, the endless multiplication of which could never add one iota to the perfection of What *is* already. (With their creation there are more *beings*, there is no more *being*.)

While we know that He is thus truly and really transcendent in His essence, we also know that He is immanent to all things by His immensity, more intimate to them than they are to themselves, in order continually to give them being and movement. We know that as all mutability pertains to things, not to Pure Act, which alone specifies His knowledge and His love, absolutely nothing would be changed in Him had He not created things, and yet He really knows them and loves them since they fall, as contingent terms attained in fact though not as specifying objects, under the very knowledge by which He knows Himself, the love by which He loves Himself, the will by which He necessarily wills His goodness. From this we seem to be able to catch a glimpse of how the evil which He permits—which supposes the existent creature and its voluntary deficiency, and is of itself only the lack of a due good—can be known by God without having God as its cause, since the creature has the first initiative in the line of evil, as God has in the line of good. And, on the other hand, we can vaguely descry how His loving of His creatures to the point of introducing them, as other selves having with Him that community of life which is proper to friends, into the unchanging love that He has of Himself and into His unchanging joy—*Enter into the joy of your Lord*—is so profound a characteristic of the deity that Christian revelation was needed to give it to us as a proper name of God: *Deus caritas est.*

So it is that integral realism first knows things, intelligible subjects subsisting outside the mind, in order to mount to the transintelligible cause of things, infinitely transcendent and sovereignly personal.

This sovereign personality is at once that which removes Him most from us—the inflexible infinite confronting my mere manhood—and brings us

---

41   In that sense we can allow Kierkegaard's expression that God is *infinite subjectivity.*

closest to Him, for incomprehensible Purity has a countenance, a voice, and has set me face to face before It, that I may speak to Him and He respond. The light of His countenance is sealed upon us. "What is man that thou shouldst magnify him? Or why dost thou set thy heart upon him? Thou visitest him early in the morning; and thou provest him suddenly. How long wilt thou not spare me, nor suffer me to swallow down my spittle? . . . Thy hands have made me and fashioned me wholly round about. And dost thou thus cast me down headlong on a sudden? . . . But yet I will speak to the Almighty: and I desire to reason with God. . . . Who would grant me a hearer, that the Almighty may hear my desire; and that he himself that judgeth would write a book, That I may carry it on my shoulder, and put it about me as a crown? . . . Then the Lord answered Job out of a whirlwind, and said: Who is this that wrappeth up sentences in unskillful words? Gird up thy loins like a man. I will ask thee, and answer thou Me."[42] All mysticism is a dialogue. A mysticism addressed to an anonymous interlocutor without personality would by that very fact own itself to be a lie. Though still unable to name the Father, the Son, and the Holy Ghost, metaphysics should attain to the recognition of the Divine Personality as its natural and necessary terminus. It misses its end, betrays itself, it is unforgivable, if it does not do so. This is what St. Paul, when he condemned the *sapientes hujus mundi*, called "holding truth captive" and "fainting away in their own thoughts."

Since God is sovereignly personal, the notion of creation makes sense: He is the absolute cause, by His intelligence and His liberty, of the entire being of that which is not Himself. The notion of sin makes sense. To mar that order according to which the nature of what is requires free wills to regulate themselves, is to wound God Himself in what He wills and loves necessarily, namely, justice, and in what He wills and loves freely, namely, created things and wills (and once they exist, there is a justice which concerns them, an order which they require by nature, and which positive law, divine or human, can achieve). The notion of revelation makes sense: He can speak to us by the human instruments of His choice. The notion of grace makes sense: He can bring us into a participation of His very deity and His personal life, and make of us His friends.

The Way of Knowing and the Way of Non-Knowing

23. Since our concept of being, and our concepts of all perfections belonging to the transcendental order, cannot be freed from the limitations which they connote, not as to the thing signified but as to the mode of signification or conception, whereas being itself and transcendental analogues are in God without these limitations, and therefore in a *manner*, and according to an infinity, a purity, which cannot be signified or conceived, then it is clear (and

---

42   Job vii, 17–19; x, 8; xiii, 3; xxxi, 35–36; xxxviii, 1–3.

St. Thomas, echoing the whole of traditional wisdom, continually; repeats it),[43] it is clear that *apophatic* theology, which knows God by way of negation and non-knowing, knows Him better than *cataphatic* theology, which proceeds by way of affirmation and of science.

But that implies the condition that apophatic theology, or theology by way of non-knowing, is not a pure and simple ignorance, but an ignorance which knows, for that is its proper mystery. Otherwise, the atheist who says, "There is no God," would possess the same wisdom as St. Paul. To be unable to write because you do not know the alphabet, and to be no longer able to write because the Summa you have composed now seems but straw, to ignore the rules of art because you cannot learn them or to ignore them because you bend them to your will, to hold yourself below reason because you have not yet awakened to rational life, or above reason because you have entered into contemplation, these are modes of behavior that ought not to be confused. *In finem nostrae cognitionis Deum tanquam ignotum cognoscimus*, at the term of our knowledge, says St. Thomas, quoting Dionysius,[44] we know God as unknown.

"For it is then above all," he adds, "that the mind dwells more perfectly in the knowledge of God, when it is known that His essence is above everything that can be apprehended in the present state of life. And so, though the deity remains unknown according as it is in itself, there is (to a higher degree than ever) knowledge of God according as He is."[45] *Tanquam ignotus cognoscitur.* This is not to say that He remains unknown to us. Rather, He is known by us, He Himself is known, but as remaining unknown.[46]

Since this is so, a purely conceptual apophatic theology would be just nothing at all, for negative knowledge proceeds by way of non-knowing to get beyond the limited mode of the concept. To tell the truth, there is a certain equivocity in this word, which explains its varying fortune. It leaves us suspended on the border between the rational and the mystical, and takes on

---

43   Cf. *In I Sent.*, dist. 22, q. I, a. 2, ad 1 (the expression is still more pointed in *De Potentia*, 7, 5, ad 2 and in *Sum. Theol.*, I, 13, 3, ad 2 and 12, ad 1), *Cont. Gent.* I, 30; III, 49, and the diverse texts quoted in Appendix III.

44   *Myst. Theol.*, c. 1.

45   "Et sic quamvis maneat ignotum quid est, scitur tamen quia est" (St. Thomas, *In Boet. de Trin.*, q. 1, a. 2 ad 1). Cf. *De Potentia*, 7, 5, ad 14: "Ex quo intellectus noster divinam substantiam non adaequat, hoc ipsum quod est Dei substantia remanet nostrum intellectum excedens, et ita a nobis ignoratur: et propter hoc illud est ultimum cognitionis humanae de Deo quod sciat se Deum nescire, in quantum cognoscit, illud quod Deus est, omne ipsum quod de eo intelligimus, excedere." Cf. also *De Verit.*, I, 1 and 9.

46   "Hoc ipsum est Deum cognoscere, quod nos scimus nos ignorare de Deo quid sit. . . . Et sic cognoscens Deum in tali statu cognitionis illuminatur ab ipsa profunditate divinae sapientiae, quam perscrutari non possumus. Quod etiam intelligamus Deum esse supra omnia, non solum quae sunt, sed etiam quae apprehendere possumus, ex incomprehensibili profunditate divinae sapientiae provenit nobis" (St. Thomas, *In Div. Nom.*, c. vii, lect. 4).

a different meaning according to the side from which it is viewed. Insofar as the *via negationis* announces that God is like nothing created, it is one of the ways of metaphysical knowledge or ordinary theology, and indeed its most exalted moment. But insofar as *theologia negativa* constitutes a species of knowledge, a wisdom of a higher order (and that is what is meant once it is distinguished from ordinary theology as a theology of another kind), it is nothing if not mystical experience. In order to experience mystically in that mode without mode what cataphatic theology knows, as from outside, belongs in things divine, *theologia negativa* enters into that reserve of ignorance with which the communicable science itself of these things is crowned. To say that in God there is neither composition nor imperfection nor limitation nor mutability nor multiplicity, that God is not beautiful as things are beautiful, is not as things are, does not love as we love—all that is still to formulate theses[47]

---

47   If the phrase "apophatic theology" is used to designate these negative propositions, it then refers to the *via negationis*. The latter is opposed to the *via eminentiae* but is strictly correlative to it. Both these ways are implied from the very beginning by the doctrine of the divine names. They are but parts of one and the same discursive knowledge, which is either first philosophy (natural theology) in the order of purely rational knowledge, or, in the order of the knowledge of reason elevated by faith, theology *per modum doctrinae seu cognitionis*.

Thus, in the *Summa Theologica* the *via negationis seu remotionis* is systematically employed along with the *via causalitatis* and the *via excessus seu eminentiae* in building up sacred doctrine. In particular—in conformity with the methodological principle that, in the imperfect knowledge of the essence, or of the *quid*, implied by all science set in the simple perspective of fact (*quia est*), what is, in the case of material substances, knowledge by some proximate or remote *genus* and knowledge by certain characteristic *accidents*, becomes, in the case of immaterial substances, knowledge by way of *negation* and knowledge by way of *causality* and of *eminence* (cf. *In Boet. de Trin.*, q. 1, a. 2, and especially q. 6, a. 3; and below Appendix III), questions 3 to 11 of the *Prima Pars*, which treat of things "quae ad divinam substantiam pertinent" (q. 14, proem.), are placed above all under the sign of the *via negationis* ("quia de Deo scire non possumus quid sit, sed quid non sit, non possumus considerare de Deo quomodo sit, sed potius quomodo non sit" [q. 3, proem.]; "et tunc de substantia ejus erit propria consideratio, cum cognoscetur ut ab omnibus distinctus. Non tamen erit perfecta cognitio, quia non cognoscetur quid in se sit" [*Cont. Gent.*, I, 14]; see also *ibid.*, III, 39); while in questions 14 to 26, which treat of things "quae pertinent ad operationem ipsius" (q. 14, proem.), after the doctrine of analogy has been expressly brought out (q. 12 and 13), it is the *via causalitatis* and the *via eminentiae* which predominate (without excluding the *via negationis*, to be sure, for in reality these three ways are connected, cf. *De Potentia*, q. 7, a. 5, and the *via negationis* is, as we noted in the text, the most exalted).

Two classes of texts are to be found in St. Thomas concerning the *via negationis*. The first refer to the method of negation employed, as we have just seen, in the theology that St.Thomas calls *per modum cognitionis* (I, 1, 6 ad 3). Cf. for example, *In Boet. de Trin.*, q. 2, a. 2 ad 2: "Hoc ipsum quod scimus de Deo quid non est, supplet in divina scientia locum cognitionis quid est: quia sicut per quid est distinguitur res ab aliis, ita per hoc quod scitur quid non est", and again *Cont.*

Gent., I, 14.

The second refer to the knowledge by non-knowing considered as constituting the highest kind of wisdom, in other words, to apophatic theology insofar as it signifies an order of knowledge superior to that of cataphatic theology. Apophatic or negative theology is then identified with mystical Theology, and therefore (since mystical Theology is itself identified with the *pati divina*) with Knowledge of God *per modum inclinationis* or the Wisdom of the Holy Ghost (I, 1, 6 ad 3; II–II, 45, 2). Cf., for example, the text of the commentary *In Boet. de Trin.* (q. 1, a. 2 ad 1), and that of the commentary *In Div. Nom.* (c. vii, lect. 4) cited above and again: *Cont. Gent.*, III, 49; "Et hoc est ultimum et perfectissimum nostrae cognitionis in hac vita, unde Dionysius dicit in libro de *Mystica Theologia* (c. 2) quod Deo quasi ignoto conjungimur. Quod quidem contingit dum de Deo quid non sit cognoscimus, quid vero sit, penitus manet incognitum. Unde et ad *hujus sublissimae cognitionis ignorantiam* demonstrandam, de Moyse dicitur (Exod. xx, 21) quod *accessit ad caliginem in qua erat Deus"*, and again: "quando in Deum procedimus per viam remotionis, primo negamus ab eo corporalia; et secundo etiam intellectualia, secundum quod inveniuntur in creaturis, ut bonitas et sapientia; et tunc remanet tantum in intellectu nostro, quia est, et nihil amplius: unde est sicut in quadam confusione. Ad ultimum autem etiam hoc ipsum esse, secundum quod est in creaturis, ab ipso removemus; et tunc remanet in quadam tenebra ignorantiae, secundum quam ignorantiam, quantum ad statum viae pertinet, optime Deo conjungimur, ut dicit Dionysius, et haec at quaedam caligo, in qua Deus habitare dicitur" (*In I Sent.*, dist. 8, q. 1, a.1 ad 4).

This text of the *Sentences* is still full of very obvious Dionysian echoes, and might lead one to believe in a dialectical ascent leading by itself to the *divina caligo*. In reality, for St. Thomas, there is question here of only an *appearance* of dialectic, by which I mean that the rational movement positing successively these diverse negations corresponds indeed to an intellectual awareness which accompanies and justifies, which founds on reason in the contemplative, the proper movement of contemplation; but the latter take place in virtue of the connaturality of love, not in virtue of any dialectic. We believe that this was already so, though less clearly in pseudo-Dionysius himself. The latter was very close to neo-Platonism and derived from it all his philosophical culture, and therefore conceived in a neo-Platonic mode of conceptualization a doctrinal substance that was in reality much more Paulinian than neo-Platonic. In what concerns the actual historical process, we are inclined to think that the author of the *Divine Names* and of the *Mystical Theology* could have considered himself a good Platonist, and unwittingly warp neo-Platonic terminology to make it express an experience which in reality was incompatible with it. A sort of tutelar *deportation* of terminology was thereby accomplished, thanks to which negative theology in the Christian sense of the wisdom of the Holy Ghost has, we believe, prevailed in fact (*in actu exercito*) in pseudo-Dionysius, in spite of the neo-Platonic garb so marked in him, and has incontestably prevailed among the Fathers, even when they employ certain Platonic formulas, until Christian thought, having achieved full self-mastery, was able with St. Thomas Aquinas, and then with St. John of the Cross, to constitute expressly (*in actu signato*) a speculative and practical science of this same negative theology or wisdom of the Holy Ghost, free from any neo-Platonic contamination, and in which the essential role of the connaturality of charity (hardly indicated in Dionysius, *The Divine Names*, Ch. 11, lect. 4 and 9–11 of St. Thomas) is fully recognized and brought out.

(though the propositions be negative, as may happen in any science); it is not yet to have left cataphatic theology, to have passed on to a higher kind of wisdom, so long as these truths are known only and not experienced, so long as they are only spoken of, not lived.

Apophatic theology makes sense only because it is more than cataphatic theology (as to the mode of knowing). It does not duplicate it, it ought not to be substituted for it. It is borne on its shoulders; it knows the same things better. It is negative, not because it simply denies what the other affirms, but because it attains better than by affirmation and negation, that is to say better than by communicable propositions because it experiences by way of non-knowing, the reality that the other affirms and will never be able to affirm sufficiently. If an ignorant shepherdess can be raised to such wisdom, it is true that she is ignorant of metaphysics and theology. But it is not true that she is an ignoramus. She has faith, and by faith she holds in their divine source all the truths that the theologian expounds in the sweat of his brow. And if she is ignorant of cataphatic theology there are others in the Church who are wise in it. On the ladder of knowledge, cataphatic theology is a step which of itself precedes contemplation, and which ought to lead to it. There is no more revelation for the contemplative than for the theologian. The field of his knowledge is not more extensive, his knowledge is simply more penetrating and more unitive, more divine. There is no supernaturally accessible object that can be attained by contemplation that dogmatic formulas do not proclaim, and do not proclaim infallibly, and with perfect exactitude and with absolute truth. But in the Way of attaining the very thing that dogmatic formulas teach, in its manner of knowing, mystical theology is higher than speculative theology.

24. If the wholly apophatic theology of Philo of Alexandria did not end up in a pure agnosticism, it is because it implied in reality a cataphatic theology against which, dazzled by the divine transcendence, the philosopher rashly turned in order to destroy as unworthy of the divinity the very ground that supported him, unaware that he was destroying by the same stroke the very affirmation of transcendence. In the course of the admirable progress to which it has been constrained by revealed dogma, and which began in the first centuries, and reached in Thomas Aquinas a perfect doctrinal formulation, Christian philosophy has understood ever better that pantheism and agnosticism can be simultaneously repressed only because a knowledge of the affirmative and propositional order is possible (the more hardy for its lowly position, speculatively valid and rigorously true, but ananoetic and inevitably deficient in its mode) and can signify in a proper sense[48] what is in God. There would certainly be no advantage in reverting today, in keeping with the aspiration of

---

48   That is to say, making us now in a non-metaphorical sense the perfections that are found formally and intrinsically in God. Cf. Ch. V, § 9, and M. T. L. Pénido, *op. cit.*, p. 191.

a certain modernist philosophy, to the positions of Philo. An apophatic theology which would rise at the expense of cataphatic theology reduced to a simple *as if*, or regarded as merely approximate, would vanish like smoke in proportion as it rose.

But why were the Alexandrians led, as it were in spite of themselves, to leave standing only a negative theology? Because, being absolute intellectualists, they demanded an intellectual knowledge of God, the very mode of which would be divine, not human; and at the same time they wanted the supreme and apophatic knowledge to remain intellectual in mode—to be a philosophy. It is impossible to have at the same time a philosophy which, to be true, enunciates, and a philosophy which, to be true, destroys enunciation; the one drives out the other. Thus, and as a result of this same absolute intellectualism, the tendency in them to reject or depreciate affirmative theology was linked to the fatal equivocation of the neo-Platonic apophasis, which pretends to be a mysticism, and to remain at the same time a metaphysics; to raise itself dialectically to ecstasy. In the course of history this same equivocation reappears with every return of neo-Platonism. A Nicholas of Cusa will give one hand to pseudo-Dionysius and the great mystics of the Middle Ages, and will hold the other out to Boehme and Hegel. The phrase "apophatic theology" will then designate an intellectual superknowledge raised above yes and no, in which contraries are identified; whereas in reality apophatic theology is "mystical theology" itself, the contemplation in charity of the saints.

This contemplation is essentially supernatural. There is not, as we hope to show in the next chapter, any natural mystical contemplation. But there can be, in a much more general sense, a natural mysticism or a natural spirituality, which stems from the natural love of God. Since this natural love is not sufficient by itself to make God loved efficaciously above all things, nor to connaturalize the soul to the deity, it cannot lead up to mystical contemplation properly so called; but it can inspire the desire for an unknown union which, in fact, that contemplation alone is to realize.

Whether it be directed to God known or unknown, loved as God or at least desired as supreme truth whose name is unknown, such a motion, such a mystical urge, animates every great philosophy—I mean *ex parte subjecti*: for no one is a philosopher if he does not love the absolute and desire to be united with it. But sometimes it animates the philosophy as tending towards an end which transcends philosophy, and as not intervening in its specification (since the latter depends purely on the object which here belongs to the wholly rational order), sometimes it animates the philosophy as tending towards an end immanent in the philosophy, and as intervening in order to constitute its proper object and to specify it. In the first case, the very purity of the philosophy as such will cause the risk that the value and efficacy of this urge be masked, especially to the eyes of the non-philosophical. But at least, in going beyond, it will be to an authentic and pure contemplation that the soul will be borne. In the second case, the very mix-up from which the philosophy suffers will render the presence of that urge in it more manifest and sensible. It is this exceedingly beautiful testimony rendered to eternal aspirations, which in its very failure, and at whatever cost, will always incline a metaphysician to revere a Plotinus, or the sages of ancient India. But—on the supposition that the term of the movement is also simply natural—that testimony will issue in the void; or at least, if superior influences enter into play, whether they come from the angels or from grace, it will still issue in a mixture, in which deception will play a great part.

The Superanalogy of Faith

25. If the mystical contemplation (or veritable apophatic theology) is essentially supernatural, a new principle of capital importance must necessarily supervene here, between the domain of metaphysics and that of contemplation, namely, theological faith, which is the principle of all supernatural life. And this faith itself must first proceed cataphatically, making the mysteries of the deity known to us in communicable propositions before raising us up to the very experiencing of them. To avoid anticipating too much the matter of subsequent chapters, we simply note that a third degree of analogy, or of ananoetic intellection, must be noted here. It is indeed, God as He knows Himself, the divine transintelligible insofar as it is, in itself and by itself, object—to Himself and to the blessed—insofar as it offers itself to their apprehension, which is attained by faith. But nevertheless, for all that, we do not yet hold Him in our grasp; He does not become in Himself and by Himself object for us; we do not see Him as the blessed do. He is constituted object for our understanding only according to the ananoetic or specular mode—*per speculum in aenigmate*—of which the metaphysical knowledge of God has already furnished us an example, i.e., by means of the objectification of other subjects which fall under our senses and which are intelligible in themselves for us, and whose attributes have in the deity their sovereign analogate.

But a capital difference from metaphysical knowledge intervenes here. For in the metaphysical knowledge of God, it is from the heart of the intelligible that our intellect, having discovered the ananoetic value of being and of objects which belong to the transcendental order, rises, thanks to them, to the divine analogate. On the contrary, in the knowledge of faith it is from the very heart of the divine transintelligible, from the very heart of the deity that the whole process of knowledge starts out, in order to return thither. That is to say, from this source, through the free generosity of God, derives the choice of objects and of concepts in the intelligible universe which falls under our senses, which God alone knows to be analogical signs of what is hidden in Him, and of which He makes use in order to speak of Himself to us in our own language. *No man hath seen God at any time: the only begotten Son who is in the bosom of the Father,*

He hath declared Him.[49] If God Himself had not revealed it, never would we have known that the notions of generation and filiation, or the notion of three having the same nature, or the notion of being made flesh and of personal union with human nature, or the notion of participatibility in deity by the creature and the love of friendship with it, could be valid in the proper order of the deity itself, and in regard to the intimate life of God.

26. The analogical instrument placed in our hands that we may attain to God with such notions is not only an *uncircumscriptive analogy*; it is a revealed analogy, a proxy or substitute for vision. Let us say it is a superanalogy. The mode of conceiving and of signifying is just as deficient in it as in metaphysical analogy, but what is signified—revealed, i.e., stripped of the veils proper to our natural knowledge, but presented or shown *under other veils*—is this time the deity as such, God as He sees Himself, and who gives Himself to us—obscurely and without our laying hands on Him yet, since we do not see Him. (Indeed the divine essence, which surpasses every concept, could be intellectually grasped or possessed only if it is seen by itself and without concepts.) Such ananoetic knowledge is therefore suprarational as to the uncreated object at which it terminates,[50] and remains conceptual and human as to the created objects through which it is accomplished. These created analogates form part of our carnal and most human world; what is more terrestrial than a father and a son? What notion is more common and more laden with human overtones than the notion of redeeming? Thus the superanalogy of faith is more humble than metaphysical analogy; it wears the livery of poverty. But we know from God that it attains divine secrets which metaphysics knows not. Once designated by revelation as likeness of what is hidden in God, the mind perceives that such things as paternity and filiation can be referred to the transcendental order; they have the value of analogy of proper proportionality. Thus, the names of Father, Son and Holy Ghost are not metaphorical; they designate (yet without containing or circumscribing) what the divine persons are intrinsically and formally. The word redemption is no longer metaphorical. It expresses intrinsically and formally the work accomplished by the Son of God. Under its livery of poverty the superanalogy of faith conceals a super-

---

49   John i, 18.

50   Because it does not *see* this object, it must be said of faith itself that it does not know God quidditatively. "Quamvis enim per revelationem elevemur ad aliquod cognoscendum, quod alias esset nobis ignotum, non tamen ad hoc quod alio modo cognoscamus nisi per sensibilia; unde Dionysius, *I Cael. Hier.*, dicit, quod impossibile est nobis aliter superlucere divinum radium, nisi circumvelatum varietate sacrorum velaminum. Via autem quae est per sensibilia, non sufficit ad ducendum in substantias supernaturales secundum cognitionem quid est. Et sic restat, quod formae immateriales non sunt nobis notae cognitione quid est, sed solum cognitione an est, sive naturali ratione ex effectibus creaturarum, sive etiam ex revelatione quae est per similitudines a sensibilibus sumptas" (St. Thomas, *In Boet. de Trin.* q. 6, a. 3).

natural vigor. By it we attain, in the light of the deity itself, the Divine Essence as it is naturally participatible by no creature, and as no created perfection of itself can show it to our reason. It should be added that in order to make us attain the intimacy of God the superanalogy of faith makes use not only of notions, the ananoetic value of which revelation itself discloses, so to speak, to our eyes; it also uses notions which as such cannot be transcendentalized, and whose ananoetic value, assured by revelation, remains as a result wrapped up in a metaphorical analogy. In the Apostles' Creed itself do we not say "and sitteth at the right hand of the Father"? Thus, the whole of poor human language is redeemed as it were by revelation: all the images of inspired Scripture, all the symbols of the Canticle of Canticles are brought in to bear witness to the uncreated Glory. Indeed, in one sense, as Dionysius points out, words of the lowest extraction provide the best images, since with them there is less danger than with more noble words that the divine transcendence be forgotten. St. Thomas quotes this saying of Dionysius in the article of the *Summa* where he explains that it is fitting that sacred doctrine make use of bodily metaphors. All these metaphorical terms truly—though improperly if taken literally—make known the intimacy of God, because they contain an authentically ananoetic significance (an analogy of proper proportionality) which appears when we have recourse to other terms,[51] although that intimacy is too rich for any term to suffice to express its plentitude: so that in one and the same text of Scripture there can be, says St. Thomas following St. Augustine, several literal senses.[52] Thus, taken in its maximum amplitude, according as it includes even the sacred metaphors, the superanalogy of faith extends its limits to the point that might be called parabolic analogy. The parable, in fact, is a metaphorical analogy which contains, and this is its proper mystery, an analogy of proper proportionality assignable and expressible for itself, but so inexhaustible and so overflowing with meaning that it always means more than its expression conveys.[53]

27. It is written that God made garments of skin for Adam and Eve in their exile. In like manner, through His prophets, then His incarnate Son and His Church, He has made for us garments woven of words and notions to clothe the nakedness of our mind till the day it sees Him. Thus, faith must necessarily proceed cataphatically, since it communicates to us, in virtue of the testimony of First Truth, or, in other words, in virtue of the infallible veracity of God revealing, and thanks to its being proposed by the Church, the knowledge of

---

51   "Ea quae in uno loco scripturae traduntur sub metaphoris, in aliis locis expressius exponuntur" (*Sum. Theol.*, I, 1, 9).

52   *Ibid.*, a. 10.

53   Unlike the myth, which signifies fictionally certain traits of the created, but which with regard to divine things has of itself only an entirely undetermined metaphorical value, and does not of itself contain an assignable analogy of proper proportionality.

what is hidden in the depths of the deity. How shall they understand if they are not taught? And how will they be taught if not by means of enunciations and notions? And how will they be taught infallibly, if these enunciations and notions do not signify in an analogical (superanalogical) mode, those very things which are in God? In this way it is understandable that faith attains to the deity itself, and in propositions that are rigorously true, but from afar, at a distance, i.e., thanks to the analogical process involved in the very use of notions and enunciations. To become wisdom and contemplation, knowledge by faith must, under a divine grace of inspiration and illumination—and yet always in a transluminous obscurity, which will remain as long as God is not seen in Himself—progressively leave behind this *from afar* and *at a distance*. That is to say, it must become experimental and proceed apophatically, by freeing itself from the limited mode of concepts, not by an intellectual knowledge that transcends yes and no, but by a passion of divine things that tastes and touches by way of the no the infinite depths of the *yes*.

SECOND PART

THE DEGREES OF SUPRARATIONAL KNOWLEDGE

CHAPTER VI

MYSTICAL EXPERIENCE AND PHILOSOPHY

To Reverend Father Garrigou-Lagrange

I
THE THREE WISDOMS

1. LET IT BE AGREED once and for all that, in the present instance, we understand the word "mystical experience" not in a more-or-less vague sense covering all sorts of more-or-less mysterious or praeternatural facts, or even simple religious feeling) but, rather, in the sense of an *experimental knowledge*[1] of the deep things of God, or a *suffering of divine things*, an experience which leads the soul through a series of states and transformations until within the very depths of itself it feels the touch of divinity and "experiences the life of God."[2]

On the other hand, the highest degree of the lower borders on the higher: if, in using the word "philosophy" we must think especially of the Philosophy of Nature when studying the relations between scientific experience and philosophy, in like manner in the present chapter, when we use the word "philosophy" we should think above all of metaphysics.

2. It is fitting, and this is a fundamental point, to distinguish three wisdoms properly so called; wisdom being defined as a supreme knowledge, having a universal object and judging things by first principles. The first and least elevated of these wisdoms is metaphysical wisdom, the supreme science in the purely rational or natural order. Rising above the visible things whose

---

1   To designate the *pati divina*, St. Thomas sometimes says "quasi-experience," sometimes "experience" (cf. R. Garrigou-Lagrange, *Revue Thomiste*, Nov.–Dec. 1928, pp. 469–472; A. Gardeil, *ibid.*, May–June 1929 p. 272). The *quasi* is inserted to preserve the prerogatives of divine transcendence; it in no way lessens what is properly experimental for us in infused contemplation. It is clear that an *absolutely* immediate, and therefore *perfectly* experimental knowledge of God is reserved for beatitude. But on this side of that end, a knowledge which is truly, though imperfectly, immediate can begin even here below (see below, Ch. VI, n. 42). That is why, once the necessary reservations have been made, it is permissible, as Father Gardeil points out, to make free use of the words "experience," "experimental," as, indeed, a John of St. Thomas has very often done.

2   St. John of the Cross, *Living Flame of Love*, St. 1, v. 1, Peers, III, p. 121.

ultimate reason it seeks, it recognizes by reason the existence of God, the first cause and author of nature. Starting with creatures—τοῖς ποιήμασιν[3]—and rising by way of causality to the first Principle of all being,[4] God can, indeed, be known; reason can indeed know God; so, too, can it know His existence and perfections, His unity, simplicity, His real and absolute distinctness from the world.

The knowledge of God which is thus achieved by reason constitutes first philosophy, metaphysics or "natural theology," as Aristotle called it. It is an ananoetic knowledge, or knowledge by analogy, which is by no means to be confused with metaphorical knowledge. To know God, it uses notions which we seek for in things and which we therefore conceive in their limited mode, according as they are realized in created things, but which *in themselves*, in what they signify, imply no limitation or imperfection and can, therefore, belong intrinsically, and in their proper sense, to the Uncreated as well as to the created—a knowledge refracted in the prism of creatures, yet veracious for all that.

St. Thomas, need it be said, never regarded the human intellect as in itself limited to a knowledge of the sensible, to which there would be added as an illusory prolongation, a metaphorical knowledge of invisible and spiritual things. This mocking interpretation, which is sometimes heard (words can be made to support anything), is a radical misinterpretation of his thought. If our understanding, inasmuch as it is human, is directly ordered to being as it is concretized in sensible things, still as intellect, it remains ordered to being in all its fullness. Indeed, the being which is achieved in sensible things is already an object of thought which goes beyond the sensible; in itself, it compels the mind to conceive an area of being freed from the limitations of the sensible, and to seek in this area for the highest reasons for everything else. Thus, our natural ordination to the being of things which are placed on the same level as we are, is like a bait, an enticement, which constrains us to rise to a higher level. From the point of view of speculative knowledge, as well as from the point of view of ethics, we must say with Aristotle that human nature, by what is most important in it, namely, the νοῦς, demands that man should rise above the human.

Metaphysics cannot attain the Divine Essence in itself; and, yet, it truly knows God in the divided mirror of transcendental perfections analogically common to the uncreated and to the created. In this mirror it grasps in the imperfect mode proper to finite things, realities which, brought to their pure

---

3   St. Paul, Rom. i, 20.

4   This point, as we know, was the object of a definition of the Church at the [First] Vatican Council (Denz.-Bannw., 1785–1806 and was, later, still further clarified by Pius X: "Deum, rerum omnium principium et finem, naturali rationis lumine *per ea quae facta sunt* (cf. Rom. i, 20), hoc est, per *visibilia* creationis opera, tanquam causam per effectus certo cognosci adeoque demonstrari etiam posse . . ." (*ibid.*, 2145).

state and overflowing all of our concepts, pre-exist in the incomprehensible simplicity of the infinite.

3. Above this wisdom of the natural order (metaphysics or natural theology) stands the science of revealed mysteries, theology properly so called. It develops in a rational manner and according to the discursive mode that is natural to us truths virtually contained in the deposit of revelation. Inasmuch as it proceeds according to the method and sequences of reason but is rooted in faith (from which it gets its principles—themselves borrowed from God's knowledge), its proper light is not the light of reason all by itself but the light of reason illumined by faith. For that very reason, its certitude is, of itself, superior to the certitude of metaphysics.

It does not have as its object[5] God as expressed by His creatures, nor God as the first cause or author of the natural order, but, rather, God in the guise of mystery, as inaccessible to reason alone, in His own essence and inner life. Theology is not concerned with God in those things that reason discovers within Him as analogically common with other beings. Rather, it studies God in those things that He has absolutely proper to Himself, in what belongs to Him alone, *deitas ut sic*, as the theologians say. This is the God Who will be known face to face in the Beatific Vision.

4. Deity as such, which is above being and every conceivable perfection; God considered in His proper essence and inner life, *sub ratione suae propriae quidditatis*,[6] let us say, in His inwardness; God's selfhood; these various terms, let us note, indicate an object common to the vision of the blessed, to the theological virtue of faith, and to theology. But these three knowledges attain the same object in three ways, under three formally different intelligibilities. The Beatific Vision knows Him BY and IN His very essence, *sicut in se est*,[7] according to what He is in Himself, in a way proportionate to what He is, without the mediation of any creature or concept. That is *scire de Deo quid est*, knowing His essence in itself. "Then," says St. Paul, "I shall know even as I am known,"[8] and St. John says, "We shall see Him as He is, *sicuti est*, καθὼς ἐστιν."[9] In vision, the Divine Selfhood will be grasped just as it is.

5   To avoid uselessly complicating our vocabulary, we are not taking into consideration here the distinction between *subjectum* and *objectum* of a science as it has been established by the scholastics. Cf. John of St. Thomas, *Curs. Theol.*, I P., q. 1, disp. 2, a. 11 (eleven) (Vivès, t. I).

6   Cajetan, *In Sum. Theol.*, I, 1, 7: "Deus secundum ipsam rationem deitatis" (John of St. Thomas, *Curs. Theol.*, I P., q. I, disp. 2, a. 2, n. 4 [Vivès, t. II]). God is the *primary* object of beatific vision, of faith and of theology, as well as of infused wisdom, by reason of his deity, *sub ratione deitatis*. Sometimes these also have creatures as their object, but insofar as they are referred to God and, thus, as secondary object.

7   St. Thomas also uses the expression *secundum guod in se est*. Cf. *Sum. Theol.*, II–II, 1, 2,

Faith, a substitute for vision here below, and a beginning of eternal life, knows this selfsame object *without seeing it*, giving, as it does, even in obscurity, an infallible adherence to what first Truth has revealed of itself. It is an essentially supernatural virtue, and it is suprarational because its formal motive, *Veritas prima revelans*, is itself essentially supernatural. Thus, it knows the very same thing that God and the blessed see in God in a very imperfect way, but the only way in which the revealed treasure can be communicated to the human race. In clinging to the testimony of first Truth, it attains God's inner depths, His very selfhood, *Deus secundum propriam quidditatem*,[10] without seeing it. That is the object at which it terminates, the thing at which it stops,[11] that in which it is fixed by revelation.

But this communication is made to it in the signs of language and human concepts. And how could we understand Him otherwise? God speaks our language so as to be understood by us. These means of transmitting Divine truths, these conceptual statements whereby uncreated light comes to us (and which the Church, Christ's mystical body, which tends our belief through its head assisted by the spirit of God, tailors with rigid precision) are the intermediaries through which faith passes, the medium faith uses to attain Deity. These are, as St. John of the Cross says, its *silvered exteriors*, by means of which the mind clings to the pure gold of Divine reality. Let us say that such is its object no longer taken from the point of view of the thing believed itself, *ex parte ipsius rei creditae*, but rather, from the point of view of the *signs or means* used by the believing mind, *ex parte credentis*.[12]

---

8   I Cor. xiii, 12. Concerning this expression of St. Paul, see below, Appendix VIII, last paragraph.

9   I John iii, 2.

10   Cajetan, *loc. cit.*

11   *Actus credentis non terminatur ad enuntiabile, sed ad rem* (Sum. Theol., II–II, 1, 2 ad 2). Cf. *ibid.*, I, 6 ad 2. *De Verit.*, XIV, 8, ad 5: "Veritas igitur divina, quae simplex est in se ipsa est fidei objectum: sed eam intellectus noster accipit suo modo per viam compositionis; et sic, per hoc quod compositioni factae, tanquam vere assentit, in veritatem primam tendit ut in objectum; et sic nihil prohibet veritatem primam esse fidei objectum, quamvis sit complexorum." Inasmuch as faith thus terminates in God's very quiddity taken *secundum se ipsum*, and in accordance with his indivisibility, then it must be said that reason all by itself (when stripped of all faith, even of implicit faith) does not under any guise or in any way attain the object of faith when it knows certain truths of the natural order that are implied in truths of faith, for example, God's existence and unity. "Quia, ut Phil. dicit IX Metaph., in simplicibus defectus cognitionis est solum in non attingendo totaliter" (*Sum. Theol.*, II–II, 2, 2 ad 3).

12   "Objectum fidei dupliciter considerari potest: uno modo ex parte ipsius rei creditae; et sic objectum fidei est aliquid incomplexum, scilicet res ipsa, de qua fides habetur. Alio modo ex parte credentis; et secundum hoc objectum fidei est aliquid complexum per modum enuntiabilis. . . .
     "In symbolo tanguntur ea, de quibus est fides, inquantum ad ea terminatur actus credentis, ut ex ipso modo loquendi apparet: actus autem credentis non

As we see, knowledge by analogy returns here once more in a certain way, to the extent, namely, that revelation uses human signs. It does not return as something determining the first formality under which God is constituted as object or thing known, for He is attained in virtue of His very selfhood, in virtue of what properly constitutes Him and not, as in the case of metaphysics, as a result of His analogy with things. But it does come back once more in the signs and means which place such an object within our grasp. To express the mystery of the Trinity, notions of Father, Son, Spirit, generation, procession, nature, person, must be used. They are first supplied by creatures, and by God Himself, Who makes Himself known through the Son within His bosom and through the Church which keeps and expounds the words of the Son. God joins these together in the dogmatic pronouncements of the Church—analogical concepts which the proper light of faith, *lumen infusum fidei* (something more "formal" than they, something more secretly and vitally supernatural), uses to attain God's inwardness.

As we have pointed out at the end of the preceding chapter, it is necessary to distinguish very clearly this use of analogy in the realm of faith, from its use in the realm of metaphysics. There is a capital difference which has not always been sufficiently stressed. In the case of metaphysics, analogy constitutes the very form and rule of knowledge. God is not attained in virtue of His incommunicable nature and selfhood, according to the indivisibility of His pure and simplest essence, but only according to that which is shown in His reflections (reflections that, by the way, are truthful) and in the analogical participations which things proportionate to our reason offer us of Him. His essence is not attained as such, but only inasmuch as creatures, by their very nature, speak of it to our understanding. Thus, not only is the mode of knowing human, but, in addition, the object itself as proposed to the mind and made the term of knowledge (*sub ratione primi entis*) is taken according as He condescends, so to speak, to human reason in the mirror of sensible things and by the analogy of being.[13] Metaphysics is poised at the summit of the created world, and from that vantage point, it looks upon the inaccessible entrance towards which all created perfections converge—but without seeing Him in Himself. It grasps His purest light only as it is broken up in the multiplicity of these perfections. Faith is installed in that very entrance itself, at the very heart of the Uncreated, but God has closed its eyes to Himself. And it is through the images of creatures which it remembers having seen here below that it describes His mystery. Deity as such is achieved, but without being seen and without any apprehension except by the analogies that God chooses in the created thing to instruct

terminatur ad enuntiabile sed ad rem: non enim formamus enuntiabilia, nisi ut per ea de rebus cognitionem habeamus, sicut in scientia, ita et in fide" (St. Thomas, *Sum. Theol.*, II–II, 1, 2, corp. et ad 2).

13 Moreover, in all knowledge that is acquired through our own efforts, the primary formality under which the object is constituted object is itself correlative with our way of knowing and in the same degree as it is.

us about it. And yet, because of these ananoetic means, this is still not to know the Divine Essence in itself, *scire tantum de Deo quia est;*[14] nevertheless, as regards the reality that is attained, it really is to know God in virtue of His essence or according to His own very essence. In other words, the super-analogy of faith adapts to our weakness a knowledge whose formal rule (*veritas prima revelans*) is absolutely higher. And in this way, there is, in the case of faith, a surprising disproportion, a dislocation, if I may dare to say so, between the terminating *object*, or the reality that is known—God in virtue of His innerness, His indivisible and holiest essence as revealed in the testimony of first Truth—and the manner of knowing which remains proportioned to our nature.[15]

An essentially superhuman formal object; a human mode of knowing: here lies, as we may note immediately in passing, the reason why faith will perpetually strive to exceed its own way of knowing. That is why faith, as distinct from metaphysics, will of itself place in the soul, at least radically, an unconditional desire for mystical contemplation properly so called, which, although it is contained within its own proper sphere, faith is nevertheless not adequate to procure all by itself.[16]

5. Now this God of faith, Deity as such, not seen, but believed, or attained to in the testimony of first Truth and by means of dogmatic definitions, is also the object of theology. Theology envisages it from the point of view of "virtual revelation," as it is called; in other words, from the point of view of the consequences that reason, when enlightened by faith, can draw from formally revealed principles.

This is not the place to go into any lengthy development concerning the nature of theological wisdom. All that needs to be noted is that theology is quite a different thing from a simple application of philosophy to matters of revelation: that would truly be a monstrous conception; it would submit

---

14   Cf. Ch. V, §§ 18 and 19; and below, Appendix III.
15   This is because faith is a revealed knowledge. *Deum nemo vidit unquam: unigenitus ilius, qui est in sinu Patris, ipse enarravit* (John i, 18). In this case, the primary formality under which the object is constituted object is referred, not to our way of knowing, but rather to the One who reveals and to His Own way of knowing. This is the way faith and theology are knowledges subalternated to the knowledge of God and the blessed.
16   Cf. St. Thomas, *De Verit.*, XIV, 2: "Unde oportet quod ad hoc quod homo ordinetur in bonum vitae aeternae, quaedam inchoatio ipsius fiat in eo qui repromittitur. Vita autem aeterna consistit in plena Dei cognitione, ut patet Joan. XVIII, 3: *Haec est vita aeterna ut cognoscant te solum Deum verum.* Unde oportet hujusmodi cognitioni supernaturalis aliquam inchoationem in nobis fieri; et haec est per fidem. . . ." *ibid.*, ad 1: "Fides est prima inchoatio et fundamentum quoddam quasi totius spiritualis vitae." John of St. Thomas, *Curs. Theol.* II–II, q. 1, disp. 2, a. 1, n. 9 (Vivès, t. VII, p. 28): "Fides importat motum quemdam intellectus ad visionem in qua quietatur."

revealed data to a purely human light and subordinate theological wisdom to philosophy.[17] There exists no genuine science or wisdom unless within the soul there be a genuine intellectual virtue proportioning the light of discrimination and judgment to the proper level of the object. To an object which is the depths of revealed divinity, insofar as it can be exploited by reason, there must necessarily correspond, as its light in the soul, not the light of philosophy, but a proportionate light, the light of supernatural faith taking up and directing the natural movement of reason and its natural way of knowing. Thus, theology is not a simple application of natural reason and of philosophy to revealed data: it is an elucidation of revealed data by faith vitally linked with reason, advancing in step with reason and arming itself with philosophy. That is why philosophy, far from subordinating theology to itself, is properly the "servant" of theology in the immanent use theology makes of it. Theology is free as regards philosophical doctrines. It is theology that chooses among these doctrines the one that will in its hands be the best instrument of truth. And, let a theologian lose theological faith; he still can keep the whole machinery and conceptual organization of his science, but he keeps it as something dead

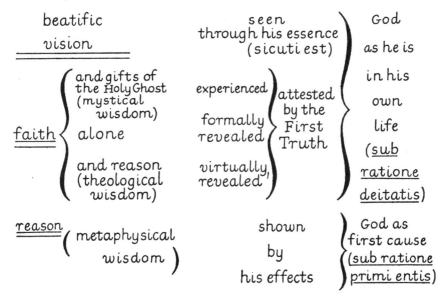

in his mind; he has lost his proper light. He is no longer a theologian except in the way that a corpse is a man. To sum up, Deity itself as seen or known quidditatively is the object of the knowledge of the blessed.[18] Deity itself as believed and formally revealed is the object of faith. Deity itself as believed and virtually revealed is the object of theology.

17   Cf. our *The Dream of Descartes*, Ch. III. On the relations between theology and faith, see F. Marin-Sola, *L'Evolution homogène du dogme catholique* (Fribourg, 1924).
18   That is the *primary* object. Cf. Ch. VI, n. 6.

6. We have said that above metaphysical wisdom there is theological wisdom. Above it, there is infused wisdom which is also called mystical theology and which consists in knowing the essentially supernatural object of faith and theology—Deity as such—*according to a mode that is suprahuman and supernatural*. In this case, according to the profound words of Denys, it is no longer a question of merely learning, but rather of suffering divine things. It is a matter of knowing God by experience in the silence of every creature and of any representation, in accordance with a *manner* of knowing, itself proportioned to the object known, insofar as that is possible here below. Faith all by itself does not suffice for that; it must be rendered perfect in its mode of operating by the gifts of the Holy Ghost, by the gift of understanding, and, above all, by the gift of wisdom. That is mystical experience; it belongs to the supernatural order; and now we must examine its conditions.

II
SANCTIFYING GRACE

7. If we would determine in a suitable way the position of mystical experience and philosophy with respect to each other, and in particular, enquire whether or not a mystical experience of a natural order is possible, we should begin by examining that mystical experience of the supernatural order itself which is vouched for by all the saints and whose reality, as well as its authenticity, is certain. We should then carry on our study in a way that is not empirical and external, but scientific, by determining its causes, its *raisons d 'être*.[19] For that purpose, it is strictly indispensable to have recourse to theology, since the means of thinking provided by philosophy alone, and, indeed, its very vocabulary, are essentially inadequate in respect to a supernatural object. This is why we have to begin with an exposition proper to the theological order, borrowed from St. Thomas Aquinas and his most faithful interpreters, and where, in order to treat mystical and supernatural experience scientifically, that is, according to its intrinsic principles (to wit, by going from remote and radical principles to more proximate ones), we shall have briefly to consider the following points:

First, the primary conditions for this experience in the ontological order (that is to say, sanctifying grace and the indwelling of the Divine Persons within the soul in the state of grace); then, in the order of exercise or operation, the manner in which this experience takes place and the means that it brings into play (that is to say, the gifts of the Holy Ghost and the knowledge by connaturality due to charity).

8. The whole theology of sanctifying grace is founded on the words of St.

---

19   See below, Appendix V, n. 1.

Peter: grace makes us sharers in the Divine Nature, *consortes divinae naturae.*[20] How can we thus be made gods by participation, receive a communication of what belongs properly to God alone? How can a finite subject formally participate in the nature of the Infinite?

Thomists give this answer: the soul is thus rendered infinite in the order of its *relation to the object.* A formal participation in Deity, which would be impossible were it a question of having Deity for its essence (for it is a pure absurdity that that which is not God should receive as its essence the very essence of God), is possible if it is a matter of having Deity as object. For a being which is not God to be raised up, in its very basic structure and in the energies from which its operations proceed, so as to have as the object of its understanding and love God Himself as He sees and loves Himself, that is, indeed, impossible to the forces of nature alone. Yet, no absolute impossibility can be detected in it. Grace bestows upon us, in a supernatural manner, a radical power of grasping pure Act as our object, a new root of spiritual operation whose proper and specifying object is the Divine Essence itself.[21]

By an intuitive vision of the Divine Essence, the beatified creature will receive—with no shadow of pantheism—infinitely more than the most daring pantheism can dream of: the infinitely transcendent God Himself, not that wretched idol-God mingled with the being of things and emerging through our efforts, which pantheism and the philosophy of becoming imagine, but the true God who is eternally self-sufficient and eternally blessed in the Trinity of Persons. By vision, the creature becomes the true God Himself, not in the order of substance, but in the order of that immaterial union which constitutes the intellectual act.

Sanctifying grace is an inherent quality, an "entitative habit" which is the very rich seed (placed in us, even here below, according to the mode of a nature or *root principle*) of that operation which is the Beatific Vision. A primary gift of love, a perfectly gratuitous gift, it is new spiritual nature grafted on to the very essence of our soul, and demands as its due to see God as He sees Himself. Just as our thinking nature has as its proportionate object the being of things material like ourselves; just as the angelic nature has as its proportioned object spiritual essences; so, too, does this supernatural spiritual principle have as its connatural object the subsistent Supernatural and render us proportionate in the depths of our being to an essentially divine object. Doubtless, it will flower into vision only at its term, but even here below, it does blossom in charity which is *the same* on earth as in heaven, even though it is in an imperfect state, for charity of itself needs to flow from vision, and here below, it issues forth from faith only as from a substitute for vision.[22] Moreover, with charity, and for charity, its inseparable property, this new nature develops within us a

---

20   "Θείας κοινωνοὶ φύσεως" (II Peter i, 4).
21   Cf. John of St. Thomas, *Curs. Theol.*, I–II, q. 110, disp. 22, a. I (Vivès, t. VI, pp. 790 ff.).
22   Cf. John of St. Thomas, *ibid.*, I–II, q. 72, disp. 17, a. 3, n. 28 (Vivès, t. VI, p. 564).

whole organism of supernatural energies—theological virtues of hope and faith, gifts of the Holy Ghost, infused moral virtues. These establish our conversation in heaven.

9. That is how grace, while leaving us infinitely distant from pure Act[23] (in the order of being), is still (in the order of spiritual operation and relation to its object) a formal participation in the Divine Nature. A seed of God: *semen Dei*.[24] There is nothing metaphorical in this, nothing merely moral: it is a "physical" reality, as the theologians say, that is, an ontological reality, all that is most positive and effective, the most solid of all realities. It is in the perspective of this radical transformation, which renders us in truth adopted sons of God and makes us live *modo aeterno* with the very life of the Eternal, that one has to place oneself to form a not-too-imperfect idea of that distinction between the natural order and the supernatural order which is at the very heart of the Catholic faith. If we had a sufficiently elevated notion of grace, many a slip in the direction of naturalism would be rendered impossible. Some, like Leibniz, more or less confuse the kingdom of grace with the realm of spirits. And that is a capital error.

There is a spiritual, metaphysical order beyond sensible nature wherein dwells not only the metaphysician, but the poet as well, and it is above all the mechanism and all the laws of the world of bodies. To this order belongs what is in the most hidden recesses of personality, namely, moral and free activity, and, more generally, voluntary activity, inasmuch as a spirit thereby envelops itself. As such, a spirit is no part of this universe (and that is why the angels do not naturally know the secrets of the heart);[25] it emerges above the whole created universe (both sensible and suprasensible), taken precisely as an artefactum, that is, as a work of art. But this world of spirits and liberty, far from enclosing within itself any formal participation in Deity, is of itself the very peak of nature understood in the quite general sense of that which has its own proper consistence insofar as it is other than God, yet it remains itself a merely natural world as long as it is not elevated gratuitously. There is still an infinite distance between that order and the order of grace which is not only above sensible nature, but above all created and creatable nature and any merely natural exercise of liberty. Charity is infinitely higher in relation to the highest created spirit than the latter is in relation to body. An act of faith or of love of a little child goes infinitely farther and is something incomparably more precious, more full of vigor and more effective than the most brilliant natural act of the highest of the angels. Pascal's famous phrase about the three orders

23　This is the sense in which it is defined in the Fourth Lateran Council, and precisely with reference to grace. "Inter Creatorem et creaturam non potest esse tanta similitudo quin sit semper major dissimilitudo notanda" (Denz.-Bannw., 432).

24　I John iii, 9.

25　Cf. John of St. Thomas, *Curs. Theol.*, I P., q. 58, disp. 22, a. 3 (Vivès, t. IV).

expresses an elementary truth of Christianity. *Bonum gratiae unius majus est, quam bonum naturae totius universi.*[26]

We have pointed out the theological reasons for this basic truth. Grace orders us to the vision of the Divine Essence, or Deity itself which is beyond being, whereas, by nature, we are ordered only to a knowledge of being in general and, in the first instance, of the being of sensible things.

It is obvious what danger lies in the slightest confusion between two formal objects. It would be to risk confusing the intellectuality we have by nature with the intellectuality we have by grace.

Doubtless by our very nature as reasonable beings, we are *capable of being proportioned* to the Divine Essence as an object of vision. But we *are so proportioned* only by grace; it is proper to grace so to proportion us—radically, by itself; proximately, by the light of glory. And that is completely supernatural. This capacity of being proportioned is nothing but our soul's obediential potency with regard to the first Agent.

In supernatural operations, two activities are joined, but not juxtaposed: the activity of nature does not initiate what grace completes; from the beginning, nature acts as elevated by grace. If the roles of nature and grace in supernatural operation, in the vision of God in heaven and in the act of theological virtues here below, were divided, then there would be a mechanical addition. No! Precisely because our very essence and our natural powers of action are themselves docility and potentiality with regard to God, our supernatural acts emanate verily from our very depths, from the very roots of our soul and of our faculties. But they so emanate only *inasmuch as* the soul and its faculties are lifted up by grace and its energies, inasmuch as they are borne by these infused qualities to possibilities absolutely inaccessible to their nature alone.

The Indwelling of the Divine Persons in the Soul

10. The effect of our being elevated to the state of grace is a new mode of God's presence within us, one that theologians call the mission of the Divine Persons and the indwelling of the Trinity in the soul.

God is present in us, at the most intimate core of our being as He is present at the most intimate core of all things, by His immensity, or in virtue of His infinite efficiency, because He gives us at each instant our being and our action. But here we are concerned with something quite other than this common presence by immensity. It is a question of a special presence peculiar to souls in the state of grace.[27]

---

26   St. Thomas, *Sum. Theol.*, I–II, 113, 9 ad 2.

27   "Divinae Personae convenit mitti, secundum quod novo modo existit in aliquo; dari autem, secundum quod habetur ab aliquo. Neutrum autem horum est nisi secundum gratiam gratum facientem. Est enim unus communus modus quo Deus est in omnibus rebus per essentiam, potentiam et praesentiam: sicut causa in effectibus participantibus bonitatem ipsius. Super istum autem modum com-

This special presence undoubtedly presupposes the presence by immensity and would not be possible without it. But of itself, and in virtue of its own proper energies, it is a *real* and *physical* (ontological) presence of God in the very depths of our being. How? In what respect? As *object*!

Not now as an efficient principle whose primary causality gives being to everything in the soul, but as term towards which the soul is inwardly turned, turned back, converted and ordered as to an object of loving knowledge.

Let us add immediately, for this is the heart of the whole question, that this is not just any knowledge and love; no! but a fruitful, experimental[28] knowledge and love which puts us in possession of God and unites us to him not at a distance, but really. For if the Divine Persons give themselves to us, it is in order that we may possess them, that they may be *ours*.[29] The gift of God is such that, according to St. Thomas' expression, it enables us freely to enjoy the

---

munem, est unus specialis, qui convenit creaturae rationali, in qua Deus dicitur esse sicut cognitum in cognoscente, et amatum in amante. Et quia cognoscendo et amando creatura rationalis sua operatione attingit ad ipsum Deum: secundum istum specialem modum Deus non solum dicitur esse in creatura rationali, sed etiam habitare in ea sicut in templo suo. Sic igitur nullus alius effectus potest esse ratio quod divina Persona sit novo modo in rationali creatura, nisi gratia gratum faciens. Unde secundum solam gratiam gratum facientem mittitur et procedit temporaliter Persona divina. Similiter, illud solum habere dicimur, quo libere possumus uti vel frui. Habere autem potestatem fruendi divina Persona est solum secundum gratiam gratum facientem" (St. Thomas, *Sum. Theol.*, I, 43, 3).

The question of the presence of grace and the indwelling of the Trinity in the soul is explained in a marvelous way by John of St. Thomas (*Curs. Theol.*, I P., q. 43, disp. 17, a. 3. [Vivès, IVl). Reference must be made, as to an essential doctrinal source, to these pages as well as to St. Thomas' articles on the mission of the Divine Persons (*In I Sent.*, dist. 14, q. I and 2; *Sum. Theol.*, I, 43). Cf. also A. Gardeil, *La structure de l'âme et l'experience mystique*, t. II, pp. 74–76; pp. 238–256; R. Garrigou-Lagrange, "L'habitation de la Sainte Trinité et l'experience mystique," *Revue Thomiste*, Nov.–Dec. 1928, pp. 449 ff.

28   "Novo modo efficitur Deus praesens mediante gratia ut objectum experimentaliter cognoscibile et fruibile intra animam" (John of St. Thomas, *Curs. Theol.*, I P., q. 32, disp. 17, a. 3, n. 10 [Vivès, t. IV]).

29   "In processione Spiritus, secundum quod hic loquimur, prout scilicet claudit in sedationem Spiritus, non sufficit quod sit nova relatio qualiscumque est creaturae ad Deum, sed oportet quod referatur ad ipsum sicut ad habitum; *quia quod datur alicui habetur aliquo modo ab illo.* Persona autem divina non potest haberi a nobis nisi vel ad fructum perfectum et sic habetur per donum gloriae, aut secundum fructum imperfectum, et sic habetur per donum gratum facientis; vel potius sicut id per quod fruibili conjungimur, inquantum ipsae Personae divinae quadam sui sigillatione in animabus nostris relinquunt quaedam dona quibus formaliter fruimur, scilicet amore et sapientia; propter quod Spiritus sanctus dicitur pignus hereditatis nostrae" (St. Thomas, *In I Sent.*, dist. 14, q. 2, a. 2, ad 2).

Divine Persons.[30] Would that be possible if they were not really and ontologically present there, offering themselves to us in our very depths?

11. Doubtless, it is only in the future life and by vision that man will enjoy this perfect possession. But God does not give Himself to us even now as an object of fruition in order that this gift should remain, in the present, just a dead letter and be wholly reserved for the future life. *Carissimi, nunc filii Dei sumus*, says St. John.[31] From this present moment we are sons of God. "Know you not that your members are the temple of the Holy Ghost, who is in you, whom you have from God: and you are not your own?"[32] Eternal life begins here and now. It begins here below and should grow unceasingly till the dissolution of the body in such a way as to realize by mystical experience and infused contemplation themselves, as far as possible on this earth, in the night of faith, in which *what we shall be has not yet appeared*,[33] that possession of God to which sanctifying grace is essentially ordained.

Thus it is clear that mystical experience and infused contemplation are, indeed, seen to be the normal, rightful end of the life of grace. They could even be said to be the summit towards which all human life tends: for, in this fallen and redeemed world wherein grace presses in on every side, human life tends towards the Christian life since every man belongs by right to Christ, the head of the human race; and Christian life itself, as we have just said, tends to the mystical life.

The Gifts of the Holy Ghost

12. Sanctifying grace and indwelling of God in the soul in the state of grace—these are the ontological foundations, the first principles of mystical experience.

But what are the proximate principles of mystical experience; in other words, how is it realized?

---

30   "Per donum gratiae gratum facientis perficitur creatura rationalis ad hoc quod libere non solum ipso dono creato utatur, sed ut ipsa divina Persona, fruatur" (*Sum. Theol.*, I, 43, 3, ad 1. Cf. *ibid.*, ad 2).

31   I John iii, 2. Cf. John of St. Thomas, *Curs. Theol.*, I P., q. 8, disp. 8, a. 6 (Vivès, t. II): "Hic autem est unio ista fruitionis inchoata, et imperfecta. Vere tamen ratione illius dicitur Deus, non solum communi modo suae immensitatis et contactu operationis et finis possessi. Nec solum hoc intelligitur fieri in gloria, sed etiam hic quando datur gratia; tum quia invisibilis missio Personarum, per quam Spiritus Sanctus personaliter datur, et non solum dona ejus, non solum fit in gloria, sed etiam quando fit sanctificatio in gratia, vel aliquod speciale augmentum (ut dicit div. Thomas, q. 43, a. 6), tum etiam quia I ad Corinth., 3, ubi dicit Apostolus: *Templum Dei estis, et Spiritus Sanctus habitat in vobis statim: si quis autem templum Dei violaverit, disperdet illum Deus*. Loquitur ergo Apostolus de statu in quo potest hoc templum violari, qui est status viae et non patriae."

32   St. Paul, I Cor. vi, 19.

33   I John, *loc. cit.*

For a theological analysis such as this, two characteristics of this experience above all others should command our attention. In the first place, it is a suprahuman mode of knowledge; in the second place, it is a knowledge by connaturality.

It is a suprahuman and supernatural mode of knowledge. The human and natural mode of knowing (natural, *mutatis mutandis*, to angels themselves) consists in knowing by ideas or concepts, and consequently, in matters that concern divine things, by analogy with created realities, for the manner in which our concepts signify is determined by them. That is why faith, even though it does reach God according to His very inwardness and His proper life, *secundum suam propriam quidditatem*, reaches Him thus only at a distance and remains a mediate knowledge, enigmatic, in the words of St. Paul,[34] in the sense that, as we have noted above, faith has to make use of formal means, proportionate to our natural mode of knowing—concepts and conceptual formulas, analogical or rather superanalogical notions.

In order to know God without any distance intervening, to the extent that it is possible here below by passing beyond the human and natural manner of concepts (and consequently, as St. John of the Cross so strongly insists, by forsaking every distinct conception and all clear knowledge),[35] not only is a movement from above absolutely required, but also a higher objective regulation; in other words, a special inspiration of the Holy Ghost. Mystical experience is a supernaturally *inspired* knowledge.

On the other hand, if it is true that mystical experience is in the normal line of development of the life of grace, then there must be within the soul in the state of grace, sails all set to receive the wind of heaven, or, to use scholastic language, permanent dispositions or habitus which guarantee the possibility (and, by rights, it is a normal possibility) of achieving this inspired knowledge. These are the gifts of the Holy Ghost, whose proper office is to make the soul *thoroughly mobile* under divine inspiration.

(So, too, in a much more general way, St. Thomas teaches that these gifts are necessary for the Christian life[36] because reason could not be a sufficient first principle for the use of suprarational and divine powers [divine in their object] such as the theological virtues are. We are like little children to whom a supernatural art, a pencil to write in heaven, has been given. God Himself must put His hand on our hand and guide the stroke.)

Thus, mystical experience is a suprahuman mode of knowledge. It presupposes a special inspiration of God and is achieved through the gifts of the Holy

---

34   I Cor. xiii, 12.
35   For it is quite clear that knowing God *without any distance intervening* and, at the same time, *clearly*, can only be realized in the beatific vision. Meanwhile, the darkness will increase in proportion as the distance diminishes. "Cuanto menos distinctamente le entienden, mas se llegan a él" (St. John of the Cross, *Cant.*, str. 1, 2nd ed., Silv., III, p. 203).
36   *Sum. Theol.*, I–II, 68, 2.

Ghost—at least, through those among them which specifically concern knowledge, namely, through the infused gifts of understanding and wisdom.

Knowledge by Connaturality

13. Mystical experience has a second characteristic: it is a knowledge by connaturality.

There are two means, says St. Thomas,[37] of judging matters of chastity; for example, either to have in our intellect moral science—a knowledge which creates within us an intellectual proportion to the truths concerning this virtue and which, if we are asked about it, enables us to answer correctly, simply referring to its object.

Or to have the virtue of chastity itself within our concupiscible appetite; to have that virtue incarnate within us and in our very bowels. This, then, enables us to answer correctly in a way that is not that of science, but of instinct, by referring to our inclination, our connaturality with chastity.

As we confront God, there is no other way of going beyond knowledge through concepts except by making use, in order to know Him, of our very connaturality, our co-nascence, as Claudel[38] would say, or our co-birth with Him.

What is it that makes us radically connatural with God? It is sanctifying grace whereby we are made *consortes divinae naturae*. And what makes this radical connaturality pass into act; what makes it flower into the actuality of operation? Charity. We are made connatural to God through charity. Charity is not just any kind of love. It presupposes sanctifying grace, of which it is the property, and it lays hold on God as He is really present within us as a Gift, a Friend, an eternal life-companion. However, it wins to God immediately as God, in His very deity, in the very intimate and absolutely proper life with which He will beatify us. Charity loves Him in Himself and by Himself.[39]

14. To go more deeply into points which theologians like John of St. Thomas[40] or Joseph of the Holy Ghost[41] explain to us on this score, would involve lengthy developments. A brief summary will suffice.

When things divine are intimately joined to us, when they have become ours and are embowelled in us through the love of charity, it is proper to the

---

37   *Ibid.*, II–II, 45, 2; cf. I, 1, 6 ad 3.

38   "Co-naissance," *L'art poétique.*

39   Cf. the texts from St. Thomas that are quoted below, Ch. VI, § 23, and Ch. VIII, §§ 10 and 11.

40   Cf. John of St. Thomas, *Curs. Theol.*, I–II, q. 68–70, disp. 18 (Vivès, t. IV). This has been translated into French by Raïssa Maritain under the title *Les dons du saint esprit* (Juvisy, 1930).

41   Cf. Joseph of the Holy Ghost, *Cursus theologiae mystico-scholasticae*, new edition (by P. Fr. Anastasio a S. Paulo) (Bruges, 1925 and years following), t. II, disp. XII and XIII.

gift of wisdom to make use of that love, that infused charity, in order to make it pass, under the special inspiration of the Holy Ghost, to the status of an *objective medium* of knowledge (*objectum quo* in scholastic terminology).[42] Then

---

42   "Et sic affectus transit in conditionem objecti" (John of St. Thomas, *Curs. Theol.*, I–II,q. 68–70, disp. 18, a. 4, n. 11).

We say that under the special inspiration of the Holy Ghost love thus passes to the side of the object and takes on an objective condition, not so as to be a known object, but, rather, a means of knowledge or *objectum quo* (cf. R. Garrigou-Lagrange, *Christian Perfection and Contemplation*, St. Louis and London, Herder, 1944, p. 315; *Revue Thomiste*, Nov.–Dec. 1928, pp. 465–566; A. Gardeil, *Structure*, t. II, p. 248; *Revue Thomiste*, May–June 1929, pp. 272–273). What we are calling here the *objectum quo* is not charity, nor wisdom taken as habitus; it is the passions which the soul actually undergoes, actual effects that serve as a real medium of knowledge under the illumination of the Holy Ghost. And in this way, God is still known through His effects (and it is necessarily so inasmuch as He is not seen through His essence), but these effects are no longer things or objects that are first known and from which the mind is elevated to God through an ananoetic process as in knowledge according to the human mode wherein God is known *by His shoulders*, as St. John of the Cross says (*Cant.*, str. 32 [19], see Ch. VIII, § 15, n. 51). They are like touches of connaturality actually experienced under the light of the Holy Ghost whereby things divine are suffered in themselves. In short, the objective intermediary in this case is neither an infused idea nor a principle of inference, it is, rather, an actual infused love that arises under the illumination of the Holy Ghost through an *objectum quo* in which and by which an experienced contact occurs between God and the soul: "Spiritus testimonium reddit spiritui nostro *per effectum amoris filialis*, quem in nobis facit" (St. Thomas, *In Ep. ad Rom.*, VIII, 16). When the soul has become love through and through without anything in it providing an obstacle to the light of the Holy Ghost, and when it fastens its knowledge upon itself, it becomes a means of perceiving God through a certain act of touch and a kind of spiritual testing. Insofar as God is known through His effects in such a suprahuman manner, He is known *immediately* or "face to face" as St. John of the Cross says (*loc. cit.*), since in this case, created effects are no longer known as a *quod* wherein, as in a mirror, a likeness of God is seen, but only as a *quo* or means of attaining God Himself. This is not an absolutely immediate knowledge (only the beatific vision is immediate in this case), but it is a knowledge of God that is truly immediate, even though imperfectly so, without passing from a created *quod*, that would be first known, to a divine *quod*. Thus, God is not only attained without reasoning, in the manner in which substance is seen "per accidens," but He is Himself touched and experienced in an obscure manner. The mystics, speaking from loftier levels of experience of that union, can describe it as "substantial touchings" and as "a touching of pure substances, that is to say, the soul and divinity" (St. John of the Cross, see below, Ch. VIII, § 15, n. 51).

If still greater precision were required, we would say that infused love and the touches of connaturality of which we have been speaking are not of themselves "formal signs" or pure *in quo's* of understanding, as the concept is, but that under the illumination of the Holy Ghost, they find themselves actually playing a role quite comparable to that of a formal sign, and this is possible because it is no longer a matter of clear knowledge but of a quite experimental, obscure and

we not only experience our love for God, but it is God Himself whom we experience by our love. "It is precisely by virtue of the gift that God has made us of Himself," writes John of St. Thomas, "and of the union that love experiences, that mystical wisdom attains things divine, made more united to us through love and more immediately touched and tasted. It enables us to perceive that what is thus felt in our affection is higher and more excellent than every consideration of the cognitive powers."[43] And again: "In its darkness faith attains God yet as He remains at a distance, inasmuch as faith is of things not seen. But charity attains God in Himself immediately, intimately uniting us to that which is hidden in faith. And so, even though faith rules love and the union with God, inasmuch as it is faith that proposes their object, yet, in virtue of this union in which love clings to God immediately, the intellect is, through a certain affective experience, so elevated as to judge of divine things in a way higher than the darkness of faith would permit. This is so because the intellect penetrates, and knows that *more lies hidden* in things of faith than faith itself reveals, ever finding there more to love and taste of in love. From this *more*, which love makes the intellect feel is hidden there, it judges more highly of things divine under a special instinct of the Holy Ghost."[44]

This is a precious text and it shows us how mystical wisdom judges the things of God through an affective experience which touches the very thing that lies hidden in faith. To the very extent that divine reality is hidden to us—being absolutely transcendent as regards every created idea—this secret wisdom experiences it: You are truly a hidden God, a savior God: and the more hidden, the more you are a savior and giver of life; the soul cherishes these dark shadows of faith because it knows they are fruitful. It knows, it feels that in them alone can it intimately taste and judge them by experience, the depths of its God. Here we have one of the theological roots of the doctrine of St. John of the Cross: "Seek Him in faith and love, and, like a blind man, these two guides will lead you along paths you know not, right into the very secret of God.[45] . . . He is hidden within you, and you do not hide yourselves as He does in order to find Him and experience Him. If anyone would find a hidden thing, he must hide himself so as to enter into that place wherein it is hidden, and when he has found it, he is just as hidden as it is.[46] . . . You ought always to hold Him as hidden, and serve Him as One hidden by hiding yourself. . . ."[47]

In brief, then, the inspiration of the Holy Ghost uses the connaturality of charity to make us judge divine things under a higher rule, under a new formal *ratio*. Thus, in the darkness of faith, we are then enabled to attain not only an

---

apophatic knowledge joining the soul to God as to someone hidden, *quasi ignoto.*

43   John of St. Thomas, *Curs. Theol.*, I–II, q. 68–70, disp. 18, a. 4, nn. 9 and 15. French translation, Ch. IV, pp. 138–39 and 143.

44   John of St. Thomas, *ibid.*, n. 14. French translation, Ch. IV, pp. 142–143.

45   St. John of the Cross, *Cant.*, str. 1, 2nd ed., Silv., III, pp. 1–202.

46   *Ibid.*, p. 200.

47   *Ibid.*, p. 203.

absolutely supernatural object—the Divine Ipseity as such—as does theological faith itself, but we do so also in a manner of knowing which is superhuman and supernatural.

> *Illustre quiddam cernimus,*
> *Quod nesciat finem pati. . . .*[48]

It should be clearly understood that we are not speaking here of a perfect experience. That is reserved for the Fatherland. Rather, we speak of an experience just begun and one that never has the point of its achievement and fulfillment in this life. Let us say that in virtue of the affective union with God dwelling within us, which is proper to this experience, charity, under the sway of the Holy Ghost, causes the experience and, by the suprarational perception of the Gift of Wisdom, the immediate, possessive knowledge of the God Whom grace had made present in the depth of the soul as a gift, as an object of possible experience and fruition. Thus, mystical wisdom realizes here below the promise, that is inscribed on the very nature of sanctifying grace, of coming to an experimental fruition of God.

This is as much as the theologians allow concerning that most hidden mystery—the experience of divine things.

Fides Illustrata Donis

15. It is obvious that this is an experience, if the word "experience" signifies the knowledge of an object as present, in which the soul undergoes an action exercised upon it by that object and perceives in virtue of this very passion. It is a vital, meritorious and free operation, but one in which the soul does not move itself (according as "to move oneself" is to put oneself in act by virtue of a previous act);[49] one in which it is moved and set into immanent action through God's grace alone operating within it as the living instrument of the Holy Ghost. He elevates it to a higher rule by suspending its human way of acting: that is why mystics describe it as a passivity and a not-acting. This experience may be said to be immediate in the sense that it does not take place through the intermediary of any image drawn from creatures, since it transcends the mode of concepts and analogy. But in another sense it is not immediate, because it is not a vision of the Divine Essence, and because in it God, as St. Teresa teaches,[50] is still known *through His effects*, that is, by the very

---

48   *Hymn of the Transfiguration.*

49   Cf. St. Thomas, *Sum. Theol.*, I–II, 9, 3, ad 1. But the soul continues "to move itself" in the sense that the act which wells up within it under the influence of operative grace proceeds in accordance with the spontaneity and immanence proper to life—and proceeds freely, as falling under the dominion that its will has over itself, and of *being able* not to be done.

50   Cf. her *Life*, written by herself, Ch. XXVII, "In the effects God produces in the soul, we understand He is present." In this text St. Teresa is speaking "of God's presence which is often made felt to people who have been favored with prayer of union and quiet," a presence she sets in opposition to intellectual vision of

effects He produces in the affections and at the very root of powers, effects which are like a taste or a touch whereby He is spiritually experienced in the darkness of faith.[51]

What, then, becomes of concepts in this case? They are not suppressed, for that would be contrary to the very nature of our intellect which needs them to be in act. So they must be there. But distinct concepts are all silent; they sleep, even as the Apostles did on the Mount of Olives. And the confused concepts which intervene, and which can remain quite unperceived, play only a material role. I mean that if mystical experience passes through them, it is not as though it were through a formal means of knowing which measures and rules the knowledge; it passes through them without being measured by them as conditions required on the side of the subject. That is why they can be as confused, as indistinct and as little discernible as you wish: the formal means and rule of knowledge are elsewhere. The connaturality of charity, under the motion of the Holy Ghost, plays the formal part. The proper light of infused contemplation only comes from the ardor of a love which burns in the night. That is why this supreme wisdom, this supernatural loving knowledge which (St. John of the Cross tells us) we can compare to a warm light,[52] is described as a renunciation of knowledge and an ignorance—*a ray of darkness for the intellect*, in the words of Dionysius. The latter calls it an apophatic, or "negative," contemplation which joins us experimentally to a hidden God who is above all knowledge, *Deo ignoto*. Finally, we see how mystical wisdom, tasting and suffering in love that very thing which faith attains in a hidden way, makes us judge and estimate in the best possible way what we know by faith. But it uncovers for us no object of knowledge which faith does not attain. It perfects faith in the manner of knowing, not as regards the object known. And how could it go further in this order than faith, which attains inwardness as such, the proper and hidden life of God? It is the God of faith who is experienced here below by His very resounding and embodiment in love, as it is the God

Christ's humanity. But what she says holds good as well for all degrees of a mystical experience of the deity on condition that it be well understood that at the highest levels there is no longer the slightest *inference* from effects to cause but an immediate knowledge of the Latter in the former.

51   See above, Ch. VI, n. 42. Cf. John of St. Thomas, *Curs. Theol.*, I P., q. 43, disp. 17, a. 3, n. 13 and 17: "Sicut contactus animae quo experimentaliter sentitur, etiamsi in sua substantia non videatur, est informatio et animatio, qua corpus reddit vivum et animatum, ita contactus Dei quo sentitur experimentaliter, et ut objectum conjunctum, etiam antequam videatur intuitive in se, est contactus operationis intimae, quo operatur intra cor, ita ut sentiatur et experimentaliter manifestetur, eo quod *unctio ejus docet nos de omnibus*, ut dicitur I Joan., IV. Haec cognitio experimentalis datur etiamsi res intuitive non videatur in se, sufficit quod per proprios effectus, quasi per tactum et vivificationem sentiatur, sicut animam nostram experimentaliter cognoscimus, etiamsi intuitive ejus substantiam non videamus."

52   Cf. below, Ch. VIII, end of § 20.

of vision who, when seen, will be likewise tasted in the future life, for the mystical experience begun here below will continue in the Fatherland.

When, in the act of infused contemplation, the gift of wisdom, under God's action, frees faith from the human mode of concept and analogy (I do not say from the conceptual formulas that express revealed truth! I say, rather, from the actual use of such distinct conceptual formulas as a formal means of knowing), it suppresses in some way, not by vision, but by the experience of love, that distance from its object, which is the case in faith all alone. And then, as Joseph of the Holy Ghost shows,[53] faith itself—attaining its object under a new formal modality due to the gift of wisdom or understanding of which it is quite incapable by itself alone—is made savory and penetrating.[54] It makes us cling by the purer and more perfect means—suprahuman means—to its ultimate object, that is, to divine reality of which the conceptual formulas are the sign, a reality which is now possessed in the unity of spirit: *Qui adhaeret Domino, unus spiritus est*.[55]

It is a disastrous illusion to seek mystical experience outside of faith, to imagine a mystical experience freed from theological faith. Living faith, illumined by the gifts, is the very principle of this experience, and, to recall the royal words of St. John of the Cross,[56] which no philosophical commentary will ever efface, it is the only proximate and proportioned means of mystical union.

III
TRANSITION TO A FEW PROBLEMS

16. It was necessary to insist on these theological considerations because it is the only way of knowing what we are talking about when we speak of the experience of divine things. But before approaching any new problems, certain explanations are necessary.

For man, there is but one spirituality in the pure and simple, the absolute

---

53   "Fides illustrata donis est habitus proxime eliciens divinam contemplationem" (*Curs. theol. mystico-schol.*, t. II, disp. 13, q. 1, § 3, n. 15). See below, Appendix V, § 4.

54   St. Thomas (III, 55, 2 ad 1) says that the apostles' faith, in seeing the Risen Christ, was a *fides occulata*, a faith that sees. . . . In contemplation there is a kind of *fides occulata* in another sense of the term, a faith that has become, as it were, experimental, no longer through the sensible light of the eyes, but, rather, through the supernatural light of the gift of wisdom, by a special illumination of the Holy Ghost *making use of the savor and connaturality of love.* . . . In contemplation and through the gift of wisdom, faith may be said to receive eyes, not positively but as a *taste* or *touch*. . . ." (R. Garrigou-Lagrange, *Christian Perfection and Contemplation*, St. Louis and London, Herder, 1944, p. 314).

55   "Ὁ δὲ κολλώμενος τῷ κυρίῳ ἓν πνεῦμά ἐστιν" (I Cor. vi, 17).

56   See below, Ch. VIII, end of § 16.

sense of the word: supernatural spirituality, that which the Holy Ghost gives, and which makes our whole life love, renders it entirely spirit. It is in this sense that St. Paul speaks of the spiritual man, and in opposing him to the "animal" or psychic man, opposes him to everything that does not belong to the order of holiness. "The sensual man perceiveth not these things that are of the spirit of God: for it is foolishness to him, and he cannot understand, because it is spiritually examined. But the spiritual man judgeth all things; and he himself is judged of no man. For who hath known the mind of the Lord that he may instruct Him? But we have the mind of Christ."[57]

We have already tried to say why this is so: "The animal or natural man receives through his senses everything that comes to him from the outside; he gathers his concepts from them by means of the activity of the intellect. Reason which transcends the senses still labors in their work-yard. Philosophy, even at its highest, is still beholden to them for their materials.

"That is why mystical language knows only two terms: life according to sense and life according to spirit: those who sleep in their senses and those who watch in the Holy Ghost. Because for us there are only two *sources*: the senses and the spirit of God.

"Man has a spiritual soul, but it informs a body. When it is a question of rising to a wholly spiritual life, his reason does not suffice; his attempts at angelism have always broken down. His only authentic spirituality is bound up with grace and the Holy Ghost."[58] We mean here spirituality in the pure and simple sense of the word, that fires and takes hold of the entire being.

But the mark of spirituality may be imprinted on only some part, either on this or that aspect of our being or our life, and it is then spirituality *of a kind*, a spirituality under a certain aspect. In that sense, there is a natural spirituality of multiple degrees and of various kinds by which the human soul bears witness to its proper essence. We find it in the speculative exercise of the intellect. Weighted down though it be, the proper activity of the scientist and the philosopher, the mathematician and the geometrician is a sort of spirituality. We find it also in the practical exercise of the intellect because the will, like the intellect, is a spiritual faculty, and there is no liberty or virtue without some spirituality. Already it is there secretly animating the humblest efforts of the peasant or artist to impose the form of reason on earthly things. But in the moral life, even as in metaphysics or poetry (the poetry of the poet or musician or of any other creator of forms), it is only when an inspiration passes into man

---

57   "ἡμεῖς δὲ νοῦν Χριστοῦ ἔχομεν." (St. Paul, I Cor. ii, 4–16). Cf. the comment of St. Thomas on the same text: ". . . In omnibus ille qui recte se habet, rectum judicium habet circa singula: ille autem qui in se rectitudinis defectum patitur, deficit etiam in judicando. Vigilans enim recte judicat et se vigilare et alium dormire; sed dormiens non habet rectum judicium de se, nec de vigilante. . . . Et ideo ab homine non spirituali spiritualis homo judicari non potest, sicut nec vigilans a dormiente."

58   *Dialogues, Roseau d'Or*, Chroniques No. 6, 1928, p. 28.

(an inspiration which, be it one descending from on high[59] or one rising from below, still remains, or can remain, of the natural order)[60] that this natural spirituality is set free for its own sake. In its highest stages, it seems bound to the natural love of God which, even though inscribed in the heart of our being, yet cannot by itself alone establish His reign over our will. (Grace and charity are needed for that.) Then it is that it seems like some sort of reflection, some kind of homesickness for the full spirituality that belongs to those who are called by St. Paul the "perfect" and the "sons of God."

We hold in particular (as was pointed out in the preceding chapter) that a mystical aspiration traverses every metaphysics; it seems (and we will return to this point in a moment) that in the final analysis, the desire—an inefficacious one—of knowing the first cause in its essence is like a secret fire in the heart of the metaphysician. He does not know what he thus desires, for the philoso-

---

59   I would like to reproduce at this point a note from our *Reply to Jean Cocteau*: "Aristotle or rather the author of the *Ethics to Eudemus*, wrote: 'It will, perhaps, be asked whether it is good fortune for anyone, who does so, to desire what he must desire and when he must do it. Without reflecting, deliberating or taking counsel, it happens that he thinks and wants what is most fitting. And what is the cause of it, if not good fortune? But what is it and how can it give such happy inspirations? That amounts to asking what is the higher principle of the soul's movements? Now it is clear that God, Who is the beginning of the universe, is also the soul's principle. Everything present within us is moved by Him. . . . Reason is not the principle of reason, something higher is its principle. Now what is superior to reason and intelligence, if not God? That is why the ancients said: Happy are those men who are led to act well without deliberating. That does not come from their will but from a principle present within them, a principle that is superior to their intelligence and will. . . . Under divine inspiration some men even foresee the future."

The ancient philosophers are not the only ones to recognize this special moving by God in the natural order, theologians also recognize it. I am reproducing here a synopsis drawn up by Fr. Garrigou-Lagrange with a view to classifying the various kinds of divine motion (*Vie Spirituelle*, July 1923, p. 419):

Our mind is moved by God
- In the Natural Order
  - To will beatitude in general
  - To be determined to a true good or an apparent good
  - By a special inspiration for example, in the poetic or philosophic order
- In the Supernatural Order
  - To turn to God, the final supernatural end.
  - To be determined in its use of infused virtues, through a special inspiration to which the Gifts of the Holy Ghost make us docile.

Cf. *Art ard Faith*, New York, Philosophical Library, 1948, pp. 121–123.

60   Concerning the problem of natural spirituality, cf. a work in preparation by Charles Du Bos, *Du spirituel dans l'ordre littéraire*; the first chapters of this work—and how wonderfully penetrating they are—have made their appearance in *Vigiles* (Nos. 1 and 4 in 1930, No. 4 in 1931).

pher as such has no conception of the Beatific Vision and of what God has prepared for those who love Him. His desire is a natural mystical desire.

17. On the other hand, there is (if the word contemplation be understood in a wide sense, as a concentrated meditation) a natural "contemplation"—the contemplation of the philosopher which, says St. Albert, "is for the perfection of the one who contemplates and consequently comes to a halt in the intellect" without "passing into the heart by love." *Contemplatio Philosophorum est propter perfectionem contemplantis, et ideo sistit in intellectu, et ita finis eorum in hoc est cognitio intellectus. Sed contemplatio Sanctorum est propter amorem ipsius, scilicet contemplati Dei: idcirco, non sistit in fine ultimo in intellectu per cognitionem, sed transit ad affectum per amorem.*[61]

This "contemplation of the philosophers," if it does not pass into the heart by love, that is to say (for these words must be understood in a very formal way) if it does not advance by the footsteps of love, *gressibus amoris,* and if it does not proceed in virtue of the union of love (and that supposes the love of charity), as has been explained already, can, nevertheless, be joined to a natural love of the object contemplated and to a heartfelt complacency in it. And this colors it with an affective and experimental hue: of itself, it is quite another thing than experience properly so called, which is immediate, and which not only attains an object intellectually contemplated, and colored by affectivity by reason of its agreement with the soul's desires, but also touches a reality lovingly contemplated, and a reality given, penetrated and known by the very love with which the soul burns and in which the soul is joined to it and given to it. Thus, as has been seen, it is the very connaturality of love which, under a special inspiration and illumination of the Holy Ghost, is the formal means of knowledge; sometimes, as regards the external and apparent signs whereby others judge these things, extrinsic resemblances may appear to exist between the two cases.

If, along with that the natural "contemplation" of which we have been speaking, a contemplation cultivated by souls in search of spiritual perfection, sets into operation natural means belonging to the moral and ascetic order (normally presupposed by contemplation properly so called), it is understandable why the discernment of the difference may be difficult despite the fundamental diversity of their essences and even though criteria are not lacking. Thus, we know for sure that animal and vegetable differ in essence, but even the biologist will hesitate to make up his mind which he is dealing with in a particular case. Let us simply note at this juncture that, taken in its pure state, the "contemplation of the philosophers" remains the highest moment in a properly human rational and discursive activity. Its stability is always precarious because, by nature, we are always on the move; it soars; it

---

61   *De adhaerendo Deo,* cap. IX. After having attributed this precious little work to John of Castel for a while, critical research once more recognizes St. Albert as its author. Cf. C. H. Scheeben, "Les ecrits d'Albert le Grand d'après les catalogues," *Revue Thomiste,* March–April 1931, p. 260, n. 3.

does not stay at rest. It has neither the inert passivity proper to subnormal states, due to temperament, sickness or imagination (for then it is a pseudo-contemplation, which rests and does not soar), nor the supernatural passivity proper to the "contemplation of the saints"—a contemplation which is, in reality, an incomparably deeper activation, from which there accrues to the soul greater flexibility and at the same time a stronger self-mastery. That contemplation soars and reposes at the same time: *et volabo et requiescam*. . . .

Is there an Authentic Mystical Experience in the Natural Order?

18. Thus, we admit, on the one hand, the existence of a natural "spirituality" (the word "spirituality" being taken in a relative sense, and on the other hand, the existence of a natural "contemplation" (the word "contemplation" being taken in a wide and improper sense). We admit there is a *natural mystical desire*, or a natural aspiration to mystical contemplation, and that there is a *natural contemplation* (in the wide sense) which, although not mystical in itself, may, however, be pressed into service by this mystical desire and thus presents itself under false pretenses.

The ground being thus cleared, we are confronted by another and a much more relevant question. Is there *mystical contemplation in the natural order*? Is there a mystical experience in the natural order? If one gives to the term "mystical experience" a vague meaning, inclusive of the diverse analogies with infused contemplation that the natural order offers us, an affirmative answer may be given and we willingly agree. It is useless to dally over a merely verbal quarrel. But the question thus understood would lose all interest. The question is: is an *authentic* and *properly so-called* mystical experience—that is to say, (1) a mystical experience which is not a counterfeit or an illusion, and (2) one which bears on God Himself and makes us experience the Divine reality is an experimental knowledge of God possible in the natural order?

19. We should, in the most categorical manner, reply "No" to this question. The whole distinction between nature and grace is here at stake.

The theological explanation given above has enabled us to note a capital truth. We ask: what is it that grace properly does? By grace, I mean that quality infused into us as a new spiritual nature, engrafted upon our first nature, a quality turned towards God to be seen face to face. What does the special presence of the three Divine Persons in a just soul as a gift and object of enjoyment properly do? We answer: IT RENDERS POSSIBLE an experience of the divine reality, and experience of God's inner depths. We ask: what do the gifts of understanding and wisdom do when, under the inspiration of the Spirit of God, they elevate the intelligence so that it may know in faith the very object of faith in a superhuman manner due to the connaturality of charity? We answer: THEY make this experience of God A REALITY. Therefore, what the supernatural properly does is to pave the way for an experimental knowledge of God.

To admit in any degree whatsoever, even in simplest inchoative form, a genuine experience of the depths of God's being on the natural level would necessarily mean either to confuse our natural intellectuality (specified by being in general) with our intellectuality as it flows from grace and is specified by the Divine Essence itself; or to confuse the presence of God's immensity (whereby God is present in all things in virtue of his created efficiency) with His holy indwelling (whereby He is present in a special way, as object, in souls that are in the state of grace); or, again, to muddle up in the same hybrid concept, the wisdom of the natural order (metaphysical wisdom), and the infused gift of wisdom; or, finally, to attribute to the natural love of God what belongs exclusively to supernatural charity. In any event, it would be to confuse what is absolutely proper to grace with that which is proper to nature. There is no "immediate grasp" of God in the natural order. A mystical contemplation (i.e., an authentic one) in the natural order is a contradiction in terms. A genuine experience of God's inner depths, a felt contact with God, a *pati divina*, can take place only in the order of sanctifying grace and through sanctifying grace.

First Objection

20. God, being sovereignly immaterial, is sovereignly intelligible, i.e., He is a pure act of understanding Himself. It is in this way that He is spiritually present in our minds. Is the immaterial presence of such an intelligible object in a created mind not enough for that mind to perceive it at least in an obscure manner?

21. No! It is not enough. (If it were enough, we would attain the formal object of the Beatific Vision at least confusedly, and we would even have the Beatific Vision while still here below, because this is a matter of perceiving God through His Essence, and it does not happen obscurely or piecemeal.) For God to be present as object, another condition is necessary: the power, the subjective vitality of the created mind, must be made proportionate to this absolutely transcendent intelligible object. It is sanctifying grace that renders the created mind proportionate to the Divine Essence as object, in respect to the radical principle of operation, but in respect to the proximate principles of the operation of vision itself, they are, on the one hand, the *lumen gloriae* (if it is a question of perfect possession), and, on the other hand, a living faith along with the gifts of the Holy Ghost (if it is a question of an imperfect and obscure possession such as may exist here below).

Second Objection

22. Every creature, St. Thomas teaches,[62] naturally loves God more than itself, although in an inefficacious manner in fallen man,[63] who cannot effec-

tively turn towards his true end without grace. Thus, there is a natural love of God distinct from supernatural charity. Now why would not this natural love of God produce in the natural order, as charity does in the supernatural order, a knowledge of God by connaturality?

23. We reply: connaturality means agreement in the same nature. Now God is the supernatural subsistent; it is absurd to suppose that we could be made connatural with the subsistent supernatural without being first made supernatural ourselves. The theological virtue of charity alone can make us connatural with God because it is a supernatural love. 1. It supposes sanctifying grace which makes us formally sharers of the Divine Nature. 2. It attains God as object of love really present within us as a gift[64] and as a friend in whose life and happiness we are destined to share. 3. Proceeding from supernatural faith which attains God according to His essence, even though obscurely and from afar (and, on the other hand, not being compelled, as the cognitive virtues are, to achieve its object through the intermediary of conceptual signs and according as it is within the intellect by means of those signs, but attaining, loving, its object according as it exists in itself), the theological virtue of charity loves God, even here below, *immediately* and *through Himself* (whereas faith does not know Him in that way); it loves God in His very Divinity, in the mystery proper to His inner life, proper to God's very essence.[65]

The natural love of God has none of these characteristics. Even supposing it capable of making us love God efficaciously above all things (and this is not the case with our fallen nature), this love, which proceeds from our essence as creatures infinitely far removed from Pure Act, and which cannot constitute a friendship properly so called between man and God,[66] nor achieve God as really present within us as a gift, a love, in fine, which can only love God through the mediation of the transcendental good (as supreme and subsistent Good)[67]—since it is ruled by an analogical knowledge in which God is known

---

62   *Sum. Theol.*, I, 60, 5; I–II, 109, 3.

63   The Church defined this point against Baius. Cf. the Bull of St. Pius V: "Ex omnibus afflictionibus" (Denz.-Bannw., n. 1034).

64   "Amor charitatis est de eo quod jam habetur" (*Sum. Theol.*, I–II, 66, 6). "Idem bonum est objectum charitatis et spei. Sed charitas importat unionem ad illud bonum, spes autem distantiam quandam ab eo. Et inde est quod charitas non respicit illud bonum ut arduum, sicut spes. Quod enim jam unitum est, non habet rationem ardui" (*ibid.*, II–II, 23, 6 ad 3).

65   "Deus qui in hac vita non potest per seipsum cognosci, potest per seipsum amari" (*Sum. Theol.*, I–II, 27, 2, arg. 2); "Charitas viae immediate Deo adhaeret" (*ibid.*, II–II, 27, 4, sed contra); "Charitas Deum immediate diligit" (*ibid.*, corp.); "Charitas est, quae diligendo, animam immediate Deo conjungit, spiritualis vinculo unionis" (*ibid.*, ad 3).

66   In the natural order, a *friendship*, properly so called, between man and God is not possible and can only exist with grace and charity (Salmanticenses, *Curs. Theol.*, t. XII, *De Charitate*, disp. 1, dub. 4. Cf. St. Thomas, *in III Sent.*, dist. 27, q. 2, a. 4; *Sum. Theol.*, I–II, 65, 5; 109, 3, ad 1; II–II, 25, 2 ad 2; 3, 26, 1).

only through the mediation of transcendental being (as First Being)—this natural love of God is incapable of rendering us properly connatural to things divine, incapable of providing a knowledge of God through connaturality, a mystical experience of the depths of God.

Undoubtedly, inasmuch as man is made, even from the natural order, in the image and likeness of his Creator, it may very well be admitted (at least on the supposition of the state of pure nature or of integral nature in which we would have been able to love God efficaciously as the Author of our nature above everything else through our natural powers alone), that this natural love, supposing that it loved God above everything else in an efficacious way, creates an active likeness, a sort of natural sympathy with God such as could be attained by starting from creatures. Whence there might follow affective complacence in the object rationally known, and even, under a special inspiration in the natural order, judgments about the divine perfections by way of inclination and instinct.

There one would find a very close analogy with mystical experience, but it would not merit the name of mystical experience any more than other analogies. For it would not entail any *experience*, properly so called, of the Divine Reality present within us, no *passion* of God suffered within the soul, no *felt contact* with God, but rather a knowledge always essentially from afar, even though affectively determined. The natural agreement or sympathy of which we have just been speaking cannot be called a true connaturality with God. Unless we muddle up our whole vocabulary, this word should be reserved for what is a formal, not merely a virtual, participation of the Divine Nature.[68] That is to say, this word should be reserved for a participation in God as God (in what is proper to Him) and not as He is the exemplar of creatures.

24. Moreover, the state of pure nature or integral nature does not exist; indeed, the possibility of loving God as the author of our nature in an efficacious way and above all else through our natural powers alone is not granted to us. That hypothesis was a fictional one and did not concern our real state. It remains none the less true that from this natural (hypothetical) resemblance a rough draft of mystical experience by way of a natural love of God is possible. Indeed such a love, inadequate though it may be in making us efficaciously prefer God to everything else, can still be intense and deep. It may even be efficacious in the ordering of our speculative aspirations, if not

---

67   God is the object of supernatural beatitude and is immediately attained through charity not as Supreme Good, but as God and in accordance with His Own very deity and life. "Naturalis cognitio non potest attingere ad Deum, secundum quod est objectum beatitudinis, prout tendit in ipsum spes et charitas" (*Sum. Theol.*, II–II, 4, 7).

68   And that is why no *virtual* participation in the Divine Nature suffices to form the basis of a friendship, in the proper sense of the word, between man and God. (Cf. *Salm., loc. cit.*, § 3, n. 50.)

in our life. It may, then, fashion within the soul that rough draft which we mentioned and that would raise the various natural analogies of contemplation which we shall consider at a later stage to a purer level of natural inspiration and spirituality.

Third Objection

25. There are Moslem, Hindu, Buddhist, and other schools of mystics. But the mystical experience to which they lay claim does not proceed from theological faith. There must, therefore, be a natural mystical experience.

26. One thing is sure: if cases of authentic mystical experience are met with in these circles, such cases arise from divine grace and from infused contemplation more or less modified in their typical forms by special conditions of development and apart from the influx of sacramental graces and the visible rays of revealed truth.[69] Everything leads us to think that such cases are encountered since we know that unbaptized persons, even though they are not stamped with the seal of unity so as to participate through the virtue of the Church in the proper work of the Church (which is the redemption continued), can nevertheless (inasmuch as they receive without knowing it the supernatural life of the self-same divine blood which circulates within the Church and of the same spirit which rests upon it) belong invisibly to Christ's Church. Thus they can have sanctifying grace and, as a result, theological faith[70] and the infused gifts. Works like those of Louis Massignon[71] and Asin

---

69 A person who has not been given a certain good as a birthright often places a higher value upon what he has been able to win for himself. From this standpoint many Christians have to take lessons in fidelity from certain pagans. But for that very reason the very prestige contemplation enjoys among spiritual people *in partibus infidelium*, the resources they have exploited to examine and pass along what they have received from it, oftentimes makes it possible for us to deceive ourselves—especially in the case where poetic expression would go much farther than experience reaches—about the level these people have successfully achieved. On the other hand, the whole "physique" that prepares the way for and goes along with contemplation (not to speak of accidental gifts that are oftentimes suspect) must, wherever human research is stretched to its utmost, stand out in particular relief. If these opinions are correct, the case of an al Hallâj would have to be deemed exceptional in its loftiness and purity.

70 That is to say, to cling with one's heart to the two primary truths in the supernatural order (a God exists Who wills my salvation and Who saves those who seek Him: "sine fide impossibile est placere Deo; credere enim oportet accedentem ad Deum *quia est, et inquirentibus se remunerator sit*" [St. Paul, Heb. xi, 6]), and, therefore, at least implicitly to other truths that are confusedly contained in these two primary truths. Cf. Fr. Schultes' study, *Fides implicita* (Regensburg and Rome, Pustet).

"An adult can only be justified by believing, in one way or another, in the redemption worked by Christ. This faith in Christ the Redeemer admits of three

Palacios[72] on Islam, present-day studies devoted to hassidism,[73] the personal testimonies of a Mukerji[74] or a Father Wallace to Hindu spirituality,[75] or even

states or, if you prefer, three different degrees: an implicit knowledge of the mysteries of the Incarnation and Redemption, such as we Christians know them; the idea of a mediator setting himself between God and men; finally, the conviction that God in His mercy has provided for the salvation of the human race in some way or other. . . . Saint Thomas, speaking of those who lived before the coming of Christ and who were saved by following the voice of conscience, says: 'Even though they did not have explicit faith (in a Mediator), they did nevertheless have implicit faith in Him, through their faith in Divine Providence, believing that God would save men by such means as pleased Him' (*Sum. Theol.*, II–II, 2, 7 ad 3). Thus, believing God saves men by means pleasing to Him is having an implicit faith in Christ, the Redeemer. It is difficult to contend that conditions have changed for those who, because they lived after Christ, have never heard mention made of him" (Eliseus of the Nativity, "L'expérience mystique d'Ibn 'Arabi est-elle surnaturelle?" *Etudes Carmélitaines*, Oct. 1931, p. 163).

At this point let us recall that, according to the Church's teaching, "Deus omnipotens omnes homines sine exceptione *vult salvos fieri* (I Tim. ii, 4), licet non omnes salventur; Christus Jesus D.N., sicut nullus homo est, fuit vel erit, cujus natura in illo assumpta non fuerit, ita nullus est, fuit vel erit homo, pro quo passus non fuerit; licet non omnes passionis ejus mysterio redimantur . . ." (1st Council of Chiersy, Denz.-Bannw., pp. 318–319; cf. Council of Trent, *ibid.*, pp. 794–795). Basing herself on St. Paul's words that Christ *died for all men* (II Cor. v, 15), the Church has condemned the following propositions: "Semipelagianum est dicere, Christum pro omnibus omnino hominibus mortuum esse et sanguinem fundisse" (D.B., 1906); "Christus dedit semetipsum pro nobis oblationem Deo, non pro solis electis, sed pro omnibus et *solis fidelibus.*" (1294); "Pagani, Judaei, haeretici aliique hujus generis nullum omnino accipiunt a Jesu Christo influxum . . ." (1295); "Extra Ecclesiam nulla conceditur gratia" (1379). Cf. R. Garrigou-Lagrange, "Prémystique naturelle et mystique surnaturelle," *Études Carmélitaines*, Oct. 1933.

71   Louis Massignon, *La Passion d'Al-Hosayn-ibn-Mansour-al-Hallâj, martyr mystique de l'Islam*, 2 vols. (Paris, Geuthner, 1922); "Le Diwan d'al-Hallâj," *Journal Asiatique*, January–March 1931 (Paris, Geuthner, 1931). al-Hallâj, the hero of Louis Massignon's basic work, can be compared with a mystic of the same lineage, Ayn al-Qudat al-Hamadani, whose *Sakwa* Mr. J. M. Benabdeljalil has published (*Journal Asiatique*, January–March 1930, Paris, Geuthner, 1930).

72   Miguel Asin Palacios, *El Islam cristiazado, estudio del "sufismo" a través de las obras de Abenarabi de Murcia* (Madrid, 1931). Ibn-Arabi's case seems to call for many more reservations than al-Hallâj's case. Mere material correspondence in the terms used gives little ground for pronouncing, even approximately, on the value of a mystical experience.

73   Cf. Horodetzki, *Ha-Hassidout-De-ha-Hassidim* (Berlin, 1922); Martin Buber, *Die Chassidischen Bucher* (1928); Jean de Menasce, *Quand Israel aime Dieu* (Paris, Plon, 1931).

74   D. G. Mukerji, *Le visage de mon frère* (Paris, Stock, 1929).

75   W. Wallace, *De l'évangelisme au catholicisme par la route des Indes* (Bruxelles, Dewit, 1921).

the works of contemporary ethnologists on the prayer of primitive peoples"[76]—all these bring precious factual confirmation to this view of the spirit. And those are but the first explorations[77] in a complicated and difficult terrain.

What we have in mind in speaking in this vein is something quite different from a syncretism, quite different, too, from a comparative phenomenist mysticism, busy as it is with effacing its essential object and levelling things of the spirit to the plane of matter. What we would like to see develop is a comparative theological mysticism working towards the discernment of various depths in properly spiritual values and towards a recognition of God's visitations; for nowhere is He left without witnesses. Only such a comparative mysticism would be competent to discern and safeguard at every point whatever is genuine because it sees in all those resemblances the traits of a single countenance instead of either peopling the world with vain images that resemble no countenance at all and which annul one another, or pretending to make a composite countenance by gathering together all the disparate elements in one and the same confusion. Because there is a true countenance, its reflections can be equitably judged. Because there is a sheep-fold, the shepherd who keeps it is also the shepherd of those *other sheep* who, without knowing it, receive of His fullness but who have not yet heard his voice. Because the Church has received the treasure of supernatural revelation in its entirety, it allows us to honor everywhere the various traces or marks or scattered fragments of that revelation. The saints who visibly belong to the Church enable us to recognize their far-off brethren who do not know Her and yet who belong to Her invisibly—St. John of the Cross enables us to do justice to Ramakrishna.[78] The perfect imitator of Christ, Paul the Apostle, is the leader of all truly spiritual men over the whole earth under whatever sky they may have flourished. And just as the virtuous man is the rule and measure of all things human,[79] so, too, in this spiritual man par excellence all genuinely mystical life finds its model and measure.[80]

---

76   W. Schmidt, *Der Ursprung des Gottesidee*, Vol. II, pt. 2 (Munich, 1929). Cf. the article of G. Horn, *Vie Spirituelle*, April 1931.

77   Cf. Louis Massignon, works quoted above and below, Ch. VIII, § 20, end of n. 28; J. Marechal, *Études sur la psychologie des mystiques* (Paris, Alcan, 1924), t. I; O. Lacombe, "Orient et Occident," *Études Carmélitaines*, April 1931. And works in which the constructive spirit is, moreover, far from being wanting, by Rudolf Otto, Friedrich Heiler, P. Masson-Oursel, M. Horten, etc.

78   We are not unaware of all that is ambivalent in the worldly destiny of a Ramakrishna whose personality does appear to be like the personality of a true contemplative, and with regard to whose school and his continuators, there is, indeed, need for considerable reserve—a fact which is scarcely surprising where the assistance of the Church's visible motherhood is lacking.

79   Aristotle, *Nicomachean Ethics*, Book X, Ch. V.

80   Deissmann (*Paulus*, 1911) and Evelyn Underhill (*The Mystic Way*, 1931) recognize the pre-eminent and universal importance of St. Paul (cf. Nicolaus von Arsenius, "Das ganz andere' in der Mystik," *Philosophia perennis*, t. II, pp. 1043 ff.).

27. Difficult though it may be, it is not impossible to distinguish genuine cases, at least as probably genuine. A critical study of expressions and testimonies, an examination of their analogies and relations with the testimony of the saints can be of help. And any love that dispossesses man of himself does not lack indications, fleeting though they be, which point to a genuine mystical experience when that love penetrates the whole being with the desire to be dissolved and to be with God:[81] a desire with a two-fold aspect, each of which is probative only in conjunction with the other.

But, on the other hand, that dubious or apocryphal cases will often crop up appears quite likely if we keep in mind that certain states, more-or-less privileged, or more-or-less powerful, of intense meditation and concentration, may present external resemblances to supernatural contemplation, and that what one might call the "physical aspect" of the inner life, or its cloak of phenomena ("the weakness of ecstasy," said St. Hildegarde), can stem from merely natural causes as well as from higher influences. In these states the natural or philosophical "contemplation" mentioned above undoubtedly plays an important role, but we do not think that for the most part it remains alone and in a pure state. When it is not aided and raised up by actual graces, and especially when its "realization" is ardently sought, while a powerful dogmatic and disciplinary control is lacking, how could it but be exposed to many admixtures and illusions: to lower influences proceeding from one's physical temperament and the imagination; as well as to certain higher influences, still of the natural or praeternatural, not the divine order, which may even be perverse.

This problem of the relations between human intellect and the separated intelligences is posited with peculiar sharpness in respect to those worlds to which the "too great love" of God has not been revealed and in which a heroic desire for spirituality comes to light. What we have in mind is not only the frauds and disguises with which the malice of fallen spirits menaces the rational animal when it tries to escape from its mediocre nature. It does not seem to us that one should rule out the notion that in a non-Christian regime certain ascetic efforts, certain sequestrations of the soul exercised upon itself, can actually tend (unknown to the subject) towards a spiritual communication with angelic nature as such, which is the same in the good as well as the bad angels, both of which contesting, for their own ulterior purposes, for this immaterial *convivium* with the human being. The care St. Thomas takes to refute the theories of Avempace, Alexander of Aphrodisias and Averroes on the possibility for man of immediately attaining the world of pure spirits[82] by an intellectual intuition, shows quite clearly the extent to which the temptation to such a communication can seduce philosophers. In the instance we have

---

81   "Desiderium habens dissolvi et esse cum Christo" (St. Paul, Philip., I, 23).
82   *Cont. Gen.*, III, 41, 42, 43, 44, 45. Cf. *Sum. Theol.*, I–II, 3, 7: "Aliqualem autem beatitudinem imperfectam nihil prohibit attendi in contemplatione angelorum, et etiam altiorem, quam in consideratione scientiarum speculativarum."

hypothetically envisaged, the human mind would find itself giving way to the attraction, not so much of seeing pure spirits and seeking its happiness therein as of receiving their help to be transported to a superhuman contemplation in which the soul would in some way mimic (in the suspension of consciousness, in a night, but a night quite different from the night of infused contemplation and the luminous cloud of Tabor) *their* way of naturally knowing themselves and the highest.

If that were so, it would be easy to understand how a kind of intellectualist mysticism, seeking ecstasy or "realization" by means of a completely metaphysical asceticism and dialectic, examples of which could be found among the neo-Platonists and gnostics and certain Oriental schools, might sometimes reach that rapture into unity of which Porphyry speaks to us in connection with his master, and so gain contact with a kind of superhuman state that seems due to collusion with a higher intellectual world. On the other hand, it is easy to understand, also, how such a metaphysical ecstasy in which human understanding impinges, as it were, upon an angelic abyss, still remains infinitely far removed from *suffering things divine*, and issues into pantheism with an almost fatal necessity.

28. It remains true, however, that genuine forms of mysticism do, of themselves, come before other forms. As regards the sacred traditions of India, we feel that, in their basic principle, the Upanishads originally depend less on philosophy than on a contemplative source and a powerful intuition, more mystical than metaphysical, of the transcendence of the Supreme Being. *Neti! Neti!* Not like that! It is neither like that, nor like that! The tragedy is that this contemplation has been prolonged by a luxuriant and hypertrophied rational discourse which, however, has never succeeded in disengaging philosophy and metaphysics in their own proper form and according to their own laws as works of human reason; and that is what they are by their very essence. Into the waters flowing from the fountainhead, streams of less pure waters have emptied their own. If, in the case of the Vedanta, pantheism is more apparent than real, suffered more than accepted;[83] and if, above all, it seems to go back to an inadequacy of conceptual techniques; if the tremendous mystical striving running through Hindu thought brings into play natural aspirations for perfect contemplation, and, as natural harbingers of that contemplation, natural processes of asceticism and intuition which constitute in regard to it a stage of expectancy, as it were, and a metaphysics which aims at preparing the way for it, then the permanent temptation which, in order to lay claim to achieving a supernatural gift by its own means, runs the risk of forcing upon this thought a choice between sovereign despair or pure abandonment as the supreme good, is an unequivocal sign that, wherever infused contemplation is not

---

83   Cf. R. P. Dandoy, "L'Ontologie du vedanta," *Questions Disputées* (Paris, Desclée de Brouwer et Cie, 1932).

granted it by grace, this striving can never arrive at a genuine mystical contemplation along the natural path.[84] The alternative is inevitable: either a genuine and supernatural mystical experience (perhaps over-burdened with adventitious elements, but that is accidental), on the one hand, or, on the other hand, a natural contemplation which does not reach the Divine reality—both, however, being capable of mingling with the other in many ways. No natural experience of the depths of God is to be envisaged here.

Does Metaphysics of Itself Demand Mystical Experience?

29. At this point, a new question must be examined. Can a mystical experience of Divine Reality be incorporated into philosophy, that is, metaphysics, in any way whatever (either because the philosophical intellect, supposing it to be able to transcend the method of concepts, would itself be capable of such an experience; or, on the contrary, because the philosophical intellect, confined to conceptual procedures alone, being incapable by its very nature of bringing the enterprise of metaphysics to a happy conclusion and essentially in need of a mystical experience in order to attain its object and perfect itself in its own line, i.e., to become a wisdom, would of itself require that it be completed by such an experience)? In other words, does the wisdom towards which metaphysical striving tends of itself require such a mystical experience, a *pati divina*?

Here, too, the answer must be, No!

Such mystical experience as would be required by the metaphysical undertaking would necessarily be either natural or supernatural. Could this be a mystical experience in the natural order? There is, we have just seen, no divine experience properly so called in the natural order. To assert the possibility of such an experience would be to compromise radically the distinction between nature and grace.

Could the mystical experience required by metaphysical activity be a divine experience in the supernatural order, infused contemplation? This sort of experience does truly exist. But to incorporate it into philosophy, to look upon it as required by the metaphysical effort itself, would be once again to muddle the orders of grace and nature, this time by making of an essentially supernatural knowledge a necessary requirement or a constructive co-principle of an essentially natural knowledge.

The dilemma is a brutal one. We do not think it is possible to escape it, whatever intermediate stages one might mark out between metaphysical knowledge and infused contemplation.

---

84   To avoid any misunderstanding that might arise from a difference in vocabulary, perhaps it is not idle to recall at this point that we understand the words *natural* and *supernatural* in the sense of Catholic theology (defined above, §§ 8 and 9), and not in the diluted sense some admit, notably various interpreters of Hinduism, in terms of which "natural" refers to empirical and sensible nature, "supernatural" to everything that transcends that nature.

No doubt there exist such intermediate stages. When philosophy of itself is thought to demand a mystical experience of things divine, certain states are included under this word mystical experience (understood in an improper way) which are not properly mystical but which nevertheless go beyond the limits of metaphysical science and of what it by essence requires. It is clear, however, that the existence of these intervening stages does not denote any demand intrinsic to the nature of philosophy to blossom forth in mystical contemplation.

The realm of metaphysics is of itself the realm of the third degree of abstraction, the world of being as being and of pure immateriality. At the penalty of endangering the value of our faculties of knowing and the value of the ananoetic process itself, which is essential to our natural knowledge of God (as well as for dogmatic pronouncements and formulas of faith), it must be admitted that the intellect, by its own exclusively intellectual means, is capable of getting a knowledge of that world, which the intellect itself by its own power of abstraction has made to exist as object. It is only by bringing the reason, the instrument of intellectual knowledge, to the supreme degree of intellectual purification, by having recourse to the most strictly abstract demonstrations, that we can arrive at sure conclusions in that order of knowing which is, strictly, the *least capable of being experienced*.

30. Is that to say that the existence of any metaphysical experience should be denied? We do not believe so—at least, when this word is properly understood (and in this way it is possible to concur in some of M. Bergson's views). Because we are spirits by what is best in us, we can have experience of things of the spirit even while we still remain on the level of nature. It is thus that we know experimentally not only the existence of our soul and of our free choice, but that we can also attain a certain obscure experimental perception of the very freedom of the spirit within us and its transcendence in respect to the whole material universe, or even (as many documents of contemporary literature attest)[85] of the nothingness immanent to all created things. On the other hand, it may happen that a truth of the natural order, such as the basic reality of being hidden beneath sensible phenomena, or the existence of the First Cause, will take on the intensity of an intuition or an immediate evidence under the influence of an actual grace. The intellect may well receive, after the manner of a sudden revelation, a knowledge of that which constitutes the proper object of the third level of abstraction. One who is very near to us one day gave us the following testimony of such a knowledge: "Before receiving the faith," that person told us, "it often happened that by a sudden intuition I experienced the reality of my own being, of the deepest, first principle that placed me outside nothingness. It was a powerful intuition and its violence often frightened me; that intuition gave me, for the first time, knowledge of a

---

85   For example, in Jacques Rivière's letters to Paul Claudel.

metaphysical absolute."[86] Or again, at the sight of something or other—a blade of grass, a windmill—a soul may know in an instant that these things do not exist by themselves, and that God exists. "Suddenly"—and I am citing the same witness—"all creatures appeared to me as symbols; they all seemed to have as their unique function to point to the Creator."

But, far from being integral parts or necessary requisites of metaphysical science, these kinds of metaphysical experiences or intuitions (whether they belong to an exclusively natural order or whether they are supernatural in their manner or production) transcend the proper sphere of metaphysics, and, without any regulation from the latter, they might even give rise to false interpretations, however true they may be in themselves. Far from being proper to the metaphysician, no discipline has a monopoly on these experiences, and it is rather amongst the poets, it would seem, that they are most often encountered. Let us not forget that it is supremely unreasonable to use what is *accidental* (*per accidens*) to judge of what is *necessary* (*per se*). Because God filled Beseleel and Ooliab with the spirit of wisdom and understanding to execute all works of sculpture and art, to engrave stones and to carve in wood, to weave tapestry and embroidery in blue and purple and scarlet twice-dyed and fine linen,[87] that is really no proof that these arts would of themselves require a mystical communication. The fact that St. Teresa, in supernatural prayer, received an infused knowledge of God's presence in everything through His creative immensity, is absolutely no proof that this metaphysical truth, accessible as it is to reason alone, would require a mystical experience in order to be known. Because all pagan philosophers have in fact shown themselves unable to elucidate the notion of creation, that does not prove that that concept is inaccessible to philosophical reason and, of itself, demands the light of revelation. Because for some men, the types of metaphysical experience of which we have just been speaking provide, on some points, a substitute for metaphysical science properly so called that does not prove that, of itself, metaphysics requires, in order to exist as a perfectly certain science and to reach being efficaciously, that it be completed by such intuitions.

31. Another degree, lying between metaphysical speculation and infused contemplation, is provided by what is called acquired contemplation, which is a kind of fruit of the exercise of meditation. We are not here concerned with the controversy which the notion of acquired contemplation has raised; but, following the Carmelite theologians and Father Garrigou-Lagrange, we do admit the existence of acquired contemplation, of which the prayer of active

---

86 In Jean-Paul's autobiography mention is made of a like intuition: "One morning, while I was still a child, I was standing on the threshold of my house and looked to the left, towards the wood-shed, when suddenly this idea came to me out of the sky like a bolt from the blue: *I am an I* and from that moment it never left me; my ego had seen itself for the first time and for ever."

87 Exod. xxxv, 30–35.

recollection described by St. Teresa in Chapter XVIII of *The Way of Perfection* seems to be the loftiest moment. But we want to point out that this contemplation, supernatural, indeed, in its object and in the virtue of faith from which it proceeds yet natural in its mode, and, by definition, quite remote from the passivity proper to the superhuman world of the gifts, cannot be called mystical; it still remains on this side of the experience in which the soul truly suffers things divine.

On the other hand, because it deals with revealed mysteries, it is absolutely outside and beyond not only metaphysical science, but the whole order of truths accessible to reason of themselves.

Consequently, we do not find in this case, either, any indication of a necessity immanent to the essence of metaphysics to transcend its own limits and integrate mystical experience within itself. There are—and this will be the burden of our final remarks—there are, we say, living relations within the soul's synergetic activity between mystical experience and philosophy; but they are there without any transfusion or any blending of their natures. Considering the nature of philosophy and the exigencies of its essence, philosophy does not of itself require mystical experience. Any intermediaries that may be found between the two fall outside the proper sphere of metaphysical science either essentially and by their object (as in the case of prayers of acquired contemplation), or by their mode, that is, in the way in which such knowledge is given to the soul (as in the case of certain experiences or metaphysical intuitions).

Natural Analogies of Mystical Experience

32. Even though an experience of things divine, properly so called, exists only in the supernatural order, do we not find even in the natural order (we have already noted this point in connection with the effects of the natural love of God) ways of knowing which are, as it were, *analogies* of that experience? Most certainly. The various kinds of metaphysical intuition or experience that we were just discussing offer examples of it. In a much more general way, moreover, every natural knowledge by way of inclination or sympathy or connaturality can be said to furnish a more-or-less remote analogy of mystical experience.

33. Where in the natural order do we find at every turn knowledge by way of inclination? In that vast realm of judgments about action: practical judgments. That is the field par excellence of knowledge by connaturality, for such knowledge necessarily intervenes in prudential judgments wherein the intellect has to judge through conformity with right will, because the object is singular and contingent. A moment ago we recalled Aristotle's phrase: *the virtuous man is the measure of human acts*; he judges human acts in accordance with the inclination of his virtue. In the classical example given by the Stagirite

and repeated by St. Thomas, the chaste man judges by inclination matters affecting chastity in consulting his own interior bent. These judgments certainly have an intellectual value and St. Thomas is careful not to belittle them. (On the contrary, he makes them the highest instrument of our moral life.) They are, however, judgments that pertain to practical intellectuality, which is shot through and through with will and appetite. They are always alien to the speculative modes of science and philosophy.

At this point let it be noted that the moral virtues—and even the natural beginnings of such virtues within us—create a certain affinity in the soul with the *spiritual order*, in the most indefinite sense of that term. In this way they can incline the intellect, with scant efficacy however, to instinctive judgments about the great truths of natural religion. That is one of the notable ingredients of the philosophy of the *vicaire savoyard*: to wit, dispositions towards these truths, aspirations towards metaphysical wisdom. It is none the less clear, however, that we are, meanwhile, far from wisdom, very far from possessing any means of making sure judgments about problems of first philosophy. On the other hand, judgments of that kind are not susceptible of certitude unless we take for granted in reality the more-or-less conscious apperceptions of common sense or spontaneous intelligence, which, of course, belong to the rational order.

34. Matters having to do with moral action are not, however, the only ones that have to be considered in the realm of the practical intellect. Knowledge by connaturality has its place among the activities of the artist, too, in matters of art and poetry.

Nor do we mean aesthetic contemplation alone—that contemplation which places us in immediate connivance with the object and in which, on a lower level, a distant image of mystical contemplation has often been, quite rightly, discerned.[88]

We mean the virtue of art itself. If in the natural order anyone has entered into a sort of agreement and, if one may dare to say so, a kind of metaphysical conspiracy with God as cause of beings, it is not the philosopher but the poet. He is the one who, after the manner of a man, also creates; his art is the grandson of God, according to Dante's expression. *"Il faut ignorer son art,"* Claudel once said, *"pour trouver au Votre quelque defaut."* The poet is, therefore, much better prepared than anyone else to understand things that are from on high, to know the various kinds of metaphysical experience we have been discussing. His proper task is to create an object that brings joy to the spirit in

---

88   The psychological process is, however, quite different in each case. Confronted by a beautiful object we first perceive the beauty before becoming connatural with the object. It is that very perception which renders us sympathetic to the object with a sympathy that will, in turn, be able to determine a knowledge (cf. *Art and Scholasticism*, n. 55). In mystical experience, on the other hand, it is connaturality that makes us perceive.

which the brilliance of a form shines forth. He perceives in things and brings forth a sign, weak though it may be, of the spirituality within them; he is connaturalized, not with God Himself, but with the mystery that is scattered in things and which has come down from God, the invisible powers at play within the universe.

Prayer, holiness, mystical experience—poetry, even pure poetry, is none of these things. But it is their most beautiful and most dangerous moral symbol.[89] Because it detects allusions scattered throughout nature, and because nature is an allusion to grace, poetry unwittingly gives us a foretaste, a hidden desire for supernatural life. A man who has never written a poem, but who is truly a poet, said to us one day: "I do not believe it is possible to be a poet and an atheist." Yet, for all that, he did not imagine that poetry should, therefore, be an integral part of philosophy.

35. Finally, to bring these observations to a close, we must not forget the most obvious and natural analogies of mystical contemplation, the ones that mystical language currently uses: human love, with all its trials and joys, with the dim though profound experience of another person which it produces—even with its most deadly madness; for things divine are so exalted and transcendent that sometimes they can find the means of showing forth some of their analogies only in the negative guises of sin.[90]

---

89   On this aspect of poetry, as well as on the distinction which should be made, when we use these words in their strictest meaning, between art as such and poetry, cf. our study "The Frontiers of Poetry," *Art and Scholasticism* (London, Sheed and Ward, 1933), p. 90, and our *Réponse à Jean Cocteau* (Paris, Stock, 1926).

90   Analogy is a very delicate matter and difficult to handle. The danger has always existed of taking an analogy between essentially distinct terms, even between terms infinitely distant from one another (so that one of the analogates is formally divine by participation and the other, perhaps, sinful), for a continuity of nature or tendency. Plato and a host of mystical heresies are testimony to that. And on that score it is necessary at the present day to point out the difficulties of a certain type of literature that usurps the name of "mystical" and runs the risk of compromising the best efforts of present-day art—efforts that are already difficult enough in themselves. "*There is but one love,*" wrote a Reverend Father, carried away by his own lofty feelings and the dialectic of the Banquet, some years ago. "We love God and man with the same heart; the object varies, as does the moving principle, but the feelings are identical (I am speaking of love, not of licentiousness). Take a human love, cleanse it of all its ugliness, all its insufficiencies, idealize it until it is ineffable, extend it to infinity, inform it with grace: if you bring such a passion to bear on the only Being capable of receiving it, you will have mystical love."

This idealism is as false as it is ambitious. If the object varies, and if grace informs it, is it not clear that a love specified by a divine object and proceeding from sanctifying grace is intrinsically different from human love, the one being supernatural *quoad substantiam*, the other being natural; one being purely spiritual, the other composed of flesh and spirit even as man himself? "Bring such a

The Song of Songs and St. Paul's teaching of the great mystery of Christ's union with the Church under the image of marriage invite us to see in the love of man and woman an image which may be impure but always retains something of its original nobility and metaphysical dignity, an image of a better and essentially holy love. There is nothing stronger among the things of earth: and yet it is a simple image, a weak and rather inconsistent image compared to the thing it signifies. If the image is so overpowered by the burden of its likeness that a creature can scarcely be truly loved without a demand for the infinite wherein human love immolates itself, why may not the trials and mutual give-and-take of such a love, the gift that love demands of those persons who constantly reveal themselves to one another, why may not these be the most direct analogy of the trials, exchanges and mutual gifts of mystical love? This, too, is worth noting: the more innocent a soul is, the less it hesitates, it seems, to use for things divine a language of symbols for that of which, in the human order, it has no experience.

Connections Between Metaphysics and Mysticism

36. One final question suggests itself: does the drawing of an absolute distinction between mystical experience and metaphysics, as we have done, suppress every organic relation between them?

Certainly not. There are vital relations between them. It is fitting to affirm the existence of those relations and to attempt to render their nature more precise. They imply at the same time: (1) *an inefficacious aspiration*; (2) *a factual*

---

love to bear on the only Being, etc. . . ." is a phrase which, if the truth be told, has absolutely no meaning—or else it signifies an error. For either that idealized passion remains natural in its essence, and then it cannot attain God as an object efficaciously loved above all else, it cannot be brought to bear on God to constitute a genuine mystical love; or else, it is supernatural in its essence (love of charity). In that case, it does not have *to be brought to bear* on God because God Himself specifies it, it bears on Him primarily and above all else. A man does love God and his own beloved with the same heart, yes; but he does not do so with the same love.

We acknowledge and appreciate the generous intentions of the author we are criticizing here, but we also feel compelled to point out that religious, happily cut off by their three vows from the tempests of the world, have something better to do than platonize about Eros. The less-protected life of the layman, struggling in this vale of tears, at least assures him of a much more reliable experience on certain subjects.

Love of charity can inform and vivify profane love; in addition, our poor psychological mechanisms can give rise to many accidental interventions and collusions between these two loves, especially in certain cases of dubious mysticism. But then it is all the more important that the essential difference between the two be well noted: the first is in no sense a "sublimation" of the second, it is a love *with a more sublime essence*, one in which the marks of profane love are found *analogically*.

dependence within the subject and by reason of the subject, of metaphysics in respect to mystical experience.

Metaphysics can be said to aspire in some way to mystical experience but without being able to achieve it and without making it, in all strictness, necessary for its own proper completion. Let my thought on this point be clearly understood. We have said that of itself metaphysics does not demand or postulate mystical experience in order that it may be constituted within its own species or have an efficacious grasp on the intelligibly real and arrive at the perfection of certitude that belongs to it in virtue of its very essence. It is, however, a general law that the lower—without for that reason quitting its own nature and its specific bounds—always tends to the higher and seeks to make contact with it: *supremum infimi attingit ad infimum supremi.* Consequently, we now say, which in no way contradicts the preceding thesis but rather completes it, that metaphysics naturally engenders in the soul a certain velleity it is unable to satisfy, a confused and indeterminate desire for a higher knowledge that is only genuinely attained in mystical experience, in the contemplation of the saints.

How can that be? First of all, because there are many problems, especially those concerning man's destiny and the conduct of the universe, that metaphysics raises but does not solve—or solves imperfectly—and whose solution, given by faith, is seen in its complete truth and fittingness only in the light of infused contemplation. And secondly, because metaphysics, like every human science, leaves us dissatisfied. Being oriented towards the First Cause and naturally desiring to know it perfectly, it is natural for it to make us desire— with an efficacious and conditional desire, but with a desire that is none the less real—to see that Cause in itself, to contemplate God's essence.[91] But it

---

91   The natural desire to know the First Cause in itself is not the supernatural desire for the beatific vision. The *specifying object* of these two desires is formally different.

In the first case, the object of my desire is the God whom I know (by reason) *as the first cause of beings* and to whom I transfer—as it were, extrinsically and in virtue of the "ascending" analogy proper to metaphysics—the designation "known in Himself or in His essence," which is borrowed from various created things that I know in this way, *but without knowing either if or how that is possible in the case of God* and by leaving the nature of such knowledge *in a state of complete indetermination.* In short, I want to know, as He is in Himself, the God *who is known to me through His effects.*

In the second case, I want to know, as He is in Himself, the God who is known to me according to His Own essence. The object of my desire is the God whom I know (by faith) *secundum suam propriam quidditatem* (and as the Trinity), the God whom I know as able to give Himself to me *according as He is the object of the divine knowledge itself,* in virtue of an unfathomable communication of which, Revelation assures me, the Divine Essence can *formally be the term,* and which, the "superanalogy" descending from faith—seeking as it does among created things for the means of designating it—tells me, consists in seeing God in His essence as I am seen by Him.

The Christian who has the notion of the mystery of the beatific vision knows that "knowing the First Cause in itself" is, in fact or materially (*identice*), the same thing that theology calls "seeing Deity face to face" or "as it is." The philosopher as such, reduced to the sole powers of reason, does not know this because he has no notion of the second term in that identity.

His desire to know the first cause in itself is an elicited desire flowing from the nature of the intelligence, elicited but quite spontaneous, indeliberate, instinctive and aroused by a knowledge of first instance which precedes reflection on the means of realizing such a desire. He will see it, upon reflection, to be conditional (or else, when he has seen that no merely human or natural process of knowing is capable of achieving God in Himself, he will be able to judge it as beyond realization. Is not the way in which Hindu thought aspires to the Nirvana testimony rendered at the same time to the natural desire of knowing God in Himself and to the intellect's despair of seeing Him in that way?).

Thus, the desire of nature to see the First Cause is conditional in that it is simply natural. That is why, if man had been placed in the order of pure nature, wherein the means of reaching a vision of the Divine Essence would have been lacking to him, that natural desire would have been frustrated (or only satisfied by lesser substitutes procuring a relative and changing beatitude) without any violation of the principle of finality which protests against the possibility of an unconditional desire of nature being in vain.

Once man is raised to the supernatural order, however, he realizes, on the one hand, that knowing the First Cause in itself is the same as seeing the God of faith face to face; and, on the other hand—since the law assures him he can attain absolute happiness—his natural desire of attaining the First Cause in itself, being perfected by grace and the desire for vision, becomes supernatural and, at the same stroke, unconditional. Then he understands that, if Nature's desire to see the First Cause could not be satisfied (even though it be through obediential power and by means of being raised to an order above the whole of nature), the principle of finality would be violated. For inasmuch as that desire is conditional as regards nature alone, it is actually unconditional for him since grace has perfected it through a supernatural desire.

We believe this manner of considering the question is quite in harmony with St. Thomas' argument (*Sum. Theol.*, I–II, 3, 8, and I, 12, 1). St. Thomas only demonstrates the possibility of man's seeing the Divine Essence—because without it a desire of nature would be vain—by proceeding as a theologian and not as a mere philosopher, by presupposing the possibility of man's attaining perfect or absolute beatitude (faith alone assures us of that, for that kind of beatitude is beyond nature, *beatitudo excedit omnem naturam creatam* [I–II, 5, 7] [cf. II–II, 4, 7, ad 2] and, consequently, reason all by itself can only bring arguments of suitability to bear on it) and, thus, only by envisaging a desire of nature made unconditional by the supernatural desire that perfects it and proceeds from the knowledge of faith. Thus *quamvis homo naturaliter inclinetur in finem ultimum, non tamen potest naturaliter illum consequi, sed solum per gratiam, et hoc est propter eminentiam illius finis* (*in Boet. de Trin.*, q. 6, a. 4, ad 5) . Vita aeterna est quoddam bonum excedens proportionem naturae creatae, quia etiam excedit cognitionem et desiderium ejus, secundum illud I *ad Cor.*, 2: "nec oculus vidit, nec auris audivit, nec in cor hominis ascendit"; et inde est, quod nulla natura creata est sufficiens principium actus meritorii vitae aeternae, nisi superaddatur aliquod supernaturale donum, quod gratia dicitur (*Sum. Theol.*, I–II, 114, 2). Cf. *Sum. Theol.*, I, 12, 4;

cannot succeed. When grace supervenes and comes to fruition within a man, it does not obtain for him that vision here below, but only a foretaste or substitute for it, to wit, an infused contemplation which fulfills the highest aspirations of metaphysics but of which metaphysics has not the slightest notion and at which it always remains astonished: a crucified wisdom, which is folly for the wisdom of pure reason. Lacking supernatural gifts, metaphysical aspirations towards a knowledge of pure vision and an intuitive possession of the absolute run the risk of leading the soul to some more-or-less deceptive substitute for infused contemplation. It can, in fine, be said that the intellect, being a perfection belonging to the transcendental order, realized in diverse degrees throughout the scale of spirits, tends with an impotent desire, to surpass the specific conditions that attach to it in the human being, wherein it exists at its very lowest level. By this we can understand that nostalgia for higher contemplation to which so many schools of philosophy bear testimony in the vast reaches of human history.

37. On the other hand, if the subject and its synergic activity are considered, it becomes quite clear that in living things, formal discontinuity does not do away with solidarity. Solidarity between energies of the human order and supernatural powers is very deep in a soul wherein the gifts of grace hold sway. There is no question but that mystical experience is absolutely independent of philosophy and gets along marvelously without it; and it is not among philosophers that great contemplatives are ordinarily found. But looking at things concretely, metaphysics is found in us to have a certain dependence on such experience—even though in itself it is independent of mystical experience as such—because it is inferior to it.

How is that? Because virtues that perfect our intellect are like so many hierarchized and solidary lights, the lower being strengthened within their own proper order by their conjunction with higher. In the same way, says John of St. Thomas,[92] inferior angels illumined by superior angels, are made stronger within themselves and in their own proper intellectual light. Thus, metaphysical wisdom is strengthened by supernatural faith and theology, even insofar as truths proper to it are concerned, truths which are demonstrable by reason alone.

Now if the lights of faith and speculative theology bring home to the philosopher with greater force, perfection, and certitude his act of purely rational adherence to objects of philosophical knowledge, such as the existence of the first transcendent cause, and even to the first principles of reason,[93] for how much greater reason ought the light of wisdom par excellence, mystical

---

I–II, 5, 1 and 5; II–II, 2, 3; *De Verit.*, q. 8, a. 1, 2, 3; *Cont. Gent.*, III, 48, 50, 51, 52, 57, 63; *Compend. Theol.*, Chs. 104, 105, 106.

92   *Curs. Theol.*, II–II, q. 1, disp. 2, a. 1, n. 24 (Vivès, t. VII).
93   Cf. John of St. Thomas, *Curs. Theol.*, I P., a. 1, disp. 2, a. 6 (n. 17) and a. 9 (t. I).

experience of the things divine, aid and purify the philosophical intellect. The example of St. Thomas himself illustrates this truth magnificently. And if it is true that the human intellect is of its very nature so weak, and is further weakened by the heritage of original sin so that it cannot attain a complete philosophic wisdom without admixture of error except with the aid of grace, then metaphysics, one might feel, could in fact only keep itself pure among men if metaphysics were from time to time strengthened from on high by the experience of things divine.

38. People oftentimes misunderstand the significance of Thomistic distinctions. The three wisdoms—metaphysical, theological and mystical—are said to be really distinct because they have different formal objects and correspond to degrees of light which are specifically distinct. Here it is a question of the proper nature of these wisdoms considered in themselves. Now inasmuch as metaphysical wisdom has a specifying object that belongs to the natural order, it does not by reason of itself, *ratione sui ipsius*, entail any intrinsically necessitating demand for mystical contemplation but only inefficacious yearning for it. In virtue of the proper requirements of its essence it does not demand any cognitive energies other than those of natural reason.

Let us not forget, however, that such wisdom exists in a subject, in a human soul. And that subject does not exist in the state of pure nature. It exists in a state of fallen nature or in the state of grace.

Metaphysical wisdom, a wisdom belonging to an order that is essentially natural, will never succeed, as a matter of actual fact, in establishing itself within us without stain of error and in avoiding all the accidents that threaten it, if no aid from above comes to assist the energies of natural reason, whether such help comes from habitual or actual grace; for our nature is weak and has been wounded. It is not enough to possess gifts of grace in order to avoid error in metaphysics. That, alas, is only too evident. But a condition can be necessary (in the present case, *morally* necessary) without, for that reason, being sufficient. Given the state of nature in which we find ourselves, if metaphysical wisdom succeeds in taking hold in man and is able to maintain itself free from fault—at least along the narrow path of a higher tradition—it is because the supernatural energies of grace, at certain times and in one way or another, will have given succor to reason.

Thus, by reason of the subject, *ratione subjecti*, by reason of a subject that is wounded in its nature and called or actually raised to the supernatural order, metaphysical wisdom clearly requires, in the normal course of things, to be strengthened by higher lights and pass onward to the wisdom of the saints. Without mentioning other differences between the Thomistic conception and Mr. Blondel's, the conflict on this score is limited, it seems to us, to this point: one explains a certain spiritual dynamism by the requirements and essential needs of knowing and philosophy, the other explains it by the conditions of the subject and the synergy in that subject of specifically distinct intellectual virtues.[94]

The fact remains that, if the distinctions are made that should be made—as we have tried to show elsewhere[95]—between the nature of philosophy and its status in the subject, we have to affirm that of itself philosophy is at once a purely rational knowledge and intrinsically depends only upon principles belonging to the natural order, and that it can only find the human conditions required for its full development in truth if it grows up under the heaven of faith.

39. And finally, let it be noted that if it is true that mystical experience is the very highest point in the life of the soul where knowledge and love bear their noblest fruit, the philosopher, the metaphysician, will certainly find the greatest possible advantage (even for his own proper object) in interesting himself in the study of so transcendent an activity. But he can do so fruitfully only if he has recourse to the light of theology, which alone is proportionate to such an object. It is a scandal to the intellect, a profound offence against the sense of order, to see psychologists and sociologists—or even philosophers and metaphysicians—lay hands on mystical experience in order to judge its nature by their own light, that is to say, to systematically misunderstand it. The philosopher needs to be initiated into one or the other of the lower sciences, to mathematics, for example, when he wants to deal with certain questions. He ought, in the same way, to borrow light from a higher science when he seeks to deal, even for his own philosophical ends, with an object that essentially surpasses philosophy.[96]

---

94   In being so limited, the conflict does not, as we have already indicated elsewhere, lose any of its gravity: for in philosophy the reasons given for a conclusion are just as important or more important than the conclusion itself (Cf. *Réflexions sur l'intelligence*, p. 86.)

95   "De la philosophie chrétienne," *Questions Disputées* (Paris, Desclée de Brouwer et Cie, 1933.

96   On this question see Fr. Maréchal's study: "Science empirique et psychologie religieuse" (*Études sur la psychologie des mystiques*, t. I, Paris, Alcan, 1924); Roland Dalbiez's articles on "Une nouvelle inteprétation de saint Jean de la Croix" (*Vie Spirituelle*, 1928: "an integral interpretation of mystical experience will be theological or it will not be integral," writes this author very justly); and also Fr. Benoit Lavaud's articles on "Psychologie indépendante et prière chrétienne" (*Revue Thomiste*, 1929) and on "Les problèmes de la vie mystique" (*Vie Spirituelle*, June 1931); Etienne Borne, "Spiritualité Bergsonienne et Spiritualité Chrétienne," *Études Carmélitaines*, Oct. 1932; T. L. Penido, "Dieu dans le bergsonisme" (*Questions Disputées*), Paris, Desclée de Brouwer et Cie, 1934.
      These pages were already in the hands of the printer when Mr. Henri Bergson's work, *Les deux sources de la morale et de la religion*, appeared. In its own way it illustrates the things we have written here and have explained at somewhat greater length in our "disputed question," *De la philosophie chrétienne*, already cited. Everything human is of interest to the philosopher. It is eminently fitting,

then, for him to meditate on that which is at the very heart of the human realm: mystical life and holiness. Yet while retaining his own proper point of view and his own way of proceeding, he should, in virtue of the demands of his object, have recourse to the information of theology, to whose scientific competency that object belongs. For in a case like this the reality he is studying is not purely natural but stems from principles beyond those of reason alone. If the unbelieving philosopher cannot admit those principles nor, as a result, the theological science founded upon them, the net result must be that his information will inevitably be deficient.

This is not the place to examine a book in which there appears, along with calm loftiness of thought, a scrupulous attention to experience, the delightful subtlety we so admire in Mr. Bergson, the same refusal to depart from radical empiricism and that "carence ontologique" (G. Marcel) with which his philosophy must be reproached. We shall confine ourselves to a few brief remarks appropriate to the subject that concerns us in this present chapter. It is not our purpose to criticize a courageous thought which, in spite of its philosophical garb, follows a pure spiritual trajectory, by the sheer concern to keep faith with its inner light. Our concern for what is true compels us, however, to set forth very clearly certain points of disagreement.

Mr. Bergson has had no difficulty in transcending the schemas of ordinary phenomenalist psychology and pointing out among the great mystics—whose "intellectual robustness" he so admires—souls that have achieved a life in some way superhuman. His book contains some singularly moving pages on this theme that disclose a more than deferential, at times even affectionate, attention to realities experienced as present and efficacious. And yet the total interpretation he himself suggests (and in which, in the absence of the proper instruments needed for a true analysis, one must be grateful for many correct views *ex communibus*) indicates that, as long as philosophy believes it must ignore the mystery of grace and the cross, it cannot attain matters of mystical life in their true nature—even when it does honor them with good faith. The question may arise as to whether or not Mr. Bergson's work, inasmuch as it is bound up with a system of ideas set forth in *Creative Evolution*, does not, in spite of everything, constitute an effort to reduce the spiritual to the biological, I mean to a biology so transcendent that it is conceived as the creative source of the universe, yet which remains biological throughout in the sense in which that word refers to the degrees of life characterized by the organic and the psychic, where life is made manifest by the animation of matter and where immanent activity is, consequently, essentially bound up with conditions of transitive action and productivity. It is true that, short of the world of grace and supernatural life, spirituality in man never transcends the biological concept except in a more-or-less imperfect way.

Since credence is given to the experience of the mystics, why not go the whole way with their testimony? When they say they are joined to their Beginning as to the life of their life they are not thinking of opening themselves to some vital impulse or to an anonymous creative urge that could only be conceived of as personal by analogy with a certain fullness of enthusiasm or emotion. Rather, they are testifying that they are turned towards the depths of a supreme personality in the fullest sense of the word, they are clinging fast to deity itself, to an infinite "denseness" of being and perfection, to a sovereignly subsistent *Other* whose existence and name they know with the utmost certitude before "negatively" experiencing the fact that He is beyond every name and every thought. Far from being disinterested in such a question, they know perfectly well, and never tire of testifying, that the principle with which they are united is "the transcendent cause of all things." They bear witness to the fact (and on that score Mr. Bergson's book seems to leave us, at the least, in an equivocal position) that their will and love are borne not towards a pure and endless surpassing, the joy in a creative drive that is completely devoid of any goal, but rather towards an infinite end. They testify that the wondrous movement which gives them life has no meaning and existence except to bear them along towards that final End wherein they will be fixed in a life without waning. They attest that their joy is not really theirs but their Lord's, and that that joy was crucified. They testify that their experience of the things of God has faith as its proximate and proportionate principle, that it is inseparable from the teaching whereby the first Truth made Himself known to them, and that, if it is obscure and only gained by love, it is still a supreme knowledge since, in such unknowing, the intellect is fed by its noblest object. They are witnesses to the fact that whereas mystical contemplation does overflow into action (for the saint's wisdom is not purely theoretical, like the philosopher's wisdom, but practical as well; it rules human life according to divine rules [*Sum. Theol.*, II–II, 19, 7]; and here, in effect, we have a general sign of the superiority of Christian mysticism), nevertheless, its "final stage" is not to "lose itself in action" and in "an irresistible urge that sweeps the soul onward into undertakings on the grandest possible scale." Among the great Christian mystics, for example among the Apostles and the founders of Orders, action is never anything more than an outpouring of contemplation, the primacy of which becomes all the more apparent as union with God becomes more perfect. Moreover, if their love is open to "the infinite" of mankind, it is because it is primarily and essentially ordered to God in Three Persons and to the person of one's neighbor. And finally, the mystics forbid us to attribute to any vital urge, marching onward to the conquest of this world, something that essentially arises from divine grace, superior to any nature that has been or can be created.

Mr. Bergson has adopted a point of view "from which," he writes, "the divinity of all men is apparent," and from which, as a result, "it is of scant importance whether Christ is or is not called a man" (p. 256). His philosophical doctrine (which dissolves all ontological values), his abandoning of practically the whole order of properly rational and intellectual certitudes within the metaphysical, moral and religious sphere, his basic omission of the fact that mystical experience presupposes the reality of its object, known naturally and supernaturally, and is nothing if it is not adherence to subsistent Truth—all these slant his theology, in spite of itself, towards a kind of thoroughgoing Pelagianism wherein distinctions that matter most are completely neglected.

If a person feels that on the subject of mysticism it is proper and fitting to listen to the mystics themselves and that the only mysticism which has fully succeeded is "the mysticism of the great Christian mystics" (p. 243), then surely it is unreasonable to reject their testimony about that which is more important to them than life itself, and to fail to listen to them when they state that mystical experience, far from having a content that may be regarded as independent of revealed faith (p. 268), is nothing but the perfect blossoming of that faith. It is at this point, as I know only too well, that the philosopher is bound to raise certain metaphysical questions and to turn to higher *sources*. But does he not prefer truth to philosophy itself and its αὐτάρκεια? He will thus be led to recognize, as we have done in the present chapter, that every genuine mysticism which has developed in a non-Christian atmosphere, since it finds its perfect exemplar in the contemplation of the saints who have germinated within the Church in unending profusion, should be looked upon as a fruit of that same supernatural life which Christ—Who is sovereignly free with His gifts—shares with souls of good will who do not visibly belong to His fold.

CHAPTER VII

AUGUSTINIAN WISDOM

A TYPICAL PROBLEM

1. IF, BY USING A PARTICULAR EXAMPLE, one would try to bring to light the sort of problem that may arise in the order of the most secret dimensions of the affairs of the spirit, that mysterious "depth" wherein the mind turns back upon itself and its own content and differentiates its works, no longer in respect to the objective degrees of abstraction and intelligibility but, rather, by the liberty of its own standpoints and its own proper purposes, the history of western thought offers to reflection the reciprocal *situation* of St. Augustine and St. Thomas as an outstanding case.

A bishop of the fourth-fifth centuries, a Scholastic of the thirteenth—not only were their eras, controversies and intellectual surroundings utterly unlike, but their tasks, too, were quite different. One was a fisher of men, the other a builder of truths. The task for the one was to bring Christian doctrine to birth, to uncover it and set it up in opposition to the wisdom of this world; for the other, it was to perfect Christian doctrine, to consolidate it in and for itself. One is a well-spring, the other a fruit.

Theirs were quite different vocations, quite different testimonies, too. The dwelling-place of the one was the heart of humanity, knowing it fully. His was to bear witness to sovereign truth with a voice from the depths of the soul; even on the purest heights of his theology we still recognize that voice. A prodigal son, a lover, a convert, a man saved from the worst errors of the flesh and the worst error of the spirit, a man whom the very experience of evil had instructed and filled to repletion before the experience of grace aggrandized him even to the touch of things divine; a man made to govern men and feed souls from generation to generation. The dwelling-place of the other was the heart of the intellect, enjoying the company of angels. And, with their tranquil and powerful gaze, he lights up for us divine secrets and reveals us to ourselves. An ever-faithful son, a chaste man, a crystal fountain wherein the waters of divine wisdom have never ceased to increase; a mind made to shine forth throughout the centuries and to teach other minds.

To compare St. Augustine and St. Thomas is not only a delicate and difficult task, but also a paradoxical one and, at first glance, impossible. The intellect has to forgo its most natural method of making comparisons, which consists in setting things side by side on the same plane, confronting one with the other in the same light, seeking points of coincidence and divergence. In this case, however, the mind must move from one plane to another, from one light to another and discover unity in the very midst of non-coincidence. *The method of Agreement, the method of Disagreement*—one is no better than the other. They both spring from the same optical illusion.

On the one hand, a comparison of Augustine's originality with that of Thomas, and vice-versa, is out of the question. Their intellectual attitudes and their systems—if St. Augustine be reduced to a system—do not coincide. On the other hand, between their wisdoms, there is not only agreement and harmony but fundamental unity. How, then, are we to resolve this antinomy? Well, without entering into the controversies that divide specialists, we would like to point out what seems to us the principle of a solution.

2. "The heart has its order; the mind has its order by premiss and proof; the heart has another.... Jesus Christ and Saint Paul follow the order, not of the mind but of charity, for they meant not to teach but to inflame. Similarly Saint Augustine. The essence of that order is digression at every point with constant reference to the main end, never losing sight of that."[1] Pascal's view requires certain clarifications, but it does suggest the essential point: a difference of order, of formal point of view, of *lumen*. Jesus Christ did not only seek to kindle a fire in the hearts of men; He meant to teach. But He taught in the order and light of divine revelation itself; St. Paul taught in the order and light of prophecy in its highest and holiest form. Both were too exalted to be satisfied with philosophizing. Like them, St. Augustine had the order of charity. However copiously he may philosophize, it is in love that he instructs and, by one and the same movement, he aims to turn the human being in a practical way to his final end. How? We will deal with that in a moment.

St. Thomas, for his part, has the order of intellect—set to work by love in order to exhale love, but carrying on its work in the pure atmosphere of objective demands (which seem cold only to those who do not love the truth). It is in the order and light of theological science and of philosophy that he teaches us—disciplines that proceed according to the mode of pure knowing.

The Gift of Wisdom Making Use of Discourse

3. What, then, is the proper source of Augustine's teaching? We think it is located on a higher plane. It is the wisdom of the Holy Ghost. I said he teaches in love. Why so, except that he teaches us in the order and light of the gift of wisdom? That is the key we have been looking for. That is the wisdom which provides him with his *point of view*; from that wisdom his thought darts out to

---

1   Pascal, *Pensées* (*vide, Pascal's Pensées*, with an English translation, brief notes and Introduction, by H. F. Stewart, D.D., New York, Pantheon Books, 1950, pp. 12 and 13).

embrace all things and ceaselessly to lead them back to their center. In the period of his philosophical intemperance, his wanderings among the sects and systems, he was seeking wisdom without knowing it. He gained it through grace alone, and without doubt one could descry from that point of view, a progressive growth and strengthening of his convert-mind. Inasmuch as he teaches in the full strength of the anointing he received, he draws all his power from that wisdom.

When I say that the fountain-head of St. Augustine's teaching, which is on a lower plane than that of St. Paul and, *a fortiori*, than that of Christ, is nevertheless more exalted than that of St. Thomas (which proceeds according to the human and rational mode, and is much more perfect in that mode), let it not be understood that St. Thomas himself was lacking in that infused wisdom. He abounded in it, just as he abounded in mystical graces. Thomas needed that wisdom to achieve his work as a theologian. But that work itself lay strictly within theology as a science (and within philosophy), which are undoubtedly wisdoms, but in the human mode, and (hence) at the same time, techniques inferior to infused wisdom. Offices and functions in the city of God are well defined. St. Thomas' teaching function, as universal as theological discipline itself, was not that of an Augustine, which was still more universal, above and beyond all technique.

4. This would be the moment to recall that the wisdom of the saints, which judges things divine by the inclination of love or connaturality, *compassio sive connaturalitas*, in virtue of the very union with God,[2] not only presupposes faith but charity as well; that it is experimental; that it is not only speculative but also practical, proceeding from union with God, guiding our activity towards such a union, regulating human life in accordance with divine rules; and, finally, that it can use discourse and fashion arguments.[3] Picture that wisdom to yourself, no longer ineffably concentrated on suffering the things of God—as happens in mystical contemplation—but majestically overflowing into communicable knowledge: not in an attempt to express in lyrics, like St. John of the Cross, or, if I may venture to say so (and without any play on words

---

2   Cf. John of St. Thomas, *Curs. Theol.*, I–II, q. 70, disp. 18, a. 1, 2, 4.

3   John of St. Thomas teaches that the gifts of wisdom and knowledge, though not of themselves discursive, still "do not always proceed without discourse: (1) because investigation and reasoning are natural to man and the gifts of the Holy Ghost do not destroy, but perfect nature; (2) because even in the case of Christ's infused knowledge the possibility of discourse and comparison of terms is admitted by St. Thomas (III, q. 1 l, a. 5), (3) because we ordinarily do not experience a light within us that makes us understand truths without discourse or comparison" (*Curs. Theol.*, *loc. cit.*, a. 5, n. 6).

Moreover, we are considering here—and in all the developments that follow—not only acts, discursive in mode, produced by the gift of wisdom all by itself, but also, and particularly, acts, discursive in mode, produced by the gift of wisdom *using acquired rational knowledge and wisdom*.

intended), in oratorical expression, as a Bérulle will do, the mystical experience itself, but rather to spread out over the whole intelligible field and take over the whole play of rational energies, to *using* all the natural instruments of knowledge with that respect, that courtesy towards nature and reason, and also that confidence, ease, boldness and sovereign loyalty which are the gifts of true spiritual liberty—such is the wisdom of an Augustine and, more generally, of the Fathers. The common wisdom of the Christian, a wisdom doubly instinctive and spontaneous—for even the least instructed of the faithful have also received the Holy Ghost and His gifts and in this light make use of their natural reason and good sense—takes on its noblest proportions, properly paternal and episcopal, in the wisdom of those great spiritual pastors; the science of the theologian, not yet set apart in its state as a specialized discipline (that was the work of the Scholastics), is contained within it as in its source, in an eminent state. (The age of techniques had not as yet begun and theology is the first great technique of the Christian world.) This supreme wisdom conquers everything, appropriates everything, carries everything along in its universal current: the spoils of the Egyptians, all the treasures of the philosophers. Let us say, just to draw a clear line of demarcation, that the treasures in question are the instruments, not precisely of the science of theology as distinguished from the science of philosophy (these were not yet made explicit in their own proper nature), but of infused wisdom, the Wisdom of the Holy Ghost which dominates and envelops them, and is bound up with grace and charity.

Thus, the mission of the Fathers of the Church is seen in all its fullness. "The Fathers and the theologians"—that expression, constantly recurring in treatises of sacred doctrine, designates two quite distinct offices. Theology is to be found in theologians in its proper nature as a specialized science whose light is reason elevated by faith. Theology is found among the Fathers under a higher state. Its light is the very light of the gift of wisdom making use of reason. It proceeds even as a doctrine in the light of sanctifying grace. It is a *holy* doctrine. There will always be new Doctors in the Church. The age of the Fathers is definitely closed. It was the age of the great pouring forth of the gifts of the Holy Ghost which was needed for the spiritual begetting, the *education* of the Church. And what is especially important in the Fathers is the purity of the waters of that impetuous flood of the Spirit, far more, certainly, than the exact polishing of each of the stones, broken off from the old philosophical rock, which it bears along.

Platonic Reason and the Gifts of the Holy Ghost

5. The philosophy which St. Augustine employed (one of the greatest religious philosophies of humanity) is unquestionably faulty, a philosophy forcibly torn away from the last defence and spiritual justification of a dying paganism. It was the neo-Platonic philosophy. (He took what he found. And

who can read Plotinus without being grateful?)[4] In Augustine, however, that philosophy is an instrument of the gift of wisdom, and as a result of the superiority and heavenly transcendence of that gift and the divine mastery with which he handles the instrument he uses, no one had a clearer cognizance of grace than he did. The gift of the Spirit, in the power of love, is absolutely primary. It illumines, distinguishes, commands, rules, measures and bestows the right of jurisdiction over everything, *spiritualis judicat omnia*; it leaps within the Christian's breast like the streams of paradise to fecundate and renew the whole field of knowledge. A human instrument, certainly in no way mediocre, but imperfect, blunted and risky, and, for its manipulation, a hand, the most perfect, fearful and pious, intelligent and understanding, strong, prudent and wise, the irresistible light of a superhuman mind—such was the wondrous paradox of the wisdom of the Christian Plato.

Should we perceive (and who has perceived it better than St. Thomas) the living *meaning*, the direction, of that wisdom, the goal to which such a spirit using such an instrument is moving—it would be the pure universe of Christian truths, the eternal depths which are shown to us, the summits from which theology takes its rise. Should we evaluate such an instrument materially, cut off from the spirit that courses through it, we would become at once involved in an endless quarrel (in a vain attempt to turn St. Augustine into a neo-Platonist) or in a literal-minded search for discrepancies between him and St. Thomas.

6. Indeed, the really remarkable feature here, and one that should be regarded as a stroke of genius, of Augustine's *saintly genius*—is the true certainty of instinct, the supernatural tact by which, whilst remaining a Platonist and in close dependence on Plotinus in philosophy, he avoids (and as much cannot be said for all his disciples!) the most dangerous snares of Platonism, at one time, by magnificently correcting his Greek masters (as, for instance, when he constructs the world of divine ideas out of the world of Platonic exemplars), at another time, by leaving unsolved questions for which the Platonic equipment does not provide a key (for instance, those many questions about the soul and its origin), at still another time, by leaving unfinished, in a state of indetermination, pathetic because it is a state of expectancy, and at the same time, one of promise and restraint, certain great doctrines of his (like his doctrine of illumination) that he could not, with the equipment at hand, bring to a higher degree of precision without falling into serious error.

But what concerns us most and what regards the main purpose of this short study, is not the Platonic tool used by St. Augustine; it is his wisdom itself, insofar as it is above all, as we have said, the gift of wisdom using reason and

---

4   "Plotinus inter philosophiae professores cum Platone princeps." St. Thomas repeats these words of Macrobius (*Sum. Theol.*, I–II, 61, 5, *sed contra*).

discourse. Such a notion enables us to understand how St. Augustine constantly philosophizes and yet is in no sense the inventor of a philosophical system; how it is that many deficiencies still do not dim his light; how it is that he stands far above philosophy, even above theological science in the strict sense of the word, and yet compasses the whole domain of theology, philosophy and practical moral science. This is, we believe, in complete accord with the wondrous doctrine on wisdom St. Augustine himself has bequeathed us, and which has passed in its entirety—with the necessary precisions and distinctions—into the Thomistic synthesis.

When St. Augustine shows that science, as distinct from wisdom (the supreme science), is the product of inferior reason and knowledge in the twilight of created things, primarily directed towards the labor of action, whereas wisdom is the product of superior reason and knowledge in the light of divine things primarily directed to the repose of contemplation;[5] when he formulates the great law, which dominates civilizations, of the inevitable choice between wisdom and knowledge—for all the riches of the latter, while good and necessary in themselves, are still ordered to the poverty of wisdom, so that to choose them as an end is a crime of covetousness and avarice, a deadly turning to perishable goods; when, in incomparable psychological analyses, he describes the economy of knowledge and wisdom in the souls of the saints, it is quite clear that St. Augustine (without, indeed, eliminating the distinction between three wisdoms—metaphysical, theological and infused wisdom—which St. Thomas was to establish later but, rather, by remaining an utter stranger to that distinction because he thinks only of setting Christian wisdom over against the false wisdom of pagan philosophers) actually centers his whole notion of wisdom on wisdom in the highest sense, i.e., on infused wisdom. The flood of his thought, finding its source in such a wisdom, always returns to it and brings his every thought back to it. He looks upon profane and sacred science (insofar as the character of science is to be found in sacred knowledge itself) as enjoying some participation in that infused wisdom when, in the Christian soul, they are subordinated to it as they should be.

---

5   It is a well-known fact that when St. Thomas enumerated the gifts of the Holy Ghost, he first (*Sum. Theol.*, I–II, 68, 4) depicted the gift of knowledge as perfecting the practical intellect and the gift of wisdom as perfecting the speculative intellect. In so doing, he was clinging in a very literal way to St. Augustine's opinion. Later (II–II, 8, 6), he realized that both the gifts of wisdom and knowledge are speculative and practical, even as faith itself: the gift of wisdom has as its proper task to judge, as though experimentally, the truths of faith from the side of divine realities; the gift of knowledge, from the side of created realities. These two positions are not, however, incompatible. As John of St. Thomas remarks (*loc. cit.*, a. 7, n. 8), even though the wisdom of the saints is at once speculative and practical, it still predominates in speculation, whereas the gift of knowledge, because it proceeds through lower causes, predominates in practical knowledge—even though it is also speculative.

The Character of Augustine's Doctrine

7. The essential difference between St. Augustine's doctrine and St. Thomas' is one of point of view and perspective. In the latter, the point of view is that of theological wisdom in the strict sense of the word; in the former, it is that of infused wisdom. With St. Thomas we track down essences; with St. Augustine we are drawn to experience Him Whom we love. We have said St. Augustine's wisdom is the gift of wisdom using discourse. If we bear in mind the properties theologians usually recognize in the gift of wisdom,[6] we will understand St. Augustine's special point of view as well as the main characteristics of his doctrine, not to mention the marvelous flavor of his style, or that supratechnical spontaneity to which we called attention a little while ago, thanks to which the instinctive baptismal wisdom of the common run of Christians recognizes itself in him. For him, true philosophy—let us say, growth in wisdom—will be understood to be a path to beatitude, the true philosopher a friend of God, *verus philosophus amator Dei*:[7] it is the wisdom of the Holy Ghost. It will also be clear that while he knew perfectly well the essential distinction between purely rational knowledge and conclusions drawn from principles of faith, he never dreamed of systematically distinguishing between philosophical and theological disciplines. He did not set up a map of intellectual disciplines; he spurred his reason, illumined by faith, towards the enjoyment of God. We shall also understand how, while more sensitive than any other man to the proper values and dignity of speculation, and rejecting with his whole being (and, as a matter of fact, without being able even to conceive) what an age lost to grace was fifteen centuries later to know as "philosophical pragmatism," this ardent lover of the intellect was able to play around with a kind of lived pragmatism with the utmost liberty—the pragmatism of eternal salvation—and to integrate the movement of the will towards its final end into his wisdom—because infused wisdom proceeds from charity.

In St. Augustine's doctrine, faith in every case universally precedes and prepares the understanding. *Crede ut intelligas.* Why should it be so surprising, then, if the understanding in question is the knowledge of infused wisdom extended by discourse to the whole humanly explorable field? This knowledge presupposes theological faith, as well as theological charity. It is absolutely essential for St. Augustine's wisdom to proceed from faith, because from the very start it tends towards experimental union with God. By the same token, St. Augustine knows by experience that the sinner's wounded reason needs to be healed by *gratia sanans*,[8] if it is actually to recover the integrity of its natural vigor, even within the very order of truths that are in themselves

---

6   Cf. John of St. Thomas, *Les dons du Saint Esprit*; French tr. Ch. IV.
7   *De Civit. Dei*, VIII, 1.
8   "Quamvis enim nisi aliquid intelligat, nemo possit credere in Deum; tamen ipsa fide qua credit sanatur, ut intelligat ampliora" (*Enarr. in Psalm.*, CXVIII, enarr. 18, n 3).

accessible to demonstrations of reason. And it is in our concrete movement towards the First Truth that he seeks to guide and instruct us.

Augustine drills into us the fact that the soul only succeeds in finding God through a return and penetration *ad intus*, by withdrawing from things and the senses to prepare for lofty ascents within itself. The reason is that it is a matter of joining, within the heart's deepest recesses, the one who dwells there as in His own temple and in whom alone the heart can find its rest, not the God of philosophers and scholars—a God that can be reached without faith—not even the God of theologians—for He can be reached without charity—but the God of the saints, the Life of Life who offers Himself to us in grace and love.

When the soul experiences God in a mystical manner, it simultaneously experiences its own nature as a spirit at the hidden-most point of its sanctified activity. This two-fold experience, produced as it is under the special inspiration of the spirit of God and through His gifts, is like the supernatural completion of that inward-directed movement proper to every spirit. Such an experience, as far as everything relating to God and the soul is concerned, is the center of gravity for St. Augustine's doctrines. If we lose sight of it, the deepest meaning of these doctrines eludes us. Under its sway from the very start, his doctrines, even when, far away from that center, they circle in an atmosphere that is itself natural, they still receive from it that indescribable note of the experimental, the delightful and lived, which characterizes them: a far-off participation, hope and promise of supreme joy. That is why metaphysical objects and their purely intelligible necessities, whose value St. Augustine takes care not to deny or belittle and whose efficacy he knows and reveres, far more than Pascal, present themselves to him only as enveloped in resonance of the soul's vibrations; that is why the rational proof of God's existence—without ever ceasing to proceed *per ea quae facta sunt* and by way of causality, without ever implying that *for us* the evidence of God precedes that of things—starts with an experience, this time a natural experience, the inner experience of the unchanging truths of reason illuminating our changing mind.[9]

As for the soul's knowledge of itself, if Augustine definitely yields to Platonic forms (which can only be defended with great difficulty) in giving philosophical formulation of his thought on this score—as well as in certain psychological theories connected with it (particularly, the theory of sensation),

---

9   Proof of God's existence by way of the sensible world also has its full value in Augustine (and on this point Pascal will deviate from him very considerably): "Ecce sunt caelum et terra, clamant quod facta sunt; mutantur enim atque variantur . . . clamant etiam quod se ipsa non fecerint . . . Et vox dicentium est ipsa evidentia. Tu ergo, Domine, fecisti ea qui pulcher es, pulchra sunt enim; qui bonus es, bona sunt enim; qui es, sunt enim. Nec ita pulchra sunt, nec ita bona sunt, nec ita sunt, sicut tu conditor eorum, quo comparato nec pulchra sunt, nec bona sunt, nec sunt" (*Confess.*, lib. XI, c. iv, n. 6). Cf. *Sermones*, CXLI, 2, 2.

the fact still remains that what he saw above all, and saw infallibly, always as a more-or-less remote participation in, and reflection of an experience, divine in its order, was the nature and spiritual privileges of the human soul whereby it is radically (but not for the state of union with the body) intelligible to itself by its substance, and knows material things only by immersing them in its own light. It will suffice for St. Thomas to specify that here below, the soul knows itself only through its acts in order, here as everywhere else, to set his doctrine straight. Undoubtedly, Augustine was forced to take too high a flight in order to make men's eyes see things in their true light, but once the substance of his psychology is grasped, it is easily integrated in its entirety—as Father Gardeil has so admirably shown[10]—into the system of Aristotelian ideas relived and, if I may so express it, *Augustinized* by the Angel of the Schools. Let us say, then, mystical wisdom is in some way the activating agent, the catalyst of Augustinian introspection, and in virtue of it that introspection appears the most wondrous instrument for discerning the spiritual in every realm. Moreover, St. Augustine's psychology never abandons the concrete; being a moral science, perhaps even more than a psychology, it proceeds in a way quite different from St. Thomas' analytical psychology.

8. In all of this we are still in a world quite different from the order of metaphysical wisdom: a realm that would be inferior to metaphysics if it were only psychology or practical knowledge, but which it would be utterly wrong to characterize in that way. It is a domain that in reality transcends metaphysics because it is, in the proper sense, the royal domain of infused wisdom, the prelude to vision, turning man back to the loving contemplation of the three uncreated Persons who dwell in him by grace. It can, then, be said with Windelband that St. Augustine's doctrine is a metaphysics of the inner life or, with Gilson, that it is a metaphysics of conversion, provided one immediately adds that such a doctrine is not a metaphysics in the proper sense of the term. Windelband's expression, and Gilson's, too, are all the more illuminating in proportion as the complete inappropriateness of the term "metaphysics" is the more fully grasped.

It is definitely apparent that St. Augustine's doctrine is *religious* both in its essence and in its mode. He does not in the least scorn or belittle scientific research into the nature of things (whether it be a matter of metaphysics or the sciences of observation). He is too great a friend of Plato's not to see the universe as a great family of essences, not to be in contact with metaphysical concepts at every moment. But he only touches them obliquely and for ends of another order. Where he examines the notion "prime matter" is in an act of thanksgiving. On no occasion does he submit the object of his researches to the specific light of purely rational speculation. The metaphysical insights in which his doctrine is so rich come down to us from a higher wisdom.

---

10   A. Gardeil, *La structure de l'âme et l'expérience mystique* (Paris, 1927).

Let us also remember that such a wisdom contains within itself, as in its source and *eminenter*, what will later be divided, among the Scholastics, as theological and philosophical disciplines, separately defined. Or, to put it more precisely, and to come to grips with the matter, let us recall that such a wisdom contains philosophy in a virtually eminent manner and theology in a formally eminent manner (for in making use of a *lumen* superior to the light of the simple theologian, in being more than theologians, the Fathers truly and properly do the work of theology). We will then realize that, as we have explained, St. Augustine's teaching is not only different from St. Thomas' in *point of view* and *habitus* of knowing; it is also different from it in *state*. In St. Thomas, the *state* is one of specific formation and actuation, the state of sciences and techniques constituted in their proper natures; in St. Augustine, it is a state of transcendent fecundity, the state of a supratechnical wisdom which enfolds the sciences in question within its own eminence, a state which, in relation to philosophic science and the scientific mode of theology, is a state of virtuality. In any case, to transfer St. Augustine's doctrine, with its properly and exclusively Augustinian characteristics, to the level of philosophical systems so as to effect an identity between the two, is to denature it by that very attempt even as animals from great undersea depths are seen to fly into a thousand pieces when brought into the open air, to the pressure earthly fauna are accustomed to breathe.

It seems fitting at this juncture to point out an equivocation in the word *Augustinism*. When used to designate St. Augustine's thought, it inevitably connotes by its ending the idea of system. In this sense, no paradox is entailed in holding that St. Augustine never taught Augustinism. It might even be asked, which Augustinism? For as many different Augustinisms have been noted—and sometimes they are antagonistic Augustinisms—as there have been Augustinian philosophers.

Augustinism and Technical Differentiations within Christian Thought

9. With the foregoing considerations in mind, it becomes clear just why the position of those philosophers to whom the history of philosophy has given the name "Augustinians" becomes debatable. To tell the truth, such a position implies, on the part of philosophy, a notable ignorance of its own limits: to ask St. Augustine for a philosophical system is to claim for philosophy and its proper light something that really comes from the light of the most exalted Christian wisdom, faith and charity. Philosophical Augustinism seems, moreover, by nature bound up with an immoderate *philosophism* that is only too obvious in the Cartesian school and somewhat more concealed in those of our contemporaries who speak disparagingly of abstract thought but only with a view to granting an excessive value to the methods of apprehension they substitute for it. But no matter what devotion a person may have to Augustine,

whatever old or new truths are derived from his treasure-house, whatever feeling for inner realities is derived from him, his spirit and thought are thereby utterly betrayed. The *Méditations touchant la philosophie première* resembles the *De Trinitate* as a dark-room resembles a poet's eye. Descartes' "attractive and bold" spiritualism, the Cartesian *cogito* (which has quite a different meaning than the *si fallor, sum!*), the ontological argument, the theory of the idea-pictures, or thought-substance, Malebranche's theo-philosophy, ontologism, occasionalism, vision in God, far from being in the remotest conceivable way authentic forms of Augustinian spiritualism, are but the residue of its rational disaggregation. An analogous process of materialization had already been experienced in theology when a Jansenius transmuted into the opaque substance of his own theological pessimism and hedonism Augustine's transparent but difficult literary expression, his all-too-savory and divinely human language concerning grace and liberty, Adam's innocence and fallen nature, delectations of the sense and those of grace.[11] We are not unaware of the fact that a theological Augustinism which does not fall into the excesses of either Jansenius or Luther, nor into the excesses of those anti-Thomist disputants by whom Luther was inspired, is possible. But we also believe that the rule which would maintain it in the line of truth is the Christian instinct of the theologian rather than the virtue of its principles of theological conceptualization taken in themselves.

The medieval Scholastic, in truth, strove in vain to draw from Augustine with Augustine's arms alone a complete theological and philosophical system. A St. Bonaventure was able to recapture St. Augustine's exalted inspiration and a ray of his wisdom, but failed to turn out a scientific work (if, indeed, he ever pretended to do so). Aristotle's arms were needed; and so, too, was St. Thomas Aquinas. In St. Thomas' day Scholastic Augustinism seemed trapped in a blind alley (and efforts it made to extricate itself after St. Thomas only served to make that state of affairs more obvious); the means of setting itself up as a science—and, as a result, the means of progressing—were clearly lacking. Only St. Thomas succeeded in truly building up theological wisdom within its own proper and specific order, building up theology as a science while, at the same time, defining the proper domain of philosophy. He alone was able to extract from Augustine, but with Aristotle's arms, not Augustine's, a science of theology and a science of Christian philosophy. For, after all, is it not with the arms of philosophy that theology is elaborated as a science? He alone was able to systematize Augustine's wisdom, theologically and philosophically, precisely because, by bringing that wisdom within the perspective of less exalted, but technically more perfect, wisdoms, which have their irreplaceable function within the economy of the Christian intellect, he had the

---

11   Cf. N. del Prado, "De gratia et libero arbitrio" (*Introductio*, February 1907, t. I, pp. lxi–lxvi).

courage to submit it to the conceptual redifferentiations necessary to change it into itself on these new planes of intelligibility.

10. Only a barren enthusiasm for the archaic could occasion any surprise at the fact that the natural progress of thought and culture was bound to bring about the liberation of philosophical wisdom and theological wisdom as special disciplines and special techniques—not separate, indeed, but distinct—as later was to happen for the natural sciences. For spiritual organisms grow just as living bodies do. And how could heterogeneous functions—functions that are mutually and vitally articulate and which correspond to diverse objects specifying spiritual activity—fail to be gradually made explicit in the course of history? The explicitation accomplished by St. Thomas Aquinas at the end of the Middle Ages was absolutely necessary.[12] Confronted with new worlds of knowledge, truths naturally accessible to reason and truths apt to be rationally liberated from the principles of faith, Christian reason was bound to arm itself with virtues suited to the task of discerning and knowing. It was bound to be able to judge of *what is* in a demonstrative fashion, in the pure light of intelligible objects and necessities, i.e., by way of science. From the very fact that in St. Augustine, theology is bound up with the discursive movement of a higher wisdom which is not in itself discursive, it still remains in a state of imperfection as far as the proper and human mode of science is concerned; in St. Thomas, theology is fully constituted in its proper mode, the human mode of reason. It has reached a state of human perfection. Set a man of science face to face with St. Augustine's teaching and he finds himself confronted with a world of religious wisdom with which his own intelligible universe cannot be articulated. If, as a believer, he clings to that doctrine, his thought is cut in two: proceeding in its very speculative development, on the one hand, according to the exigencies of a purely objective analysis, and, on the other hand, according to the movement of love towards an experience which must overwhelm him. The marvel of Thomistic wisdom, the metaphysics of being and of causes, theology as a science, is that, being set at the peak of human reason, recognizing itself inferior to the knowledge of infused wisdom but superior to every other knowledge, and distinguishing only to unite, such a wisdom establishes within the human soul an enduring coherence and living solidarity between those spiritual activities that reach up to heaven and those that reach down to touch the earth. And it does so without in the least lessening or changing them, and always with objective exactness.

---

12   Cf. Fr. M. D. Chenu's remarkable study, "La théologie comme science au XIIIe siècle," *Archives d'histoire doctr. et litt. au moyen âge*, t. II, pp. 31 ff. And, it might be added, there is no "rationalism" in the work thus accomplished by St. Thomas. To recognize the proper value of reason or nature is neither *rationalism* nor *naturalism*.

Thomas Aquinas, Augustine's Heir

11. The story goes that in Cologne, Master Albert had advised his great disciple always to follow Augustine in theology and Aristotle in philosophy. This partition, however, should be taken as applying less to the subjects dealt with than to their formal aspects. For since both the aspect of science and that of wisdom are simultaneously encountered in philosophy and theology, one may say that to treat of things divine and human, Thomas Aquinas looked to Aristotle for his scientific equipment and received from Augustine and the other Fathers and Holy Writ, the substance of his wisdom. His faithfulness to Augustine's wisdom is even more perfect than his mastery of Aristotle's technique. He corrects Aristotle, he honors Augustine as a son honors his father and, with the same devotion, offers him all the help of his youthful strength in various difficult passages (and, to be candid, there are plenty of them). And let us add, the more one shows the importance of the relation of St. Thomas to Aristotle and Greek and Arabian philosophy, on the one hand, to St. Augustine and the whole Christian tradition, on the other, the more one will show by the same stroke the astonishing originality of his genius.

Whether it be a question of beatitude or the Trinity, eternal law, the virtues and gifts, contemplation,[13] evil, providence and divine foreknowledge, predestination, or, generally speaking, any question in sacred theology, nothing is more obvious in St. Thomas' theological synthesis than his most wholehearted faithfulness to St. Augustine. Everyone knows that the main doctrine in which their agreement is manifest is the doctrine of grace. In St. Thomas we see the coming to a perfect scientific formulation of those essential truths, which affirm the distinction and union between the natural and supernatural orders, the sovereign liberty of created love, the intrinsic reality and vital character of the infused gifts within us, truths which Augustine's wisdom never ceased to proclaim against Pelagius, although in a language which is still groping. When St. Thomas teaches the motion of the human free will by grace and divine causality in such a way that the free mode of our voluntary acts is itself caused by God, and that all their goodness comes, at once, from God as first cause and from us as second cause, and that we are the first (defective) cause only of evil; when St. Thomas teaches how liberty (in the sense of autonomy) is the work of the grace of the Holy Ghost, it is the very voice of St. Augustine and of St. Paul to which we are listening. It has been rightly pointed out (and we know the cause of this difference) that the notion of nature in St. Augustine's "oftentimes too literally scriptural" theology,[14] has a much more concrete and historical meaning than it has in St. Thomas' theology: "Whereas the nature investigated by St. Thomas Aquinas is a metaphysically indestructible essence whose intrinsic necessity resists even the corruption of original sin so as to leave nature all but the graces of which

13   Cf. Fr. F. Cayré's fine book, *La contemplation augustinienne* (Paris, 1927).
14   A. Gardeil, *La Structure de l'âme et l'expérience mystique*, t. I, p. xxx.

sin deprives it, along with the powers sin weakens or perverts, Augustine describes under the title 'nature' the factual state which is determined by sin, and what in this state warrants the hope that man can escape it; and it leaves no doubt in our minds that these two attitudes are not, in the final analysis, dogmatically contradictory. St. Augustine does not exclude St. Thomas Aquinas in this central theme of all Christian philosophy, rather he prepares the way for him and calls for him. But in our opinion it could not be maintained that the plane on which these two explanations move is the same."[15] This is our opinion, too. Yet it is well to add that this difference is purely modal, that St. Augustine taught as clearly as possible the ontological value of the distinction between nature and grace,[16] and that he clearly affirmed that distinction even for the state of innocence;[17] and since, according to Augustine, grace is the root of Adam's supernatural prerogatives, bodily immortality, for example, it is also supernatural;[18] grace is positively and intrinsically ordered to the beatific vision which is not due to any created intellect, even angelic;[19] even in the angels, grace is distinct from nature (*simul condens naturam et largiens gratiam*).[20] Yet again, Thomistic theology simply explains according to its own proper mode and perspective the substance of Augustinian thought.

12. But St. Thomas has also transferred into his own philosophic synthesis—and to a much greater extent than is often believed—if not the way of conceptualizing that thought, at least its essential elements.

It is this thought that may be recognized as made more precise, developed and perfectly pointed up in that metaphysical masterpiece, the Thomistic

---

15   E. Gilson, *Introduction à l'étude de Saint Augustine* (Paris, 1929, p. 298).

16   Cf. *De gratia et libero arbitrio*, c. XIII, n. 25: "Numquid natura est gratia? Nam et hoc Pelagiani ausi sunt dicere, gratiam esse naturam, in qua sic creati sumus, ut habeamus mentem rationalem, qua intelligere valeamus, facti ad imaginem Dei, ut dominemur piscibus maris et volucribus caeli et omnibus pecoribus quae reptunt super terram. Sed non haec est gratia, quam comnendat apostolus per fidem Jesu Christi. Haec enim naturam etiam cum impiis et infidelibus certum est nobis esse communem; gratia vero per fidem Jesu Christi eorum tantummodo est, quorum at ipsa fides." *De Praedest. Sanctorum*, c. V, no. 10: "Posse habere fidem, sicut posse habere charitatem, naturae est hominum; habere autem fidem, quemadmodum habere charitatem, gratiae est fidelium. Illa itaque natura, in qua nobis data est possibilitas habendi fidem, non discernit ab homine hominem; ipsa vero fides discernit ab infideli fidelem." *Enarr. in Psalm.* XLIX, enarr. 2: "Manifestum est ergo, quia homines dixit deos, ex gratia sua deificatos, non de substantia sua natos . . . Qui autem justificat, ipse deificat, quia justificando filios Dei facit. *Dedit* enim *eos potestatem filios Dei fieri* (Joan, I, 12). Si filii Dei facti sumus, et dii facti sumus; sed hoc gratia est adoptantis, non naturae generantis."

17   Cf. R. Garrigou-Lagrange, *Communications à la semaine augustinienne de Rome* (April 24, 1930).

18   Cf. *De Correptione et gratia*, c. XI, n. 29: "Quid ergo? Adam non habuit Dei gratiam? Immo vero habuit magnam, sed disparem."

19   *De Trinit.*, lib. XIV and lib. XV (especially c. iii).

20   *De Civit. Dei*, lib. XII, c. ix.

doctrine of analogy and the divine names. For on this score, Augustine thinks in Plotinian fashion but only by leading Plotinus in the direction of a cataphatic theology required by Revelation; he not only teaches that God is immutable, eternal, immense, infinitely simple, that He is all He has,[21] Truth, Life, Beauty, Wisdom, but he also knows He is personal, aware of Himself and His work,[22] *Deus non aliquid nesciens fecit*,[23] that He has done everything through His will, *causa omnium quae fecit, voluntas ejus est*,[24] that He is Being Itself, *ipsum esse subsistens*, as St. Thomas will say; *Deum nihil aliud dicam esse, nisi idipsum esse*.[25] The Augustinian proof of God's existence is likewise found equivalently in St. Thomas' *quarta via*,[26] at times St. Thomas even seems to evoke it under its own form,[27] even though, frankly, we do not believe that its formulation could remain the same in St. Thomas (which undoubtedly explains why, instead of developing that proof *ex professo*, St. Thomas is content, rather, to allude to it). As a result, indeed, of what is, in fact, the main difference between St. Augustine and St. Thomas in the philosophic and noetic order—to wit, as Father Gardeil[28] has so well shown, the substitution of efficient causality, the dominant Aristotelian-Thomistic note, for *participation*, the dominant Augustinian note—the eternal truths, whose value not only of ideal necessity, but also of illuminating virtue Augustine indistinctly envisaged, made him go straightway to God, the first Truth and subsistent Light; whereas, St. Thomas,

---

21   "Quae habet haec et est, et ea omnia unus est" (*De Civit. Dei*, lib. XI, c. x). As Mr. Gilson so correctly notes, this formula contains, in germ at least, the medieval doctrine of the non-distinction, in God alone, between essence and existence. (Cf. *De Trinit.*, lib. XV, c. xiii, n. 22.)

22   Charles Boyer, *L'idée de vérité dans la philosophie de Saint Augustin* (Paris, 1921, p. 108).

23   *De Civit. Dei*, lib. XI, c. x.

24   *Enarr. in Psalm.* CXXXIV, enarr. 10.

25   *De Moribus Ecclesiae*, XIV, 24. Cf. *De Trinit.*, lib. I, c. i, n. 2: "Quae vero proprie de Deo dicuntur, quaeque in nulla creatura invenientur, raro ponit scriptura divina; sicut illud quod dictum est ad Moysem: Ego sum qui sum, et: Qui est, misit me ad vos." Texts like that, as well as *De Trin.*, lib. V, c. i, n. 2, and *Confess.* lib. XI, c. iv, n. 6 (cited above, n. 9), contain virtually the whole Thomistic doctrine of the divine names and analogy.

26   Cf. R. Garrigou-Lagrange, *Dieu, son existence et sa nature*, 5th. ed., p. 296. (Cf. also J. Maritain, *Approaches to God*, New York, Harpers, 1954, p. 57. Tr.)

27   Particularly in the following text from the *Summa Contra Gentiles*, whose importance Mr. J. Sestili has quite rightly underscored: "Veritates intellectae fundantur in aliquo aeterno. Fundantur enim in ipsa prima Veritate, sicut in causa universali contentiva omnis veritatis" (II, 84).

28   A. Gardeil, *La structure de l'âme et l'expérience mystique*, t. II, Appendix II. (In this section Fr. Gardeil is commenting on and generalizing a thesis expounded in Mr. Gilson's study, "Pourquoi Saint Thomas a critiqué Saint Augustin," AHDLMA, t. I, 1926–1927.) As regards the notions *creation* and *formation* in particular, we believe, however, that Mr. Gilson's remarks are correct (*Introduction à l'étude de Saint Augustin*, p. 258).

recognizing as he did our agent intellect as the active light of our understanding, would, we believe, have had to pass (if he wanted to develop the
Augustinian proof itself) through this created illuminating cause, which we
bear within us, in order to rise to the First Cause whose virtue it participates
and thus find the supreme reason for those eternal truths in that very First
Truth and thence conclude from the truth in our mind to a first foundation for
it in the real order.

Notwithstanding the fundamental difference in philosophic sign of which
we have just spoken, it should be said, in accord with Father Boyer's excellent
studies, that the whole substance of the Augustinian doctrine of truth has
passed into St. Thomas, by means of the general transposition and the many
slight readjustments consequently required. Indeed, it is evident[29] that the
Aristotelian structure of metaphysics and natural philosophy found their
completion in the Thomistic synthesis only in virtue of an Augustinian cor-
nerstone, I mean to say, the doctrine of creative Ideas. For it is in God Himself,
in the creative Ideas that illumine the angels before causing things, that the
created world finds the highest principle of its order and movement.
Augustine not only traced out the broad lines of a theory of creation, but his
exemplarism supplies a full consistency, a supreme metaphysical boldness
unknown to Aristotle's analytical circumspection, to the conception of the
world which St. Thomas was to develop.

We have mentioned but a few characteristic traits. One would have to give
an infinite number of examples if one wanted to point out all the Augustinian
riches assimilated by St. Thomas' thought, and all the manifestations of
veneration the Angelic Doctor accorded St. Augustine's authority even in the
smallest details.[30] The more one studies both of these doctors the better is the
statement of Father Gardeil verified: "The positions on which they differ can
be counted; it is impossible to number those in which they agree. . . . The dumb
ox has devoured the whole spiritual substance of the eagle of Hippo . . . he has
made it, as much as Aristotle, the proper substance of his own mind."[31] If the
essential values of St. Augustine's thought are considered in their integrity, it
must be admitted, as we have explained, that the sole metaphysical systematization of that thought which remains *essentially* Augustinian is the Thomistic
synthesis.

Thomism and Augustinism

13. How foolish it is to oppose Thomism and Augustinism (I mean St.

---

29   Mr. Simeterre stressed this point in his lectures at the Institut Catholique de Paris.
     Unfortunately, they are not published.
30   On the sole authority of Augustine, St. Thomas admits that Moses was transito-
     rily raised up to the beatific vision. Cf B. Levand, "La vision de Dieu ici-bas,"
     Revue Thomiste, Jan.–Feb. 1929, pp. 75–83; May–June 1930, pp. 253–256.
31   A. Gardeil, *La structure de l'âme et l'expérience mystique*, t. 1, pp. xxix–xxx.

Augustine's Augustinism) as though they were two opposed systems! The first is a system, the second is not. Thomism is the scientific state of Christian wisdom; among the Fathers and in St. Augustine that wisdom is still in its source. There is no opposition between the spring and the waters of the plain. It is not *apart from* Thomistic wisdom, and as if the spring caused the river to overflow, that the ceaseless flood of Augustinian inspiration reaches us in its purity. His inspiration presided over the formation of the Thomistic synthesis; it passed into that synthesis, and is bound to continue to pass into it and stir it to new growth, for St. Thomas' doctrine is destined to go on growing for ever. No doubt, after invisible meanderings, streams deriving from the source may spring up alongside the main stream; they are destined to swell its waters. No doubt "Augustinian" systems will always continue to be elaborated in opposition to Thomism: to tell the truth, however, they will only be witnesses to the laziness of Thomists, slow-downs they have caused in the pursuit of that work of universal assimilation and illumination so powerfully begun by their master. Despite the delays and the obstacles, that work must normally continue. Those "Augustinian" philosophers who, in spite of the inconsistency of their systematic position, by recapturing something of the vigor of St. Augustine's intuition, show forth the value of neglected truths or extend our knowledge of inner realities, will be unconsciously working for the philosophy of St. Thomas.

Augustine's inventive audacity, more disposed than the theological prudence of St. Thomas to take risks in the region of the probable, sought to attain some understanding of the very succession of events in human history: basing himself on Scripture, St. Augustine created the philosophy of history, or, let us say more exactly (for the lights of faith are necessary here), *the wisdom of history*. And, in our opinion, his feeling for the irreversibility of historical becoming, of the movement and development of the world in the sense of time, is one of the most precious jewels of the Augustinian heritage. In that connection we feel there is a whole area to be taken back from Hegel and reclaimed for Christian wisdom. Will Thomistic thought, stimulated by Augustine's spirit, one day enrich itself with those conjectures in the matter of the exegesis of history, which a reflective examination of culture can scarcely do without? It would appear that the *Discours sur l'histoire universelle* has to be rewritten, and a more modern continuation to the *City of God* would be of great assistance.

Besides, it is important to understand that the state of incompleteness in which we see the so-called Augustinian school, or the manifold attempts to form an Augustinian school of philosophy, do not promise renewal or progress. Such incompleteness is of itself rather a sign of imperfectibility. How can an organism grow that does not even succeed in establishing itself? It is precisely because Thomism has been formed as a science with well-defined systematic equipment, which is also (but in another sense) incomplete, that it is capable of endless progression and growth. Far from telling us that since St.

Thomas everything has been done, it says that as long as history shall last and bring new problems to light, so long will more still have to be done than has as yet been accomplished.

Let us recall what we have already put forward regarding the wisdom of the Fathers and theologians. One might imagine that, by reason of the height of their spiritual level, it was fitting that the Middle Ages should accomplish their thousand-year task under the headship of the Fathers and, above all, of St. Augustine. Our own epoch has a spiritual outflow that is not so free, but it has more perfect instruments, better means of verification, surer techniques. It has a different job to do. It is fitting that Christian thought should now put forth its effort under the more direct leadership of the Theologian par excellence.

14. Call the wisdom of a St. Augustine Christian philosophy, if you wish, or, in a more general sense, call it Christian wisdom, i.e., infused wisdom making use of reason and discourse—definitions of names are free. This "philosophy," which essentially presupposes faith, charity, the gifts of the Holy Ghost, the whole supernatural order, is not that work of exploring the natures of things in which those whom we usually call philosophers engage, nor does it possess the means, once we rise above the spontaneous certitudes of ordinary reason, of judging demonstratively and assigning *raisons d'être* to truths which are of themselves accessible to unaided powers of our mind. It lacks a properly philosophical instrument. But once that instrument is born in the mind, it has its specifying object, the intelligibility of things, it has its own proper rules and light, the rules and light of natural reason, not of the infused gifts.

In order that the names we use may correspond with realities, we should call *Christian philosophy* a philosophy properly so called, a wisdom defined as a perfect work of reason, *perfectum opus rationis*,[32] and which on the side of its object is in harmony with revealed truths—and on the side of its subject, in vital contact with the supernatural forces whose philosophical *habitus* is distinct but not separated in the Christian soul. It is enough for this philosophy to be true in its own order to find itself in harmony with revealed truth. For then, while displaying "the rigor of its own rational demands in all their integrity," while pursuing a method that is not theological but purely and strictly philosophical, it will produce "a conception of nature and reason open to the supernatural,"[33] confirmed by data natural of themselves, and not

---

32   St. Thomas, *Sum. Theol.*, II–II, 45, 2.

33   M. D. Chenu, *Bulletin Thomiste*, Jan. 1928, p. 244. We believe that by distinguishing between the implications of Christian philosophy *ex parte objecti* and *ex parte subjecti*, the truth Fr. Chenu's remarks contain (*loc. cit.*) can be reconciled with the truth of Mr. Gilson's observations (*Introduction à l'étude de Saint Augustin*, p. 302, n. 1). Regarding the order followed by St. Thomas, he follows the theological order as a theologian, not as a Christian philosopher. Moreover, in his commen-

repugnant to data supernatural of themselves contained in the deposit of Revelation. But because the human subject cannot, in fact, arrive at the whole body of the supreme truths naturally knowable, without aid from on high, this philosophy needs for its development within the subject, to grow in vital connection with faith which, without entering into its texture, nor serving as a positive criterion, plays, in respect to it, the role of an extrinsic regulating principle, *veluti stella rectrix*—along with theology (which corroborates it by using it as an instrument) and the Wisdom of the Holy Ghost (which also strengthens it in the Christian's soul).

Here St. Augustine reminds us of what Thomists are tempted to forget when they let Thomism grow weak within themselves, namely, that in respect to the conditions of its existence, Christian philosophy needs to live and spiritualize itself by contact with the living faith and the experience of a Christian soul, to enter in its own way into the anguish and the peace of the work of redemption, to be fortified from on high by contemplation. St. Thomas reminds us of something that Augustinians seem to forget from the very start, namely, that Christian philosophy, in itself and in its intrinsic structure as a rational wisdom, is strictly independent of the dispositions of the subject and can only be ruled by objective necessities and intelligible constraints.

15. What we have said about St. Augustine's wisdom should be said likewise, as we have already noted, about the wisdom of the other Fathers. If one wished to go into refinements—undoubtedly presumptuous—and seek out what marks Augustine from among all the others, it would perhaps be necessary to add that his proper characteristic lies in the fact that the splendor of his gift of knowledge[34] is no less prodigious than that of his gift of wisdom, whence his privilege of so profound a supernatural knowledge, not only of divine things but also of the human heart and the complexities of the creature.

---

taries on Aristotle he found an opportunity to follow, as a philosopher (and as a Christian philosopher), the philosophical order. Concerning the notion "Christian philosophy," see E. Gilson's exposition to the French Society of Philosophy (meeting of March 21, 1931), his two volumes on *The Spirit of Medieval Philosophy*, Régis Jolivet's works, *Essais sur les rapports entre la pensée grecque et la pensée chrétienne* (Paris, Vrin, 1931), and *La philosophie chrétienne et la pensée contemporaine* (Tequi, 1932), and our little work, *De la philosophie chrétienne*. Concerning Augustinism and its most authentic meaning, see F. Cayré, *Les sources de l'amour divin d'après Saint Augustin* (Paris, 1933), and, above all, the author's Introduction. The doctrinal agreement pointed out in these pages is of great value to us.

34   Here it is a matter of mystical *knowledge*, a knowledge that penetrates the creature with a loving light due to connaturality with divine things produced by charity, a knowledge that corresponds to the beatitude of "those who weep." Cf St. Thomas Aquinas, *Sum. Theol.* II–II, q. 9; John of St. Thomas, *Les dons du Saint Esprit*, tr. R. Maritain, Ch. IV.

CHAPTER VIII

ST. JOHN OF THE CROSS, PRACTITIONER OF CONTEMPLATION

I
COMMUNICABLE KNOWLEDGE
AND INCOMMUNICABLE KNOWLEDGE

1. WHEN WE SEE GOD face to face, we shall have supremely clear and limpid intellectual knowledge of the Divine Essence. This knowledge will, however, be incommunicable because, on the one hand, the Divine Essence itself will actuate our intellect immediately, without the mediation of any *species* or idea (for no idea, angelic or human, could adequately represent the Divine Essence); while, on the other hand, it is by means of ideas or concepts that our knowledge is communicable.

With the exception of this absolutely privileged case of the beatific vision, which is at once both strictly intellectual and strictly experimental, intellectual knowledge in heaven and on earth is communicable by its very nature. Its proper mystery is precisely this communicability. It is not communicated like material things, a coin passing from hand to hand. It obviously demands a vital, personal, irreplaceable act—an immanent act of thought on the part of the receiver as well as on the part of the donor. But this act is governed and specified by objects which are transmitted precisely by means of ideas and which are valid for both donor and receiver.

But besides this communicable knowledge, which takes place through ideas, there is another knowledge whose object is the concrete as such and which arises from experience: this is incommunicable knowledge. In acquiring it we can, no doubt, have masters and guides; but in this case they do not impart to us the objects of knowledge themselves. What they do transmit is a store of cognitions, counsels and rules which we need in order to have a certain experience, in itself, inexpressible, as is every experience. When such knowledge has God for its object, then it is infused contemplation. It subsists in heaven where, John of St. Thomas tells us, an affective experience, a sort of taste or touch of God by means of the gifts of the Holy Spirit, accompanies and reflects vision in such wise that faith will cease, but not mystical experience, which remains, as does charity—proceeding in this life from faith but, in the future life, from vision.

2. To our mind, St. John of the Cross is the great Doctor of this supreme incommunicable wisdom, just as St. Thomas Aquinas is the great Doctor of the highest communicable wisdom. It is in function of the delicate and admirably instructive relations existing between the Doctor of Light and the Doctor of Night that we shall, in this chapter, examine certain aspects of the spiritual teaching of John of the Cross.

In doing so we shall not adopt the historical point of view and investigate the influences he underwent, the reading he did and the texts he quoted. Intelligently and soberly conducted, such studies are incontestably useful. But by themselves they do not much enrich the intellect. This would be especially true and our labors would be worse than useless if their purpose, like that of a learned chemist, were to measure the intellectual ingredient entering into the composition of the saint's thought, or to watch the synthesis of this thought operating *in vitro* in the retort of history. History gives us valuable information about the material conditions in which a man's thought has developed, but it can never effect the synthesis of that thought. A St. John of the Cross, like St. Thomas, profited from everything he read and from the most diverse authors; he read St. Gregory and St. Bonaventure,[1] Baconthorpe and Michel de Bologne, as much as and more than he read St. Thomas himself However true that may be, the important question is not whether or not he read St. Thomas. The question is whether, and to what degree, his testimony taken in its objective meaning agrees with the testimony of St. Thomas, also taken in its objective meaning. From this point of view it would be better had he read St. Thomas much less than he undoubtedly did read him, better indeed had he never read St. Thomas at all! The results of confronting these two doctrines would not be any the less meaningful. It is the differences in point of view and situation, differences which must be known prior to such a comparison, that we shall try especially to point out here.

II
THE SPECULATIVE ORDER AND THE PRACTICAL ORDER

3. To do this, we had best begin by stressing a notion which, in our opinion, governs the whole discussion, the notion of practical science.

In the SPECULATIVE ORDER the mind, considering the world of existence, evokes from this world universes of intelligibility which are increasingly pure, increasingly detached from matter: the universe of mathematical sciences, the universe of metaphysics. Then, coming back to the world of existence considered as such, the mind takes as its concern human action going on in that worldy[2] and, philosophizing, this time in the PRACTICAL ORDER, seeks to know,

---

1   We know that he recommended the writings of these two great masters of the spiritual life to his novices.

2   "Speculativum" solum importat et attingit objectum secundum rationem quid-

no longer for the sake of knowing but for the sake of acting; it seeks to acquire, respecting an object which is something practical (an act to be done), a science which proceeds in a practical manner in regard to its own finalities and the conditions of the object, but nevertheless remains *speculative or explanatory in mode* in regard to the general or fundamental cognitional equipment, and considers the universe of action and operative values from the point of view

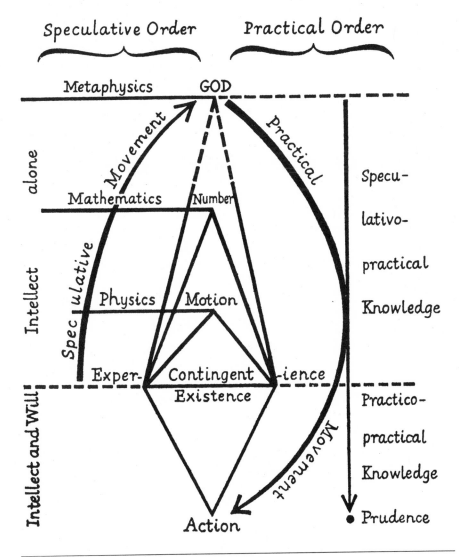

ditatis suae, et eorum quae quidditatem consequuntur, ideoque respicit veritatem abstrahendo ab exercitio existendi. At vero practicum respicit objectum, ut stat sub exercitio existendi . . ." (John of St. Thomas, *Curs. Theol.*, I P., q. 1, disp. 2, a. 10, n. 5).

of their *raison d'être* and the intelligible structures immanent in it.[3] That is what Aristotle called practical philosophy: ethics, economics, etc. Many important observations might be made on the subject of practical philosophy, whose nature is so misunderstood by moderns. It could be pointed out that practical philosophy has nothing to do with the degrees of abstraction characteristic o the speculative sciences; it cuts right through the whole field of knowledge, from the metaphysical heavens from which it is suspended, to the world of experience, on which it must needs rest. It could also be pointed out that since, in this order, ends play the role of *principles*, practical philosophy is not limited to prescribing, as Kant would have had it. It is a science, it knows. But it does not completely and truly know its object, which is something to be done, unless it knows how it should be done.[4] Thus, despite the major role experience plays in it, the knowledge that constitutes practical philosophy is not knowledge of simple observation. It is also, and essentially, a regulative science, a normative science.[5]

The only point we want to bring out here is that practical philosophy does not suffice to regulate action. It knows in a theoretical, speculative, explanatory way things which need not only to be explained but also to be done. It gathers into a scientific system all the knowledge necessary to regulate action from afar, that is, all the rules for action which the intellect can discern by adapting to practical use an equipment and a mode of discerning the true which is typically speculative. The most expert and competent philosopher in ethical matters can be disconcerted by the smallest act to be done, and he can himself lead an immoral life.

4. Let us add, however, that although there are two perfectly distinct types of philosophical science corresponding to the speculative order and the practical order, theological science on the contrary, because of its eminence, includes within its unity both the speculative and the practical order.[6] Moreover, since as a matter of fact man acting here on earth is not the abstract subject, the pure and simple subject of human nature considered by philosophy, but exists in determinate concrete conditions universally affecting his nature (I mean in the concrete state of fallen and redeemed nature), it actually pertains not to a practical philosophy, unless it be illumined by theology, but to the

---

3   See Appendix VII, II.

4   "De operabilibus perfecta scientia non habetur nisi scientur inquantum operabilia sunt" (St. Thomas Aquinas, *Sum. Theol.*, I, 14, 16, sed contra).

5   On this capitally important point of doctrine, see pages 130–136 and 172–182, in the collective work *Clairvoyance de Rome*.

6   Cf. *Sum. Theol.*, I, 1, a. 3 and 4. As Cajetan forcefully remarks, it is not "by way of aggregation" but in the very indivisibility of its essence that theology is both formally and eminently speculative and practical. (Cf. John of St. Thomas, *Curs. Theol.*, I, q. 1, disp. 2, a. 10). However, it is more speculative "because it treats more principally of divine things than of human acts. For it deals with the latter insofar as man is ordained by them to the perfect knowledge of God in which eternal beatitude consists" (St. Thomas, *loc. cit.*, a. 4).

practical part of theology to regulate our actions from above. However, our remarks about the theoretical and speculative way in which practical philosophy studies its practical object (human acts) remain equally true of theology in its practical function. The theologian considers and regulates human acts in a speculative and purely intellectual manner. We may say that this is a *speculatively practical science*. It is from the point of view of this science that St. Thomas deals with moral affairs: human activity and the supreme activity which is mystical contemplation. His teaching is situated within theological doctrine, within a science which is speculative and explanatory in its mode. And if we are looking for a sure and certain speculative elucidation of mystical theology, as of other supernatural mysteries, we should address ourselves to him before all others.

Practically Practical Science

5. But in dealing with the requirements of the practical as such, practical knowledge cannot stop at this point. It is like a great intelligible flux which gradually becomes particularized and narrows down more and more as it flows, until it comes in contact with the concrete and singular act to be done *here and now*, within the indefinite variety of contingent circumstances. In immediate contact with action, because immediately regulative of action, right practical knowledge is no longer what we call wisdom, scientific knowledge, because at this level its object is not only a practical object to be done, but that practical object taken in its very singularity, in its relation with the ends actually willed by my incommunicable person—and that is not an object of *science*. Right practical knowledge, as the immediate regulator of action, is the virtue of prudence. It judges and commands what is to be done here and now. As we know, this virtue is both intellectual and moral; it is connected with the moral virtues and necessarily presupposes the rectitude of the will. In this field the intellect does not work alone, but depends upon the will and its dispositions. It is in relation to the direction of the *agere* and to the rectitude of the will that its judgment is true or false.[7]

And now a question arises. Is there not an intermediate zone of knowledge between prudence and speculatively practical science? Explicating the principles of St. Thomas,[8] we would answer: Yes! There is practical science in the strict sense of the word. We may call it *practically practical* science. This is a science because even though it is much more particularized than moral

---

7   Cf. St. Thomas, *Sum. Theol.*, I–II, 58, 5: "Utrum intellectualis virtus possit esse sine morali," and 57, 5, ad 3: "Verum intellectus practici (in prudentia) accipitur per conformitatem ad appetitum rectum." In a particularly important commentary, Cajetan writes concerning this latter article: "Veritas intellectus speculativi consistit in cognoscere, veritas autem intellectus practici in dirigere." See also *Art and Scholasticism*, IV, 3.

8   See Appendix VII.

theology or ethics, even though it considers the details of cases, it nevertheless moves within the universal and the *raisons d'être* as within its proper object. But as to the fundamental equipment of knowledge itself or as to the structure of notions and definitions, its procedure follows a wholly different mode than does ethics or moral theology. The very method of science is reversed. The whole mode of science here is practical. What does that mean? It means that there is no question here of explaining and resolving a truth, even a practical truth, into its reasons and principles. The question is to prepare for action and to assign its proximate rules. And, since action is a concrete thing which must be thought in its concretion before being posited in being, knowledge here, instead of analyzing, composes; I refer to the fashion in which the relation of truth is established between this knowledge and its object. It gathers together everything that is already known, all the explanations, principles and *raisons d'être* (but in order to organize them all from new points of view which provide what is needed to posit the concrete act, as they are furnished directly by experience, whose role here is primary). It is in this wholly characteristic sense that Thomists teach that practical sciences (practically practical) proceed *modo compositivo*[9] like art and prudence. Moreover, just as prudence and art presuppose the rectifying of the appetite (the latter in the order of the workman's ends only, the former in the order of human ends as such),[10] these practical sciences too (because in the line of what is to be made they are identical with art itself and in the line of what is to be done they are linked to prudential experience and in some measure take on its conditions)[11] imply and presuppose,[12] in order to judge truly, the right dispositions of the will and a certain purification of the appetite with respect to the ends with which they are concerned.

6. We are inclined to believe that philosophers, especially in modern times, have often seriously neglected the importance of these sciences which belong to a wholly different order than their own. There is a science of the practitioner as such which is irreducible to a knowledge that is speculative in mode, and whose dignity and importance are truly great for culture. I am not speaking

---

9   In the practically practical sciences the compositive or "actuating" mode invades the intimate structure of knowledge, although in a less fundamental way than in prudence: the notional instruments, the ways of apprehending and judging become fundamentally practical (cf. below, § 13) and the relation of truth, on which the fundamental regulation of knowledge depends, no longer belongs to the purely intellectual order: let us say that truth is taken here according to *dirigere* itself, as founded on *cognoscere*. See Appendix VII.

10   Cf. Cajetan, *In Sum. Theol.*, I–II, 57, 5, ad 3 (*Art and Scholasticism*, new ed., pp. 77–79).

11   See Appendix VII, II.

12   To a lesser degree than prudence, however, for it is not the function of the practical sciences, as it is of prudence, to determine the last practical judgment here and now, and to lead to the *imperium*.

only of the vast universe of knowledge connected with the professions, whether it be that of the engineer, the doctor, the banker, the architect, the artisan or the army commander, in whom a practical science is always incorporated with art properly so called. I am speaking also of the moral order, of the knowledge of man. Among many great moralists, Confucius, for example, we find more of a practitioner's science than a philosopher's science. It is likewise with many great statesmen. Which brings us back to one of the fundamental theses of this book: there are in the world of the mind structural differentiations and a diversity of dimensions whose recognition is of the greatest importance. Serious misunderstandings can be avoided only by assigning to each type of thought its exact situation in this sort of transcendental topography. The differences of which we speak here have to do with the "fourth dimension," according to which the mind diversifies its knowledge-values in line with its own proper finalities. From this point of view we believe it is an error to attribute to psychology, the speculative science of the human being, the profound studies and discoveries made by so many deeply intuitive men, from Montaigne and Pascal to Nietzsche, from Shakespeare to Racine and Baudelaire, from Swift or Meredith to Balzac and Dostoievsky. These powerful observers of men are not merely observers, they are not "psychologists"; properly speaking, they are moralists—not philosophers but practitioners of the science of morals. No doubt, they do not concern themselves with this science taken as a whole, right down to the formulation of its rules and precepts. They deal, above all, with the experimental matter of this science (sometimes sadly defective from the point of view of its regulative truths). What they do study is really the dynamism of the human being, the use of free will, and, consequently, man's situation in face of his ends. Thus, the accuracy and depth of their views do not depend only upon their keenness of sight, but also upon their idea of good and evil and the dispositions of their heart toward a sovereign good. They draw upon admirable psychological riches but within a knowledge which is the practically practical science of human action,[13] not psychology. That is precisely why they are not psychologists but moralists— because their psychology goes incomparably farther than all the psychology of laboratory or university.

The Practical Science of Contemplation

7. It is important to understand that, with respect to that most eminent of actions, to wit, the passion of things divine and contemplative union with God, there is not only a speculatively practical science which is the science of the

---

13   An analogous remark could be made about speculatively practical knowledge. Deliberately and with profound perspicacity, St. Thomas put into the second part of the *Summa* many explanations and psychological analyses which, to a superficial glance, would seem better placed in the (wholly speculative) treatise *De Homine*.

theologian, but that there is also a practically practical science which is not so much interested in telling us what perfection is, as leading us to it. This is the science of the master of spirituality, the practitioner of the soul, the artisan of sanctity, the man who stoops to our wretched hearts, which he wants at all costs to lead to their supreme joy. In this practical science of contemplation St. John of the Cross is the master.

In the works of St. John of the Cross two things are to be distinguished: his inspired poems and the commentaries in which he gives us his teaching. In his poems, written under divine inspiration, he expresses his own mystical experience in limpid and lyrical symbols, and to the full extent that human language can express the inexpressible, which is to say quite inadequately. At such times he thinks only of singing.[14] In his commentaries, written at the request of his spiritual daughters, he sets forth a doctrine, he teaches. This doctrine, which is a practical doctrine,[15] is the teaching that is incorporated within that practical science which proceeds by combining proximately regulative notions directed towards concrete action. In the writings of St. Teresa, who never allows herself to speak like a doctor, but whose doctrine is glorified by the Church, we have rather the descriptive and experimental elements of such a science. But in the writings of St. John of the Cross, this science exists with all its dimensions, so much so that the theorist of the sciences can find nowhere else so perfect an example of practical science. For practically practical science depends on speculatively practical science; the practical science of contemplation depends on moral theology. And St. John of the Cross was

---

14   Although perhaps the very fact that he was given the grace and divine impulse to sing of his experience contained germinally the virtual intention (unknown to him) of teaching the paths of the spirit. *Contemplationem aliis tradere* is the Carmelite vocation according to Fr. Jerome of the Mother of God; it is eminently the vocation of St. John of the Cross. And charisms are given *ad utilitatem aliorum*. So the distinction we are making here should not be too strongly pressed. The lyrical expression contains within itself, in a wholly implicit and indeterminate state, a first movement of expansion toward others.

We should recall here that before writing his *Exposition* for Anne of Jesus in 1584, St. John of the Cross added four, and then five verses to the original thirty verses of the canticle written in 1578 in the prison of Toledo. To Madeleine of the Holy Spirit, admiring the lively and subtle expressions in his poem, he said: "My daughter, sometimes God gave them to me, sometimes I sought them myself" (Silverio, *Obras de S. Juan de la Cruz*, t. I, p. 325; cf. Louis de la Trinité, *Études carmélitaines*, Oct. 1931, p. 10). But this does not prevent the poem from proceeding primarily, as the saint testifies in his prologue to Anne of Jesus, from "fervor of love for God," from inspirations above and beyond every human explanation, from the Spirit of the Lord "Who aids our weakness."

15   He is perfectly well aware of this himself. He teaches the "pure and sure road of union," *el puro y cierto camino de la union* (Ascent of Mount Carmel, Prologue, Silv., II, p. 7; Peers, *The Complete Works of St. John of the Cross* [London, 1934], Vol. I, p. 12). He "would fain speak in some way that may be profitable" to souls. (*Dark Night of the Soul*, Bk. I, Ch. vii, Silv., II, p. 386; Peers, I, p. 370.)

not only a wonderful contemplative, he was also a good theologian, which is why this practical science is found in him in its perfect state.

8. This is a good place to ask ourselves what relations exist between this practical science and theology. If we take the word "theology" in the very general sense of sacred doctrine[16]—including the whole organism of our knowledge of the mysteries, faith itself, the theological discursus and the gifts of knowledge, understanding and wisdom—then the practical science we are discussing here is evidently a part of theology thus understood. But understanding the word "theology" in the strict sense in which we have taken it heretofore, as science of the virtually revealed, proceeding according to the speculative mode, it seems clear that this practical science is to be distinguished from theology. A man may lose charity and remain a (sufficient if not eminent)[17] theologian, even in matters of mystical theology, if he has theological faith and reasons well. But although St. Teresa preferred a very learned and not so holy confessor to a very saintly and not so learned one (for she was guided less by the confessor than by the Holy Spirit), how could one be expert in this guidance of the Holy Spirit, and have practical concrete knowledge of the paths that lead souls to infused contemplation if one has no experience of it oneself—experience which supposes charity?

Therefore this science, which is practical not only in its object but also in its mode, and which, based on faith and presupposing experience of divine things, uses theological principles to guide souls along interior paths, remains distinct from theology taken in the strictest sense of the word. Nevertheless, it is most closely bound to it. For even when it treats of human acts and man's pilgrimage to his final end, theology undoubtedly does so according to a speculative mode, seeking reasons and explanatory structures. Yet, it is practical in an eminently formal sense, as we have seen, and is thereby in continuity with the sciences which most intimately regulate action. So, in short, we may conclude that just as the practical intellect is an extension of the speculative

16   Cf. St. Thomas, *Sum. Theol.*, I, 1, 1. Likewise, it is by giving a very general meaning to the word theology that we call infused contemplation "mystical theology."

17   The theological *habitus* of itself necessarily presupposes theological faith; but unlike the gift of wisdom it does not necessarily presuppose charity. This is why it may remain substantially in the sinner. Cf. John of St. Thomas, *Curs. Theol*, I P., q. 1, disp. 2, a. 2 and 8. But it does not seem possible that a theologian could be eminent without being strengthened by the gift of wisdom and having some experience of the realities about which he reasons. "Etenim sive docendo sive scribendo hic divina pertractat, praeclarissimum dat theologis documentum illius quae inter sensus animi et studia intercedere debet necessitudo maxima. Nam, quemadmodum regionem aliquam longinquam bene habere cognitam non dicitur qui ejus descriptionem quamvis subtilem cognoverit, sed qui aliquamdiu ibidem vixerit, sic intimam Dei notitiam sola scientia pervestigatione nullus assequitur, nisi etiam eum Deo conjunctissime vivat" (Pius XI, Encycl. *Studiorum ducem*). (Cf. R. Garrigou-Lagrange, *De Revelatione*, Vol. I, p. 21.)

intellect, but wherein new principles (dispositions of the appetite) necessarily enter in, so the practical science of the interior paths of the spirit is a practical extension of theology wherein mystical experiences and the gifts necessarily enter in. And the very clear distinction that must be acknowledged between them does not go so far as to make two specifically different *habitus* of them; for the practical science in question should be considered as a particular development of the theological *habitus*.[18]

But to return from this digression. We know now—and this is precisely the point I wanted to make—we know exactly how to situate St. John of the Cross and St. Thomas in relation to each other. St. Thomas, as we said above, is the pre-eminent Doctor of dogmatic and moral theology, he is especially the Doctor par excellence of the *speculatively* practical science of contemplation and of union with God. St. John of the Cross is the pre-eminent Doctor of the *practically* practical science of contemplation and union with God. The former explains and makes us see, the latter guides and leads us; the former casts every intelligible light upon being, the latter leads liberty through all the nights of renunciation; by his teaching mission, the former is a demonstrator, the latter, a practitioner of wisdom. It is this point of view, the point of view of practical science, which we must adopt in order to understand the teaching of St. John of the Cross.

III
THE MEANING OF HUMAN LIFE

9. Practically practical knowledge presupposes speculatively practical knowledge. So before examining the spiritual doctrine of St. John of the Cross in its practicality, it would be advisable to examine the theological presuppositions of this doctrine. In so doing, we cannot but observe the deep and essential agreement between the thought of St. John of the Cross and that of St. Thomas even—and this is all the more striking—when John's sources and language do not seem to depend upon the Thomist school. On this subject we would like to stress two particularly important points;[19] the first concerns the

---

18   Cf. John of St. Thomas, *Curs. Theol.* I P., q. 1. disp. 2, a. 10, n. 17: "Respondetur theologiam non esse prudentiam proxime et formaliter, sed directive et architec-tonice. . . . Et cum dicitur, quod non datur scientia practica, nisi habeat adjunctam prudentiam, respondetur quod scientia quae tantum fundatur in principiis naturalis ordinis non est practica, sed distinguitur a prudentia; quae vero habet pro principiis res fidei, illa etiam est practica, habetque rationem prudentiae non proxime formaliter, sed regulative, quatenus explicat fidem, quae dirigere potest prudentiam, non solum ut speculativa est, sed ut practica. Et cum dicitur quod potest aliquis esse theologus, et valde imprudens, et peccator, respondetur quod tunc manet theologia sine exercitio practico et extensione actuali ad res practicas, non tamen sine essentiali ratione practici."

19   We could stress many other points concerning, for example, the dependence of

human understanding and rational *discursus* upon the senses (which notion, Aristotelian in origin, is fundamental in the thought of John of the Cross; it explains why his position on the subject of the natural activity of our spirit, and on meditation, is removed as far as possible from Platonism); the efficacy of grace and the liberty of creative and sanctifying love; the relations of charity to the gifts and virtues; the distinction between the presence of immensity by which God is in all things, and the presence of grace, by which He dwells in the souls of the just; and so on. On this last point (cf. above, Ch. VI, n. 27), see the capital text in the *Ascent of Mount Carmel*, Bk. II, Ch. v (iv): "In order, then, to understand what is meant by this union whereof we are treating, it must be known that God dwells and is present substantially in every soul, even in that of the greatest sinner in the world. And this kind of union is ever wrought between God and all the creatures, for in it He is preserving their being so that if union of this kind were to fail them, they would at once become annihilated; and would cease to be. And so, when we speak of union of the soul with God, we speak not of this substantial union which is continually being wrought, but of the union and transformation of the soul with God, which is not being wrought continually, but only when there exists that likeness that comes from love; we shall therefore term this the union of likeness, even as that other union is called substantial or essential. The former is natural; the latter supernatural.

"... as we have said, God is ever in the soul, giving it, and through his presence preserving it within its natural being, yet He does not always communicate supernatural being to it. For this is communicated only by love and grace, which not all souls possess and all those that possess it have it not in the same degree, for some have attained more degrees of love and others fewer.

"Wherefore, as has already been explained, the more completely a soul is wrapped up in creatures and in its own abilities, by habit and affection, the less preparation it has for such union; for it gives not God a complete opportunity to transform it supernaturally. The soul, then, needs only to strip itself of these natural dissimilarities and contrarieties, so that God, Who is communicating Himself naturally to it, according to the course of nature, may communicate Himself to it supernaturally by means of grace" (*Silv.*, II, pp. 81–82; Peers, I, pp. 80–81).

Some difficulties have been raised about the following text from Ch. xv (xiii): "when the soul has completely purified and voided itself of all forms and images that can be apprehended, it will remain in this pure and simple light, being transformed therein into a state of perfection. For though *this light never fails in the soul*, it is not infused into it because of the creature forms and veils wherewith the soul is veiled and embarrassed; but if these impediments and these veils were wholly removed . . . the soul would then find itself in a condition of pure detachment and poverty of spirit, and, being simple and pure, would be transformed into simple and pure Wisdom, which is the Son of God. For the enamored soul finds that that which is natural has failed it, and it is then imbued with that which is Divine, both naturally and supernaturally, so that there may be no vacuum in its nature" (*Ascent*, Bk. II, Ch. xv [xiii], Silv., II, p. 135; Peers, I, p. 129, 4). This text (from which the word *naturally* was omitted by the first editors) must evidently be understood within the general teaching of the saint and finds its natural commentary in the explanations previously given by him in Ch. v. As we have just seen, he explains there that although divine light is *never absent from the soul* ("according to the course of nature," Ch. v) because God is present to it

end and meaning of human life, and the second has to do with theological faith.

10. For St. John of the Cross, as for St. Thomas Aquinas and the whole Christian tradition, the final end of human life is transformation in God, "to become God by participation,"[20] which is fully achieved in heaven by the

by His creative immensity, the "transformation of the soul with God by love" can be produced only when grace renders God present in the soul according to the union of likeness (or, as St. Thomas says, accordingly as the known and loved is in him who knows and loves. *Sum. Theol.*, I, 8, 3). Only because the soul has thus received "from God this rebirth and adoption which transcends all that can be imagined" (Ch. v) can it remove the veils and obstacles due to creatures and abide in poverty of spirit. That is the condition presupposed by everything the saint says in Ch. xv, and that is why, although the soul supernaturalized by grace and "already surrendered to love" is emptied of the "natural," the Divine immediately permeates it naturally (according to the substantial "union that is ever wrought between God and all the creatures" by which He already dwelt in the soul) and supernaturally, according to the union of grace and love.

This doctrine is taken up again and explained in the Spiritual Canticle, 2nd redact., st. 11 (eleven), Silv., III, pp. 245–246.

20   *Ascent*, Bk. II, Ch. v (iv), n. 7, Silv., II, p. 84 (Peers, I, p. 82); *Dark Night*, Bk. II, Ch. xx, n. 5; Silv., II, p. 492; *Living Flame of Love*, st. 1, line 1, Silv., IV, p. 9 (iii); st. 2, line 6, Silv., IV, pp. 44–45 (151–152); *Canticle*, st. 27 (22), Silv., III, p. 132; st. 38 (39), Silv., III, pp. 171–172. Cf. *Spiritual Sentences and Maxims*, § 132: "What God wants is to transform us into gods, and to give us by participation what He Himself is by nature. . . . He is like fire which changes everything into fire" (Ger., III, p. 31).

We generally quote the works of St. John of the Cross from the edition of Rev. Fr. Silverio de Santa Teresa. The chapter numbers of the *Ascent of Mount Carmel* are not the same in Gerardo and Silverio. The number in parentheses indicates the chapter number in the Gerardo edition. (The English translations have been checked, wherever possible, with Allison Peers' translation of St. John of the Cross. Tr.)

Our quotations from the *Living Flame* are taken from the first redaction; the number in parentheses represents the corresponding pages in the second redaction, which differ from the texts quoted only in a few matters of form that do not affect the thought.

Unless noted to the contrary, quotations from the *Spiritual Canticle* are taken from the first redaction. The number in parentheses indicates the corresponding stanza in the second redaction. When a passage from the second redaction is quoted, then the number in parentheses refers to the first redaction.

Textual criticism must settle the debate about the two canticles. Arguments of internal criticism drawn from the opposition of theories, may lead to serious probabilities (against the authenticity of the second Canticle). To our mind, however impressive they may be, these arguments do not go so far as demonstrative certitude. We have to keep in mind the liberty proper to wise men: the Son of Man is master even of the Sabbath; a St. John of the Cross is master of his text and is free to recast it in order to make certain truths more understandable, or to draw new meanings from it, even if this amounts to a general change in perspective. That is a simple possibility, but the rules of logic require that we do

beatific vision and beatific love, and fulfilled here below, in faith, by love. The supernatural love of charity, by which we love God and creatures with a properly divine love, makes us one with God and causes us to be one same spirit with Him. *Qui adhaeret Deo, unus spiritus est.* "The end of all actions and

---

not overlook it. On this question see the different opinions of Silverio de Santa Teresa (*Cant.*, t. III, Appendices, pp. 499 ff.), Eugenio de San José (*Archivo Carmelitano*, 1931), Gabriel de Ste. Marie-Madeleine (*Études Carm.*, April 1934) on the one hand, and on the other hand Phillipe Chevallier (*Le cantique spirituel*, critical text, 1930; "Le cantique spirituel interpolé," *Vie Spirituelle*, July–August 1926 ff.), Jean Baruzi (*Saint Jean de la Croix et le problème de l'expérience mystique*, 2nd ed., 1931, Bk. I), Louis de la Trinité (*Études Carm.*, Oct., 1931 ff.). The upshot is that, although the apocryphal character of Canticle B is not proven, at the present stage of research it at least seems probable. Regarding the question of the authenticity of the second version of *The Spiritual Canticle*, the work of P. Gabriel de Ste. Marie-Madeleine (*Études Carmelitaines*, April 1934) seriously upsets the negative thesis of Dom Phillipe Chevallier.

But there is another and no less important question: that of knowing where the *materials* with which Canticle B was constructed come from. It can be easily understood, in the present hypothesis, that the compilers, with the boldness characteristic of those days, cleaned and pruned, corrected or glossed passages judged to be dangerous, and that they also added either connecting passages, or passages intended to justify changes they had introduced into the plan of the work. But there is much other material, not included in either one of these categories, which is found in the Second Canticle although it does not appear in the first, and which fully agrees with the thought of the Saint as revealed in other texts, and with the spontaneous eloquence characteristic of his style. It seems unlikely that this material was fabricated out of sheer taste for falsehood and for the pleasure of inserting passages after the manner of St. John of the Cross who is, moreover, a very difficult author to imitate. The only psychologically satisfying explanation would seem to be that the passages in question were fragments of letters written by the Saint, or notes taken down during his instructions, perhaps during oral commentaries on the *Canticle*. Thus, the purpose of the compilers of Canticle B would have been to preserve precious materials by enshrining them in a work whose plan they recast with ill-advised piety. Dom Phillipe Chevallier (*Vie Spirituelle*, July–August 1926) has given a typical example of a similar procedure: the subject is the *Vrays Entretiens* of St. Francis de Sales, published in 1629 through the efforts of Ste. Jeanne de Chantal. The latter made important suppressions, pruned, trimmed and interpolated fragments of sermons and letters into the original text. "Three of the *Vrays Entretiens* were not actually delivered in the convent parlor but were taken from sermons in manuscript." She added no passages of her own invention fashioned after the style of Francis de Sales! Such would be the case with Canticle B if, with Dom Chevallier, Baruzi, Rev. Louis de la Trinité, we consider it apocryphal. That is why we do not believe that, even though we be convinced that it is a posthumous compilation, we need purely and simply reject it and thus sacrifice the many admirable texts it contains. What is necessary and sufficient, it seems to us, is that in using a text from Canticle B (and not suspected of belonging to the justifications written by a foreign hand) we mention its origin so as to warn the reader of the merely probable attribution of this text to St. John of the Cross.

human affections," writes St. Thomas,[21] "is the love of God, that is why there is no measure regulating that love; it is itself the measure and measures everything else, and can never be too great. The interior act of charity has the *ratio* of an end because the highest good of man is that the soul adhere to God, in accordance with the words of the Psalmist, 'It is good to cling to God. . . .' " And St. John of the Cross writes, "As love is union of the Father and the Son, even so also is it union of the soul with God."[22]

Perfection consists in charity, says St. Thomas[23] again. The perfection of divine love is commanded of all, undoubtedly not as a term to be immediately attained, but at least as the end to which everyone must tend each according to his condition. *Estote perfecti*—seek the perfection of charity which is a perfection of heaven, the *raison d'être* of our life. "At eventide they will examine thee in love," cries St. John of the Cross.[24] And again: "After all, it was for the goal of this love that we were created."[25] It is our supreme reward on this earth, for love "confers no *payment* save of itself,"[26] "the soul that loves God must not claim nor hope for aught else from Him save the perfection of love."[27] Before seeing God in heaven as he sees us, the highest achievement of our life here below is to love God "as much as He loves us." Despite human frailty, such is the state of souls who have attained to spiritual marriage. Attaining during their mortal life—I mean in a state of increasingly rapid motion and progress—that *equality of love* with God which is consummated in the blessed, these souls truly unite heaven and earth within themselves. *Le amara tanto como es amada.* No stronger words have been spoken, illumining our darkness as with a lightning flash, because—as is the wont of John of the Cross—they unveil in a concrete way the highest goal accessible to us here on earth, before the dissolution of this poor flesh. They show us, if I may so speak, our penultimate end, our end on earth, and the end of this perishable existence itself.[28]

---

21 *Sum. Theol.*, II–II, 27, 6, corp. and ad 3.
22 *Cant.*, st. 12 (13), Silv., III, p. 61; Peers, II, p. 74.
23 *Sum. Theol.*, II–II, 184, 3.
24 *Spiritual Sentences and Maxims* (Andujar MS.), § 57, Silv., IV, p. 238 (Peers, III, p. 247).
25 *Cant.*, 2nd redact., st. 28 (19), Silv., III, p. 362 (Peers, II, p. 346).
26 *Cant.*, st. 9, Silv., III, p. 48 (Peers, II, p. 62).
27 *Ibid.*, p. 49 (Peers, II, p. 63).
28 *Cant.*, st. 37 (38), Silv., III, p. 167. We shall come back to this point in the next chapter and in Appendix VIII. But let us note here that, although the second Canticle shifts to the side of the future life the verses describing this equality in its full force and breadth, it nevertheless affirms the possibility of this equality here below. This possibility stands whether it be a question of the equality of love which begins with the spiritual betrothal, "by calling Him her brother, she denotes the equality which there is in the betrothal of love between the two before they attain to this estate (of spiritual marriage)" (*Cant.*, 2nd redact., st. 22, Silv., III, p. 323; Peers, II, p. 143. This passage is identical in the first edition, st. 27, Silv., p. 135); "This kiss is the union whereof we are speaking, wherein the soul is made

11. In beatitude we shall be deified by intellection. But this very vision will be the crowning effect of love, the hand by which it will grasp its good, and in the delights of exultant love this vision will blossom.[29] Furthermore, here below, where we do not know God by His essence but by His effects, no pure knowledge is able to unite us to God immediately and without an intervening distance. But love, on the contrary, can. "God, Who in this world cannot be known in Himself, can be loved in Himself" and "immediately,"[30] as the

---

equal with God through love. Wherefore she has this desire, asking to be given the Beloved that He may be her brother, which phrase signifies and makes equality" (*Cant.*, 2nd redact., st. 24, Silv., III, p. 331; Peers, II, p. 92. This passage is identical in the first edition, st. 15, Silv., p. 82); or whether the question concerns the equality of love proper to spiritual marriage: "For the property of love is to make the lover equal with the object of his love. Wherefore, since its love is now perfect, the soul is called the Bride of the Son of God, which signifies equality with Him, in the which equality of friendship *all things of both are common to both.* . . ." (*Cant.*, 2nd redact., st. 27, Silv., III, p. 356; Peers, II, p. 341).

In any event, whether the second redaction of the Canticle be considered authentic or apocryphal, the doctrine of an equality of love beginning on earth and highest term of the soul's aspirations here below, is essential in St. John of the Cross. This is attested, among other confirmations, by the texts from the *Living Flame* which are to be found in Ch. IX, §§ 12–16.

29 St. John of the Cross is in full agreement with St. Thomas when he considers beatitude as consummated by love. (Cf. *Cant.*, 2nd redact., st. 38 (37), Silv., III, p. 412.)

According to St. Thomas (and St. John of the Cross professes the same doctrine; see, e.g., *The Dark Night*, Bk. II, Ch. xx, n. 5, Silv., II, p. 492 and many other passages) beatitude is constituted formally and essentially by vision (cf. *Sum. Theol.*, I–II, q. 3, a. 4 and 8). That by which the creature possesses God as his good is the act of understanding. But the immensity of joy entailed by such an act reaches its fullness in the will and therefore, in the will, that beatitude is consummated, "quia scilicet ipsum gaudium est consummatio beatitudinis" (a. 4).

In the *Spiritual Canticle*, st. 13 (14), St. John of the Cross speaks of the greatest delights of the soul, which are "en el entendimiento, en que consiste la *frucion*, como dicen los teologos, que es ver a Dios" (Silv., III, p. 71). Were someone to question the words "en que consiste la frucion," "wherein fruition resides," claiming that it is not Thomistic to situate fruition in the intellect and not in the will, we could answer that, as a result of the mutual inclusion of the spiritual faculties "quod est in voluntate est etiam quodammodo in intellectu," so that "affectus animae . . . sunt in intellectu . . . sicut principiatum in principio, in quo habetur notio principiati"; "unde et Philosophus hoc modo loquendi utitur in III *de Anima*, quod voluntas in ratione est" (St. Thomas, *Sum. Theol.*, I, 87, 4, c, ad I and 3). Actually, St. John of the Cross simply wanted to point out that, as Fr. Garrigou-Lagrange rightly remarks (*Vie Spirituelle*, Oct. 1, 1930, p. 25), the intellect, seat of the beatitude which consists in seeing God, is in heaven the principle of that fruition.

30 *Sum. Theol.*, I–II, 27, 2; II–II, 27, 4. Cf. I–II, 62, 3: It belongs properly to charity to produce with God "unionem quamdam spiritualem per quam quodammodo transformamur in illum finem." Cf. above, Ch. VI, §§ 14 and 23.

Angelic Doctor profoundly remarks. And again: "The love of charity has for its object that which is already possessed,"[31] to wit, He who has already given Himself by grace. And what does the Catholic faith say? That God is love, as St. John proclaimed. Οτι ὁ θεὸς ἀγάπη ἐστιν. We are to understand that, even though God has many proper names, and though to Moses He called Himself *He who is*, and although Greek Wisdom knew His name as *Thought thinking itself*, the Gospel reveals to us an even more secret name, by showing us that He is *subsistent Love*. As love He transforms us into Himself; this is the name that holds all His secrets with us. These truths which we stammer out were the very breath of life to St. John of the Cross. That is why he said "there is no better or more necessary work than love."[32] "God is pleased with naught save love."[33] That is why the idea that pure knowledge or pure understanding could be the means proportionate to union with God, seemed to him to be absurdity itself. That is why he is convinced, with all Christianity, that contemplation is not its own end but remains a means (the most excellent of means and already united to the end) for the union of love with God, and that it is itself a knowledge of love, a "loving attentiveness to God."[34]

We are here at the antipodes of neo-Platonic intellectualism. And we are here at the very heart of the theology of St. Thomas.[35] We must add, we are also very far from certain modern interpretations of St. John of the Cross. This doctrine is a commentary on a Canticle because it explains the *moments* in a dialogue of love, at whose end the lover and the beloved are but one voice,[36] truly one in a unity not of substance but of love: "Two natures in one spirit and love."[37]

Theological Faith

12. The second theological presupposition we would like to stress refers to the nature of theological faith. A famous verse from the Spiritual Canticle has to do precisely with this subject, and St. John of the Cross explains it very clearly in his commentary.

> O crystalline fount. If on that thy silvered surface
> Thou wouldst of a sudden form the eyes desired
> Which I bear outlined in my inmost parts!

31 *Sum. Theol.*, I–II, 66, 6: "Amor charitatis est de eo quod jam habetur."

32 *Cant.*, 2nd redact., st. 28 (19), Silv., III, p. 361; Peers, II, p. 346.

33 *Ibid.*, 2nd redact., st. 27 (18), Silv., III, p. 356; Peers, II, p. 341.

34 "Advertencis amorosa a Dios, sin especificar actos" (*Living Flame*, st. 3, line 3, §6, Silv. IV, p. 66 [173]; Peers, I, p. 116); Cf. *Ascent*, Bk. II, Ch. xiii (xi), Silv., II, p. 120; etc.

35 Cf *Sum. Theol.*, II–II, 180, 1; I–II, 68, I to 6; II–II, 45, 2.

36 "He gives her a voice [*the song of the sweet philomel*] that she may sing to God with Him" (*Cant.*, st. 38 [39]; Peers, II, p. 179).

37 "Consumado este spiritual matrimonio entre Dios y el alma, son dos naturalezas en un espiritu y amor de Dios" (*Cant*, st. 27 [22], Silv., III, p. 132; Peers, II, p. 140). Cf. below, Ch. IX, §§ 10 and 12.

The *crystalline fount* is faith "because from it there flow to the soul the waters of all spiritual blessings"; it opens within us the source of living water which is the Holy Spirit; it is like crystal "because it has the properties of crystal in being pure in its truths and strong and clear, free from errors and natural forms."[38]

The "silvered surface" are the propositions or articles of faith. "It must be noted," explains the Saint, "that faith is compared to silver with respect to the propositions which it teaches us, and the truths and substance which they contain in themselves are compared to gold; for that same substance which now we believe, clothed and covered with the silver of faith, we shall behold and enjoy in the life to come, fully revealed and with the gold of the faith laid bare. . . . But when this faith shall have come to an end, which will be when it is perfected through the clear vision of God, then the substance of the faith will remain, stripped of this veil of silver, and in color as gold."[39]

Finally, the "eyes, desired" are the very substance of faith itself, the divine eyes, divine truths considered in themselves, those living truths which the soul possesses in itself, but only "outlined," because they are veiled in faith (and which, we may note, will in eternal life be not only the reality seen but also, as it were, the very eyes by which we see, since it is *by themselves* that they will be known).

This is the very same doctrine that St. Thomas sets forth in the *Summa Theologicae*,[40] when he distinguishes within faith the *reality* in which it terminates (namely, God Himself in the interiority of His essence, the same God Who is seen by the blessed), and the *mode of knowing* (which is proportioned to our nature and reveals this divine reality to us only through the appearances of objects that are first attained by the concepts and names which are our natural means of knowing, and which God, through the ministry of His Church, uses to tell us of Himself in human language).

The capital importance of this doctrine with respect to mystical theology is immediately evident. Mystical theology's whole impetus and desire is to grasp, by freeing itself of the human and imperfect mode of multiple ideas, this same object, this same divine reality to which the light of faith unites us by using these ideas as a means proportionate to our nature. Thus contemplation on this earth is essentially knowledge *by faith*, since only supernatural faith attains to divine reality in its proper life; and it is knowledge in a *suprahuman mode*, wherein faith surpasses its natural mode of knowing, beyond distinct ideas, to experience its object. And how could this be done except by love, which inviscerates us within things divine and itself becomes the light of knowledge, in that purely and ineffably spiritual awareness given by the Holy Spirit acting through His gifts?

---

38   *Cant.*, 11 (12), Silv., III, p. 52; Peers, II, p. 65.
39   *Ibid.*, p. 53; Peers, II, p. 66.
40   *Sum. Theol.*, II–II, 1, 2, c, and ad 2. Cf. Ch. VI, § 4.

As we shall emphasize again, at the end of this chapter, this is truly the thought of St. John of the Cross, and it is in full agreement with Thomistic theology. How does he continue his commentary upon this verse of the Canticle, in which the soul aspires to see suddenly appear the desired eyes which it bears etched in its heart? Before the beatific vision, to which the soul so aspires, there is an anticipation in which these desired eyes begin to appear. To the *first outline* of things divine which faith imprints upon the heart *is added another which is the work of love*. And by virtue of the "union of love" the image of the Beloved is so "completely and vividly pictured" in the soul that He is truly in the soul and the soul in Him, and "each lives in the other, and the one is the other, and both are one through the transformation of love." In the words of St. Paul, "I live but not I, it is Christ who lives in me."[41] As St. John of the Cross explains at length elsewhere, it is in and by this union of love—and always in and by faith—that contemplation touches and experiences divine things.

IV
THE "PRACTICALITY" OF ST. JOHN OF THE CROSS' VOCABULARY

13. We come now to the properly and essentially practical character of the teaching of St. John of the Cross, which we have stressed from the outset. Here again, we shall not become involved in endless enumerations, but content ourselves with two particularly significant examples, one of which concerns the vocabulary of St. John of the Cross and the other his doctrine of the void.

In the first place, the most important thing to note is that the sciences which we have called *practically practical* make a wholly different use of concepts than do the *speculative* or *speculatively practical* sciences; not only as to their determining finalities and procedure in discourse, but also as to the manner in which the concepts themselves are fashioned and recast, signify and grasp the real and, if I may so speak, make intelligible cross-sections of things. Let us say that in the speculative sciences concepts have their bare abstractive and intelligible value. In these sciences the question is to analyze the real into its ontological or empiriological elements. In the practical sciences, on the contrary, concepts incorporate a whole progression of concrete harmonics; here the question is to assemble the means, the dynamic moments by which action comes into existence. Whence it follows that in these two orders of knowledge concepts that have the same name (one of which is the projection of the other into another noetic sphere) are differently related to the real.

Thus, two differences of principle are to be noted between the conceptual vocabulary of St. John of the Cross and that of scholastic theology: the language of St. John of the Cross refers to mystical experience; it refers to a practical

41   *Cant.* st. 11 (12), Silv., III, p. 55; Peers, II, p. 68.

science. This language of practical science is what we have just tried to describe. Now the language of mysticism has been very well shown[42] to be necessarily other than the language of philosophy. In mystical language, hyperbole is not an ornament of rhetoric but a means of expression rigorously required to signify things exactly; for what it purports to express is sensible experience itself, and what experience! Philosophical language proposes to speak of reality without touching it, mystical language seeks to divine reality as if by touching it without seeing it.[43] How many misunderstandings would be avoided if these two orders were properly distinguished! The misfortune of some mystics, like Eckhart, is to have confused them.

Once again, these differences are not accidental. They relate to the requirements of the specifying objects of the conceptual lexicon concerned. I am not saying that it is impossible to pass from one to the other. I am not saying that the formulas of a mystical writer, or of a practical doctor, are not big with speculative values and, from this point of view, cannot be judged ontologically true or false. The intellect goes from one conceptual vocabulary to another, as it goes from Latin to Chinese or to Arabic. But it cannot apply the syntax of one to the other, it cannot judge the ontological value of a mystical formula or of a practically practical statement except by taking into account the modifications which they must undergo in being translated to the ontological level.

14. St. John of the Cross describes contemplation as *non-agere*,[44] whereas St. Thomas defines it as the *highest activity*.[45] And yet they agree with each other. One takes the ontological point of view, and from this point of view, there is no higher activity than to adhere vitally to God by infused love and infused contemplation, under the influx of operating grace. The other takes the point

---

42   Cf. R. Garrigou-Lagrange, *L'amour de Dieu et la Croix de Jésus*, Introd.; *Lettre postulatoire* addressed in the name of the Angelican College by the Revs. Hugon and Garrigou-Lagrange to the Sovereign Pontiff, June 14, 1926, with a view to obtaining the title of Doctor of the Universal Church for John of the Cross (*Analecta O.C.D.*, Oct.–Dec. 1926: "St. Thomas notes (*in Isaiam* c. 5 & 13) that hyperbole exists in the Scriptures. Thus, when Our Lord says: If thy eye scandalize thee, pluck it out; if thy hand, cut it off. Mystical style is not scholastic style; the only error would be to defend as scholastically true propositions which are true only in the mystical language where hyperbole is used."

43   For example, the mystic, in describing his experience of what created being is before God, would say that the creature is *nothing*, that it is nothing at all. Yes, but these expressions have a mystical, not an ontological meaning. If we are looking for their ontological *foundation* we will find it formulated in this way by St. Thomas, in a text of enormous metaphysical significance: "Prius enim inest unicuique naturaliter quod convenit sibi in se, quam quod solum ex alio habet. Esse autem non habet creatura nisi ab alio, sibi autem relicta in se considerata nihil est: unde prius naturaliter inest sibi nihil quam esse" (*De Aeternitate Mundi*).

44   *Living Flame*, st. 3, line 3, Silv., IV, pp. 65–75.

45   *Sum. Theol.*, II–II, 179 and 180. On this point see Raissa and Jacques Maritain, *De la vie d'oraison* (Rouart, 1925), n. III.

of view of mystical experience itself, and from this point of view, the suspension of every activity in the *human mode* appears to the soul as non-activity. Not to move oneself, to cease from all particular operation, to be in supreme act of attentive and loving immobility, which is itself received from God—is this not to do nothing, not, of course, in the ontological sense, but in the psychological and practical meaning of the word?

15. Likewise St. John of the Cross says that certain divine touches in which the soul savors *eternal life* are experienced in the very substance of the soul, as opposed to its powers or faculties;[46] or again, that the joy of the Holy Spirit penetrates to the very substance of the soul, inaccessible to the senses and the devil.[47] But the context clearly shows that he is not opposing substance to powers[48] in the philosophical sense. For him, the question bears on the degrees of interiority of the divine operations. And when divine action, having first touched the substance of the soul,[49] touches the faculties in their deepest roots

---

46   *Living Flame*, st. 2, line 5, Silv., IV, p. 37 (143) and p. 38 (144). "Toque de sustancia, es a saber, de sustancia de Dios en sustancia del alma . . ." "Y asi el alma, segun sus potencias y su substancia goza." In his commentary on the second line, the Saint tells us that "this is a touch of the Divinity in the soul, without any form or figure whether formal or imaginary" (*ibid.*, pp. 32 and 137; Peers, III, p. 43). And again "Oh, delicate touch, Thou Word, Son of God, Who through the delicateness of Thy Divine Being, dost subtly penetrate the substance of my soul, and, touching it wholly and delicately, dost absorb it wholly in Thyself in Divine ways of sweetness which have never been heard of in the land of Canaan, nor seen in Teman!" (*Ibid.*, line 3, pp. 36 and 141; Peers, p. 47).

47   *Living Flame*, st. 1, line 3, Silv., IV, p. 14 (113): "Porque en la sustancia del alma donde ni el centro del sentido ni el demonio puede llegar, pasa esta fiesta del Espiritu Santo." Cf. *Cant.*, st. 13 (14), Silv., III, p. 70: ". . . las virtudes y gracias del Amado, las cuala mediante la dicha union del Esposo embisten en el alma, y amorisisamente se communican y tocan en la sustancia de ella."

48   It is enough to recall that he wrote, "God here purges the soul according to the substance of its sense and spirit and according to the interior and exterior faculties" (*Dark Night*, Bk. II, st. 1, line 1. Ch. VI, Silv., 11, p. 428; Peers, I, p. 411), to understand that for him the word "substance" has a wholly experimental and concrete meaning which does not always or necessarily include the meaning given it in the ontological analysis used by philosophers. For John of the Cross, this word means what is deepest, most fundamental, most hidden. Cf. St. Teresa, *Interior Castle*, Mansion IV, Ch. II; Peers, II, p. 237: "When it is His Majesty's will and He is pleased to grant us some supernatural favor, its coming is accompanied by the greatest peace and quietness and sweetness within ourselves—I cannot say where it arises or how. . . . I do not think that this happiness has its source in the heart at all. It arises in a much more interior part, like something of which the springs are very deep; I think this must be the center of the soul. . . ." (Tr. Allison Peers, *Complete Works of Saint Teresa*, New York, Sheed and Ward, 1946, Vol. 2, p. 237).

49   According to the Madrid edition (1630) of the *Spiritual Canticle*, verse 13 (14), Silv., III, p. 70, divine action reaches the substance of the soul by means of the

and they, being thus supernaturally moved, become so spiritualized that they allow a glimpse of the soul's depths to shine through, as it were, then it is not the naked substance which acts or knows by itself; the soul does indeed know and act by its powers,[50] and by the gifts and infused love, but in so intimate a center—at the secret nexus where the soul's powers are rooted—that no particular action is produced by these powers, which are actuated from their very depths *in darkness and in concealment*,[51] and absolutely no sign indicates to the angels what is going on in the deepest recesses of the heart.

will ("asi tambien el toque de las virtudes del Amado se sienten y gozan en el tacto de esta alma, que es en la sustancia de ella *mediante la voluntad*"). Is this an editor's commentary? In any event, the Saint writes further on (*ibid.*, p. 71), "Porque este toque de Dios satisface grandemente y regala la sustancia del alma, *cumpliendo suavemente su appetito* . . ."; it is thence that the divine action passes to the understanding ("una subidisma y sabrosisima inteligencia de Dios y de sus virtudes, *la cual redunda en el entendimiento de toque que hacen estas virtudes de Dios en la sustancia del alma*," *ibid.*, p. 70).

50 *Cant.*, st. 13 (14), Silv., III, p. 71: "this most subtle and delicate knowledge enters with marvelous sweetness and delight *into the inmost substance of the soul*." Which, as the Saint immediately explains, means that what is thus "understood" is "naked substance, stripped of accidents and imaginary forms" (cf. also, farther on, p. 72: "esto que el alma entiende, porque sea sustancia desnuda . . .") and that this knowledge is communicated to the "*understanding that is called by philosophers 'passive' or 'possible*,*'* because it receives it passively, doing naught on its own behalf" (Peers, II, pp. 82–83). This last phrase (and there are many others) shows that St. John of the Cross soared high above philosophy and that he was not troubled by any excessive solicitude for strict technical exactness in this realm.

51 *Dark Night*, Bk. II, Ch. xxiii, Silv., II, p. 506; Peers, I, p. 481. Cf. p. 505: "The reason for this is that, as His Majesty dwells substantially in the soul, where neither angel nor devil can attain to an understanding of that which comes to pass, they cannot know the intimate and secret communications which take place there between the soul and God. These communications, since the Lord Himself works them, are wholly Divine and sovereign, for they are all substantial touches of Divine union between the soul and God." See this whole page. See also *Cant.*, st. 32 (19), Silv., III, p. 150; Peers, II, p. 157. St. John of the Cross speaks there of "the touch of pure substances—that is, of the soul and the Divinity." The context shows that here again the word substance has a more experimental than speculative meaning: on the one hand it has to do with a union which completely escapes the sensitive part, and with graces "so lofty and substantial and so *intimate*" that the senses can know nothing of them (pp. 150–151; Peers, II, p. 157). On the other hand, the soul does not then know God "by his effects and works" (St. John of the Cross means that the soul does not know God by His effects as by things from whose knowledge we proceed to the knowledge of their *causa*"; he obviously does not intend to inquire here whether infused love—an effect produced by God in the soul—serves as the *means [quo]* of this knowledge of the "face of God." See above, § 14). The soul knows God "without any kind of intermediary in the soul, through certain contact thereof with the Divinity" (*in virtue of the union itself*, John of St. Thomas will say). And that this contact of substance with substance is itself experienced only on condition that the soul's powers be actuated has clearly been said by the Saint several lines above. Let us

16. Do we need another example? What St. John of the Cross calls pure faith[52] in nakedness of spirit is theological faith, indeed, dogmatic faith, but it is not theological faith isolated by ontological analysis according to its species from the other energies of our supernatural organism; it is living faith, [53] one with the charity which informs it and the gifts which illumine it,[54] the loving, wise and fertile Faith which acts concretely in the life of a holy soul; it is by reference to the mixture of the natural and sensible ingredients that this faith is pure. Thus, St. John of the Cross will say that by faith we love God without seeing Him;[55] and whereas a speculative theologian like John of St. Thomas will rightly affirm that faith all by itself, that is without the gifts, cannot contemplate,[56] St. John of the Cross, the mystical Doctor, will state with no less truth that faith alone, i.e., the concretely taken faith of which we have been speaking, enveloping within itself love and the gifts, is the proximate and proportionate means of contemplation.[57]

reread the whole beginning of this passage (Silv., p. 150; Peers, II, pp. 156–157): "It is as though the soul were to say: "Dear Spouse of mine, withdraw Thee into the inmost part of my soul communicating Thyself to it after a secret fashion and manifesting to it Thy hidden wonders, which are far removed from mortal eyes.' *And look with thy face upon the mountains.* The *face* of God is His Divinity and the mountains are the faculties of the soul—memory, understanding and will. Thus it is as though she were to say: Illumine my understanding with Thy Divinity, giving it Divine intelligence; and my will, giving and communicating to it Divine love; and my memory, with Divine possession of glory. Herein the soul prays Him for all that for which she may pray, since she is not now being content with knowledge and communication of God from behind, such as God granted to Moses (Exod. xxxiii, 23), that is, with a knowledge of Him by His effects and works; but she desires to see the face of God, which is essential communication of His Divinity, without any kind of intermediary in the soul, through certain contact thereof with the Divinity. This is a thing far removed from all sense and accidents, inasmuch as it is the touch of pure substances—that is, of the soul and the Divinity." So it is clearly a question of substantial contact between the soul and Divinity and this takes place because the latter has fully invaded the powers of the soul and is attained, not by proceeding by inference from effects to the Cause, but in virtue of the very union of love which causes the presence of the Divine Essence in the substance of the soul to be spiritually perceived and possessed.

52   Cf. *Ascent of Mount Carmel*, Bk. II, Ch. i (Ger., *Introd.*) Silv., II, pp. 67–68; Ch. xxiv (xxii), Silv., II, p. 203; *Dark Night*, Bk. I, Ch. xi, Silv., II, p. 400; etc.

53   Cf. *Avisos y Sentencias*, §100, Ger., III, p. 27: "Todas las aprehensiones y noticias de cosas sobrenaturales no pueden ayudar al amor de Dios tanto cuanto el menor acto de Fe viva y Esperanza, que se hace en desnudez de todo eso."

54   "En la otra vida es por medio de la lumbre de gloria, y en esta por medio *de la fe ilustradisima*" (*Living Flame*, st. 3, line 3, Silv., IV, p. 91 [201]).

55   "la Fe, en la cual amamos a Dios sin entenderle" (*Cant.*, Prologue, Silv., III, p. 5).

56   John of St. Thomas, *Curs. Theol.*, I–II, q. 68–70, disp. 18, a. 1, n. 12. *Les dons du Saint Esprit*, tr. R. Maritain, Ch. I, § 12. Cf. above, Ch. VI, § 4.

57   On this capital point, which St. John of the Cross does not tire of stressing, see R. Garrigou-Lagrange, *Perfection chrétienne et contemplation*, t. II, pp. 38–44;

17. Finally, we know that St. John of the Cross constantly makes use of the Augustinian division of the higher faculties into *understanding, memory and will*, as did the Franciscan writers whom the Carmelites of the Reform were much wont to read. And actually—even though from the point of view of speculative and ontological analysis the bipartite division into *intellect* and *will* is the only one conformed to the real—from the point of view of practical analysis, which distinguishes the powers of the soul not according to their essential ontological articulations, but according to the subject's principal concrete modes of activity with respect to his ends, the Augustinian division is the right one, it is this division that is in conformity with reality, with *that* reality.

From this point of view, there is every reason to distinguish three principal functions in the subject taken as a living whole: sometimes he turns towards objects in order that he may know them in themselves—and this is understanding (which, in the concrete vocabulary of St. John of the Cross, includes the senses and the imagination, whence the intellect draws all its ideas); sometimes the subject turns towards things insofar as he has experienced and will experience them, insofar as they concern him and touch his personal experience, have practical value for him, weave the web of the ever-increasing past which, as Bergson says, constantly crowds the present in order to take it over—this is the memory (including from this point of view, not only knowledge but affection and appetivity); sometimes the subject turns toward things to desire and love them, and to move toward them, and then they become his interior weight—this is the will. That is why almost all mystical writers have, with good reason, adopted the Augustinian division which is traditional among them; that is why, from his practical point of view, St. John of the Cross had to make the three theological virtues correspond to the three terms of this division, and relate Hope to memory, Faith to understanding and Charity to will. He was thus enabled to expound the profoundest of views upon the relations of the virtue of hope to memory and the purification of the latter by the former.

But none of this entails the slightest incompatibility with the views developed by St. Thomas, in the ontological order, upon the number of the soul's faculties and their specification. Father Crisogono is entirely right in remarking that Baconthorpe, along with St. Thomas Aquinas, assigned hope to the will. And, he adds, he knows of no scholastic who departed from this doctrine,

Crisogono de Jesus Sacramentado, *San Juan de la Cruz, su obra científica*, 1929, pp. 320 ff. Rev. Crisogono gives more than twenty textual references to the Saint: *Ascent*, Bk. I, Ch. ii (Ger., I, p. 38); Bk. II, Ch. iii (p. 106); Ch. iii (p. 109); Ch. vii (p. 127); Ch. viii (p. 132); Ch. ix (p. 135); Ch. x (p. 139); Ch. x (p. 141); Ch. xiv (p. 172); Ch. xvii (p. 195); Ch. xxii (p. 229); Ch. xxii (p. 230); Ch. xxviii (p. 259); Bk. III, argum. (p. 269); Ch. xi (p. 299). *Dark Night*, Bk. I, Ch. xi (Ger., II, p. 38), Bk. II, Ch. ii (p. 55); Ch. xxi (p. 123); *Cant.*, st. I, line 1 (Ger., II, p. 177); st. 12, declar. (p. 221), *Living Flame*, st. 3, line 3, § IX (Ger., II, p. 454).

and, consequently, St. John of the Cross, by his manner of expressing himself on this subject, "broke with the whole tradition of the schools."[58] Moreover, from the point of view of ontological analysis and scholastic theology, the idea of situating theological faith in the memory would clearly be indefensible. Is it credible that St. John of the Cross did not perceive so patent a point of doctrine, or that he wanted to invent on this point a new theological theory, he who was never interested in treating such matters speculatively? He is not speaking as a scholastic theologian, but as a practitioner in the things of the spirit. It was because he clung to the point of view of the "practically practical" science of human acts that he made these teachings on the memory[59] so important (and so powerfully original) a part of his work, and that he takes his place with St. Augustine among those who have penetrated most deeply into the psychology of the memory.

The Doctrine of the Void

18. Since all human means, whatever they may be, are disproportionate with respect to possessing God in his own life, the best thing the creature can do is to cast himself off, rid himself of self, renounce his own proper operations and make a void within himself. This central thesis of St. John of the Cross would be absurd were God not supernaturally present in the soul (and it is a question of a soul already called in a proximate manner to contemplation), were God not there knocking at the gate, to invade the soul wholly, to replace all it has lost by a better life which is the life of God Himself, the torrent of His peace. A mad courage, heroic confidence corresponding in the very order of the spirit to the "insane" love of God, All-holy, such is the basic character of the spirituality of St. John of the Cross. "Nothing, nothing, nothing," as he said to Ana de Penalosa, "even to leaving one's skin and all else for Christ."

What? Was he not aware that grace completes nature and does not destroy

---

58   Crisogono de Jesus Sacramentado, *op. cit.*, p. 122. Farther on (pp. 330–331) Fr. Crisogono rightly points out the practical importance of St. John of the Cross' teachings on Hope—against Quietism which was to develop later in France and Spain, and whose errors the Saint (like Ruysbroek before him) was already denouncing in the false mystics and *illuminati* of his day.

59   The modern reader will find in those teachings many remarks to which his acquaintance with contemporary literature will make him particularly responsive. "All the greatest deceptions which are caused by the devil, and the evils that he brings to the soul, enter by way of knowledge and reflections of the memory . . ." cries St. John of the Cross. "I would that spiritual persons might clearly see how many kinds of harm are wrought by evil spirits in their souls by means of the memory, when they devote themselves frequently to making use of it, and how many kinds of sadness and affliction and vain and evil joys they have, both with respect to their thoughts about God, and also with respect to the things of the world; and how many impurities are left rooted in their spirits" (*Ascent*, Bk. III, Ch. iv (iii), Silv., II, pp. 251–252; Peers, I, p. 237).

it? He knew it much better than we do. We are now at the crux of the apparent antinomy between the *ontological* language of theology and the *practical* and *mystical* language of a St. John of the Cross or of the *Imitation of Christ*. St. John of the Cross is not laying hand upon the ontological order and upon the perfecting, the enrichment, the superelevation which nature received from grace: he supposes this order and all truths concerning it. He is preaching neither mutilation nor suicide, nor the slightest ontological destruction of the least vein in the wing of the smallest gnat. His point of view is not that of the structure of our substance and its faculties: it is the point of view of our ownership of ourselves in the free use and moral exercise of our activity. And there he asks for everything. There we must give all.[60] The death he preaches is very real, more subtle and more delicate than material death and destruction, a vitally active and efficacious death, savored, free, which strikes to the heart of our most immanent activity, is accomplished in and by it, grows with it, adheres to it in deepest intimacy. This death is called *self-surrender*. This death does not obliterate sensibility, it refines and makes it more exquisite; it does not harden the fibers of being, it softens and spiritualizes them, it transforms us into love.

Remember that grace is not added to nature like a roof or a façade on a monument; it grafts divine life on to nature, penetrates and superelevates the soul in its very essence as well as in its faculties, enabling it to perform divine works proceeding wholly from grace and wholly from our natural powers, but now superelevated by grace. What does this mean, if not that at the term of our growth the initial principle of all our acts, the principal agent, the head of our internal government, must no longer be ourselves but the Spirit of Christ in us?[61] This is not possible without a radical dispossession. As owners of

---

60   Concerning the *Spiritual Sentences and Maxims* addressed to the Carmelites of Beas, see Appendix IX.

61   Cf. *Ascent of Mount Carmel*, Bk. III, Ch. ii (i), Silv., II, p. 244; Peers, I, pp. 220, 301: "When at last God possesses the faculties and has become the entire master of them, through their transformation into Himself, it is He Himself who moves and commands them divinely, according to His Divine Spirit and will; and the result of this is that the operations of the soul are not distinct, but all that it does is of God, and its operations are Divine, so that, even as St. Paul says, he that is joined unto God becomes one spirit with Him (I Cor. vi, 17). Hence it comes to pass that the operations of the soul in union are of the Divine Spirit and are Divine. And hence it comes that the actions of such souls are only those that are seemly and reasonable, and not those that are ill-beseeming. For the Spirit of God teaches them that which they ought to know, and causes them to be ignorant of that which it behooves them not to know, and to remember that which they have to remember, with or without forms, and to forget that which they should forget, and it makes them love that which they have to love, and not to love that which is not in God. And thus all the first motions of the faculties of such souls are Divine and it is not to be wondered at that the motions and operations of these faculties should be Divine, since they are transformed in the Divine Being." "all the first motions of the faculties of *such souls* are divine," said St. John of the

ourselves we shall have eclipsed ourselves. Love desires nothing so much as this, for it is the seal of our union with the God we love and of our transformation in Him. Nothing is more desired by our spiritual nature, since in this perfect poverty the soul becomes perfectly free, the more deeply "self-causing" (*causa sui*) because it has forgone being principal cause. But nothing more completely strips humanity and empties it of self, nothing exacts more radical purification and suffering.

This is why the practical realization of the axiom "grace perfects nature and does not destroy it" is accomplished only by the mystical, not ontological, agony and death of this same nature. Let us die the death of angels, said St. Bernard. In human nature (wounded ever since the first sin and gnawed to its depth by concupiscence), this death cannot be achieved without those great uprootings in the night of the senses and the night of the soul—unless the seed fall to earth and decay. Then do we not remain alone, then do we bear fruit. "To the end that God may of His own accord work Divine union in the soul, it is necessary to proceed by this method of disencumbering and emptying the soul, and causing the natural jurisdiction and operations of the faculties to be denied them, so that they may become capable of infusion and illumination from supernatural sources. . . ."[62]

But the law of suffering goes even farther. For the soul already raised to transforming union and whose suffering from then on (according to the testimony of the saints) can come only from God Himself, not from creatures, is more than ever athirst for suffering, St. John of the Cross tells us.[63] For the fact of it is that the very grace which transforms us is the grace of our crucified Head, and that, being associated with His work, which is to die for the world, we are transformed from splendor to splendor.

Indeed, in all this supernatural striving, from the first stammerings within us of the grace of conversion, we must renounce very real, and—if one may so speak—terribly ontological goods; is not even the most paltry pleasure, in the words of Aristotle, the metaphysical fruit of act? There are many joys not so paltry that we leave for Christ; we would love Him very little did we not forgo, for His sake, things truly good and beautiful. And that is a kind of universal destruction; for it is almost as difficult, sometimes even more difficult, to detach ourselves from what we might have or might have had than from what we have (for the fact remains that we have at least had the latter). That self-surrender of which we were speaking a while back demands proofs;

Cross. "All the first movements of nature are right and good," Jean Jacques Rousseau will cry (*First Dialogue*). A comparison of these two statements gives us the measure of the great abyss separating Christian wisdom from its naturalistic counterfeit.

62   *Ascent*, Bk. III, Ch. ii (i), Silv., II, p. 241; Peers, I, p. 227. Cf. *Living Flame*, st. 2, line 6, Silv., IV, p. 44 (150–151).

63   Cf. *Cant.*, st. 35 (36), Silv., III, p. 161; see below, Ch. IX, § 11.

the twisted and torn limbs of the martyrs, the bloody destruction of the great Victim upon the cross, point out what kind.

However, as we have already insisted, what is primarily necessary is the interior stripping indissolubly linked to charity; dispossession of the self: the remainder is, so to speak, added by way of superabundance. In us, the reality of this remainder, whatever is ontological in what God by His law, His inspiration or His providence asks us to renounce, is only the ontological reality of a certain use of our liberty and our powers, which yields to a higher and more divine use. The ontological reality of which we are thus deprived is very important to our affectivity, it matters deeply to our flesh. There is not the slightest mutilation, but, on the contrary, incomparable enrichment in sacrificing it for love, which is worth more than all else and whose ontological perfection is incomparably higher.[64] The perfection, not only moral, but metaphysical, of the human creature was never and will never be more fully achieved than when the most beautiful of the children of men was immolated upon the wood of the cross.

This, then, is the concrete meaning of the theological axiom: nature is not destroyed but perfected by grace. Whoever hears the words *Be ye perfect* must not expect his nature to be "perfected" in any more comfortable fashion. Should one entertain such expectation, even though it be only by diminishing his natural desires in order to cultivate them in peace, he will succeed only in atrophying his nature in order to suffer less. What, then, is there to complain about? What more does nature need than the eight beatitudes? It certainly does not wish for more, it wishes for less. That is why St. John of the Cross so passionately reproaches those who fear to suffer, for their lack of ambition and magnanimity. When self-annihilation and suffering achieve their full dimensions, as in the Doctor of Night himself, then do love and perfection achieve theirs, too. To be sure, a hundred-fold reward is promised us even on this earth. But only on the conditions which have been already set down: "Since I have taken up my abode in nothing, I find that nothing is wanting to me."

19. From this eminent example we can see how the speculative science and the practical science of Christian realities are in harmony, even while they speak a different language and are apparently opposed to each other. At the same time, we understand how wrong it would be to vitiate the one by transferring to it the formulas of the other just as they are; for this would give rise, on the one hand, to a sort of Jansenist or Lutheran theology teaching that nature is essentially corrupt and grace is its enemy and, on the other hand, it

---

64 Immediately proportioned as it is to eternal life, charity is, speaking absolutely and ontologically, what is most perfect in man, not only in the line of merit and virtue but in the line of being itself; it is metaphysically more perfect than the highest intellectual virtues on this earth; it is inferior in metaphysical degree only to the light of glory, which rules it in heaven. Cf. John of St. Thomas, *Curs. Theol.*, I–II, p. 67, disp. 17, a. 3. n. 25–29.

would result in a kind of pagan or naturalistic ascetic which would teach that perfection is simply an athletic development of natural activities crowned by grace, and that Christ chose the thorns in order to leave us the roses.

Analogous observations could be made concerning the "contempt for creatures" professed by the saints. Practically, the Saint sees that creatures are nothing compared to Him he loves and the End he has chosen: nothing can be done about it, they are worthless for him in comparison with his love. This is a lover's contempt for that which is not his beloved, that is to say in this case, Love itself. To give Him "all the substance of his house"[65] is nothing. "For love of Him I have lost everything, treat everything else as refuse, if I may have Christ to my credit. . . . Him I would learn to know and the virtue of His resurrection, and what it means to share His sufferings. . . ."[66] And by a marvellous reflex, the more he despises creatures as rivals of God, as objects of a possible option against God, the more he cherishes them in and for Him Whom he loves, as loved by Him and made truly good and worthy of being loved by the love which creates and infuses goodness in all things.[67] For to love a being in God and for God—I am speaking here of the love of friendship, not the love of concupiscence—is not to treat it simply as a means or occasion to love God, which amounts to dispensing oneself from loving him (and at the same time ceasing truly to love God, who is truly loved only when we love His visible images, too); to love a creature in and for God is to love this being and consider him as an end, to desire his good because he deserves to be loved in himself and for himself, I mean *according as this very merit and this dignity as end* flow from the sovereign Love and sovereign Lovableness of God. They are thus fused in God and, at the same time, placed beyond all quarrels and vicissitudes. Not to stop short at the creature—that is the guarantee that the creature will be loved unfailingly, transfixed in the root of its lovableness by the arrow which pierces it. In this way the paradox becomes comprehensible: that in the end the Saint embraces in a universal love of friendship and piety—a love incomparably more free, but also more tender and happier than the love of concupiscence of the voluptuary or the miser—everything that passes in time and all the weakness and all the beauty of things, everything he has given up.

He has the right to despise creatures. The philosopher, the theologian do not have that right. Here, again, it would be completely wrong to give a speculative meaning to the formulas of a John of the Cross. There is no worse philosophy than a philosophy that despises nature. A knowledge that despises what is, is itself nothing; a cherry between the teeth holds within it more mystery than the whole of idealist metaphysics. A philosophical distortion of

---

65   *Canticle of Canticles*, viii, 7.
66   Philip. iii, 8–10 (Knox trans.)
67   "Amor Dei est infundans et creans bonitatem in rebus" (St. Thomas, *Sum. Theo.*, I, 20, 2).

the maxims of the saints cut off from love, in which alone these maxims have their meaning, would lead one to think that creatures are nothing so that one might love nothing, and to humiliate them before God in order to give oneself the right not to render them their due. . . .

Finally, to come back to our consideration of semantics and the mind's power to vary the meaning of its signs to suit its own ends, let us note that whereas speculative language, because it considers the pure object of the intellect, is an essentially ontological language, practical and mystical language (if it is to be accurate) must, of necessity, be predominantly psychological and affective, because it considers things in relation to, and even as invliscerated in, the acting subject.[68] Particularly with respect to the relation and union of the soul with God, some formulas of the mystics, which are absolutely rash if understood theologically, assume their true meaning when it is acknowledged that love has its own autonomous mode of expression.[69]

---

68   "The vocabulary of the mystics is not ontological, but affective, individual rather than personal" (Louis Massignon, "L'expérience mystique et les modes de stylisation littéraire," *Chroniques du Roseau d'Or*, 1927, no. 4).

St. John of the Cross himself writes that "it would be ignorance to think that sayings of love understood mystically, such as those of the present stanzas, can be fairly explained by words of any kind. For the Spirit of the Lord Who aids our weakness, as St. Paul says, dwells in us and makes intercession for us, with groanings which cannot be uttered, pleading for that which we cannot well understand or comprehend, so as to express it ourselves. For who can write down that which He reveals to loving souls wherein He dwells? And who can set forth in words that which He makes them feel? And lastly, who can express that which He makes them desire? Of a surety, none; nay, indeed, not the very souls through whom He passes. And it is for this reason that, by means of figures, comparisons and similitudes, they allow something of that which they feel to overflow and utter secret mysteries from the abundance of the Spirit, rather than explain these things rationally. These similitudes, if they may not be read with the simplicity of the spirit of love and understanding embodied in them, appear to be nonsense rather than the expression of reason" (*Cant.*, Prologue, Silv., III, pp. 3–4; Peers, II, pp. 23–24).

69   To proceed directly to the most difficult case to defend (if, indeed, it be defensible), a most particularly thorny problem of interpretation is posed by a certain Angelus Silesius, for example, when he says:

> *Ich weiss, dass ohne mich Got nicht ein Nu kann leben;*
> *Werd ich zunicht, er muss von Not den Geist aufgeben.*

(I know that without me God cannot live for an instant; were I annihilated, He would necessarily cease to be.)

> *Dass Gott so selig ist und lebet ohne Verlangen*
> *Hatt er sowohl von mir als ich von ihm empfangen.*

Or again:

Gott ist so viel an mir, als mir an ihm gelegen.
Sein Wesen helf ich ihm, wie er das meine hegen, etc.

All of these formulae are manifestly scandalous if taken as statements of philosophical or theological doctrine. God could not annihilate the possibility of an ant without beginning by destroying His own essence, for the possibility of things is only the multiform participability of the Divine Essence itself, eternally seen by Divine Intellection. But without the shadow of change within Himself, He could have not created the universe nor the humanity of Christ, for the effective positing of creatures outside of nothingness depends upon His sovereign liberty. Not to distinguish the possible creature from the existing creature is the very basis of Spinozism.

Still, it could be that while speaking in this pantheistic fashion, Angelus Silesius was thinking of something quite different from pantheism. He himself says so in the preface to the *Cherubinic Traveler.* We do not have to believe it, but what interests us is, under what conditions it would it be possible to believe it. Taking these *distichs* as words uttered not in the order of being and intelligibility to express the nature of objects, but in the order of love to express the subject's experience, they could appear as a delirium of human words incapable of expressing in any other way the unity of the spirit lived by love. Translated into ontological language and understood in the light of the eternal predestination they thus presuppose, they would signify that the soul loved by God and chosen as His forever is God's good and this good cannot be lost. And the truth corresponding to them in the ontological order and constituting their foundation (in the sense in which a real being is the foundation of a being of reason) is that the love by which God freely loves creatures is the very love by which He necessarily loves Himself; contingence here would be only on the side of the created term, not on the side of the divine act, which is identical with the Divine Essence. Thus, *supposing* that this creature *were chosen* from all eternity, it is quite true that it could no more lose its election than God could lose His existence.

Actually, Johann Scheffler's vocabulary is that of Böhme; if the preceding remarks are valid, we would have to admit (and this is in no way impossible) that the same vocabulary has different values in these two cases: in the latter they have an especially speculative value; in the former, a more especially affective one. This is a consideration which makes it particularly difficult to pass judgment; but it is well known that the discernment of spirits is a difficult task, and the judging of such matters is not always necessary, at least for the philosopher who has enough to do handling doctrines.

The fact remains that if Angelus Silesius is orthodox, as Dr. Seltmann claims he is (*Angelus Silesius und seine Mystik,* Breslau, 1896), he expressed himself in paradoxes which are sometimes heretical in themselves and in their literal sense. Thus he appears to be a border-line case, at the extreme limits of the kingdom at whose center stands St. John of the Cross. Angelus Silesius published the *Cherubinic Traveler* in 1657, four years after his conversion, but we may with likelihood suppose that he had written it before that time and that it had been for him still a Protestant, a sort of anticipated avowal of his catholicism of heart, for he was even at that time reading St. Gertrude, St. Mechtilde, St. Bridget and Tauler with great predilection. Everything didactic and conceptually constructed in his astonishing poem shows it to be a type of expression or stylization of mystical experience in which the retrospection and the profound recasting

V
MYSTICAL CONTEMPLATION

20. There is evidently a question about which it is particularly important to get St. Thomas Aquinas' and St. John of the Cross' views. It is the question of the nature of mystical contemplation itself. Their respective teachings on this point are in strict accord. For both, contemplation is an experimental knowledge of love and union. And the principles developed by Thomistic theologians—a John of St. Thomas, a Father Chardon—are those which best enable us to understand the incomparable teaching of John of the Cross.

The doctrine of St. Thomas, to which St. John of the Cross explicitly refers,[70] may be summarized in these words: charity, as it increases, transforms us in God, whom it attains immediately in Himself,[71] and since this increasingly perfect spiritualization cannot be achieved without its repercussions in knowledge, because spirit is interior to itself, the Holy Spirit uses this very loving transformation in God, this supernatural connaturality, as the proper means to delectable and penetrating knowledge which, in turn, renders the love of charity as possessive and fruitful as is possible here below. This is the very same teaching as that of St. John of the Cross; it is to this teaching that the

required to put such experience into words are carried to the extreme. And although this mode of expression is essentially related to the order of affection and love it nevertheless reveals that mystical experience has here undergone the treatment of speculative preoccupation to the very limit.

Angelus Silesius' most beautiful lines remain cold didactic and poetic jewels; they are not pure testimony surging out of the fire. The versification of St. John of the Cross is more learned, yet his testimony is absolutely pure, direct and blazing. This shows that what matters is not the simplicity of the instrument but the simplicity of the spirit using it. It was by using the technique prepared by a Garcilaso de la Vega that Divine Inspiration produced in the greatest of mystical writers the written words which least alter the ineffable substance they contain.

The case of Angelus Silesius was brought up here only to make clearer a whole order of problems in spiritual semantics (pointed out and studied by Louis Massignon in most remarkable fashion. Cf. *Essai sur les origines du lexique technique de la mystique musulmane* [Geuthner 1922]; *Le folklore chez les mystiques musulmans* [Melanges Rene Basset, 1923]; *L'expérience mystique et les modes de stylisation littéraire*, quoted above, n. 68). By its very contrast with the case of St. John of the Cross, this case verifies the general law that the more a mystic allows the taste for human knowledge and discursive speculation (philosophical or theological) to creep into his incommunicable experience itself, or into the retrospective grasp he tries to get of this experience in attempting to express it, the more he risks going astray, either in his mode of expression only, or in his thought itself. Mystical experience stimulates speculation; in its very substance it is free of it.

70 Cf. *Dark Night*, Bk. II, Ch. xvii, Silv., II, p. 477; Peers, I, p. 456.
71 See above, Ch. VIII, §§ 10 and 11. Similarly, St. John of the Cross says: "Porque solo el amor es el que une y junta al alma con Dios" (*Dark Night*, Bk. II, Ch. xviii, text quoted below, Ch. VIII, n. 83).

divinely profound, rich, subtle and precise explanations of the whole life of contemplation which he gives us according to the mode of practical science are referred. For him, as for St. Thomas, contemplation is the very experience of this union to which all else is preordained. It is not only for love, it is *by* love: "God never grants mystical wisdom without love, since love itself infuses it."[72] "The delectable science . . . is mystical theology,—the secret science of God, which spiritual men call contemplation; this is most delectable since it is science through love, which love is its master and that which makes it to be wholly delectable."[73] It is produced by love itself, by the supernatural love of charity which causes us to enter into the intimate life of the divine Persons and which, under the superior guidance of the Holy Spirit, pierces to the depths of God, τὰ βάθη τοῦ θεοῦ,[74] and thus gives to faith penetration and savor, freeing it thereby from the human mode of our reason.

Because this love flows from faith which alone, in its superhuman obscurity, unites our intellect to the abyss of Deity, the supernatural Subsistent, we must affirm that faith, i.e., living faith "formed" by charity and enlightened by the gifts of the Holy Spirit,[75] is the very principle of mystical experience, the sole "proximate and proportionate" means of divine union. St. John of the Cross never tires of repeating this.[76]

That is why contemplation itself is a night wherein the soul forgoes the use of distinct ideas and all formulated knowledge, passes beyond and above the human mode of concepts to undergo divine things in the infused light of faith by means of love and all the effects God produces in the soul united to Him by love. And this is, as Dionysius says, like a ray of darkness for the intellect.[77] "In the army of Gideon . . . all soldiers had lamps in their hands, which they saw not, because they had them concealed in the dark pitchers; and when these pitchers were broken, the light was seen. Just so does faith, which is foreshadowed by these pitchers, contain within itself Divine Light; which when it is ended and broken, at the ending and breaking of this mortal life, will allow

---

72	*Dark Night*, Bk. II, Ch. xii, Silv., II, p. 456; Peers, I, p. 437; cf. Bk. II, Ch. xvii: "La contemplacion . . . se infunde en el alma por amor" (Silv., II, p. 477).
73	*Cant.*, st. 18 (27), Silv., III, p. 99; Peers, II, p. 109. Cf. Prologue: "mystical theology, which is the science of love, and wherein these verities are not only known but also experienced" (Silv., III, p. 5, Peers, II, p. 25). St. John of the Cross remarks here, with exquisite tact, that the mystical wisdom itself to which Anne of Jesus was given the grace to be raised "deep within the bosom of love," disposes the mind in the absence of technical preparation to understand explanations belonging to the purely intellectual order of scholastic theology.
74	St. Paul, I Cor. ii, 10.
75	Cf. above, Ch. VIII, n. 54.
76	*Ascent*, Bk. II, Ch. ix (viii), Silv., II, p. 101; Peers, I, p. 98. See above, Ch. VIII, n. 57.
77	"Contemplacion, la cual es en esta vida, como dice San Dionisio, rayo de tiniebla" (*Cant.*, st. 13 [14], Silv., III, p. 73; Peers, II, p. 84. Cf. *Ascent*, Bk. II, Ch. viii [vii]), (Silv., II, p. 100; Peers, I, p. 87).

the glory and light of the Divinity, which was contained in it, to appear. It is clear, then, that if the soul in this life is to attain to union with God and commune directly with Him, it must unite itself with the darkness whereof Solomon spake, wherein God had promised to dwell, and must draw near to the darkness of air wherein God was pleased to reveal His secrets to Job, and must take in its hands, in darkness, the jars of Gideon, that it may have in its hands (that is, in the works of its will) the light, which is the union of love, though it be in the darkness of faith, so that, when the pitchers of this life are broken, which alone have kept from it the light of faith, it may see God face to face in glory."[78]

"Say not, therefore, 'Oh! the soul can make no progress, for it does nothing.' For if it is true that it is doing nothing, then, by this very fact that it is doing nothing I will now prove to you that it is doing a great deal. For, if the understanding is voiding itself of particular kinds of knowledge, both natural and spiritual, it is making progress, and the more it empties itself of particular knowledge and of the acts of the understanding,[79] the greater is the progress of the understanding in its journey to the highest spiritual good. 'Oh,' you will say, 'but it understands nothing distinctly, and so it cannot be making progress.' I reply to you that it would rather be making no progress if it were to understand anything distinctly. The reason of this is that God, towards Whom the understanding is journeying, transcends the understanding and is therefore incomprehensible and inaccessible to it; and thus, when it is understanding, it is not approaching God, but is rather withdrawing itself from Him. Therefore the understanding must withdraw from itself,[80] and walk in faith, believing and not understanding. And in this way the understanding will reach perfection, for by faith and by no other means comes union with God; . . . Since the understanding knows not what God is,[81] it must of necessity walk

78   *Ascent*, Bk. II, Ch. ix (viii), Silv., II, p. 103; Peers, I, pp. 99–100.
79   "A los actos de entender." "Entender" corresponds to the Latin *intelligere*. The Thomistic texts to be adduced for commentary on this passage of St. John of the Cross are: "Secundum statum praesentis vitae . . . non possumus intelligere substantias separatas immateriales secundum seipsas" (*Sum. Theol.*, I, 88, 1), and: "Per substantias materiales non possumus perfecte substantias immateriales intelligere" (I, 88, 2); cf. *Cont. Gen.*, III, xlv.
80   We would also comment on this passage by using the articles in which St. Thomas explains how, in faith, the intellect is as a captive ("et inde est quod intellectus credentis dicitur esse captivatus, quia tenetur terminis alienis et non propriis [II Cor. x, 5] *In captivitatem redigentes omnem intellectum*" [*De Verit.*, XIV, 1]) in a captivity that sets it free ("bonum intellectus est ut subdatur voluntati adhaerendo Deo: unde fides dicitur intellectum expedire in quantum sub tali voluntate ipsum captivat" [*De Verit.*, XIV, 3, ad 8]).
81   "No puede saber como es Dios." Cf. St. Thomas, *Sum. Theol.*, I, 2, 1: "Nos non scimus de Deo quid est," we cannot know about God what He is in Himself. "Quidquid intellectus noster apprehendit minus est quam Dei essentia, et quidquid lingua nostra loquitur minus est quam esse divinum," writes St. Thomas in his commentary on the *Divine Names* (cap. 5, lect. 1); and this is also

towards Him in submission.... In the contemplation of which we are speaking, wherein God, as we have said, infuses into the soul, there is no necessity for distinct knowledge, nor for the soul to perform any acts of the understanding, for God, in one act, is communicating to the soul light and love together, which is loving and supernatural knowledge, and may be said to be like heat-giving light, which gives out heat, for that light also enkindles the soul in love; and this is confused and obscure to the understanding, since it is knowledge of contemplation, which, as St. Dionysius says, is a ray of darkness to the understanding."[82]

21. Let us read again the description of contemplation given in the *Dark Night of the Soul*:[83] This dark contemplation (is described as 'secret' since, as we have indicated above, it is mystical theology, which theologians call secret wisdom, and which, as St. Thomas says, is communicated and infused into the soul through love.[84] This happens secretly and in darkness, so as to be hidden from the work of the understanding and of the other faculties. Wherefore, inasmuch as the faculties aforementioned attain not to it, but the Holy Spirit infuses and orders it in the soul, as says the Bride in the Songs, without either its knowledge or its understanding, it is called secret. And, in truth, not only does the soul not understand it, but there is none that does so, not even the devil; inasmuch as the Master Who teaches the soul is within it in its substance, to which the devil may not attain, neither may natural sense nor understanding.

"And it is not for this reason alone that it may be called secret, but likewise because of the effects which it produces in the soul. For it is secret not only in the darknesses and afflictions of purgation, when this wisdom of love purges

---

what St. John of the Cross will say of the need to divest oneself of every distinct idea in order to be united to God in faith.

82   *Living Flame*, st. 3, 2nd redact., Silv., IV, pp. 181–183 (72–73); Peers, III, pp. 186–187. The Saint goes on to say that "as far as concerns the soul's performance of natural acts with the understanding there can be no love without understanding, but in the acts which God performs and infuses in the soul, as in those of which we are treating, it is different, for God can communicate Himself in the one faculty and not in the other. Thus He can enkindle the will by means of a touch of the heat of His love, although the understanding may have no understanding thereof, just as a person can be warmed by a fire without seeing the fire." This and similar texts are not at all opposed to St. Thomas' teaching that love universally follows knowledge. For while, on the one hand, St. Thomas teaches that the degree of love is not necessarily proportioned to that of knowledge, he says, on the other, as does John of the Cross, that when God supernaturally inflames the will without illumining the understanding, a knowledge is always presupposed—that of faith.

83   Bk. II, Chs. xvii and xviii. Peers, I, pp. 456–458.

84   "Propter hoc Gregorius (*Hom. 14 in Ezech.*) constituit vitam contemplativam in charitate Dei" (*Sum. Theol.*, I–II, 180, 1).

the soul, and the soul is unable to speak of it, but equally so afterwards in illumination, when this wisdom is communicated to it most clearly. Even then it is still so secret that the soul cannot speak of it and give it a name whereby it may be called; for, apart from the fact that the soul has no desire to speak of it, it can find no suitable way or manner or similitude by which it may be able to describe such lofty understanding and such delicate spiritual feeling. And thus, even though the soul might have a great desire to express it and might find many ways in which to describe it, it would still be secret and remain undescribed . . . Jeremiah . . . after God had spoken with him . . . knew not what to say save 'Ah, ah, ah!' . . . Pure contemplation . . . is indescribable . . . for which reason it is called secret.

"And not only for this reason is it called secret, and is so, but likewise because this mystical knowledge has the property of hiding the soul within itself. For, besides performing its ordinary function, it sometimes absorbs the soul and engulfs it in its secret abyss, in such a way that the soul clearly sees that it has been carried far away from every creature and has become most remote therefrom; so that it considers itself as having been placed in a most profound and vast retreat, to which no human creature can attain, such as an immense desert, which nowhere has any boundary. . . . It not only shows it how base are all properties of the creatures by comparison with this supreme knowledge and Divine feeling, but likewise it learns how base and defective and, in some measure, how inapt, are all the terms and words which are used in this life to treat of Divine things, and it is impossible, in any natural way or manner, however learnedly and sublimely they may be spoken of, to be able to know and perceive them as they are, save by the illumination of this mystical theology. . . . This road whereby the soul journeys to God is as secret and as hidden from the senses of the soul as the way of one that walks on the sea, whose paths and footprints are not known, is hidden from the senses of the body. The steps and footprints which God is imprinting upon the souls that He desires to bring near to Himself, and to make great in union with His Wisdom, have also this property, that they are not known.[85] . . . This secret wisdom is also a ladder. . . . The principal characteristic of contemplation, on account of which it is here called a ladder, is that it is the science of love. This, as we have said, is an infused and loving knowledge of God, which enlightens the soul and at the same time enkindles it with love, until it is raised up step by step, even unto God its Creator. For it is love alone that unites and enjoins the soul with God."[86]

22. It would be madness to want to attain to such knowledge of God by our own powers and "rudimentary acts."[87] For such knowledge is supernatural

85   *Dark Night*, Bk. II, Ch. xvii, Silv., II, pp. 477–482; Peers, I, pp. 459–460.
86   *Ibid.*, Ch. xviii, Silv., II, p. 484; Peers, I, pp. 460 and 462. The texts in which St. John of the Cross thus describes contemplation as an *infused, loving knowledge* are innumerable.

not only with respect to the virtues it brings into play and in respect to its objects, but also in respect to its mode.[88] The soul is therein acted upon beyond what it can do by itself, even as perfected in the supernatural order by the three theological virtues. In other words, God is here the principal Agent. "God works all this and the soul of its own power does naught therein."[89] "Let such as these take heed and remember that the Holy Spirit is the principal agent and mover of souls and never loses His care for them; and that they themselves are not agents, but only instruments to lead souls in the rule of faith and the law of God, according to the spirituality that God is giving to each one."[90] God is the principal agent in this matter, and the guide of its blind self. He will take it by the hand and lead it where it could not of itself go (namely, to the supernatural things which neither its understanding nor its will nor its memory could know as they are); then its chief care will be to see that it sets no obstacle in the way of the guide. . . . And this impediment may come to the soul if it allows itself to be led by some blind guide; and these blind guides that might lead it out of its way are three, namely, the spiritual director [he who has no knowledge save of hammering souls and pounding them like a blacksmith],[91] the devil, and its own self.[92] What other formal reason for the "passivity" of the mystical states than that God, in such work, is the cause or principal agent? (And John of the Cross uses the word in the precise meaning given it in the theory of instrumental causality.) "In this state the soul must never have meditation imposed upon it, nor must it perform any acts, nor strive after sweetness or fervor; for this would be to set an obstacle in the way of the principal agent, who, as I say, is God. For God secretly and quietly infuses into the soul loving knowledge and wisdom without any intervention of specific acts, although sometimes He specifically produces them in the soul for some length of time. And the soul has then to walk with loving awareness of God, without performing specific acts, but conducting itself, as we have said, passively, and having no diligence of its own, but possessing this simple, pure and loving awareness, as one that opens his eyes with the awareness of love."[93] Since God is the principal agent in the work of contemplation, which nevertheless is an eminently vital and immanent operation, it is easy to

---

87   "Modos rateros" (Living Flame, st. 3, line 3, Silv., IV, p. 64 [171]; Peers, III, p. 75).

88   "The soul continues to receive these blessings passively and after the supernatural manner of God, and not after the manner of the natural soul" (Living Flame, st. 3, line 3, Silv., IV, p. 67 [174]; Peers, III, p. 78). This is the very doctrine of the "suprahuman mode" of the gifts, as set forth by St. Thomas in his Commentary on the Sentences.

89   Living Flame, st. 1, line 3, Silv., IV, p. 12 (114); Peers, III, p. 24.

90   Ibid., st. 3, line 3, Silv., IV, p. 71 (179); Peers, III, pp. 82–83.

91   Ibid., p. 70 (178), Peers, III, p. 82.

92   Living Flame, st. 3, line 3, Silv., IV, p. 63 (171); Peers, III, pp. 74–75. All these pages bear fervent witness to the pity inspired by the Saint by long experience of the damage and delays caused in souls by ignorant and presumptuous directors.

93   Ibid., p. 65 (173); Peers, III, pp. 76–77.

understand the essential role attributed by St. John of the Cross to the special impulse of the Holy Spirit.[94] For him, it is the Holy Spirit who marks the passage from the natural mode to the supernatural mode: *Breathe through my garden and let its odors flow.* And St. John of the Cross points out that the soul does not say "breathe into my garden," but "through my garden." "There is a great difference between these two expressions. To breathe into the soul is to infuse into it grace, gifts and virtues; to breathe through the soul is for God to touch the virtues and perfections which have already been given to it, refreshing them and moving them, so that they may diffuse wondrous fragrance and sweetness."[95] Divine *South wind that awakenest love* releasing the fragrance of the budding virtues as it stirs among them. "In this breathing of the Holy Spirit through the soul which is His visitation of her in love, the Spouse, Who is the Son of God, communicates Himself to her after a lofty manner.... Wherefore it is greatly to be desired that every soul should pray for this breath of the Holy Spirit to breathe through its garden and for the flowing of its Divine odors."[96]

A few pages before, St. John of the Cross, echoing St. Thomas, insists upon the connection between the virtues in charity (their garland is "bound together by this hair of love ... in such a way that, if it were to break in any place, then ... they all would be lost") and adds: "Even as the breeze stirs the hair and causes it to flutter upon the neck, even so does the breeze of the Holy Spirit move and excite strong love that it may make flights to God; for without this Divine wind, which moves the faculties to the practice of Divine love, the virtues work not, neither have any effect, although they be in the soul."[97] The soul in question here has already attained to spiritual betrothal, and its virtues are moved instrumentally by the Holy Spirit. When it has attained to spiritual marriage, it will have "invoked and obtained the breeze of the Holy Spirit ... which is the proper disposition and means for the perfection of this estate."[98] Moreover, "when she possesses in perfection the seven gifts of the Holy Spirit in the manner wherein she is able to receive them" the soul "likewise possesses the seven degrees or cellars of love." Finally, "when the soul attains to perfect possession of the spirit of fear," which is "the last of the seven gifts,"—whereby she began to be raised to wisdom—"she has likewise in perfection the spirit of love."[99] Similarly, St. Thomas teaches that the gifts increase together, and

94 The soul cannot receive these inner communications "if the Spirit of the Spouse cause not this motion of love within her" (*Cant.*, 2nd redact., st. 1–7 [26], Silv., III, p. 293; Peers, II, p. 282).
95 *Cant.*, st. 26 (17), Silv., III, p. 127; Peers, II, p. 135.
96 *Ibid.*, pp. 128 and 129, Peers, II, pp. 136–137.
97 *Cant.*, st. 22 (31), Silv., III, pp. 113–114; Peers, I, p. 122.
98 *Cant.*, st. 27 (22), Silv., III, p. 131; Peers, II, p. 102.
99 *Ibid.*, st. 17(26), Silv., III, p. 91; Peers, II, p. 102. An attempt has been made to interpret this passage to mean that for St. John of the Cross, the gift of fear was the highest gift (*Bulletin Thomiste*, May–June 1930, p. 90). As Father Garrigou-Lagrange has had no trouble showing that (as was admitted thereafter, *Bulletin Thomiste*, January 1931, p. 10) to do this would be gratuitously to attribute to the

that "the gift of fear is perfect in a soul only if charity and the gift of wisdom are perfect in it."[100] In all this, and every time he speaks of science and wisdom, as, for example, when he adopts and makes classic Tauler's doctrine on the three signs characteristic of the soul's entry into the "mystical state," St. John of the Cross is in full agreement with the teaching of Thomistic theology on the gifts of the Holy Spirit and on the entry of contemplative souls into the habitual governance of the gifts.

In his concrete and savory language, nourished by Holy Writ, he most frequently calls the action of the gifts "the anointings of the Holy Spirit."[101] Here again, we may observe the strictness with which the laws proper to the vocabulary of practical science are shown forth in his work. Ontological analysis of the organism of the virtues and infused gifts is not what primarily interests him; it is their concrete interplay and the experience of their sweetness; and what other word than the one he has chosen could better make manifest that the motions, by which the Holy Spirit as principal agent directs the soul and raises it to a supernatural *manner* of living its supernatural life, are impulses of love? "The interior blessings that this silent contemplation leaves impressed upon the soul without its perception of them are, as I say, inestimable; for they are in fact the most secret and delicate anointings of the Holy Spirit, whereby He secretly fills the soul with riches and gifts and graces, for, after all, being God, He acts as God."[102] The blazing criticism St. John of the Cross levels at spiritual directors who absolutely insist upon imposing discursive meditation is motivated precisely by the fact that these directors trespass on the Holy Spirit's domain, and set obstacles in the way of His action upon those souls which are already under the habitual governance of the gifts.[103]

Saint an inadvertence diametrically opposed to all his teaching on wisdom, *juge convivium*.

    Others have also tried to find a disagreement between St. Thomas and St. John of the Cross in that the latter reduces the passions to four principal ones, and not to eleven, as St. Thomas does. But this is to forget article 25, 4 in the I–II, where St. Thomas says that among the eleven passions the four enumerated by Boethius, joy, sorrow, hope and fear, are the principal ones *ut completivae aliarum*.

100   R. Garrigou-Lagrange, "St. Thomas et St. Jean de la Croix," *Vie Spirituelle*, October 1, 1930, p. [27].

101   Rapid reading, stopping short at words without penetrating to things, might lead one to believe that St. John of the Cross speaks very little of the gifts. Actually, he is always speaking about them, but in words other than those used by a speculative theologian. Is it surprising that in the great Doctor of "secret wisdom," science also be disguised? Once more, if we expect to find in him speculative science *with its own language*, we are foredoomed to misunderstand him.

    It would be no less naive to be surprised that St. Thomas does not speak the language of practical science and that the "nights" do not appear in his vocabulary.

102   *Living Flame*, st. 3, line 3, Silv., IV, p. 69 (177); Peers, III, pp. 80–81.

Careful examination makes clear that, in its most fundamental features, its absolutely primary characteristics, the spiritual doctrine of St. John of the Cross appears, more than any other, as a practical explanation of the theology of the gifts. From beginning to end, St. John of the Cross remains obstinately attached to the essential supernatural. His whole teaching claims and insists that what belongs essentially to the domain of the grace of virtues and gifts must be shielded from the usurpations of the charisms. And although he leads souls to the supreme degree of love and mystical union, it is not by the shorter, but less sure,[104] path of extraordinary favors and gratuitously given gifts, but

---

103   "The state of beginners (i.e., in the vocabulary of Thomistic theology, souls who have not yet come under the habitual guidance of the gifts) comprises meditation and discursive acts" (i.e., acts and exercises, discursive in conjunction with the imagination), *Living Flame*. st. 3, line 3, Silv., IV, p. 64 (171–172); Peers, III, p. 75.

    But souls which the Holy Spirit has led into the contemplative life have by that fact passed beyond meditation and attempts to force them to return to it can do them serious harm. "These anointings, then, and these touches, are the delicate and sublime acts of the Holy Spirit, which, on account of their delicate and subtle purity, can be understood neither by the soul nor by him that has to do with it, but only by Him Who infuses them, in order to make the soul more pleasing to Himself. These blessings, with the greatest facility, by no more than the slightest act which the soul may desire to make on its own account, with its memory, understanding or will, or by the application of its sense or desire or knowledge or sweetness or pleasure, are disturbed or hindered in the soul, which is a grave evil and a great shame and pity. Ah, how serious is this matter, and what cause it gives for wonder, that the evil done should be imperceptible, and the hindrance to those holy anointings which has been interposed should be almost negligible, and yet that this harm that has been done should be a matter for greater sorrow and regret than the perturbation and ruin of many souls of a more ordinary nature which have not attained to a state of such supreme fineness and delicacy. . . . When the work of so delicate a hand as this of the Holy Spirit has been thus roughly treated, who will be able to repair its beauty? Although this evil is so great and serious that it cannot be exaggerated, it is so common and frequent that there will hardly be found a single spiritual director who does not inflict it upon souls whom God is beginning to draw nearer to Himself in this kind of contemplation" (*Living Flame*, st. 3, line 3, 2nd redact., Silv., IV, pp. 177–178; Peers, III, p. 182); (cf. 1st redact., Silv., IV, pp. 69–70; Peers, III, p. 81).

104   We agree with Rev. Fr. Garate, who is followed by Abbé Saudreau and Rev. Fr. Garrigou-Lagrange, that *the shortened way* spoken of by St. Teresa (*Castle*, Mansion V, Ch. III) designates the beginning of ecstasy, and, more generally, gratuitously given graces, which sometimes, but not necessarily, accompany infused contemplation. Cf. our "Question sur la Vie mystique et la contemplation," *Vie Spirituelle*, March 1923, p. 644.

    Today the doctrine generally accepted by the best theologians is that all souls, by the fact that they are called to heavenly beatitude, are also commonly called in a general way to enjoy the beginnings of beatitude on earth by means of infused contemplation. This doctrine is in entire accordance with the teaching of St. John of the Cross. (Cf. *Living Flame*, st. 2, line 5, Silv., IV, pp. 39–41 [145–147].) It is not especially addressed to those whom extraordinary graces help to

rather by the normal way of the virtues and gifts, those gifts infused in every soul in the state of grace,[105] because, as St. Thomas explicitly teaches in the

---

advance more rapidly (but not without danger) along the path of the spirit. The only means it requires are living faith, the organism of supernatural gifts with which every soul in the state of grace is provided, and the whole asceticism of the virtues (described in the *Ascent of Mount Carmel* with the special characteristics it assumes with respect to the contemplative life and which continues throughout all spiritual progress). From this point of view, this teaching applies to all who seek Christian perfection, whatever their particular path may be: "as well suited to one kind of person as to another if they desire to pass to detachment of spirit" (*Ascent,* Prologue, Silv., II, p. 11; Peers, I, p. 15). But it is addressed to them at a certain point in their journey, after they have reached a certain degree of progress. From this point of view, St. John of the Cross speaks only to souls whom the divine life has already stirred up and who, having already striven in meditation (which they eventually lay aside) and in asceticism (which they never lay aside), hear themselves called by name, and proximately, to contemplation. The Saint himself stresses this in several instances: "this first night (of the senses) pertains to beginners, occurring *at the time when God begins to bring them into the state of contemplation* (*Ascent,* Bk. I, Ch. i; Silv., II, p. 13; Peers, I, p. 18); cf. *ibid.,* Bk. II, Ch. vi (v), § 8 (Silv. II, p. 89); Ch. vii (vi), § 13: "But let us now address the understanding of the spiritual man, and particularly that of the man whom God has granted the favor of leading him into the state of contemplation (for, as I have said, I am now speaking to these in particular), and let us say how such a man must direct himself toward God in faith, and purify himself from contrary things, constraining himself that he may enter upon this narrow path of obscure contemplation" (Silv., II, p. 96; Peers, I, p. 93); *ibid.,* Bk. III, Ch. ii (i), §§ 1 and 2: "This would be true if we were seeking here only to instruct beginners, . . . But we are here giving instruction to those who would progress farther in contemplation, even to union with God. . . ." (Silv., II, p. 241; Peers, I, p. 226). But few reach the goal, for the union he preaches is a "rare and heroic" deed: "como esta alma habia de salir a hacer un hecho tan heroico y tan raro, que era unirse con su Amado divino . . ." (*Dark Night,* Bk. II, Ch. xiv, Silv., II, p. 466; Peers, I, p. 446). It has been very justly pointed out that "it would be an extremely dangerous error to apply the rules laid down by the mystical Doctor to every soul, without discrimination, from its very first steps in the interior life." (C. H., *Abrégé de toute la doctrine mystique de saint Jean de la Croix,* Preface, p. vi.) To recommend heroic passivity, which is the soul's highest renunciation to one who is working on his own, and is not deprived *by God* of "the human mode" of acting, would be to ruin his whole spiritual life. It is a mark of quietism to put oneself in such a state of passivity, thus usurping divine action. Like Ruysbroeck, St. John of the Cross was a merciless opponent of quietism and it was to guard against it, especially against the quietism of the *alumbrados,* that he insisted so much upon the authentic signs betokening the dawn of mystical life.

105 Obviously, he is not unaware that extraordinary favors of the charismatic order can intervene to help the soul in its progress (this is the "shortened way" of which we spoke above). But it is not his purpose to treat of these things. For "studying different kinds of rapture and ecstasy and of other issuings forth and subtle flights of the spirit," he explicitly refers us to the writings wherein St. Teresa has "left notes admirably written upon these things of the spirit," which notes he

Summa,[106] they are necessary for salvation. Let the organism of supernatural energies which the soul requires for salvation develop, grow and reach maturity, and holiness is the result.[107] St. John of the Cross bases all his teaching upon these truths, he never tires of inculcating and explaining them in all sorts of ways; his doctrine is pre-eminently a practical theology of contemplative gifts.

Contemplative Purity and Poverty of Spirit

23. I would like to show further how the very purity with which St. John of the Cross maintains, more rigorously than any other mystic, the transcendence

hopes soon will be printed (*Cant.*, st. 12 (13), Silv., III, p. 59; Peers, II, p. 72, § 6). In this connection we might say that perhaps we have, in the controversy about "acquired" and "infused" contemplation, one more occasion to appeal to the general principle of the differences between the speculative vocabulary and the practical vocabulary. From the practical, descriptive, concrete point of view, we might call "acquired" contemplation that which is gained progressively by the development and growth of the grace of the virtues and gifts, and "infused" contemplation that which is received by means of extraordinary graces. But from the speculative and ontological point of view it is evident that the first type is no less "infused" than the second since, after a transitional period which is the fruit of all preceding activity (in which the soul induces recollection by its own initiative but in which the gifts begin to exert their influence predominantly—a period which corresponds to Bossuet's "prayer of simplicity" and the "habit" engendered by meditation of which St. John of the Cross speaks in the *Ascent of Mount Carmel*, Bk. II, Ch. xiv (xii), Silv., II, pp. 122–123; Peers, I, p. 118), this contemplation is "acquired" only at the moment when the Holy Spirit acts in the soul as principal agent and when the soul, far from acting by itself, has only to receive the supernatural knowledge of love thus infused within it. Cf. the *Question* cited in the preceding note (*Vie Spirituelle*, March 1923, pp. 641–642). As for admitting with some that the three signs of the *Ascent of Mount Carmel* (Bk. II, Ch. xiii [xi], Silv., II, pp. 119–120) and the *Dark Night* (Bk. I, Ch. ix, pp. 389–393) mark the passing either to infused contemplation or to a so-called acquired contemplation developing parallel to infused contemplation—this to our mind would be to dismember the whole doctrinal synthesis and thought of the Saint.

106 *Sum. Theol.*, I–II, 68, 2.
107 It is in this sense that the teaching of St. John of the Cross ties up with the doctrine of salvation. (This sense is quite different from Baruzi's interpretation [*op. cit.*, p. 652], which is altogether foreign to both the teaching and spirit of the Saint; for even in "pushing mystical thought to its limits," St. John of the Cross would never have considered the "theopathic state—which however remains infinitely rare— as the sole condition for a true love of the soul for God and of God for the soul".) His is not a doctrine of *salvation* but a doctrine of *perfection* (and he knew very well that the perfect cooperate in the salvation of others, *adimplentes ea quae desunt passionum Christi*). But although it is not necessary to have attained perfection in order to be saved; it is nevertheless necessary to be turned or oriented toward it, if it is true that the perfection of charity comes under the law (a precept, not a counsel), not as matter or something to be immediately realized, but as an end to which everyone must tend according to his condition. (Cf. R. Garrigou-La-grange, *Perfection chrétienne et contemplation*, Vol. I. Ch. iii, a. 5.

of the holy and "secret wisdom" of infused contemplation with respect to metaphysical and theological speculation, bears conspicuous witness to his fundamental accord with St. Thomas. The severity with which he dealt with the desire for special knowledge and the taste for revelation is well known. Let us reread the admirable passage in the *Ascent of Mount Carmel* in which he explains why, since Christ's coming, all partial revelation is thenceforth useless.

"The principal reason why in the law of Scripture the enquiries that were made of God were lawful, and why it was fitting that prophets and priests should seek visions and revelations of God, was because at that time faith had no firm foundation, neither was the evangelical law established; and thus it was needful that they should enquire of God and that He should speak, whether by words or by visions and revelations, or whether by figures and similitudes or by many other ways of impressing His meaning. [108]

"But now that the faith is founded in Christ, and, in this era of grace, the evangelical law has been made manifest, there is no reason to enquire of Him in that manner, nor for Him to speak or to answer as He did then. For, in giving us, as He did, His Son, which is His Word—and He has no other—He spoke to us all together, once and for all, in this single Word, and He has no occasion to speak further. And this is the sense of that passage which St. Paul begins, when he tries to persuade the Hebrews that they should abandon those first manners and ways of converse with God which are in the law of Moses, and should set their eyes on Christ alone: In the old days God spoke to our fathers in many ways and by many means, through the prophets; now at last in these times he has spoken to us, with a Son to speak for Him. (Heb. i, 1) And this is as though he had said: That which God spake of old in the prophets to our fathers, in sundry ways and diverse manners, He has now, at last, in these days, spoken to us once and for all in the Son. Herein the Apostle declares that God has been, as it were, dumb, and has no more to say since that which He spake aforetime, in part, to the prophets, He has now spoken altogether in Him, giving us the All which is His Son. Wherefore he that would now enquire of God or seek any vision or revelation, would not only be acting foolishly, but would be committing an offence against God, by not setting his eyes altogether upon Christ, and seeking no new thing or aught beside. And God might answer him after this manner, saying: If I have spoken all things to thee in My Word, which is My Son, and I have no other word, what answer can I now make to thee, or what can I reveal to thee which is greater than this? Set thine eyes on Him alone, for in Him I have spoken and revealed to thee all things, and in Him thou shalt find yet more than that which thou askest and desirest. For thou askest locutions and revelations, which are the part; but if thou set

---

108   *Ascent*, Bk. II, Ch. xxii, § 3; Peers, I, p. 173. This text may be compared with what St. Thomas says in *Sum. Theol.*, II–II, 1, 7 (*Utrum secundum succesionem temporum articuli fidei creverint*).

thine eyes upon Him thou shalt find the whole; for He is My complete locution and answer, and He is all My vision and all My revelation; so that I have spoken to thee, answered thee, declared to thee and revealed to thee, in giving Him to thee as thy Brother, Companion and Master, as ransom and as reward. For since that day when I descended upon Him with My Spirit on Mount Tabor, saying This is My beloved Son, in whom I am well pleased; hear ye Him, (Matt. xvii, 5) I have left off all these manners of teaching and answering and I have entrusted this to Him. Hear Him; for I have no more faith to reveal, neither have I any more things to declare. For if I spake aforetime, it was to promise Christ; and if they enquired of Me, their enquiries were directed to petitions for Christ and expectancy concerning Him, in Whom they should find every good thing (as is now set forth in all the teaching of the Evangelists and the Apostles), but now, any who would enquire of Me after that manner, and desire Me to speak to him or reveal aught to him, would in a sense be asking Me for Christ again, and asking Me for more faith, and be lacking in faith which has already been given in Christ; and therefore would be committing a great offence against My beloved Son, for not only would he be lacking in faith, but he would be obliging Him again first of all to become incarnate and pass through life and death. Thou shalt find naught to ask of Me or to desire of Me, whether revelations or visions; consider this well, for thou shalt find that all has been done for thee and all has been given to thee,—yea, and much more also,—in Him."[109]

24. In thus condemning the desire for special revelations and everything *extraordinary* in the spiritual life, in prescribing that the soul never reflect upon the clear and distinct things supernaturally impressed upon it, that it never appropriate them to itself, that it renounce, even in the highest charismatic communications, the sensible and intelligible particular to turn toward the pure substance of faith and let the pure spiritual itself act within the soul, St. John of the Cross is simply applying his general principles, his unyielding will never to let the soul stop at anything less than God Himself. But at the same time and by that very fact, he maintains mystical contemplation in its absolute purity, free of any parasitic curiosity, from all desire or purely human exercise of the intellect—absolutely free of the accoutrements and gear of human wisdom. *Quoniam non cognovi litteraturam.*

This most sublime of wisdoms is a wisdom of the poor; in itself and in the order of knowing it is all poverty and nudity of spirit. Naked wisdom, divine joy, wisdom and joy crucified.

If to know is what you want—and knowledge must be desired—study metaphysics, study theology.

If divine union is what you want, and you succeed in attaining it, you will know a great deal more, but precisely in the measure that you go beyond

---

109   *Ascent*, Bk. II, Ch. xxii, Silv., II, pp. 183–185; Peers, I, pp. 173–175.

knowledge—and in such a dispossessed fashion that you should in truth say: *I was reduced to nothing and I knew no more.* Beyond knowing? That is to say, in love; in love transilluminated by the Spirit, compenetrated by intelligence and wisdom. *For now my exercise is in loving alone.*

If renunciation of knowing in human mode is prerequisite to this supreme knowing, the reciprocal consequence is that knowing in human mode does not find its own perfection in that supreme knowing. Do not ask St. John of the Cross for lessons in metaphysics; ask Aristotle. St. John of the Cross himself tells us to do so. For everything not pertaining to the domain of contemplation in the union of love and nakedness of spirit, for all the regions of knowledge less lofty than this divine summit, he charges us to have recourse to reason. In those realms we are expected to see, not to close our eyes but to open them, and there St. John of the Cross wants us to keep our eyes wide open. By perfecting reason, faith and the gifts only help us to open them the wider. St. John of the Cross respects nature, its order, its limits. Why is it not good to question God about particular things, why do these indiscreet queries displease God, even when He answers them? "The reason for this is that it is lawful for no creature to pass beyond the limits that God has ordained for His governance after the order of nature. In His governance of man He has laid down rational and natural limits; wherefore to desire to pass beyond them is not lawful and to desire to seek out and attain to anything by supernatural means is to go beyond these natural limits."[110] *Above* nature, *above* reason—yes, that is where John of the Cross leads us: into the supernatural order, into the suprarational denseness of divine wisdom and faith. *Outside* of nature, *outside* of reason—no, he does not want that, he abhors the unreasonable.[111] The order of grace does not abolish, does not violate the boundaries of nature; it elevates nature whither nature unwittingly aspires to rise in aspiring to its own perfection, where nature groans because it is not, with a groaning which springs from that reserve of radical obedience and potentiality before its Author which is instinctive in its very being.

110　*Ascent*, Bk. II, Ch. xxi, Silv., II, pp. 172–173; Peers, I, p. 163.

111　In this he was the good pupil of the great Reformer of Carmel. This horror of the unreasonable, this profound respect for the natural order is one of St. Teresa's most significant characteristics. In this regard we might recall how wisely she acted when something to be done was pointed out to her by supernatural communication: "While I was praying it was said to me from our Lord, that I must not fail to go (to found a convent at Pastrana). When I heard this, although I saw strong reasons for not going, I dared not do otherwise than I was used in similar matters, that is, to be guided by the advice of the confessor. So I sent for him *without telling him what I had heard in prayer*: for I am always better satisfied not to do this, but to beseech the Lord to give them light according to what they can know of their own knowledge; and His Majesty when He desires a thing to be done puts it into their heart. This has often happened to me: and so it was now, for taking all into consideration, he thought I had better go and so I determined to go . . ." (*Foundations*, Ch. xvii, Peers, III, pp. 79–80).

Thus, the division is perfectly clear, the distinction assured, between knowing that is supernatural in mode and must proceed under the rule of the Holy Spirit, and knowing in human mode which proceeds according to the rule of reason: reason alone, in matters of philosophy and metaphysics; reason superelevated by faith, in theological matters. Consequently, to ask metaphysics to lead to the highest contemplation would, therefore, only betoken a vast ignorance both of metaphysics and of contemplation; to consider reason as inefficacious, of itself, in metaphysics unless it be vivified by a knowledge by mystical connaturality, is no less an offense against the essential order of things. St. John of the Cross forearms us against such weaknesses as much as St. Thomas does. Inversely, while mystical authors, when they forget the Apostle's great dictum: *sapere sed ad sobrietatem*, often give in a bit to the temptation to speculate (I mean in the mystical order), and seek to interrogate their holy wisdom concerning particular problems, making it leave its repose and incline towards theological or philosophical discourse (where it can do no more than help reason grope blindly toward dazzling bewilderment, or itself depend on interpretations that are sometimes rash) St. John of the Cross sees only a diminution and a renunciation of the purely divine, a danger of illusion in this intermingling (sometimes very beautiful in the poetic order) of mystical night and human lights, which often stems only from an as yet undifferentiated moment in the progress of thought, but sometimes from confusion and, in its aberrant forms, leads to illuminism and theosophy.

This purity, which I have tried to describe, this inflexible discipline of spirit, this profound respect for distinctions and essential connections and for the order established by God, is the most stirring and venerable sign of the fundamental agreement that unites together St. John of the Cross and Thomas Aquinas, not only in the doctrine they taught, but in the doctrine lived and, if I may so speak, in the very configuration of their sanctity.[112]

---

112 As we have written elsewhere (*St. Jean de la Croix*, Pere Bruno de Jesus-Marie, Preface pp. xxi–xxii), "accidental and *reducible* divergencies between witnesses confirm the veracity of their testimony, by showing that their agreement was not premeditated. As both St. John of the Cross and St. Thomas were adept in both acquired and infused wisdom (for the author of the *Spiritual Canticle* received from his Salamancan masters and had acquired by himself solid knowledge of theology, and the author of the *Summa Theologica* lived in the light of mystical contemplation) but had different missions to perform, both bear witness to the same living truth, one from the point of view of mystical experience, the other from the point of view of theological science. And the fundamental agreement of St. John of the Cross with St. Thomas is all the more significant because the former is not at all interested in playing the role of scholastic theologian, but only in singing what he knows divinely, and then expounding in his commentaries the practical science of the path that leads to such wisdom (not without referring, when necessary, to scholastic theology) because this practical, lyrical and concrete movement of his thought, bristling with psychological intuitions, is at the opposite pole to the mode of scholastic exposition; because when differences in

point of view entail apparent contradictions in the way in which something is conceived, he does not even think of explaining these differences or of trying to establish harmony (which for him is taken for granted) between his language and the language of speculation. Disciple of the best scholastic tradition in theology, but pupil of the Holy Spirit in contemplation, and writing only of 'experimental science as he experienced it,' his function was not to continue the teaching of St. Thomas, after the manner of a commentator, but to confirm it after the manner of a witness."

CHAPTER IX

TODO Y NADA

To Charles Henrion

1. AT A CERTAIN DEGREE OF DEPTH and concentration, all things, even those most distant from the spirit considered in its true substance, seem to take on as it were a spiritual mode of being. Taking the word "spiritual" in this analogical and very broad sense, there may be said to be in things a sort of spiritual density, independent of the proper quality of the values involved but highly important to the efficiency of a soul, a work or a world. For good or evil a certain immaterial weight, function of this density, carries everything to its proper place, closer to the center of history in proportion as the invisible mass thus moved is greater. For this reason, some men, very light in the manner of their thought or action, fulfil a grave density and weigh heavily on the course of events.

It is not good that the leaven buried in the dough rises to the surface and becomes inert. The profound imbalance of the modern world is betrayed by the fact that, taking the average state of culture and the ordinary regimen of human life, the spiritual density of the true has for several centuries become lighter than that of the false. And in these days it looks as though the weight of the scales had effectively shifted.

Classical man draped in his selfishness at the foot of the Cross, a purely natural equilibrium, order, peace, beatitude, possession of the earth by wealth and by the *Mathesis* which religion confirms and eternal rewards will crown— such was the big lie which a vigorous civilization and an admirable art, at the peak of its perfection, had made us believe in the early days of modern history. Jansenism tried to react, but did so by asking the Christian soul to revere mystery with a ravaged reason—and therefore still within the human norm, though shattered (and this is altogether different from the norm of the divine). It oppressed the soul with glory and narrowed the embrace of the arms of the Crucified. . . .

Christian naturalism became normal and conscientiously practicable, legitimate, honest and certain; genuine Christianity tended to be considered as impracticable and in any event inhuman; and this was the way in which civilization, Christian only in name, bogged down in the carnal and lost its ancient weight of charity. The love of so many tremendous saints barely sufficed to prevent the dissolution of the Christian world. And as to the message which this world was charged to deliver, it was not delivered, the cries of the poor were raised in vain.

During that time—for there is no escaping the angels—an inverse phenomenon was taking place, and today it is becoming tangible; the more the Christian world watered down its substance, the more the world, that world ruled by the Prince of this world, concentrated its own. Today it seems as if all the alembics of the invisible are working to transmute things human to a state of quintessence. From art and poetry, as from the life of the senses, from vice and sin, from dreams, from money and from death, it is spirit, pure spirit which is given off and it stinks in our nostrils. A spirituality of the flesh, an ascesis and a martyrdom of the passing moment subjugate souls. The new wine of the Holy Spirit is rejected; it is by alcohol that souls get drunk and die, while the devil distributes his drug, black or white, and his other sacraments to his precious victims. Meanwhile, many Christians, looking down from their heights in judgment upon their benighted brethren, make an honest effort to live righteously, even to uphold the interests of the Almighty, while they consider theology as arrogant, asceticism as superfluous, contemplation as dangerous and the precept "Be ye perfect" as supererogatory. They are battling froth on the crest of the waves.

2. Such is the imbalance of which we spoke at the beginning of this chapter, and whose consequences can be readily foreseen. There can be no redemption without the shedding of blood. But, alas, every lamb that is put to death is not a paschal lamb, every baptized Christian led to slaughter is not a martyr. But mighty portents have arisen on the far horizon of our most happy Europe. Atheism, become the religion of the state, condemns everything that is not content with this earth. And thought seeks still further pretexts for dealing death, while, in fact, it is for the crime of rebelling against this negative religion that many have already been immolated. A blessed day is breaking when man may die for God alone; not for the nation, not for humanity, nor for revolution, nor progress, nor science, but for God alone. More cynical and brutal than the education by omission with which western liberalism has stifled childhood, a painstaking pedagogical surgery is operating on souls to extirpate from them the image of God. And despite everything, this image will be reborn: a poor child who believes he is an atheist, if he truly loves what he takes to be the face of goodness, has turned to God without knowing it. It is with deep respect that we speak here of the Russian people and the spiritual tragedy in which it is involved. That such a world of naiveté and violence, of faith and abnegation be delivered over to the false miracles of material grandeurs and of a spirit, denying the spirit, must be for some purpose of tremendous purification. This is not the place to ask whether, in the social realm, nature, too long outraged by covetousness and egoism, wanted at any cost to find an outlet for the

demands of justice—her dishonored soul. We are considering here only the spiritual aspect of things. Once unleashed in history, sinister influences are fated endlessly to multiply their effects. But how shall we not believe that at the same time there will appear, rising from the cleared soil of human nature thus plowed and harrowed, renewals of grace, divine regenerations which will perhaps justify in some unpredictable way the religious hope which a Soloviev or a Dostoievsky had in the destiny of their people? Meanwhile the Church prays for it lovingly; but for the men of our time, cold as the dead, indifferent, not indeed to what pertains to business and plunder in this tremendous venture, but to what belongs to the soul, do they, I say, hear Russia telling them how flesh and blood do in their fashion the work those who have the name of Christian have neglected? Do they understand what spiritual density, what deep ascetic violence, Marxism and hatred of a world held to be accursed by history, must have assumed in the invisible universe of a Lenin's heart, in order to burst forth so tellingly? God has warned us that He does not put up with lukewarmness. On God's threshing-floor, what has been so thoroughly ground under heel can only be cleared away by harsh means.

Nevertheless, on every side, even where grace is disguised, where man does not yet know the true name of the divinity at work within him, it seems as though genuine spirituality yearns to remobilize its energies, and the world itself seems to urge souls to turn toward the spirit. Not, indeed, in order to disclaim temporal works, for love itself compels us to turn our hands to the works of time, but rather to put first things first. Works done for the common good of the world by one who does not first seek the secret of heroic life bear little fruit.

If we seek instruction in the things of the spirit, the mystical Doctor will teach us. He knows the pathways on the mountain where God dwells, the mountain luxuriant with grace, the mountain of compact wisdom and good-ness. For those who commit themselves to this journey "in the nakedness of spirit" he has drawn a map of the ascent of Mount Carmel.[1]

---

1   The symbolic representation we follow in our explanation is the one given at the beginning of the original edition of *Subida del Monte Carmelo* (Alcala, 1618). It is reproduced in the Silverio edition (*Obras de san Juan de la Cruz*, Burgos, 1929, t. II). The first sketch drawn by St. John of the Cross for the Carmelites of Beas and reproduced in the work of Fr. Bruno of Jesus and Mary (*Saint Jean de la Croix*, Paris, Plon, 1929, p. 260) was later completed and corrected by the Saint himself (Testimony of Madeleine of the Holy Spirit. Cf. Silverio, t. 1, p. 136). This final version of the Saint's work is very probably found in the drawing in the *editio princeps*, at least as to its general disposition and the text of its legends (which is the most important thing). The well-spaced hills, the trees and flowers, the coats of arms, show that the drawing was copied and touched up for this edition by a rather heavy-handed professional, whose signature, *Diego de Abstos fecit*, appears in the upper corner on the left. But that does not affect it from the point of view of doctrine. We might note that Chapter XIII of the first book in the *Ascent of Mount Carmel* refers to this symbolic drawing and agrees better with the latter's

3. A fundamental feeling seems to permeate all the work of St. John of the Cross. It is a feeling for the double and almost untenable paradox of the condition of man and the works of God, the sense of disproportion overcome of the joining of extremes, of annihilation as the condition of superabundance, of death as the condition of supreme action. The sense of the Cross, of that Cross whereon the mystery of the Incarnation was consummated.

St. John of the Cross has not the tragic sense of life, for the tragic as such is without issue and in him, on the contrary, everything rushes and hurtles toward a blessed and radiant, but superhuman issue which is beatitude itself, the transfixed heart of the living God. For him, everything takes on that supernatural straining of earth toward heaven which the figures painted by Greco picture for our bodily eyes. Whereas in the speculative wisdom of St. Thomas Aquinas, in which everything is knitted together at the heights of first Truth, it is unity above all else that is revealed to us, explaining, and reconciling, ordering and justifying all the disparity—even thus did Angelico paint the heavenly dances—in the practical wisdom of St. John of the Cross, wherein everything is knitted together at the level of the human heart, it is disparity which is revealed to us, in order that, vanquished by love, it may lead us to unity. Only Christian wisdom can truly reach from one extreme to the other—wedding peace, security, joy and all that belong properly to the divine condition, to the agony of desire, the bloody sweat, the death for sin which are the truth of the human condition. "Who will deliver me from this body of death?" says St. Paul; and "It is not I who live but Christ liveth in me. I can do all things in Him who strengtheneth me."

4. There are two wrong roads, and they are broad. On these the soul loves itself with a proprietary love. The *road of the misguided spirit* leads to earthly goods. *The more I sought them, the less I found myself. I cannot climb the mountain for having taken a wrong road.* This is the road of death.

The road of the imperfect spirit claims to lead to heavenly goods and may perhaps do so. But it does so by seeking creaturely satisfactions in them. *Because I sought them I have them less than if I had mounted by the path. I delayed the longer and rose less high because I did not take the path.* This is a road of servitude.

---

second form. See also Bk. III, Chs. ii (i) and xv (xiv). Hoornaert's translations of the legends are not completely satisfactory.

Some readers may, perhaps, be surprised that St. John of the Cross resorted to graphic representations to explain spiritual realities. They forget that, according to Dionysius, that which is beyond expression can be represented in the simplest pictures, and furthermore, that the Saint must have smiled a bit while making his drawing. Others may think that this is a rather naive mnemonic. But really it is something quite different, a graphic poem deplorably overinked by the meticulous academicism of a copyist, but the quality of whose first sketch was very pure and stirring (cf. the *Ascent* published in Bruno of Jesus and Mary, *loc. cit.*).

The right road is the *path of perfection*. It passes almost imperceptibly between the two hills of egoism on whose flanks wind these two carriage roads. It climbs right straight up. It is narrow. *Quam arcta est via.* It widens out only farther on. On it the soul loves itself as emptied of self, that is, it hates itself, and detaches itself from all things. It has consented to lose itself, decided to remit its spirit—which is to die—into the hands of the Beloved. This path leads to the land of Carmel, to God perfectly loved for Himself and above all else. *The glory and honor of God dwells alone on this mountain-top. Thou shalt be, by so much, more as thou shalt have willed to be less.* This is the road of liberty. The sole road of liberty.

The end of the journey is transformation into God, which is begun here below by grace, faith and love, and will be consummated in vision. It is a matter of going to that place where the Son is. (He is in the bosom of the Father and He is on the Cross.) It is a matter of becoming one single spirit with God. "God communicates Himself most to that soul that has progressed farthest in love; namely that has its will in closest conformity with the will of God. And the soul that has attained complete conformity and likeness of will is totally united and transformed in God supernaturally."[2] This is given to those who are "born again through grace" and who have received from God "this rebirth and adoption which transcends all that can be imagined."[3]

The soul is like to a window in which light dwells by nature. If, strengthened by grace, it rids itself of every obstacle, every stain, every veil of creatures, it will become light by participation. "God communicates to it His supernatural Being, in such wise that it appears to be God Himself, and has all that God Himself has. . . . The preparation of the soul for this union, as we said, is not that it should understand or experience or feel or imagine anything . . . but that it should have purity and love. . . ."[4] Ultimately "the understanding of the soul is now the understanding of God; and its will is the will of God; and its memory is the memory of God; and its delight is the delight of God. And the substance of the soul, although it is not the Substance of God, for into this it cannot be changed, is nevertheless united in Him and absorbed in Him, and is thus God by participation in God."[5]

The value of contemplation is not only, not so much, that it is a life of knowledge, but above all that it is a life of love, and, as it were, the space wherein spiritual love unfolds to its fullest dimensions. Therein knowledge is demanded by love, and by knowledge, love shares a common life with Him who is Spirit; knowledge proceeds from love which, through a God-given instinct, experiences God. The property of spirit is to be within itself: how should not the unity of spirit effected by the adhesion of love between God and the soul re-echo in knowledge? Contemplation is the very experience of

2   *Ascent of Mount Carmel*, Bk. II, Ch. v (iv), § 4; Silv., II, p. 82; Peers, I, p. 80.
3   *Ibid.*, § 5; Silv., II, p. 83; Peers, I, p. 81.
4   *Ascent of Mount Carmel*, Bk. II, Ch. v (iv), §§ 7 and 8; Silv., II, p. 84; Peers, I, p. 82.
5   *Living Flame*, st. 2, v. 6; Silv., IV, p. 45 (152); Peers, III, p. 57.

union; it is by the union of love that the soul experiences and touches the divine. Taught by love, contemplation "is very delectable" for "all that love does is delectable."[6] Indeed, "naught is obtained of God save by love."[7] To become God by participation is to become love. "[The] perfect [soul] is wholly love."[8]

5. Can this be asked of the most complex and weakest of creatures, of a garrulous animal, of a glutton who unceasingly devours the meager intelligibility of visible things and the delights of the moment, of a wounded nature, pierced with a taste for evil and concupiscence, whose self-love is a barrier to love? Quick! Let him be buried deep in the ground, let him die, let the juices of the soil dissolve him, else he will remain alone; the seed planted in the dunghill of his heart will never germinate. John of the Cross is in a hurry; he does not want to waste a minute. Because no one has felt more keenly than he the enormous chaos separating the extremes that must be joined, no one has more vividly brought to light the prodigious dynamism of the life of a Christian. Those ladders and escalades which mystical writers so often describe make all too feeble an image. The whole substance is in travail, groans and melts away in order to spring up into life everlasting. And the invisible movement must ceaselessly accelerate. Pity those sentimental souls who, shedding a tear over the courage it takes not to leave their sins behind, think it would be more comfortable to believe in God and that one turns Christian to find a tranquil shelter.

Nothing, nothing, nothing, nothing, nothing: this is the path of St. John of the Cross. *Understanding and repose,—not this, nor that. Consolations and knowledge,—not this, nor that. Joys and honors,—not this, nor that. Security and liberty,— not this, nor that. Glory and enjoyment,—not this, nor that.* Nothing.

Upon the mountain, nothing.

If it is a matter of transforming the human being into love, bringing him to have the manners of God, one cannot be astonished at the destructions which are entailed. It is all too clear that a dialectical catharsis after the manner of Plotinus is here radically insufficient; this only digs an intellectual void which, in respect to the very being of the subject, is nothing but a superficial erosion. The purification which St. John of the Cross teaches and which is accomplished by God digs infinitely deeper, to the very sinews of being. It leaves us nothing of our own, not even the walls of the container. Everything is surrendered, everything is lost. The creature, made from nothing—and this is what Plotinus never knew—must be reabsorbed into nothingness, know and live it. It dies that it may begin to live in God's way—it dies again to act in God's way, to enter into the work of the Savior.

---

6   *Cant.*, st. 8 (27); Silv., III, p. 99; Peers, II, p. 109. Cf. above, Ch. VIII, § 20.
7   *Cant.*, 2nd ed., st. I; Silv. III, p. 204; Peers, II, p. 201.
8   *Cant.*, 2nd ed., st. 27 (18); Silv., III, p. 356; Peers, II, p. 340.

In slaying, thou has changed death into life.[9]
"Be ye perfect as your heavenly Father is perfect." "He who hateth not his life for my sake cannot be my disciple": these two sayings echo from earth to heaven, and say rigorously the same thing.

The Way to Arrive at Everything[10]

In order to arrive at that which thou knowest not,
Thou must go by a way that thou knowest not.

In order to arrive at that wherein thou hast no pleasure,
Thou must go by a way wherein thou hast no pleasure.

In order to arrive at that which thou possessest not,
Thou must go by a way that thou possessest not.

In order to arrive at that which thou art not,
Thou must go through that which thou art not.

The Way to Possess Everything

In order to arrive at knowing everything,
Desire not to know anything in anything.

In order to arrive at having pleasure in everything,
Desire to have pleasure in nothing.

In order to arrive at possessing everything,
Desire not to possess anything in anything.

In order to arrive at being everything,
Desire not to be anything in anything.

The Way Not to Impede the All

When thou thinkest upon anything,
Thou ceasest to cast thyself upon the All.

For, in order to pass from the all to the All,
Thou hast to deny thyself wholly in all.

---

9   Cf. *Living Flame*, st. 2, v. 6 (Peers, III, p. 140). *Matando, muerte en vida la has trocado.*
10   Cf. *Ascent of Mount Carmel*, Bk. I, Ch. xiv (Peers, I, pp. 62–63).

And, when thou comest to possess it wholly,
Thou must possess it without desiring anything.

For, if thou wilt have anything in all,
Thou hast not thy treasure purely in God.

Such conduct would be insane were it not instigated by God. He it is Who, by giving us grace, plants in us a seed of Himself. He it is Who guides the toil of our willing. He it is Who, when we have come under the habitual regime of the gifts of His Spirit, takes pains to complete our purification and to raise us, by the ways of passivity, to the heights of contemplation. "When, therefore, the soul considers that God is the principal agent in this matter. . . ."[11] "And that is impossible with natural ability alone. The truth, I repeat, is that God must place the soul in this supernatural state; but the soul, as far as in it lies, must be continually preparing itself; and this it can do by natural means, especially with the help that God is continually giving it."[12]

6. The rigor of the means employed must be understood in the light of the goal envisaged. The love of creatures, far more rarely attained in its full perfection (its perfection even of death and sin) than is divine love, strews its path with thousands of abortive attempts. Many, too, are the half-hearted efforts, the lovers who have failed and fallen by the wayside, along the road to divine love. One of the sorrows of a Christian is to think that, by his deformities (for what is less gracious than an embryonic saint, distorted with egoism and imperfect virtues?), he runs the risk of making divine love the subject of blasphemy among men. Poor wretch, he knows very well that only saints progress beyond the larval state, they alone are elegantly formed. St. John of the Cross wants no larvae. He tirelessly repeats that the excellence of the love of God, into whom the soul must be transformed, is the measure of the stripping which the senses must undergo. Even the imperfect spirituality of profane wisdom demands a certain measure of this sort of stripping; is it surprising that a divine spiritualization should require a still more radical stripping of the senses?

The teaching of St. John of the Cross on this point is all the more solid because his conception of human nature is wholly Aristotelian. For him man is not a pure spirit using a body; his natural life, even in the spiritual order, thrusts its roots into the senses and is exercised only through the shaping of images. Wherefore, as practitioner of the things of the soul, he groups the senses, the working of reason and discursive meditation all under the same heading. For, with respect to the being of God, all that is the region of unlikeness.

---

11   Cf. *Living Flame*, st. 3, v. 3; Silv., IV, p. 63 (170); Peers, III, p. 176. Cf. Ch. VIII, § 22.
12   *Ascent of Mount Carmel*, Bk. III, Ch. xxi, § 13; Silv., II, p. 246; Peers, I, p. 232.

He does not ask us to suppress the activity of the senses, any more than the Gospel, in speaking of those who have "made themselves eunuchs for the kingdom of God," prescribes mutilation. He loved the beauties of the country-side, which helped him to pray; he had a most delicate sensibility; he was one of the greatest poets of Spain and of the world; sometimes he complained; he had a deep tenderness for his brother Francis, the poor mason, and a great love for his spiritual sons and daughters. But he demands absolute renunciation in the use of notions, as well as of sensory attractions. Use them as though you were not using them. Later, on the mountain, all will be transfigured. Meanwhile, we must begin by losing all: such is the law of the path to God. In the material or physical order, to renounce everything is impossible and to renounce some determinate things by poverty, chastity and obedience, is the privilege of a few. But in the order of the spiritual, the renunciation of all things is required of all who wish to be perfect. There are no two ways out of the lamentable struggle of a spirit rooted in the senses, which communicates to them its infinity of desire. Give all, poor men; how much easier to give all than to give half. Everything we hold on to is a cancer gnawing at our entrails.

7. The senses bring two impurities in their train: one which is contrary to the life of the virtues, and which the soul conquers by the right use of its faculties and of the senses themselves; the other which is contrary to the contemplative union; the soul overcomes it by passing beyond the senses. To cure the first impurity, the ascesis of St. John of the Cross recommends two remedies. "He said that there are two ways of resisting vices and acquiring virtues. The one is common and the less perfect, which is when you endeavor to resist some vice, sin or temptation by means of the acts of virtue which conflict with [it]. . . .

"There is another way . . . which is easier, more profitable and more perfect. According to this, by its loving analogical movements and acts alone, without any other exercises whatsoever, the soul resists and destroys all the temptations of our adversary and attains virtues in the most perfect degree. This . . . becomes possible after this manner.

"When we feel the first movement or attack of any vice, such as lust, wrath, impatience or a revengeful spirit when some wrong has been done to us, we should not resist it by making an act of the contrary virtue, in the way that has been described, but, as soon as we are conscious of it, we should meet it with an act or movement of analogical love directed against this vice, and should raise our affection to union with God, for by this means the soul absents itself from its surroundings and is present with its God and becomes united with Him, and then the vice or the temptation and the enemy are defrauded of their intent, and have nowhere to strike. For the soul, being where it loves rather than where it lives, has met the temptation with Divine aid and the enemy has found nowhere to strike and nothing whereon to lay hold, for the soul is no longer where the temptation or enemy would have struck and wounded it. . . . It has escaped. . . . In this way there is begotten in the soul a wondrous and heroic virtue, which the angelic doctor, St. Thomas, calls the virtue of a soul that is perfectly purged."[13]

To heal the second impurity which comes in the wake of the senses and which prevents the union of love and contemplation by a mist of creatures, there is but one remedy: night, the void. St. John of the Cross deals most fully and completely with this purification (which belongs properly to mystical theology) in his teaching on the Night of the Senses. This is a two-fold night, both active and passive,[14] or rather perhaps a twilight into which those souls penetrate who have heard the call to contemplation (and the Saint speaks only to these). In the one case, the soul exerts itself on its own initiative, turning down the taste of the senses and the force of their attractions, lulling the appetites to sleep. In the other case, God works in the soul, purifying it Himself with an incomparably greater efficacy. Without this divine scouring of the passive night, the soul would never be cleansed of those all-too-visible stains which are imperceptible to it: of the desire for consolation, the spiritual presumption, sensuality, impatience, avarice, gluttony, envy and sloth which are the ordinary faults of apprentices in perfection. Distinguishing spiritual realities from sensible representations, passing beyond phantasms, beginning

---

13   *Testimony of St. Eliseus of the Martyrs*; Silv., IV, pp. 349–350; Peers, III, pp. 309–310.

14   It is important to note that the active nights treated in the *Ascent of Mount Carmel* and the passive nights treated in the *Dark Night of the Soul* are two concomitant aspects of the same life and the same progress (just as the two works comment upon the same verses); "And thus, as the soul, for its own part, enters into this renunciation and self-emptying of forms, so God begins to give it the possession of union; and this God works passively in the soul, as we shall say, *Deo dante*, when we treat of the passive night of the soul." (*Ascent*, Bk. III, Ch. ii [i], Silv., II, p. 246; Peers, I, p. 232.) The *Ascent* explains what the soul (which has already passed through meditation and is proximately called to contemplation) must do for its part in this progress; the *Night* explains what God does. In both places St. John of the Cross asks of the soul "courage and the perseverance that comes from courage" (*Spiritual Sentences and Maxims*, Andujar MS., § 3, Silv., II, p. 232; Peers, III, p. 241), in one case courage to undertake, in the other, courage to endure.

      Why did not St. John of the Cross treat both aspects of spiritual progress at the same time and prefer to study the active series and the passive series separately? In our opinion, the reason is that there is no fixed correspondence between the various successive moments of these two correlative series: the various moments of the second series can anticipate or come after those of the first, at the good pleasure of the free initiatives of God.

      However, if we want to correlate the two series in a general way (*ut in pluribus*), it is our opinion that the passive nights should be put somewhat farther along in the temporal line than the active nights (which prepare and dispose the soul for the passive nights). As for the third night spoken of in Bk. 1, Ch. ii of the *Ascent*, it is described in the *Spiritual Canticle* (spiritual betrothal and marriage) and in the *Living Flame*.

to know itself and to understand that the divine will fill it just insofar as it is empty, the soul begins also to glimpse the peace of God, enters into the prayer of quiet, the beginning, the tiny beginning of infused contemplation.

8. This dark night of the senses "serves rather to accommodate sense to spirit than to unite spirit to God."[15] In the rare souls whom God sees are not too pusillanimous to be called to higher purification, this night is complicated by special suffering and temptations. Then for some appears the angel of Satan or the spirit of fornication, sometimes the spirit of blasphemy, sometimes the spirit of vertigo, to bar the entrance to the night of the spirit. This night is also two-fold, active and passive, as dense and dark as the shades of midnight before the eternal morning of vision. In the active night of the spirit the contemplative soul purifies its understanding by faith, not only by remaining in darkness as to creatures but also by refusing every distinct light, by rejecting, when it seeks God in prayer, all representations it might make for itself about God and spiritual things. This is what the soul has to do here, this is its action: to reject everything that is unlike the divine. For no created thing, no conceivable thought, no distinct idea, nothing which the understanding can grasp in this life, can serve as a proximate means for divine union. The only proper and proportionate means of union is pure faith, faith vivified by charity and made penetrating and savorous by the gifts of the Holy Spirit. Let the soul concentrate its forces upon one general and pure act: "Be still and see that I am God."[16] In the same way, the soul purifies its memory by hope, stripping itself of all things, abandoned, but God becomes its whole support. It purifies its will by charity, risking for love everything it loves, renouncing all goods that are not God, even spiritual goods, raising the sacrificial life over the very pledge of all the promises it has received.

But God for His part works all by Himself in the fullness of His initiatives. This is the passive night of the spirit, the "horrible night of contemplation" which is infused contemplation itself; like the Cross of Jesus, a place of supreme torments and the beatitudes of peace. There is no longer a question of accommodating the sense to the spirit, but rather the created spirit to the uncreated Spirit. In this agony of its very substance is consummated the meeting of extremes, of which the mystical Doctor has so terrible an intuition. Human measures no longer have any value. In this superhuman atmosphere all human perceptions are confounded, take on incomprehensible proportions. A divinely pure light pierces the dark and impure soul. It feels persecuted by God as by an enemy, it no longer has any foothold, it longs for death, no one has the slightest pity on it, "so it believes and so it is."[17] The divine grinds it, dissolves its spiritual substance and absorbs it in deep and absolute

---

15   *Dark Night*, Bk. II, Ch. ii, § 1; Silv., II, p. 416; Peers, I, p. 400.
16   Ps. xiv, 11.
17   *Dark Night*, Bk. II, Ch. v, 37; Silv., II, p. 425; Peers, I, p. 408.

darkness; it is as if it were swallowed alive by a beast; digested in the dark depths of its belly. To remove the human rust at the center of the soul, must it not be made red-hot in the fire like an empty cauldron, and be in some manner destroyed and annihilated "since these passions and imperfections have become connatural to it"? "Of such souls one could truly say that they 'go down alive into hell.' "[18] In this way do the passive purifications of the spirit remove the deep inveterate stains, as old as Adam, which are woven into our very selves, "the natural coarseness every man contracts from sin," and the actual imperfections, all of which constitute the flaws of the proficient. Like love and by it those purifications melt the heart for love is there and love does all. Stripped, transformed, transparent, inflamed with love in the darkness: filled by a light that is supernaturally simple; pure, general, detached from every particular intelligible—the soul has become apt to "search all things, yea the deep things of God."[19] "And this is the characteristic of the spirit which is purged and annihilated with respect to all particular affections and objects of the understanding, that in this state wherein it has pleasure in nothing and understands nothing in particular, but dwells in its emptiness, darkness and obscurity, it embraces everything with great adaptability, to the end that those words of St. Paul may be fulfilled in it: 'Having nothing and possessing all things.' For such poverty of spirit as this would deserve such happiness."[20]

9. I realize how rash it is to attempt to summarize in a few lines a teaching of such incomparable plenitude, transcending all philosophy, and so run the risk of falsifying. But it was necessary to point out the principal stages in the spiritual journey described by St. John of the Cross. Now the soul is at ease; it is free to roam. It has passed through the Gate. "And it will go in and come out, and it will find pasture." It is no longer correct to say that its path has widened; the narrow path opens on to the infinite breadth of spiritual liberty: *Here there is no more road. Because for the just man there is no law.*

This is the very teaching of St. Paul. [21] There is no law for the just, because he has become the law itself, and more than the law, the king. He is like the hardened criminal, he has nothing more to lose; he has lost his very soul, hidden in the light of the Trinity. Love has destroyed him and given him rebirth, buried him and raised him to life along with the great Phoenix of the five wounds. Activated by the Spirit of God and become the son of God because in him grace has borne its fruit, because, having renounced his human

---

18 *Dark Night*, Bk. IV, Ch. vi, § 6; Silv., I, p. 430; Peers, I, p. 412. *Et descendant in infernum viventes*, Ps. liv, 16. Cf. Job xvii, 16; xx, 13.

19 St. Paul, I Cor. ii, 10.

20 *Dark Night*, Bk. II, Ch. viii, § 5; Silv., II, pp. 440–441; Peers, I, p. 422.

21 Rom. x, 4: "Finis enim legis, Christus"; Gal. iii, 24: "Itaque lex paedagogus noster fuit in Christo"; v. 18: "Quod si Spiritui ducimini, non estis sub lege"; 23: "Adversus hujusmodi non est lex"; II Cor. iii, 17: "Ubi Spiritus Domini, ibi libertas"; Rom. viii, 14: "Qui Spiritu Dei aguntur, ii sunt filii Dei."

personality for God, he has in some manner put on the personality of God; marching "straight forward. Whither the impulse of the spirit was to go . . . and they turned not when they went."[22] He announces peace upon the mountains, he is disconcerting and elusive, a bright cloud borne along by a breath; he judges all, and men treat him as refuse but cannot judge him.[23] He magnifies God because God has become, in him and by him, what God alone can be, and what He wants to be in us: Supreme Liberty moving without obstacle another liberty and taking complete possession of it, making a man will what He wills (for the man no longer wills anything but the good), what they both will, for the two wills are no longer practically distinguishable: God and the Saint have exchanged hearts. "Thou knowest not whence he cometh and whither he goeth. So is every one that is born of the Spirit."[24]

Liberty and spirituality are two strictly correlative terms. Liberty, gratuitousness, availability, avoidance of the social and of opinion, no more beaten track, no more bonds, yes, no more law! But the mistake is to look for all this in the flesh. The law is the only way to transcend the law, providing that love pass through it. Christ was heard because of His obedience. Liberty is not in the spirit of poetry, or the spirit of mathematics, or the spirit of earthly nourishment, but in the Holy Spirit who sanctifies and sacrifices.

"The things also that are of God, no man knoweth, but the Spirit of God."[25] Upon the mountain of perfection it is the Spirit of God who illumines and vivifies. Spirit of filial fear, the spirit of piety, spirit of understanding, spirit of counsel, spirit of fortitude, spirit of knowledge, spirit of wisdom; by the seven gifts which it touches off and animates in the soul, the Spirit brings the soul to mystical union and exhales within it the sweetness of God:

> *Breathe though my garden*
> *That its perfumes may breathe forth.*

The fruits of the Holy Spirit, chastity, continence, modesty, strength of faith, meekness, benignity, kindness, patience, long-suffering, peace, joy, the tenderness of charity—such are the final and delectable products super-abounding on those heights. The four cardinal virtues, inferior to the gifts and which are to wisdom as a gate-keeper who opens the door before the king, are inscribed upon slopes of the mountain. On the crest, higher than the gifts, are faith, hope and charity which attain God and bind man to his center. There, too, is security, which the soul has found with liberty, because in the beginning it said to them: neither this, nor that. Since I have rooted myself in nothing, I find that nothing is lacking to me. He who is reunited in the depths of his being with the Life of

---

22   Ezekiel i, 12.
23   "Spiritualis autem judicat omnia; et ipse a nemine judicatur" (I Cor. ii, 15).
24   John iii, 8.
25   I Cor ii, 11.

all life, dwelling in him by grace, thenceforward possesses all things. *When I did not seek Him with self-love, He gave Himself to me without being sought.*

"Mine are the heavens and mine is the earth; mine are the people, the righteous are mine and mine the sinners; the angels are mine and the Mother of God and all things are mine; and God Himself is mine and for me, for Christ is mine and all for me. What then, dost thou ask for and seek, my soul? Thine is all this, and it is all for thee."[26]

Divine Silence. Divine Wisdom. Unity of life, unending communication of the goods of friendship; perpetual feast when the prodigal returned is drunk with wisdom; where, in the Father's kingdom in the inward heaven of the divinized soul, the Son drinks with the sons the new wine of eternal bliss. *Secura mens quasi juge convivium.*[27]

10. When the night of the soul has been sufficiently deep, when the soul's substance has been sufficiently dissolved, *cupio dissolvi et esse tecum,* then the soul's desire: *to be with Thee,* becomes felt and palpable; it is the invasion of peace. In the state which St. John of the Cross calls spiritual betrothal, contemplation becomes luminous. It is the moving twilight. Without seeing God in his essence, the soul nevertheless experiences that He is all, in transpiercing glances, in knowledge stripped of all accidents and images, and whose sweetness sometimes penetrates to the very marrow of its bones. But peace is not yet complete because God's visitations remain intermittent and the soul is still exposed to the terrors of the devil.

The perfect peace promised by Jesus is given in the transforming union of spiritual marriage. "For even as in the consummation of marriage according to the flesh the two become one flesh, as the Divine Scripture says (Gen. ii, 24) even so, when this spiritual marriage between God and the soul is consulted, there are two natures in one spirit and love."[28] The soul then possesses the unlimited rights of a bride; God reveals to her all His secrets. Terrible is the strength of the soul entirely subject to God's will! It shares in some manner in the impassibility of the angels; the waters of sorrow can no longer slake it, even its contrition for its sins, which is perfect, no longer distresses it; devils no longer dare assail it; it seems identified with peace itself. "The soul in such a condition is in a certain manner as Adam was in the condition of innocence, when he knew not what evil was; for it is so innocent that it understands not evil, nor judges aught as evil; and it will hear things that are very evil, and will see them with its eyes, and will be unable to understand that they are so, because it has no habit of evil whereby to judge it."[29] Confirmed in grace, it

---

26   *Spiritual Sentences and Maxims* (Andujar MS.), Silv., IV, p. 235; Peers, III, p. 244.
27   Prov. xv, 15.
28   "son dos naturalezas en un espiritu y amor, segun dice San Pablo. . . ." (*Cant.,* 2nd ed., st. 22, Silv., III, p. 320; Peers, II, p. 308; 1st ed., st. 27, *ibid.,* p. 132; Peers, II, p. 140).
29   *Ibid.,* 2nd ed., st. 26 (17); Silv., III, pp. 348–349; Peers, II, p. 334. Cf. *Living Flame,*

"becomes God by participation[30] insofar as may be in this life." And all the time it is annihilated, perfectly empty, yes, of all that is not the truth of God and love. "For my heart has been inflamed, and my reins have been changed; and I am brought to nothing and I knew not. *Et ego ad nihilum redactus sum et nescivi.*"[31]

11. These things are set forth in the *Spiritual Canticle* and in the *Living Flame*; in our account of them we have made use of the saint's own expressions. No century has lacked holy souls who have experienced these things, souls without whom all our goods on this earth would long since have been dissipated. Their experience echoes that of St. John of the Cross. We would like to quote here an especially instructive page from some very valuable notes upon the spiritual marriage written some fifty years ago by a member of the Society of Jesus, but published only recently—for such works are not too plentiful. "The soul in this blessed state," wrote Father Rabussier,[32] "comes to have the habit of possessing everything it can desire in view of God, and not only for itself but for the greater good of souls. . . . In this conformity of will the person united in spiritual marriage experiences even this: when the thought of something he desires comes into his mind, to test it, he needs only to withdraw into the heart of this prayer; if the desire springs from there, it is an evident sign that God wants to fulfil it; if not, this desire vanishes of itself. Little by little, this habit of possessing everything begets a certitude, surpassing all else, that that for which God gives the greatest desire will be done. Even this future (*will* be done) is not quite exact, for this habit goes so far as to experience and see clearly that all is done and decided by the very fact of this prayer.

"Thus . . . when more than one soul has entered into full possession of this prayer, and the Holy Spirit, with admirable design, inspires them with unanimous desires converging toward the same end, there results an irresistible force. . . . It is a great misfortune when among a great many souls at the head of the apostolate there is not one who has attained to this prayer; then, the saints teach us, a country declines and Providence seems to dispose all things in favor of the wicked and against the good. . . .

"But how is it that such dominion belongs to the prayer of spiritual

---

st. 2, v. 6: "And finally, all the movements and operations which the soul had aforetime, and which belonged to the principle of its natural life, are now in this union changed into movements of God" (Silv., IV, p. 45 [152]; Peers, III, p. 57). Cf. above, Ch. VIII, n. 61.

30   *Cant.*, st. 27 (22); Silv., III, p. 132, Peers, II, p. 140.
31   Ps. lxxii, 22.
32   *Revue d'Ascetique et de Mystique,* July 1927, p. 289. Rev. Fr. Rabussier died in 1897. These notes were written for Mme. Cecile Bruyère, abbess of St. Cecile of Solesmes, when she was preparing her work, which has since become a classic, on *L'Oraison d'après la Sainte Ecriture et la tradition monastique.*

marriage, when so many millions of saints and angels confirmed in grace cannot chain up the devil nor triumph over sinners? Here we must advert to the fact that God works within the framework of order, that heaven and the Church on earth are distinct from each other. Just as the heat of a single star could melt all the ice on earth, and yet we have winter, just as you need a point of contact to move the arm of a lever, so God wants every heavenly action on earth to have a point of contact, and this point of contact is the saints who are still on their pilgrimage in this life. . . ."

This contemplative goes on to explain that in the state of spiritual marriage, suffering (the suffering of prayer, due to divine action and which in this state is nothing but a sharing in the redemptive Passion) can co-exist with completely pure and inadmissible peace.[33] Such a soul "has the supreme bliss of being able to suffer only by the hand of God." "This suffering strikes to the depths of the soul where the prayer of spiritual marriage abides, the locus of the pain of eternal damnation for the damned. We have also said that this profound suffering in no way disturbs their peace. Yes, even then there is always a substratum of gladness, because the springing up anew of the infinitely deep source of spiritual marriage is always there at will."

Let us enter further into the thicket, said St. John of the Cross. Let us enter into this "deep thicket" of wisdom and of mysteries and marvels without number, into this vast "thicket of wisdom and knowledge of God"[34] which is the mountain of God and of which David spoke: Mons Dei, mons pinguis; mons coagulatus. "And thus the thicket may be understood . . . as signifying trials and tribulations insomuch as they are a means of entrance into the thicket of the delectable wisdom of God: for the purest suffering causes and entails the purest knowledge, and, in consequence, the purest and loftiest joy which comes from deepest penetration. So, not content with any manner of suffering, the soul says: Let us enter farther into the thicket. Wherefore Job, desiring this suffering, said: Who will grant that my petition may be fulfilled and that God may give me that for which I hope, and that He who began me may diminish me and let loose His hand and cut me off, and that I may have this consolation, that He will afflict me with grief and will not pardon or relieve me? Oh, that it might be perfectly understood how the soul cannot attain to the thicket of the wisdom and riches of God, save by entering into the thicket of many kinds of suffering and by setting thereupon its consolation and desire! And how the soul that of a truth desires wisdom first desires truly to enter farther into the thicket of the Cross!"[35]

---

33   Cf. St. Teresa, Interior Castle, Mansion VII, Ch. iii, pp. 339 ff. "The second effect [of spiritual marriage] is a great desire to suffer. . . . Their conception of glory is of being able in some way to help the Crucified. . ."; see also Ch. iv, ibid., p. 344. The already mentioned work of Mme. Cecile Bruyère (Ch. xix, pp. 370 ff.) contains remarkable passages upon the sufferings peculiar to the state of perfect union.

34   Cant., st. 35 (36); Silv., III, p. 60; Peers, II, p. 166.

The blessed repose of the soul transformed is not a repose of immobility for it has not yet attained its end; this repose is the stability of triumphant movement and desire, whose vehemence multiplies unceasingly. The soul wants to love God as she is loved by Him: to equal divine love is her sole preoccupation. "Until she attains so far, the soul is not content, nor would she be content in the next life if [as St. Thomas says in *opusculo de Beatitudine*] she felt not that she loves God as greatly as she is loved by Him."[36] She can die of thus desire.[37] She has become love entirely, she no longer does anything but love:

> *Nor have I now other office*
> *For now my exercise is in loving alone.*

12. This equality of love, which will be complete and consummated only in the future life, begins at the time of the spiritual "betrothal": "By calling Him her brother, she denotes the equality which there is in the betrothal of love between the two...."[38] Then the soul in its exchange of love with God, allowing none of the grace offered to it to go to waste, so to speak[39] (whereas we, when a whole river is offered to us, use but a drop), then the betrothed soul gives back God measure for measure, as much of love at each moment of its progress as it receives of loving advances and attentions from the eternal will by which God wills all men to be saved. But now, to that sort of equality, which is as a condition or prerequisite disposition, another is added: the privilege of consummated union.

The soul's act of love is finite and measured, like the soul's degree of charity; and the love with which God loves the soul is also finite and measured as to its term (for God does not love all things equally).[40] But in itself and in its

---

35　*Cant.*, st. 35 (36); Silv., III, p. 161 (402–403); Peers, II, 167. Cf. *Living Flame*, st. 2, v. 5; Silv., IV, pp. 40–41 (147); Peers, III, pp. 52–53: "Oh, souls that seek to walk in security and comfort! If ye did but know how necessary it is to suffer and endure in order to reach this lofty state, and of what great benefit it is to suffer and be mortified in order to reach such lofty blessings, ye would in no way seek consolation, either from God or from creatures, but would rather bear the cross, together with pure vinegar and gall."

36　*Cant.*, 2nd ed., st. 38 (37); Silv., III, p. 411; Peers, II, p. 391. See above, Ch. VIII, end of § 10, and below, Ch. IX, n. 75.

37　Cf. *Living Flame*, st. 1, v. 6; Silv., IV, p. 23; Peers, III, p. 35; and especially the 2nd ed., Silv., p. 127; Peers, III, p. 135.

38　Cant., st. 27 (22); Silv., III, p. 135; Peers, II, p. 143. Cf. st. 15, p. 82 (Peers, p. 92): "This kiss is the union whereof we are speaking, wherein the soul is made equal with God through love. Wherefore she has this desire, asking to be given the Beloved that He may be her brother, which phrase signifies and makes equality."

39　Cf. below, Appendix VIII.

40　"Cum amare sit velle bonum alicui, *duplici* ratione potest aliquid magis, vel minus amari. Uno modo ex parte ipsius actus voluntatis, qui est magis, vel minus intensus. Et sic Deus non magis quaedam aliis amat, quia omnia amat uno et

substance, *ex parte ipsius actus voluntatis*, His love is infinite; as a matter of fact, it is with the same eternal and subsistent love with which God loves Himself that He loves creatures as finite and contingent terms (and when they join the ranks of the blessed, they enter into His own joy: *intra in gaudium Domini tui*). In this infinity how can divine love be equalled? "And as the soul sees the truth of the vastness of the love wherewith God loves her, she desires not to love Him less loftily and perfectly...."[41] This is the mystery proper to the espousals. However difficult it may be to understand and correctly to recount, the teaching of St. John of the Cross on this point is formal. We shall try to pick out its principles.

"He who is joined to the Lord is one spirit," says St. Paul. *Qui adhaeret Domino, unus spiritus est.*[42] From the point of view of entity, in the register of the proper being of things, there is always a duality, nay, say an infinite distance between the soul and uncreated love. But there is another order than that of entity, and it is to that order that St. Paul makes allusion in his words: "one spirit," he says, not "one single being." This is the order of love as love, considered not in its ontological constituents of essence and existence (for there it is considered as being but in the absolutely proper reality of the immaterial intussusception by which the other within me becomes more me than myself. It is said that the formal effect of love is that beloved be to me as I am to myself, or, as another myself.[43] If the immaterial activity of knowledge is to become the other as other, the immaterial activity of love is to lose oneself in the other as the self, to alienate myself in the reality of the other[44] to the extent that he becomes more me than I am myself.[45] It is in this that love is "ecstatic"—*in amore amicitiae affectus alicujus simpliciter exit extra se*[46]—and that

---

simplici actu voluntatis, et semper eodem modo se habente. *Alio modo ex parte ipsius boni, quod aliquis vult amato. Et sic dicimur aliquem magis alio amare, cui volumus majus bonum, quamvis non magis intensa voluntate. Et hoc modo necesse est dicere, quod Deus quaedam aliis magis amat. Cum enim amor Dei sit causa bonitatis rerum, ut dictum est, non esset aliquid alio melius, si Deus non vellet uni majus bonum, quam alteri" (Sum. Theol., I, 20, 3).*

41   *Cant.*, st. 37 (38); Silv., III, p. 16; Peers, II, p. 172.

42   I Cor. vi, 17.

43   "Cum aliquis amat aliquem amore amicitiae [this is the only kind of love we are discussing here], vult ei bonum, sicut et sibi vult bonum; unde apprehendit eum ut alterum si, inquantum scilicet vult ei bonum, sicut et sibi ipsi, et inde est, quod amicus dicitur esse *alius ipse*; et Augustinus dicit in IV *Confess.*: Bene quidem dixit de amico suo, *dimidium animae meae*" (St. Thomas, *Sum. Theol.*, I–II, 28, 1). Cf. *ibid.*, ad 2: "Amans se habet ad amatum, in amore amicitiae, ut ad seipsum."

44   "Cognitio perficitur per hoc, quod cognitum unitur cognoscenti secundum suam similitudinem sed amor facit, quod ipsa res, quae amatur, amanti aliquo modo uniatur, ut dictum est: unde amor est magis unitivus quam cognitio" (*Sum. Theol.*, I–II, 28, 1, ad 3). Cf. *Réflexions sur l'intelligence*, pp. 125–127.

45   This is what St. Thomas calls "complacentia amati interius radicata" (*ibid.*, a. 2). And again: "Amatum continetur in amante inquantum est impressum in affectu ejus per quamdam complacentiam" (*ibid.*, a. 2, ad 1).

it melts the heart, *ut amatum in ipso subintret*,[47] and is the cause of everything the lover does.[48]

The mystery of cognitive union and of the true compels the philosopher to conceive a "being of knowledge" and an *esse intentionale* which is not entitative being or being of nature. The mystery of the union of love and of the good compels him to conceive an *intentional being of love*[49] which is not entitative being either.[50] In the beatific vision the created intellect and the uncreated essence remain entitatively distant to infinity, and yet the soul, in its supernatural activity of knowledge, becomes God according to the intentional being of knowledge. In the spiritual marriage the created will and uncreated love remain entitatively distant to infinity, yet the soul, in its supernatural activity of love, loses or alienates itself in God Who, according to the being or actuality of love, becomes her more than herself, and is the principle and agent of all her operations. The Saint himself has, with eloquent wisdom, summed up this

---

46 "Quia vult amico bonum, quasi gerens curam et providentiam ipsius propter amicum" (St. Thomas, *Sum. Theol.*, I–II, 28, 3).

47 *Sum. Theol.*, I–II, 28, 5, sed contra.

48 *Ibid.*, a. 6.

49 We are calling the immaterial *esse* according to which the spirit of love proceeds "intentional" being by analogy with the intentional being according to which the mental word proceeds. But it must be understood that, in this case, intentionality plays an entirely different role than it does in knowledge, because of the proper function of the will, and because of its immateriality which is, indeed, no less pure in itself but less separated from things and wholly turned toward their concrete state (cf. *Sum. Theol.*, I, 82, 3). Unlike the intentional being of knowledge, the intentional being of love is not an *esse* in virtue of which the one (knower) becomes the other (the known): it is an *esse* in virtue of which the other (the beloved), spiritually present in the one (the lover) as a weight or impulse, becomes to him as an other self. This is an immaterial *processus* but entirely different from that of knowledge.

50 St. Thomas points this out in saying: "processio verbi attenditur secundum actionem intelligibilem. Secundum autem operationem voluntatis invenitur in nobis quaedam alia processio, scilicet processio amoris, secundum quam amatum est in amante: sicut per conceptionem verbi res dicta vel intellecta est in intelligente" (*Sum. Theol.*, I, 27, 3).
   So there is a certain immaterial being proper to the union of love, according to which the beloved is in the will of the lover, just as there is a certain immaterial being proper to cognitive union, according to which the known is in the intellect of the knower. In the latter case, that presence is by mode of likeness wherein the knower becomes the known; in the former, this presence is by mode of impulsion and motion, and the beloved becomes the principle of action, the "weight" of the lover (*ibid.*, a. 4). The great Thomists have admirably deepened and developed the questions concerning the being of knowledge; fruitful principles for a similar development concerning the intentional being of love and the spiration of love can also be found in their works. (Cf. John of St. Thomas, *Curs. Phil. Phil. Nat.*, Ia P., q. 13, *de Fine*: *Curs. Theol.*, Ia P., q. 27, disp. 12, a. 7 and qq. 36–38, disp. 15, a. 3, 4 and 5.) But this development itself is yet to be made.

whole matter in a passage we have already quoted: "there are *two natures in one spirit and love of God.*"[51]

"In this state, therefore, the soul can perform no acts, but it is the Holy Spirit that moves it to perform them. Wherefore all its acts are divine. . . ."[52] and although they come from Him, they belong to the soul likewise, for God works them in the soul with its own aid, since it gives its will and consent thereto."[53] But it is not only the moving and efficient action of God upon the soul that must be considered here. The reason why the divine action burgeons and blossoms in the soul, unhindered by any obstacle arising from the nothingness of the creature, is because simultaneously and under this same action (in the order of formal causality) the soul is transformed into God. Not transformed, as we have already seen in speaking of sanctifying grace and the indwelling of God in the soul,[54] by an entitative changing of its being into the being or substance of Deity, or, indeed, in a simply moral sense; no, the transformation is effected in a "physical" or ontological manner, but in order of the relation of the soul to God as object, inasmuch as by grace the soul is made capable of God and turned towards God *to see and to love* as He sees and loves Himself.[55]

Here is achieved in its fullness that of which sanctifying grace is the principle and root. This complete transformation takes place in two different ways: either "the beatific life, which consists in seeing God, and this is to be attained by means of the natural death of the body," or "perfect spiritual life, which is the possession of God through the union of love."[56] Thus, according to the Saint's own teaching and testimony, it is necessary to recognize, before the ultimate end of human life, fixed for eternity by the beatific vision a sort of anticipation of that glory in time itself, a possession of God even here below

---

51   "Consumado este espiritual matrimonio entre Dios y el alma, son dos naturalezas en un espiritu y amor de Dios" (*Cant.*, st. 27 [22]; Silv., 111, p. 132 [320]).
(Cf. above, Ch. IX, § 10, and Ch. VIII, § 11.) (Peers, II, p. 308.) St. Teresa, *Interior
Castle*, Mansion VII, Ch. II, Peers, Vol. II, pp. 335–336: "It is impossible to say
more than that, as far as one can understand, the soul . . . is made one with God.
. . . It is here that the little butterfly to which we have referred dies, and with the
greatest joy, because Christ is now its life."

52   *Living Flame*, st. 1, v. 1; Silv., IV, p. 8 (111); Peers, III, p. 2.

53   *Ibid.*, v. 3, p. 12 (114); Peers, III, p. 24.

54   See above, Ch. VI, §§ 8 and 10.

55   The soul lives a divine life because the object of some of its operations is God in
his own essence. "And as each living creature lives by its operation, as the
philosophers say, having its operations in God, through the union that they have
with God, the soul lives the life of God and its death has been changed into life."
Living Flame, st. 2, v. 6; Silv., IV, p. 44 (151); Peers, III, p. 56.

56   *Living Flame*, st. 2, v. 6; Silv., IV, p. 43 (150); Peers, III, p. 55. As was explained
above (cf. Ch. VI, § 14), this "union of love" is *possessive* because, thanks to the
gifts of understanding and wisdom and by the special inspiration and illumination of the Holy Spirit, the loving transformation of the soul into God is itself the
formal means of the experimental knowledge of God, the passion of things
divine.

which takes place by love. Love outstrips understanding: *cucurrit Petro citius.* . . . And is this not already true of time as of eternity?[57] The payment which the intellect will receive only in the future life (because it cannot transform the soul in God until she sees Him, after the separation of soul and body), love can receive in this present life, because for the soul to be transformed into God it is enough that the soul love God, but love Him so much as to separate the soul from herself.

Consequently, according to St. John of the Cross, the transformation we are discussing is effected by love and in the line of what we call "the intentional being of love." For it is love alone that unites and joins the soul with God."[58] "Love unites the soul with God, and, the more degrees of love the soul has, the more profoundly does it enter into God and the more it is centered in Him. . ."[59] Therefore do I entreat that which Thou desirest me to entreat, and that which Thou desirest not, that desire I not, nor can I desire it, nor does it pass through my mind to entreat it . . . and my judgment comes forth from Thy countenance."[60] *De vultu tuo judicium meum prodeat . . .*[61]

There is a sort of heterogeneity between spiritual marriage and the states preceding it: both St. John of the Cross and St. Teresa strongly emphasize this difference in nature. In the state of spiritual betrothal the soul "has attained to the possession of God through grace of will"[62] in accordance with the entire rectitude and conformity of its will, its own will. But these "are all preparations for the union of marriage" and have "nothing to do with the favors and delights of marriage": for in the latter "the soul not only possesses God through grace but through union"—with all the strength and sweetness of His own will and through the "communication of persons, and union"[63]—as is the case in marriage. At each phase of the progress of the life of grace, the Divine Persons, says St. Thomas, are sent to the soul.[64] But now they have been sent and given to the soul definitively and in their fullness so that on earth, before the final transformation produced by death, no new mission can take place.

But as the *Living Flame* and the *Canticle* attest, all this is more than ever accomplished by love, in the life of love and according to the *esse amoris.* Spiritual betrothal was as yet the transformation of love in the process of becoming, or the final dispositions for this transformation; spiritual marriage

---

57   See above, Ch. VI, § 8.

58   *Dark Night*, Bk. II, Ch. viii; Silv., II, p. 484; Peers, I, p. 462. Cf. above, Ch. IX, § 4, and Ch. VIII, §§ 10 and 21.

59   *Living Flame*, st. 1, v. 3; Silv., IV, pp. 13–14; Peers, III, p. 64; 2nd ed., p. 115: "By means of love (mediante el amor) the soul is united to God. . . ." Peers, p. 124.

60   *Ibid.*, st. I, v. 6, pp. 27–28 (132); Peers, III, p. 39.

61   Ps. xvi, 2.

62   "Ha llegado a tener a Dios por gracia de voluntad" (*Living Flame*, st. 3, v. 3; Silv., IV, p. 61 [168]; Peers, III, p. 72).

63   *Ibid.*

64   *Sum. Theol.*, I, 43, 3. Cf. above, Ch. VI, § 10.

is this transformation consummated: "a total transformation in the Beloved."[65] We know of no sensible parallel for this opposition of *fieri* and *factum esse* except in the order of substantial change; but we must note that what is true there of the being of nature or entitative being, is verified here of the immaterial being of love, wherein the principle of gravity of a whole spiritual universe is as it were "transessentiated" into another spirit (it remains the same entitatively; it becomes another spiritually). This is why St. John of the Cross here resorts to the classical example of the flame and the wood.[66] The wood becomes fire, but as long as it retains its own humidity it sputters, smokes, steams and weeps wet drops; it transforms itself, it is being transformed. But when it has been reduced to glowing coals or pure flame, then it is transformed (the fact that the wood thereby loses its entitative being is the defect in this comparison, in which entitative being is the only kind of being involved). The Saint uses another metaphor which does not involve substantial change, but which is just as inadequate: "It is as when the light of the star or of the candle is joined and united with the sun, so that that which shines is not the star or the candle but the sun, which has absorbed the other lights in itself."[67] And St. Teresa: "It is like rain falling from the heavens into a river or spring; there is nothing but water there and it is impossible to divide or separate the water belonging to the river from that which fell from the heavens. Or it is as if a tiny streamlet enters the sea, from which it will find no way of separating itself. . . ."[68] However deficient these comparisons may be, it is clear that as long as love has not completely transformed the soul, the latter lives with its own life, progressively divinized no doubt, but always enclosed within its created limitations, always finite (not only as to its entitative structure, as it will always be, but as to the union of love itself which causes the soul's operations and is as the breath of its liberty). . . . The soul is a whole which makes exchanges with the Whole. But when the transformation of love is accomplished and all within it that does not breathe of love has vanished; then the soul is in some manner the Whole, the very infinity of God's life which erupts in it as if the whole sea were to flow into a river, I mean a river of love surging with vital operations and able from its very source to become one single spirit with the sea. The whole universe, says Thomas Aquinas, can be contained in its least part, if that part has the power of knowledge.[69] The eternal and infinite life of God can fill the least of his creatures if that creature

---

65   *Cant.*, st. 27 (22), v. 1; Silv., IV, p. 132 (320); Peers, II, p. 140.

66   *Living Flame*, st. 1, v. 4; Silv., IV, pp. 16–20 (119–124); Peers, II, p. 140; *Cant.*, st. 38 (39), v. 5; Silv., III, p. 176 (423); Peers, II, p. 81.

67   *Cant.*, st. 27 (22), V. 1; Silv., III, p. 132 (321); Peers, II, p. 140.

68   St. Teresa, *Interior Castle*, Mansion VII, Ch. II (Peers, II, p. 335). "In spiritual marriage," writes St. Alphonse of Ligouri, "the soul is transformed in God, and is made one with Him, as a pitcher of water when poured into the ocean is but one with it" (*Homo apost.*, appendix I, no. 18).

69   *De Verit.*, q. 2, a. 2.

is loving and gives full rein to the Love who loved it first. *I live, now not I; but Christ liveth in me.*

13. These principles will, I believe, enable us to understand in its full force[70] the teaching of St. John of the Cross concerning the spiritual marriage. His doctrine appears here under three inseparable aspects.

To love is to give; first and essentially, in the sealed abyss of immanent activity, it is to give all of oneself. What the espoused soul gives, she gives by her act of finite love, and inseparably, undiscernibly, by infinite Love itself, she loves God with the same love with which He loves her, and with which she loves herself. How can that be? It is the effect of the union of love itself such as we have tried to explain it. Uncreated love has become, according to the immaterial being of love, the principle and agent of all that the soul does.

"The will of the soul that is converted into the will of God is then wholly the will of God, and the will of the soul is not lost but becomes the will of God. And thus the soul loves God with the will of God, which is also her own will; and thus she will love Him even as much as she is loved by God, since she loves Him with the will of God Himself, in the same love where with He loves her, which is the Holy Spirit Who is given to the soul, even as the Apostle says: *Gratia Dei diffusa est in cordibus nostris per Spiritum Sanctum qui datus est nobis. . . .*[71] He shows her how to love Him as He loves Himself . . . transforming her in Himself, and thus giving her His own love, as we said, wherewith she may love Him, therefore He is really showing her how to love,—that is He is placing an instrument in her hands, telling her how to use it, and continually using it with her, and thus the soul now loves God as much as she is loved by Him . . . therefore the love of them both is one love. Wherefore the soul is not only instructed in loving, but is even made mistress of loving, united with the Master Himself and consequently satisfied. For she is not satisfied until she comes to this love which is to love God perfectly, with the same love wherewith He loves Himself, but this cannot come to pass perfectly in this life, although

---

70   "Sometimes," writes Fr. Poulain, "the mystics indulge in exaggerations of language in their impotence to depict how elevated this participation is. They will say that one thinks with the eternal thought of God, loves with His infinite love, wills with His will. They seem to confuse the two natures, divine and human. Thus, they describe what *they believe* they feel; like astronomers they speak the language of appearances (*Des Grâces d'Oraison*, 5th ed., p. 282. The italics are the author's. Cf. *ibid.*, pp. 288–289). We hope to show here that to exonerate St. John of the Cross from every shadow of pantheism or confusion of the two natures, it is not necessary to admit that, when he is teaching the highest mysteries of the union of love to first Truth, he indulges in *exaggerations* and speaks the *language of appearances* and describes not what he feels but what he *believes* he feels, in short that he is like the astronomers, in the order of appearance, not of what is, when he witnesses to the supreme realities he experiences. How strange to put appearance at the end of mystical wisdom, as at the end of a telescope!

71   Rom. v, 5.

in the estate of perfection, which is that of spiritual Marriage . . . it may come to pass after some manner."[72]

14. Thus, the espoused soul loves and gives by infinite love itself; it is by infinite love that the soul operates according to the intentional being of love, the while it operates according to the entitative being by its own finite acts. And what does it so give? Not only itself and its all, but that which is its all more than its all, its inward self and its life more than its own life and inwardness. For God has given to the soul, as to a true spouse, rights over Him, made her the proprietor of His goods; she may dispose of them, give them to whomsoever she will. Thus, she gives God to God; her act of love, measured and finite in itself, gives to God, by the infinite love of God, the infinite Himself, an immeasurable gift. This gift evidently must not be understood as of the entitative order, as if the soul had the power of exercising an act upon God and adding to His perfection, enriching God's being by its own being; for this would be absurd. It is a very real gift, but a gift which is effected in the pure line of the being or actuality of love, of the wholly immanent immaterial activity which takes place without involving the slightest entitative mutation (for it is *actus perfecti*) and achieves what matters most in the world, within the closed universe which the soul is to herself.

"For although this is not so as perfectly as in the next life, the soul is, as it were, a shadow of God. And in this way, since the soul, by means of this substantial[73] transformation, is the shadow of God, it does in God and through God that which He does through Himself in the soul, in the same way as He does it. For the will of these two is one; and (thus the operation of God and that of the soul) are one. And even as God is giving Himself to the soul with free and gracious will, even so likewise the soul, having a will that is the freer and the more generous in proportion as it has a greater degree of union with God, is giving God in God to God Himself, and thus the gift of the soul to God is true and entire. For in this state the soul truly sees that God belongs to it, and that it possesses Him with hereditary possession, as an adopted child of God, by rightful ownership, through the grace that God gave to it of Himself, and it sees that, since He belongs to it, it may give and communicate Him to whomsoever it desires; and thus it gives Him to its Beloved, Who is the very God that gave Himself to it. And herein the soul pays all that it owes; for, of its own will, it gives as much as it has received (of Him. And since in making this gift to God it gives) to the Holy Spirit that which is His in a voluntary surrender, so that He may be loved as He deserves. And herein is the inestimable delight (and fruition) of the soul: to see that it is giving to God that which is His own and which becomes Him according to His infinite Being. For although it is true that the soul cannot give God Himself to Himself anew, since

72   *Cant.*, st. 37 (38); Silv., III, pp. 167–169; Peers, II, pp. 173–174.
73   "Substantial" in the sense of the absolutely fundamental transformation of love.

He in Himself is ever Himself, yet, insofar as the soul is itself concerned, it gives perfectly and truly, giving all that He had given to it, to pay the debt of love. And this is to give as he has been given to it, and God is repaid by that gift of the soul. . . . And this He takes with gratitude, as something belonging to the soul that it gives to Him anew . . . and surrenders Himself to it anew. . . . And so at this time there is a reciprocal love between God and the soul, in the agreement of the union and surrender of marriage, wherein the possessions of both, which are the Divine Essence, are possessed by each one freely, and are possessed likewise by both together in the voluntary surrender of each to the other, wherein each says to the other that which the Son of God said to the Father in St. John: *omnia mea tua sunt, et tua mea et clarificatus sum in eis . . .*[74] That gift can evidently be made by the soul, although it is greater than its capacity and its being; . . . This is the great satisfaction and contentment of the soul, to see that it is giving to God more than it is (in itself and more than) it is itself worth. . . . In the next life this comes to pass through the light of glory, and in this life through most enlightened faith."[75]

---

74   John xvii, 10.
75   *Living Flame*, st. 3, w. vv. 5–6; Silv., IV, pp. 89–91 (200–201). The bracketed words are from the second edition.
      In an article in *Vie Spirituelle* (July 1, 1931), Dom Phillipe Chevallier rightly remarks that in these pages of the *Living Flame* wherein is explained with what values (con extranos primores . . .) the soul makes its gift, St. John of the Cross refers to the opusculum *"de Beatitudine"* (expressly quoted in *Cant*. B, Silv., III, p. 411; cf. above, end of § 11). "St. John of the Cross has drawn upon that work, making his own choice among the 'values,' recognizing in those which he chose something apt to convey his experience on earth." Following Dom Chevallier, let us quote the passage in question from this opusculum, which was long attributed to St. Thomas Aquinas and which Mandonnet's work has now placed among the apocrypha. "The glorified soul will love God by God, that is by the Holy Spirit. Not only is all that the creature does as creature imperfect, but the Lord Jesus has asked this for His faithful when He said to the Father: I have taught them Your name (by faith), I will teach them it (by vision) so that the love with which You have loved Me may be found in them."But the love with which the Father loves the Son is eternal and immeasurable: He loves by the Holy Spirit which is the *Nexus* between them. The gloss tells us "The very Love with which the Father loves the Son abides in all the just, by Him the glorified soul loves God and is loved by God; or, as St. Augustine says, the soul which has no rest except in God for Whom it is created, would never have true or complete repose if it did not return to its Creator the like in love."
      "When God loves the soul," says St. Bernard, "it is an eternity Who loves, an immensity Who loves, Someone whose greatness is without bounds and whose wisdom is unlimited. So the soul must return an immense and eternal love in order that it may be able to be completely at rest in God. This can only be done by the Holy Spirit of whom the Apostle tells us: 'The charity of God is poured forth in our hearts by the Holy Ghost Who is given to us' (Rom. v, 5)."
      The Gloss remarks further: "The love of God is God and at the same time a gift of God. And because God has loved us in order that we might love Him in return,

15. Finally, St. John of the Cross says—(and we come now to that almost inexpressible "breathing of the Air" which to discuss is inevitably to lessen[76] what is most mysterious in the Saint's teachings and, as it were, the luminous cloud of this Tabor)—the espoused soul is associated in a certain manner with the operations of the Trinity. The Holy Spirit, in producing in it "most delicate touch and feeling of love" (which is this breathing, by which it "may love God perfectly"), raises the soul so that "she may breathe in God the same breath of love that the Father breathes in the Son and the Son in the Father, which is this same Holy Spirit that they breathe into her in the said transformation."[77] Clearly, once again, the Saint is not using the language of the speculative theologian; there is absolutely no question here, from any point of view, of an entitative participation of the creature in the uncreated act of love by reason of which the Holy Spirit proceeds from the Father and the Son. It would be nonsense to suppose that a creature could contribute in any way in producing a Person in God.[78] St. John of the Cross is speaking about something else entirely, and that is why he insists upon the ineffability of the mystery on which he touches.

He has given us the Holy Spirit. If the virtue of charity were the measure of our love for God in the heavenly life, the all-wise God would have given us His Holy Spirit in vain.

"Formerly the Master of the *Sentences* was of this opinion; contemporary thinkers have another opinion; you may think as you please. But it remains that God gave His Holy Spirit so that the soul of the blessed might return to Him the like in love and thereby find in Him unalloyed repose."

76   "Of that breathing of God I should not wish to speak, neither do I desire now to speak; for I see clearly that I cannot say aught concerning it, and that, were I to speak of it, it would seem less than it is." (*Living Flame*, st. 4, vv. 4–6, Silv., IV, p. 102 [212]; Peers, III,p .) Such a statement makes discussion of these matters a bit awkward. However, we are somewhat reassured by the thought that the remarks we wish to make here are not intended to lessen in any way the mystery of such a union. They aim only to show in what register the Saint's language must be understood. As we have pointed out above (Ch. VIII) his language is mystical, not ontological, and desires above all and at all costs to witness to the experience of love.

77   *Cant.*, st. 38 (39); Silv., III, p. 171; Peers, II, p. 176.

78   The teaching of St. John of the Cross has nothing to do with Eckhart's proposition that "everything proper to the divine nature is also proper to the just and divine man; he does everything God does; with God he creates heaven and earth, is generator of the eternal Word and, without such a man, God would not know what to do." This proposition was condemned by the Church (Denz.-Bannw., n. 513). As theorist and maker of systems, Eckhart uttered a theological enormity from which St. John of the Cross remained alien for the very reason that he strictly adheres to what alone is warranted by his experience. As we explain in the text, St. John of the Cross does not say, in any way, that the soul is associated in an entitative manner, even by participation, with the divine processions. The participation of which he speaks relates to the to *union of love*, to *the unity and transformation of love*.

When he recalls the sacerdotal prayer of Christ: "Father, I will that where I am, they also whom Thou hast given Me may be with Me: that they may see My glory"[79] which is to say, adds the Saint, I will "that they may work in Us by participation the same work which I do by nature, namely, breathe the Holy Spirit";[80] when he thus explains that we are called as associates of the divine nature, having become "gods by participation, equals of God and His companions,"[81] to do works in God's measure, to "perform in Him, in company with Him, the work of the Most Holy Trinity, after the manner whereof we have spoken,"[82] he means that the Father, wishing us to be one as They are one, the Son in us and He in the Son, and loving us as He loved the Son,[83] will bestow upon us "the same love as to the Son, though not naturally, as to the Son, but as we have said, by *unity and transformation of love*. Neither is it to be understood here (any more than in St. John) that the Son means to say to the Father that the saints are to be one thing in essence and nature, as are the Father and the Son; but rather that they may be so by union of love, as are the Father and the Son in unity of love."[84]

It happens solely in the order of the union of love, in the pure immanence of an act inwardly referring the soul to the Trinity as object, an act perfecting the soul and bringing it to perfection within itself without being exteriorized, and not insofar as she is and acts, but only as loving, in such wise that another becomes her soul's center, her weight and her all, that the spouse, crowned with the seven gifts, penetrates to the bosom of the trinitary life without the essence of the Three undergoing or ever being able to undergo the slightest entitative contact. God eternally saying to the creature: "Touch Me not," but also saying: "I will espouse thee to Me forever."[85] "Thou hast wounded My heart, My sister, My spouse,"[86] "I am thine and for thee, and I delight to be such as I am that I may give Myself to thee and be thine,"[87] and raising it to the kiss of His spirit, wholly penetrating the substance of the soul with His "delicate touch" in virtue of the union of love.[88] The soul may be said to breathe forth the Spirit of love with the Father and Son inasmuch as, turned toward

79   John xvii, 24.
80   *Cant.*, st. 38 (39); Silv., III, p. 172; Peers, II, p. 177.
81   "De donde las almas esos mismos bienes poseen por participacion, que el por naturaleza, por lo cual verdaderamente *son dioses por participacion, iguales y companeros suoys de Dios*" (*ibid.*).
82   *Ibid.*, p. 173; Peers, II, p. 178; "O souls created for these grandeurs and called thereto; What do ye do? Wherein do ye occupy yourselves? Your desires are meannesses, and your possessions miseries. O wretched blindness of the eyes of your souls. . . ."
83   John xvii, 22–23.
84   *Cant.*, st. 38 (39); Silv., III, p. 172; Peers, II, p. 177.
85   Osee, II, 19.
86   *Canticle of Canticles*, IV, 9.
87   *Living Flame*, st. 3, v. 1; Silv., IV, p. 52 (159); Peers, III, p. 63.
88   Cf. Ch. VIII, § 15; *Living Flame*, Peers, III, p. 47.

the Father and Son as objects of her love, she loves them (the while the Holy Spirit receives absolutely nothing from her) with the same love which in God breathes forth the Holy Spirit and in the same sense in which it "gives God to God." The soul breathes this Spirit of love in a very real manner as to what belongs to her and to her own loving transformation, but in a manner in no way real as to any inconceivable effect. Thus is the soul itself transformed into the Spirit by the union of love. "For it would not be a true transformation if the soul were not united and transformed into the Holy Spirit, as well as in the other two Divine Persons, albeit not in a degree revealed and manifest, by reason of the lowliness and condition of this life.... But the soul that is united and transformed in God breathes God in God with the same Divine breathing with which God, while in her, breathes her in Himself, which, as I understand, was the meaning of St. Paul when he said: 'Because ye are the sons of God, God sent the Spirit of his Son into your hearts, crying Abba, Father,[89] crying in prayer to the Father.'[90] 'The soul now loves God, not through itself, but through God Himself; which is a wondrous brightness since it loves through the Holy Spirit, even as the Father loves the Son, as St. John says: May the love wherewith Thou hast loved Me be in them and I too in them."[91]

16. "There thou wouldst show me that which my soul desired. . . ." That is how man attains to his penultimate end, the highest point attainable during this life of the eternal life to come begun here below, where he loves God as he is loved by Him and as God loves Himself,[92] ready from then on to pass without hiatus or break, upon the dissolution of his body, to the ultimate transformation which will give him possession of his Beloved unveiled. "The lover cannot be satisfied if he feels not that he loves as much as he is loved,"[93] to love God *as* He loves us, that is with His own love. In the equality of love of the eternal nuptials begun on earth, we see accomplished in its fullness and to the highest degree the evangelical precept: "Be ye perfect as your heavenly Father is perfect," that is, be perfect with His perfection, or with His love. And

---

89   Gal. iv, 6
90   *Cant.*, st. 38 (39); Silv., III, p. 171; Peers, II, p. 176.
91   *Living Flame*, st. 3, vv. 5–6; Silv., IV, p. 91; Peers, III, p. 103. Cf. st. 4, vv. 4–6, *ibid.*, p. 102; Peers, III, p. 113.
92   "Como el se ama," *Cant.*, st. 37 (38); Silv., III, pp. 166, 168; Peers, II, pp. 172–174; "con el mismo amor que el se ama," *ibid.*, p. 169. As a gloss on the Sanlucar manuscript is careful to note, the expression "I do not mean to say that the soul loves God *as much as* He loves Himself," (*ibid.*, p. 168; Chevallier, *Cant.*, p. 303), obviously does not mean that the soul, with its creaturely love, can love God as much as He is lovable. It means, in the sense already given, that it can "give God to God," and love Him "with the will of God Himself, in the same love wherewith He loves her, which is the Holy Spirit Who is given to the soul" (*Cant.*, st. 37, § 2). For God loves us by the same eternal act of love by which he loves himself: *amarle como el se ama* means exactly the same thing as *le amara tanto como es amada.*
93   *Cant.*, st. 37 (38); Silv., III, p. 167; Peers, II, p. 172.

it is also the supreme fulfillment of the third request in the Lord's prayer: that the will of the Father be done on earth as it is in heaven, that is to say, that we may live by His will and by His love.

It is very remarkable and of the greatest consequence that, at this summit of the spiritual life and of mystical experience the soul emerges expressly into the depths of the holiest mystery of Christian revelation, "transformed in the flame of love, wherein Father, Son and Holy Spirit commune with it."[94] The reason is that from the very outset, its contemplation—if it is authentically mystical—has proceeded from a living faith and from supernatural gifts and has led the soul, not to the One of the philosophers, not to God unknown as if from without and by His effects, but to God attained in His own divine essence, to the Deity Itself and as such, who in His absolutely proper and intimate life, is a Trinity of Persons, a resplendent and tranquil society of Three in the same indivisible essence and light of love. In these last pages we are thus led back to the doctrine on mystical experience set forth in the preceding chapter. Essentially supraphilosophical, because its proximate and proportioned principle is faith illumined by the gifts, mystical experience tends from the beginning to loving and fruitful knowledge of the three uncreated Persons. "The knowledge of the Trinity in unity," says St. Thomas Aquinas, "*is the fruit and end of our whole life.*[95] And St. Augustine: "*The realities we will one day enjoy are the Father, and the Son and the Holy Spirit.*"[96]

This leads immediately to another conclusion. How can the supreme perfection of mystical experience, its blossoming into the state of spiritual marriage, be possible to souls to whom the mystery of the Trinity has not been

---

94   *Living Flame*, st. 1, v. 1; Silv., IV, p. 10 (112); Peers, III, p. 22.

95   *In I Sent.*, dist. 2, *expositio textus*. Cf. *ibid.*, dist. I, q. 2, a. 2: "Una fruitione fruimur tribus Personis."

96   *De Doctr. Christ.*, lib. I, cap. v. The basic error of theosophical doctrines (if by theosophy we understand the deviation of a mysticism which, forgetting the sobriety necessary even to wisdom, *sapere, sed sapere ad sobrietatem*, actually gives metaphysics precedence over contemplation, and this in the order of the sacred mysteries themselves), an error found in Bohme, and very clearly expressed by Valentine Weigel, is to consider knowledge of the Trinity of Persons as exoteric knowledge of God and relative to creatures, whereas knowledge of the One, and of the Urgrund; leads to the very depths of deity. In this view metaphysics (a pseudo-metaphysics) really precedes divine revelation and supernatural wisdom; and this is the very inverse of the truth. Jean Baruzi commits an error of the same order on the subject of St. John of the Cross himself (*Saint Jean de la Croix et le problème de l 'expérience mystique*, 2nd ed., Paris, 1930, p. 675). When the contemplative knows God through love, with a knowledge higher than any distinct concept, more highly one in its mode, it is the divine Trinity that he thus knows, and the unity of the essence, at the same time and in the same act. This is attained by a supernatural experience which infinitely surpasses all philosophy. When Ruysbroeck insists upon the unity in which the contemplative is immersed, he is speaking of the unity thus attained, albeit his formulas are not always beyond reproach.

explicitly revealed? Undoubtedly, more-or-less veiled forms are possible, corresponding to the different typical phases of normal mystical progress. But the fact remains that spiritual marriage is of itself a state explicitly related to the intimate life of the Trinity. Unlike preceding states it is accompanied by explicit and formal experience of the Trinity in unity. St.Teresa, for her part, attests this in the strongest possible fashion. But while she speaks conformably to her personal experience, she testifies simultaneously and without distinction, to the substance of this experimental union and the special mode in which she experienced it: "It is brought into this Mansion by means of an intellectual vision in which . . . the Most Holy Trinity reveals Itself, in all three Persons."[97] Now, according to St. Thomas, intellectual vision stems from the gift of prophecy;[98] it is a lofty grace, charismatic and supererogatory as such, with respect to the essentials of the mystical state; so it should not be surprising that the vision spoken of by St. Teresa is not always granted to souls who have attained to spiritual marriage.[99] However, this does not authorize us to consider also as accidental the essential fact that the consummated union is an experimental union to the Persons of the Trinity themselves.

To say, "*mystical experience of the life of the Trinity*" in the supreme degree of infused contemplation, is not to say, "*intellectual vision of the Trinity*." Between these two notions there is a very marked difference. The latter belongs to the order of the charismata, the former to the order of the grace of virtues and gifts. Here we must take the testimony of St. John of the Cross to clarify that of St. Teresa,[100] for he is not only giving an account of his personal experience, he is

---

97   St. Teresa, *The Interior Castle*, Mansion VII, Ch. I; Peers, II, p. 331.

98   *Sum. Theol.*, II–II, 174, 2 and 3.

99   "In this degree some persons have a continual intellectual vision of the Holy Trinity. St. Teresa even says that this is always so. Nevertheless it seems that this does not happen to all the souls who have undergone the transformation in God and from then on possess that which forms the basis of the spiritual marriage" (A. Poulain, *Des Grâces d'Oraison*, 5th ed., p. 23).

100   Fr. Poulain notes (see the preceding note) that St. Teresa says it is always so for those who have reached the Seventh Mansion: in another place she says that this was granted her as "an extraordinary privilege" (*Interior Castle, loc. cit.*, Peers, II, p. 331). Is this contradictory? If we make use of a distinction which she herself has not made here, we can understand that it is always so *as regards infused contemplation*, and that that was given to her, personally, in an extraordinary way, *as regards the charisma of intellectual vision*. In any event, it is with respect to experimental knowledge of the divine Persons through infused contemplation, abstracting from the charismatic mode which may be adjoined, that we should take her testimony and grant it universal value, when she writes: "It sees these three Persons, individually and yet, by a wonderful kind of knowledge which is given to it the soul realizes that most certainly and truly all these three Persons are one Substance and one Power and one Knowledge and one God alone; so that what we hold by faith the soul may be said here to grasp by sight although nothing is seen by the eyes, either of the body or of the soul, for it is no imaginary vision. Here all three Persons communicate Themselves to the soul and explain

teaching the practical science of the mystical way. And his testimony is quite clear: the texts we have quoted from the *Canticle* on the subject of the breathing of love leave no doubt about it. How could Father Poulain write that in the *Canticle* and the *Living Flame* St. John "was content to point out a very lofty contemplation of the divine attributes"?[101] To say that the soul is associated with the Trinitary life, that it is called to "perform in God, in concert with Him, the work of the Most Holy Trinity," and to "breathe in God the same breath of love that the Father breathes in the Son and the Son in the Father, which is the same Holy Spirit that they breathe into her in the said transformation"; to say that it must be united and transformed "in the Holy Spirit as well as in the other two Divine Persons," is not "to be content to point out a very lofty contemplation of divine attributes."[102] *Intellectual vision of the Trinity* is not essential to the spiritual marriage. But *mystical experience of the life of the Trinity*, insofar as it can proceed only from the essential principle of infused contemplation—I mean from faith enlightened to the highest degree by the gifts of understanding and wisdom, from *fe illustradisma*[103] as St. John of the Cross says apropos of spiritual marriage—such experience is one of the essential privileges of this state of transformation. While it requires, and because it requires, the highest knowledge on this earth of the abyss of unity, this state is explicitly and formally related to the life of the Trinity: such is the doctrine of St. John of the Cross. Dionysius the Carthusian gives the same teaching;[104]

to it those words which the Gospel attributes to the Lord,—namely that He and the Father and the Holy Spirit will come to dwell with the soul which loves Him and keeps His commandments" (*op. cit.*, pp. 331–332).

101 *Op. cit.*, p. 283.

102 See above, Ch IX, § 5. "And this is for the soul so high a glory, and so profound and sublime a delight, that it cannot be described by mortal tongue, nor can human understanding, as such, attain to any conception of it" (*Cant.*, st. 38 (39); Silv., III, p. 171; Peers,II, p. 176). "And though this can be perfectly fulfilled only in the next life, nevertheless, in this life, when the estate of perfection is reached, a clear trace and taste of it are attained, after the manner we are describing, albeit, as we have said, this cannot be expressed" (*ibid.*, p. 173; Peers, II, p. 178).

103 *Living Flame*, st. 3, vs. 5–6; Silv., IV, p. 91 (201); Peers, III, p. 102. Cf. above, Ch. VIII, n. 54, and Ch. IX, § 14.

104 "Then shall it be given to you to see everything given to us by faith in all sweetness and truth, with the understanding of a purified soul penetrating the motives and secret reasons of the mysteries. Then, bathed in deific light, you shall be able constantly and serenely to enter into contemplation of the inaccessible glory of the august Trinity, to consider the processions and relations of the divine Persons *ad intra*, their mutual love and the joy they have in each other; the ineffable glance by which they contemplate each other, their eternal and immutable essence, supremely glorious and beatifying. Then, in the presence of the infinity and immensity of God, all creatures will seem small and narrow to you and in God alone will be all your consolation and all your love" (Dionysius the Carthusian, *Flame. div. amoris*).

Angela de Foligno testifies similarly: "It seems to me that I hold and lie in the midst of this Trinity which I see so darkly" (from Mme. Cecile Bruyère, *La vie*

and if we are looking for modern witnesses, the testimony of Father Rahussier[105] and Mother Cecile Bruyère[106] are formal on this point. This is, the reason why we believe that, no matter how high a mystical experience springing from a merely implicit supernatural faith may rise outside the visible membership in the Church of the Incarnate Word, it never rises to this point.

17. Having reached the highest degree of divine union, the soul can do nothing which in itself is better and (apart from positive obligation) nothing more useful and fruitful than to contemplate and love God in solitude.

"For so long as the soul has not reached this estate of Union of love it must needs practice love, both in the active life and in the contemplative; but when it reaches that estate it befits it not to be occupied in other outward acts and exercises which might keep it back however little from that abiding in love with God, although they may greatly conduce to the service of God; for a very

spirituelle de l'oraison, p. 350).

105   "The soul has purchased this earthly paradise during the immense perturbations, the hell and the complete desert of ecstatic prayer; it has found the road to this promised land where, in incomprehensible bliss, it can truthfully say from now on: "It is no longer I who live, it is the thrice-holy Trinity who lives in me, and I live in the Holy Trinity."

"It can be said, indeed, that in the prayer of spiritual marriage, the soul enters into the spirit and life of God, as God enters into the soul of man. This is a most striking truth. . . . And in this depth, in this inner sanctuary of God, this soul is united and unites itself to the essential secrets of the Three Divine Persons and shares in their perfections" (*Revue d'Ascétique et de Mystique*, July 1927, p. 284).

106   Speaking of spiritual marriage she writes: "In the act of contemplation, the contemplative perceives things eternal, not by ordinary vision but by real experience. God reveals Himself and reveals Himself as He is, that is, one and triune. The soul is, in fact, brought into perfect union by a very lofty knowledge of the august and most holy Trinity. Our Lord's words at the Last Supper are realized entirely and in their full force. *Ad eum veniemus, et mansionem apud eum faciemus.* Not only do the three divine Persons reveal their presence in the soul, but they dwell there in such manner that although the soul does not always feel their presence with the same clarity, yet she feels herself to be in this divine company most of the time. This is so typical a characteristic of the third degree of the unitive life that St. Dionysius begins his treatise on mystical theology by an invocation to the Holy Trinity which should be read in the context itself. . . . *The soul lives in close and conscious union with the three divine persons."*

And concerning the saints of the Old Law, she adds: "The great patriarch Abraham, whom Scripture shows us to have been raised to such close familiarity with God, had the Trinity revealed to him when he received the Lord under the form of three angels whom he saluted as if they had been but one alone; and this example is not unique in the Old Testament, when, nevertheless, truths, and particularly the mystery of the most august and serene Trinity, were still veiled in shadows. This is not surprising: God condescending even then to raise some chosen souls to the higher regions and unveiling himself to these souls, taught them to know Him as He is, in essence one, and in persons, three" (*La vie spirituelle et l'oraison*, pp. 343–346).

little of this pure love is more precious in the sight of God and the soul, and of greater profit to the Church, even though the soul appear to be doing nothing, than are all these works together. For this reason Mary Magdalene, although she wrought great good with her preaching, and would have continued to do so, because of the great desire that she had to please her Spouse and to profit the Church, hid herself in the desert for thirty years in order to surrender herself truly to this love, since it seemed to her that in every way she would gain much more by so doing, because of the great profit and importance there is to the Church in a very little of this love. . . . After all, it was for the goal of this love that we were created."[107]

---

107 *Cant.*, 2nd ed., st. 28 (19); Silv., III, p. 362; Peers, II, p. 346. Cf. Chevallier, *Cant.*, p. 182. This text does not contradict the testimony of Father Eliseus of the Martyrs who reports that the teaching of St. John of the Cross upon the superiority of the mixed life, in which contemplation overflows into action (without being diminished), is the same as these of St. Thomas Aquinas. "He would also say that love for the good of one's neighbor is born of the spiritual and contemplative life. . . . For the Rule aims at making persons observe the mixed and compounded life so that they may embrace and include within themselves two lives, the active and the contemplative one. This mixed life the Lord chose for Himself because it is the most perfect. And the state and method of life of the religious who embraces it is the most perfect of its kind" (*Spiritual Sayings*, Silv., IV, p. 351; Peers, III, p. 312). "With this reservation," adds Father Eliseus, "that at this period he found it better not to speak abroad among religious this conception which was his own; because the number of religious was too small, and in order not to disquiet them; it was fitting rather to insist on the contemplative life until the number of brothers should be greater."

When St. Thomas, and St. John of the Cross after him, assert the superiority of the mixed life, they take their position from the point of view of the state of life, the type or kind of life. Of itself, the state of the mixed life is evidently best, since it entails a "plus" in which contemplation overflows, thus multiplying the kinds of good; it is the state which most resembles Christ's kind of life. (Let us add that the souls placed in this state which, while being the highest, sanctions and sanctifies, as to the works proceeding *per se* from contemplation, the humble regimen of mutual service and interaction naturally required by the economy of human life will generally fulfill their duties rather badly and inadequately as long as they have not attained to sanctity. The episcopal state is the state of acquired perfection; one must be a saint to fill it adequately.)

In the text on St. Mary Magdalene which we have quoted, St. John of the Cross approaches the problem from another angle. He no longer considers the nature of the kind or state of life taken in itself, he considers the case of a soul that has admittedly reached the fullness of love and attained that degree of union in which it is really co-operatrix with Christ. Its contemplative life has its whole perfection wholly within itself and its pure immanence, like the life of God *ad intra*. It does not need to overflow into action, to issue into works, except by reason of one of those duties of one's state of life which make up the warp of human life (the duties of a bishop, a doctor, a father, etc.), precisely because this activity is supererogatory with respect to the substance of perfection (something like production *ad extra* is supererogatory with respect to the Divine perfection).

Purely and perfectly spiritual, free from all egoism as well as from every animal or biological" vestige (by which I mean a life still centered in the proper interests of the individual or the species), such a love, in which two natures are but one spirit, two persons one same love, is inseparable from the penetrating sweetness of a wisdom which is in some manner substantial and from experimental knowledge of the divine Persons; and thus it brings the human being to the highest degree of knowledge accessible here below.

In this detachment the spiritual soul
finds its quiet and repose; for since

it covets nothing, nothing wearies it
when it is lifted up, and nothing

oppresses it when it is cast down, for
it is in the center of its humility;

since, when it covets anything, at that very moment
it becomes wearied.[108]

No longer considering the diverse states of life but only what is purely and simply the best and most useful thing that can be done by a soul which has attained this degree of divine union, St. John of the Cross would say: it is to give all its time to love in contemplation. Except for obligations imposed by the duties of the state of life or by service to the neighbor, which would in one way or another make one lead a mixed life, this soul should do nothing but love God in solitude.

The fact remains, however, that the love for souls and their salvation is inseparable from the love of God. "And,'" says Father Eliseus of the Martyrs, "when he expounded the words of Christ Our Lord: *Nesciebatis quia in his, quae Patris mei sunt, oportet me esse?* he said that that which is of the Eternal Father must be here understood of nothing else than the redemption of the world, and the good of souls, wherein Christ Our Lord uses the means foreordained by the Eternal Father. And he would repeat that marvelous phrase written in confirmation of this truth by Dionysius the Areopagite: *Omnium Divinorum Divinissimum est cooperari Deo in salutem animarum.* That is, that the supreme perfection of any souls in their rank and degree is to progress and grow, according to their talent and means, in the imitation of God, and the most wondrous and divine thing is to be a co-operator with Him in the conversion and conquest of souls. For in this there shine the very works of God, and to imitate Him in them is the greatest glory. For this reason Christ Our Lord called them works of His Father and cares of His Father" (*Spiritual Sayings*, Silv., IV, p. 351; Peers, III, p. 312). But, for a soul which has achieved the fullness of union, the means which is in itself the best for this co-operation for the salvation of souls is still the contemplative activity of love. In such activity the soul possesses virtually the perfection of the mixed life, but actualizes it only if a special motive makes this necessary. So, by an apparent paradox, the most perfect soul should not, unless it be, as it were, required thereto from without, engage in the works *ad extra* implied by the most perfect state.

108   *Ascent of Mount Carmel*, Bk. I, Ch. xiii; Peers, I, p. 63.

APPENDIXES

APPENDIX I

THE CONCEPT[1]

1. The doctrine concerning the concept and its function, which we expounded in Chapter III in accordance with the teaching of John of St. Thomas, was treated more concisely in my *Réflexions sur l'intelligence* (Ch. II). That doctrine has been made the target for a criticism formulated by Father M. D. Roland-Gosselin in the *Revue des Sciences Philosophiques et Théologiques* (April 1925). In reviewing my book (*Bulletin Thomiste*, November 1935), Father Blanche made a very penetrating study of the question, and defended it against the criticisms made by Father M. D. Roland-Gosselin, while he himself sought some *via media* between Father Roland-Gosselin's position and mine. We trust that the rather more complete explanations given in this present work (Ch. III, § 16) will be such as to dissipate certain misunderstandings. However, it is important to go into the question more deeply because what, in principle, is here at stake is the whole Thomistic noetic and the whole debate between realism and idealism. Indeed, we are of the opinion that the doctrine synthesized by John of St. Thomas is the only one that allows a coherent understanding of the nature and function of the concept without making it a terminus *quod*, known first of all as object. Further, to consider the concept as a terminus *quod*, known first of all as object—something that would make a thing known because, it resembles it—constitutes one of those alterations of Scholasticism which prepared and, in a sense, made unavoidable the Cartesian theory of ideas[2] and, subsequently, the modern idealistic noetic.

If, precisely in respect to the intelligible elements delivered to the mind in the act of understanding,[3] there is an identity between the essence, attained as object, and the concept in its intentional function, how, asks Father Roland-Gosselin,[4] can the concept be a *formal sign*? To him "it appears impossible to aim to fuse into one" these two principles of solution. In short, he thinks that "a choice must be made between relation of identity and relation of sign."

St. Thomas did not think that such a choice was imperative. The texts that are cited below (Appendix I, § 3) clearly indicate this, especially the text from *Quodlibet*

---

1   Cf. the letter of R. P. M. D. Roland-Gosselin to the author and the reply to the same, *Bulletin Thomiste*, April 1933.

2   We have given some references on this point in *Three Reformers* (new ed., 1929, n. 48). See also E. Gilson, *Commentaire sur le discours de la méthode* (Paris, Vrin, 1925, especially pp. 318–323); Roland Dalbiez, "Les Sources scolastiques de la théorie cartesienne de l'être objectif" (*Rev. d'Hist. de la Philosophie*, Oct.–Dec. 1929); L. Noel, *Notes d'épistémologie thomiste* (1925, pp. 11, 35, 119); and our *The Dream of Descartes*.

3   It is quite clear, as Father Blanche has so well noted (*Bulletin Thomiste*, Nov. 1925, p. [5]), that it is only from this point of view that we say the presentative form and known object constitute but one nature.

4   *Art. cit.*, pp. 201–202.

8, a. 4, which is a crystal-clear expression of the thesis of the "relation of identity" which we have defended. It is this thesis which seems to Father Roland-Gosselin to be rather obscure. Neither did John of St. Thomas think that choice was imperative, and he explicitly affirms these two principles together. The relation of "identity" in reference to the intelligible constituent does not rule out the relation of sign because it is not a question of identity pure and simple or in all respects.[5] As a matter of fact, it is the very relation of sign which, in order to possess the purity and effectiveness demanded in this incomparable universe, the universe of knowing, requires the relation of "identity" (in respect to the intelligible constituent). It is because an instrumental sign is not a pure sign, because its primary and essential function is not *to make known*, that we refuse to look upon the concept as a simple instrumental sign. For the instrumental sign is itself first and foremost a *thing*, and only secondarily does it function as a sign; it is *known first* as object and only after that does it "make known." The concept must be a formal sign, i.e., precisely as *species* it must be *nothing but* sign; it is a pure *"maker-known."* It therefore must consist in being a pure representer or vicar of the object, possessing no trait of nature, no quidditative note, that is not a note and trait of the object. *There* is the relation of "identity" demanded by the relation of sign itself. We have never affirmed anything but that sort of identity, and to charge us with having taught an absolute identity or an identity in all respects between concept and object would be to fight a shadow. Only in the case of the uncreated Word is such an identity encountered.

Father Roland-Gosselin thinks that we do not sufficiently emphasize the fact that the concept is a *"similitudo* rei intellectae," and that we are inclined "to dissimulate or belittle (I do not say suppress) the part played in intellectual knowledge by the resemblance between the concept and the reality."[6] Actually, quite the reverse is true. We are so insistent upon that resemblance that we claim that the concept is not only a thing which resembles the object: that is to claim far too little for it! We claim that it is the very likeness of the object, the very similitude and the pure similitude of the thing understood. In so doing, we are considering the concept not in its entitative character and as accident of the soul, *secundum suum esse in,* but rather in its intentional function and as vicar of the object, *secundum suum esse ad.* Thus, we claim that the concept is "identical" with the object, *in reference to the intelligible constituent or quidditative traits.* Yet it is still a sign and therefore differs from the object signified in that the object exists or can exist not only in the mind, where it is known, but also *extra mentem in esse naturae* as identical with the thing (from which it is not really distinct); while the concept in its very function of *species,* exists *in esse intentionali.* (And, in its entitative being, the concept is an accident of the soul and differs *ut res* from the object signified.)

2. All of this is explained in detail and with great clarity in the main texts of John of St. Thomas so familiar to every Thomist—texts that are much too lengthy to reproduce here: *Curs. Phil., Log.,* II P., q. xxii, a. 1 and 2; *De Anima,* q. iv, a. 1; q. vi, a. 2 and 3; q. x, a. 2; q. xi, a. 1 and 2; *Curs. Theol.,* I P., q. xviii, disp. 2, a. 2, diffic. 1 (Vivès, t. III); q. xxviii, disp. 12, a. 5 and 6 (Vivès, t. IV).

If the words *signum formale* and *signum instrumentale*[7] are not themselves,

---

5   Cf. John of St. Thomas, *Log.,* II P., q. 22, a. 1, *dico primo,* ed. Reiser, t. I, p. 696.
6   *Art. cit.,* p. 201.
7   As well as the terms *conceptus mentalis* and *conceptus objectivus,* which are used to

literally, in the writings of St. Thomas, the distinction they express is obviously inherent in his doctrine; and in distinguishing between *signum formale* and *signum instrumentale* the commentators are simply making explicit what is most fundamental to his noetic. John of St. Thomas' interpretation of the texts of his master which he appeals to in this connection is obviously inevitable as far as the value and necessity of this distinction is concerned. Although it may appear "labored,"[8] it is so only on a particular point of vocabulary, that is, in establishing whether the word "sign" is used by St. Thomas himself in reference to the concept in its proper (not metaphorical) sense. Furthermore, as Father Blanche has established with remarkable precision,[9] we must agree that John of St. Thomas is right on this point—after all, he very prudently only offers his affirmative conclusion as more probable.[10] Besides, it does seem that the word "sign," when applied to the concept, is not a word that leaps to the tongue, that is, a word born in the very process of elaborating the theory of the concept. It is, rather, if I may say so, an imported word, a word corresponding to a didactic and reflexive preoccupation of thought which re-examines this theory in order to test and verify it. For that very reason, it marks a step forward in technical exposition because, in the case of the concept, it obliges one to definitely exclude the notion of "instrumental sign," which the current usage of the word "sign" tends to evoke.

In addition, let us remark parenthetically, it is clear that in such a discussion as this the *primum necessarium* is to have recourse to the text of St. Thomas and to establish an exact interpretation of the vocabulary he used. But if, for that reason, one were to neglect or reject the explanations and developments introduced by his great disciples, that would be to reduce Thomistic philosophy to an archaeological discipline, to refuse it, from the very outset, recognition as a living philosophy, growing with time and constantly placing itself in a position to reply to newly raised questions. Moreover, one would thus be deprived of luminous insights highly useful in avoiding faulty interpretations. This is all the more true considering that, in putting questions to St. Thomas regarding problems that have arisen in the realm of dialectical explicitation[11] only since his time, pure literalism, under the guise of material exactitude, would prove to be a fallacious method which, when properly used, could only lead to the conclusion—fortunately a modest one—that the question in hand is obscure and, in the last analysis, it is a waste of time to bother about it.

---

indicate another distinction.

8   M. D. Roland-Gosselin, *art. cit.*, p. 202, n.

9   F. A. Blanche, *Bulletin Thomiste*, Nov. 1925, pp. [3–4].

10   John of St. Thomas, *Log.*, II P., q. 22, a. 1; Reiser, I, p. 694.

11   Thus, it seems that St. Thomas was much more concerned with the relation between the *extramental thing* and the presentative form thanks to which it is made object than with the relation between the presentative form and the object itself taken as such. That is why, as we will see later, it often happens that he deals with the concept not by distinguishing between *mental concept* and *objective concept*, but rather by speaking of it, at one time, in the sense of mental concept (*intentio intellecta* could then be translated as "the mental aim") and, at another time, in the sense of objective concept (*intentio intellecta* could then be translated as "the object aimed at mentally"). This is to say, he speaks of the concept by thinking of the mental concept not precisely as specics but from the point of view of the *object* it presents to the mind.

3. But let us close this parenthesis and see what St. Thomas tells us about the "relation of sign" and the "relation of identity."

a) As regards the relation of sign, he writes in the *De Veritate* (q. 9, a. 4, ad 4) that the concept can be called a sign in the *wide* sense (i.e., a known which makes known—but such that thought does not first stop at the sign and then pass over to the thing signified:[12] "Communiter possumus signum dicere quodcumque *notum in quo* aliquid cognoscitur, et secundum hoc forma intelligibilis potest dici signum rei quae per ipsam cognoscitur; et sic angeli cognoscunt res per signa. . . ." Cf. *De Verit.*, q. 4, a. 1, ad 7: "Verbum interius per prius habet rationem significationis quam verbum exterius"; *in I Sent.*, d. 2, q. 1, q. 3: "inquantum in re extra animam est aliquid quod respondet conceptioni animae, sicut significatum signo"; and also *Quodlib.*, IV, a. 17.

On the other hand, the main text in which St. Thomas shows that the *species intelligibiles* are not the object (*quod*) but the pure means (*quo*) of knowing (*Sum. Theol.*, I, 85, 2) does not hold true only for the *species impressa* but, obviously, is equally applicable to the concept.[13] If species were *quod intelligitur*, there would not be any knowledge of things but only of that which exists in the soul; moreover, contradictories would be simultaneously true inasmuch as the judgment of the understanding would then deal only with the way in which the understanding was affected in each case. This argument clearly concerns the intelligible forms which are the terminus and fruit of intellectual apprehension as well as the impressed species which are its principle and seed. In fact, the argument applies even more forcibly to the former since the *species impressae* only deal with intelligibility (in act) and are not known in the act of intellection, while concepts, on the other hand, concern intellection in act; they are known (although they are not known *ut quod* except in a second act, an act of reflection). It is of the concept, above all, that St. Thomas can say: "Quia intellectus supra seipsum reflectitur, secundum eamdem reflexionem intelligit et suum intelligere, et speciem, qua intelligit. Et sic species intellectiva secundario est id quod intelligitur: sed id quod intelligitur primo, est res, cujus species intelligibilis est similitudo,"[14] because it is not the *species impressa*, but the concept that is first grasped in reflection. The *ad 1*, moreover, expressly refers to the *similitudo* or *forma* whereby the intellect in act is the object of intellection in act, and that identification holds good for the intellect in second act (through the concept) as much as, and even more than, it does for the intellect in first act (through the *species impressa*). The same may be said for the *ad 2*. Thus, the term *species intelligibilis* (which in St. Thomas' vocabulary designates what is later called the *species impressa*) in this article does not exclude the concept or *species expressa*, at least insofar as the concept is precisely *species* or *similitudo*; on the contrary, it actually includes it.[15] The *species intelligibilis* is opposed (*ad 3*) only

---

12   "Signum proprie loquendo (i.e., sign in the strict sense. Cf. F. A. Blanche, *loc. cit.*) non potest dici nisi aliquid ex quo deveniatur in cognitionem alterius quasi discurrendo."

13   See below, Texts 8 (b) and 13.

14   Cf. the text from the *Contra Gentiles* quoted below: "Aliud est intelligere rem et aliud est intelligere *ipsam intentionem intellectam*, quod intellectus facit dum super opus suum reflectitur."

15   Cf. *Cont. Gent.*, IV, 71: "Intentio intellecta . . . non [est] in nobis res intellecta." *De Verit.* 2, 6 (St. Thomas, making use of a comparison with the mirror [as a simple metaphor that must not be pushed too far] explains that in the operation of abstraction the *phantasma* is not *sicut objectum cognoscibile*, but *sicut medium cognitionis*. "Unde intel-

to the *objects* which the mind, by and in the concept, forms for itself and presents to itself, or composes and divides. Further, for St. Thomas, logic is a *scientia de intentionibus*. That is to say, the direct object of intellectual apprehension is not the concept or the *intentio intellecta* (otherwise, logic would be the whole of science), but, rather, the *res*. This he declares in the clearest possible manner: "*Aliud est intelligere rem et aliud est intelligere ipsam intentionem intellectam, quod intellectus facit dum super opus suum reflectitur*: unde et aliae scientiae sunt de rebus et aliae de intentionibus intellectis" (*Cont. Gent.*, IV, 11).

It is precisely because the concept is at once sign and *quo* (pure means) that the Thomistic school has been led to elaborate the notion of formal sign as well as that of the *terminus in quo* ("notum in quo" are St. Thomas' words in the text from the *De Veritate* quoted above). It is thus that the followers of St. Thomas approach the special difficulties of the theory of the concept, and so examine the more profoundly the nature of the concept. If, in the beginning, there may have been certain fluctuations of vocabulary, still all the great commentators are in substantial agreement on this theory, a theory brought to a very high point of scientific precision by John of St. Thomas.

b) As regards the relation of "identity" (in reference to the intelligible constituent), let us first recall the following text: "Similitudo intelligibilis per quam intelligitur aliquid secundum suam substantiam oportet quod sit ejusdem speciei, *vel magis species ejus*; sicut forma domus, quae est in mente artificis, est ejusdem speciei cum forma quae est in materia, vel potius species ejus" (*Cont. Gent.*, III, 4). That is a very significant text in respect to the meaning of the word *species*. The *species* is a representation of the thing because it is in the mind, *in esse intelligibile* and in order to *intelligere*, the very same principle of specification which specifies the thing in order for it to exist, and *in esse naturali*.

Above all, let us carefully take note of two texts in which St. Thomas states in an exact and literal fashion what we have only repeated after him:

"Unde species intelligibilis est similitudo ipsius essentiae rei, *et est quodammodo ipsa quidditas et natura rei* secundum esse intelligibile, non secundum esse naturale prout est in rebus" (*Quodlib.*, VIII, a. 4). *Quodammodo* refers to a difference in state or *esse*. On the other hand, it is clear that what is true of the similitude *qua*, at the beginning of intellection, is also true of the similitude *in qua*, at its termination. St. Thomas himself expressly asserts that, too:

"Nec tamen substantia Filio data desinit esse in Patre, quia nec etiam apud nos desinit esse propria natura in re quae intelligitur, ex hoc quod *verbum nostri intellectus ex ipsa re intellecta habet ut intelligibiliter eamdem naturam numero*[16] con-

lectus noster non directe ex specie quam suscipit fertur ad cognoscendum phantasma, sed ad cognoscendum rem cujus est phantasma." And that holds not only for the phantasm, a formal sign in the sensible order, but also very clearly for the concept, a formal sign in the intellectual order [Cf. *Sum. Theol.*, I, 85, 2, ad 3]).

16 As Father Blanche remarks, following Silvester of Ferrara, the expression "eadem numero" in this context does not signify individual identity since nature as such abstracts from individuality. "In this case it only signifies that the nature has exactly the same constitutive characteristics in the 'word' of the intellect as in the thing" (*art. cit.*, p. [5]).
"Ipsummet objectum numero, quod est in re entitative, ingreditur intra intellectum intelligibiliter et in esse intentionali seu repraesentativo," says John of St. Thomas (*Curs. Theol.*, I P., q. 27, disp. 12, a. 6, n. 18; Vivès, t. IV, p. 130). And again: "Processio intelligibilis non est elaboratio imaginis per modum picturae et artis, sed per modum

tineat" (*Cont. Gent.*, IV, 4). The word of our intellect contains in an intelligible way *the same nature, without numerical* distinction, as is contained in the thing known; that could not be stated more definitely or more forcibly. And that is the very doctrine we have maintained. The mental word, according to its entitative being, or its *esse in*—as accident of the soul—is distinct *ut res* from the nature of the thing known. But according to its intentional being, or its *esse ad*—and this is proper to it as *species*—the mental word is, in reference to the intelligible constituent, the very nature of the thing known, and it contains the very nature of the thing known without numerical distinction, i.e., it is a pure likeness essentially relative to that nature and according to it the knower intentionally becomes in second act something other than he is. One cannot say, "It's beyond me," or find any contradiction in that notion unless he also gets lost in the Thomistic notion of knowledge: *cognoscens intentionaliter fit (vel est) aliud a se.*

4. It would be to the point, however, to explain once more and as clearly as possible the articulations of the doctrinal synthesis established by John of St. Thomas and which I have once again taken up. (For the sake of clarity in the discussion which follows these paragraphs, I shall number these different steps with Roman numerals.)

i. *Ens reale*, the direct object of the intellect, does not imply actual existence. It is that which exists or *can exist* outside the mind, in the "thing" (actual or possible).

ii. This *thing* can be considered either as something which exists or can exist for itself (a thing as thing), or as something that exists or can exist for the mind—something attained by it and made present to it (thing as object).

iii. The *object* is one with the thing and differs from it only by a virtual distinction of reason. But far from exhausting the entire intelligibility of the thing, the object is only one or other of the intelligible determinations that may be distinguished within it (in other words, it is the thing as "objectifiable" under this or that aspect).

iv. Such an intelligible determination is that which is immediately signified (the formal object) by the concept, a presentative form engendered within the mind. The very same immanent act whereby the intellect knows the object (becomes it intentionally) is also vitally productive of the concept. In other words, by one single and identical act, the mind *conceives* (gives birth to) the thing in the concept and *perceives* it as object.

v. The concept is not the thing intellectually perceived. Otherwise there would be no science of things, but only of concepts, and contradictions would be true at one time. (Cf. above, Appendix I, § 3 (*a*)).

vi. The concept is a *mediator*; by and in it the object is brought into the womb of the mind in the state of ultimate intellectual actuation. Thus, our intellect attains things only according as its concepts render them present to it. The manner of our understanding corresponds to the more-or-less complete, or the more-or-less defective way in which the thing is objectified in the concept.

vii. It is as *pure means* that the concept is a mediator. It is not something perceived, which resembles the thing; it is the thing's very likeness itself, taken formally (the similitude of that which is objectified of the thing). Thus, the concept

---

naturalis expressionis et emanationis in esse intelligibili, in quo petit non solum similem, sed eamdem naturam seu objectum in se exprimere, et formare, quae est in ipsa re intellecta, sed non in eodem esse entitativo, sed in esse intelligibili . . ." (*ibid.*, p. 139, n. 29)

is the objectified nature itself but as *quo* or means, not as *quod* or object; in reference to its intelligible constituent, the objectified nature is the same in both the thing wherein it exists with a real existence and in the concept wherein it exists with an intentional existence.[17]

"Unde conceptus seu verbum apud nos, est res non intelligibilis, sed *intellecta in actu in esse intentionali*; et ea necessitate ponitur, qua ponitur objectum intellectus in actu intus." (Cajetan, *In Iam*, q. 27, a. 1) (Cf. on the theory of knowledge in general, the main texts: *In Iam*, q. 14, a. 1; q. 55, a. 3; q. 79, a. 2).

Thus the concept is a pure likeness of a pure image[18] which, as regards the intelligible nature, is one with the object it presents. In virtue of the status of the concept as pure image (as opposed to just any image), the general principle enunciated by Aristotle in his *De Memoria et Reminiscentia* is verified: "the movement towards the image *as image* and the movement towards the thing are but one single and the same movement." (St. Thomas, *Sum. Theol.*, III, 25, ad 3)

viii. The concept is not a pure means in the sense of a principle or fertilizing seed, like the presentative form which is received (*species impressa*); it is a pure means as *term* or fruit (*species expressa*, presentative form which is uttered). But since this produced term—term *quod* in respect to intellection as productive—is a pure means in respect to intellection as intellection, it does not arrest in itself the intellection which fulfills itself in it. By the fact that understanding is completed in it as in a *quo* which makes known, by that very fact is understanding achieved in the object as in the *quod* which is known. Whence we have the expression *in quo*, an expression which in no way destroys or diminishes the force of the word *quo* as applied to the concept,[19] but only makes it more precise, and signifies that the act of understanding indivisibly includes, at once and by the same token, both the concept signifying and the object signified.[20]

---

17   Species "ita pure repraesentat id quod formaliter est in objecto, quod materialem ejus entitatem exuunt, et ita sunt ipsum objectum formaliter et pure repraesentative" (John of St. Thomas, *Phil. Not.* III P. De anima, q. 6, a. 2). "Species impressa . . . est ipsamet quidditas objecti, quatenus totum quod in objecto invenitur realiter, transfertur ad speciem repraesentative. . . . Species impressa ita est virtus objecti ad eliciendam cognitionem et formandum verbum quod formaliter in se habet esse intentionale, in quo convenit in eodem esse intentionali, licet non sit ita formatum et expressum sicut in ipso verbo." (*ibid.*, a. 3).

18   In God, the Word is identical in nature with the Father in real being, not in intentional being. Yet the Word is called the image of the Father by St. Paul Coloss. I, 15) Cf. *Sum. Theol.*, I, 35, 1 and 2.

19   *Quo* can either be understood in general, in the sense of a *pure means* (and then the concept is a *quo* just as the *species impressa* is), or in particular, in the sense of a means by which (as from a *principle*) the act of intellection is produced (and then the word only suits the *species impressa*, whereas the concept is *in quo*, a means in which, as in its *term*, the act of intellection is completed).

$$Quo\ (pure\ means) \begin{cases} Quo\ (principle) \\ In\ quo\ (term) \end{cases}$$

According to the terminology used by St. Thomas in a text from the *De Veritate*, III, 2, which I shall quote below, the *species impressa* could be called the *primum quo* (the principle of the act of intellection), and the concept the *secundum quo* (the term of that act).

20   The term *species quod* used by Father Simonin ("La notion d'*intentio*," *Rev. des Sc. Phil. et Théol.*, July 1930, p. 456) does not seem to me quite in conformity with Thomistic

Thus, although it is attained by means of or through the mediation of the concept, the real object is *immediately* attained in the sense that no *quod* mediates it.[21] "Prima intellecta sunt res extra animam, in quae primo intellectus intelligenda fertur."[22]

ix. All this amounts to saying that the concept is a *formal sign*. Like every sign, it is a *praecognitum*,[23] but in this case it is not only necessary to say that the sign is first known, with a simple priority of nature and not of time, but it should be added that it is first known *formaliter*, in virtue of its being the actualizing form of knowledge—and not foreknown *denominative* as an object attained by knowledge.[24] Insofar as it is an object, it is only attained as an afterthought and in a secondary fashion, by a reflexive act (and that implies the formation of a new concept). The concept bathes in actual understanding; it is the act of understanding itself which produces it. It is the first to be actuated by actual intellection, but in order to communicate undivided and at the same stroke, that actuation to the object. For it is in the concept that the intellect in second act is the object. Since the concept is the intelligible form *in which* the object exists intentionally and makes itself known, its proper existence is the act of understanding itself, taken from the side of term, the *intelligi intrinsecum*[25] in act as affecting the object through that

---

terminology. At any rate, to conform to St. Thomas' doctrine, the term can only signify *species quod* as the term that is produced, and not *species quod* as object known. As Cajetan's text, quote below in xi shows so clearly, there is an essential difference between "species seu intentio *quam* intellectus intelligit (ut *intentio* est rei)" and "species seu intentio *ut quod* intelligitur (sc. ut *objectum*)." The whole Thomistic theory of the concept could even be said to hang on this difference.

If you say the object is a *quod*, but is not the object known, and it is a term known only "as representing the object," then you are saying exactly the same thing as I am, namely, that the concept is *quod* as product and *in quo* as known.

21   "Et haec species expressa dicitur conceptus seu verbum tanquam quid formatum ab intellectu, et locutum seu dictum ab ipso, ut ubi objectum attingat tanquam in medio formaliter repraesentante, non ut in medio prius cognito: nec enim prius attingitur conceptus, et deinde objectum, sed *in ipso immediate res cognita attingitur*, sicut media specie impressa objectum unitur, quin attingatur ipsa species" (John of St. Thomas, *Curs. Theol.*, I P., q. 27, disp. 12, a. 5 [Vivès, t. IV, p. 94]).

In ananoetic intellection there is a mediating *quod*, the analogate primarily attained by us. But that analogate is itself immediately attained, in the sense pointed out here.

22   St. Thomas, *De Potentia*, q. 7, a. 9.

23   The *species impressa* is a *quo* to which the name *pure sign* or *formal sign* does not belong since it is only at the beginning and not at the term of intellection. Furthermore, as a consequence of this, it is not *praecognita* in any way whatever, even in the purely formal sense in which the concept is first known. Only the phantasm and concept can be called formal signs. Cf John of St. Thomas, *Log.*, II P., q. 22, a. 2 (Reiser, I, p. 704); a. 3.

24   Ad solvandum proprietatem signi sufficit salvare, quod sit praecognitum, quod in signo formali reperitur, non quia sit praecognitum *ut objectum*, sed *ut ratio et forma*, qua objectum redditur cognitum intra potentiam, et sic est praecognitum formaliter, non denominative et ut res cognita" (John of St. Thomas, *Log.*, II P., q. 22, a. 1; Reiser, I, p. 695). These few lines from John of St. Thomas are fundamental; if they are understood, the whole thing is, understood. They are the key to the question. Cf. below, §§ (4)(c), 5(13)(a), and R. Garrigou-Lagrange, *Communication to the Thomistic Congress at Rome*, 1925, p. 220.

25   Cf. John of St. Thomas, *Log.*, II P., q. 22, a. 2 (Reiser, I, p. 707). St. Thomas says in very clear terms in the *Summa Contra Gentiles* (lib. IV, cap. xi: Esse verbi interius concepti

very form. Thus, the concept is the *intentio intellecta* and, even as *species* or *intentio* (and not merely in respect to the object it presents), it can be called "primo et per se intellectum"; but what is known under the rubric *quod* is the object. Cajetan explains this point as concisely as possible and in admirably formal language: "Conceptiones ut intentiones sunt *quas* [intellectus] intelligit: et hoc ideo quia . . . conceptus praesentat rem objective; *significari autem et sciri res extra primo, et conceptiones non ut res, sed ut intentiones sunt rerum extra, idem est:* quia idem est motus animae in imaginem ut imago est, et in rem, ut dicitur in De Memoria et Reminiscentia" (*In*, I, 85, 2). As *species*, the concept is *so little a thing* or *object* that to say it is attained by understanding is precisely to say *that the thing*, and not it, *is known as object*. It is known (in the direct act of understanding) only insofar as it is the actualizing form of the understanding of the object.

x. We signify our concepts to others by spoken words. And that is so because in order to make known to others the very objects we know, we communicate to them the same means, the same formal sign, that we ourselves use to know these objects. It is our concepts, then, that we communicate to them by those instrumental signs, which are spoken words, or by gestures; our concepts exclusively inasmuch as they present the object; our mental concepts exclusively inasmuch as the object of the concept or the objective concept is delivered to us by means of them. This is so precisely because the concept, the term *quod* of understanding as productive, is the term *in quo* of understanding as intellective: when we name the thing, we signify the concept which is at one and the same time the actualizing form that our understanding needs, and the spiritual manifestation of that self-same intellection.

Thus, too, while spoken words signify the concept of the thing, they also signify its *definition* (at least its nominal definition), i.e., the complex of characteristic notes that mark it off from everything else and constitute its *objective notion or ratio* (cf. *Sum. Theol.*, I, 85, 2 ad 3. See below, *Texts*, § 1 and § 13 (c)). It is also apposite to note that it is not so much simple names that we communicate to others as statements or judgments. In other words, what we communicate is *our* composition or separation of *things* presented to our mind by our concepts. In short, while we signify our concepts through language, it is the things themselves that we are signifying, as Cajetan said a little while ago (see above, Appendix I, § 4, ix), just as by our concepts it is things that we know directly and immediately as object. "Voces significant . . . ea quae intellectus sibi format ad judicandum de rebus exterioribus" (*Sum. Theol., loc. cit.*).

xi. The expression "mental word" applies not only to the concept as we have considered it up to this point, but also to the complex products fashioned by the intellect, for instance, definition and division (which have to do with the mind's first operation) and proposition (which has to do with the second).

In definition and division, there is a complexity which is the result of our own work; but the conceptual complex that is thereby set up continues to signify simply one object, one thing (actual or possible). On the other hand, in the proposition and the judgment, one object is constructed by us along with another with which we assert it is or is not identical in reality. This assertion is properly due to us; it is ours, even as this union or separation is ours. That is why truth or error can only exist in the judgment (and, before that, in the definition insofar as it implies a

---

sive intentionis intellectae est ipsum suum intelligi."

judgment of compatibility), for they indicate a relation of conformity or non-conformity between our intellect and the existing thing (either as actually or possibly existing). Therefore, the mental word thus constituted by an enunciation makes, on this account, two with the thing. But each of the concepts thus united or separated is but one (in reference to the intelligible constituent, or as *quo*) with the thing or object. The mental word in question makes known what *I think* (composition or division) of the things (as they are made objects of understanding in act in my concepts of the subject and predicate).

If, when speaking of the mental word and its distinction from the thing, St. Thomas ordinarily cites definition and enunciation rather than the simple concept, it is precisely because in these cases there is something that is entirely our own (the mental composition), and this makes the distinction clearer than the mere difference of state or *esse* between concept and object would.[26]

Father Roland-Gosselin wonders how our interpretations can be reconciled "with the Thomistic theory of judgment, since the judgment also forms part of the mental word."[27] I believe my interpretation finds one of its strongest confirmations in this very theory.[28] xii. The human intellect must regulate itself by things which precede it in being. For that reason, the proper task of the concept is to bring to mind an object of which it is the vicar or *likeness* and by which it is measured. If, however, it is a matter of the creative idea, then the case is quite different. By creative idea, I mean the divine ideas, of which the innate angelic *species* are a created participation, and which at the lowest possible level, the human artist's working-idea imitates with the maximum of imperfection. For the creative idea as such[29] preceded the thing (which is no longer to be known, but to be made, and which is known before it exists on its own). In this case, the idea is *purely form and not formed*[30] (I mean, as regards the divine ideas, it is the form of a *possible* thing which is known by a knowledge of simple intelligence). As the inner term of the act of understanding it is always an "*in quo*," but this time it also advances to the rank of a "*quod*";[31] not, however, as a model-object, an idol of the created thing that we might imagine within the bosom of the creative mind and of which the thing-object, the creatable or created *ideatum*, would be a transfer or a double. This time, the inner term of the act of understanding is the uncreated and unlimited form that must determine the thing-object or the creatable or created *ideatum*, which, in turn, is thus exhaustively attained by means of a term or object *quod*

---

26 Cf. *De Verit.*, III, 2: "Species (sc. impressa) qua intellectus informatur ut intelligat actu, est primum quo intelligitur; ex hoc autem quod est effectus in actu per talem formam operari jam potest formando quidditates rerum et componendo et dividendo; unde ipsa quidditas formata in intellectu, vel etiam compositio et divisio, est quoddam *operatum* ipsius, per quod tamen intellectus venit in cognitionem rei exterioris; et sic est quasi *secundum quo* intelligitur."

27 *Art. cit.*, p. 203.

28 The point has already been touched upon in *Réflexions sur l'Intelligence*, Ch. II, § 10.

29 "Forma separata *ad quod* aliquid formatur. . . . Forma quam aliquid imitatur ex intentione agentis" (*De Verit.*, III, 1).

30 Cf. John of St. Thomas, *Curs. Theol.*, I P., q. 15, disp. 1, a. 1, n. 3 (Vivès, t. III).

31 "Si quis consideret ideam operati esse in mente operantis sicut quod intelligitur, non autem sicut species qua intelligitur, quae est forma faciens intellectum in actu" (*Sum. Theol.*, I, 15, 2). "Sapientia et ars significantur ut quo Deus intelligit, sed idea, ut quod intelligit" (*ibid.*, ad 2). "Idea non habet rationem ejus quo primo aliquid intelligitur, sed habet rationem intellecti in intellectu existentis" (*De Verit.*, III, 2, ad 9).

which is the infinite Divine Essence itself, for as much as being the object of the Divine Intellection, it is known in the many facts of its imitability, in the infinite multitude of analogies that the finite, creatable thing can have with it.[32] On this score, John of St. Thomas[33] explains that the artistic or operative idea, which serves us as an analogate in conceiving the divine ideas, is neither the concept in its function as vicar of the thing that informs the intellect (a *medium quo* of knowledge), nor the object known (*conceptus objectivus*), but the concept, indeed, though precisely as, in the artist, it forms, vitally and within itself, and leads on to its ultimate determinations, a known object (known according to the very ways of realization) which precedes the extramental thing and which, when posited in existence, will be that extramental thing. And insofar as it contains and presents the object to the mind in this fashion, the operative idea is *quod intelligitur*. Let us say there are two "moments of reason" to be considered here: first, in its common function as concept or presentative form informing the intellect, the artist's concept is the specifier of his knowledge just as the Divine Essence is the specifier of the Divine Intelligence (but the Divine Essence is the object *quod* that is known, whereas the concept in its ordinary function as concept is only the *medium in quo* of knowledge). Second, the artist's concept as an operative concept, forms in his mind, contains and expresses, as object known, the thing to be made even before it exists in its own nature (it is thus that it is a *quod*). Even so, the Divine Essence, known in its imitability and according to the multiplicity of its relations of reason to things that can be created, is the medium in which both the creatable things and these very relations themselves are attained as known objects (cf. *Sum. Theol.*, I, 5, 2 ad 2). Thus, it is the privilege of operative knowledge and, in a unique way, of creative knowledge, for the idea to be at once a means *in quo*, and an object *quod*, by reason of a content that precedes the thing.

It is a truly remarkable fact that Descartes, on his own confession, chose by preference the word *idea* (which, in strict Scholastic terminology, was reserved for operative and creative ideas) to designate the concept whereby our human thought knows things, because this term "idea" was already used by philosophers "to signify the forms of the perceptions of the divine mind."[34] Thus, Descartes transferred to the speculative human concept the schema which the Scholastics had drawn up for the creative idea. This schema was poorly understood at that, owing to a material interpretation of the notion of exemplar, for which it seems that Scholastic pedagogy was primarily responsible. In the summary placed at the

32   "Idea in Deo nihil est aliud quam Dei essentia" (*Sum. Theol.*, I, 15, 1, ad 3). "Essentia Dei est idea rerum non quidem ut essentia, sed ut est intellecta . . . cum proportione creaturae fiendae ad ipsam divinam essentiam, secundum quod deficit ab ea, vel imitatur eam. . . . Ipsa divina essentia, cointellectis diversis proportionibus rerum ad eam, est idea uniuscujusque rei" (*De Verit.*, III, 2). "Una prima forma, ad quam omnia reducuntur, est ipsa essentia divina secundum se considerata; ex cujus consideratione divinus intellectus adinvenit, ut ita dicam, diversos modos imitationis ipsius, in quibus pluralitas idearum consistit" (*ibid.*, 3, 2, ad 6). "Ideae plurificantur secundum diversos respectus ad res in propria natura [possibiliter] existentes" (*ibid.*, 3, 2, ad 7).
33   Cf. John of St. Thomas, *Curs. Theol.*, I P., q. 15, disp. 1, a. I (Vivès, t. III).
34   "Ostendo me nomen ideae sumere pro omni eo quod immediate a mente percipitur . . . Ususque sum hoc nomine, *quia jam tritum erat a Philosophis ad formas perceptionum mentis divinae significandas*, quamvis nullam in Deo phantasiam agnoscamus . . ." Reply to the third objections [V], ed. Adam-Tannéry VII, 181. Cf. *The Dream of Descartes* (Philosophical Library, New York, 1944, tr. M. L. Andison, pp. 109–111).

head of the *Meditations*,[35] he speaks of the idea of "a very ingenious and artificial machine" which is to be found in any worker's mind and says that the worker's knowledge is the cause of its "objective contrivance." Was not the world-machine for him a created *copy* of the "objective contrivance" of the ideal world present in the mind of the Divine Worker? But even in the case of human art, the creative idea is not a model set before the mind, of which the work of art is a copy (such a model is only completed *when the work itself is made*, either in our mind, or in matter; in our mind, as a poem or sonnet is completed when nothing remains but to transcribe it on paper, in matter, as in the case of a picture or statue). In the case of human art, the role of "creation" (understood in an improper and diluted sense) is, of course, very weak; the creating process is necessarily immersed in the whole of what comes to us from things through our cognitive and representative activity. The creative idea *as such* is, in our thought, an utterly spiritual and simple moment of intellection which, in relation to the work, is transcendent and unlimited, and by which the representations and images that are, as it were, the first materials of the work, are themselves formed. This is a very imperfect imitation of the properly creative idea which from the very first instant achieves every single detail of the thing. But because that creative idea is the uncreated form of the thing in question (since the Divine Knowledge has the Divine Essence as its only specifying object, and the creative idea is the Divine Essence itself insofar as it brings the creatable thing or the thing already created to the Divine Knowledge), it is, as it were, a secondary term and materially attained.

Descartes had but to transform the relation (as he understood it): creative idea to created *ideatum*, into the relation: cognitive idea to known *ideatum*, in order to come to his notion of the idea as an object *quod*.

5. Let us now reread the main texts of St. Thomas which have to do with the concept, placing each in its proper reference to the various steps we have just distinguished. We shall see that where difficulties seemed to crop up, such difficulties are only apparent. We shall also see how definitely St. Thomas refuses to recognize presentative forms as the immediate object of thought, and asserts that they are *ut quo*, not *ut quod*, and that the concept is *formed* or uttered in order that the nature of the thing, the object of the intellect, may be perceived (cf. §§ 5 (*b*), 8, 12, 13, 14, 16, 17).

The texts grouped together in the first three paragraphs are of interest to us chiefly from the standpoint of terminology. After that come the texts which are most important from a doctrinal point of view. It is well to point out, in respect to the words "ratio" (see § 1), "intellectus" (see § 2), "intentio intellecta," an inevitable intermingling of the vocabulary proper to logic with the vocabulary proper to metaphysics, and psychology. As a matter of fact, these three terms originally belonged to the vocabulary of logic (which has to do with the known precisely as known in the soul), and in that context they designate first of all the object of the concept (as reflexively envisaged in the mind). But then they migrated (especially the third one, very rarely the first) into the vocabulary of metaphysics (which has to do with the operations and means of knowledge taken in their relation to extramental being). In that context, they designate the concept itself by which, and in which, the object is known. This self-same concept is also indicated by the words

35   Adam-Tannéry, ed., VII, 14.

"conceptio intellectus" and "verbum mentis." But with these two terms the inverse phenomenon has somehow or other occurred. They properly belong to the vocabulary of metaphysics and psychology. But at the same time, they can be understood from the point of view of logical reflexion, which attains in the mind the thing known as known. Consequently, they sometimes merely designate what later will be called the *conceptus mentalis* (concept in the ordinary sense of the word), i.e., the intelligible likeness by and in which the object is known; at other times, they designate at once and principally what later will be called the *conceptus objectivus*, the object of the concept or the object considered as such. As we have already pointed out,[36] St. Thomas was more concerned with the relation and distinction between the concept and the thing, than with the relation and distinction between the *conceptus mentalis* and the *conceptus objectivus* (itself distinct from the thing *ratione*).[37] And so those texts in which the concept is given as *quod primo et per se intellectum est* may be interpreted in two ways: either[38] as referring to the objective concept (*quod*), (or the mental concept taken as the objective concept it presents to the mind); or as referring to the mental concept itself (*in quo*), which, first, is *quod* (insofar as it is something produced), and second is foreknown *formaliter* (see above § ix), (as the intellectualizing form of the object, having as its proper act of existing the very intellection of the object).[39]

TEXTS

1. [*In Sent.*, 1254–56]

a) "Ratio prout hic sumitur nihil aliud est quam id quod apprehendit intellectus de significatione alicujus nominis: et hoc in his quae habent definitionem, est ipsa rei definitio, secundum quod Philosophus dicit, IV Meta. text 11: *Ratio quam significat nomen est definitio* . . .

Ratio qualitatis est id quod significatur nomine qualitatis; et hoc est illud ex quo qualitas habet quod sit qualitas . . .

Et sic patet quod ratio sapientiae quae de Deo dicitur, est id quod concipitur de significatione hujus nominis, quamvis ipsa sapientia divina definiri non possit.

Nec tamen hoc nomen *ratio* significat ipsam CONCEPTIONEM, quia hoc significatur per nomen rei; sed significat intentionem hujus conceptioni, sicut et hoc nomen *definitio* et alia

COMMENTS

The word "ratio" in St. Thomas' vocabulary is seen in this text—and the same is true of the word "intellectus" ("the thought about," see below 2; cf. *conceptus*, "the conceived"), and of the word "intentio intellecta" ("the mental aim when thought about," see below §§ 7 and 8), to be originally a *nomen secundae impositionis*, a reflexive and logical name which first of all designates the object of the concept (what later will be called *conceptus objectivus*) *taken as known or as existing in the mind*, in other words as the object of a second mental aim. That is the reason why the noun "ratio" does not signify the *conceptio animae* or the *similitudo rei* (whereby the thing is known and which is signified by the thing's name). The word "ratio" has to do with the reflex aim which grasps this conception and its content in the mind. Moreover, this *ratio*, thus exist-

---

36   Cf. above, Appendix I, n. 4.
37   Cf. below, § 6 (a).
38   Cf. below, §§ 6, 7 (*b*), 10, 11 (*a*), 12 (*c*), 15 (*b*), and 15 (*b*) n.
39   Cf. below, Texts 6, 7 (*c*), 8, 10, 11 (*b*), (*c*), 12 (*d*), 13 to 17.

nominasecundae impositionis . . .

Ratio . . . dicitur esse in re inquantum in re extra animam est aliquid quod respondet conceptioni animae, sicut significatum signo.

ing in the mind (cf. *De Potentia*, q. 7, a. 6: "istae autem diversae rationes in intellectu nostro existentes . . ."), is said to be in the thing inasmuch as there is something in the thing corresponding to the *conceptio* of the soul, just as the thing signified corresponds to the sign, in other words, to the extent that ihe *conceptio* (synonym for *verbum mentis*), whose content, as secondarily and reflexively envisaged, this *ratio* designates, is the likeness of the extramental thing (and not the fabricator of a being of reason).

As so often happens in other instances, so too, it happens here that the metaphysician or theologian has recourse to logical notions to settle a question that is not logical but ontological. Here the question concerns the plurality of perfections attributed to an infinitely simple God. (This is, in fact, the subject of this article from the *Sentences*: "Whether the plurality of notions—*rationum*—whereby the divine attributes are distinguished from one another is only in the mind or in God as well.")

b) There follows the distinction between real being and being of reason.

Aliquando hoc quod intellectus concipit, est similitudo rei existentis extra animam, sicut hoc quod concipitur de hoc nomine "homo"; et talis conceptio intellectus habet fundamentum in re immediate, inquantum res ipsa, ex sua conformitate ad intellectum, facit quod intellectus sit verus, et quod nomen significans illum intellectum proprie de re dicatur.

Aliquando autem hoc quod significat nomen non est similitudo rei existentis extra animam, sed est aliquid quod consequitur ex modo intelligendi rem quae est extra animam; et hujusmodi sunt intentiones quas intellectus noster adinvenit. . . .

In this case it is a matter of logical beings of reason.

c) Ratio dicitur esse in re, inquantum significatum nominis, cui accidit esse rationem, est in re; et hoc contingit proprie quando conceptio intellectus est similitudo rei."
(*In I Sent.*, dist. 2, q. 1, a. 3).

2. [*De Potentia*, 1259–1263]
a) "Rationes nominum quae sequuntur conceptiones intellectuum." (*De Potentia*, q. 7, a. 6).
b) "Intellectui respondet aliquid in re dupliciter. Uno modo immediate, quando videlicet intellectus concipit formam rei alicujus extra animam existentis, ut hominis vel lapidis,

c) Alio modo mediate, quando videlicet aliquid requiritur actum intelligendi, et intellectus reflexus supra ipsum considerat illud. Unde res respondet illi considerationi intellectus mediate, id est mediante intelligentia rei . . ." (*De Potentia*, q. 1, a. 1, ad 10).

3. [*De Potentia*]
a) "Ex hoc quod intellectus in seipsum reflectitur, sicut intelligit res existentes extra animam, ita intelligit eas esse intellectas; et sic sicut est quaedam CONCEPTIOintellectus vel RATIO, cui respondet res ipsa quae est extra animam; ita est quaedam conceptio vel ratio, cui respondet res intellecta secundum quod hujusmodi; sicut rationi hominis vel conceptioni hominis respondet res extra animam; rationi vero vel conceptioni generis aut speciei, respondet solum res intellecta" (*ibid.*, q. 7, a. 6).
b) Omnes rationes [perfectionum divinarum] sunt quidem in intellectu nostro sicut in subjecto: sed in Deo sunt ut in radice verificante has conceptiones." (*ibid.*).

4. [*Quodlibet* V, 1271]
a) Secundum Augustinum, XV De

[*Significatum nominis* is the *object* which the noun signifies in signifying the concept *primo et per se*. And it happens to this object to be the *ratio* insofar as it is the object of a reflexive glance grasping it in the mind precisely as known.]
[In this case, *intellectus* designates the *object* or the thing signified by the concept.]

[Here, on the other hand, *intellectus* is a synonym for *conceptio intellectus* or *verbum mentis* (the mental concept), because something properly corresponds *in re*, "sicut significum signo" (see § 1), to the *conceptio intellectus*.]

[Refinements to bear in mind in connection with the object of Logic, and in connection with the indirect relation of Logic to reality.]

In this text, the word "ratio" has itself become a synonym for *conceptio intellectus* (concept, or mental word, *in quo*), while at the same time always connoting the object of the concept *ut quod*.

[This object of the concept exists within us as known and as contained in the concept; it is in God, as in the reality in which it exists outside the mind, which (reality) corresponds to the concept we form of it.]

Inasmuch as it is produced or uttered,

Trinit., verbum cordis importat quoddam procedens a mente, sive ab intellectu. Procedit autem aliquid ab
intellectu, inquantum est constitutum
per operationem ipsius.

Est autem duplex operatio intellectus. . . . Una quidem quae vocatur
indivisibilium intelligentia, per quam
intellectus format in seipso definitionem, vel conceptum alicujus in-
complexi. Alia autem operatio est
intellectus componentis et dividentis,
secundum quam format enuntia-
tionem. Et utrumque istorum per operationem intellectus constitutorum
vocatur verbum cordis, quorum
primum significatur per terminum incomplexum, secundum vero significatur per orationem.

b) Manifestum est autem quod omnis
operatio intellectus procedit ab eo secundum quod est factus in actu per
speciem intelligibilem, quia nihil operatur nisi secundum quod est actu.
Unde necesse est quod species intelligibilis, quae est principium operationis intellectualis, differat a verbo
cordis, quod est per operationem intellectus formatum;

c) quamvis *ipsum verbum possit dici
forma vel species intelligibilis [species im-
pressa]*, sicut per intellectum consti-
tuta, prout forma artis quam
intellectus adinvenit dicitur quaedam
forma intelligibilis" (*Quodlib.*, V, a. 9).

5. [*De Potentia*]
a) "Intelligens autem in intelligendo
ad quatuor potest habere ordinem:
scilicet ad rem quae intelligitur,
                                    ad
speciem intelligibilem, qua fit intellectus in actu,
                    ad *suum intelligere*
                                    et ad
conceptionem intellectus.

"constituted by the operation of the
intellect," and inasmuch as, for this
reason, it contains the object, the concept is *quod*—as will be seen later (cf.
§ viii above).

Cf. § XI.

See § 7 (b) below.

[It is the *species impressa* that is the
principle of this operation.]

[*species expressa*]
The word, as thought about or as the
intrinsic term of the intellective act, is
a term *in quo*, a form, or, if we may say
so, the intentional matrix by reason of
which the object is brought to a condition of actual understanding (cf. further on §§ 6, 8, 12, 13–17).

It is the thing that is really the object
(*quod*) of understanding. Cf. § ii and v
above. Here it is a matter of the *species
impressa.*

Quae quidem conceptio a tribus praedictis differt.

b) A re quidem intellecta quia res intellecta est interdum extra intellectum; conceptio autem intellectus non
est nisi in intellectu. [See i, ii and v
above].

Cf. §§ i. ii, v above.

Et iterum conceptio intellectus ordinatur ad rem intellectam sicut ad finem; *propter hoc enim intellectus
conceptionem rei in se format ut rem intellectam cognoscat.*

Cf. § iv above. Note the typical formula: "The intellect forms the conception of the thing within itself so as to
know the thing it has understood (*intellecta*)."[40] See later on §§ 7 (d), 8 (f)
and 17.

c) Differt autem a specie intelligibili:
nam species intelligibilis qua fit intellectus in actu, consideratur ut principium actionis intellectus; cum omne
agens agat secundum quod est in actu;
actu autem fit per aliquam formam,
quam oportet esse actionis principium.

The intellect is put into first act by the
species impressa (see § 7 [b]); it passes
into second act in producing the concept.

d) Differt autem ab actione intellectus:
quia praedicta conceptio consideratur
ut terminus actionis, et quasi quoddam per ipsam constitutum.

Cf. § viii.

Intellectus enim sua operatione format rei definitionem vel etiam propositionem affirmativam vel negativam.

Cf. § xi.

Haec autem conceptio intellectus in
nobis proprie *verbum* dicitur: hoc enim
est quod verbo exteriori significatur:
vox enim exterior neque significat ipsum intellectum, neque speciem intelligibilem, neque actum intellectus; sed
intellectus conceptionem qua mediante refertur ad rem.

Cf. §§ x, xi.
Cf. § vi.

Hujusmodi autem conceptio, sive
verbum, qua intellectus noster intelligit rem aliam a se, ab alio exoritur, et
aliud repraesentat.

Oritur quidem ab intellectu per

Cf. § v.

---

40 Cf. *Quodlib.*, V, a. 9, ad 1: "Intellectus intelligit aliquid dupliciter, uno modo formaliter,
et sic intelligit specie intelligibili qua fit in actu, alio modo sicut instrumento quo utitur
ad aliud intelligendum, et hoc modo intellectus verbo intelligit, quia format verbum
ad hoc quod intelligat rem." The intellect forms the word in order to think or perceive
the thing intellectually (*intelligere*)."
    Let us note in this text, following Fr. Blanche (*art. cit.*, p. [3]²) and John of St. Thomas
(*Log.*, II P., q. 22, a. 3, *Solvuntur argumenta*), that the word "instrument" does not signify
"instrumental sign" but simply means in general ("medium internum in quo").

suum actum; est vero similitudo rei
intellectae.[41]

e) Cum vero intellectus seipsum intelligit, verbum praedictum, sive conceptio, ejusdem est propago et
similitudo, scilicet intellectus seipsum
intelligentis. Et hoc ideo contingit,
quia effectus similatur causae secundum suam formam: *forma autem intellectus est res intellecta.*

Cf. § viii.

It is the object itself which is the form
of the intellect by means of the concept. Cf. §§ vii and viii above.

Let us call to mind at this point that
"St. Thomas has never made understanding consist in the intellect's being (entitatively) informed by the
word or representative quality, but
rather in its being (intentionally) informed by the object or *res intellecta*"
by means of the word as vicar of the
object and *medium quo* of knowledge
(John of St. Thomas, *Curs. Theol.*, I P.,
q. 27, disp. 12, a. 5, n. 11). As I noted in
my *Réflexions sur l'intelligence* (p. 67),
it is a capital mistake to confuse the
(intentional) information of the intellect by the object, thanks to the concept, with the (entitative) information
of the intellect by the concept; one is
surprised to find this error in Suarez.
John of St. Thomas (*loc. cit.*) forcibly
protests against this confusion.

Et ideo verbum quod oritur est similitudo rei intellectae, sive sit idem quod
intellectus, sive aliud.

Cf. § VII.

f) Hujusmodi autem verbum nostri
intellectus est quidem extrinsecum ab
esse ipsius intellectus (non enim est de
essentia, sed quasi passio ipsius),

The mental word is *quasi passio intellectus* according to its entitative being.

non
tamen est extrinsecum ab ipso intelligere intellectus, cum ipsum intelligere
compleri non possit sine verbo prae-
dicto" (*De Potentia*, q. 8, a. 1).

Cf. § ix.

---

41   "Verbum semper est ratio et similitudo rei intellectae (*Comm. in Joann.*, I, 1). "Verbum
      interius conceptum est quaedum ratio et similitudo rei intellectae" (*Cont. Gent.*, lib.
      IV, c. XI). Cf. § 8 (a).

6. [*De Potentia*]

a) "Id autem quod est per se intellectum non est res illa cujus notitia per intellectum habitur,

cum illa quandoque sit intellecta in potentia tantum, et sit extra intelligentem, sicut cum homo intelligit res materiales, ut lapidem vel animal aut aliud hujusmodi:

cum tamen oporteat quod intellectum sit in intelligente, et unum cum ipso.

b) Neque etiam intellectum per se est similitudo rei intellectae, per quem informatur intellectus ad intelligendum impressa. . . . Haec . . . similitudo se habet in intelligendo sicut intelligendi principium, . . . non sicut intellegendi terminus.

c) Hoc ergo est primo et per se intellectum As contained in the concept, the object quod intellectus in se ipso concipit de re intellecta,[42]

This *per se intellectum* is at once (see below,(c)) the objective notion or *ratio* which came up for discussion in i; or the object of the concept (taken as known in the mind), as well as the *conceptio intellectus* in which that object has been attained. The thing known (cf. §§ i and ii), taken as thing (and as that to which "being known" comes as an extrinsic denomination), is at the same time distinct from both (cf. §§ iii, iv and v).

That is true of the object of understanding (cf. § iii) as well as of the concept of that object, and precisely by reason of the necessity of this concept.

In this case it is a matter of the *species impressa*.

As contained in the concept, the object of the concept (or *ratio* in the logical sense) is a known *quod*. As mental concept or species presenting that object to the mind, it is a *quod* which is produced and an *in quo* of knowledge (see above the remarks on § 4). It is thought or known (*per se intellectus*) as the intentional form for which to exist is to be in a state of actual intellection, by reason of which the thing is known.

"Primo et per se intellectum," when applied to the mental concept, therefore, does not designate an object of

---

42   In this text—often quoted but not always properly understood—St. Thomas seems to be thinking mainly of the objective concept when he talks of the word, or at least of the mental concept taken in its content in relation to the objective concept (the *quod* that is known). But as we point out in our comments, this same text can also be understood of the mental concept considered as such, provided it is interpreted by taking into account everything known from other texts about St. Thomas thought on the question. "Certainly, the doctrine expressed in this place," notes Fr. H. D. Gardeil (*Bulletin Thomiste*, Oct. 1931, p. 361), "should be taken into account in order to establish the authentic theory of the word, but there are other places in which St. Thomas speaks of the word in different terms, and after all this text does not give us the most balanced expression of the doctrine."

sive illud sit
definitio, sive enuntiatio, secundum
quod ponuntur duae operationes intellectus in III de Anima. Hoc autem
sic ab intellectu conceptum dicitur
verbum interius, hoc enim est quod
significatur per vocem; non enim vox
exterior significat ipsum intellectum,
aut formam ipsius intelligibilem, aut
ipsum intelligere, sed conceptum intellectus quo mediante significat rem;
ut cum dico, homo, vel homo est animal.
d) In intellectu nostro aliud est intelligere et aliud est esse. Et ideo verbum
conceptum in intellectu nostro, cum
procedat ab intellectu inquantum est
intellectus, non unitur ei in natura, sed
solum in intelligere" (*De Potentia*, q.
9,a. 5)

7. [*Summa Contra Gentiles*, 1258–1260]
a) "Res exterior intellecta a nobis in
intellectu nostro non existit secundum
propriam naturam, sed oportet quod
species ejus sit in intellectu nostro per
quam fit intellectus in actu.
Existens autem in actu, per hujusmodi
speciem sicut per propriam formam
intelligit rem ipsam . . .

Ipsum intelligere . . . manet in intelligente, secundum quod habet relationem ad rem quae intelligitur, ex eo
quod species praedicta, quae est principium intellectualis operationis, ut
forma, est similitudo illius.
b) Intellectus per speciem rei formatus
. . .

knowledge attained *ut quod* but,
rather, that in which (*in quo*) intellection is achieved. It is that which is
brought to intellection in act as the
actualizing form *in esse intelligibili*, in
other words, the formal sign (cf. § ix
and §§ 8 and 12).
Cf.§ xi.

The word conceived of that which the
intellect perceives; for us, it makes the
object nown in act, and it reveals both
the knowledge and the known; in God
it reveals the knowledge and the
known, only.

Cf. § ix.

The thing does not exist in our mind
according to its natural esse, but intentionally thanks to the *species impressa*.

It is the thing itself which is the object
(*quod*) of understanding (cf. §§ ii and
iii).

[intentionality of the *species*]

This is a formation (not *in esse entitativo*, but *in esse intelligibili*) by the species insofar as it has an intentional

intelligendo format in signo quamdam *intentionem rei intellectae, quae est*

ratio ipsius quam significat definitio . . .

c) Haec autem intentio intellecta, cum sit quasi terminus intelligibilis operationis, est aliud a specie intelligibili quae facit intellectum in actu, quod oportet considerari ut intelligibilis operationis principium, licet utraque sit rei intellectae similitudo.
d) Per hoc enim quod species intelligibilis, quae est forma intellectus, est similitudo rei exterioris, requiritur quod intellectus intentionem, formet illius rei similem, quia quale est unumquodque talia operatur; et ex hoc quod intentio intellecta est similis alicui rei, sequitur quod intellectus formando hujusmodi intentionem rem illam intelligat (*Contra Gent.*,lib. I, c. 53).

existence and as it is the vicar of the object.[43]
This "mental aim" at the object which the mind forms within itself is (from the viewpoint of the logician who reflexively attains the conceptus objectivus) the *ratio* of the thing or its objective notion (see above §§ 1–3; cf. § iii) expressed by the definition (cf. § x). And when it is taken in this way, as objective concept, it is intellecta ut quod.
To the eye of the metaphysician and the psychologist, it is in the likeness of the object (cf. § viii) that intellection is completed as in its term, i.e., the word or mental concept. In this respect, it is *intellecta*, thought or known in act, not as a *quod* but *formaliter ut quo* (cf. § ix). This is an immaterial and intentional information. And it is a likeness in the most formal meaning of the word (cf. § vii), a likeness which, in the case of the concept, the term of intellection, should be called, "formal sign" (cf. § ix): "informing such an intention (intellection in act), the mind *perceives* the thing *intellectually.*" See § 5 (b), 8 (f), 17.

8. [*Summa Contra Gentiles*]
a) Dico autem intentionem intellectam

A most important text. St. Thomas is

---

43 That is true of the *species impressa* as well as of the *species expressa* (see above, § 5 (e)). Cf. John of St. Thomas, *Phil. Not.*, III P., q. 6, a. 3: "Denique videri potest in quodlib. VIII, a. 4, et contra Gent., cap. 49, ubi speciem non solum vocat similitudinem quidditatis, sed quod etiam sit ipsa natura, et quidditas rei in esse intelligibili quod utique stare non potest sine vero et proprio esse intentionali." It is very surprising to read in an article by Fr. M. D. Simonin ("La notion d'*intentio,*" *Rev. des Sc. Phil. et Théol.*, July 1930, pp. 456–457) that "the *intentio intellecta* alone is in *esse intentionali* . . . Only the word, the term of understanding belongs to the intentional order." If such an assertion were taken literally, it would utterly destroy the whole Thomistic doctrine of knowledge at one stroke of the pen. The author refers to *Summa Theologiae*, I, 78, 3. But that article precisely explains that sensation demands an *immutatio spiritualis per quam intentio formae sensibilis fiat in organo sensus.* This amounts to saying that the *species impressa* present in the sense-organ by reason of a "spiritual immutation" belongs to the intentional order. He refers also to *Summa Theologiae*, I, 56, 2, ad 3. But in this article, it is precisely a matter of the innate *species impressae* that are the principles of intellectual operation in the angel; and they belong to the intentional order.

id quod intellectus in se ipso concipit de re intellecta.

Quae quidem in nobis neque est ipsa res quae intelligitur, neque est ipsa substantia intellectus,

sed est quaedam similitudo concepta intellectu de re intellecta, quam voces exteriores significant;

unde et ipsa intellectio verbum interius nominatur[44] quod est exteriori verbo significatum.

b) Et quidem *quod praedicta intentio non sit in nobis res intellecta, inde apparet quod aliud est intelligere rem et aliud intelligere ipsam intentionem intellectam, quod intellectus facit dum super suum opus reflectitur*: unde et aliae scientiae sunt de rebus et aliae de intentionibus intellectis.

c) Quod autem intentio intellecta non sit ipse intellectus in nobis, ex hoc patet quod esse intentionis intellectae in ipso intellectu consistit, non autem

defining *intentio intellecta*; it is that which the intellect *conceives* or gives birth to within itself through the thing intellectually grasped. It is the concept in the fullest etymological force of the term, the fruit *conceived* by and in the intellect and *conceived of the thing*, i.e., signifying it, and differing from it by the fact that it is (inasmuch as it is its formal likeness) *ut quo*, and not *ut quod* (cf. §§ iv, v. vi, viii).

This *intentio intellecta* is the same as the mental word and it is that which the name signifies (cf. § x).

In this text the intentio in question is clearly seen to be intellecta because it is that by which ("*quo*") intellection is completed, not because it is known *ut quod*. It is intellecta in this latter sense only as the object of Logic and Psychology. St.Thomas is here making use of the same argumentation as in the *Sum. Theol.* (cf. above, Appendix I, § 3)—a clear indication that that article in the *Summa* holds for the concept as well as for the *species impressa*.

The *esse* of the concept as such is the very immanent act of intellection itself, the *intelligi intrinsecum* (cf. § ix).

---

44   Cf. § 8 (f). According to these texts, it is evident that *intentio intellecta* and *verbum mentis* are synonymous. I think, along with Fr. Simonin (*art. cit.*, p. 460[2]), that the word *intentio* refers to the way of being characteristic of intellection and, in a more general way, of knowledge. But whereas it is true that the word *intentio intellecta*, by reason of its affinities with the terminology of the logician (already pointed out above, p. 398), designates the mental aim taken from the standpoint of its content or object, none the less it could not be said purely and simply that the *intentio* is "the known object as such" (*ibid.*, p. 457), "the object of knowledge considered as such" (*ibid.*, p. 460). I feel that anyone who takes the trouble to weigh all the texts and follow the present discussion in detail will agree with me. The object is the content of the concept or what the concept presents to the mind; it is not the concept itself or the *intentio intellecta* itself as synonymous with *verbum*. The expression *intentio intellecta*, when the psychologist or metaphysician uses it, designates the concept and connotes the content, or object, of the concept.

        In a general way, *intentio* designates the "mental aim" both in the sense of the object aimed at and in the sense of the form by which the act of aiming takes place. Thus, the *intentio* in the sensible order is sometimes the *intentio formae sensibilis* present in the organ of the external sense (I, 78, 3), i.e., the *species sensibilis* itself (in this case it is obviously not the known object). At other times, it is the aspects of the object and not accessible to external sense—useful, harmful, past, etc.—but perceived by the inner senses.

esse intellectus nostri, cujus esse non est suum intelligere . . .
d) Esse autem verbi interius concepti sive intentionis intellectae est ipsum suum intelligi . . .
e) Quum intellectus noster seipsum intelligit, aliud est esse intellectus, et aliud ipsum ejus intelligere; substantia enim intellectus erat in potentia intelligens antequam intelligeret actu. Sequitur ergo quod aliud sit esse intentionis intellectae, et aliud esse intellectus ipsius, quum intentionis intellectae, esse sit ipsum intelligi. Unde oportet quod in homine intelligente seipsum, verbum interius conceptum non sit homo verus, naturale hominis esse habens, sed sit homo intellectus tantum, quasi quaedam similitudo hominis veri ab intellectu apprehensa . . .

f) Intellectus intelligendo concipit et format intentionem sive rationem intellectam, quae est interius verbum (*Con. Gent.*, lib.IV, c. 11).

9. [*De Veritate*, 1256–1259]
a) "Verbum intellectus nostri . . . est id ad quod operatio intellectus nostri terminatur, quod est ipsum intellectum quod dicitur conceptio intellectus;

sive

Thus, Berkeley's formula fits the concept.

The *esse* of the concept is, therefore, other than the *esse* of its object.

When man thinks "himself," the object of his concept is the man that exists in nature; the concept itself is only man existing in the mind as thought about, as a likeness by which and in which that object is known (cf. § vii).

If the expression "formal sign" is not used by St. Thomas, the whole doctrine of the concept as a formal sign is, none the less, contained in brief form in this page from the *Summa Contra Gentiles*.
Cf. §§ 5 (b), 7 (d), 17. The intellect *forms* the concept in perceiving the thing.

This text finds its natural interpretation in the preceding text. The concept is the term of intellection (cf. § viii); it is *ipsum intellectum*, the thing thought about itself, the term of intellection in act. However, as has already been explained in Text 6, this *intellectum* designates at one and the same time both the objective concept or *ratio* and the mental concept properly so called (in this latter case, however, it does so in a secondary way). This mental concept, as that which is produced or given forth, is *ut quod*; but as thought and known, it is *ut quo formaliter*, as has already been shown in the preceding text (cf. § ix).
To form the concept is *to form the quid*

sit conceptio significabilis per vocem incomplexam, ut accidit quando intellectus format quidditates rerum;

sive

per vocem complexam, quod accidit quando intellectus componit et dividit.

b) Omne autem intellectum in nobis est realiter progrediens ab altero; vel sicut progrediuntur a principiis conceptiones conclusionum, vel sicut conceptiones quidditatum rerum posteriorum a quidditatibus priorum, vel saltem sicut conceptio actualis progreditur ab habituali cognitione: et hoc universaliter verum est de omni quod a nobis intelligitur, sive per essentiam intelligatur, sive per similitudinem; ipsa enim conceptio est effectus actus intelligendi; unde etiam quando mens intelligit seipsam, ejus conceptio non at ipsa mens, sed aliquid expressum a notitia mentis" (*De Verit.*, q. 4, a. 2).

dity of the thing, to bring it to the highest level of intentional actuation in the concept.

"Omne intellectum": in this text, it is a question of every *term of understanding in act* in the sense determined above (*the known quod*), reflexively attained for the logician, but from the point of view of direct knowledge the *quod* brought forth, the simple *quo* or in *quo* of intellection), since those "conceptions" are under discussion which are "the effect of the act of intellection" and since even that which is known by its essence, mind, for example (to use, hypothetically, Augustinian language as St. Thomas so often happens to do in the *De Veritate*), is known in and through such a conception.

10. [*De Veritate*]
"Conceptio intellectus est media inter intellectum et rem intellectam, quia ea mediante operatio intellectus pertingit ad rem: et ideo conceptio intellectus non solum est id quod intellectum est, sed etiam id quo res intelligitur:

Cf. § vi.

"Id quod intellectum est," i.e., the term of intellection in act. This term is *ut quod* with reference to intellection taken as an action productive of the mental word, and as it contains the object within itself and brings it to final intelligible actuality (cf. § 6). At the same time, however, it is *ut quo* or *in quo* with regard to intellection of the object (this is the way John of St. Thomas understands this text).[45] (Cf. [*e it*

ut

sic id quod intelligitur possit dici et res ipsa, et conceptio intellectus" (*ibid.*, ad § 3).

§ ix.) When I am thinking "man," I understand what I am thinking about (*conceptem intellectus*) and I understand a certain nature which is independent of my thought (*rem ipsam*).

---

45   "Quia non est terminus in quo ultimate sistit cognitio, sed quo meadiante fertur ad cognoscendum objectum extra, ideo habet esse signum formale, quia est cognitum intrinsecum, id est ratio intrinseca cognoscendi [. . .] tanquam in quo continetur res

11. *[De Veritate]*
a) "Verbum interius est ipsum interius intellectum, . . . scilicet id quod actu consideratur per intellectum" (*De Verit.*, q. 4, a, 1).

b) "Verbum interius per prius habet rationem significationis quam verbum exterius" (*ibid.*, ad 7).

c) Interius verbum significat omne illud quod intelligi potest, sive per essentiam sive per similitudinem intelligatur" (*ibid.*, ad 9).

The same observations as on the two preceding texts The word is "what is actually considered by the intellect" insofar as it is *said* or *produced* or *expressed* by the intellect within itself. It is the *quod* which is known if it is taken from the point of view of its content or as object of the concept ("the objective concept").

The word, taken precisely as mental concept, is *quod* insofar as it is produced. It is *quo* (*in quo*) from the standpoint of the very intellection of the thing, since it is the sign of the latter (as has already been stated in the reply to objection 7 in the same article); it is a sign of such a kind that it makes known what is known "through its essence."

In addition it should be noted that when St. Thomas is speaking of the human word apropos of his treatise on the Trinity, he considers a word uttered chiefly out of indigence, "propter necessitatem objecti," and in order to form an intellection in its ultimate act, in its relation of analogy to another Word, uttered solely out of superabundance and to make manifest the known. Whence, in those writings wherein his vocabulary is still not perfectly lucid, there are texts which could lead to misunderstandings if they were not examined with sufficient care. But in the *Summa Theologiae*, St. Thomas' vocabulary will be in perfect focus and set more completely free from the logician's "second intentions." Let us recall certain formulae from the Prima Parts, q. 34;

12. *Summa Theologiae*, I^a Pars, 1266–1268.

---

cognita intra intellectum. Et sic eadem cognitione per se attingitur conceptus et res concepta. . . . Et quia est id *in quo* res seu objectum redditur proportionatum et immaterializatum per modum termini, ideo dicitur ipse conceptus cognosci ut quod, non tanquam res seorsum cognita, sed *tanquam constituens objectum in ratione termini cogniti.*" (John of St. Thomas, *Log.*, II P., q. 22, a. 2; Reiser, I, p. 705).

a) "Primo et principaliter interior mentis conceptus verbum dicitur."

That is the sense in which, according to John Damascene "verbum dicitur [Cf. vii] naturalis intellectus motus, secundum quem movetur, et intelligit, et cogitat, velut lux et splendor."

Cf. § vii.

Dicitur *figurative* verbum id quod verbo significatur vel efficitur (*Sum Theol.*, I, 34, 1).

Only in an improper way is the thing signified by the word (ipsa res quae intelligitur, cf. § 8 (a)) called "word."

b) Cum dicitur quod verbum est notitia, ... accipitur notitia ... pro eo quod intellectus concipit congnoscendo" (*ibid.*)

Cf. § iv.

c) "*Dicitur* enim non solum verbum sed res quae verbo intelligitur vel significatur.

Cf. § vii.

Sic ergo uni soli Personae in divinis convenit dici eo modo quo dicitur verbum; eo vero modo quo dicitur res in verbo intellecta, cuilibet Personae convenit dici. . . . Sicut intellectus hominis *verbo quod concipit intelligendo lapidem*, lapidem dicit.

Cf. § viii.
The word is, indeed, *ut quod* insofar as it is the term which is produced; the thing is *ut quod* insofar as it is the known object (known by and in the term that is produced).

d) *Dicere* et *intelligere* differunt. *Nam intelligere importat solam habitudinem intelligentis ad rem intellectam: in qua nulla ratio originis importatur, sed solum informatio quaedam in intellectu nostro, prout intellectus noster in actu per formam rei intellectae* . . .

Cf. § ix.
What is said here of the *forma rei intellectae* should be understood of the mental word (wherein the intellect is actuated in second act) as well as of the *species impressa* (which actuates the intellect in first act).

Sed dicere *importat principaliter habitudinem ad verbum conceptum: nihil enim est aliud dicere quam proferre verbum. Et, mediante verbo, importat habitudinem ad rem intellectam, quae in verbo prolato manifestatur intelligenti.*"

e) Verbum autem in mente conceptum, est repraesentativum omnis ejus quod actu intelligitur. Unde in nobis sunt diversa verba secundum diversa quae intelligimus" (*Sum Theol.*, I, 34, 3).

Cf. §§ vi, viii, ix.

13. [*Summa Theologiae*, Ia Pars.]
a) "Haec opinio (sc. quod species intelligibilis est ipsum quod intelligitur)

Cf. §§ v–ix, xx.

manifeste apparet falsa ex duobus.

"Primo quidem, quia eadem sunt, quae intelligimus, et de quibus sunt scientiae: si igitur ea, quae intelligimus, essent solum species, quae sunt in anima, sequeretur, quod scientiae omnes non essent de rebus, quae sunt extra animam, sed solum de speciebus intelligibilibus, quae sunt in anima: sicut secundum Platonicos omnes scientiae sunt de ideis; quas ponebant esse intellecta in actu.

"Secundo, quia sequeretur error antiquorum dicentium quod omne quod videtur, est verum; et sic quod contradictoriae essent simul verae; si enim potentia non cognoscit nisi propriam passionem, de ea solum judicat: sic autem videtur aliquid, secundum quod potentia cognoscitiva afficitur; semper ego judicium potentiae cognoscitivae erit de eo quod judicat, scilicet de propria passione, secundum quod est: et ita omne judicium sit verum; puta, si gustus non sentit nisi propriam passionem, cum aliquis habens sanum gustum judicat mel esse dulce, vere judicabit; et similiter si ille, qui habet gustum infectum, judicit mel esse amarum, vere judicabit: uterque enim judicat secundum quod gustus ejus afficitur; et sic sequitur quod omnis opinio aequaliter erit vera, et universaliter omnis acceptio.

ET IDEO DICENDUM EST QUOD SPECIES INTELLIGIBILES SE HABET AD INTELLECTUM, UT QUO INTELLIGIT INTELLECTUS . . .

Similitudo rei intellectae, quae est species intelligibilis, est forma secundum quam intellectus intelligit; sed quia intellectus supra seipsum reflectitur, secundum eamdem reflexionem intelligit et suum intelligere et speciem qua intelligit.[46] ET SIC SPECIES

This is one of the chief texts, as is the one from the *Summa Contra Gentiles*, quoted as § 8. It is perfectly clear and leaves no loophole.

As we have shown above (Appendix I, § 3), it applies to the concept or mental word as well as to the *species impressa*, although the concept, in contradiction to the *species impressa* (as has been explained in §§ viii and ix), is intellectually perceived precisely as making the object known (in this sense, Cajetan, in his commentary on this article, ad 3, calls it "intentio quam intellectus intelligit *ut intentio* est rei extra"), still, unless it be done reflexively, the concept cannot be perceived as object—as the *known quod*—any more than the *species impressa* can. The argument developed by St. Thomas in the present article holds in both cases with the same force and necessity.

Again, let us note that, as the *species impressa* is *similitudo rei intellectae*, so is the concept (cf. above, §§ 5 (d), 7 (b), 8 (a)); St. Thomas himself also calls it *species intelligibilis* (§ 4 (c)) and *passio intellectus* (§ 5 (f)). Everything that is said here of the *similitudo rei intellectae*, the *species intelligibilis* or *propria passio potentiae* holds for the concept as well as of the *species impressa*. If the concept were the object known, *ipsum quod intelligitur*, the intellect would judge only of its own passion, and all opinions would be equally true.

Finally, the texts we shall quote under the three following numbers, inasmuch as they could be grouped as satellites around this last one (*Cont. Gent.*, lib. II, c. 75; *In de An.*, lib. III, lect. 8; *Comp. Theol.*, c. 85), and inasmuch as they are texts in which St. Thomas is

---

46   Cf. *De Verit.*, q. I0, a. 9: "Actio intellectus nostri primo tendit in ea quae per phantasmata apprehenduntur et deinde redit ad actum suum cognoscendum; et ulterius in species et habitus et potentia et essentiam ipsius mentis."

INTELLECTIVA SECUNDARIO EST ID QUOD INTELLIGITUR: SED ID, QUOD INTELLIGITUR PRIMO, EST RES, CUJUS SPECIES INTELLIGIBILIS EST SIMILI-TUDO." (*Sum. Theol.*, I, 8, 2).

b) "Intellectum est in intelligente per suam similitudinem. Et per hunc modum dicitur, quod intellectum in actu est intellectus in actu: inquantum similitudo rei intellectae est forma intellectus."(*ibid.*, ad 1).

c) "Non ergo voces significant ipsas species [sc. impressas], sed ea, quae intellectus sibi format ad judicandum de rebus exterioribus" (*ibid.*, ad 3).

14. [*Summa Contra Gentiles*]
"Secunda ratio deficit ex hoc quod non distinguit inter id quo intelligitur et id quod intelligitur. Species enim recepta in intellectu possibili non habet se ut quod intelligitur; cum enim de his quae intelliguntur sint omnes artes et scientiae, sequeretur quod omnes scientiae essent de speciebus existentibus in intellectu possibili: quod patet esse falsum. Nulla enim scientia de eis aliquid considerat, nisi naturalis [psychology] et metaphysica [critique]; sed tamen per eas quaecumque sunt in omnibus scientiis cognoscuntur.

"*Habet se igitur species intelligibilis recepta in intellectu possibili, in intelligendo, sicut id quo intelligitur; sicut et species coloris in oculo non est id quod videtur sed id quo videmus.*

"*Id vero quod intelligitur est ipsa ratio rerum existentium extra animam*; sicut etiam et res extra animam existentes visu corporali videntur; ad hoc enim inventae sunt artes et scientiae ut res

they are texts in which St. Thomas is arguing against the proponents of the unity of the possible intellect, also hold in the case of the concept, as much as, and even more than in the case of the *species impressa*.

If the object known in second act is the intellect in second act, insofar as the likeness of the thing that is known (the concept) is the *form of the intellect*, it is because the concept is known only as form or intrinsic reason of the knowledge of the thing (as John of St. Thomas has constantly stated), and not as object.

Words do not signify the *species impressae* (nor *species expressae* taken as things or objects). As Cajetan points out at the end of his commentary on this article, the concept is signified (as it is known) not as *quod* or object, but as *quo* or as making the object known (by way of definition or enunciation).

St. Thomas is arguing in the same way as in the preceding text to show that the *species intelligibilis* is not *ut quod*, but *ut quo intelligitur*. The objection may be stated thus: if there are as many intellects as human beings, the species intelligibiles would be individuated in those intellects; consequently, they could not be intelligible forms, inasmuch as the intelligible is universal, not individual. The question is the same, and the reply holds in identically the same way for both the concept and the *species impressa*. In both cases, a species that is individual according to the being it has in the subject (but a species that is spiritual and, hence, intelligible) makes known a universal *object quod*.

in suis naturis cognoscantur. . . .

"Quod enim dicit scientiam in discipulo et in magistro esse numero unum, partim quidem vere dicitur, partim autem non; est enim numero una quantum ad id quod scitur, non tamen quantum ad species intelligibiles quibus scitur, neque quantum ad ipsum scientiae habitum."(*Cont. Gent.*, II, 75).

15. [*Comm. in de Anima* (1270?)]
a) "Manifestum est etiam, quod species intelligibiles, quibus intellectus fit in actu, non sunt objectum intellectus. Non enim se habent ad intellectum sicut quod intelligitur, sed sicut quo intelligit.

"Sicut enim species, quae est in visu, non est quod videtur, sed est quo visus videt; quod autem videtur, est color, qui est in corpore; similiter QUOD INTELLECTUS INTELLEGIT EST QUIDDITAS, QUAE EST IN REBUS: NON AUTEM SPECIES INTELLIGIBILIS, NISI INQUANTUM INTELLECTUS IN SEIPSUM REFLECTITUR.

"Manifestum est enim, quod scientiae sunt de his quae intellectus intelligit. Sunt autem scientiae de rebus, non autem de speciebus, vel intentionibus intelligibilibus, nisi sola scientia rationali. Unde manifestum est quod species intelligibilis, non est objectum intellectus, sed quidditas rei intellectae . . .

b) "Non enim est species intelligibilis ipsum intellectum sed similitudo ejus in anima: et ideo si sunt plures intellectus habentes similitudinem unius et ejusdem rei, erit eadem res intellecta apud omnes" (*In III de Anima*, lect. 8).

The *object* or the *quod* that is intellectually known is numerically the same for the master as well as for the pupil; such is not the case for the species they use; they are *ut quo*.

This text is likewise a very important one. As in the two preceding texts, it holds for the concept as well as for the *species impressa*. The fact that there are as many likenesses of the object as there are different intellects does not prevent those intellects perceiving the same object, because these likenesses are only *ut quo*, not *ut quod*. The case is the same whether it is a question of the likeness which is the principle of intellectual opposition or of the likeness-term (the latter being a formal sign as distinct from the former, cf. § ix). *The species are not the object of the intellect: the quiddity of the thing is its object.*

The species is not *ipsum intellectum*; it is rather its likeness in the soul. Thus, when St. Thomas (cf. above §§ 6, 7, 9, 10, 11) says the concept is *primo et per se intellectum*, it is either because the concept is, in that case, not taken as species (but as objective concept)[47] or

---

47 It is worth noting that in the following text St. Thomas writes intellectum or res intellecta for constituted or formed by the operation of the intellect. In this place, it is obvious that he is thinking of the concept (constituted or formed by the operation of the intellect), taking it to mean, not the species or mental concept, but as objective concept or the object itself known in the concept (intellectum, which is identical with the res intellecta, being distinguished from it only by a distinction of reason cf. §§ ii–iv): "Species [impressa] se habet ut principium formale quo intellectus intelligit.

16. [*Compendium Theologiae*, 1272].

"Concedimus idem esse intellectum ab omnibus hominibus, *dico autem intellectum, id, quod est intellectus objectum; objectum autem intellectus non est specics intelligibilis, sed quidditas rei.*

"Non enim scientiae intellectuales omnes sunt de speciebus intelligibilibus; sed sunt de naturis rerum, sicut etiam objectum visus est color, non species coloris quae est in oculo.

"Quamvis igitur sint plures intellectus diversorum hominum, non tamen est nisi unum intellectum apud omnes, sicut unum coloratum est, quod a diversis inspicientibus videtur . . .

"Intellectum intelligens per eas sc. per species intelligibiles suum objectum reflectitur supra seipsum intelligendo ipsum suum intelligere, et speciem qua intelligit" (*Compend. Theol.*, cap. 85)

17. [*Comm. in Joannem*, 1270–1272].

"Illud ergo proprie dicitur verbum interius quod intelligens intelligendo format.

"Intellectus autem duo format, secundum duas ejus operationes: nam secundum operationem suam quae dicitur indivisibilem intelligentia, format definitionem; secundum vero operationem suam quae componit et dividit, format enuntiatonem vel aliquid hujusmodi: et ideo illud sic formatum et expressum per operationem intellectus, vel definientis, vel enunt

because "intellectum" is not taken in the sense of known object, but in the sense of formal sign of the object.

Here is just one more clear confirmation of the doctrine expounded in the three preceding texts. No *species intelligibilis* is *quod*; no *species intelligibilis* (concept or *species impressa*) is *intellectum* in the sense of being the object of the intellect.

This *intellectum*, the same for everyone, is the object of the concept (paragraph III) or the conceptus objectivus. The mental concept or the concept as species is not quod or the known object but, rather, that by which the intellect perceives its object.

Let us bring this discussion to a close with that admirable text from the commentary on St. John wherein St. Thomas has given the clearest and most definitive statement of his thought.

What the intellect forms in perceiving is the mental word (cf. §§ 5 (b), 7 (d), 8 (f)).

What the external sound signifies is that which the intellect has formed, i.e., the mental concept (definition or proposition, cf.§ xi) insofar as it presents the object. And that concept or mental word, even though it is *quod* insofar as it is something that is *produced* or *uttered*, is in turn a pure means as regards the intellect's *perceptive* ac

Intellectum autem, sive res intellecta, se habet ut constitutum vel formatum per operationem intellectus: sive hoc sit quidditas simplex, sive sit compositio et divisio propositionis" (*De Spirit. Creaturis*, a. 9, ad 6).

iantis, exteriori voce significatur. Unde Philosophus dicit quod ratio quam significat nomen est definitio.

"*Istud ergo sic expressum, scilicet formatum in anima, dicitur verbum interius: et ideo comparatur ad intellectum non sicut quo intelligit, sed sicut in quo intelligit; quia* IN IPSO EXPRESSO ET FORMATO VIDET NATURAM REI INTELLECTAE" (*In Joann.*, cap. I, 1.)

tivity. However, it is not a means, as is the *species impressa*, at the beginning of the intellectual operation (*ut quo*), but, rather, at the term of that operation (*ut in quo*). In other words, it is *quo* as the term whereby the object is brought to the state of actual intellection and as that in which the *intelligere* of the object is completed (cf.§§ viii and ix).

Since it has been formed and expressed by the intellect within its own bosom, *it is that in which the intellect sees the nature of the thing known.* The word *videt* expresses quite clearly that the operation which is performed by means of the concept is a *perceptive* or *intuitive* operation—perceptive of the nature *of the thing that is known.*

In short, "Verbum interius conceptum est quaedam ratio et similitudo rei intellectae" (*Cont. Gent.*, IV, 11), "quoddam mente conceptum quo homo exprimit mentaliter ea de quibus cogitat." (*Sum. Theol.*, I–II, 93, 1 ad 2), et quod "intellectus in se format ut rem intellectam cognoscat" (*De Potentia*, q. 8, a. 1); "intellectus formando hujusmodi intentionem, rem intelligit" (*Cont. Gent.*, I, 53); "in ipso expresso et formato videt naturam rei intellectae" (*In Joan.*, I, 1).

APPENDIX II

ON ANALOGY

"Analoga proportionalitatis [propriae] dicuntur quorum nomen commune est, ratio vero significata eadem secundum similitudinem seu convenientiam proportionum [et in utroque formaliter et vere praesens]."[1] The sense in which the analogue belongs intrinsically and formally to each of the analogates is purely and simply diverse (*ratio significata est simpliciter diversa*), yet the same under a certain aspect (sed eadem secundum similitudinem *proportionum*), in that it implies like relations to terms that are alike even though essentially different—relations that are registered in the very nature of the analogical concept.

The pages in Chapter V devoted to the analogy of being and the transcendentals are not an exposition *in forma* of the doctrine of analogy. They are simply an attempt to shed a little light on certain particularly important aspects of the doctrine from the point of view with which we are concerned, to wit, the critique of metaphysical knowledge. That is why we only retained the last of the diverse sorts of analogy recognized by logicians (that result from a division whic is itself analogical)—analogy of attribution, metaphorical analogy, analogy of proper proportionality[2]—for this last one is metaphysical analogy in the highest sense of the word, and there is an advantage in dealing with it alone in order to work with a *pure case*. As Cajetan says, it alone constitutes a true analogy, the others being called by that name only in an improper manner. Moreover, if analogy of attribution is often mingled with analogy of proper proportionality, it is only in virtue of the analogy of proper proportionality that the analogy of attribution, in such mixed cases, permits us to attain attributes (in things known analogically) that are predicated of those things intrinsically and formally. Of itself, an analogy of attribution only permits us to attain a form found intrinsically in the prime analogate, *in aliis vero extrinsece et per denominationem* (John of St. Thomas, *Log.*, II P., q. 13, a. 4).

Now let us try to characterize these three kinds of analogy as definitely as possible:

In analogy of attribution (when it functions in its pure state, without being linked up with an analogy of proper proportionality), one has to do with a concept which is UNIVOCAL IN ITSELF (concept # 1: "healthy" said of a living organism) but which the mind *uses analogically* by transferring it to other subjects (concept # 2: "healthy" said of climate), in which case it designates something which is made known by its relation to the object of thought signified in itself by concept # 1 (a

---

1   John of St. Thomas, *Log.*, II P., q. 13, a. 3.
2   We are using these designations so as to fall in line with common usage. In a more correct terminology (cf. A. F. Blanche, *Rev. des Sc. Phil. et Théol.*, January 1921), we would say *analogy of reference* instead of "analogy of attribution," and *analogy of proportion* instead of "analogy of proportionality."

climate is "healthy" because it is a *cause* of health—of the health of the organism). It is immediately evident that, under these conditions, an analogy of attribution, when it is all by itself, does not enable us to attain the thing analogically known *in accordance with what is properly signified by the concept*. It enables us to do that only when it is linked with an analogy of proper proportionality. In such mixed cases, as John of St. Thomas explains it (*loc. cit.*), there is *formally* an analogy of proper proportionality and only *virtually* an analogy of attribution.

In metaphorical analogy one has to do with a concept which is UNIVOCAL IN ITSELF (concept # 1: "eagle" said of a bird) and which the mind uses analogically by transferring it to other subjects (concept # 2: "eagle" said of an orator) wherein it designates something made known by the *likeness between the relation* which that subject (the orator) has to a certain term (sublime eloquence), and the relation which the object properly signified by concept # 1 (the bird) has to another term (lofty flight). It is clear that, under such conditions, metaphorical analogy (analogy of *improper* proportionality) never enables us, by itself, to attain the thing analogically known *in accordance with what is properly signified by the concept*.

In analogy of proper proportionality one has to do with a concept which is ANALOGICAL IN ITSELF ("knowing" said of sense and intellect, "being" said of the creature and of God), and which designates, in each of the subjects of which it is said, something made known by the *likeness between the relations* which one of these subjects (sense) has to the term (knowing) designated in it by that concept, on the one hand, and the relation which the other subject (intellect) has to that term (knowing) likewise designated in it by the same concept, on the other hand. It is immediately evident that under these conditions (the concept being in that case analogous of itself), an analogy of proper proportionality does enable us to attain the thing analogically known *in accordance with what is properly signified by the concept*. In this case, what is signified by the concept, inasmuch as it is one (even though it is so only in a unity of proportionality), is intrinsically and formally in each of the analogates.

Thus, the *essential* difference between analogy of proper proportionality and the other two becomes quite apparent. When Cajetan, discussing analogy of proper proportionality, writes that analogical concepts are concepts that are first univocal and then made analogical ("omnia enim fere analoga proprie, fuerunt prius univoca, et deinde extensione, analoga communia proportionaliter illis quibus sunt univoca et aliis vel alii, facta sunt"),[3] that does not mean that we make something analogical which was not so in itself from the first, but rather that the mind, after having first used such concepts univocally and without realizing that they were analogical, later discovers that they are really analogical. But they were analogical from the very outset; they are analogical *of themselves*. (We would like to make this "gloss" on page 93 of T.-L. Pénido's book to which we refer below.) That is why an analogical concept (with an analogy of proper proportionality) is one in a certain respect, in a unity of proportionality, whereas in analogy of attribution and metaphorical analogy there is not even that kind of imperfect unity: "*illa analoga non sunt unius conceptus, sed plurium habentium aliquam connotationem inter se* (et non, sicut aequivoca, a casu)" (John of St. Thomas, *loc. cit.*, and art. 5). The concept "healthy," denoting a quality of the climate, and the concept "healthy," as referred to the organism, are two different concepts; the first of them connotes

---

3   Cajetan, *De Nom. Anal.*, cap. XI, ed. de Maria, p. 278.

the second and results from transferring the second to a subject to which it does not belong as far as the thing it properly signifies is concerned.

The question of analogy has given rise to numerous studies. In this place, we mention only those to which the interpretation we deem authentically Thomistic and which is taken for granted in the reflections we have set forth in our text, can in some way be referred as to its source: Cajetan, *De Nominum Analogia; in Iam,* q, 13; John of St. Thomas, *Log.,* II P., q. 13, a. 3, 4, 5; R. Garrigou-Lagrange, "Dieu, son existence et sa nature; La première donnée de l'intelligence d'après saint Thomas" (*Mélanges Thomistes,* 1923); Le Rohellec, "De fundamento metaphysico analogiae" (*Divus Thomas,* Plac., 1926–1927); A. Gardeil, "La structure analogique de l'intellect" (*Revue Thomiste,* 1927); J. M. Ramirez, "De Analogia secundum doctrinam aristotelico-thomisticam" (*La Ciencia Tomista,* July 1921–January, 1922); and the excellent book of T.-L. Pénido, *Le rôle de l'analogie en théologie dogmatique* (Paris, 1931).

As regards the *princeps analogatorum* we share the opinion of Pénido,[4] Garrigou-Lagrange and Le Rohellec—and it is the opinion of Cajetan and John of St. Thomas as well. In analogy of attribution there is a *princeps analogatorum* whose notion is included in that of all the other analogates ("forma principalis analogati debet poni in caeterorum definitione, quae ab illa denominantur")—because all those analogates are only made known through the diverse relations they have to the supreme analogate (and, when the analogy of attribution is in its pure state, it is a concept which is univocal in itself, but used analogically by the mind). The same is not the case in analogy of proper proportionality. In this case, the supreme analogate is the one of which the analogous term is said primarily *quoad se,* not *quoad nos.* Uncreated being is the supreme analogate of being. Moreover, its notion is not included in the notion of the other analogates ("non debet unum poni in definitione aliorum," John of St. Thomas, *loc cit.,* a. 4).

On the other hand, we feel that T.-L. Pénido has not made sufficient use of John of St. Thomas' penetrating remark that in mixed cases (cases in which analogy of attribution and analogy of proportionality are linked together), analogy of attribution is only *virtual.* When from the existence of created being we conclude to the existence of its uncreated Cause, we are already (even though we are not yet aware of it) bringing the analogy of proper proportionality into play. For such a reasoning implies that the notion of *cause* is itself analogous by an analogy of proper proportionality; and in addition it implies that the uncreated being to which the reasoning concludes and the created being from which it sets out are called by the

---

4   F. A. Blanche's reply to T.-L. Pénido (*Rev. de Phil.,* Jan.–Feb. 1932) will prove very interesting reading. In analogy of proper proportionality, the inferior analogates share in the prime analogate (*princeps analogatorum*) in different degrees: Fr. Blanche has quite rightly insisted on this point. But it does not follow that the prime analogate should enter into the notion or definition of the others—even though it were only a participated principle.

On the other hand, if there is *quoad nos* (because our knowledge stems from experience) a prime analogate which is not the *princeps analogatorum,* it should not enter into the notion or definition of the other analogates either. It is by reaching the analogue itself dianoetically, by this inferior analogate (cf. above, Ch. V, §§ 10 and 13), that we know ananoetically the superior analogates. Only in this way is it possible to understand that the stigmata of created perfections, through which we have a concept of uncreated Being, while they necessarily affect our mode of knowing, affect it alone, and in no wise do they affect the thing signified by our concept.

same name, "being," not only because the first is the cause of the second, but because what is signified by the concept "being" is found in both according to a likeness of proportions. From the fact that the relation of causality lies at the basis of analogy of attribution, between effect and cause, it does not follow that analogy of attribution is formally used each time the path of causality is followed to establish "the existence of the source" of created perfections (*op. cit.*, p. 146).

APPENDIX III

WHAT GOD IS

"Cum enim dicimus, quod cognoscimus esse et non quidditatem, assueti peripateticis sermonibus, intendimus, quod scimus de illis terminare quaestionem *an est*, quae de esse quaerit, et quod nescimus de eis terminare quaestionem *quid est*, quae quidditatem scrutatur: etsi secundum aliquod praedicatum quidditativum terminare illam noverimus; notitiam illam *quia* et non quidditativum vocamus sequentes Aristotelis vestigia, qui notitiam rei per communia, notitiam *quia* in Posterioribus Analyticis appellat. Et propter hoc ea notitia proportionaliter negatur de quidditate a Thomistis in proposito, quae affirmatur de esse; quia notitia de propria quaestione quidditatis non haberi dicitur, notitia vero de propria quaestione ipsius esse non caremus" (Cajetan, *In de Ente et Essentia*, cap. VI, q. 15, ed. de Maria, p. 204).

Scire de aliquo quid est is to know how to treat the question: "In what does the essence of the thing consist?" according to its proper requirements, and thus to know how to define the thing by its essential predicates and how to assign the reason (*ratio*) of its properties. "Sic ergo quaestio *quid est* et quaestio *propter* quid redeunt in idem subjecto, quamvis differant ratione.[1] . . . Idem est scire *quid est*, et scire causam quaestionis *an est*; sicut est idem scire *propter quid*, et scire causam quaestionis *quia est*.[2] . . . Quaerere *propter quid* est, nihil aliud est quam quaerere *quid* est.[3] . . . Unde scientiae speculativae non sunt de ipsis essentiis substantiarum separatarum. Non enim per scientias demonstrativas possumus scire quod quid est in eis; quia ipsae essentiae harum substantiarum sunt intelligibiles per seipsas ab intellectu ad hoc proportionato; non autem congregatur earum notitia, qua cognoscitur *quod quid est* ipsarum, per aliqua priora. Sed per scientias speculativas potest sciri de eis an sint, et quid non sunt, et aliquid secundum similitudinem in rebus inferioribus inventam."[4] This is why knowing *quid est* consists, as we have pointed out,[5] in knowing "in the register or perspective of the *raison d'être*" or in knowing what the thing is *in itself*. This is the way *scire de aliqua re quid est* must be translated. To render this rigorously technical and didactic expression purely and simply by the phrase "to know what the thing is" would be completely ambiguous for, unlike the Latin phrase it purports to translate, this English phrase does not designate a special type of knowledge by way of the *raison d'être* and the quidditative definition. *Scire de Deo quid est* can only consist in seeing God face to face.

---

1   St. Thomas, *In Anal. Post.*, lib. II, lect. 1, n. 8.
2   *Ibid.*, lect. 7, n. 2.
3   *Ibid.*, lect. 7, n. 8.
4   *Ibid.*, lect. 41, n. 8.
5   See above, Ch. II, § 9, and Ch. V, § 19.

On the other hand, St. Thomas will say[6] that we know the essence of God in a certain way (by analogy) without knowing *de Deo quid est.*

Scire de aliquo quia est is to know how to deal with the proper requirements of the question: "Does the thing exist?" even when we do not know the thing's nature except by means of what it has [univocally or analogically] in common with other things (*per communia*). This is not at all the same as knowing nothing in any way about the thing's nature; it is not to know it *in itself* and through its essential predicates, even to its ultimate difference. "Aliud est cognoscere quidditatem, seu cognitio quidditatis, et aliud est cognitio quidditativa, seu cognoscere quidditativa. Cognoscit enim leonis quidditatem quicumque novit aliquod eius praedicatum essentiale. Cognoscit autem quidditative non nisi ille, qui omnia praedicata quidditativa usque ad ultimam differentiam novit, etc."[7] Only he knows God *quidditative* who sees the Divine Essence. But to know *that God is* as St. Thomas knew it—knowing the meaning of His name whose existence we thus confess—is to bend beneath an immensity of knowledge which attains the Divine Nature without seeing it, and to acknowledge oneself conquered by one's object.

Our knowledge of God does not go beyond *quia est,* but while it does not surpass *quia est* it knows what God is in a way which (although imperfect with respect to beatific vision—the only knowledge of God according to *quid est* and seen from the perspective of the *raison d'être*—) admits of the most varied degrees of noetic wealth, short of the supreme degree.

Included in the knowledge of *quia est* are our metaphysical knowledge of God (and of spirits), the angel's natural knowledge of God,[8] the supernatural knowledge through faith which the angel had of God at the moment of his trial, the supernatural knowledge of God which faith gives us and which bears on the deity as such but which is given to us by means of created and material analogates, knowledge through infused contemplation itself, which is but the peak of the knowledge through faith. "Quia igitur intellectus noster secundum statum viae habet determinatam habitudinem ad formas, quae a sensu abstrahuntur, cum comparetur ad phantasmata ut visus ad colores, ut dicitur in III *De Anima,* non potest ipsum Deum cognoscere in hoc statu, per formam quae est essentia sua, sed sic cognoscitur in patria a beatis . . . Unde reliquitur quod solum per formam

---

6   *Sum. Theol.,* I, 13, 2, ad 3; ad 2.

7   Cajetan, *In de Ente et Essentia, loc. cit.,* ed. de Maria, p. 193. "Cum autem," Cajetan continues, "cognoscamus intelligentias esse substantias, et esse intellectuales, etc., liquet quod earum quidditates cognoscimus: unde hoc in dubium non vertitur; sed quaestio est, an quidditative cognoscere eas possimus, et penetremus scilicet usque ad ultimas earum differentias." Some of St. Thomas's expressions, which might at first be misinterpreted, are best understood by keeping Cajetan's explanations in mind. The reason why St. Thomas writes (*In Boet. de Trin.,* q. 6, a. 4): "Quidditas autem substantiarum separatarum non potest cognosci, per ea quae sensu percipimus, ut ex praedictis patet, quamvis pervenire possimus per sensibilia ad cognoscendum hujusmodi substantias esse, et aliquas earum conditiones," is that in his vocabulary *cognoscere quidditatem* is to know the quiddity *in itself,* right through to its ultimate difference, what Cajetan calls "cognoscere quidditatem quidditative." Likewise, when St. Thomas writes: "De Deo quid sit penitus manet ignotum" (*Cont. Gent.,* III, 49), this technical expression *quid sit* designates the essence *secundum quod in se est* (cf. *Sum. Theo.,* I, 13, 8, ad 2; cf. 13, 2, ad 1); and the Divine Essence *secundum quod in se est* remains completely unknown this side of vision.

8   Cf. *Cont. Gent.,* lib. III, cap. 49.

effectus cognoscatur. Effectus autem est duplex, quidam qui adaequatur virtuti suae causae, et per talem effectum cognoscitur *plene* virtus causae, et per consequens quidditas ejus; alius effectus est qui deficit a praedicta aequalitate, et per talem effectum non potest comprehendi virtus agentis, et per consequens nec essentia ejus, sed cognoscitur de causa tantum quod est. Et sic se habet cognitio effectus, ut principium ad cognoscendum de causa an est, sicut se habet quidditas ipsius causae cum per fonnam suam cognoscitur. Hoc autem modo se habet omnis effectus ad Deum: et ideo non possumus in statu viae pertingere ad cognoscendum de ipso, nisi quia est. Et tamen cognoscentium quia est, unus alio perfectius cognoscit, quia causa tanto ex effectu perfectius cognoscitur, quanto ex effectu magis apprehenditur habitudo causae ad effectum, quae quidem habitudo in effectu non pertingente ad aequalitatem suae causae, attenditur secundum tria, scilicet secundum progressum effectus a causa, et secundum hoc quod effectus consequitur de similitudine causae suae, et secundum hoc quod deficit ab ejus perfecta consecutione, et sic tripliciter mens humana proficit in cognitione Dei, quamvis ad cognoscendum quid est non pertingat, sed an est solum . . . In hoc autem profectu cognitionis maxime juvatur mens humana, cum lumen ejus naturale nova illustratione confortatur: sicut est lumen fidei et doni sapientiae et intellectus, per quod mens supra se in contemplatione elevatur, inquantum cognoscit Deum esse supra omne id quod naturaliter apprehendit. Sed quia ad ejus essentiam videndam penetrare non sufficit, dicitur in seipsum quodammodo ab excellenti lumine reflecti, et hoc est quod dicitur *Genes.* XXXII, super illud: 'Vidi Dominum facie ad faciem,' in glossa Gregorii: 'Visus animae, cum in Deum intenditur, immensitatis coruscatione reverberatur.'" (*In Boet. de Trin.*, q. I, a. 2).

Farther on (q. 6, a. 3), after explaining the conditions of knowledge in the register of the *quid* ("Ad hoc quod de re aliqua sciamus quid est, oportet quod intellectus noster feratur in ipsius rei quidditatem sive essentiam, vel immediate, vel mediantibus aliquibus, quae sufficienter ejus quidditatem demonstrant," *sufficienter*, that is to say in such a way that the quiddity is known in its ultimate difference), and after showing that neither by way of likeness, causality, natural knowledge, nor revelation ("quia divinae revelationis radius ad nos pervenit secundum modum nostrum, ut Dionysius dicit") can we come to know the essence of God and of immaterial substances, St. Thomas continues: "*Est tamen sciendum, quod de nulla re potest scire an est, nisi quoquomodo de ea sciatur quid est, vel cognitione perfecta, vel cognitione confusa.*" And he explains how this imperfect knowledge of the nature of immaterial substances occurs. Unlike the imperfect knowledge which serves as the starting point for our investigation of material nature by furnishing us with a knowledge of "some proximate or remote genus" to which the thing belongs, and of "certain exterior accidents," [9] the imperfect knowledge of the nature of immaterial substances takes place by *negation* of what these substances are not (which replaces knowledge of the genus[10]) and by the relation of *causality* or *eminence* (*excessus*) which they have with respect to sensible substances (which takes the place of knowledge of accidents).

The *De Potentia*, q. 7, a. 5, contains very definite explanations of this point. We really should quote the whole article, but we shall limit ourselves to this long passage: "Intellectus autem noster cum a rebus creatis cognitionem accipiat,

9   *In Anal. Post.*, lib. II, lect. 7, n. 6.
10   Cf. *Cont. Gent.*, lib. I, cap. 14.

informatur similitudinibis perfectionum in creaturis inventarum, sicut sapientiae, virtutis, bonitatis et hujusmodi. Unde sicut res creatae per suas perfectiones aliqualiter, licet deficienter, Deo assimilantur, ita et intellectus noster harum perfectionum speciebus informatur.

"Quandocumque autem intellectus per suam formam intelligibilem alicui rei assimilatur, tunc illud quod concipit et enuntiat secundum illam intelligibilem speciem verificatur de re illa cui per suam speciem similatur: nam scientia est assimilatio intellectus ad rem scitam. Unde oportet quod *illa quae intellectus harum specierum perfectionibus informatus de Deo cogitat vel enuntiat, in Deo vere existant*, qui unicuique praedicatarum specierum respondet sicut illud cui omnes similes sunt.

"Si autem hujusmodi intelligibilis species nostri intellectus divinam essentiam adaequaret in assimilando, ipsam comprehenderet, et ipsa conceptio intellectus esset perfecta Dei ratio, sicut animal gressibile bipes est perfecta ratio hominis. Non autem perfecte divinam essentiam assimilat species praedicta, ut dictum est; et ideo licet hujusmodi nomina quae intellectus ex talibus conceptionibus Deo attribuit *significent id quod est divina substantia*, non tamen perfecte ipsam significant *secundum quod est, sed secundum quod a* nobis intelligitur. Sic ergo dicendum est, quod quodlibet istorum nominum *significat divinam substantiam*, non tamen quasi comprehendens ipsam, sed *imperfecte*: et propter hoc, nomen *Qui est*, maxime Deo competit, quia non determinat aliquam formam Deo, sed significat esse indeterminate. Et hoc est quod dicit Damascenus (lib. I, *Orthod. Fidei*, cap. xii), quod hoc nomen *Qui est* significat substantiae pelagus infinitum.

"Haec autem solutio confirmatur per verba Dionysii, qui dicit (cap. I *De Div. Nom.*, a medio), quod *quia Divinitas omnia simpliciter et incircumfinite in se ipsa existentia praeaccipit;* ex *diversis convenienter laudatur et nominatur. Simpliciter* dicit, quia perfectiones quae in creaturis sunt secundum diversas formas, Deo attribuuntur secundum simplicem ejus essentiam; *incircumfinite* dicit, ad ostendendum quod nulla perfectio in creaturis inventa divinam essentiam comprehendit, ut sic intellectus sub ratione illius perfectionis in se ipso Deum definiat.

"Confirmatur etiam per hoc quod habetur V *Metaph.* (com. 21), quod simpliciter perfectum est quod habet in se perfectiones omnium generum; quod Commentator ibidem de Deo exponit."

Names signifying, although only ananoetically, "*id quod est divina substantia*" do indeed tell us in some manner what God is. Consequently, although on this earth we cannot in any degree or in any way know God as He is in Himself (this is exclusively reserved for the beatific vision), it is clear that we can, nevertheless, know what God is in a more-or-less imperfect, but always true, fashion. This we can do either by metaphysics, which attains God analogically *sub ratione entis primi*, or by faith, theology and infused contemplation which attain the deity as such veiled by created analogates (see Ch. V, § 26). To render "quid est ipsius Dei semper nobis occultum remanet" (*De Verit.*, 2, 1, ad 9), "de Deo quid sit penitus manet ignotum" (*Cont. Gent.*, lib. III, c. 49), by translating "We do not know God in *any way*, in *any thing*, in *any degree*,"[11] is to expose the reader to serious misconceptions.

Thus, in cases where the original expression has a technical or didactic meaning which a word-by-word translation does not render, literal or quasi-literal transla-

---

11   A. D. Sertillanges, Member of the Institute, *Renseignements téchniques*, which follow after his translation of the treatise on God in the *Sum. Theol.*, t. II, p. 383. Italics are the author's.

tions may only appear to be exact. Does that justify an author who, recently coming across a French phrase which he was not able to recognize as a quasi-literal[12] translation of a passage from the *Summa Contra Gentiles*, taking scandal at it as if it were a heresy?[13] However that may be, if we keep in mind St. Thomas's explicit explanation of the expression *scire de aliquo quid est* ("Tunc intellectus dicitur scire de aliquo quid est, *quando definit ipsum, id est quando concipit aliquam formam de ipsa re quae per omnia ipsi rei respondet*. Jam autem ex dictis patet quod quidquid intellectus noster de Deo concipit, est deficiens a repraesentatione ejus; et ideo quid est ipsius Dei semper nobis occultum remanet," *De Verit.*, II, 1, ad 9), we can see that the passage from the *Summa contra Gentiles* (lib. I, c. 30): "Non enim de Deo capere possumus quid est, sed quid non est, et qualiter alia se habeant ad ipsum," is simply a summary of the doctrine St. Thomas constantly teaches in like terms wherever he treats of the divine names, and which we referred to above in respect to the commentary on the *De Trinitate* of Boethius.

This teaching is admirably summarized in the *Summa Theologiae*, Ia P., q. 13. We would like to draw attention to the fact here that in the second article St. Thomas states, as he does in the text of the *De Potentia* quoted above: "quod hujusmodi quidem nomina *significant substantiam divinam, et praedicantur de Deo substantialiter*, sed deficiunt a repraesentatione ipsius . . . Divinam substantiam significant, imperfecte tamen, sicut et creaturae imperfecte eam repraesentant. Cum ergo dicitur Deus est bonus, non est sensus, Deus est causa bonitatis, vel Deus non est malus: sed est sensus, *id quod bonitatem dicimus in creaturis, praeexistit in Deo, et hoc quidem secundum altiorem modum.*"

In the *ad 1* he explains further: "Damascenus ideo dicit quod haec nomina non significant quid est Deus, quia a nullo istorum nominum exprimitur quid est *perfecte*. Sed unumquodque *imperfecte eum significat*, sicut et creaturae imperfecte eum repraesentant." And in the *ad 3*: "Essentiam Dei in hac vita cognoscere non possumus secundum quod in se est; sed COGNOSCIMUS EAM *secundum quod repraesentatur in perfectionibus creaturarum.*" Cf. *ibid.*, a. 8, ad 2: "Secundum quod naturam alicujus rei ex ejus proprietatibus et effectibus cognoscere possumus, sic eam nomine possumus significare. Unde quia substantiam lapidis ex ejus proprie-tate possumus cognoscere secundum seipsam, sciendo quid est lapis: hoc nomen lapis ipsam lapidis naturam, secundum quod in se est, significat; significat enim definitionem lapidis, per quam scimus quid est lapis: ratio enim quam significat nomen est definitio, ut dicitur in IV *Metaph.* (lect. XVI). Sed ex effectibus divinis divinam naturam non possumus cognoscere *secundum quod in se est, ut sciamus de ea quid est; sed per modum eminentiae et causalitatis, et negationis*, ut supra (q. 12, a. 12) dictum est. Et sic hoc nomen Deus significat naturam divinam. Impositum est

---

12 We say "quasi-literal" for in strictly literal translation "non de Deo capere possumus quid est" should be rendered, "we cannot grasp *of God what He is*" and not, "we cannot grasp *what God is.*" To translate it in that way would preserve at least the form of a Latin expression whose didactic and technical character is known to every reader familiar with the scholastic vocabulary.

13 *Vide* Father Blaise Romeyer, *Archives de Philosophie*, t. VI, cahier 4, pp. 254–258, 267 (on the subject of Rev. Fr. Sertillanges' phrase: "Nous ne savons pas ce que Dieu est, mais seulement ce qu'il n'est pas et quelle relation soutient avec lui tout le reste," which is a quasi-literal translation of the text from the *Summa Contra Gentiles* quoted above). Father Romeyer has taken this up again in Vol. VII of the *Archives*, 3rd supplement, pp. 11–15.

enim nomen hoc ad aliquid significandum supra omnia existens, quod est principium omnium, et remotum ab omnibus." Such texts say everything that is to be said and, while noting the technical meaning of *scire de aliquo quid est*, they show clearly that according to St. Thomas, although we cannot know the essence of God as it is in itself, nevertheless we do know it, although in an imperfect way.

Finally, let us reread the two following texts from the *De Potentia* and the *Summa Theologiae*. To the objection "Utrum in Deo sit substantia vel essentia idem quod esse. Et videtur quod non. Dicit enim Damascenus, in I lib. *Orth. Fidei*, (cap. I and III): *Quoniam quidem Deus est, manifestum est nobis: quid vero sit secundum substantiam et naturam, incomprehensibile est omnino et ignotum*. Non autem potest esse idem notum et ignotum. Ergo non est idem esse Dei et substantia vel essentia ejus," St. Thomas answers: "Ad primum ergo dicendum, quod ens et esse dicitur dupliciter, ut patet V *Metaph*. (lib. X, text. 13 and 14). Quandoque enim significat essentiam rei, sive actum essendi; quandoque vero significat veritatem propositionis, etiam in his quae esse non habent; sicut dicimus quod caecitas est, quia verum est hominem esse caecum. Cum ergo dicat Damascenus quod esse Dei est nobis manifestum, accipitur esse Dei secundo modo et non primo. Primo enim modo est idem esse Dei quod est substantia: et sicut ejus substantia est ignota, ita et esse. Secundo autem modo dicimus quoniam Deus est, quoniam hanc propositionem in intellectu nostro concipimus ex effectibus ipsius." (*De Potentia*, q. 7, a. 2, ad 1; cf. ad 11.) "Esse dupliciter dicitur. Uno modo significat actum essendi. Alio modo significat compositionem propositionis, quam anima adinvenit conjungens praedicatum subjecto. Primo igitur modo accipiendo esse, non possumus scire esse Dei, sicut nec ejus essentiam; sed solum secundo modo. Scimus enim quod haec propositio, quam formamus de Deo, cum dicimus, *Deus est* vera est. Et hoc scimus ex ejus effectibus; ut supra (q. 2, a. 2) dictum est." (*Sum. Theol.*, I, 3, 4, ad 2). St. Thomas is here answering an objection which declares that the *esse* of God is not identical with His *essence*, because the Essence of God is clearly manifested to us only in vision, whereas the existence of God is clearly manifested to us even here on earth. He answers that what is clearly manifested to us here below is the truth of the proposition: "God is," which can be proved from creatures. (In other words, this is the copulative *esse* by which, constrained by the evidence of the proof, we join in our mind the predicate "existing" to the subject "God."[14] This *esse* is different from the one which signifies the act of being, since we can say: "Blindness is," whereas blindness as such does not exercise the act of being. To say that "Blindness is in a man" is only to affirm that "A man is blind," to join the predicate blind to the subject man.)

On the contrary, the *esse* signifying the act of being and attributed to God in this same proposition: "God is," or "God has *esse*," exceeds our knowledge for the same reason as does the Divine Essence with which it is strictly identical. And, like this Essence, it is known by analogy and by a defective mode of conceiving.

Such is clearly the meaning of these texts in St. Thomas. It is impossible to find that meaning in an interpretation like the following: "In this proposition: God is, *the verb to be does not signify real being*, being considered as an attribute: it is only

---

14   In propositions *de secundo adjacente* the word "is" functions both as copula and predicate. The proposition "Deus est" is strictly equivalent to "Deus est existens"; the composition of subject and predicate evidently takes place only in the mind and in no way affects the simplicity of the Divine Essence.

the logical link in a true proposition and is used in a sense *which would be equally authentic* in a thing without real existence, as when we say 'Blindness is.'" The author of the commentary from which these lines are taken[15] seems here to forget that precisely when we say "Blindness is," we affirm only the logical bond between a predicate (blind) and a subject (some man)[16] because blindness is a being of reason, whereas in the case of God, who is not a being of reason, we affirm, in saying that He is, *both this logical link and the perfection, act of being,* attributed by means of this link to the subject *of the proposition as a real esse and all that is most real,* known by analogy. The same is true of existence as is true of life, of goodness, of unity, etc.[17] These are predicates which we attribute to God without thereby positing in God any composition of subject and attribute, for this composition belongs to the purely logical order and concerns only our thought. Cf. *De Potentia,* q. 7, a. 4; *Sum. Theol.* I, q. 13, a. 2 ("Hujusmodi autem nomina . . . praedicantur de Deo substantialiter"); a. 6; a. 12 ("Propositiones affirmativae possunt vere formari de Deo").[18] Although in God there is no quality or determination added to His substance, we can predicate these names of Him in the concrete, according to a defective mode of signifying which of itself alludes to non-subsisting determinations (I, 13, 1, *ad* 2 and *ad* 3). And although the manner of signifying is deficient, the name which by its very indetermination most eminently befits Him: *Qui est* (*ibid.,* a. 11) is the first of these names attributed to God in the proper sense and as a perfection that is most real. "Ego sum qui sum" (Exod. iii, 14), the revealed utterance itself attributes to God (*ego*) by means of the verbal copula (*sum*) existence (*qui sum*) as constituting its essence.

If, in this proposition: God is, the verb "to be" signified only the logical copula and not real being (attributed as a predicate by means of the copula), how could St. Thomas in the same article (q. 7, a. 2) of the *De Potentia,* attribute real being to God by affirming that God *is being itself, "est ipsum esse"* (ad 8) and that the being of God is distinguished from every other being *per hoc ipsum quod est esse per se subsistens (ad 5)?*

He himself explicitly declares that the intellect attributes *esse* to God: "Intellectus attribuens esse Deo, transcendit modum significandi, attribuens Deo id quod significatur, non autem modum significandi" (*ad* 7). And he is evidently not speaking of the being which belongs to the verbal copula when he writes: "*Hoc quod dico esse est actualitas omnium actuum, et propter hoc est perfectio omnium perfectionum" (ad 9).*

---

15   A. D. Sertillanges, member of the Institute, *Renseignements téchniques,* following on his translation of the treatise on God in the *Sum. Theol.,* t. II, p. 383. Italics ours. Cf. T.-L. Pénido's criticism of these same positions in his book *Le rôle de l'analogie en théologie dogmatique,* pp. 170–182; and Rev. Garrigou-Lagrange, *Dieu, son existence et sa nature,* 5th ed., pp. 513–568.

16   Cf. *In Metaph.,* lib. V, lect. 9, nn. 895–896.

17   "Dicit Augustinus in VI (cap. 4) *De Trinitate:* 'Deo hoc est esse, quod fortem esse vel sapientem esse, et si quid de illa simplicitate dixeris, quod ejus substantia significatur.' Ergo omnia nomina hujusmodi significant divinam substantiam." (*Sum. Theol.* I, 13, 2, *sed contra.*)

18   "Sed quamvis intelligat ipsum sub diversis conceptionibus, cognoscit tamen quod omnibus suis conceptionibus respondet una et eadem res simplex. Hanc ergo pluralitatem quae est secundum rationem, repraesentat per pluralitatem praedicati et subjecti, unitatem vero repraesentat intellectus per compositionem."

Doubtless, in attributing being to God, we do attribute to Him a name drawn by us from creatures, which are what we first know;[19] but as the meaning of the word, being, like wisdom and goodness is said of God before being said of His creatures. Thus it is completely ambiguous to say, "He who is . . . is but the name of a creature."[20] "Quantum ad rem significatam per nomen, per prius dicuntur [hujusmodi nomina[21]] de Deo quam de creaturis: quia a Deo hujusmodi perfectiones in creaturas manant."[22]

It is perfectly clear that God is not *one of the beings* which share *ens commune;* He is outside the order *of beings,* "voluntas divina est intelligenda extra ordinem entium existens, velut causa quaedam profundens totum ens et omnes ejus differentias" (St. Thomas, *In I Periherm.,* lect. 14, n. 22). But precisely because He is the cause of *ens commune,* which is the being common to the ten categories and the *subject* of metaphysics (cf. *In Metaph.,* Proeemium, and above, Chap. V, § 13, n. 19),[23] He is Himself, in His perfect incommunicability, subsisting Being itself, *Deus est ipsum esse per se subsistens. (Sum. Theol.,* I, 4, 2; 44, 1).

Let us conclude that we should not say, purely and simply: "We do not know what God is," but rather, "We do not know what God is *in Himself.*" Nor should we say purely and simply, "We know what God is," but rather, "We know imperfectly what God is, *without being able to grasp His essence in itself.*"

It was with much reluctance that we have had to criticize certain expressions of Father Sertillanges here. It was not our intention to accuse him of "semi-agnosticism" as Father Romeyer did. In so serious a matter, wherein incorrect expressions may so easily obscure correct thought, such an accusation should not be hastily brought against so well-informed a philosopher. Father Sertillanges has an acute sense of the transcendence of Pure Act, but the vocabulary he uses in order to bring out this transcendence, and which he borrows either from a language less developed and less scientific than that of St. Thomas or from technical expressions of St. Thomas which lose their exact meaning in translation,[24] is apt to lead to serious misunderstandings. Ambiguity is not a philosophical instrument and the conciliation of Thomism with certain modern systems would be too dearly paid for were it to be bought at the price of equivocal language.

---

19 "Hoc nomen *Qui est* nominat Deum per esse inventum in creaturis, quod exemplariter deductum est ab ipso" (St. Thomas, *In I Sent.,* dist. 8, q. 1, a. 1, ad 2); which is why, like every form of human language, "imperfecte signficat divinum esse." (*ibid.,* ad 3) "Quantum ad impositionem nominis, per prius a nobis imponuntur creaturis, quas prius cognoscimus" (*Sum. Theol.,* I, 13, 6).

20 A. D. Sertillanges, *op. cit.,* p. 384

21 Metaphorical names, on the contrary, are first said of creatures, even as to what is signified by the name (*Sum. Theol.,* I, 13, 6).

22 *Sum. Theol.,* I, 13, 6. *In I Sent.,* dist. 22, q. 1, a. 2, *solutio* and ad 2.

23 Cf. also *In I Sent.,* dist. 8, q. 4, a. 1.

24 Furthermore, his translations are sometimes incomplete; for example, "Our intellect . . . defines (a thing) when it conceives about this thing, an intellectual form corresponding to its nature . . . Thus God always remains hidden to us" (*op. cit.,* p. 382), where the text has: "Intellectus . . . definit (aliquid) quando concipit aliquam formam de ipsa re quae *per omnia* ipsi rei respondet . . . Et ideo *quid est ipsius Dei* semper nobis occultum remanet." (*De Verit.,* q. 2, a. 1, ad 9).

APPENDIX IV

ON THE NOTION OF SUBSISTENCE
First Version

1. The notion of subsistence is one of the most difficult and most controversial in Thomistic philosophy. We should like to set forth some reflection concerning the metaphysical value of this notion, which will, we hope, show its connection with the principles of the doctrinal synthesis of St. Thomas.

If we take exact account of the special conditions which the doctrine of potency and act assumes in the case of essence and existence, we can see that the notion of *subsistence* as a substantial mode is not Cajetan's invention but rests upon the fundamental principles of Thomistic thought, and upon what must be considered—if not as St. Thomas' own discovery (for the neo-Platonists, and Avicenna after them, had already suggested or taught the real distinction between essence and existence in creatures[1]), at least as the truth singled out by him, with incomparable lucidity, to be the foundation of the whole metaphysical edifice—I mean of the extension of the Aristotelian doctrine of potency and act to the relation of essence to existence.

What is altogether unusual about this case is this: an essence, which is completely achieved in its line of nature, is potency with respect to the act of existing, of being placed *extra causas*.

In all other cases where we have to deal with the potency-act—couple, for example, in the case of a faculty in relation to its operation—there exists between the potency and the act, which are in the same line, a proportion such that, all the conditions being given, the act received in the potency can be received only in it, and is strictly adapted to it alone because in itself it limits that act to itself, to the exclusion of every other potency. It is *its* act, *its* actuation, *its* determination.

In the special case of which we are now speaking, it is a whole order which is potency in respect of another order. Essence and existence belong to two different orders, and essence is in potency with respect to existence.

It cannot properly be said here that the act is received in a potency because the words "to be received in a potency" relate to an act which itself is posited in existence as a determination of that potency's own reserves of determinability.

Consequently, it should rather be said here, that it is the act which, if it does not receive, at least holds essence up and sustains it by causing it formally to be. In other terms, if I may be allowed to put it so, there is a sort of transcendence of the act of existing by reason of which (not being the achievement of a potency *in the*

---

1   Cf. Cajetan, *In de Ente et Essentia*, q. 12 (ed. de Maria, p. 154); Mandonnet, "Les premières disputes sur la distinction réelle entre l'essence et l'existence," *Revue Thomiste* (1910); M. D. Roland-Gosselin, "Le De ente et essentia de saint Thomas d'Aquin," *Bibliotheque Thomiste* (1926), pp. 135–205.

order proper to that potency—for existence is not the achievement of essence in the order of essence: it does not form part of the order of essence), the potency which the act achieves, considered with respect to its quidditative constituents, *has not in itself anything by which to make* ITS OWN the act in question.

Considering any substantial nature exclusively in its quidditative constituents, it is made to exist *per se*; it is made to possess existence in itself, not in another thing. But if we consider the act of existing, it becomes clear that since, according to a universal principle, it is potency which limits act, there is nothing in this act taken in itself which limits existence to this particular potency rather than to another one; and if we view essence itself exclusively in its quidditative constituents, there is, as we have just seen, nothing in it either which limits or appropriates this act of existing to itself alone, to the exclusion of any other essence. It summons existence, but existence is not one of *its* determinations. Existence is not a quidditative determination; existence does not form part of the line of essence; it is not a determination of essence. By a unique paradox, it actuates essence and it is not an actuation of the reserves of potency within essence.

Consequently, nothing stands, metaphysically, in the way of its being joined with another substantial essence in the act of existing; under this aspect it is *unterminated*. Nevertheless, it cannot exist (and act) except it be terminated. Existence must be *its own*. Briefly, every (substantial) finite essence (really distinct from existence) requires to be terminated on the side of existence, face to face with existence, in such fashion that it *cannot* be joined to another substantial essence in order to receive existence. When it is thus terminated, it will limit existence to itself and to its own finitude. It will be terminated in this fashion by a substantial mode which is precisely *subsistence*, and which is not a quidditative constituent of essence any more than the point which terminates a line is itself an extent, a segment of the line. On the one hand, this subsistence is not one of the quidditative constituents of essence, and, on the other hand, it is not yet existence. Its proper office is to terminate substantial essence, to bring it to pass that the essence be rendered incommunicable—by which it is to be understood *not to be able to communicate with another substantial essence in the existence that actuates it*; to cause it to be divided off from every other, not only as regards *that which* it is (as individual substance), but divided off from every other *in order to exist*.

2. What we have just said relates to finite or created (substantial) essences, which are precisely *actuated* by existence. In order to have a more complete analogical notion of subsistence, we may say that its formal effect is to make the (substantial) nature or essence so possessive of existence that it cannot communicate in the act of existence with anything which is not itself,[2] or which it is not already.[3] There is, it seems to us, better ground for defining subsistence in this manner than for defining it as that which renders a nature incommunicable *to another suppositum* (for it is precisely the setting up of the suppositum that is the question here, and

2   Substance can communicate with accidents in the act of existing, there can be a concurrence of substantial nature and accidental nature in the created suppositum because an accident is "of" a substance.

3   In the hypostatic union, the Word can communicate His Divine Existence to the human nature of Christ, there can be a union of Divine Nature and created (substantial) nature in the uncreated Person, because God is *eminently* human nature and all things.

consequently, the notion of suppositum should not be used to define it). Let us examine three eminent cases where it applies.

The first case concerns the philosophically attainable truth that *God is personal*. In saying this we mean that God subsists *ut quod* in a way that is really and essentially distinct from everything which is not He, that He possesses His own existence in the absolute singularity and the absolute independence of His nature without this existence's being communicable to another nature in any fashion which would make the Divine Nature enter in any way into composition with that nature. But this distinction exists in virtue of the Divine Nature itself ("Judaei et Gentiles non intelligunt essentiam distinctam nisi ab his quae sunt alterius naturae, quae quidem distinctio fit per ipsam divinam essentiam"),[4] and it is only as a perfection which the very notion of pure act requires to be present in this nature that the philosopher thus recognizes absolute subsistence in God (cf. John of St. Thomas, *Curs. Theol.*, I P., q. 32, disp. 14, a. 2, Vivès, t. IV).

The second case is that of the *mystery of the Trinity*. Here, incommunicable by reason of their relative opposition, three relative Subsistences or Personalities possess one and the same singular nature and one and the same singular existence; and that very absolute subsistence we have been discussing as well as the super-abundance by reason of which Divine Existence (along with the Divine Nature itself) is thus possessed in common, is bound up with the perfectly proper possession of this existence by that nature, by reason of which the Divine Existence is thus possessed in common by Persons who are really identical with the Divine Nature, each of whom is God. This is another title—which only revelation can reveal to us—by which the notion of subsistence is realized *in divinis* ("apud nos hypostasis intelligitur ut distincta ab eo quod est ejusdem naturae, a quo non potest distingui nisi per relationem tantum").[5]

The third case is the *mystery of the Incarnation*. Because the subsistence of the Word is an infinite subsistence, It can receive in Itself the human nature of Christ, a created substantial *quo* (without a created personality) which subsists and exists by the Divine Subsistence and the Divine Existence themselves (and that without the Divine Nature entering into composition in any manner with the created nature, for it is *in rationi puri termini personalis* that the subsistence of the Word is united to Christ's human nature). But this is a *privilege of the infinite subsistence* of a Person whose nature is identical with His existence and is eminently all things. ("Hoc autem est proprium divinae personae propter ejus infinitatem, ut fiat in ea concursus naturarum, non quidem accidentaliter, sed secundum subsistentiam.")[6] In what concerns created natures, on the contrary, we must say—precisely because subsistence enables them in their very finitude to imitate in some manner the self-sufficiency of divine beings—that none of them, once sealed in its own subsistence, can exist in common with any other nature whatsoever. No hypostatic union is possible with an angelic or a human person. By the fact that it is finite and that there are others, it excludes those others from the existence which actuates it, itself, and which properly belongs to it.

---

4   St. Thomas, *De Potentia*, q. 8, a. 4, ad 4.
5   *Ibid.*
6   St. Thomas, *Sum. Theol.*, III, 3, 1, ad 2. Cf. John of St. Thomas, *Curs. Theol.*, III P., q. 3, disp. 6, a. 1, nn. 9–11 (Vivès, t. III, p. 167).

3. If we admit the real distinction between essence and existence, we must then distinguish between the two modes of "individuation," if we may so speak: individuation properly so called, which belongs to the order of essence, the ultimate concretion in the line of nature itself, and another sort of "individuation," the ultimate determination or delimitation in itself, relating this time to existence and excluding the possibility that this nature, individuated in its line, communicate in the act of existing with another nature (as the human nature of Christ, individual but lacking its own subsistence, is united to the Divine Nature in the act of divine existing, or as two distinct individual things can be united in the special act of existing which consists in being seen or known). Thus, subsistence appears as a sort of individuation of the essence *with respect to the order of existence*, leaving the line of nature to face up to something altogether different, to make the leap into existence; a sort of individuation by whose means the essence, individuated in its own line, *appropriates* to itself alone the existence it receives.

This can be expressed in another way: the essence individuated in its own line is *closed upon itself*; and if it is complete (which is not the case of the separated human soul, which is incomplete in the very line of essence, since it needs to inform a matter), if it is complete it constitutes a closed WHOLE *in the quidditative order*; we say that it is terminated *in ratione speciei seu naturae*. This is the case with the human composite, the human soul united to the body. But in order that it be terminated with respect to existence, to confront existence (and operation), that does not suffice. It is a closed WHOLE *in the order of the aptitude to exist* (*by itself*) only when it is terminated *in ratione substantialitatis*, when it has received that substantial mode which is subsistence. Then it is not only a principle *quo*, it is a principle *quod*; it is not *that by which a man is what he is*, it is *this man*, you or I (and that which exists is *you* or *I*); it is not only apt to exist by itself, it is apt to have this existence *as its own*; it is in condition to limit existence to itself, to be a closed whole for the purpose of existing. Only when it possesses this last metaphysical complement does it have the ultimate disposition to receive existence. *Habet jus ad esse per se et separatim.* (The rational soul is thus terminated by subsistence, *in ratione substantialitatis* "before" being complete *in ratione specie*, since the body subsists with the subsistence of the soul.) These remarks show that subsistence adds nothing (any more than existence does) to the quidditative order in its own line. *From the point of view of quidditative construction, or in that which constitutes them intrinsically as intelligible objects*, there is no more in a hundred subsistent thalers than in a hundred possible thalers. Otherwise (if to be subject as subject changed anything in the subject as thinkable, or as object), all knowledge of subjects would be false, since they cannot be known except as thinkable, or as objects. (In this sense St. Thomas says that actual existence is *extra genus notitiae*.)[7] But subsistence adds something utterly real, most real of all, to the quidditative order—outside the proper line of this order. It makes what is *such*, to be *I*; it makes a certain depth of reality and intelligibility to be also a depth for itself. And subsistence, like existence, has an intelligible content, a thinkable quiddity. There is more in reality *and in my thought* in one hundred subsisting thalers than in a hundred thalers simply conceived and defined in their nature; but this more is extrinsic to their quidditative construction. When I think one hundred subsisting thalers (or one hundred existing thalers), I think of two united quiddities: and the second does not extend

7   *De Verit.*, III, 3, ad 8.

the constitutive notes of the first any more than the point extends the line. That is why philosophers find it difficult to understand this notion, of capital importance though it may be, of subsistence, which adds to a nature, to a *quo*, a certain thinkable depth, something very real (namely, to be a *quod*, to hold itself in being) without adding any note, either essential or accidental *in the line of nature itself*.

ON THE NOTION OF SUBSISTENCE
Further Elucidations (1954)

The first draft of the Note on the Notion of Subsistence contained in Appendix IV of *The Degrees of Knowledge* appears in all previous editions. It has been reprinted in the present edition since it represents a certain typical approach to the problem which has seemed true to us now for a long time, and also because it has furnished one of the themes discussed in the recent controversies on the problem. At present, however, we consider that it requires revision, not in its fundamental insights, but in regard to certain corollaries against which the criticisms addressed by Father H. Diepen seem to be justified.[8]

Father Diepen, moreover, is quite correct in suspecting[9] that the philosophical considerations in question have been inspired by reflection on the Theology of the Incarnation, especially by reflection on the thesis of the Thomistic school which affirms that just as there is but one subsistence, that of the Verbum, in Christ, so also there is but one existence, the uncreated existence of the Verbum, in virtue of which exists also the human nature assumed by Him. Father Diepen attacks this thesis of "the ecstasy of existence" (according to which the human nature of Christ, deprived of its own existence, is enraptured so to speak in the eternal *esse* which holds it outside nothingness).[10] He maintains that the human and created nature has been actuated in Christ by a human and created existence, and asserts that on this point Cajetan and all the great Thomists of the school have forced the thought of their master. After carefully weighing them, it now seems to me that Father Diepen's arguments can hardly be refuted. But when the same author, in explaining how there is nevertheless only one personal *esse* in Christ, as St. Thomas formally teaches, endeavors to show that the created existence of the human nature concurs with the uncreated existence of the Verbum in that personal *esse*,[11] then the least we can say is that it remains very obscure as far as we are concerned.

Not being a theologian by profession, it is no business of ours to take sides in

---

8 Father H. Diepen, "La Critique du Baslième selon saint Thomas d'Aquin," *Revue Thomiste*, 1950 and 1950, II. Particularly does the author seem right in noting (p. 115), against what we wrote in the first draft, that the act of existing "is of itself perfectly adapted and accommodated to the essence which is its formal principle; so perfectly that it can be joined to no other essence in the actuation of the latter."
   Whence it follows that it ought to be considered "an impossibility for one essence to be joined to another essence in a common actuation, hence in an act of existing in so far as it is the actuation of the essence. (Cf. also *ibid.*, p. 304.)

9 *Ibid.*, p. 117.

10 This thesis is defended in particular by Father R. Garrigou-Lagrange, *De Christo Salvatore*, (Turin, 1946, pp. 314 ff.). Father Diepen's criticism of it is presented in the *Revue Thomiste* (1950, II).

11 *Revue Thomiste*, 1950, II, pp. 521–524.

this debate and to choose between the Thomism of Father Diepen and the Thomism of Cajetan, John of St. Thomas, Gonet, Billuart and Garrigou-Lagrange. If, moreover, we have recourse to the texts of the Angelic Doctor himself, we are not freed, at least at first sight, from the difficulty. For we find on the one hand that he teaches:

"Sic igitur cum humana natura conjungatur Filio Dei hypostatice vel personaliter, et non accidentaliter: consequens est quod secundum naturam humanam non adveniat ei novum esse personale, sed solum *nova habitudo esse personalis praeexistentis* ad naturam humanam, ut scilicet persona illa jam dicatur subsistere non solum secundum divinam naturam, sed etiam secundum humanam" (*Sum. Theol.*, III, 1, 2); and again: "Illud esse aeternum Filii Dei, quod est divina natura, *fit esse hominis*, in quantum humana natura assumitur a Filio Dei in unitatem personae." (*ibid.*, ad 2).

But, on the other hand, he declares in an opusculum of which the authenticity is today recognized,[12] and which antedates the Third Part of the *Summa Theologiae* by a few years:

"Sicut Christus est unum simpliciter propter unitatem suppositi, et duo secundum quid propter duas naturas: ita habet unum esse simpliciter propter unum esse aeternum aeterni suppositi. *Est autem aliud esse hujus suppositi*, non inquantum est aeternum: sed *in quantum est temporaliter homo factum*. Quod esse, etsi non est accidentale, quia homo non praedicatur accidentaliter de Filio Dei, ut supra habitum est, non *tamen est esse principale sui suppositi, sed secundarium*. Si autem in Christo essent duo supposita, tunc utrumque suppositum haberet proprium esse sibi principale, et sic in Christo essent simpliciter duo esse." (*De Unione Verbi Incarnati*, a. 4).

In any case, simply as a philosopher we may learn a lesson from the mishap to which theology exposed us in the first version of our discussion of the notion of subsistence. Henceforth, while we shall always recognize the fact that it is the theology of the Hypostatic Union which has led philosophy to become aware of the problems concerning the person and subsistence, we will abstain from linking our philosophical reflections on subsistence to a particular theological theory, especially to one subject to controversy and which may eventually be discredited, and force ourselves to proceed on a basis and within a frame of reference that is purely philosophical.

The following three are the fundamental considerations on which, in our opinion, we must rely:

In the first place, it is things, subjects, *existents* that we experience. From these existents our intelligence disengages by abstraction essences—"suchnesses" or intelligible "structures." These are the object of its first operation (simple appre-

---

12   If previously we did not take into account the *De Unione Verbi Incarnati*, it was because, relying on Cajetan, we doubted its authenticity. But contemporary criticism following Fr. Pelster now maintains that authenticity to be definitely established. Hence, even if the text of article 4 is the only one of its kind in the work of St. Thomas, it is proper nevertheless to emphasize with Fr. Diepen (*art. cit.*, pp. 296–297) the incontestable importance of such an ἅπαξ.

hension) and of eidetic vision. Though these essences are found in a state of universality in our mind, where they are known as such, they exist really in things—in a state of singularity, as individual natures. To deny or to put in doubt this extramental reality of (individuated) essences would be to put in doubt the noetic value of the human intelligence.[13] But for a sufficiently attentive analysis what is the absolutely precise and "pure" data of the intelligence as far as essences are concerned? Because they are derived from existents by the operation of the intelligence, they do not appear as the existents themselves made present to us, but quite precisely as something immanent in the existents and which determine the existents to be what they are. The intelligence seizes them and gives them to us as *that by which* the things, subjects, or existents, are such or such. Hence, in its very notion, essence is a principle *quo*.

In the second place, essence is potency in relation to existence, to the act of existing, which is act and perfection par excellence. Essence is form or act in a certain order (the order of specification), but potency or capacity in another (the order of exercise) or in relation to *esse*. Between essence and existence there is a relation analogous to that which we observe between the intelligence and the act of intellection, the will and the act of volition.

> "Esse rei consequitur principia essentialia rei sicut operatio virtutem."[14]
> "Sicut enim potentia se habet ad operationem ut ad suum actum, ita se habet essentia ad esse."[15] "Sicut autem ipsum esse est actualitas quaedam essentiae, ita operari est actualitas operativae potentiae. Secundum enim hoc utrumque eorum est in actu: essentia quidem secundum esse, potentia vero secundum operari."[16]

In the third place, there is an intuition of existence, which is the first act of any authentic metaphysics, and in virtue of which, within the very analogy to which we have just referred between the *esse* in relation to essence and the act of intellection or of volition in relation to the intellect or the will, the *esse* is perceived quite precisely—even as in their own order intellection and volition—as an *exercised act*,[17] exercised by the thing or the existent subject, or as an activity in which the existent itself is engaged, an energy that it exerts. Existence is therefore not only received, as if by *esse* essences were pinned outside nothingness like a picture hung on a wall. Existence is not only received, it is also *exercised*. And this distinction between existence as received and existence as exercised is central for the philosophical theory of subsistence. It was not made explicit in the first draft of this Note, which was thus open to the criticisms of Father Diepen. Truly—one can rightly maintain—since it is the potency to *esse*, essence as such suffices by that very fact to limit, appropriate or circumscribe to itself the existence that it *receives* (in order to bring the subject to existence). But to exercise existence something besides the bare essence is necessary, namely, the supposit or person. *Actiones sunt suppositorum*, actions are proper to supposits, and especially and above all the act

---

13   Cf. our *Introduction Generale à la Philosophie*, pp. 141–155.
14   *In II Sent.*, dist. 15, q. 3, a. 1, ad 5.
15   *Ibid.*, q. 79, a.1.
16   *De spiritualibus creaturis*, a. 11.
17   Cf. H. Diepen, *art. cit.*, p. 303.

of exercising existence. In other words, to exercise the existence the essence must be completed by subsistence and thus become a supposit.

By way of parenthesis, we might note that a consideration of the *esse* proper to operations and more generally to accidents, brings remarkable confirmation to the necessity of distinguishing between existence as received and existence as exercised. In effect, the nature is the radical principle *quo*, powers or faculties the proximate principle *quo*, of operations. It is the supposit (*quod*) which produces or accomplishes them. What does this mean if not that the supposit exercises the diverse accidental *esse* which are proper to its diverse operations—as well as the diverse accidental *esse* proper to its powers or faculties? But neither the faculties nor the operations *exercise* the (accidental) existence proper to them.[18] They are activated by it, they *receive* it in the substance in which they inhere and "to which" they belong, they do not exercise it. It is the supposit that exercises existence—its own substantial *esse* and the accidental *esse* of its operations. And so we have here a similar situation in that the *esse* which is *received* by the accidents is not *exercised* by them, but is *exercised* by the supposit.

In regard to the substantial *esse*, it is received by the nature and (by means of the nature) by the supposit. It is *exercised* by the supposit.

It was no mistake to insist on the most important significance of the difference of order between essence and existence and of the "transcendence" so to speak of existence in relation to essence. But what inference should be drawn from that? Since existence by its very notion demands as we have just seen, that it be not only received but exercised, and since this exigency, pertaining as it does to the existential order, places us outside and beyond the order of essence, it must be said that (substantial) essence or nature can *receive* existence only by *exercising* it, which it cannot do as long as it remains in its own essential order. In other words, it can receive existence only on condition of being drawn at the same time from the state of simple essence and placed in an *existential state* which makes of it a *quod* capable of exercising existence. This *state* which completes, or rather sur-completes the essence—not at all in the line of essence itself, but in relation to a completely other order, the existential order—and permits the essence (henceforth supposit) to *exercise* existence, is precisely subsistence.

Nor was it a mistake to affirm that if existence is received by the essence as act by potency, it is by (the existence) *itself holding* (not certainly efficient causality, but by formal or intrinsically activating causality) the essence outside the realm of simple possibility,[19] since the *esse* is not received by the essence as in a pre-existing

---

18   When the faculties pass into act they exercise (in a secondary fashion and as instruments of the supposit) their operations and the accidental *esse* proper to the latter. But precisely as powers or faculties they do not exercise their own accidental *esse*, which is exercised only by the supposit from which they emanate (and which uses them as instruments only when they pass into act). Nor do the *operations* exercise their own accidental *esse*. The latter, like themselves, is exercised by the supposit (principally) and by the faculties (instrumentally).

In short, it is only when an accident (such as an active power or a *habitus* . . .) is actually used by the supposit to produce an operation that it exercises—secondarily and instrumentally—an accidental *esse* (that of the operation). In all other cases it is the supposit alone which exercises the *esse* of the accidents, which is received but not exercised by them. In this we have one of the characteristic signs of the fact that there is only analogy between substantial *esse* and accidental *esse*. Any other conception of accident makes it an additional little substance.

subject which would thus already be in existential act. The essence which receives existence holds from it—in what concerns the existential order—absolutely all its actuality, in short is nothing without it. But what must be inferred from that? Exactly the same as in the preceding observation. Since existence is by its very notion an exercised act, the essence can be so held outside the realm of simple possibility only on condition of being at the same time carried by subsistence to the state of subject or supposit capable of *exercising* existence.

And so the proper effect of subsistence is not, as we thought at the time of the final drafting of this Note, to confer on the individuated essence or individual nature an additional incommunicability (this time in relation to existence) or to make it limit, appropriate, or circumscribe to itself the existence it received, and hence prevent its communicating in existence with another essence or receiving existence conjointly with another essence; it is simply to place it in a state of *exercising existence*, with the incommunicability proper to the individual nature. The individual nature does not receive a new incommunicability from the fact of subsistence. Facing existence as a subject or supposit capable of exercising exist- ence, it is enabled to transfer into the existential order, to exercise in existence itself the incommunicability which characterizes it in the order of essence and as an individual nature distinct from any other. This is not a new kind of incommuni- cability, but the promotion onto a new plane of the incommunicability which defines singularity. Subsistence renders the essence (become supposit) capable of existing *per se separatim*,[20] because it renders an individual nature (become suppo- sit) capable of exercising existence.

It appears, then, that subsistence constitutes a new metaphysical dimension, a positive actuation or perfection, but under the title of a *state* (according as a "state" is distinguished from a "nature") or of a terminative mode. Thus do we under- stand, with, however, certain important modifications, the position of Cajetan.[21] Let us say that the state in question is a state of *active exercise* which by that very fact makes the essence pass beyond the order of essentiality (terminates it in this sense) and introduces it into the existential order—a state by reason of which the

---

19   On this point, as with regard to the transcendence of existing, we are happy to be in
      agreement with Fr. M. Corvez ("Existence and Essence," *Revue Thomiste*, 1951, II). And
      with him we hold that we may believe that the fear . . . that in writing *holds, sustains
      the essence"* we have "unconsciously envisaged efficient causality, is without founda-
      tion" (*ibid.*, p. 324, n. 1).

20   Cf. *Sum. Theol.*, III, q. 2, a. 2, ad 3.

21   Some precisions may be useful here. If, for us, subsistence terminates nature, it is not
      as we for a long time believed following Cajetan, as a *terminus purus*. With Fr. Diepen
      we think that this substantial *mode* or *state* is a positive reality or a positive perfection
      added to the nature (but not in the line or order of nature), and that between
      subsistence and essence there is a real distinction (cf. Diepen, *art. cit.*, *Revue Thomiste*,
      1950, I, pp. 104–105, 110–111). But, for us, this positive reality is defined by the notion
      of *state of exercise* rather than by state of independence or of possession of self by the
      self (which belongs to person, not to supposit in general); and it does not result from
      the nature without any causality being required for it (as Fr. Diepen grants following
      Cajetan, *ibid.*, pp. 108 and 110); it is an actuation received by the nature under the
      efficient causality of the First Cause, at the very instant that the latter makes the nature
      exist—an actuation which belongs to the existential order and does not confer any
      specification, but which, like existence itself, approximates formal causality without
      being a form properly so called (see later, note 33 to page 466).

essence so completed faces existence not in order only to receive it, but to exercise it, and constitute henceforth a center of existential and operative activity, a subject or supposit which exercises at once the substantial *esse* proper to it and the diverse accidental esse proper to the operation which it produces by its powers or faculties.

And when the subject or supposit is a person, subsistence, from the fact that the nature which it "terminates" or "sur-completes" is an intellectual nature— whether a pure spirit, or a spirit animating a body (in which case the body subsists by the subsistence of the spirit)—brings with it a positive perfection of a higher order. Let us say it is then a state of active *and autonomous* exercise, proper to a whole which envelops itself (in this sense that the totality is in each of its parts), therefore interior to itself and possessing itself. Such a whole, possessing itself, makes its *own* in an eminent sense or reduplicatively, the existence and the operations that it exercises. They are not only *of it*, but *for it*—for it as being integral parts of the possession of the self by the self characteristic of the person. All the features we have just indicated belong to the ontological order. They refer to the ontological depths of subjectivity. Precisely here lies the ontological basis of the properties of the person in the moral order, of the mastery that it has over its acts by free choice, of its aspiration to liberty of autonomy, of the rights it possesses— these latter in reference to goods which are due to it as pertaining to what we have elsewhere[22] referred to as the sphere of its possession of itself by itself and of its mastery of itself, or its auto-determination.

From all this it is clear that the conception we are here proposing, and the very distinction between existence as received and existence as exercised, is understandable only in the light of the axiom *causae ad invicem sunt causae*.

From the side of formal causality, it is by reason of the existence received by the essence—or because the essence is actuated by *esse*—that the supposit exists.

And from the side of dispositive causality (material causality), it is on condition that subsistence carries the essence beyond its own order and constitutes it a supposit capable of *exercising* existence, that the essence receives *esse* and is actuated by it.

In other words, it is by being received by the essence that existence is exercised by the supposit, and it is by being exercised by the supposit that existence is received by the essence. Subsistence plays (but in an absolutely different order) a role analogous to an "ultimate disposition," or is, so to speak, a kind of ultimate disposition for the exercise of *esse*. This involution of causes is at the core of the problem.

Finally, we have pointed out that St. Thomas establishes a relation of analogy between the couple essence and *esse* and the couple active potency and operation,[23] and we have stated that it is the supposit or person that *exercises* existence (its own substantial *esse*) and exercises its operations, as well as the accidental *esse* proper to them.[24] We shall now note the difference between these two kinds of exercise. The supposit has an efficient power over its operations. These latter emanate from it and are produced by it: by means of its active potencies or faculties. Though, when it is a question of the perfectly immanent operations of intellection and volition, such operations, inasmuch as they are of themselves not predicamental

---

22   Cf. *Neuf leçons sur les principes premiers de la philosophie morale*, p. 165.
23   See above, pp. 454 and 460.
24   See above, pp. 460 and 461.

"actions" but "qualities" and kinds of super-existence, are more properly exercised and lived than produced.

But with regard to existence, the supposit obviously enjoys no efficient power. Its *esse* is neither produced by it nor does it emanate from it. If it can be said that the supposit actively exercises existence, it is in the more profound sense—and this is the privilege, and the mystery, of the act of existing—that for *esse*, to actuate the supposit is (in virtue of the divine action compenetrating it) to be the fundamental and absolutely first activity of the supposit in its substantial intimacy and depths—activity eminently *its own* when the supposit is a person—by which it is other than nothing.

The views put forward in the preceding pages constitute an emended version of our position concerning subsistence, this time elaborated from a purely philosophical perspective without depending on any particular theological thesis. Nothing now prevents our crossing, for a moment, the threshold of a domain not our own and returning, by way of a brief intrusion into the theological controversy mentioned at the beginning, to the texts of St. Thomas which we have cited, so as to test in their context the validity of the philosophical notions we have just used. Perhaps it will devolve that if we use instrumentally the notions in question, these texts admit an interpretation bordering on that of Father Diepen, but nevertheless different, and which mediates in a certain way the positions of the eminent Benedictine theologian and those of the great Dominican Commentators.

Our remarks are situated in the context of the articles of Father Diepen already cited. And it is in the form of questions subject to the judgment of theologians that we submit them. We would like to know whether, in order to have the best chance of understanding the thought of St. Thomas, it might be best to express it in the following fashion.

1°. Just as there is in Christ only one single *subsistence*, so also there is only one single *personal existence* (*esse personale* is St. Thomas' expression; that is to say, the *esse* in virtue of which the supposit as such or the person as such exists). And this unique personal existence is the Divine Existence, as the great Commentators maintain.[25]

---

25   This thesis, in our opinion, manifestly derives from the article of the *Tertia Pars* from which we quoted a few lines at the beginning and which we quote more fully here:
"Illud esse quod pertinet ad ipsam hypostasim, vel personam secundum se, impossibile est in una hypostasi vel persona multiplicari; quia impossibile est quod unius rei non sit unum esse . . . Si contingeret quod post constitutionem personae Socratis advenirent Socrati manus; vel pedes, vel oculi, sicut accidit in caeco nato, ex his non accresceret Socrati aliud esse, sed solum relatio quaedam ad hujusmodi; quia scilicet diceretur esse non solum secundum ea quae prius habebat, sed etiam secundum ea quae sibi postmodum advenerunt. Sic igitur cum humana natura conjungatur Filio Dei hypostatice vel personaliter, ut supradictum est, et non accidentaliter; consequens est quod *secundum humanam naturam non adveniat ei novum esse personale*, sed solum nova habitudo esse personalis praeexistentis ad naturam humanam, ut scilicet persona illa jam dicatur subsistere non solum secundum divinam naturam, sed etiam secundum humanam." (*Sum. Theol.*, III, q. 17, a. 2).
"*Illud esse aeternum* Filii Dei, quod est natura divina, *fit esse hominis*, inquantum natura humana assumitur a Filio Dei in unitatem personae" (*ibid.*, ad 2).
Cf. *Ibid.*, q. 19, a. 1, ad 4: "Esse pertinet ad ipsam constitutionem personae; et sic quantum ad hoc se habet in ratione termini, et ideo unitae personae requirit unitatem ipsius esse completi et personalis." And *Comp. Theol.*, cap. 212: "Si esse accipiatur

2^0. There is, however, in Christ, as he says in the *De Unione Verbi Incarnati*, and as Father Diepen maintains, a created *esse*, by which the human nature is actuated, as it demands to be insofar as it is potency in regard to the act of existing.

3^0. But this *esse* is only *received* by the human nature, it is not exercised by it (since in no case is it the nature, but the supposit, which exercises existence). Nothing human exercises this human *esse*. It is exercised (secondarily) by the pre-existing Divine Person, without entering for all that in any way into the constitution of the *esse personale* of Christ.

4^0. If in effect the created and human *esse* of the human nature is exercised by the Person of Christ it is in a way similar to that by which are exercised the multiple *esse* of the operations that this Person produces by the instrumentality of the human nature, without this created *esse* received by the human nature contributing anything to the *esse* in virtue of which absolutely speaking, the Person of Christ exists, and which is eternal.

5^0. Thus the created and human *esse* does not at all concur in the constitution of the *esse personale* of Christ. And yet, being the substantial *esse* of a nature in which the Incarnate Word subsists, and being exercised by the Person of Christ, it is sovereignly *possessed* by that Person, it is sovereignly *His*; and that is why St. Thomas can call it *esse secundarium sui suppositi*.[26] It is a substantial *esse* which belongs to the Divine Person, which is His, but which does not enter into the constitution of the *esse personale* of this Person, or of the *esse* in virtue of which it exists as person, and which is the uncreated existence. We can say that by this existence of the human nature, which it exercises and possesses, which is its own, the Divine Supposit exists humanly. But from this existence of the human nature it receives absolutely nothing in order to exist purely and simply, or to exist as supposit, to *exist personally*.[27] In other words, the created existence of the human nature is integrated or "attracted," just as that nature itself, to the *ens personale*, to the subsistent whole (the accidents themselves and their accidental *esse* most certainly are!)[28]—but it cannot be integrated into the *esse personale* of Christ, concur in the constitution of the existence—eternal and uncreated—in virtue of which the subsistent whole exists *both as supposit and as person*.

6^0. Although it be a substantial and not an accidental *esse*, the created and human *esse* of Christ would thus not compromise the unity of Christ as subject (*aliquid*) and as person (*aliquis*), nor the unity of the *esse personale* any more than do the multiple *esse* of the accidents, powers and operations, which emanate from the human nature. On the other hand, if the humanity were joined to the Son of God *accidentaliter*—and if in saying "this man" I designated a human subject accidentally united to the Divine Word—the temporal and created *esse* proper to the human nature would obviously constitute another *esse personale* than the divine *esse personale*. But it is *hypostatice* or *personaliter* that the humanity is joined to the

---

secundum quod unum esse est unius suppositi, videtur dicendum quod in Christo sit tantum unum esse." And it is clear that for St. Thomas this *unum esse* is the pre-existing existence of the Word, the eternal and un-created existence.

26   *De Unione Verbi Incarnati*, a. 4 (quoted above).

27   Cf. *Sum. Theol.*, III, q. 3, a. 1, ad 3: "Non enim ex natura humana habet Filius Dei quod sit simpliciter, cum fuerit ab aeterno; sed solum quod sit homo." *Cont. Gent.*, IV, c. 49, ad 4: "Verbum Dei per solam naturam divinam *simpliciter esse habet*, non autem per humanam naturam; sed per eam habet quod sit hoc, scilicet, quod sit homo."

28   Cf. *Comp. Theol.*, cap. 211: "Accidens *trahitur* ad personalitatem subjecti."

Son of God; so that in saying "this man," it is the uncreated Person, the Divine Word Itself, that I designate. [29] Hence, what occurs is only a new relation (*nova habitudo*)—to the human nature—of the pre-existing *esse personale*—it becomes the *esse personale* of "this man," that is to say, of the Divine Supposit which subsists henceforth according to this human nature also, and no longer only according to the Divine Nature;[30] and the temporal and created *esse* proper to the human nature, while being a substantial *esse* sovereignly *possessed* by the Divine Supposit, remains outside the *esse personale* by which the latter exists—eternally—as supposit.

7⁰. In this way it becomes quite clear, we believe, in what very precise sense St. Thomas teaches in the *De Unione Verbi Incarnati* that the temporal and created *esse* of Christ is not in the same relation as the *esse divinum* with the eternal supposit,[31] and that it is *secundarium*.[32] It is, if I may say so, a simple temporal and created echo—in the human substance of Christ—of His uncreated personal existence. It is received by a human nature without human subsistence, it is exercised by an uncreated supposit which pre-exists it and for whose existing as supposit, or personally (for its existing *simpliciter*), it in no way contributes.

And it is also clear that these positions of the *De Unione Verbi Incarnati* in no way contradict the doctrine which, we believe, springs obviously from the *Summa Theologiae*, and according to which the unique *esse personale* of Christ is the eternal *esse* of God.[33]

---

29   Cf. *Cont. Gent.*, IV, c. 9, ad 10: "Ipsum Verbum supponitur cum dicitur *hic homo*." And *Sum. Theol.*, III, q. 16, a. 9: "Oportet quod in hoc quod dicitur: *iste Homo*, demonstrato Christo, designetur suppositum aeternum."

30   Cf. *Sum. Theol.*, III, q. 17, a. 2, corp., and ad 2 (quoted above).

31   "Esse humanae naturae non est esse divinae. Nec tamen simpliciter dicendum est quod Christus est duo secundum esse: *quia non a aequo respicit utrumque esse suppositum aeternum*." (*De Unione Verbi Incarnati*, a. 4, ad 1).

32   *Ibid.*, a. 4, corp.

33   As for the very notion of subsistence, which we have tried to clarify above, we see, if we pass from the philosophical plane to that of theology, that St. Thomas, in his doctrine on the Hypostatic Union, teaches that the human nature of Christ has no subsistence of its own. This created subsistence is replaced by the uncreated subsistence of the Word. Does St. Thomas' teaching on this point indicate that the uncreated subsistence acts as subsistence for the human nature by divinely conferring on it the completion which created subsistence, of which this nature is deprived, would confer on it? Or does it indicate that the uncreated subsistence *renders useless* the human nature's being perfected or completed by such a completion? For our part, we believe that it is the second interpretation that is better founded. In other words, a human nature, on which this mode or state in which subsistence consists is not at all conferred, is assumed, possessed and used by the eternally subsisting Person of the Word.

It seems to us that in this way a more satisfactory account is given of the fact that the Divine Subsistence "terminates" the human and created nature of Christ without entering into composition with it and plays an informing role in regard to it. It terminates it in the sense that this human nature cannot exist without a subsistence which assumes it and possesses it, but this subsistence which assumes it and possesses it and in virtue of which a pre-existing Whole makes it a part of itself, does not perfect it itself and render it itself subsistent, it dispenses it from subsisting, or from being itself achieved and completed by that mode or state in which subsistence consists. Thus, on the one hand, the humanity, become nature and part of the Divine Supposit, and principle *quo* of the life and operations accomplished through it, becomes for the eternal *esse* of that supposit the term of a new relation, inasmuch as it is with the

A final remark can be made on the subject of the Thomist theory of subsistence or of supposit. It is the supposit that *lives* and *acts* only *by nature*. Hence, it follows that Christ the Person, who is Divine, lives and acts at once in two totally distinct orders: on the one hand, in virtue of the Divine Nature with which it is identical; on the other hand, in virtue of the human nature which it has assumed.

If we meditate on what St. Thomas has written on this subject,[34] we are led, we believe, to the following positions: the Incarnate Word lives and acts according as He is God, or in virtue of the Divine Nature, within the uncreated Trinity. He lives and acts according as He is man, or by His human nature, among us on earth. In His terrestrial life He has lived and acted in all things by His human nature and its operations—acting also to be sure by His Divine Nature but precisely insofar as it uses, as instrument, the human nature and human operations (*super hominem operabatur ea quae sunt hominis*, as Pseudo-Dionysius said).[35] It is by His humanity, or always humanly, always by the exercise of His human operations—moved by the divinity more perfectly than any purely human man could be—that the Son of God has accomplished everything He did here below, has spoken, acted, suffered, accomplished His divine mission.

Hence it follows that the uncreated divine science that He possessed as God did not enter into His human knowledge and His terrestrial life.[36] And according as He was man that which pertained to His state as *comprehensor* was reserved, so to say, for heaven by reason of the exigencies of His state as *viator*. Even the share of His human soul in the Divine Life—the beatific vision which it enjoyed here below—remained a paradise above, sealed off from its faculties. The vision, says St. Thomas, did not reverberate from the superior part of the soul in the inferior part, nor from the soul into the body, "*dum Christus erat viator non, fiebat redundantia gloriae a superiori parte in inferiorem, nec ab anima in corpus.*" [37] For, indeed, the beatific vision, being of itself strictly ineffable, shone on the highest part of the soul without being expressed in any concept or communicable idea.

We ask ourselves, or rather we ask theologians, if the conclusion to be drawn from this is not that the supreme evidence that Christ, in His human soul, had of

---

eternal *esse* (*esse personale*) that *iste homo*, this man, this divine subject which has humanity, exists. On the other hand, the human nature of Christ receives a human and created existence (*esse naturae*) without itself being rendered capable (by subsistence, and as a supposit) of exercising this existence, because it is the eternally pre-existing supposit which, making use of it as a principle *quo* of activity, itself exercises the human and created act of existing proper to the human nature, as it exercises also the human operations accomplished by means of the latter, and the accidental *esse* which are proper to them.

34   See especially *Sum. Theol.*, III, q. 19, a. 1.

35   Quoted by St. Thomas, *Sum. Theol.*, III, q. 19, a. 1, ad 1. In the *ad 2* St. Thomas explains that "operatio quae est humanae naturae in Christo, inquantum est instrumentum Divinitatis, non est alia ab operatione divinitatis; non enim est alia salvatio qua salvat humanitas Christi et divinitas ejus." Cf. q. 43, a. 2.

36   Cf. *Sum. Theol.*, III, q. 9, a. 1: "Christus cognovit omnia per scientiam divinam operatione increata, quae est ipsa Dei essentia: Dei enim intelligere est sua substantia, ut probat Philosophus. Unde hic actus non potuit esse animae humanae Christi, cum sit alterius naturae. *Si igitur non fuisset in anima Christi aliqua alia scientia praeter divinam, nihil cognovisset*: et ita fuisset frustra assumpta; cum omnis res sit proper suam operationem" (*ibid.*, ad 1). Cf also *ad 3*.

37   *Sum. Theol.*, III, q. 46, a. 8; cf q. 14, a. 1, ad 2, and q. 15, a. 5, ad 3.

His own divinity by the beatific vision did not pass into the experience of Himself proper to the *homo viator* in the form only of an absolute certitude or knowledge which was sur-conscious or super-conscious (I mean retained at the supreme spiritual point of consciousness), and neither signifiable in concepts nor communicable? And that, in His human soul, it was by His infused and prophetic knowledge employed as an instrument by His own Divine Nature and His own Divine Science that He knew with *communicable and reflexively conscious knowledge* that He was the Incarnate Word? May not the same things also be said of the knowledge He possessed of His redemptive mission?

It seems to us that these considerations, whether they simply express, or extend by inference, the positions of St. Thomas, remain quite close to the Gospel text, and assist us in understanding, for example, how the Son of God was pleased to call Himself the Son of Man, and that He could say the Father was greater than He, and complain on the Cross of being abandoned by God. It also seems to us that these considerations show how Thomistic principles throw light more profoundly than do the hypotheses correctly criticized by Father Diepen,[38] on the problems that contemporary minds, having a particularly lively sense of the Savior's humanity, have raised concerning the human psychology and psychological consciousness of Christ.

---

38   Cf. H. Diepen, "La Psychologie humaine du Christ selon Saint Thomas d'Aquin," *Revue Thomiste*, 1950, III.

APPENDIX V

ON A WORK OF FATHER GARDEIL

1. In Chapter VI we tried to point out the principal articulations of a study of mystical experience, conducted in a speculative manner, that is, by investigating its causes and *raisons d'être*. It was this point of view of a strictly scientific analysis that the late lamented Father Gardeil took in his book on *La Structure de l'âme et de l'expérience mystique*. This theological work, written under the twin lights of St. Augustine and St. Thomas, seems to us one of the most notable of contemporary attempts to examine the question in a truly scientific fashion—much more so than those works of "scientific psychology" which apply to mystical experience rules of investigation inspired by the positivist and phenomenist conception of science and which only succeed in assembling empirical data (although they do, none the less, use methods of material verification which are most useful and productive).

After the classic works of a Joseph of the Holy Spirit and especially of a John of St. Thomas (of whom the Salmanticenses used to say that there is no need to add anything to his teaching on the gifts of the Holy Spirit, but only to meditate upon it), Father Gardeil's profound and penetrating book and Father Garrigou-Lagrange's two very accurate studies (*Perfection chrétienne et contemplation* and *L'Amour de Dieu et la Croix de Jésus*) must be considered as the most important contributions to this subject. We want to express here and now our deep gratitude to these two masters: to Father Gardeil, regrettably deceased while we were putting the final touches to this book, and to Father Garrigou-Lagrange, who has for a long time borne the weight of a triumphant battle for the essential theses of the mystical theology of St. Thomas.

In a note (*Structure*, Vol. II, p. 155), Father Gardeil kindly referred to some remarks we made to him about his articles while they were appearing in the *Revue Thomiste* (Nov.–Dec. 1929) and we were preparing the present chapter. I would like to indicate briefly the points which, in my opinion, need still further discussion, despite the valuable explanations contained in the author's "Examen de Conscience" (*Revue Thomiste*, 1928 and following years).

2. *The Soul's Self—knowledge*. In *Revue Thomiste* (Nov.–Dec. 1929) Father Gardeil has made his position on the soul's self-knowledge quite clear, as against Father Romeyer's interpretations. However, we are of the opinion that it cannot be said (cf. *Structure*, Vol. II, pp. 94–121) that the soul's habitual or radical knowledge of itself, inasmuch as it is a spirit, is *partly actualized* in its reflection on its acts. This knowledge is, in fact, shackled and prevented by its state of union with the body.[1]

---

[1]   Cf. John of St. Thomas, *Curs. Phil.*, t. III, *De Anima*, q. 9, a. 1, Vivès, p. 436; *Curs. Theol.*, Vivès, t. IV, disp. 21, a. 2, n. 13, Fr. Garrigou-Lagrange, *Angelicum*, Jan.–Mar. 1928, pp. 37–54; E. Peillaube, *Revue de Philosophie*, May–June, Sept.–Oct., Nov.–Dec. 1929.

This impediment cannot be half removed; it subsists as long as the soul is not separated. Furthermore, it is here a matter of an intelligible information of the intellect by the substance of the soul in the role of a *species*, and we cannot see how such radical knowledge of the self could be partly and obscurely actualized. If it is actualized, that can only come about by an intuitive vision of the soul's essence, a vision which we clearly do not have in this life.

In order to preserve the substance of the profound views which Father Gardeil sets forth on this important subject, we believe that it suffices to consider the structure of the soul *ut mens*, and the radical self-intellection we are discussing as the metaphysical condition and the primary basis for the power of perfectly reflecting upon its acts, which the soul possesses as spiritual and which alone is the proximate reason for the self-knowledge we experience on this earth.

We would not say that there is "fusion of knowledge of the soul by its act *vis a fronte* with the actualization (entirely relative as it is) of the habitual knowledge of the soul by the soul *vis a tergo*."[2] We would prefer to say that although the radical intelligibility of the substance of the soul objectively informing the intellect is never, even partially, actualized in the state of union, yet the soul in reflecting upon its act knows it to be its *own* because this act is present to the soul (after the manner of a habitus, says St. Thomas),[3] as the principle of cognitive operation, and with a presence that is intelligible in act when the intellect is formed by the form of the object now become its own proper form. Thenceforward, owing to the direct operation by which it judges things, the soul knows—germinally or in first act, not yet effectively—its own presence and existence; and when it reflects upon its direct act of knowledge, it grasps immediately—this time in ultimate act and expressly—(cf. above, Ch. III, n. 20) not only the psychological content, which then becomes its reflex object, but also itself as present and actually existing, I mean itself as principle of this act. The soul thereby knows nothing more about this principle than that it immediately experiences its existence and that it is principle of this act, and this gives assurance of the identity of the knower and the known since what is thus reflexively known is known only as that which knows. From this, we can see how the act of direct knowledge, when reflexively grasped (and in its experienced connaturality with all the soul's previous experience of itself), appears straightway to the soul as its own, or as emanating from that whose existence it experiences reflexively by turning back upon this act.

Thus, while the soul is united to the body, the act of self-knowledge has no "essential" content, capable of making known (by signs) *that which the self is* whose existence is thus perceived, other than those very operations of the subject, or the reflexively perceived flux of its consciousness. (This is why the apparent splitting of personality is possible, when a subject is unable to group together in the same psychic synthesis, everything belonging to him as his own. This would be inexplicable if the soul, in grasping its act reflexively, at the same time partially actualized—*vis a tergo*—its radical knowledge of itself through its essence.) But in this flux or more-or-less deep phenomena making known and qualifying the self, in this empirical *quid*, the *existence*, the *quia est* of the soul as principle of these operations is immediately grasped as possessed and experienced in act. *Ego sum* is inseparably given with *ego cogito*; it is the same reflex perception: "In hoc enim

2   A. Gardeil, *Mélanges Thomistes*, 1923; cf. *Structure*, Vol. II, p. 117.
3   St. Thomas, *In I Sent.*, dist. 3, q. 5, ad 1; *De Verit.*, q. 10, a. 8 and a. 9.

aliquis percipit se animam habere, et vivere, et esse, quod percipit se sentire et intelligere, et alia hujusmodi vitae opera exercere."[4]

It is important, I believe, to note well that my experimental knowledge of my soul (or rather of my substance, which is, in fact, soul and body, but is grasped by means of a spiritual activity, an activity of the soul alone) belongs to the purely existential order and implies the presentation to the mind of no other *quid* than my operations reflexively perceived in their emanation from their principle. Whence it follows that I cannot during this life experience my soul or my substance in its essence; a *quidditative* experience of the soul is possible only for the separated soul (which is exactly what St. Thomas says in the capital text governing this whole question, *De Verit.*, q. 10, a. 8). But it also follows that the more I give my attention to the existential experience of my soul, the more I will tend to neglect the diversity of objects and acts the reflexive apprehension of which is nevertheless the condition of this experience. Using different terms, Father Gardeil has brought this progressive separation to light in a remarkable manner (*Structure*, Vol. II, p. 114; *Revue Thomiste*, Nov.–Dec. 1929, p. 526). We might add that this, it seems, could be the starting point of a possible interpretation of certain natural states imitating or prefiguring authentic mystical experience. It is not impossible that a certain natural mysticism could apply itself methodically to the stripping off of particular images and representations, in the hope that, on the verge of the unconscious, as Bergson would say, it might achieve an evanescent grasp of the pure existence (unsignifiable in itself) of the soul's substance. But (supposing that the beginnings, at least, of such an experience were posssible), since no content of the "essential" order, no *quid* would in any event be attained, it is patent that in these circumstances philosophical thought reflecting upon these attempts would inevitably run the risk of confusing the self ("atman") with the supreme Principle.

[In a study of the notion of intellectual intuition (*Philosophia perennis*, t. II, pp. 711 ff.), Father Roland-Gosselin has very clearly set forth the classical thesis that the soul knows itself only through its operations and by means of its intentional information by the species through which it first knows things. Although, as we have pointed out, there are grounds for thinking that Father Gardeil has gone too far in one direction, we would be committing the opposite error were we to deny that we do have a genuine experience of the self (an obscure experience, not an intuition in the strict meaning of the word). For by means of the species of the object known and by the act of intellection, the intellect and the soul are themselves in act and therefore intelligible in act, illumined by the very light of the intellective operation itself. The intellect is illumined as to its existence and its essence, inasmuch as to be the principle of such operations is the very definition of essence; the soul is illumined only as to its existence and as ordered to this act (cf. Ch. III, n. 45). Consequently, *precisely insofar as they exist as* (radical and proximate) *principle* of this operation, the intellect and the soul can come immediately within the scope of the reflex apprehension, which thus knows them experimentally without needing any other internal principle of determination than their presence and the species by means of which the direct act is specified. Such an experimental apprehension of the soul, not by its essence but by its acts, can be said to be immediate in this sense, that the reality it attains is not known by any other intermediary than its own actuation; the object of direct knowledge is present only

---

4   *De Verit.*, q. 10, a. 8. Cf. above, Ch. III, § 3; Ch. III, n. 45; Ch. III, n. 111.

as a necessary condition for the mind's return upon itself. And, as Father Roland-Gosselin correctly observes (*ibid.*, p. 720), just as its *species* does not prevent the soul, which has become intelligible in act by means of this species, from being immediately known precisely insofar as it knows. Thus, we truly have an experience of the singular existence of our soul; I mean to say, by and in its operations, and our concept of ourselves is an experimental concept.]

3. *The word "intentional."* Father Gardeil uses the word "intentional" in quite a different sense than the one in which we use it in this work and which is, we believe, the sense currently accepted in the School. For him (cf. *Revue Thomiste,* Nov.–Dec., 1931, pp. 842 ff.), "intentional" essentially implies a tendency to a distant object, and consequently knowledge is all the less intentional the more it is experimental or intuitive—less at a *distance*; a truly experimental and possessive act of knowledge could not be intentional. For us, on the contrary, intentionality belongs properly to all created knowledge (only Divine Knowledge is not intentional, because God is by Himself all things). In intuition par excellence, I mean in the beatific vision wherein God is known possessively and with no distance intervening, since His very essence plays the role of species, does not the soul become, is it not, *intentionally* God? When the angel knows himself intuitively by uttering a concept in which he expresses his whole substance, is he not *intentionally* himself? Finally, in that intuition, the lowest in itself but the first for us, does not the sense become *intentionally* the object which it nevertheless knows in the presentiality of its action upon the sense-organ? What is essential to intentionality is not distance from the object, but the mode of existence which this word implies, and according to which a subject is something other than it is by its being of nature.

Clearly the word "intentional" may be otherwise defined. Definitions of words may be freely chosen. But the foregoing remarks seemed to us necessary in order to avoid ambiguity.

4. *The "immediate" experience of God and Faith illumined by the gifts.* The "immediate" experience of God (see above, Ch. VI, n. 83, and Ch. VI, § 15) possible in this life at the highest degree of mystical union, is referred (*Structure*, t. II, pp. 238–264) to the gift of wisdom. This conforms to the great theological tradition reviewed in a masterly fashion by Father Gardeil in an article on the gifts of the Holy Ghost in the *Dictionnaire de théologie catholique*. But the gift of wisdom is inferior to the theological virtues; its specifying object is not God Himself *secundum suam propriam quidditatem*; therefore, during our pilgrimage here on earth it is at the service of faith. How, then, could it go farther than faith, "succeed where faith fails," and lead us to the experience of union while *abstracting from faith* ("when, without excluding faith, but in abstracting from it, the soul has stripped itself of every activity of which it is the first efficient principle")?[5] It is faith itself, perfected by the gifts, which succeeds where faith alone fails.

If the objections raised in *Structure* (t. II, pp. 152–181) against the possibility of experimental and fruitful knowledge with no distance intervening, by means of *fides illustra donis*, were valid, that would be the end of mystical experience. (Mystical contemplation which is not experimental to at least some degree, would be nothing. Infused contemplation is experimental from the outset, but imperfectly

---

5   *Structure*, t. II, p. 262.

so, because it is only imperfectly passive and incompletely subject to the govern-ance of the gifts. However, as it becomes more and more perfectly passive and more completely an exercise of the gifts so does it become more and more intimate and "immediate.")[6] But there is nothing insurmountable about the objections raised by Father Gardeil. John of St. Thomas fully explains that the gifts bring a superior regulation or specification to the soul's activity and perfect the theological virtues themselves, not as to their formal object (than which there is nothing higher), but as to their mode. And St. Thomas teaches that one and the same act can proceed from several habitus conjointly exercised, the formal object of one being subordinate to that of the other.[7] On the other hand, not only does faith have secondary acts (*percipere, judicare*) over and above its principal and sovereign act which is to *believe* (cf. *Structure*, t. II, pp.169–170), but this sovereign act itself, taken in its most formal aspect (as adhesion to the First Truth not yet seen in itself), can be rendered more perfect—not indeed as to its object, but as to its mode. In other words, it is true that the proper effect of the *lumen fidei* applied to dogmatic formulas is this act which (signifying its human mode as well as its substance) we call "faith," meaning assent to certain statements on the authority of a truthful witness. But when the soul, inspired and enlightened by the Holy Ghost, uses as formal means of knowing, not concepts, but loving connaturality, this same proper effect is still "faith," but in a more mysterious and more sublime mode, *modo supra humano*, I mean *adherence in darkness* to the very substance of what love attains immediately, to the very substance of that *plus* spoken of by John of St. Thomas (see above, Ch. VI, § 14) surpassing all formulable knowledge.—"Tametsi *credere* simpliciter et absolute sumptum sit separabile a *contemplari*, credere *illustratum* separabile a *contemplari* non est," writes Joseph of the Holy Spirit[8] and he invokes the precious testimony of St. Bonaventure (*Breviloquium*, V, 4) at least as Thomas of Jesus read it (*De Oratione divina*, t. I, c. IV): "Loco citato explicat Seraphicus Doctor triplicem gradum fidei infusae dicens sic: *Primus est credere simpliciter*. Ecce tuum *credere*, quod toties repetis. *Secundus, intelligere, et penetrare credita*. Vides fidem non jam solummodo credentem, verum etiam credita penetrantem? *Tertius, videre intellecta*. Vides fidem non solum penetrantem, sed videntem. Audi quo-modo haec ab eodem habitu fidei fieri valeant: *In primo gradu*, prosequitur Bonaventura, *reaedificatur anima per virtutes morales et theologales in secundo: per habitus donorum redditur expedita: in tertio vero per habitus beatitudinum dicitur videre intellecta juxta illud: Beati mundo corde, quoniam ipsi Deum videbunt. . . .*" "Habet enim eadem fides," concludes Joseph of the Holy Spirit, "illos tres actus differentes. Primus correspondet fidei ut fides est. Secundus, fidei ut illustrata simpliciter est. Tertius correspondet fidei ut magis illustrata est" (*loc. cit.* n. 23). And it is in this that the gift of wisdom perfects the mode of faith, makes it penetrating and fruitful and suppresses, as far as is possible here below, its distance from its object. As we explain in Chapter VI, the soul does not actually use the formulas of faith as formal means of knowing; it allows concepts to slumber, but it does not "abstract from

---

6   We also think that the disparity set up by Fr. Gardeil between the words "mystical contemplation" and "mystical experience" (*Revue Thomiste*, May–June 1932) is artifi-cial and does not correspond to the testimony of the mystics themselves.

7   Cf. *Sum. Theol.*, II–II, 4, 3, ad 1; Garrigou-Lagrange, *Perfection chrétienne et contempla-tion*, 6th ed., t. II, p. 109.

8   *Curs. Theol.*, t. II, disp. 13, q. 1, § 4, n.^{0} 21.

faith." Faith, the *lumen fidei*, enters more than ever into play; thus perfected in its mode by the gift of wisdom, it is the proximate and proportionate means of contemplation.

Finally, although generally it is not the function of love to effect the *unio realis*, nevertheless the love of charity presupposes the real union effected by sanctifying grace and thus "concerns what is already in some manner possessed." And although, on the one hand, this love of charity itself, considered alone and without the gifts, cannot render knowledge properly experimental and fruitful, but can only bring about affective complacency and sweetness, to wit that "experience improperly so-called" of which Father Garrigou-Lagrange speaks (*Perfection* p. [111–112]), and which is not yet a fruition of the object, on the other hand, it belongs properly and precisely to the gift of wisdom to make use of the *unio affectiva* proper to such a love already radically possessive, and of the effects of this union as a means of knowing and, so to speak, raising loving connaturality to play (as does the Divine Essence itself in the beatific vision) a role analogous to the one which an impossible *species* of the deity would play, and so to procure an experience properly so called of the Divine Object, in such a manner that knowledge and love then become truly fruitful (albeit always imperfectly so, during this life). (Cf. John of St. Thomas, *Curs. Theol.*, I–II, q. 60–70, disp. 18, section 4, n. 14.)

That is why we are maintaining here that mystical experience, even in its highest degrees (abstracting from the effects of charismata which are accidental), is achieved by means of *fides illustrata donis* (magis illustrata), "por medio de la fe ilustradisima."[9] And we think that what Father Garrigou-Lagrange has said is right: "Infused contemplation is an act proceeding from the gift of wisdom, or the gift of understanding, as from its proximate formal and elicitive principle, the while it proceeds (*concomitanter*) from the infused virtue of faith as from its radical principle; in this sense we may say: it proceeds from infused faith as to its substance and from the gift of wisdom or knowledge as to its superhuman mode.[10] Or with Joseph of the Holy Ghost: "Fides illustrata donis est habitus proxime eliciens divinam contemplationem."[11] Thus, we can see that the act elicited by the gift of wisdom, conjointly with faith, is something quite other than a simple intellectual "attitude" of renunciation (as it is put in *Structure*, t. II, p. 262), but is indeed a true intellectual fruit, a "proper product" of infused knowledge. And so, we also perceive the marvelous unification which mystical contemplation brings to the soul: under the motion and illumination of the Holy Ghost one and the same infused act, bringing peace to the whole soul, is produced by both intellect and will, by faith, by charity and by wisdom: by faith as to its essentially Divine Object; by charity as to its formal object; by the gift of wisdom as to its experimental mode.

---

9   St. John of the Cross, *Living Flame*, st. 3, v. 3, Silv., IV, p. 91; Peers, II, p. 102. See above, Ch. II, § 16, and Ch. IX, § 14.

10   *Perfection chrétienne et contemplation*, 6th ed., t. 1, p. 411; cf. t. II, pp. [109–111].

11   *Loc. cit.*, § 3, n. 15.

APPENDIX VI

SOME CLARIFICATIONS

When reduced to an exact logical diagram (an *exacte epure logique*, to use Mr. Blondel's way of speaking), every system of the type which we may be permitted to call Blondelian inevitably encounters the dilemma posed in Chapter VI, § 29. We pay our due respects to Maurice Blondel's deeply religious inspiration. A great many of his ideas strongly appeal to us, at least in their positive aspects. But we think that their philosophical systematization, their organization into a body of doctrine, contributes a debatable *ensemble*, because the internal logic of such a system tends to integrate into the essential needs of philosophy elements which, of themselves, postulate the supernatural and, at the same time, proclaim the insufficiency of the intellect when confronted by the proper object of philosophy.[1]

The order in which Mr. Blondel's thought would find its rightful place is apologetics. In apologetics the object for which reason strives to gain recognition is a supernatural object. There, proofs proposed by reason produce their effect (a practical effect) only through a rectification of the will and when reinforced by the solicitations of grace, often by some foretaste of mystical graces. There, man called upon to decide in favor of his final end, definitively understands that without religion, without the entire supernatural organism, no action has any meaning for him.

But, as Blondel knows full well, apologetics and philosophy are not the same thing. In his work *Le Problème de la philosophie catholique* (Paris, Bloud, 1932) it is striking to see how far he goes to insist that he is not an apologist and desires to be only a philosopher (this has been his constant theme, ever since the defense of his thesis on *l'Action*), even at the very time when he is himself emphasizing the kinship of his method with the apologetic method of Cardinal Deschamps, whose method has at least the merit of being and wanting to be what it is.

The thought of a Pascal can be delivered from the errors to which its transformation into a philosophical system would give rise, because Pascal, apologist and mystic, almost constantly soars above philosophy.[2] But the philosophical systematization in which Blondel's thought is cast is essential to it.

Granted that the intellect taken in itself suffices in speculative matters, it is, however, all too true that many act as though they were the intellect taken in itself; whereas, actually, without the help which comes either from religious faith, or from a well-attested doctrinal tradition, or from rectitude of will and heart, it usually takes too great an effort for man to think straight: on this quite practical

---

1   Cf. our *Réflexions sur l'intelligence*, Ch. III. Truth obliges us to say that, as long as Blondel holds to his position on the nature of "notional" knowledge, his desire to rejoin St. Thomas will remain ineffectual.

2   Cf. *Réflexions sur l'intelligence*, Ch. IV.

point, it must be acknowledged that Blondelian philosophy is right. No doubt, too, metaphysical wisdom is lofty and not easily accessible. But we should beware lest, in appealing, in philosophical matters, to mystical experience or to anticipations thereof, we seek to bridge a void, to remedy an alleged essential impotence of speculative reason (a notion which was really bequeathed to us by Kant). For, in so doing, we inevitably run the risk of mingling by a sort of osmosis, the nature of mystical experience with that of philosophy, that is, of distorting both of them.

We particularly run the risk of distorting metaphysics by mistaking its proper object, which is a "speculable" object, accessible in itself to our natural powers, and by misunderstanding its proper means, which is speculative reason and its conceptual processes. No matter how much we love the intellect, if we say that it cannot in itself attain the *real*, lay hold on being, without the help either of action and the will, or of knowledge by love and mystical connaturality, then we either unwittingly play upon a verbal equivocation or we destroy metaphysics. It is a verbal equivocation to say *"attain the real or lay hold on being"* when we mean only that the intellect cannot get an *experimental* grasp of being taken in its extramental, concrete and singular existence; as a matter of fact, the intellect actually does not obtain such knowledge except with the help of the appetite, which tends to its object as it exists in the concrete; but philosophy has never pretended to deliver being to us in that way, nor does the intellect pretend to procure for us such an experimental grasp of things by itself alone. On the other hand, it would be destructive of metaphysics to say that the intellect is incapable by its very nature of attaining the real and laying hold on being by itself alone, in the sense that by itself it cannot obtain, by solely and exclusively intellectual means, an absolutely true and certain (although abstract) grasp of being—a grasp of being, in our mind, which effects, in a perfectly sure, constraining and stable manner, the agreement of our judgments with what is. This would be simply to assert the impotence of the intellect and—while intending to save them—to destroy the certitudes proper to metaphysics.

In the case of mystical experience, the internal logic of Blondel's system leads, as we have already noted, to still another dilemma. The experience of God postulated by the impotence of the conceptual intellect in the metaphysical line would either be a *natural* experience of God—and there is none, unless we want to confuse the order of nature with that of grace—or else it would be a *supernatural* experience of God, and here again the distinction between grace and nature is compromised.

In a study entitled "Le probleme de la Mystique" (*Cahiers de la Nouvelle Journée*, n. 3) Maurice Blondel alludes to various criticisms which have been made of his philosophy and, in this connection, draws up "exact diagrams" of some doctrines opposed to his own. We must admit that, particularly insofar as it concerns us, we are discouraged by the many confusions and amazing misunderstandings which crowd this study.[3] That *loc. cit.* § 5 is concerned with our views, we finally realized

---

3   Such mishaps are not infrequent with philosophers. In his book, *Le problème de la philosophie catholique*, Blondel also misunderstands Etienne Gilson's position on the notion of Christian philosophy, as we have noted elsewhere (*Revue Neo-Scolastique*, May 1932).

from a few quotations, although not from the text, wherein we discovered no trace of our thought. Let a few points be here noted for the record.

1. We have never thought that, in the natural order, knowledge by connaturality can of itself constitute only "a sort of bargain-basement counterfeit, a vicarious and subalternate function which must be relegated, like a lackey, to the servants' quarters" (p. 29); that it is "without intellectual character and without any real import" (p. 29); that it is "not even a knowledge" (p. 28); that it constitutes "the world of feeling of our inferior nature, without any possible intellectuality" (p. 37), reducing us to "the purely sensitive and animal level" (p. 35). All that is pure nonsense.

We have always taught that knowledge by connaturality has its place and role in the natural order, even that it is strictly indispensable in the field of action and of the virtue of prudence; that it is very properly a knowledge, and therefore something intellectual, valid and true although obtained by recourse to affective and appetitive powers and to the virtues of action and thereby *by means not exclusively intellectual*. As if to say "knowledge by connaturality" were to say "non-knowledge"! As if to make use of the reverberations of the good in the appetite in order to make a judgment were not to judge, not to perform an intellectual act susceptible of *truth and falsity*! As if the virtue of prudence, the while it is a moral virtue, were not also an intellectual virtue! As if the practical intellect were not the intellect!

Only when this knowledge, wrenched from its proper functions and from the whole immense field of *non-scientific* certitudes with which it enriches human life, is set up as the organ of *metaphysics* and *philosophy*, as the means of arriving at full doctrinal certitudes about God and the world of beings, have we declared that it can provide nothing but an *infra-rational substitute*—an infra-rational substitute *for philosophy*. (Cf. *Réflexions sur l'intelligence*, pp. 116–120.) We are forced to stigmatize as a complete distortion of our thought the effort to extend to the whole field of knowledge by connaturality what we have said about a certain arbitrary use of such knowledge on a special and well determined point. (A distortion which is, of course, unintentional, and we regret it all the more because of our respect for the person of Maurice Blondel and for his intentions; but a false imputation made in good faith is none the less a false imputation.)

2. Never have we said, thought, nor given the slightest occasion for thinking this enormity: that God is "an ideologue, a contemplator of essences, indifferent to those singularities which are the beings of flesh and blood" (p. 34). Nor have we ever professed disdain for concrete reality, contempt for action (p. 35), or affirmed "the baseness of action" (p. 29), or judged that persons and their acts are unimportant and passing, whereas the world endures (p. 35), or deemed that "to come to God we must definitely spurn all those individual beings that are mixed up in our lives, all that entails and promises resurrection of the flesh, all that must in comprehensive charity be embraced in our thought and heart as man and Christian" (p. 38).

This "exact outline" is the exact *contrary* of our thought. We have said that Divine Knowledge bears upon the singular and that it is *our knowledge* which, because of its inferiority, bears of itself only upon the universal. This does not mean that we do not have a knowledge of the singular (even an *intellectual* knowledge, although it be indirect and by reflection upon the senses). For that matter, all knowledge is not necessarily scientific.

We have said that it is important never to confuse formal objects. We have said that action has its dignity and speculation has its dignity and that while the contemplative life is superior to the active life, the most perfect life is that wherein action

flows from the superabundance of contemplation. We have said that individual acts are of such importance that moral science (precisely because it directly bears upon only the universal) does not suffice directly to regulate conduct, and that the intellect must be perfected in this order by a special virtue (prudence), which directly bears upon concrete reality and the singular. We have taught the primacy of charity in human life—charity, which has to do with singular persons, God and our neighbor, and which is above all human science, even above infused wisdom. We have asserted that this infused wisdom, which is wisdom supreme and bears especially upon a person (or more exactly upon three Persons), depends upon charity, not upon philosophy. Because "the active, moral and ascetic life" stems directly, not from speculative knowledge but from the practical intellect, where, then, have we said that his life is "imperfect and *un-intellectual*, an obstacle to contemplation" (p. 38)? On the contrary, it prepares the way for contemplation, inasmuch as it establishes the reign of charity in the soul. "The knowledge which will be *evacuated*," writes Blondel, "is the knowledge which is not knowledge of the individual" (p. 35). On the contrary, St. Thomas teaches that knowledge acquired during this life remains in the separated soul according to the universal *species* preserved in the intellect—although this does not prevent knowledge of the singular, there also. What will be *evacuated* is the imperfect (discursive) mode of the act of knowing (*Sum. Theol.*, I, 89, 4, 5, 6). But would one not imagine that, in face of vision, any philosophy acquired here on earth, if it remains in heaven, will be somewhat eclipsed? Philosophers will leave their hats at the door.

3. According to Blondel, we show that the "supreme vision of Christ" is "solely concerned with the multiple diversity of those ideal and general types, scorning the 'accidents' which constitute individuals or singular persons" (p. 32). This is a strange misapprehension. In the particular passage of the book (*Réflexions sur l'intelligence*, III, n. 1) to which Blondel alludes, we said not a word about Christ's *supreme vision*. What we were discussing—and this is something else altogether— was his *infused knowledge*, which implies a great number of *habitus* (as many as there are known essences) and notions (infused, not abstract). Any reader of the IIIa *Pars* knows that for St. Thomas, several distinct types of knowledge exist simultaneously in the soul of Christ, nor do we suppose that so expert a philosopher as Blondel could confuse Christ's *infused* (human) *knowledge* with the *beatific vision* by which, even during this life, he saw the Divine Essence immediately and in it all created things to the very depths of their individuality.

As to "individuals or singular persons," is it necessary to note that no Thomist has ever dreamed of considering *substances* (πρῶται οὐσίαι) as being "constituted by accidents"?

4. Nor have we ever proposed to "turn away the intrusions of curiosity and

human effort from the most secret domain of grace" (p. 36), that is to say, if we understand it correctly, to deny to reason (armed with suitable principles and lights, in other words, theological reason or philosophical reason which has recourse to theological information in order to penetrate farther than empirical appearances) the right to examine, insofar as that is possible, the mystery of infused contemplation. We only say—and this is quite different—that the very work of infused contemplation is itself a supernatural act: $1.^0$ essentially, or as to its specifying object; $2.^0$ in its mode, since *infused* contemplation is a free and vital act of our powers superelevated by grace, an act which the soul produces "passively," as all the mystics have remarked, under the influence of operating grace, and which infinitely surpasses all the efforts and "curiosity" of reason and philosophy, and even all efforts of our supernatural energies used by us as principal agent. For this contemplation is infused and not acquired; and it is not within our power to put ourselves into the passive state (without running the risk of the quietist *simili*); we can only dispose ourselves to it.

5. Blondel asks that if in the natural order there is no "real knowledge" (read "non-abstractive, experimental, immediate knowledge") of spiritual beings and God "where, then, is the congenital and fundamental realism of the intellect?" (p. 37). But it is Blondel, it would seem, who conceives this realism of the intellect after the type of realism of the will (which tends to things related to the subject according to their external existence, in their concrete individuality) . Our teaching, on the contrary, is that the intellect's natural realism tends to things from the point of view of the essence, both to carry them into the mind by decanting their universal value (which for the human intellect occurs only through abstraction) and yet by attaining them indirectly in their singular conditions of existence by reference to the sensible. We are speaking here about requirements connatural to our intellect itself. If we try to enter more deeply into the knowledge of individuals as such, we do so in order to face up to another demand, and first of all because we love them: it is love, then, which, for its own ends, uses the intellect to penetrate to the heart of the being it loves.

On the other hand, we do indeed think that the "divine real, as such," by which we may understand deity to be seen in itself and experience, is "the constitutive object of the supernatural" (p. 37). But it precisely is not "the inevitable object of the mind" (p. 37); the created intellect has as its formal and specifying object only being, and tends naturally to God only from this angle (as cause of what is). That is why "its natural desire" to know the first Cause in its essence remains, insofar as it is natural, both conditional and inefficacious. The intrinsic superelevation of grace is needed in order that our intellect may have as its connatural term God to be seen in Himself and in His Essence, that is, the object of the Divine Intellect himself.

6. As to the thesis *malum ut in pluribus in specie humana*, and the thesis affirming the purely intellectual connaturality of speculative virtues with their object, we do indeed hold them, but St. Thomas professed them before we did (as he did the doctrine discussed above concerning the infused knowledge of Christ); they express his very thought. And it is somewhat surprising to see Blondel, in his belief that he is aiming only at our poor self, accuse the Angel of the Schools of "striking

Christ to the heart" with respect to the first thesis (p. 39), and, with respect to the second, accuse him of making an "intrepid assertion" which is both "gratuitous and unintelligible" (pp. 33 and 34 n.). This unintelligibility would perhaps disappear for one who appreciated the true value of the Thomistic doctrine of the habitus.

APPENDIX VII

"SPECULATIVE" AND "PRACTICAL"

I
On the Proper Mode of Moral Philosophy[1]

1. By the very fact that practical knowledge is like a continuous movement of thought inclined toward concrete action to be posited in existence, its practical character, present from the beginning, is progressively intensified and, in *prudence*, becomes wholly dominant. There it is all pervasive, and although the prudential judgment always implies a knowing, its proper truth does not consist in knowing what is, but in directing what is to be done. (Cajetan, in I–II, 57, 5: "Veritas intellectus speculativi consistit in cognoscere, veritas autem intellectus practici in dirigere; cf. *Art and Scholasticism*, IV, 3.) So long as there is *science*, on the contrary, knowledge always remains speculative to some degree; and in the order of practical knowledge, it is *moral philosophy* that represents its most *scientific* degree.

Moral philosophy proposes to regulate action *from afar*, and therefore, to act *from afar* upon the will through knowledge itself. It is in view of this end that it organizes its materials into a practical context and discovers the ontological articulations which are concerned with action by adapting to its practical end a conceptual equipment, to wit, those modes of defining and judging which are typically speculative. Unlike prudence, which consists formally in *directing* and not in *knowing*, the truth of judgments in moral philosophy consists formally in knowing, I mean *knowing* as the foundation of *directing*.

This is why we have said (Ch. VIII, § 3) that moral philosophy proceeds in a practical manner as to its proper finalities, the conditions of its object, and, therefore, its proper law of argumentation; and that its mode remains, nevertheless, speculative and explanatory as regards the general or fundamental equipment of knowledge. From this aspect moral philosophy is considered strictly as philosophy or *speculatively practical* knowledge, as opposed to strictly practical knowledge such as it exists in practically practical moral sciences, and to the highest degree in prudence. A text from John of St. Thomas throws the speculative mode of moral philosophy into strong, perhaps too strong, relief (*Log.* II P., q. 1, a. 4, *sub fine*): "Scientia moralis potest dupliciter considerari: uno modo, ut etiam includit prudentiam; alio modo, ut eam excludit et solum versatur circa cognitionem virtutum speculando . . . Si secludat prudentiam, et solum tractet de materia virtutum definiendo, dividendo, etc., est speculativa, sicut fit in Theologia, in Prima Secundae. Nec utitur principiis practicis, aut modo practico, id est ut moventibus et inclinantibus affective, sed praecise speculativis, quatenus cognos-

1   Cf. Yves Simon, *Critique de la connaissance morale*, Paris, Desclée de Brouwer et Cie, 1934 (*Questions Disputées*).

cunt naturam virtutum et prudentiae in ratione veri, ut in Ethicis, et in tota Prima Secundae videri potest; et ita bene potest aliquis esse insignis Philosophus ethicus et Theologus, et imprudens peccator." It is because moral philosophy thus proceeds *speculabiliter, non operabiliter*, breaking up human acts and their very morality according to the intelligible constitutives which explain them and making use of the necessary and evident principles proper to it (cf. St. Thomas, *In Ethic.*, lib. I, lects. 3 and 11; lib. VI, lects. 1 and 7), that moral philosophy remains a science properly so called, able as Alamannus says (*Sum. Phil.*, III P., q. 1, a. 5) to "deducere certas et infallibiles conclusiones, per respectum ad opus, ex primis naturaliter cognitis" (cf. *Sum. Theol.*, II–II, 47, 15; *In III Eth.*, lect. 2, 8).

However, lest a hasty reading of the above-quoted text of John of St. Thomas lead us astray, and lest we imagine that moral philosophy is a purely and simply speculative science, a metaphysics or a psychology of the virtues, we must remember that, as St. Thomas repeatedly teaches, the reason why practical philosophy is distinguished essentially from speculative philosophy, is that it is from the very outset directed toward operation (cf. Aristotle, *Eth.*, II, 2; St. Thomas, *In Ethic.*, lib. I, lects. 1 and 2; *In Metaph.*, lib. II, lect. 2) and considers the operable *insofar as it is operable*. Thus, the formal reason (*ratio*) under which it attains its object, the scientific task to which it is ordered, the spiritual light animating and directing it, are other than those proper to the speculative sciences. It is distinguished from these latter "ex ipso intrinseco ordine ad objecta, ex quo una notitia habet respicere tantum veritatem secundum se in abstracto, altera secundum ea, quae requiruntur ut ponantur in exercitio existentiae" (John of St. Thomas, *Curs. Theol.*, I P., q. 1, disp. 2, a. 10, n. 5).

From this point of view, it must be said that moral philosophy itself proceeds according to a practical and compositive mode (since *modus et finis scientiae se concomitantur*, as Cajetan says, *In Iam*, 14, 16; for, if ethics is distinguished from speculative philosophy by its *ratio formalis sub qua*, why should it not also be distinguished from it by its *mode of knowing*?). As we have already said, the mode of knowing is to be understood as practical and compositive *in respect to the conditions of the object known* (human acts), which object is considered in relation to its ends and in its practical values, and referred to the first principles of synderesis. For this reason, moral philosophy is oriented from the beginning toward the operable taken as such, and toward the positing of acts in existence: hence, the proper characteristics of moral philosophy which we have pointed out in Chapter VIII; hence, its proper law of argumentation, directed toward the concrete synthesis of action;[2] and hence, it results that it is a normative science, that it necessarily takes into account not only what is but what should be, and that it involves the consideration of ends, especially of the final end (for, in the practical order, ends play the same role as principles in the speculative order).

But the fact remains that what moral philosophy thus prepares and gathers up in view of operations to be directed from afar, is knowledge whose structure is wholly intellectual,[3] whose truth implies neither regulation by right appetite nor affective motion, and which examines its different objects according to the laws of ontological analysis, *dividendo et resolvendo*, in order to grasp their intelligible

---

2   Ex universalibus principiis ad particularia, in quibus est operatio" (St. Thomas, *In Metaph.*, lib. VI, lect 1., n. 1145).

3   It is *scientia intellectualis*, ἐπιστήμη διανοητική, ". . . circa causa et principia" (*ibid.*).

constituent. Thus, in moral philosophy the mode of science is not practical but speculative *as to the fundamental equipment of knowledge and as to the structure of notions and definitions*. We are dealing here only with a first degree of the adaptation of intellectual equipment to a practical end. In the practically practical sciences, on the contrary, and in prudence, the very structure of this equipment is modified, as we have explained in Chapter VIII, §§ 3 and 13. Although truth in moral philosophy does not consist purely and simply in *cognoscere* as it does in speculative philosophy, it does at least consist in *cognoscere* as the foundation of *dirigere*; whereas, in practically practical science truth consists in *dirigere* indeed, but as based upon *cognoscere*, and in prudence, it consists formally simply and solely in *dirigere* itself. This we believe is the correct interpretation of the text of John of St. Thomas which we quoted at the beginning of these remarks.

From these remarks it can be seen how the operable thing can be considered, precisely as operable, in three different ways: from the point of view of knowledge, considered above all as knowing, or considered as already operating also, or considered above all as operating. It can also be seen how true it is to say that moral philosophy proceeds *modo practico* in respect to the conditions of the object known and the process of reasoning, and *modo speculativo* in respect to the means themselves, of apprehending and judging.

We might note here that the expression "practically practical" should be understood in a more-or-less strict fashion—quite strict in the case of prudence, more broadly in the case of the practically practical sciences.

II
General Remarks about the Speculative and the Practical

1. For the distinction between the speculative and the practical the following texts may be consulted: St. Thomas, In Metaph., lib. II, lect. 2; In Ethic., lib. I, lects. 1 and 3; In Polit., lib. I, lect. 1; Sum. Theol., I, 1, 4; In Boet. de Trin., q. 5, a. 1; In Anal. Post., lect. I; In III de Anima, lect. 15; Sum. Theol., I, 14, 16; De Verit., 2, 8; 3, 3. John of St. Thomas, Log., II P., q. 1, q. 4; Curs. Theol., t. I, I P, q. 1, disp. 2, a. 10.

2. When you try to group these texts together in a single synthesis it is a delicate task to interpret them properly owing to the multitude of cross-currents between the speculative and the practical, and the diversity of degrees within the practical itself. As St. Thomas constantly repeats, after Aristotle, it is by the ends they seek (to contemplate an object, to do something) that the speculative and the practical differ. But the very ordination to a practical end can itself affect knowledge to very different degrees. Furthermore, what noetics is concerned with is the ordination of knowledge itself to a practical end. But a complication arises from that fact in the last three texts listed above—which are the classical texts upon this question— St. Thomas is dealing with a particular problem: is divine knowledge speculative? And consequently, he speaks of what is speculative or practical *ex fine*, while thinking of the actual ordination or non-ordination of the knowing subject to a practical end. In other words, he is thinking of the *actual use* which the subject makes of his knowledge, and that depends upon the latter's free will and could not enter into the specification of his *habitus*[4] (cf. Cajetan, *In Iam*, 14, 16; John of St.

---

4   Except where prudence is concerned. Unlike art, prudence extends to actual perform-

Thomas, *Curs. Theol., art. cit.*, n. 15). Keeping this in mind, and thus avoiding further complications, we can set up the following diagram, showing the division of knowledge from the point of view of the speculative and the practical.

3. The following texts may serve as a commentary on this diagram:

END		OBJECT	MODE	SCIENCE	EXAMPLES
To know	for the sake of knowing	*of pure speculation*	*speculative*	speculative	Speculative philosophy	
For the sake of acting	to direct action from afar	*of operation*	" (as to the structure of ideas)	specu- latively practical	Moral philo- sophy	Theo- retical medicine
	to direct action from nearby		"	*practical*	practically practical	Practical moral sciences	Practical medicine
	to direct action immediately		" (to the highest degree)		Prudence	

1^0. *In respect to the end and the object*: "Theoricus sive speculativus intellectus in hoc proprie ab operativo sive practico distinguitur, quod speculativus habet pro fine veritatem quam considerat, practicus autem veritatem consideratam ordinat in operationem tanquam in finem: et ideo dicit Philosophus III *de Anima*, quod differunt ab invicem fine, et in II *Metaphysic.* dicitur, quod finis speculativae est veritas, finis operativae sive practicae, actio. Cum igitur oportet materiam fini esse proportionatam, oportet practicarum scientiarum materiam esse res illas quae a nostro opere fieri possunt, ut earum cognitio in operationem quasi in finem ordinari possit. Speculativarum vero scientiarum materiam oportet esse res quae a nostro opere non fiunt, unde earum consideratio in operationem ordinari non potest sicut in finem, et secundum harum rerum distinctionem oportet scientias speculativas distingui" (St. Thomas, *In Boet. de Trin.*, q. 5, a. 1.—"[Cognitio . . practica efficitur] per extensionem speculativae ad opus," *De Verit.*, q. 2, a. 8 [Cf. *Sum. Theol.*, I, 79, 11; *In de Anima*, lib. III, lect. 15, 433a14–15]).

2^0. *In respect to the mode*: "In cognitione practica artifex excogitat formam artificii, et scit per modum operandi (. . .) Tunc consideratur res ut est operabilis, quando in ipsa considerantur omnia quae ad ejus esse requiruntur simul." (*De Verit.*, q. 3, a. 3). "Scientia potest dici speculativa primo ex parte rerum scitarum, quae non sunt operabiles a sciente, sicut est scientia hominis de rebus naturalibus, vel divinis. Secundo quantum ad modum sciendi ut puta, si aedificator consideret domum definiendo et dividendo, et considerando universalia praedicata ipsius. Hoc siquidem est operabilia modo speculativo considerare, et non secundum

---

ance; for, not to use prudence *hic et nunc* would be imprudence. Cf. *Sum. Theol.*, I–II, 57, 4 and 5.

quod operabilia sunt. Operabile enim est aliquid per applicationem formae ad materiam, non per resolutionem compositi in principia universalia formalia . . ." (*Sum. Theol.*, I, q. 14, a. 16. "De operabilibus perfecta scientia non habetur, nisi sciantur in quantum operabilia sunt" (*ibid., sed contra*).

It should be noted that in this question 14, a. 16, when he speaks of scientific knowledge in the *speculative mode* of an object of operation, St. Thomas is not thinking of what we are here calling speculatively practical knowledge, e.g., moral philosophy. As Cajetan remarks ("per speculativam ex modo tantum, id est de objecto operabili modo speculativo, non intelligitur scientia de operabili in universali, . . . sed intelligitur scientia de operabili scrutans non quomodo res fiat, sed quid est"), he is thinking of a *purely speculative knowledge* of an object which happens to be operable in other respects. It is thus that God knows the things He makes or can make with a knowledge that is not only practical but also speculative, and which corresponds supereminently to our purely speculative knowledge of these same objects.

Thus, in taking over from St. Thomas the distinction between science which is practical in its object and speculative in its mode, and science which is practical both in its *mode* and its *object*, some of his disciples applied it differently. Consequently, they call *"mode"* of knowing—practical in the first case; speculative still, in the second—the classical distinction between the knowledge typical of prudence (or art or practical science) and the knowledge characteristic of moral philosophy. (Examples of this procedure may be found in John of St. Thomas [see above, in the first part of this appendix], Goudin [*Philosophia thomistica*, III P, praeamb.: "Prudentia est recta ratio agibilium ut *hic et nunc formaliter agibilia sunt*, praecipiendo quid agendum sit, concedo; *ut in communi scibilia sunt, speculando* rectum et honestum, nego. Id enim proprium est scientiae morali"], Gredt, [*Elementa*, Log. Proeem., n. 103]). We have already explained in the first part of this appendix, how in one view this still speculative mode of moral philosophy (speculative as to the equipment of knowledge, not as to the condition of the object known) does not prevent it, as Goudin says (*loc. cit.*), from being *scientia omnino practica*, from the fact of its essential ordination to a practical end.

This distinction between the speculative (in respect to the means of knowledge) mode of moral philosophy and the practical mode of strictly practical sciences, and especially of prudence, makes it possible to reconcile easily apparently opposed statements found in the writings of the ancients, where, on the one hand, they vigorously distinguish between moral philosophy and prudence and, on the other hand, insist upon the specifically practical character of moral philosophy and its continuity (not in essence but in tendency or direction) with prudence.

At the beginning of the article (*Log.*, II P, q. 1, a. 4) from which the text quoted above is taken, and which overemphasized the speculative character of moral science, John of St. Thomas writes: "Practicum et speculativum exigunt diversa principia in ipsa formali ratione cognoscendi siquidem principia speculativa procedunt *modo resolutorio*, et solum tendunt ad manifestandum veritatem secundum connexionem et dependentiam a principiis formalibus talis veritatis, principia autem practica, neque resolvunt, neque illuminant veritatem quantum ad sua formalia principia et quidditatem, quasi abstrahendo ab existentia, sed applicant et ordinant illam ad ponendum in esse, et ita procedunt *modo compositivo* . . . Et sic magis distant in ratione cognoscendi et illuminandi principia practica et

speculativa, quam duo speculativa, quae diversas species scientiae constituunt."
(See also *Curs. Theol.*, I P., q. 1, disp. 2, a. 10, n. 5.)

These remarks obviously apply to moral philosophy as well as to prudence and
the strictly practical sciences, since moral philosophy is from the outset divided
off from the whole order of speculative philosophy. Yet they must be applied to
moral philosophy otherwise than to prudence, since the latter is distinguished
from moral philosophy as practical knowledge from science. This two-fold fact is
explained by the distinction between the *speculatively practical* and the *practically
practical*.

3⁰. *In respect to speculative philosophy and practical philosophy*: "Cum enim philosophia vel artes per theoricum et practicum distinguuntur, oportet accipere distinctionem eorum ex fine, ut practicum dicatur id quod ordinatur ad operationem,
theoricum vero quod ordinatur ad solam cognitionem veritatis" (*In Boet. de Trin.*,
q. 5, a. 1, a. 4). "Sapientis est ordinare . . . Secundum autem diversos ordines quos
proprie ratio considerat, sunt diversae scientiae. Ordo enim quem ratio considerando facit in proprio actu pertinet ad philosophiam rationalem seu Logicam . . .
Ad philosophiam autem naturalem seu Physicam pertinet considerare ordinem
rerum quem ratio humana considerat sed non facit: ita quod sub naturali philosophia comprehendamus et metaphysicam. Ordo autem actionum voluntariarum
pertinet ad considerationem moralis philosophiae" (*In Ethic.*, lib. I, lect. 1. Cf. *In
Metaph.*, lib. II, lect. 2; *Sum Theol.*, I, 1, 4).

4⁰. *In respect to prudence and art*: "Scientia moralis, quamvis sit propter operationem, tamen illa operatio non est actus scientiae, sed actus virtutis, ut patet V
Ethic. Unde non potest dici ars, sed magis in illis operationibus se habet virtus loco
artis" (*In Boet. de Trin.*, q. 5, a. 1 ad 3). "Cum medicina dividitur in theoricam et
practicam non *attenditur divisio secundum finem*. Sic enim tota medicina sub practica
continetur, utpote ad operationem ordinata; sed attenditur praedicta divisio secundum quod ea quae in medicina tractantur, sunt propinqua vel remota ab
operatione. Illa enim pars medicinae dicitur practica, quae docet modos operationis ad sanationes, sicut talibus apostematibus sunt talia remedia adhibenda.
Theorica vero dicitur illa pars quae docet principia ex quibus homo dirigitur in
operatione, sed non proxime, sicut quod virtutes sunt tres, et quod genera febrium
sunt tot. Unde non oportet si alicujus activae scientiae aliqua pars dicatur theorica,
quod propter hoc illa pars sub speculativa scientia ponatur" (*In Boet. de Trin., ibid.*,
ad 4). This text shows very clearly that for St. Thomas moral philosophy, which
differs from speculative philosophy *secundum finem*, also belongs to the practical
order and has, with prudence (and the other practically practical moral sciences),
a relation analogous to that which theoretical medicine has with practical medicine. As Cajetan writes, *In Iam*, 14, 16: "scientia de operabili, sive sit per principia
proxima operationis, sive per principia remota et universalia operationis, sub
eodem membro cadit."

5⁰. *In respect to the degree of certitude*: "Quanto aliqua scientia approprinquat ad
singularia, sicut scientiae operativae, ut medicina, alchimia et moralis, minus
possunt habere de certitudine, propter multitudinem eorum quae consideranda
sunt in talibus scientiis, quo quodlibet si omittatur, frequenter erratur, et propter
eorum variabilitatem" (*In. Boet. de Trin.*, q. 6, a. 1, *ad sec. quaest.*).

4. It would also be well to note that certain apparent difficulties can arise from

the elasticity of the scholastic vocabulary which, for example, may sometimes stretch the meaning of *scientia practica* (obviously in a very improper sense) to include prudence itself: (Cf. *In III Sent.*, d. 33, q. 2, 5, ad 1; d. 35, q. 1, a. 3, q. 2, ad 2.)

The effective continuity of the whole order of the practical might offer some justification for this elasticity of vocabulary. The more we meditate on the moral teaching of St. Thomas, the more we are aware that this concrete continuity is therein constantly presupposed (without prejudice to the differences in nature between the faculties or *habitus* concerned). From moral philosophy to the prudential act, one single concrete intention traverses the whole order of practical thought, which becomes less and less "science" the more it becomes "practical," as we tried to show in the diagram on page 484. This is why the ancients not only sometimes assimilated prudence, which is contra-distinguished from science into practical science, but also and inversely sometimes extended moral philosophy to include prudence.

This continuity also explains why the ancients included in moral philosophy all wisdom concerned with human acts, in the same way as they included in *philosophia naturalis* all wisdom concerning the things of nature. We believe that just as the progressive differentiation of the sciences has brought out a clearer and clearer distinction between the experimental disciplines and the philosophy of nature, so likewise, and without breaking the effective continuity of the practical order, a similar difference should be recognized between moral philosophy and the practically practical moral sciences.[5] The mode which is *practical and compositive*, not only in respect to the conditions of the object known but also *in respect to the very structure of the means of apprehending and judging*, characterizes not only *prudence*, which immediately governs the act to be done *hic et nunc* by a judgment and command appropriate to the absolute individualization of the concrete case, but it also characterizes (although to a lesser degree) a *science* of human action whose object, unlike that of prudence, is to organize universal truths, and yet which proceeds to do so, not *per principia remota operationis* as moral philosophy (which it presupposes) does, but *per principia proxima operationis*.[6] Consequently, it must depend on practical principles in its fundamental equipment and in its very knowledge-value; its means of knowledge must be fundamentally impregnated with practicality and it will yield that complete and assured truth proper to science only when it presupposes in him who teaches it an authentic experience of the concrete term to which it directs those who are taught. As such, this experience does not stem from communicable wisdom; it depends upon the prudential judgment itself, wherein speculative principles and criteria are completed by regulations that issue from moral virtues and rectitude of will.[7]

This notion of strictly practical science was developed by St. Thomas rather in

---

5   Thus, in many faculties of theology there has been added to the course in *speculative moral theology*, in which are explained the subjects treated by St. Thomas in Ia–IIae and IIa–IIae, a course in practical moral theology, conceived from the point of view of the theology of St. Alphonsus Ligouri.

6   Such is the case, for example, with the *Praxis confessarii ad bene excipiendas confessiones* of St. Alphonsus.

7   No doubt rectitude of will is *even more* necessary for prudence, which alone considers singular cases *hic et nunc* and alone reaches right down to the *imperium*. But for the reasons we have just pointed out, it is also necessary for practically practical science.

the line of the *factibile* or of artistic *making* and *apropos* of art. But the explanation we are discussing here is necessary if the nuances of the real are to be respected and it is in complete conformity with the principles and spirit of his doctrine. When we recognize that such a science has also a place in the line of the *agibile*, of human *action*, we see more clearly the continuous movement of thought which passes from ethical considerations to the positing of the prudential act, and at the same time we see more clearly the difference in mode between moral science, in which the intellect alone enters into play, and that science in which the intellect works in conjunction with the experience proper to prudence and with the inclinations of the appetite. That is why we insisted so strongly upon the importance of practically practical science in the case of St. John of the Cross. Analogous remarks should suitably be made about that very great practical, as well as speculative, moralist, St. Alphonsus Ligouri. The teaching of these saints is, to our mind, a much purer example of practically practical moral science than are certain works on casuistry, which can be reproached for being both too speculative in mode and tending to misunderstand the absolutely irreducible role of the virtue of prudence in the proper regulation of human acts—a virtue which no science could ever replace, because only prudence can judge infallibly of the contingent itself.

5. Prudence is clearly a *habitus* specifically distinct from either speculatively or practically practical moral science, since an ignorant man can be prudent in his personal conduct and since, strictly speaking, prudence (like the other moral virtues) supposes only the first naturally known principles of practical reason and information derived from experience (*Sum. Theol.*, I–II, q. 58, a. 4; II–II, q. 47, a. 3, 6, 14 and 15). It does, however, need to be enlightened by moral science by taking counsel, and in some cases (for example, when a man has to counsel or direct others) it requires science in the subject itself.

As we have indicated above, we think that, on the other hand, strictly practical moral science supposes prudence (and therefore the other moral virtues), if not in respect to the experimental material and partial truths it can gather up, at least for its complete truth and scientific certitude. For such a science is an extension of moral philosophy into the practical field as such. How, then, could it be stabilized in the practically true were it not centered in prudence and in experience of prudential conduct? St. John of the Cross and St. Alphonsus were able to produce absolutely sure practical doctrine only because they were not only learned but prudent and experienced.

Is this practical science a *habitus* distinct from moral philosophy or theology? Certainly it is not a habitus specifically distinct from theology. For theology, being as it were a certain impression in us of the science of God and the blessed, is in its very essence *eminenter (et formaliter) practica*, and there is less difference between the practically practical and the speculatively practical than there is between the practical and the speculative. The practical science of which we speak should be considered as a special development of the theological *habitus*.

On the other hand, in the philosophical order,[8] in which *habitus* are more

8   We do not think that, in the state of fallen and redeemed nature, a complete moral wisdom of the purely philosophical order is possible, be it speculative or practical in mode. But we do think that, by illumination from theology and *subalternation* to it, an entirely true philosophical wisdom of human acts is possible and, in the same rational

distinct, we regard it as probable that such a practical science constitutes a *habitus* specifically distinct from that of moral philosophy. For although the fundamentally speculative structure of the means of knowledge used by moral philosophy does not suffice to classify this latter in the speculative order, for the reason that these means are themselves involved in the typical movement of a knowledge which is characterized, first and foremost, by its practical finality, the fact remains that within the *genus*, practical, a different notional structure and a different mode of defining should denote a specific diversity (cf. Ch. VIII, §§ 13–18). Therefore, we do not think that it is enough to say that the strictly practical moral sciences are simply particular developments of the *habitus* of moral philosophy. They must differ specifically from this *habitus*, just as arithmetic and geometry, the philosophy of nature and the experimental natural sciences (cf. above, Ch. IV, n. 69), prudence and its associated virtues, respectively, differ specifically from each other.

Finally, in what concerns the line of the *factibile* or the work of art, if we reflect, on the one hand, that art is more purely intellectual and less "voluntary" than prudence and is fulfilled in the act of judging, not of commanding what is to be made, and, on the other hand, that logic and, as St. Thomas adds in his commentary on the *De trinitate* of Boethius, the other sciences of the *trivium* and *quadrivium*, are both speculative sciences and (speculative) arts at the same time, we shall reach the conclusion that the *practical science* of the work to be made and (practical) *art* are not two distinct *habitus* but rather two formal aspects of the same *habitus*. However, one of these aspects may be more marked than the other in different particular cases; the *art* aspect predominates, e.g., in a Moussorgsky, or in some physician who frequently cures his patients and seems to work by rule of thumb; the *science* aspect predominates in a da Vinci, or in a physician who is more learned but effects fewer cures. Yet the "theoretical" part and the "practical" part of one and the same art (like medicine, cf. above, § 1 and table) stem from the same specific *habitus*, whereas in our opinion, moral philosophy and the practically practical moral sciences are specifically different *habitus*.

---

line, a practically practical moral wisdom (which would differ from the practically practical science of the theological order not, of course, by an effective direction impressed on human acts, but by the mode or style of those considering it. Whether they be faithful to all its requirements, or whether they err more or less gravely, this is the practically practical moral wisdom from which stem a Pascal, a Joubert, a Manzoni, a Nietzsche, an Emerson . . .).

APPENDIX VIII

"LE AMARA TANTO COMO ES AMADA"

In Chapters VIII and IX there was question of the equality of love between God and the soul which St. John of the Cross considered possible even in this life at the summit of the spiritual life (spiritual betrothal and marriage). We pointed out the very clear difference which distinguishes the state of betrothal from the state of spiritual marriage. We also noted that the equality of love which begins with spiritual betrothal and is common to the state of betrothal and the state of marriage is of another kind than the equality of love proper to spiritual marriage. In the state of betrothal, love becomes equal on both sides in this sense: that the soul renders to God measure for measure a love of charity (created love) equal to the love, measured or finite not in itself but as to its *terminus*, with which God loves His creature. To this first equality, which takes place "by the grace of conformity of will" and which is a "disposition for the union of marriage" (see above, Ch. IX, end of § 12) a second is added with spiritual marriage. Then it is a love without measure that the soul renders to God, and it is within the very immensity of divine love that the equality occurs, since it is by the uncreated love itself that the soul loves God, thus giving to God God Himself (cf. Ch. IX, §§ 12–16).

In this appendix we would like to return to the equality of love as it begins with spiritual betrothal, in order to examine certain questions it raises, and to show how the practical science of St. John of the Cross agrees on this point with the speculative doctrine of St. Thomas. With regard to the equality of love to which the soul aspires, the second redaction of the Canticle invokes the authority of St. Thomas *In opusc. de Beatitudine* (cap. 2, Silv., III, p. 411). It is to the same opuscule, today considered apocryphal, that the Saint refers implicitly in the *Living Flame*, when he is treating of the same subject (see above, Ch. IX, n. 75) . In our opinion, since St. Thomas looked at things from the standpoint of essences, and in his very formal technology used words according to their maximum force, he would not have employed the expression "equality of love." But though the terminology of the two Doctors is different, we believe there was no disagreement in their thought either with regard to the second equality of love, as we saw above (Ch. IX), or with regard to the first of which we are now speaking especially.

Let us note that though to *see* God as He sees us is not possible here below, it does not follow that to *love* Him as He loves us (this expression being properly understood), is equally impossible here below. Love can go beyond knowledge (cf. *Sum. Theol.*, I–II, 27, 2, ad 2: "Contingit quod aliquid plus ametur quam cognoscatur, quia potest perfecte amari etiamsi non perfecte cognoscatur"). Whether it be ruled by faith or ruled by vision it remains the same love. *Caritas numquam excidit.*

Granting that charity is purified in Purgatory without any merit, since to merit is proper to the state of *via*; granting, on the other hand, that the degree of charity of the glorified soul corresponds to the degree to which it is loved by Him who predestined it, it is necessary to conclude that a soul that enters beatitude without passing through Purgatory, without needing purification, has loved God here below (even if it be only at the instant of death) as much as it was loved by Him. It has been, in other words, even if only at that instant, perfectly faithful to the grace received. This is precisely the case of those—*que son pocos*—who have reached the ninth degree of divine love, which is "the degree of the perfect." They are already entirely purified by love (*ya por el amor purgadisimos*), and at death do not pass through Purgatory.[1]

It is clear, moreover, that for St. John of the Cross, the soul that has arrived at "equality of love" with God, so that it would not pass through Purgatory should death intervene, continues always and more than ever to grow in charity as long as it remains on earth. (For during its terrestrial life the soul is more loved to the degree that it receives more, since it receives new graces only because it is more loved. Thus, the equality in question refers only at the moment of death to the final degree corresponding to the glory to which the soul is predestined. That is why the soul, though being in the plentitude of peace, always aspires, and knows that to love God as much as He loves it "cannot be *perfectly* in this life."[2]) Here below this equality of love signifies only that the soul does not cease to correspond perfectly to the ever greater and more abundant graces it receives.

It is likewise obvious that as long as the soul is united to the body it cannot be constantly in the state of supreme actuation of its *habitus* of charity. Even the perfect must pay tribute to sleep, and to everything which derives from sleep in our terrestrial condition. "If the soul," St. John of the Cross writes, "never leaves the sublime state of marriage once God has raised it to that state, the union is not always actual as to the powers, it is so only for the substance. . . . The union of the powers . . . is not without intermissions in this life, such a thing is impossible."[3] And so this equality of love itself is not constantly in act here below (it is precisely in this that it is perfectly realized only in heaven).

Consequently, there is no disagreement between the fact that St. John of the Cross attributes an equality of love (begun here below, definitive and completed in the other life) to spiritual "betrothal" and "marriage," and the fact that St. Thomas teaches that in the state of *via*, charity can (and ought) always to increase (II–II, 24, 4) and that here below the human heart cannot be *always actually* borne in its entirety to God (*ibid.*, 8).

The Angelic Doctor describes the perfection compatible with the present life as a state in which "there is excluded from the heart of man not only whatever is contrary to charity, but also everything that would hinder the movement of the heart from being totally directed towards God" (*Sum. Theol.*, II–II, 184, 2). To an attentive consideration this terminology, purposely as moderate as possible, will be seen to signify in another way the very same thing as the ardent language of

---

1   *Dark Night*, Bk. II, Ch. xx, Silv., II, pp. 491–492.

2   *Cant.*, 1st redact., str. 37, Silv., III, p. 169. Cf. *Living Flame*, 2nd redact., st. I, v. 3, Silv., IV, p. 117: "The habitus of charity can be as perfect in this life as in the next, but not in its operation nor its fruit; though the fruit and operation of love grow to such an extent in this state that they become exceedingly like those of the other life." See also the accurate comments of Fr. Silverio (t. III, *Appendices*, pp. 509–511).

3   *Cant.*, 1st redact., st. 17 (26), Silv., III, pp. 94–95 (tr. Chevallier).

the Mystical Doctor. Such an exclusion of every obstacle of love, when it is complete and perfect and so supposes an absolutely eminent degree of fidelity to grace, is the very equality of love which according to St. John of the Cross begins with spiritual betrothal[4] and is accompanied, in the state of marriage—that is to say when the transformation of love is already fully accomplished—with the "communication and union of the persons," in which the soul gives God Himself to God.

Finally, let us note that if we consider, not this second kind of equality of love, in which the soul loves God by the love with which He loves Himself and with which He loves it, but the equality of which we are here speaking, and which concerns the love elicited by the soul itself, then to say that in heaven we will love God perfectly as He loves us, and that this equality of love can begin already here below, is not to affirm between the one love and the other a parity *under every respect*, for a certain disparity will always remain, in this sense: that God loves us to the very degree that there is goodness in us (infused in us by His creative and vivifying love), while we can never, even in heaven, love Him as much as He is lovable, that is to say in an infinite manner (cf. *Sum. Theol.*, II–II, 184, 2). But we will render to God, in love, all that we receive from Him: *si ex tota se diligit creatura, nihil deest ubi totum est.* Similarly St. Paul says that in heaven we will know God as He knows us ("videmus nunc per speculum in aenigmate, tunc autem facie ad faciem; nunc cognosco ex parte, tunc autem cognoscam sicut et cognitus sum" (I Cor. xii, 12). And yet there will not be parity *under all respects* between the one knowledge and the other, for God knows us to the very extent that we are knowable, while we will never be able, even in heaven, to know Him to the extent that He is knowable, in other words to *comprehend* Him (cf. *Sum. Theol.*, I, 12, 7).

---

4   One should recall what St. Bernard says: "Conformandae ipsi (Verbo) in quo? In charitate. Talis conformitas maritat animam Verbo, cum, cui videlicet similis est per naturam, similes nihilominus ipsi se exhibet *per voluntatem, diligens sicut dilecta est.* Ergo si perfecte diligit, nupsit. Vere spiritualis sanctique connubii contractus est iste: Parum dixi contractus: complexus est. Complexus plane ubi idem velle et nolle idem, unum facit spiritum de duobus. . . . Non plane pari ubertate fluunt amans et amor, anima et Verbum, sponsa et sponsus, Creator et creatura non magis quam sitiens et fons. Quid ergo? Peribit propter hoc et ex toto evacuabitur nupturae votum, desiderium suspirantis, amantis ardor, presumentis fiducia, quia non valeat ex aequo currere cum gigante, dulcedine cum melle contendere, lenitate cum agno, candore cum lilio, claritate cum sole, charitate cum eo qui charitas est? Non. Nam etsi minus diligit creatura, quoniam minor est, tamen si ex tota se diligit nihil deest ubi totum est. Propterea sic amare nupsisse est" (*Super Cantic.*, sermo 83). These texts cited by Fr. Crisogono (*op. cit.*, t. 1, p. 381) in his chapter on "The Degrees of Union with the Infinite" wonderfully illuminate the equality of love in question here, an equality which begins with spiritual betrothal and which is common to the state of betrothal and to the state of marriage.

APPENDIX IX

THE "CAUTELAS" OF ST. JOHN OF THE CROSS[1]

When John of the Cross in his *Spiritual Warnings*, addressed to the Carmelite nuns of Beas, tells them to tear out by the roots all attachment to their families, does anybody imagine that he is here contradicting the common teaching of the Church and in particular that of St. Thomas, on the love we owe our parents? On the contrary, he takes that teaching for granted. I mean that he knows that those to whom he is speaking are in no more danger of falling into insensibility than the contemplatives, to whom he is teaching the way of emptiness, run the risk of lapsing into quietism. He is sure of the souls to whom he is talking; they are above nature, not below it; fully prepared for the demands of the perfect life, they can bear the Gospel in the most divine and secret meaning its letter conceals. "If any man come to me and hate not his father, and mother . . . he cannot be my disciple."[2] John of the Cross: "The first [caution] is, preserve an equal love and an equal forgetfulness of all men whether relatives or not. . . . Look upon your kindred as strangers. . . . Do not think about them; have nothing to say about them either good or bad. Avoid them as much as you possibly can."

These prescriptions should be taken in their strictest sense and without the least watering-down. But they must be understood. They do not call for exterior detachment only; they require an inner and radical detachment, a complete death. But it is to be a basic renunciation of *proprietorship* in, the *purely natural exercise of*, our feelings, and, thanks to that renunciation, a higher love will quicken those feelings. It is not to be a radical destruction of the *ontological reality* of those feelings, if such an expression may be used. Between these two deaths, there is the whole vast difference between the superhuman and the inhuman. With a view to growing in the life of the spirit the disaster of abandoning oneself to the second so as to become tough and cold-hearted is as great as refusing the first, for that is but to refuse the perfection of love and the price that must be paid for it; "the saints," said the Curé of Ars, "had limpid hearts."

John of the Cross is addressing his *Canticles* to souls that have decided to leave all else behind for love, souls that have already entered into the path of the spirit;[3]

---

1   These pages are taken from the Preface to a book of Fr. Bruno de Jésus-Marie, *Saint Jean de la Croix* (Paris, Plon, 1929). Cf. Fr. Bruno, *St. John of the Cross* (Sheed and Ward, London, 1932, ed. Fr. B. Zimmerman, Introduction, pp. xx–xxii).

2   Luke xiv, 26: "Si quis venit ad me, et non odit patrem suum, et matrem, et uxorem, et filios, et fratres, et sorores, adhuc autem et animam suam, non potest meus esse discipulus."

3   And he addresses them to souls that *are pledged by vows to the purely contemplative life;* souls whose activity as well as whose affections should pass through God to reach the creature (not merely the creature in general, but this and that one *nominatim*, in keeping with the order of charity and preference God allows). If they are faithful to

his own mission, his flaming secret, is to bring them straight to their goal without losing a split second. He knows that along the path such souls travel, even the most legitimate natural affections (and especially attachment to their own families) set up one of the greatest roadblocks unless these souls be radically dispossessed of them. (And St. Philip Neri thought exactly the same, for he commanded his disciples to cut themselves off completely from their relatives.[4] And how many religious remain mediocre, more-or-less deaf to the Spirit of God, and oftentimes to the voice of the Church because even in the cloister they are still too tightly *bound* to family affections and prejudices!) His harshest warnings simply apply St. Thomas' gloss on St. Luke ("One's closest relations must be hated for God's sake, that is if they turn us away from God"[5]) to their particular cases, and they do so in a totally spiritual sense. The soul can only achieve the highest charity (wherein it loves itself perfectly in, and for, God) if it hates itself[6] (i.e., if it dispossesses itself of the natural love it bears itself in virtue of its personal well-being, with a view of subordinating that love utterly to supernatural charity).[7] Again, the soul must not destroy its lawful love for relatives, but it must completely subordinate that love to charity and, as far as possible, tear from itself all feeling of proprietorship. Then, and then only, will it succeed in perfectly loving its own in and for God, loving them also as its own but only according to God and in a supernatural and incomparably deeper way. "Detach your heart from both the former and latter," St. John of the Cross writes in the same place. "You must, in some way or other, even detach yourself from your parents, *fearing lest flesh and blood come to life again through the natural love that always exists between the members of the same family and which it is always fitting to mortify so as to arrive at spiritual perfection.*"

These lines, so exact and so carefully shaded, give the true meaning of this first warning, as has quite rightly been noted.[8]

---

the graces of this vocation, they will love with far greater order, delicacy and tenderness, but precisely because that very same love has been required of them do they give it back to God: greater and more active than ever, it is theirs no longer, for they have been dispossessed of it.

4   "Gallonius only had permission to go and see his family, living in Rome, once each year. Baronius will never again go back to Sora. Consolini, the beloved disciple, had two brothers and a sister: 'he never took up pen to write them a line, and he never opened his mouth to find out if they were dead or alive'" (G. Rabeau, "La fantasie comique et la grace de Dieu, saint Philippe Neri," *La Vie Spirituelle*, July–August 1929, p. 215). The author quite correctly points out that from Philip's day to our own the role of the family in social life has changed completely. A powerful and an oppressive force in the sixteenth century, it is today socially very weak and threatened ever more and more. A legitimate inference to be drawn from such considerations is that "if Philip were alive today," he would have recourse to means much less rigorous, but not that "he would have thought the exact opposite" (*ibid.*). The laws of inner detachment and spiritual progress do not change.

5   *Sum. Theol.*, II–II, 26, 2 (sed contra). Cf. 26, 7, ad 1.

6   "If any man come to me, and hate not . . . yes and his own life also. . . ." (Luke xiv, 26).

7   Cf. St. Thomas Aquinas, *Sum. Theol.*, II–II, 19, 6; 19, 8 ad 2. Cf. above, Ch. I, n. 8.

8   Fr. de la Trinité, "Precautions spirituelles. Avis et Maxims de saint Jean de la Croix," *Le Carmel* (Sept. 15, 1925, p. 218). "The saint's way of living," the author adds, "should itself be sufficient to put us on the alert against the generalizations of extreme rigorism: in the midst of founding the convent at Duruelo, he brought his mother, his brother, Francisco de Yepes, and his sister-in-law and entrusted to them certain menial jobs connected with the building of the convent. Again, he loved the Car-

If St. John of the Cross had been compelled to sketch the general laws of ethics and of the hierarchy of duties, is it conceivable that he would have expressed himself otherwise than St. Thomas did in articles 7 and 8 of question 16 of the *Secunda Secundae*? If St. Thomas Aquinas had been forced to bring souls like these, consecrated to God, to saintliness, can anyone doubt that he would have given them (in another tone, perhaps, and in quite a different style) the self-same counsels John of the Cross gave to his sisters at Beas?

---

melites at Beas with an affection that did not preclude his having legitimate prefer-ences precisely because it was a thoroughly spiritual affection; as prior at Segovia, and, consequently, at the very close of his heroic career, he was pleased to call for his well-beloved brother and keep him near him." Father Bruno has done well to bring all these exquisitely natural traits to light. It is curious to note that St. John of the Cross (who, moreover, found himself in much different conditions, not having to work in the very midst of a crowded world as did St. Philip Neri) had outward severities much less rigorous than the kindliest and most humorous of the saints, this chapter on relations with our neighbor being put aside.

INDEX OF NAMES